MW01040891

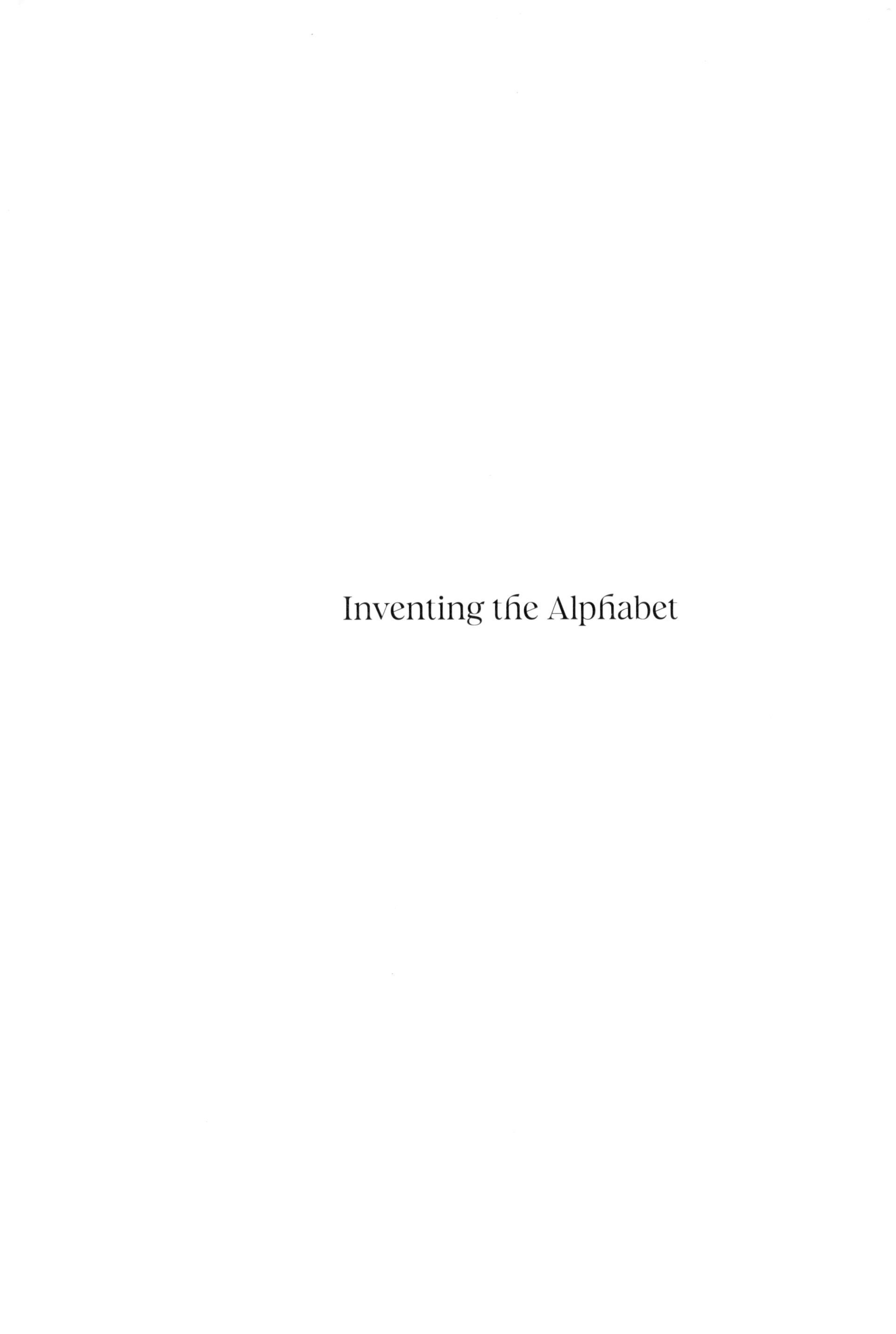

Inventing the Alphabet

Invent

the

ing

Alphabet

Johanna Drucker

THE ORIGINS OF LETTERS FROM ANTIQUITY TO THE PRESENT

The University of Chicago Press
CHICAGO AND LONDON

The University of Chicago Press, Chicago 60637
The University of Chicago Press, Ltd., London

Published 2022
Printed in the United States of America

31 30 29 28 27 26 25 24 23 3 4 5

ISBN-13: 978-0-226-81581-7 (cloth)
ISBN-13: 978-0-226-81580-0 (e-book)
DOI: https://doi.org/10.7208/chicago/9780226815800.001.0001

Library of Congress Cataloging-in-Publication Data

Names: Drucker, Johanna, 1952– author.
Title: Inventing the alphabet : the origins of letters from antiquity to the present / Johanna Drucker.
Description: Chicago : University of Chicago Press, 2022. | Includes bibliographical references and index.
Identifiers: LCCN 2021043203 | ISBN 9780226815817 (cloth) | ISBN 9780226815800 (ebook)
Subjects: LCSH: Alphabet—History.
Classification: LCC P211 .D76 2022 | DDC 411—dc23
LC record available at https://lccn.loc.gov/2021043203

♾ This paper meets the requirements of ANSI/NISO Z39.48-1992 (Permanence of Paper).

Contents

Introduction

Few human systems have as long a history of continuous use as the alphabet. Few play such a major role in the production or transmission of knowledge and culture. With the exception of character-based writing (Chinese, Korean, and Japanese), the alphabet in its many variations is the chief writing system in use today, and yet few of its users pause to consider its origins or history. When and where did the letters come into being? How did they spread and change in the course of their near-global expansion? How can letterforms invented nearly four millennia ago undergird global communication in the present? These are topics that hardly make it into academic discussions, let alone ordinary conversation.

However, this study is not an addition to the number of authoritative books on alphabet history.[1] Classics such as Isaac Taylor's *The Alphabet* (1883) and David Diringer's *The Alphabet: A Key to the History of Mankind* (1947) have been joined by many contemporary works.[2] Instead, this work is a contribution to the intellectual history of this topic. Who knew what when about the alphabet? And how did the way they knew it—through texts, images, inscriptions, or artifacts—affect their conception of the identity and origin of alphabetic writing? As a *historiography*, this account traces the ways knowledge and belief shaped the understanding of alphabetic writing.

Many basic misconceptions exist in this field. Ask the average literate person about the alphabet and often the response is, "Which alphabet? Our alphabet? You mean the Greek alphabet?" In fact, the alphabet was invented only once, by Semitic speakers in the ancient Near East. Alphabetic scripts all derive from the same root; as they spread, their letterforms were modified. Even scripts as visually distinct as Arabic, Cyrillic, Latin, Greek, Hebrew, Devanagari, Tamil, and Gheez have a common source. This root emerged nearly four thousand years ago in a cultural exchange between Egyptians, Canaanites, and other speakers of the Afro-Asiatic language group of which Semitic languages form a branch. The factual details of alphabetic innovation are increasingly well documented, supported by knowledge of ancient languages and the study of inscriptions. Physical evidence of the early alphabet has been carefully mapped onto the geography of archaeological sites that track transmission throughout the Mediterranean in the second millennium BCE.

Writing, a broader category than alphabetic script, was invented in several forms in human history and includes hieroglyphics in Egypt, cuneiform in Mesopotamia, various linear scripts in Crete, the glyphs and characters of New World systems, the Indus valley, and Easter Island. Of these, only character-based writing survives today. This type of writing was an independent invention in ancient China, whose earliest known inscriptions are dated to about 1600 BCE. Writing may have sprung into being and been lost at other times. But with the exception of Egyptian and Mesopotamian writing, these systems are completely separate from the history of the alphabet. Notation systems for counting with tallies or marks, or tracking the motions of the stars and planets, have even longer histories than writing. Other systems of record keeping—wampum, quipu, bark painting, calendars, and abstract marks—also have independent histories. But no other system of writing has been so persistent and so pervasive as the alphabet—or, arguably, so potent in its global effects.

The intellectual imagination required to create a relationship between spoken language and written notation is one of the most profound achievements of humankind. Alphabetic writing differs from pictographs, tokens, or glyphs, for instance, and even early hieroglyphics, because those signs symbolized things, quantities, or concepts. The predominant early scripts in Egypt were hieroglyphics, hieratic (a cursive form of Egyptian writing), and in Mesopotamia, cuneiform. As later versions of these scripts began to correlate with sound, notation systems in the ancient Near East became simpler. A reduced set of nonpictorial written signs helped lay the foundation for the emergence of the alphabet. Significant analytic skill was required to understand that speech had elemental sound units—whether understood as syllables, phonemes, consonants, or vowels—that could be reduced to a manageable number and then represented by a stable set of signs. The way this occurred, by what process or motivation, is impossible to recover in full detail, but the early alphabet was the expression by Semitic speakers of the analysis of the sounds of their language. This accomplishment is what permitted the alphabet to develop, spread, and be adopted by speakers of many different languages who used its signs for their own speech.

Contemporary methods of scholarly work have established an empirical foundation for the basic account of alphabet history. But until the end of the nineteenth century, the physical evidence on which alphabet history could be traced was scant. Only a handful of inscriptions from the earliest periods of formation was available. In the twentieth century, this situation changed dramatically. Now it is possible to show when and by what steps the earliest Proto-Sinaitic and Proto-Canaanite scripts of the second millennium BCE led to consolidation of the Phoenician script around 1000 BCE. Debates about the specific details of this process of formation are still ongoing. But the movement of the alphabet southward into Arabia and North Africa, northwest into Asia Minor, west through the islands of the Aegean and the Italian and Iberian peninsulas, east into the mountains of the Caucasus, and across the Indus valley into India and Southeast Asia is well mapped. Most modifications to the alphabet occurred slowly, but in other cases (usually later), deliberate interventions were made. For instance, in the fourth century, Mesrop Mashtots created the Armenian version of alphabetic script, and in the ninth century, St. Cyril designed the variant that bears his name. These scripts were built on the same template (keeping the sequence, names, and sound values, or "powers," of letters) as the earlier alphabet on which they were based, but the graphic characters were altered. The Vai syllabary and the Cherokee syllabary are independent inventions, both created in the early nineteenth century, but they drew on established principles of sound notation and were inspired by alphabetic principles. Changes in the form of individual letters, or the overall look of a script, are sometimes the result of adaptations to the requirements of specific languages, or to materials and tools. Ink, paper, metal, stone, clay, and papyrus all have qualities that support certain styles of mark making over others.

Despite the modifications the alphabet has undergone, the visual forms of the original script are still discernible in the shapes of many of the letters. The schematic forms of early alphabetic signs remain. With a persistent echo and on a daily basis, these forms connect us to our past across a span of nearly four thousand years. Even in those parts of the world that use character-based scripts, the alphabet plays a role in internet infrastructure and design. Alphanumeric notation is the basis of Unicode, the international standard controlling text display on our digital screens.

This project is fundamentally bibliographic in nature, tracking lineages of citation, copying, and transmission through which "the alphabet" is constructed as an idea. The question, What is the alphabet? is answered differently in various historical periods and intellectual frameworks as new evidence on which to produce an answer appears. The processes by which misconceptions come into being—like the one about the Greek alphabet with which this discussion opened—are part of that long history of knowledge production and transmission. Earlier versions of alphabet history include mythic tales and partial truths that attribute its origins to the finger of God, to the writing of the stars, to the Jews in their wanderings in the Sinai, to the Egyptian god Thoth, and to the Phoenicians. These examples of historical knowledge of alphabet origins are grounded in a combination of belief and available evidence, part of the intellectual legacy that contributes to present understanding.

Alphabet historiography offers a fascinating case study of the history of Western thought. It also provides insights into the way the materiality of knowledge production and transmission engenders intellectual conceptions. For instance, *textual descriptions* do not provide examples of the *visual forms* of alphabetic characters they describe. *Physical artifacts* and ancient inscriptions may not be immediately legible. Establishing the *lineage of objects* in relation to the historical past requires multiple archaeological methods. The properties of evidence shape the historical arguments.

Though the *history* of the alphabet can now be documented with some degree of accuracy, the *historiography* of the alphabet remains largely unknown. In many other fields, the canonical texts would be identified and studied, even if they are eclipsed. A student of Western philosophy certainly knows the works of Plato and Aristotle, Descartes, and Kant and other major references into the present. Similar lists could be compiled for astronomy, physics, history, and poetics. But who is familiar with Hrabanus Maurus, Johannes Trithemius, Teseo Ambrogio, Angelo Rocca, Thomas Astle, Edmund Fry, Charles Forster, Isaac Taylor, Frank Moore Cross, and Joseph Naveh—or has any idea of their writings on the alphabet? The authors just mentioned were crucial. Each copied and cited the works of others until the trends or beliefs in them were overshadowed by others, or put aside as obsolete. Some are still vital to debate. In this project, those intellectual traditions and frameworks of belief are identified and described explicitly—they are the foreground rather than the background of the story.

I began this study decades ago. In 1980, in my first semester as a graduate student at the University of California, Berkeley, I encountered Baron van Helmont's *Alphabeti vere naturalis Hebraici* (The natural Hebrew alphabet; 1667) on the open stacks in Doe Library. Bound in the original vellum, the book fit into the palm of my hand and exploded the limited horizons of my understanding. I had no idea what I was looking at or why the figures in the book depicted speech organs in a sliced view of a head wearing a crown of Chaldean and Hebrew letters. I did not know what Chaldean letters were. My search to understand this book—along with a host of others in proximity to it on those shelves—and the intellectual traditions of which it was a part has been a continuing line of my research ever since.

FIGURE I.1 Baron van Helmont, *Alphabeti vere naturalis Hebraici* (1667). Note the versions of the Hebrew letter *daleth* arranged in the crown, the shape of the organs of speech, and the letters in the framed area at the bottom. *From top left:* modern square Hebrew, its immediate precedents, a "lunette" version, and other variations. Public domain.

My earlier book *The Alphabetic Labyrinth: The Letters in History and Imagination*, published by Thames and Hudson in 1994, concentrated on visual and graphic expressions of the letters and the values projected onto them as images. *Alphabetic Labyrinth* described *what was known or assumed* about the letters as graphic forms at different points in time. But *Inventing the Alphabet* describes *how we know what we know* about this history. The difference between "what" and "how" is the difference between the study of things and the study of production of knowledge about those things.

Each chapter in this study is concerned with a particular technology of knowledge transmission (classical and biblical texts, medieval copying, compendia, antiquarian objects, tables, archaeological and paleographic methods). The chapters follow a chronological trajectory, though many of these approaches overlap and endure in the present. The interpretation of classical or biblical accounts of the alphabet's origins are not finished, nor are discussions of antiquarian artifacts or archaeological methods. Explanations of the past change over time, and yet in each moment, the explanation is bounded by a horizon of understanding specific to that moment.

These histories do not necessarily invalidate each other, nor are they strictly sequential. The historians of each period provide a complete and valid explanation of the past as they understood it. No attitude of superiority to scholars of the past—antiquarians, mystics, or forensic experts—makes sense. Current models of the past will also be superseded, as the limits of the knowledge on which they are based are exposed. Scholarship is always produced in historical relation to its methods. The alphabet, with its rich cultural history, is an ideal topic on which to explore the ways that historicity participates in the conception of objects of knowledge. The alphabet has been invented continually out of our historically defined and limited understanding. Archaeological methods, digital analytics, linguistic sophistication, and paleographic techniques appear to provide a complete idea of the alphabet and its origins, but later historians may see beyond the horizons of current methods and beliefs.

On a personal note, I want to acknowledge that had my graduate mentor, Bertrand Augst, not perceived and supported my work beginning in fall 1980, I might never have become a scholar. My beloved stepmother, Jane Drucker, provided crucial input by reading every chapter in this text in at least two versions, calling attention to the structure of argument and many details. Henry Rosen deserves recognition for his meticulous perseverance in obtaining images and permissions. To Susan Bielstein, profound appreciation for support across three decades and many projects, including this one.

ONE

When Did the Alphabet Become "Greek"?

The Old Testament account that describes writing as a Divine gift to Moses might seem the obvious starting point for historical reflection on knowledge of the alphabet. But, in fact, the earliest continuously transmitted text that mentions the alphabet was written by the Greek historian Herodotus in approximately 440 BCE. His passages come forward intact and have been cited continuously in alphabet studies, providing a touchstone for research even in the twenty-first century. Herodotus made clear that the Greeks did not invent the alphabet but received it as a gift from Cadmus and the Phoenicians. Precise details of where and exactly when the alphabet was transmitted to Greece and in what form are still matters of research. But the misconception that the alphabet is Greek was not based on any ancient writer's text. The claim was the result of cultural politics within twentieth-century classical studies where crucial questions were posed about the date at which the Greeks began to use the alphabet and the state of literacy in their culture at the time. These questions were used to differentiate the Greek alphabet from its Semitic sources. Examining the scholarship that draws on classical references from the fifth century to the present provides an answer to the question of *when* the alphabet came to be thought of as a Greek invention as well as *why*. Paying attention to the classical authors, Herodotus in particular, is the way to begin.

The alphabet is much older than Herodotus and arrived in Greece several hundred years earlier than his account, but the basic points in his description of the historical events he describes are not disputed. The key passage from Book V of *The Histories* is frequently presented in this short version (excerpted from the authoritative 1922 Loeb Classics translation):

> These Phoenicians who came with Cadmus . . . brought with them to Hellas, among many other kinds of learning, the alphabet, which had been unknown before this, I think, to the Greeks. As time went on the sound and the form of the letters were changed.
>
> At this time the Greeks who were settled around them were for the most part Ionians, and after being taught the letters by the Phoenicians, they used them with a few changes of form. In so doing, they gave to these characters the name of *Phoenician*. I have myself seen Cadmean writing in the temple of Ismenian Apollo at Boeotian Thebes engraved on certain tripods and for the most part looking like Ionian letters.[1]

Herodotus named writing and letters, called them to attention, recognized their importance, and established their borrowed pedigree in terms that remained in play for centuries to come. He described the exchange between the Phoenicians and the Ionians and then followed with testimony of his eyewitness observation of this "Cadmean writing" in a temple at "Boetian Thebes." The word used by Herodotus in the original Greek to describe writing was *grammata*, letters. The Latin word *alphabetum* had its earliest documented use centuries later, in the work of Tertullian, a second-to-third-century Roman Christian author from Carthage.[2] Greek grammarians used different terms for oral and written letters—*stoicheia* and *grammata* respectively—thus indicating they made a distinction between the sounds and their graphic inscription.[3]

Because it was a *text*, Herodotus's passage had certain limitations. Specifically, it could not *show* the script that was being discussed—it did not instantiate the particular Phoenician letters it referenced. Nor did it pin down the precise moment or place of this cultural exchange. "At this time" and "into Hellas" were vague terms even if Ionia and Boeotia are identifiable regions in Asia Minor and the Greek mainland respectively. Nonetheless, the date and location of nearly every ancient inscription found in the Greek islands or mainland has been assessed against this text in an attempt to pin down where and when the transmission took place. For instance, in the mid-twentieth century, the classical scholar Lilian Jeffery used Herodotus's references to organize research findings in her 1961 landmark study, *Local Scripts of Archaic Greece*.[4] Her empirical methods weighed evidence within the framework of the ancient texts to assess dates of early inscriptions.

Many details about the Greek reception and modification of the Phoenician alphabet are still debated—such as when the left to right direction of writing became standardized in Greece. While Herodotus and other classical authors described transmission of the alphabet as a complex process of cultural exchange, the accumulation of evidence—archaeological and artifactual—continually shifted the meaning of these ancient texts. To appreciate these arguments, their history needs to be traced, including discussions of the role of Egypt and the identity of the Phoenicians in the ancient world as they were gradually redefined in early modern scholarship from the seventeenth century onward.

HERODOTUS, THE LONGER TEXT

The more complete version of Herodotus, Book 5, 57–59, contains a preliminary passage with numerous specific references that are now obscure, as well as an additional sentence about materials:

> 57. Now the Gephyraean clan, of which were the slayers of Hipparchus, is said by themselves to have come at first from Eretria, but my own enquiry shows that they were some of the Phoenicians who came with Cadmus to the country now called Boeotia; and in that country the lands of Tanagra were allotted to them, where they settled. The Cadmeans having been first expelled thence by the Argives, these Gephyraeans were in turn expelled by the Boeotians and betook themselves to Athens. The Athenians received them as citizens of their own on set terms, debarring them from many practices not here deserving mention.[5]
>
> 58. . . . Thus also the Ionians have from ancient times called papyrus-sheets skins, because formerly for lack of papyrus they used the skins of sheep and goats; and even to this day there are many foreigners who write on such skins.[6]

The additional details in this passage expand references to the identity of people (the Gephyraeans, synonymous with Cadmeans or Phoenicians), place from which they came (Eretria), sites of contact (Boeotia, Tanagra, Athens), and writing support (papyrus and skins). These are all pertinent for gleaning historical information from the account.[7]

Ionia is located in Asia Minor, on the western coast of modern Turkey, while Boeotia, in central Greece, was the site of an ancient city named Thebes (far from its namesake in Egypt). Eretria was located close to Boeotia, across the gulf of Euboea. Archaeological finds support it as a site of trade and exchange, mainly among Greeks, in the eighth century BCE, but flourishing in the sixth century BCE. Herodotus uses the terms Cadmeans and Gephyraeans interchangeably and records that they were by turns expelled by the Argives and Boetians from their temporary settlements.[8] These statements do not answer questions about the original homeland of the Phoenicians, just that they were not Greek and had come from the East. Extensive Phoenician trade routes were well established by the ninth–eighth centuries BCE, as Herodotus would have known. The ancients understood their own identity within a myriad of cultural exchanges among shifting populations. But if Herodotus's geography was explicit, his timelines were vague. Herodotus telescoped events that occurred over centuries into a single narrative. Still, he was not confused about the source of the alphabet. The date of transmission is crucial to understanding the Greek contribution to alphabetic writing—and to the experience of literacy prior to its arrival—and later scholars have engaged systematically with archaeological research that was not available to Herodotus.

Early forms of writing had been created in the older Mycenaean and Minoan civilizations that preceded the emergence of classical Greece. The collapse of this well-developed Bronze Age Greek culture sometime after 1200 BCE is generally considered the endpoint for the use of its writing systems. Linear A seems to have appeared early in the second millennium BCE within the Minoan civilization and has never been fully deciphered. Linear B, derived from Linear A, was adopted by Greek-speaking people in Mycenae, perhaps as early as 1600 BCE.[9] Another Minoan writing system that consists of hieroglyphic signs, probably inspired through frequent contact with the Egyptians, has also never been deciphered. Minoan inscriptions have been found as far east as Ugarit, Cyprus, and the Syrian coast but not on the Greek mainland. As all these earlier writing systems ceased to be used by 1100 BCE, it seems unlikely they had any direct relationship with the development of later literacy in Greece. Any argument that a memory of literacy remained that facilitated adoption of the alphabet would be difficult to prove without physical or textual evidence—which is lacking for a period of at least three hundred years, possibly longer.[10]

The Phoenician alphabet became stabilized around 1050 BCE, but the earliest alphabetic inscriptions found in Greece date to several centuries later, raising questions about whether trade and context occurred in this interval but simply did not involve writing. The early Greek inscriptions, by contrast, should show signs of modification and transformation that fit the time gap for deviation from Phoenician models of the letters. Estimates on how much time would have been required for these changes factor into dating the inscriptions and characterizing the Greek culture in which these changes took place. A late adoption would signal that Greek culture advanced independently of Asiatic influence while an early one suggests a slower process in a less literate environment. The timing of adoption is thus linked to judgments about cultural development.

Though Herodotus remains the ancient authority most cited in alphabet history, other classical authors offered an array of observations that have also been repeated across the last two millennia. Most had very little additional evidence in the form of objects or inscriptions on which to base their opinions, but their texts served as references, passed through traditional historical sources. When archaeological and epigraphic methods began to focus on actual inscriptions, the ancient accounts provided a historical framework for evaluating such evidence. Without the classical texts, the modern revisions and discoveries would lack the resonance and richness of tradition. But nowhere in this intellectual lineage did any author claim the alphabet was a Greek invention until the nineteenth century, and that fact itself is significant.

THE CANON OF CLASSICAL TEXTS

The passages from classical authors on the origins of writing and the alphabet form a standard list. Once this bibliographic lineage became established in printed texts, the same citations appeared in published works from the sixteenth century to the present, even if the value given to them changed.[11] Later scholarship recycled texts from antiquity that were themselves filled with citations and paraphrase, such as writings by Josephus, Eusebius, Clement of Alexandria, and others who formed a reference corpus for historians.

This canonical lineage even persists in the work of a twentieth-century authority, Godfrey Driver. In his 1948 publication, *Semitic Writing from Pictograph to Alphabet*, Driver provided a succinct summary of these classical sources. Their discussions of the origins of writing locate it in Egypt and the Near East. Plato (writing more than half a century after Herodotus) "named an Egyptian called Theuth as the inventor of letters, and the Syrian Philo Byblius in the 1st century A.D. only repeated this legend. . . . Tacitus, too, was of this opinion."[12] These authors were concerned with *writing*, not specifically the alphabet (in spite of the occurrence of the word *letters*). Driver noted that the classical authors were divided on their allegiance to a Phoenician or Egyptian origin, though they carefully distinguished between the activities of invention and transmission of an already existing system. All were united in their conviction that the alphabet brought into Greece was invented in the Near East. For instance, the passage in Tacitus's *Annals*, Book II, written around 109 CE, read:

> The Egyptians, in their animal pictures, were the first people to represent thought by symbols: these, the earliest documents of human history, are visible to-day, impressed upon stone. They describe themselves also as the inventors of the alphabet from Egypt; they consider the Phoenicians, who were predominant at sea, imported the knowledge into Greece, and gained the credit of discovering what they had borrowed. For the tradition runs that it was Cadmus, arriving with a Phoenician fleet, who taught the art to the still uncivilized Greek peoples. Others relate that Cecrops of Athens (or Linus of Thebes) and, in the Trojan era, Palamedes of Argos, invented sixteen letters, the rest being added later by different authors, particularly Simonides.[13]

Very little in this account differs from the information in Herodotus, though Simonides and Palamedes, responsible for the additional letters added by the Greeks, were named. Tacitus correctly ascribed the derivation of the Roman alphabet from that of the Etruscans, who had been exposed to both Greek forms and, independently, to the original Phoenician sources. His remarks anticipated work by the nineteenth-century German scholar Adolf Kirchhoff, who mapped these developments.[14] Herodotus had written his *Histories* at a moment not long after the Latin alphabet had appeared. But Tacitus was part of a cosmopolitan Roman world and was writing more than five centuries later, with many additional historical accounts on which to draw. Tacitus could distinguish between the pedigree of the Greek and Roman descendants of Phoenician scripts, and his work showed that alphabetic writing had come to be understood as the outcome of a process of slow transformation and modification, not as the circulation of an unchanging system. His distinctions made evident that the Romans did not see themselves as descendants of the Greeks, nor were they indebted to them for their writing system, which was referred to as Punic (a variant of the word Phoenician).

Another classical source cited by Driver was a Greek historian who lived in the first century BCE: "Diodorus Siculus held that the Syrians were the inventors of the alphabet . . . and by Syrians he perhaps meant Assyrians in accordance with the statement of the elder Pliny."[15] The term Syria had been used by Herodotus. Some scholars believe he was using it to refer to central Turkey, but in the Roman period it designated a region closer to the one it now occupies in the Levant. In Book 5 of his *Natural History*, Pliny the Elder, a first-century Roman, repeated the story of the Phoenicians, and in Book 7 of his work, he amplified this account by saying that "the letters were 'found' by the Assyrians" and that Cadmus was the one who brought these letters to Greece.[16] Pliny repeated the standard account with some variation in (abundant) details: "During the Trojan war Palamedes added four letters and after him Simonides . . . invented four more. Aristotle held that the original ancient letters were eighteen in number and that Epicharmus, not Palamedes, added two, as per the testimony of Hermolaus Barbarus. In addition, the 1st century writer Critias, as well as Lucan, supported the idea of Phoenician invention. Furthermore, Suidas, a Greek lexicographer, and Photius, in the 9th century, were also supporters of this version, though the latter added a figure named 'Agenor' as its inventor."[17]

Pliny's version does not challenge Herodotus's but merely fleshes out details and adds more evidence. These are founding texts that form an account of history as a chain of citations. Driver also referred to the Jewish historian Eupolemus, who, "in the second century A.D., claimed Moses as the inventor of the alphabet, claiming to glorify his race."[18] By the Common Era, an expanded view of the origin of alphabetic writing added more references, each embellishing the story with more information about sources in the ancient Near East. But none disputed that the Greeks had received the alphabet as a gift.

To a twenty-first-century reader, many of the names beyond Herodotus, Plato, and Pliny are obscure. But to Western authors from the Renaissance onward, steeped as they were in the Greek and Latin classics, these writers are familiar. The same names and excerpts were mentioned and discussed in each work that touched on the topic of alphabet origins. Alphabet scholarship followed an established pattern, beginning with a discussion of the ancients who clearly saw the Greeks as recipients, not inventors, of the letters.

CITATION PATTERNS IN EARLY MODERN STUDIES

By the seventeenth century, scholarship on the history of writing had become extensive and the focus on origins had shifted squarely to the ancient Levant. The ambitious title of Claude Duret's 1613 book, *Le thrésor de l'histoire des langues de cest univers* (The treasure of the history of languages of this universe) gives a hint of its scope and claims.[19] Duret's work on the history of writing remained a much-cited source for other authorities in the centuries that followed. Duret cited Siculus to describe the confusion into which the origin of the letters had fallen on account of historical events: "The Egyptians assert that they were the first to invent letters, the paths of the stars, geometry, and other arts and sciences."[20] His paraphrase of Siculus continued, describing the time when "Aten, son of the Sun was in Egypt and taught Astrology to the Egyptians, and then Greece was ruined by the deluge, many thousands of men perished, and the memory of the letters was forgotten, which supports the argument that after many centuries had passed one guesses that Cadmus, son of Agenor, was the one who first introduced the letters to Greece, so that the Greeks, by common error and ignorance, imagine it was his invention."[21]

Attributions of the invention of writing were becoming more complex. In *De prima scribendi* (The first writing; 1617), another major authority of the same period, Hermannus Hugo, also cited Siculus to insist that the Greeks always praised Cadmus for this gift.[22] Some decades later, in 1662, Thomas Godwin, author of a lengthy study of Roman history that went into more than a dozen editions, cited the usual witnesses, such as Pliny and Diodorus Siculus. But Godwin introduced another authority, an ancient sixth-century BCE Etruscan king, Servius, whose careful statements contained considerable wisdom: "Writing in no nation came to its perfection on a sudden, but by degrees. The opinions of the ancients concerning the Authors and inventors of letters are different."[23] Godwin's list went on: "Some say Cadmus brought them into Greece, others say Palamedes. . . . Some say Rhadamanthus brought them into Assyria, Memnon into Aegypt, Hercules into Phrygia, Carmenta into Latium. Some say the Phoenicians had first knowledge and use of the letters."[24] Godwin's statements further complicated the history by distributing credit to multiple individuals across a wide geographic area. Godwin included another frequently cited text from the *Pharsalia* of the poet Lucan:[25]

Phoenicians first (if story be believed)
Dared to record in characters; for yet
Papyrus was not fashioned, and the priests
Of Memphis, carving symbols upon walls
Of mystic sense (in shape of beast or fowl)
Preserved the secrets of their magic art.[26]

Lucan's verse also reappeared with regularity, attributing priority for characters to the Phoenicians and for symbolic signs and monumental writing to the Egyptians. Though authors cite the same list of classical authorities in the multitude of volumes that touch on alphabet history from the sixteenth through nineteenth centuries, not all were in agreement about the origins of letters—or the identity of the Phoenicians.[27] Guillaume Postel, the sixteenth-century Cabalist, asserted that the Greeks got the letters from the Hebrews, who were the same as the Phoenicians. Postel drew on many classical authorities, including Pliny the Elder and Eusebius, in support of his argument that the letters were Chaldean.[28] This term is used to describe Paleo-Hebrew, on the basis of the letter names, which had no sense in Greek (where *aleph* became *alpha*, *beth* became *beta* and so on). The regular reference to Herodotus and other classical authors demonstrated unquestioned confidence in textual evidence. The modern scholars believed the ancients, even when they contradicted each other or were at odds with biblical passages.

These citations create elaborate lineages and demonstrate the entangled conditions of scholarship in alphabet studies in the early modern period, such as a work by the esteemed English antiquarian John Jackson. His text, *Chronological Antiquities* (1772), became an essential reference for anyone writing about ancient history in English in the century after its publication.[29] Jackson aligned the Phoenicians and Egyptians with the race of Ham, an attribution for African peoples linked to the mythic distribution of the earth among the sons of Noah following the Flood (Japhet and Shem took the other portions). For readers of Jackson's *Antiquities* this terminology "the race of Ham" would have been fully legible. The ancients, Jackson noted, ascribed writing to Hermes, Thoth, or Taaut, thus giving the Egyptian origin its due. Jackson conflated the identities of Hermes and Thoth despite the difference in their Greek and Egyptian names, an accepted interpretation of these mythic figures. But he also cited an author named Sanconiatho, a Phoenician historian reputed to have lived in the time of Solomon. Sanconiatho's texts were preserved only through fragments cited in the work of the third-to-fourth-century figure Eusebius, who noted that Philo of Byblos had translated his works out of the Phoenician language. Jackson further shored up Sanconiatho's reputation by noting that the third-century Neoplatonist philosopher Porphyry (also a Phoenician) had said that Sanconiatho got the information for his ancient history from "the public Registers of Cities, partly from the sacred records of the Temples,

[and] lived in the Reign of Semiramis, Queen of Assyria, who reigned before or about the Time of the Trojan War."[30]

This series of associations is highly elaborate. Jackson's readers were expected to be familiar with ancient history, and to know these references. But the citations also demonstrate the extent to which the Phoenician origin of writing had been tracked back into the Near East, to the cities of Tyre and Sidon and the older history of the Assyrian Empire—which Semiramis was reputed to have ruled in the ninth century BCE. This level of detail was standard practice in the scholarship of the early modern period and similarly entangled passages could be taken from many authors beginning with the seventeenth century.[31] A major goal of antiquarians like Jackson was to sort out the relationship between the "sacred" (i.e., biblical) and "profane" (i.e., classical) accounts of ancient history, and the interweaving of classical texts with biblical passages was in the service of reconciling these textual traditions.

These examples demonstrate the persistence of standard classical references within the lineage of alphabet studies. But while each of the figures mentioned by earlier authorities—Pliny, Diodorus, Tacitus, Lucan, Sanconiatho, and so on—continues to be acknowledged even in the present, the author whose work commanded greatest attention was still Herodotus.

HERODOTUS AMONG THE ANTIQUARIANS

No subsequent writer has doubted the authority or dependability of Herodotus's text—and that it recorded some version of actual events, whether presented in mythic guise or not. The textual lineage of Herodotus's *Histories* is well documented, and a fairly stable version of the work can be tracked to manuscript fragments from the tenth century.[32] Across 2,500 years, Herodotus's tale was passed from generation to generation, as intact and reliable as any passage in the Western corpus from antiquity. As noted, the passage made an appearance in nearly every account of the history of the alphabet produced into the Common Era and in printed sources from at least the sixteenth century into the present. The specific meaning of each bit of Herodotus's text has been studied extensively, even recently. These studies remain crucial in understanding the process through which the alphabet spread from the eastern part of the Mediterranean to become a global writing system. Herodotus has been cited in establishing historical fact but also perverted to support different arguments from those of its author—even used to support the idea of the alphabet as a Greek innovation.

By the seventeenth century, Herodotus's text began to be situated within multiple geographies and temporalities that were subject to discussion: Is the Thebes of Boeotia the same as the Thebes of Egypt, and what is the connection? Who are the Ionians? When did Kadmos (Cadmus) arrive? And how might this historical account match the biblical histories of Adam, Moses, the Decalogue, and the Deluge as milestones in an equally compelling set of references about writing and its origin, dissemination, and variation? The questions became complex and the evidence amplified.

Herodotus's passage said a great deal about the ways Greeks thought about themselves within cultural exchanges among various people whose identities were clearly distinct, even if many aspects of their history were obscure. When Plato, nearly a century later, ascribed the origins of writing (notably, not the alphabet) to the Egyptian god Thoth (Theuth), he introduced a more multifaceted concept of language development. Plato knew full well that writing was an import, like many other aspects of Greek culture, such as knowledge of astronomy, geometry, architecture, and timekeeping. The Greeks never thought of themselves as independent from influences and exchanges with other cultures in their world.

The status of alphabet studies in the seventeenth century can be discerned by turning to Edward Stillingfleet's *Origines sacrae* (Sacred origins; 1662), in which he conflated the invention of the alphabet with that of writing generally. However, he provided a rich inventory of the alphabet's variations among peoples, stating that it was

> deservedly called by Galileo, *admirandarum omnium inventionum humanarum signaculum*, the choicest of all humane inventions. And had we no other evidence for the great obscurity of ancient history, the great difference as to the first inventor of letters, would be a sufficient demonstration of it. For almost every Nation hath had a several Authors of them: The Jews derive them from Adam or Moses; the Egyptians attribute their invention to Thoyt or Mercury; the Grecians to Cadmus, the Phoenicians to Taautus, the Latins to Saturn, others to the Aethiopians: And lest the Pygmies should be without their enemies, some think they were found out *a gruum volatu*, from the manner of the flying of cranes. Thus it hath happened with most Nations, what was first among themselves, they thought to be the first in the world.[33]

With some wit, he added "that the Greeks, who had writing late, are most aggressive in claiming it as their own."[34] He then qualified this claim, "This we are certain of, the Grecians had not the use of letters among them till the time of Cadmus, the Phoenicians coming into Greece, whither he came to plant a Colony of Phoenicians there."[35] Stillingfleet provided an interesting interpretation of the standard passages. His understanding of the cultural exchanges of the ancient world was evident as he explained that the name Cadmus is from a Hebrew word meaning "the East." But also Stillingfleet understood the relative perception of historical time and commented on it, saying that you could not get a history of antiquity from the Greeks, since "they think something so modern in comparison as Cadmus coming into Greece is thought by them a matter of so great antiquity."[36] Stillingfleet's chronology was linked to Creation and biblical timelines, and he attempted correlations between the era of Cadmus's father, the sometimes-mentioned

Agenor, and the figures in the Old Testament. This commentary on Herodotus was, as always, premised on the idea that his text was accurate.

Typical for the seventeenth and eighteenth centuries, Stillingfleet cited other classical authorities in support of Herodotus, "Philostratus, Critias in Athenaeus, Zenodotus in Laertius, Timon Philasius in Sixtus Empiricus," in a display of erudition.[37] He then invoked the highly renowned modern scholar Joseph Scaliger, and in turn, that author's discussion of the "Ionick" letters, the full alphabet of which, twenty-four letters, was completed through the additions of Palamedes and Simonides (as per already cited passages). He also noted that the Greeks had agreed to adopt the Ionic alphabet as their official alphabet, an action taken in Athens in 403 BCE.[38] He decried the Greeks' "want of timely and early records to digest their own history."[39] Stillingfleet's modern canon in support of his arguments was not extensive, though again it was one held in common among other authors concerned with the same material such as Gerardus Vossius, Samuel Bochart, and Scaliger—figures often now forgotten but much cited at the time.[40]

A century later, Thomas Astle, who also made important contributions to antiquarian methods, made his own systematic survey of classical sources in his *The Origin and Progress of Writing as well Hieroglyphic as Elementary* (1784).[41] In addition to those authors discussed above, Astle included three that have not had much attention so far. The first was the above-mentioned Sanconiatho, a possibly mythic Phoenician historian, whose lost work is mainly preserved in a few fragments cited by Eusebius. The second was the Egyptian priest Manetho, whose third-century *History of Egypt* provided a much-used chronology. The third was Berosus, the third-century Babylonian author of *History of Chaldea*. Of Sanconiatho, Astle said that he "derived his first books of the Origin of Gods and Men, from writings ascribed to Taaut the first Hermes" and further "He [Taaut] invented letters . . . either in the reign of Uranus, or Cronus; and staid in Phoenicia with Cronus."[42] Astle drew on published authorities in an attempt at a comprehensive presentation of evidence, and his list of classical as well as modern authors was composed of familiar names.

While still engaged with classical texts, Astle, like Stillingfleet, wrestled to align biblical and classical chronology. Herodotus, though present, was not the only source. Astle expanded the discussion of the Phoenicians, suggesting that the country was composed not only of the maritime cities of Palestine (the term then in use for the region) but also of Judea and the country of the Canaanites and Hebrews. He invoked Herodotus to shore up the Semitic identity of the Phoenicians, "also designated the Hebrews or Jews, because according to him the Phoenicians were circumcised while the Tyriens, Sidonians, did not observe this custom."[43] He invoked multiple Roman authorities to support the standard Phoenician tale, noting that the Greeks got their "history of the gods from the Phoenicians and Egyptians" as well as their writing.[44] He took note of the differences between the version of human history recorded by Sanconiatho ("This author makes mankind live in Phoenicia") and by Moses, which "seems to be grounded upon a very different tradition belonging to the first ages."[45] The blurring and comparison of classical and biblical histories was conspicuously present, but he said that without doubt, the letters were invented "in Phenicia by TAAUT, who lived in the twelfth of thirteenth generation after Creation. This same Taaut is called Thoth by the Egyptians."[46] Writing and the alphabet were again conflated. The theory of Egyptian origins will return in various forms, but the letters and hieroglyphic writing were, of course, not the same.

In Astle's tightly woven text, Herodotus's statements fitted into a web of references and information. Like that of other antiquarians, Astle's pursuit of the "original" alphabet led him into examination of much evidence about Hebrew and its relation to other languages. But the account of the transmission to the Greeks was taken as a given. Astle considered the Greek-Phoenician exchange to have occurred long after the crucial moment of original invention and spoke of "the alphabet" transmitted by Cadmus without too much detail. Astle, a student of written forms, was astutely clear on another point he shared with Tacitus. Astle believed that the letters from which the Etruscan (and hence the Roman) alphabet were derived came independently from an early common source from which the Greek, then Gothic, Coptic, Russian, Illyrian, and so on emerged as another branch. These latter he correctly believed were all descended from the Ionic script, the eastern variety of Phoenician. Another century would pass before the fuller understanding of the differences among the archaic variants of the Greek alphabet could be dated with physical evidence provided by inscriptions, but the assumptions made by Astle were in large part correct and demonstrated increased understanding of the multiple phases of Greek and Italian developments in alphabetic letterforms.

Though published just sixty years after Astle's major work, P. Austin Nuttall's *A Classical and Archaeological Dictionary in the Manners, Customs, Laws, Institutions, Arts etc. of the Celebrated Nations of Antiquity and of the Middle Ages* belonged to a completely different intellectual era.[47] This 1840 study offered a contrast in scholarly method and tone and showed how rapidly the lineage of alphabet bibliography became codified. The antiquarian frameworks were still present in the familiar list of authoritative sources for the work: Sanconiatho, Berosus, Manetho, Homer, Herodotus, Diodorus, Strabo, Xenophon, Pliny, and Josephus, alongside Godwin and Astle, in a thicket of others. But Nuttall had moved out of mythology and biblical chronologies. He organized his entry on Phoenicia within a modern timeline. In his assessment, the Phoenicians were involved in major trafficking by sea from about 2000 BCE, and he put a precise date of about 1493 BCE on Cadmus's emigration to Boeotia where he "introduces the Phoenician letters into Greece; founds Thebes."[48] Again, the details of Cadmus's role were taken straight from Herodotus but now with modern calendar and timekeeping. Nuttall's dates were too early, and have been modified by later historians. But the tale told by Herodotus persisted with admirable stability until questions about the identities of the Greeks and the Phoenicians began to arise.

IDENTITY POLITICS

Into the nineteenth century, no writer had questioned the cultural identity of the Phoenicians. Their language and writing were related to Hebrew, as were their customs, which seemed to make sense given their geographic proximity to the Jews (whose emergence as a distinct group is sometimes placed as early as the fifteenth century BCE at the time assumed for Abraham's covenant with God, the founding instance of the Jewish religion). The Phoenicians were Semites. They did not practice Judaism, but their language and script were indeed aligned with that of other Semitic speakers of the region. In the nineteenth century, new reflections on the identity of the Greeks began to surface, with a distinction made between the ancient Helladic inhabitants of the Greek mainland and islands, and the later Greeks.

In 1852, the British writer Edward Pococke published a book titled *India in Greece*. In this tract, he argued for a direct connection to an Indo-European past of the Hellenes. Pococke was extending the work of philologists, particularly Franz Bopp, whose work on Sanskrit had helped establish a common root for Indo-European languages. This development had radically altered the view of European languages and also (correctly) distinguished them from the Afro-Asiastic languages of the ancient Near East. The alphabet may have been brought by Semitic-speaking Phoenicians, but it was adopted by Greeks whose language was fundamentally Indo-European. The origins of the Greek culture were encoded in its language, Pococke argued, and in place-names, evidence that they had arrived through early migrations from India, across Iran and Asia Minor. Pococke was particularly focused on the term Pelasgian, as the designation for the earliest settlers of Hellas—a term he claims was inherited from Sanskrit *before* the Greek language was in existence.[49] Pococke's etymologies were used to connect the mythology and identity of the Pelasgians to the imagery and culture of ancient India (as the source for wheeled chariots, for instance). He believed the evidence of this could be found by linking the meaning of ancient place-names to their Sanskrit roots.[50]

Pococke's work inscribed a racial identity onto the Hellenes as a people. By giving the Greeks an Indian origin for their culture and language, Pococke created distinctions that would not have occurred to Herodotus. The fifth-century historian had used the term Ionian within his own context where it designated one of the groups of Greek people, the Hellenes who lived in the eastern mainland and islands near Turkey, while the term Pelasgic was used to refer to the people who had inhabited the Greek region before them.[51] Pelasgic is generally taken to mean "sea people" and to describe a wide range of groups in the Mediterranean. Pococke's ideas are related to a theory of a fierce chariot-driving Asian steppe people, the Yamnaya, as third millennium BCE invaders into Europe sometimes used to justify the "Aryan" origins of Greece.

EVIDENCE OF EARLY GREEK INSCRIPTIONS

Advances in Greek and Phoenician paleography gradually made it possible to address more precisely when and where the legendary Cadmus might have arrived in Greece and what specific version of alphabetic script might have been transferred to its inhabitants. By the nineteenth century, the combination of physical evidence and systematic scholarship allowed Herodotus's narrative to be examined analytically.

When Hugh James Rose had published his *Inscriptiones Graecae vetustissimae* (The oldest Greek inscriptions) in 1825, he had had fewer than a hundred examples to draw from.[52] Almost sixty years later, in 1883, the outstanding British scholar of the alphabet Isaac Taylor published a comprehensive two-volume work that drew on the plentiful work of the "great German epigraphers: Bockh, Franz, Mommsen, and Kirchhoff."[53] Acknowledging the slowness of British scholars in catching up in the field, Taylor praised German scholarship, saying that it could now "determine the approximate date and place and origin of inscriptions."[54] Taylor began by noting the agreement among the "unanimous tradition of classical writers" about the Phoenician source of the Greek alphabet. But then he expanded on the usual story, suggesting that Cadmus had gone first to Thera, which was inhabited by Carians, who were Greeks originally from southwest Anatolia. Cadmus left a colony on that island but then went with the rest of his mariners to Thasos and Boeotia where they taught the Hellenes writing. Taylor believed that Thera contained the "most ancient of all existing monuments of Greek epigraphy," while the colony at Boeotia, in the cities of Thebes and Corinth, he dated to about the twelfth century BCE, before the Trojan War.[55] These dates would have coincided with the composition of the epics of Homer (between the twelfth and eighth centuries BCE), but they are no longer accepted. The earliest inscriptions on Thera are now dated to the seventh and sixth centuries BCE with others on the Greek mainland at about 750 BCE.[56] The close formal resemblance to Phoenician letterforms from the previous century is marked and matches estimates of the time required for modification from one script to the other.[57]

Taylor drew on larger historical understandings for this timing, suggesting that the establishment of Phoenician colonies had been prompted in part by a flood of refugees from the collapsing Hittite empire coming into their coastal cities sometime in the twelfth century BCE. Phoenician presence in the Greek islands and mainland did not last more than about two hundred years, by Taylor's account, and they left the areas in which they had settled by about the tenth century BCE. Other scholars have put forth the possibility that Phoenician contact may have begun in the tenth century BCE, familiarizing the Greeks with ideas of alphabetic writing. But no conclusive evidence for sustained early contact necessary for transmission has been found.

The process of modifying the original Phoenician letters into the Greek alphabet would, in Taylor's opinion, have required two to three centuries at minimum and could have lasted as long as four or five. Taylor referenced the remarkable Egyptian monument, Abu Simbel, well up the Nile, which carried "memorials written in many alphabets by countless travelers of all ages who have visited this spot."[58] Among these were Greek inscriptions left by soldiers working for an Egyptian king, Psammetichus, and written sometime before the seventh century BCE. If common soldiers could write a message and scratch their names and dates of visiting the site, this implied that alphabetic writing was widespread across the Greek population by this time, not a novelty. The alphabet of these inscriptions contained the letters of modern Greek—including six vowels, and three new letters unknown in Semitic systems, written in a direction from left to right. Taylor drew on highly specialized scholarly publications that documented the development of the Greek alphabetic well beyond the mythic versions of classical accounts. The "when" of transmission was increasingly refined by this new evidence and scholarship.

Another still-cited authority of the nineteenth century was the German classicist Adolf Kirchhoff. In his 1867 publication, Kirchhoff mapped the different scripts of archaic Greece in a system still referenced by the colors he used to refer to certain geographic areas: red (Western), blue (Eastern), and green (the islands). He used these to distinguish those inscriptions that were closer to Phoenician and had no supplemental letters from those that had advanced toward the full Greek alphabet.[59] Kirchhoff's maps of multiple points of contact and transmission, and a relatively early time frame, still left a gap between the earlier Mycenaean and Minoan writing systems and those of alphabetic script. Kirchhoff's work did not address the question of whether the Greeks "remembered" the lessons of literacy from the Mycenaean period. When Taylor drew on the work of Kirchhoff, he took up his division of the Eastern and Western forms of Greek script and described with even more granularity the arrival of letters into Greece through multiple routes. The marked distinction between these Eastern and Western branches of Greek is detectable through certain letters (the lambda, for instance, is conspicuously different), suggesting two different sources of transmission. The Boeotians of central Greece, mentioned by Herodotus, seemed indeed to have obtained their letters from Tyronian or Sidonian traders while the Greeks to the east, in Ionia, in Asia Minor, had received theirs from the nearby Semitic tribes in Lycia and Cilicia during and after the sixth century BCE. Taylor made a close study of inscriptions and authoritative sources to propose that the trade routes through which systems of weights and measures had come from two different Babylonian traditions might be similar to those for transmission of the alphabet. Taylor and Kirchhoff suggested that Semitic culture had reached Greece by two separate channels—by land from Asia Minor and by sea to the islands and mainland.[60] Both routes had brought alphabetic scripts derived recently enough from a common source to share formal characteristics and structure.

Herodotus's account was not disproved by this discussion, merely extended and modified. The dating of inscriptions in these various regions also supported the Cadmean legend, since Boeotia was still regarded as the place where the alphabet had taken hold in Greece, even though no ancient inscriptions had been found there at the time that Taylor was writing. Taylor emphasized that the Ionian inscriptions, from which the alphabet was ultimately adopted in Athens, showed "an orderly sequence of chronological developments to standard Greek" while "non-Ionian inscriptions find no place in any such sequence. They evidently belong to a separate alphabetic type, in many respects the more archaic of the two, and which, though displaced in Hellas, survived in the alphabet of Italy, and thus became the parent of the existing alphabets of Western Europe."[61] Taylor ended with a description of three phases of adoption of the Phoenician alphabet by the Greeks. In the first phase, the script forms were very close to the Phoenician or Cadmean originals; in the second, a proliferation of local scripts prevailed.[62] But by the third phase, the prototypes of the two "classical alphabets of Europe" had become distinct—one that led to the Etruscan, Umbrian, Oscan, and Roman scripts of Western Europe, and the other, the Ionian, that gave rise to the scripts of the East—Romaic, Coptic, Slavonic, and so on (again, an observation already recorded by Tacitus in the first century). Taylor characterized the first phase of encounter as one between the commercial traders and the "semi-barbarous Greeks."[63] In the process of exchange, the Greeks became alphabetized.

Taylor's observations were further complicated by reflections on whether an illiterate culture could adopt an alphabet, a theme that persists in current discussions. The conceptual development required to grasp the connection between sound and sign depended on an analytic understanding of the sounds that constitute speech. As already mentioned, literacy had developed in Mycenae with the formation of Linear B around 1400 BCE, but knowledge and use of that writing system had disappeared with the collapse two hundred years later. In the intervening centuries, the Greeks on Crete and in the southern part of the Greek mainland who had made use of these syllabic scripts had apparently lost their knowledge of literacy. Again, no consistent records from the centuries before the appearance of Phoenician-inspired inscriptions from the seventh or eighth century have been found to substantiate an earlier transfer.

With Taylor's conspicuously modern, empirically grounded, and authoritative contribution in place, the study of Greek (and Semitic and other) alphabets was on firm ground. Taylor did not identify "the alphabet" as "Greek," but described the process of transmission and modification through which the Greeks had received and adapted the Phoenician script. This would appear to be the end of the matter, but other agendas arose with regard to the characterization of the Greek adoption of the alphabet.

MODERN STUDY OF ARCHAIC GREEK SCRIPTS

When the distinguished twentieth-century classicist Lilian Jeffery published her monumental study, *Local Scripts of Archaic Greece*, in 1961, she dedicated much of her first chapter to addressing Herodotus's text, even though it had been written two and a half millennia earlier. She noted that among the classical authors, "only Herodotus stands the test of time."[64] His text provided the intellectual scaffolding within which Jeffery's exhaustive scholarly study of all known ancient Greek inscriptions was framed. Jeffery wanted her exhaustive analysis of inscriptions from the eighth through early fifth centuries BCE to be correlated with his account. The evidence of the inscriptions and the historian's text had different kinds of authority, but neither could be discounted in trying to determine where and when the Greeks adopted the letterforms they transformed into their alphabet.

Jeffery was a paleographer and historian, not a literary scholar. She attended to the words of Herodotus for their historical information. Like Kirchhoff and Taylor, she had paid careful attention to geography to establish the chronology of transmission through paleographic, textual, and historical evidence. Time, place, and the form of inscriptions were all crucial.

Jeffery classified the physical evidence of characters scratched into pottery shards, stone, and metal surfaces, trying to work out where and when the Phoenician-based alphabet had come to be part of Greek culture. Many questions had to be answered to solve these quandaries. The alphabet was developed to record a Semitic language with a consonant-based sound system. As an Indo-European language, Greek requires explicit vowel notation for clarity. But Jeffery noted that vowel notation was a weak point of argument for making hard distinctions between Phoenician and Greek alphabets. Certain letters (notably the *waw* and *yod*) were sometimes given vocalic values in Semitic languages.[65] In addition, the changes in the original Phoenician letters and the emergence of local variations needed to be accounted for in terms of time from adoption. Changes in the direction of writing and individual letterforms had to be explained as well.

For Jeffery, as for Taylor and others before her, the pressing question was how an illiterate Greek culture could make use of a new technology without some prior understanding. The gap of time (at least three centuries) between the Mycenaean collapse in the twelfth–eleventh century BCE and the adoption of Phoenician letters in the seventh had always posed a problem. The conditions for cultural exchange between a literate and nonliterate people needed to be sustained long enough for the idea of writing and its practice to take hold and for the alphabet to be taken up in Greek communities. The contact could not have been casual and ephemeral; it had to be persistent. A bilingual settlement would have provided ideal conditions for this transfer, one that was not a mere trading site but a place of continuous cohabitation.[66]

In discussing Herodotus's assertion that a Phoenician dynasty existed in Thebes, she countered with a frustrating admission that no traces of Phoenician occupation had been found there, even though the palace was named for Kadmos. Thebes, she said, focused on inland trade, not outside, and contact with the Phoenicians would have been limited. Herodotus's account started to break down under the weight of evidence and her analysis. Jeffery combined analysis of linguistic, archaeological or geographic, and paleographic evidence to test the passage from Herodotus but also assessed her evidence against it.

In her search to find a location with geographic position and cultural conditions that could have fostered the alphabet's transmission, she shifted attention to other possibilities. She considered the Doric islands of Crete, Thera, and Melos. She concluded, also in keeping with Kirchhoff, that the inscriptions found there were closer to North Semitic originals than any of the other local scripts. Though ivories found in Crete made a direct connection with Syria through trade, the island was an unlikely site of transmission by virtue of lack of sustained Phoenician settlement. Rhodes had been described by Diodorus as a "Settlement of Kadmos's followers."[67] But the island did not have physical evidence of a settlement. Over and over, Jeffery weighed the literary and historical information against the archaeological, seeking a match between what the physical evidence suggested about development and what the classical texts reported. Her resolution of this dilemma came in a surprising form, with the idea that a Greek settlement on the Phoenician coast may have been the site of transmission. She then identified Al Mina in Syria as the possible site. Transferring the location of cultural exchange to Greeks in the Levant was a radical move. This solution left open the question of how transmission to the Iberian peninsula, Italy, North Africa, and other sites around the Mediterranean were to be integrated into the model of exchange, since they, like Greece, were sites of similar absorption and modification. But the idea that the transmission of the alphabet originated in a place that had a bilingual community was a powerful argument.

Jeffery was against an early date of transmission, stating that if "writing were known in Greece from the early eighth century or earlier, it is extraordinary . . . that the practical instinct for marking should have lain dormant for so long."[68] If the Greeks had had the alphabet, wouldn't they have used it? Ultimately, Jeffery's training as an epigrapher played a key role in her assessment: "Where general similarity seems greatest, there the date of introduction is set."[69] In her opinion, careful comparison of letterforms between archaic North Semitic and the earliest extant Greek provided the only solid foundation for dating. Therefore, her conclusion was that Greeks in a colony on the Syrio-Phoenician coast in the middle of the eighth century provided the source site.

Her evidence and arguments did not coincide exactly with those of Kirchhoff or Taylor, each of whom suggested multiple points of contact and transmission and a more gradual, localized process of modification throughout Greek territories. Herodotus's account guided her discussion even as she came to conclusions that undermined some specific features of his version. Jeffery wanted to reconcile the evidence of physical artifacts with considerations of the necessary cultural conditions and contexts of exchange.

THE EGYPTIAN HYPOTHESIS

While Herodotus's text was the crucial account of cultural transmission of the alphabet, Plato's assertion that the Egyptians were the inventors of writing remained highly influential. The international exchanges on which Greek culture were based were apparent to the ancient philosopher, as well as to later scholars. Among these was Athanasius Kircher, the seventeenth-century Jesuit polymath, who argued strongly for an Egyptian origin to the alphabet. The sophistication of hieroglyphics was evident in Renaissance Europe when ancient writing from the Near East was still virtually unknown (cuneiform was barely known until the late eighteenth century). Though vague in particulars, Plato's insights and Kircher's musings have been supported in part by later research and the Egyptian contribution factors into current theories, though not precisely as they imagined.

In the *Phaedrus*, written in the fifth century BCE, Plato attributed the invention of writing to the Egyptian god Thoth (Teuth) and acknowledged the role of Egypt in the formation of Greek culture. Though mythological in character, the Thoth reference contained a kernel of important evidence, as presented in a long passage from Champollion-Figeac, elder brother of the famous decipherer of the Rosetta stone:

> Plato, who had visited Egypt, places in the mouth of Socrates the following sentence: "I have learned that, in the environs of Naucratis, a city of Egypt, there was an ancient god, to whom the bird called the ibis was consecrated; his name was Theuth. He is said to have been the first inventor of figures and the science of calculation, of geometry, and of astronomy, and also of the game of chess, and of letters. Thamus was then king of all Egypt, and resided in the great city of Upper Egypt which the Greeks call the Egyptian Theses, the god of which was called Ammon. Theuth went to this king, and explained to him his discoveries, telling him that he must spread the knowledge of them among the Egyptians." Theuth has to explain to the king which of these inventions are useful and which are not. When he comes to the letters: "Great king," said he, "this science will render the wisdom of the Egyptians greater, and will give them a more faithful memory, it is a remedy against the difficulty of learning

and retaining knowledge." "Wise Theuth" replied the king, "some are more apt at discovering arts, and others at judging in what degree they may be useful or injurious. Thou, father of letters, hast allowed thyself to be blinded by thy inclination, till thou seeist them different to what they are. Those who learn them will leave to those strange characters the care of recalling to them all that they should rather have confided to memory, and they will themselves preserve no actual recollection of them. Thus, thou hast discovered not a means of memory, but only of reminiscence. Thou givest to thy disciplines the means of appearing wise without really being so; for they will read without the instruction of masters, and think themselves wise upon many things, when, in fact, they will be ignorant, and their intercourse will be insupportable." Plato says Theuth, or some divine man, separated the voice sounds into vowels, mixed, and mutes.[70]

Diodorus Siculus gave a similar account of the invention of writing and preserved the tradition current in his time that "Hermes (Thoth) was the first who fixed the precise articulation of the common language, and who gave names to great numbers of objects which previously had no fixed appellation, and who discovered the art of tracing letters."

Kircher enthusiastically supported the Egyptian version of the origins of the alphabet. Writing in the mid-seventeenth century, Kircher would have had little idea of the ancient civilizations of the Tigris-Euphrates valley, except from biblical sources, or of the long process of development that had contributed to the formation of the alphabet. But the age of Egyptian writing and culture (architecture, sculpture, painting, religion) eclipsed any other of which there was evidence. His interest in Egyptian language had manifested itself first in published form in 1636 with the *Prodromus Coptus* (Coptic forerunner).[71] Though Coptic script was a version of the Greek alphabet, the Coptic language was an ancient Egyptian member of the Afro-Asiatic family that included Semitic. We see here a reverse transmission. The Coptic derivative of Greek writing, modified from a Semitic original for an Indo-European tongue, was taken up for a non-Indo-European, Afro-Asiatic language. Kircher recognized that the Coptic language was ancient Egyptian but believed that its written signs showed commonality with Hebrew, Latin, and Greek script forms. In particular, he identified the hieroglyphic for *mu*, or water, as a possible origin for the letter *M*.[72] Citations of Kircher's opinions and contributions kept the Egyptian hypothesis alive as an explanation of alphabet development.

MAKING THE ALPHABET GREEK

In the early 1930s, a young American scholar, Milman Parry, broke new ground in classical studies with a thesis that suggested that Homer's epic poems could be analyzed in terms of distinctions between oral and written approaches to composition.[73] The thesis had an enormous impact on the study of Homeric verse but also became a touchstone for discussions of orality and literacy, classical language, and, by extension, the dating of transmission of the alphabet to Greece. Parry's career was brief. He died in an untimely accident, and his work was edited and published posthumously. But his arguments continued to be cited as foundational, and his basic findings about poetic structure were accepted as accurate.

Parry argued that Homeric verse had features that were designed to make the poems memorable in an era that did not have writing. He identified what he termed "formulae"—short units of sound and word patterns—which were repeated throughout the verses. The structure was quite different from that of later Greek composition, such as the essays of Plato, he argued, which had been composed in written form. In *The Cratylus*, Plato made the argument that writing would destroy memory, a point used by Parry to support his thesis. The techno-deterministic arguments in Plato's comments on writing were used and reused across millennia.

But Parry's work also opened a door to debates about literacy and orality. In support of his thesis, he pointed out that the term used for poet in Homeric verse is "singer." In search of a living tradition that embodied these oral traditions and features, Parry studied a community of southern Serbian poets. In the supposed similarity between the still-extant tradition of the Serbian epic oral verse and those of the ancient poet, Parry found his proof that the oral structure of the epics meant that they could have existed without writing. Parry therefore suggested a very late adoption of the alphabet into Greece, one that arrived in a highly developed literary culture.

The "barbaric" stage of Greek development was banished by Parry's thesis. The Greek alphabet was no longer an outcome of cultural exchanges—slow, localized transformations and multiple modifications—but instead a singular fully formed technology to serve an already sophisticated culture. The alphabet in this argument was characterized as an autonomous, intact, uncomplicated technology, a set of signs useful for a developed thought and language. To serve Parry's agenda, the alphabet that the Greeks developed had to be given a distinct and unique identity. It could not be seen as an offshoot of the Semitic scripts but instead understood as an *actual* alphabet rather than a *proto*-alphabet. The explicit notation of vowels, essential for an Indo-European language like Greek, became the defining feature of a fully distinct writing system in this argument.

The alphabet was thus made to fit into a conceptual paradigm rather than being considered as part of a longer cultural process. This rhetorical move allowed the Greek form of writing to be called "the alphabet" while Semitic sources were disparaged as incomplete formations. The distinction was founded on a mistaken assumption that Semitic alphabets were not based on the analysis and representation of the sounds of speech because they did not explicitly note vowels. But though the requirements for representing Greek and other Indo-European languages forced modifications, the structural principles on which a writing system represented sound did not change from the Semitic sources to the Greek adoption. Parry never provided an explanation for how the Greek version of the alphabet appeared in its fully modified form without transitional stages.

A CHANGE IN PHOENICIAN IDENTITY

Closer to the present, the conception of the identity and history of the Greek alphabet was distorted by scholarly beliefs that altered the standard interpretation of Herodotus's text. The racialized politics of this bear directly on the issue of "when" the alphabet became Greek.

Rhys Carpenter's influential article, "The Letters of Cadmus," contributed to the reinterpretation of Herodotus after it appeared in the *American Journal of Philology* in 1935. Carpenter began by suggesting that "Cadmus the Phoenician maybe belonged to mere legend or actual tradition" though he went on to say that "ancient literary testimony on Cadmus agrees fundamentally with this Herodotus version."[74] However, Carpenter was not content to stop with this observation. He reported on recent scholarship and findings, citing a Professor J. L. Myres who, in his Sather lectures titled "Who Were the Greeks," "calculated that Cadmus came to Thebes about 1400 BC."[75] Then he noted that an archaeological site dug by Antonios Keramopoullos in Cadmea, named for the legendary founder of Thebes, contained inscriptions that could not, in his opinion, be earlier than the sixth century. He described the late inscriptions as writing that "could have been legible to Herodotus," the fully modified Greek alphabet, far from the Phoenician prototypes.[76] Carpenter attempted to reconcile the disparate dates of this evidence by assigning an early arrival to the mythic Cadmus, ignoring the reality that the Phoenician alphabet was not even in stable form until the middle of the eleventh century BCE. Carpenter was (again) asserting that the Greeks had been "twice-literate." They had known Cretan linear script, well publicized through the work of Sir Arthur Evans, which belonged to the late Helladic period, 1400–1200, while the second period of literacy was considered to have begun in the second half of the eighth century. The novel aspect of Carpenter's argument was to suggest that it was this ancient Helladic writing, the Linear script of Crete, that Cadmus had imported (rather than Phoenician): "Since the locality is right, the environment is right, the date is right, why should we not accept the Greek folk-memory as a true tradition and, taking the Herodotean phrase, call this Helladic writing 'Cadmean letters'?"[77] The answer to that question was simple: Linear B had no relation in form or structure to the Semitic alphabet of the Phoenicians. But this did not stop Carpenter from making the argument.

He went on, stating that a second wave of literacy, also brought about by contact with Phoenicians, was a completely separate event. However, he said, "Herodotus combined them into a single effect for the good and sufficient reason that Cadmus was traditionally a Phoenician."[78] Carpenter argued that the study of the early writing, by which he meant the Linear B he was identifying as Helladic, "yielded nothing whatever to suggest any Semitic strain or influence."[79] While that is true, he extended this to assert that there were no Phoenician associations with Thebes, the site of exchange with Cadmus, which Carpenter also characterized as completely Helladic—that is, early Greek. Then he dismissed the entire Phoenician identification. "Why did the Greeks apply the name *Phoenician* to the Semitic inhabitants of the North Syrian coast-towns . . . ?" he asked.[80] He claimed that "they called themselves Sidonim" and did not even have a term "Phoinikes."[81] While the Phoenicians did identify themselves as Canaanites, Herodotus had used the former term.

Arguing that the "true Cadmean letters" were not the scripts of the seventh or sixth century BCE, Carpenter shifted the label, with its now modified Phoenician identity, back onto Linear B.[82] He went on: "Only in the sense, then, that Cadmus was a non-Semitic and non-Syrian Phoenician (which agrees with his genealogical connections, which are neither Syrian nor Semitic), were the Cadmean letters a 'Phoenician' script."[83]

By dismissing Cadmus from the late diffusion of writing and associating him with the early script, Carpenter essentially separated the earlier phase of original "Helladic" literacy on Greek territories and writing from the later adoption. The second wave was alphabetic but grafted onto an already fully literate culture. Furthermore, by placing the source of the Semitic alphabet away from the Greek mainland and islands and toward a site in Asia Minor or the Levant, the later transmission could be understood without cultural mixing. If the transfer of the alphabet were casual, if it had occurred through minimal contact rather than settlements on their own soil, then the racial purity of the Greeks could be preserved despite their acquisition of a foreign technology associated with Semitic people. All of this distorted the identity of Cadmus, who, by all other accounts, was a Semitic Phoenician who visited Greece in the seventh century BCE.

In his 1990 publication, *Cadmean Letters*, Martin Bernal sharply criticized the dating scheme in Carpenter's work as "scientific confidence and positivism in disciplines on the fringes of natural science."[84] Bernal built on substantial paleographic evidence to assess the dates of transmission and development. A late transmission date would suggest that the Greeks be characterized as a "superior" culture that developed independently, already literate when the alphabet arrived. An earlier transmission suggested their capacity for literacy emerged slowly and under influence from their neighbors to the east. The concept of a fully autonomous Greek culture became privileged in these debates, a notion that had not been present in Herodotus's time.[85]

Carpenter and Bernal were both dealing directly with the classical texts, with Herodotus in particular, and with the ways textual, or literary, transmission of knowledge could be distorted even as it served to preserve historical memory. But where Carpenter bent the historical facts in Herodotus's account, Bernal worked to demonstrate its accuracy.

CURRENT SCHOLARSHIP

Recent scholarship takes into account the details of Herodotus's description while adding new considerations based on language analysis, cultural study, and paleographic evidence. Given the differences between the Semitic languages from the Levant and the Indo-European tongues of Greece, Italy, Spain, and other European regions, the modifications of the alphabet made sense. Vowel notation, so often used as the way to make a hard break between earlier alphabets and the Greek, is not unknown in the notation systems that precede it. The analysis of language into sounds, and use of that analysis to assign values to marks so they could notate spoken language, was well advanced in the Near East. An Ugaritic syllabary, found in inscriptions at Ras Shamra, was the equivalent of writing alphabetic syllables in cuneiform. This could be compared with using Morse code or shorthand to write alphabetic letters. The understanding of language structure, fundamental to phonetic writing, was in place before Greeks adopted the alphabet. That was the intellectual breakthrough that made alphabetic notation possible, even when an alternative set of graphic signs is used to represent these features of speech.

In *Greek Writing from Knossos to Homer* (1997), Roger Woodard arrived at the conclusion that the transmission from the Phoenicians to the Greeks could not have happened earlier than about 1050 BCE. Like Jeffery, he argued that bilingualism would have been a prerequisite for transfer and that sustained cultural contact would have been required.[86] Woodard agreed with Jeffery that Al Mina on the Syria coast was a candidate that met all requisite criteria.

The notion that the alphabet was adopted for the purpose of writing down Homeric verse still has its advocates. For them, the alphabet of the Greeks is distinct, unique, and sufficiently differentiated from its original sources to justify constant reiteration of the idea that they "invented the alphabet" even though this argument falls apart under examination of historical evidence.[87]

Woodard also suggested that the adoption of the alphabet would have been facilitated if the Greeks were already literate. According to his argument, scribes were accustomed, at the very least in Cyprus, to spelling Greek with the syllabic Cypriot script.[88] The Cypriot syllabary remained in use until well into the eleventh century BCE, and thus the dates of its diminished use coincided with exposure to the stable form of the Phoenician alphabet. The argument that the benefits of the alphabet over the syllabary would have been sufficient to cause the one to replace the other is hard to prove, even if it is grounded in logic. Woodard, like other more recent scholars, was interested in a more subtle approach to the relationship of Greek and Phoenician, one that recognized the preexisting knowledge on which writing systems—syllabaries and alphabets—operated. The hard and fast division of a "full" writing system of vocalic notation and a "primitive" one consisting only of consonants did not hold in Woodard's view. He recognized that an understanding of the relation between writing and sound would have been necessary for the adoption of the alphabet, an argument for continuity and change rather than rupture and radical change.

These politics of alphabet history remain active, even though the conflation of language identities and racial ones is built on bias and ignorance. In a 2008 article, Lukasz Niesiolowski-Spano cited several authorities in support of the idea that the "Philistines," a non-Semitic Greek-speaking group, might be the conduit for the alphabet to Greece.[89] This argument's "starting point was the assertion that the mythological figure of Kadmos, to whom the process of alphabet transmission was attributed, need not be identified as the personalization of the Phoenicians, but could be seen as the symbol of a 'Greek-speaking' population from Levant, i.e. Philistines."[90] Indeed, evidence exists that these people settled on the Levantine coast after the Mycenaean collapse—but no inscriptions exist to attest to their use of an earlier writing system or to their role in its spread.

The fundamental fact of the transmission of the alphabet to the Greeks is clear. But questions of precisely when are not resolved. If it was as early as 1400–1200 BCE, then it took place before the Phoenician system was stable and left an unexplained gap in which no inscriptions appear for three to four hundred years. Transmission could have been as late as the eighth century BCE, in colonies in Asia Minor or northern Syria, or in contact fostered in Phoenician settlements in the Greek islands and mainland, though little archaeological evidence exists for the latter. The general consensus is for a later transmission in one or more locations of sustained cross-cultural contact, probably the settlements in Asia Minor or the Levant in the eighth–seventh centuries BCE and then to Greece by land and sea.

In a comprehensive 2018 article, Willemijn Waal summarized the archaeological, epigraphic, and linguistic evidence to arrive at a well-supported argument for a period of transmission that began in the eleventh century BCE. Waal's discussion is framed by the statement that in general the "Semitists overall tend to favour an earlier transmission date (11th–9th century) than the classicists."[91] Waal's discussion revisits these arguments, beginning with Carpenter's article, by examining discussions about letterforms and directions, the presence or absence of various characters within the alphabet, the location of inscriptions, and the correlation of alphabet and languages.

Waal also draws on the work of the Semiticist Joseph Naveh that compares the earliest Greek inscriptions with those of various stages of alphabetic development. Naveh's argument, as stated by Waal, is that there is "more resemblance between the Greek letter forms and the Proto-Canaanite inscriptions than the later cursive Phoenician writing."[92] This formal evidence supports an earlier transmission as does the variability of direction of Greek inscriptions (direction was standardized as right to left in Phoenician script by the eighth century), variations among individual letters, and use of word dividers (points or lines). Accounting for these features, as well as for other variations, leads Waal to conclude that the standardization of the Greek alphabet took several centuries and occurred across a distributed set of locations from the coast of Asia Minor through the Greek mainland and islands. In essence, Waal's argument counters the characterization offered by Carpenter that it would be "unthinkable" to imagine that the culturally advanced Greeks, as an "intensely active people," needed more than fifty years to take up and modify this "wonderful invention" as it spread "along the seaways of enlightened Hellenic thought."[93] Instead, Waal argues, these developments "are likely to have occurred in phases over the course of a substantial period of time, most likely several centuries, which would explain the regional diversity."[94]

CONCLUSION

"Since ancient Greek times, the peoples of Western culture have been . . . the children of alphabetic letters."[95] Published in 2016, this statement by Laurence DeLooze reiterates the ongoing mythology of the Western alphabet as a Greek invention. This misperception came late in the 2,500-year history of alphabet studies. Most scholars have remained convinced of the accuracy of Herodotus's text. Other classical authors make clear that the Greeks were well aware that the alphabet, like many other forms of knowledge and technology, was borrowed from other cultures. History remained largely a matter of textual information well into the seventeenth century. Herodotus and Plato, among others, were important because they provided records of earlier witnesses against which to corroborate new evidence. If Herodotus had done nothing more than to name writing—and as a consequence, make it into an object of attention and study—his contribution would have been significant. But multiple generations of commentary and reassessment make his words a vital touchstone. They serve as versions of history whose authenticity, though not to be taken literally in all details, is still useful. In the mixed attributions of origin to the Phoenicians as the source of the script that becomes the Greek alphabet, and the Egyptians as the cultural crucible within which writing arises, considerable recognition of the cultural mixing from which the alphabet sprang is recorded. The Afro-Asiatic roots of Western culture are well preserved in the classical authors, and the Greeks as well as the Romans were keenly aware of the richness of Egyptian and Asiatic precedent on which their own cultures were based. The urge to deny that history, which plays out repeatedly at intervals in the literature on the alphabet, will be taken up again in Chapter 9, where the most virulent denials of this past are couched in terms of erudition that barely masks their motivation: characterizations of literacy are used to establish a biased hierarchy of cultures.

Biblical texts pertaining to the origins of the alphabet were also repeated across centuries. Their authority is likewise respected and contested. The Greeks knew they were not the inventors of the alphabet, and to them its origin was a mystery. Godwin, cited above, makes this clear in his citation of a third-to-fourth-century text of Eusebius, "But upon better grounds it is thought, that Moses first taught the use of letters to the Jews, and that the Phoenicians learned them from the Jews, and the Grecians from the Phoenicians."[96] That is the next chapter in alphabet studies.

TWO

Divine Gifts

Original Letters, Moses, and the Tablets at Mount Sinai

The work of Herodotus and other classical authors prompted generations of scholars to assess when and where the alphabet had arrived in Greece. With equal persistence—but greater awe for the miraculous quality of the invention—passages from the Old Testament and work of biblical historians inspired other questions: What might the "original" letters on the Tablets given to Moses have been—Hebrew, Chaldean, or Samaritan? When Moses received the written Law, how could he read without instruction? And how could Adam's son Seth have inscribed the legacy of his father's wisdom on pillars of brick and stone so many generations before the Divine gift on Mount Sinai? Unlike the scholars in the classical traditions, those investigating these issues would not be able to resolve them by finding archaeological evidence. No amount of searching the rocks of the possible site of Mount Sinai is likely to unearth the evidence of tablets inscribed by the finger of God, even if many well-documented inscriptions play a role in sorting myth from historical reality. But questions of faith, belief, and textual authority pushed the quest for the "original of letters" into the present, along with research into other verifiable aspects of the biblical past in relation to alphabet studies.

The passages in Exodus describing God's gift to Moses on Mount Sinai are dramatic but sparsely narrated. Still, the nineteenth-century master

Gustave Doré mobilized his graphic skills to render the scene vividly, replete with lightning, wind, and an awed populace greeting Moses as he is about to smash the Tablets. If the Greeks understood the receipt of the alphabet in terms of cultural exchanges and peoples, the Jewish historians made a far more ambitious claim about its Divine origins. Miraculous and inspirational, this tale has its own textual lineage, as do other key passages about the alphabet in biblical tradition.

The passages in the Old Testament are repeatedly cited to explain the *origin* of the letters. Their influence continues in present efforts to reconcile historical fact and traditional accounts. The passages in Exodus were taken literally by many scholars into the nineteenth century (and at least figuratively by some into the present). Ultimately, their authority rests on grounds of faith. Either one believes in an actual Moses and a Divine gift or one does not. Still, the field of biblical archaeology (a phrase used to describe much of the site exploration done in the ancient Near East in the nineteenth and early twentieth centuries) contains many attempts to verify references in the Old Testament. Empirical research to locate the site of Moses's ascent and to identify the "original of letters" persists.[1] Secular and religious scholars have participated in the search to determine the historical foundations of the story of Exodus and other biblical tales.

Despite their differences, both the classical and biblical sources are *textual* methods of knowledge transmission and rely on passages much cited, repeated, retranslated, and subject to multiple interpretations. Each tradition conceives of the alphabet differently. The classical writers understood the alphabet as a *technology of notation* for the transcription of language. The biblical texts assert that because of their Divine origin the letters have great powers. The two concepts could not be more distinct. They provide radically different stories of the invention—and identity—of the alphabet. So, though the historical accuracy of classical authors was continually reassessed against textual and physical evidence, the biblical texts about the origin of writing were initially examined through logical arguments developed to refute or support these accounts.

The biblical passages were reframed as scholarly paradigms shifted. Initially taken as received texts, they were accepted without question in late antiquity and the medieval period. In the Renaissance, they were analyzed in the context of mystical traditions, particularly the Cabala as it becomes part of Christian scholarship. Somewhat later, they were put into relation to physical evidence by antiquarians looking for confirmation of the biblical past. By the eighteenth century, rational approaches to history and the experience recorded by travelers provided a geographically specific framework of examining inscriptions and linking them to biblical texts. This was then extended by archaeological, linguistic, and paleographic methods. As the scholarship commenting on the biblical tales developed, citation piled on citation until the sheer mass of its accumulated weight became overwhelming and the issues of what Moses knew or how the alphabet originated were

FIGURE 2.1 Gustave Doré, *The Holy Bible*. Illustration from Exodus showing Moses about to break the Tablets (London: Cassel, Petter, and Galpin, 1866). Public domain.

nearly lost in a thicket of references to ancient and modern authorities. Even in the present, some tensions arise from attempts to relate biblical accounts and archaeological evidence for the "original" letters.

THE CRUCIAL PASSAGES

The description of the gift of the Tablets to Moses by God occurs in a few brief passages of Chapters 19 and 24 of Exodus, taken here from an early twentieth-century English translation of the authoritative Masoretic text:

> Chapter 19: 5–6 "Now therefore, if ye will hearken unto My voice indeed, and keep My covenant, then you shall be Mine own treasure from among all peoples; for all the earth is Mine; 6 and yet shall be unto Me a kingdom of priests, and a holy nation."
>
> Chapter 19: 20 "And HaShem called Moses to the top of the mount; and Moses went up."
>
> Chapter 24: 4 "And Moses wrote all the words of HaShem, and rose up early in the morning, and builded an altar under the mount, and twelve pillars, according to the twelve tribes of Israel."
>
> Chapter 24: 7 And he took the book of the covenant and read in the hearing of the people;
>
> Chapter 24: 12 And HaShem said unto Moses: "Come up to Me in the mount and be there; and I will give thee the tables of stone, and the law and the commandment, which I have written, that thou mayest teach them."[2]

These verses made clear not only that the Law was written but also that Moses knew spontaneously how to read and write when so commanded by Divine authority. These passages focus on the Decalogue, the Ten Commandments inscribed on the stone tablets. However, within the historical tradition that derives from the first-century Roman-Jewish scholar Josephus Flavius, another story about the early use of writing also persists—that of Adam instructing his son Seth to make two "inscribed pillars" to preserve wisdom.[3] So powerful was the influence of Josephus that this story was treated as if it existed on biblical authority, even though it did not. Both texts were cited repeatedly, often within detailed chronologies that begin with the date of Creation. In later scholarship that reckoned with modern time frames, such chronologies were used to compare archaeological evidence and biblical accounts.

Much of the medieval and Renaissance rabbinic literature in which these passages were debated was produced within linguistically and culturally distinct communities, but when the late medieval development of the mystical tradition of the Kabbalah (Cabala is the generally accepted spelling for Christian scholarship in this field) emerged in twelfth-to-thirteenth-century Spain, the Jewish tradition crossed into the work of scholars writing in Latin. While Kabbalistic textual sources did not repeat the story of Moses, they contributed to debates about alphabet origins. Invoking the mystical tradition, in which the letters of the alphabet were considered Divine and endowed with powers, they brought its precepts into the broader discussion.[4] A separate study would be needed to address the interpretation of the story of Moses within the Hebrew rabbinic tradition, where the chief concern was with the nature of God and what it meant for the Jewish people to receive the founding gift of the Law.[5] But in the literature on the study of the alphabet, authors focused on whether the letters on the Decalogue were written in Hebrew and on the Kabbalistic vision of the alphabet's role in Creation.

BIBLICAL TEXTS AND EARLY HISTORIANS

The trail of debates about Moses usually begins with reference to a few sections in the work of the Hellenistic scholar named Eupolemus, considered the earliest Jewish historian, who probably lived in in the second century BCE. However, as is common in such lineages, Eupolemus's actual text does not survive. His discussions of Moses are preserved only as citations in the writings of the first-century BCE Greek scholar (and Roman slave) Alexander Polyhistor. Polyhistor is in turn mainly available through citations in Eusebius, the third-century CE writer whose work is also largely passed on through citation in other sources. For instance, the relevant text of Eupolemus is one of six fragments preserved by Polyhistor and then copied by Clement of Alexandria (d. 215 CE) and, a century later, by Eusebius (b. 260 CE). These multiple levels of embedded citations lead to rote repetition of certain statements and passages taken directly from the *Stromata* of Clement.[6] An excerpt reads: "And Eupolemus, in his book On the Kings in Judea, says that 'Moses was the first wise man, and the first that imparted grammar to the Jews, that the Phoenicians received it from the Jews, and the Greeks from the Phoenicians.'"[7] For Jewish historians and early Christian writers of antiquity, Moses was a historical figure, about whom specific facts were known that could be stated without qualification. Centuries later, the Divine gift was subject to other considerations. For instance, the medieval encyclopedist Isidore of Seville, in his comprehensive seventh-century *Etymologies*, included these analytic passages about the alphabet:

> The Latin and Greek letters seem to be derived from the Hebrew, for among the Hebrews the first letter is called "aleph," and then "alpha" was derived from it by the Greeks due to its similar pronunciation, whence A among Latin speakers. A transliterator fashioned the letter of one language from the similar sound of another language (i.e. derived the names and shapes of letters

> of similar sound from the "earlier" language); hence we can know that the Hebrew language is the mother of all languages and letters. But the Hebrews use twenty-two characters, following the twenty-two books of the Old Testament; the Greeks use twenty-four. Latin speakers, falling between these two languages, have twenty-three characters. The letters of the Hebrews started with the Law transmitted by Moses. Those of the Syrians and Chaldeans began with Abraham, so that they agree in the number of characters and in their sounds with the Hebrew letters and differ only in their shapes.[8]

Isidore did not question the role of Moses as source of the letters and transmitter of the Law, but his longer discussion of the letters included their names, number, and sound. He took into account the Syrians and Chaldeans and linked them to Abraham, a connection that made sense geographically.[9] Abraham had come from Chaldea to Canaan, from the lands of Mesopotamia to those of the Levant. Isidore had some knowledge of these areas, and of various forms of ancient writing, and though cuneiform would not have been known in his period, his references extended beyond Hebrew. Isidore's discussion of Moses was crucial since his *Etymologies* provided one of the most influential compendia of medieval knowledge.

JOSEPHUS AND THE SON OF ADAM

Aside from the biblical texts, the most cited of ancient Jewish authorities is the first-century Roman-Jewish scholar Flavius Josephus (37–100 CE). His work *Jewish Antiquities* provided a major source for knowledge of the Jewish people. Furthermore, his place in early modern scholarship was assured by the attention paid to him by the influential and highly renowned sixteenth-century scholar Joseph Scaliger. Scaliger's erudition and language skills expanded European views of history beyond the classical tradition to include the ancient cultures of Egypt and the Near East. He acquired knowledge of the Semitic languages—Hebrew, Arabic, Syrian, and Persian—in addition to Greek and Latin and thus became one of the main conduits for texts in these languages in a period when few scholars in Europe were acquainted with them.[10] Scaliger's major work, *Opus novum de emendatione temporum* (New work of the Amendment of Time; 1583), focused on the ways the reckoning of time had been done in antiquity, work that had a direct bearing on alphabet studies.[11]

Had Josephus hired a publicist to revive his career more than a millennium and a half after his death, he could not have found one better than Scaliger, who said bluntly: "Josephus is a highly truthful author in his history and indeed more reliable than any other author, and very faithful."[12] Scaliger's attestation to Josephus's credibility, and his citation of Josephus's work, assured that his passages describing Moses, the Decalogue, and the legendary account of Adam and the pillars of Seth were brought to the attention of modern scholars. Neither the Old Testament passage nor Josephus's paraphrases could be tested by archaeological remains. However potent they were as symbols, the pillars of Seth and the Tablets of Moses did not exist physically. Eventually, the paleographic inscriptions in the Sinai, as well as on routes that might have been followed on the passage from Egypt, were (and are) used in attempts to corroborate biblical accounts. But for many centuries, texts were the sole evidence for debating the identity of the Hebrew alphabet and its claim to being the "original" alphabet of humankind.

Many historians considered Josephus a biased witness—he had switched sides to ally with the Romans during the Jewish uprising in the first century CE, so his loyalties to Jewish identity were sometimes questioned. But rather than discuss the authenticity and reliability of Josephus's text, most authors cited him as the main source for certain legends, and these versions became part of the received tradition. For instance, discussion of the inscribed pillars appeared in a passage from Josephus just after he spoke of Seth as a man "of an excellent character."[13]

> That their inventions might not be lost before they were sufficiently known, upon Adam's prediction that the world was to be destroyed at one time by the force of *fire*, and at another time by the violence and quantity of *water*, they made two pillars: the one of brick, the other of stone: they inscribed their discoveries on them both: that in case the pillar of brick should be destroyed by the flood, the pillar of stone might remain, and exhibit those discoveries to mankind: and also inform them that there was another pillar of brick erected by them. Now this remains in the land of *Siriad* to this day.[14]

The searches for this pillar and the site of Siriad were accompanied by questions about the form of script in the inscriptions and how Seth might have been instructed in its use—since Adam lived almost sixteen centuries before Moses.[15] If, as the major biblical texts argued, Moses was the first to have writing, and in particular, Hebrew script, from God, then whatever Seth wrote had to be qualified in some way for the Bible to be consistent. Logical questions and chronological calculations were crucial to this analysis. But as the notion of mystical origins folded into the scholarship, the forms of the letters also came into the discussion. The universal belief in Hebrew as the original alphabet prevailed until the sixteenth century, when the rediscovery of Samaritan briefly introduced doubt by offering an alternative possibility. In addition, the gradual realization that square Hebrew was a relatively modern invention (from the second–first centuries BCE) raised questions about what letters might have been the "original" ones. Ideas about Hebrew drew on the Jewish tradition of Kabbalah, adding another dimension to the stories of Adam, Seth, Abraham, and Moses. In this mystical tradition of Jewish thought, the creation of the alphabet is a Divine act but also a cosmological one. It occurs independently from the story of Moses, whose receipt of the letters becomes a second act in the larger drama.

DIVINE CREATION IN KABBALAH / CABALA

In the classic, early text of Jewish Kabbalah, the *Sefer Yetzirah* (*Book of Creation*), the letters of the alphabet were given a major role in bringing the world into being. The date of composition of the *Book of Creation* remains unclear, though it is generally placed somewhere between the second century BCE and the first centuries of the Common Era on the basis of linguistic form and resemblance to Gnostic teachings. The book is linked to an unspecified "ancient" rabbinic lore and Jewish mysticism, but no early manuscripts exist.[16] The earliest reliable commentaries were in the tenth century, but in the twelfth–thirteenth centuries, it became a touchstone for mystical Jewish practices in Spain and then beyond. The work contained features of much older traditions, such as the division of the letters into "three classes of vowels, mutes, and sonants," a division that appeared in Hellenistic texts.[17] Traditionally the text was attributed to Abraham, but the habit of claiming great antiquity was a common trope to cloak the book in a mysterious past that gave it an aura of great authority. Magical practices of many kinds invoked angels, sigils (string letters), signs, and alphabetically related symbols that dated back to the early decades of the Common Era. Not all of these were derived directly from the Kabbalah or its texts, even if they became linked to its teachings.

The *Book of Creation* was concerned with the most important aspect of God's work—the making of the world out of nothing. Not surprisingly, therefore, it contained a key to many intricate patterns that aligned number symbolism with primary elements, in schemes of perfect order and revelation: "Ten are the numbers, as are the Sefirot, and twenty-two the letters [of the Hebrew alphabet], these are the Foundation of all things."[18] The text described ten categories—beginning with spirit, then air, water, fire, the depth and directions of the earth—that take on primal and mystical values. Among these, the second is air, in which the letters appear: "Air emanated from the spirit by which He formed and established twenty-two consonants, stamina. Three of them, however, are fundamental letters, or mothers, seven double and twelve simple consonants; hence the spirit is the first one."[19] This symbolism was both explanatory and revelatory, showing the alphabet as elemental and generative within a finely wrought scheme of Divine Creation. The desire to imbue the letters of the alphabet with Divine powers was central to Kabbalistic thought, which shared features of other mystical traditions from the Hellenistic world—including Pythagorean symbolism and Gnosticism that linked the Greek ideas of the letters to elaborate cosmic schemes. These systems of belief recognized—and attempted to reckon with—the profound power of the alphabet as a dynamic force.

The mystical tradition of the Kabbalah bequeathed two crucial concepts to the alphabet. The first was that the Hebrew letters were derived in the initial stages of God's creation of the world. The second was that they were evident in the constellations, an idea concretized in the sixteenth-century publications of Guillaume Postel's *De originibus seu de Hebraicae lingua* (On the origin of the Hebrew nation and tongue; 1538) and continued a century later by Jacques Gaffarel in *Curiositez inovyes sur la sculpture talismanique des Persans, horoscope des patriarches, et lecture des estoiles* (Unbelievable curiosities of talismanic sculpture of the Persians, the horoscope of the patriarchs, and the reading of the stars; 1650).[20] Their works on the origins of the Hebrew letters included a graphic celestial map (invented by Postel and copied a century later by Gaffarel), showing the direct derivation of the alphabet.[21] Showing that the letters were written in the stars confirmed their Divine status—the alphabet was literally the writing of God in the book of nature. Because the celestial script had been written by God, these characters were accepted without question. In the sixteenth and seventeenth centuries, Paleo-Hebrew and its forms were largely unknown, or perhaps these authors would have discerned *those* forms in the stars. The dates of the emergence of modern Hebrew letters and the composition of the early Kabbalistic texts may have been close in time, but the older Paleo-Hebrew letters had a much longer history that predated the mystical texts by centuries.

This concept of the alphabet as a Divine gift, one filled with potency, and the power of letters, had a surge of popularity among Christian Cabalistic writers in the Renaissance inspired by Pico della Mirandola and Johannes Reuchlin. Reuchlin's writings were a major conduit for knowledge of the Kabbalah into non-Hebrew-speaking European culture in the Renaissance. His *De arte Cabalistica* (Cabalistic art), published in 1530, remained among the most consistently referenced titles in the field, particularly for scholars reading and writing in Latin, until interest in mystical explanations of history waned in the early eighteenth century.[22] Occult and Jewish esoteric thought continued to have a focus on the alphabet, but notions of Divine origin in celestial configurations gradually became peripheral to alphabet studies.

For Christian scholars to engage with Jewish mysticism required mastery of Hebrew. Both Pico and Reuchlin were skilled Hebraists, as well as advocates for Hebrew scholarship. The bulk of Reuchlin's work addressed the possibility of conceiving of the existence of Christ within the *Book of Creation*, in particular by a transformation of the Tetragrammaton, the sacred name of God in Hebrew letters, by addition of a fifth letter.[23] The alphabet played a major role as a key to occult knowledge and mystical truth. Reuchlin's interest in Hebrew was religious and humanistic—he sought confirmation of faith as well as knowledge of traditions that linked Christian thought to the older history of Jewish sages. In 1500 "the number of Christians who knew Hebrew was infinitesimal" but by "1550, Hebrew instruction was available at every major university."[24] This transformation can be attributed in part to the efforts of Reuchlin, who is credited with the founding of many university chairs in Hebrew in the early sixteenth century. In 1511 he wrote a passionate defense of Jewish learning, *Recommendation Whether to Confiscate, Destroy and Burn All Jewish Books*, when a threat to burn Jewish texts was issued as an edict by Maximilian I.[25] His love for the language was suffused with mystical belief: "When reading Hebrew I seem to see God Himself speaking when I think that this is the language in which God and the angels have told their minds to man from on high. And so I tremble in dread and in terror, not, however, without some unspeakable joy."[26] The Jewish Kabbalah and Christian Cabala promoted mystical belief in the alphabet as a Divine creation.

One of the more original among the Christian scholars who took up Cabalistic thought was Baron van Helmont. Helmont pushed his quest for the "natural" letters, those closest to God, to a biological as well as an astronomical inquiry. In his book *Alphabeti vere naturalis Hebraici* (The natural Hebrew alphabet; 1667), he included images of Chaldean letters alongside Hebrew characters.[27] Helmont's goal was to show that the forms of letters were mirrored in the organs of speech, thus guaranteeing their "naturalness" on multiple levels—from the stars, the finger of God, the organs of the mouth, and sacred meaning and form intertwined. The aim of understanding the Bible in terms of the *natural* Hebrew alphabet was a key. If Hebrew was Divine, why wouldn't it be the pattern for all manner of things, and most of all, the Scriptures themselves and the embodied production of speech? Helmont felt that even the Jews had forgotten the value of the letters as the fundamental building blocks of the universe.[28] This was a core belief of the *Sefer Yetzirah*. Gottfried Leibniz, who strove in the seventeenth century to find a universal character, an alphabet of human thought, was a supporter of Helmont's and even ghostwrote a book for him on the topic.[29] The Christian Cabala had absorbed a conviction about the origin of writing that became part of the persistent lore of the alphabet as a Divine invention—but one in which Moses did not appear.

CITATIONS FROM ANCIENT TO EARLY MODERN

However, scholars continued to engage with the question of Moses's role. In late antiquity and the early Middle Ages, these speculations had been found in the works of Eusebius and Isidore of Seville. Both exerted considerable influence on Renaissance writers, who almost invariably supported the idea that Moses was the conduit through which the Hebrew letters had appeared. Among the most frequently cited are the fifteenth-century philosopher Pico della Mirandola, the sixteenth-century Hebraicist Abraham de Balmes, and the seventeenth-century historian Hermannus Hugo.[30] Pico's *Heptaplus*, published in 1489, was one of the first texts to bring Jewish Kabbalistic thought into Latin and to engage with its esoteric principles; in it the theory of Divine origins of the letters was combined with a study of Moses's initiation into wisdom.[31] Balmes, in his influential, philosophically oriented Hebrew grammar (1523), described the superiority and priority of Hebrew letters as the first alphabet.[32] Hugo avoided mention of Moses but still argued for Hebrew as the original script.

The question of how Moses could read (or write) the Tablets was particularly vexing to early modern writers who accepted the Bible as historical fact. One of the first English texts published on the topic of the alphabet was that of Alexander Top. In *The Olive Leafe* (1603), Top asserted the antiquity of the Hebrew letters with absolute authority, stating that "mine only endeavour shall be to calculate their birth day."[33] Top culled every commentary on the biblical texts that he could find in support of arguments about letters and writing, even including discussion of Cain, whom he said, was *marked* by God (in other words, written on with a sign). Top constructed logical arguments around these points, saying the "Lord's writing been vaine, if men could not read the Marke."[34] Top sifted analytically through the texts, figuring out when and how "these little Figures" had been wrought. As conclusive evidence of early Creation, Top observed that in the first week the works done by God numbered twenty-two and that the letters were produced in a "correspondent summe." Hebrew writing, Top went on to say, could not have been invented by humankind as it surpassed all other accomplishments (a sentiment that was echoed many times in the centuries ahead). Only "Almighty God, who would scarcely be thought at leisure to attend to little things" could have "vouchsafed to write or carve these forms most seriously with his owne finger."[35]

Hugo was a contemporary of Top's, and his 1617 text, *De prima scribendi*, was devoted entirely to writing's history.[36] Hugo assigned Hebrew primary place but also put forth the suggestion that the letters might be Adam's invention, and that *he* might have gotten them from God.[37] Hugo's sources were a combination of ancient and modern: Eusebius, Polydorus, Pliny, and Lucan among the former and a group of figures who feature largely in sixteenth-century texts on the topic of the alphabet among the latter: Guillaume Postel, Theodore Bibliander, Joseph Scaliger, and Angelo Rocca, librarian at the Vatican.[38] All were canonical figures in alphabet studies and appeared in Hugo's lists of authorities to support arguments about the specific letters of the original alphabet.

Bibliander's 1548 publication, *De ratione communi omnium linguarum & literarum commentarius* (On the general relation of all languages and letters), showcased his extensive linguistic knowledge through comparison of various ancient languages and their derivation of one from another. His extensive citations provided a useful inventory of scholarship on the topic. Citing the twelfth-century biblical scholar Moses Kimchi and Reuchlin, the groundbreaking Renaissance Hebraist and Cabalist, Bibliander asserted the priority of Hebrew as the original tongue. He also hedged his bets, asserting that the forms of the earliest alphabet were a matter of speculation. Herodotus was his source for discussing the four main dialects of Greek (Attick, Aeolicam, Doric, Ionic), but he tracked the development of a surprising number of languages—Egyptian, Aethiopic, Chaldean, Latin, Hebrew, Arabic, Armenian, Turkish, Persian, Lithuanian, Prussian, Tartar, Serbian, Dalmation, Etruscan, and Canaanite—the last of which he identified (correctly) with Hebrew. While biblical sources were cited throughout, Bibliander also drew on Pythagoras, Plato, and Cicero to support the "sidereal" origins of letters in the positions of the stars, reinforcing this concept with a non-Kabbalistic origin.[39] Rocca's *Bibliotheca Apostolica Vaticana* (The Vatican Apostolic Library; 1591), a compendium of exemplars from the Vatican Library, provided evidence in the form of an exhaustive bibliography supporting the statement that Moses had invented the oldest Hebrew letters. These were scholars for whom *textual authority* was *the only authority*, even as they were increasingly replete with graphic exemplars also passed directly from one source to another. Rocca, for instance, produced a remarkable table of scripts.

These many details demonstrate that questions of alphabet origins were a major preoccupation of the sixteenth and early seventeenth centuries. The state of scholarly practice in the period was exemplified in the way that citations became a tangle of abbreviations, quotes, excerpts, and intellectual shorthand. Works like those of Hugo or Bibliander were not written for a broad public, or with widespread audiences in mind, but rather as erudite studies of theological and intellectual questions. Sources are often referred to in abbreviation (e.g., "Eus. *Prae.*" for a work by Eusebius) or nonstandard or Latinized name spellings with which it was assumed scholars would be familiar.[40] Bibliander, Reuchlin, and Hugo compiled scholarship that stretched into earliest antiquity to justify their assertion that Hebrew was the original tongue. The materials on which they drew included many theological texts and commentaries that would have been part of their training in Church and classical literature.

Hugo had expressed scant interest in Cabalistic and mystical musings, while others, such as his predecessors Pico and Reuchlin, or Hugo's important contemporary Claude Duret, made little distinction between magical and historical traditions. Duret's exhaustive 1613 publication, *Le thrésor de l'histoire des langues de cest univers*, was a mélange of magical and historical information drawn from every available source.[41] In Duret's assessment, the origin of the letters was always associated with Divine work, not through the finger of God on the Tablets, but as the writing in the heavens: "The Hebrews, as the first people in the universe, showed that figure of their Hebrew letters, expressed and engraved in the Heavens, according to the position of fixed stars."[42] Duret was again borrowing from the Cabalistic tradition by way of Postel, whose definitive 1538 publication, *De originibus seu de Hebraicae linguae & gentis antiquitate* (On the Origin of the Hebrew language and nation), was his source for the idea of celestial configurations as the origin of the letters.[43] The association with Cabala linked Duret's discussion to an even earlier author, St. Augustine, whose passage in *The City of God* said "that in the primitive church he had seen books composed by Adam that on account of their great antiquity were not received or approved by the Christians."[44] These supposedly referred to Cabalistic commentaries on the *Sefer Yetzirah*, or *Book of Creation*, with references to the angel Raziel and others, suggesting that this text was evidently known in Augustine's time (the fourth–fifth centuries).[45] In Duret, the idea of this Divine alphabet was extended by the authority of so many other writers that to begin to list them all would be impossible—Duret's thousand-plus-page work contained on average fifteen to twenty citations per page that are often obscure or partial.[46]

Many authors trying to sort out the questions of the origins of writing and the alphabet were content simply to present all the available evidence rather than to reach definitive conclusions.[47] Still, the persistent question remained: What were the original letters? The suggestion that Moses had used two types of characters—the ones written by God and the others "called Samaritan" that were used for profane purposes—began to feature in the early modern debate.[48] The Samaritan script had emerged from obscurity and into the consciousness of Western scholars in the sixteenth century.[49] The version of the Pentateuch preserved in the Samaritan community appeared to be older than the Greek translation from the third to the second century BCE, known as the Septuagint, which had provided the oldest continuous textual tradition.[50] The discovery—or rediscovery—of the Samaritan text and script had raised questions by the early seventeenth century that begged to be resolved. By making a distinction between Divine and profane scripts, Samaritan could be assigned a complementary role without posing a challenge to the sanctity of Hebrew.

EIGHTEENTH CENTURY: DANIEL DEFOE, THE NOVELIST'S ACCOUNT

These lineages of citations and arguments continued into the eighteenth century when one of the richest discussions of these questions was written by a renowned novelist. In a text published in 1726, Daniel Defoe composed a passionate discussion of the "originals of letters."[51] Defoe's language was vivid, and his arguments complex as well as erudite. The full title of Defoe's work laid out the dimensions of the argument in wonderful eighteenth-century prose, *An Essay upon Literature, or An Enquiry into the Antiquity and Original of Letters Proving That the Two Tables, Written by the Finger of God on Mount Sinai, Was the First Writing in the World; and That All Other Alphabets Derive from the Hebrew, with a Short View of the Methods Made Use of by the Antients, to Supply the Want of Letters Before and Improve the Use of Them, After They Were Known*. Though brief, Defoe's essay delivered on the promises of this title.

Defoe began by posing a few questions, such as whether or not there was a time before writing or whether the peoples in the antediluvian world had the use of letters. Moses, he said, was not so remote in time from the last days of Noah.[52] As the author of the Pentateuch, Moses was the first historian, and his accounts of the letters provided our first knowledge of writing. "Scripture," Defoe continued, was "the oldest as well as the truest account of these things in the world."[53] This contrasted radically with his attitude toward Herodotus, Pliny, or other ancients whom he treated as mortal figures with the same capacity for error as modern writers while Moses drew on Divine authority.

Defoe believed that since the Decalogue was the earliest writing, and the letters in which it was written were made by the finger of God, that the children of Israel would never have changed them. But they had to have had writing before they received this gift or "how else could the Children of Israel read it?"[54] Thus the familiar conundrum troubled him as it had bothered nearly every writer who commented on the story.

Defoe considered the Phoenicians the "antientest People in the World" next to the Egyptians but did not allow them priority with regard to the invention of writing.[55] Phoenician coinage, he claimed, had no inscriptions.[56] He also discounted the claims of China and Japan to great antiquity, dismissing as false their calculations proving the world was eleven thousand years old and their monarchy seven thousand. Having thus dismissed the competition, he returned to question Cadmus's role, "for even who this Cadmus was is a doubtful thing."[57] With impeccable logic, Defoe returned to the assertion that as all these other claims were false or dubious, writing had to have been God's invention and gift. The date of this gift was linked to Moses on the basis that all kinds of things would have been written down if writing had existed earlier. Here Defoe's imagination as a novelist comes into play as he suggests that had writing been available, the story of Noah and his drunkenness would have been recorded in a full account since "Noah did not stop at once drinking Wine to excess, as it signify'd in the Text, but that he grew [became] a grievous Drunkard, a kind of habitual Sot etc."[58] In addition, if there had been writing, then Venus would have been exposed as an "everlasting Whore, an insatiate impudent Strumpet."[59] The perversity of using mythological references to legitimate biblical history seemed not to have troubled Defoe.

Defoe dated the story of the Exodus precisely to the year 2515, when Moses was eighty.[60] Many familiar authorities showed up in Defoe's account: Pliny and St. Augustine, as well as St. Jude, and then Sir Walter Raleigh, who had produced a detailed chronology of the first era of the world in 1614.[61] Sifting through one account after another, Defoe summarized and either dismissed or engaged their points. He approved of St. Augustine, for instance, because of his assertion that "the Hebrew Letters began from the Law given to Moses."[62] He reinforced this assessment by citing yet other authorities: "The vulgar Opinion of us Christians, . . . and also of the Hebrews Is, that the Hebrew Letters had Moses for their Author, which Eupolemus and also Atrapanus, and other prophane Writers also do assert."[63]

The historical details had gotten more and more complicated in the seventeenth century with the realization that modern and ancient Hebrew were not the same. Though the evidence was only a handful of coins, it was clear that the modern square Hebrew letters did not match ancient ones.

This transformation needed an explanation. The accepted wisdom of the late seventeenth century was that the Jews had had two sorts of writing in ancient times. The early Mosaic script had been brought into Canaan by Abraham and taken to Egypt by Jacob. Seven centuries later, according to biblical chronology, the Jews lost their writing during Babylonian exile. Ezra the scribe was given credit for producing a new script after release of the Jews from captivity. This standard account provided an explanation for the difference between modern Hebrew and ancient script. But precisely what ancient script Defoe might have had in mind at this point is unclear since he did not mention either Samaritan or Chaldean as the original alphabet. While he dutifully cited Josephus's story of the pillars of Seth, he did not try to sort out the chronological relation of their earlier writing to that of Moses.

Defoe's imagination was also captured by the idea of antediluvian writing, evidence of which he gleaned from other writers. Among them was the early seventeenth-century scholar James Bonaventure Hepburn, who, he claimed, "insisted on Enoch's being the Father of Antediluvian literature."[64] In the New Testament, St. Jude had implied that Enoch wrote accounts in a book. Furthermore, examples of the letters from Adam, Enoch, and Noah had been presented by various other authors Defoe cited, including Thomas Bang in *Exercitationum literariarum* (Literary exercises; 1657), in whose publication a long list of alphabets appeared.[65] The legendary Book of Enoch and its script were renowned among occultists, and Defoe conscientiously cited the existing sources to keep his account comprehensive.[66]

Ultimately, Defoe came to the following conclusion:

> It is sufficient, after all, that we have an Original, a Pattern in the Mount, which we know was handed to Moses, from the Finger of God, and that no History gives any Account that can be depended upon, or is more rational than this, that all the pretended Knowledge of Letters before it, is without Ground, or so much as Probability; and so far were they from having left any Remains behind them, of that Knowledge, that their Posterity valued themselves infinitely upon that dull unperforming, as we may call it, Dumb Language of Hieroglyphicks, and Images of Creatures, making the Brutes Speak for them, when at the same Time they knew not how to form any proper Character for Words, or to which the Sound of Words might be appropriated.[67]

But even with this elaborate argument, Defoe could not resolve the basic contradictions that lingered: if writing did not exist before Moses received the Tablets, then how could he and the children of Israel read the Laws?

EIGHTEENTH CENTURY: THE MODERN HISTORIANS

The early modern writers, including Defoe, grounded their approach to history in models of ancient chronology dating back to Eusebius. History was treated as a series of distinct events but not necessarily as a process of development. As the notion of progress began to inform alphabet studies, it became clear that writing, languages, and scripts were not simply invented once and preserved unchanged into the present. In the inquiry into the origin of letters, two British scholars are particularly notable, the first, Anselm Bayly, for his focus on writing, and the other, John Jackson, for his prominence as an antiquarian.[68]

By the eighteenth century, knowledge of ancient languages had broadened considerably, and investigations of origins had to address many claims about Assyrian, Chaldean, and Samaritan sources among others in describing a full historical sequence. In 1758, Bayly stated the usual formulation quite succinctly in *An Introduction to Languages*: "God writ the Law called the Ten Commandments with his own Finger; that is, he was the sole Author of that Writing."[69] That clear statement might have been sufficient for earlier scholars, but Bayly's explanation demonstrates a shift toward discussions of progress, or, as he termed it, the "Order and Derivation of Languages." He stated: "The Hebrew, hence the Chaldee and Syriac, Chananistish [Canaanite], Phenician, Punic, Ethiopic, Arabic, and in Part the Persia; the Languages now spoke in Syria, Mesopotamia, Arabia, Armenia, and Abyssinia are thought to carry in them great remains of the Chaldee."[70] Bayly's elaboration of the lineage of languages and their related histories was in part informed by the work of Bishop Brian Walton, whose polyglot Bible had been printed almost a century earlier in nine languages using multiple scripts.[71] Even if Hebrew was the original alphabet, the ancient writing of the Assyrians mentioned by Pliny had to be accounted for, as did the connection between Samaritan and Hebrew. The term Chaldean referred to a version of Syriac considered to be of great antiquity since Chaldea was the land from which Abraham had come.

One small excerpt from Bayly is enough to show how these scholars sorted through their bibliographic evidence, attending first to the ancient authors and then to the modern: "The Origin of Letters some ascribe to one Nation, and some to another, as Pliny to the Phenicians, Egyptians and Assyrians; Plato, Barbaros, that is, Foreigners whom he sometimes calleth Syrians, Chaldeans, and sometimes Egyptians; Diodorus Siculus to the Cretans and Syrians, as doth also Eusebius, meaning by Syrians, the Hebrews, and in particular their Law-giver Moses: In this agree also many antient Writers, as Eupolemus and others cited by Eusebius; Clemens Alexandrinus; St. Augustine, and amongst the moderns Dr. John Owen; Gale; Sir Charles Wolseley, Mr. Johnson, and many others."[72] On the crucial question of the Divine gift, he said, there "seem to be no sure Proofs either from Facts, Tradition, or the History of Moses." But "God at Mount Sinai gave unto a chosen People Laws inscribed with his own Hand. No Time seemeth so proper from whence to date the Introduction of Letters among the Hebrews, as this."[73] He went on to observe that Moses was educated in the wisdom of the Egyptians, and if he had known writing he would not have needed God's assistance at Sinai.[74] Bayly, like many others, was convinced that the invention of writing was beyond human capacity. And this led him back to arguments for the Divine gift:

> First, reason may shew us how near to an Impossibility it was, that a just and proper Number of convenient Characters for the Sounds in Language should naturally be hit upon by any Man, for whom it was easy to imitate and vary, but not to invent; and therefore Livy justly ascribeth the Discovery of Letters *miraculo & divinitati*. Secondly, from Evidence of the Mosaic History it appeareth that the Introduction of Writing among the Hebrews was not from Man, but God; Thirdly, there are no evident Vestiges of Letters subsisting among other Nations till after the delivery of the Law at Mount Sinaie, nor then among some till very late.[75]

Regarding the specific forms of Hebrew, Bayly stressed another line of argument. If the letters were written by God, "with his own finger," the Jews would never have parted with that alphabet afterward. A people does not give up a Divine gift. In addition, he said, "That the beauty of the Hebrew Characters is so pleasing to the Eye, of such geometrical Proportion, beyond any other in the World" was also evidence of its Divine origin.[76] The letters Bayly was describing were the modern "square" Hebrew letters, with their elegant strokes and qualities, not the (also quite exquisite) Paleo-Hebrew of ancient antiquity, samples of which Bayly would have been able to see only on a handful of coins.[77]

A near contemporary of Bayly's, John Jackson was a scholar of formidable reputation, whose work was broader in scope and historical ambition than that of his colleague. In *Chronological Antiquities* (1772), Jackson noted that "the Annals of the Jewish Nation have been corrupted over time" and that "the true Mosaic Chronology of Scripture is, by divine Providence, preserved in the uncorrupted *Greek Translation* of the Old Testament, which was made by learned Jews also contained in the *Jewish Antiquities* of Josephus, taken from an uncorrupted Hebrew copy."[78] Jackson dismissed the claim that Seth "invented the Hebrew letters" as "groundless."[79] He went on to say, "Moses, in his history of the antediluvian Ages, makes no mention of Letters, so no Foundation for the Jewish Traditions of their being invented by Seth or Enoch or any Patriarch of those times. If Moses had any account of the letters being found out in that early period, he could not have failed making mention of the Author of so wonderful and useful an invention," especially since he told of the invention of far less useful things, such as the tent and the harp.[80] Jackson dismissed the Chaldean myth of Oannes's teaching the letters a thousand years after Creation as "a Fable" and asserted that the letters had to have been invented after the dispersion of human beings in the Flood.[81] The Chaldeans, however, had written records to show "that Letters had been known and used among them at least 2234 Years before the Christian Era, and undoubtedly they had them long before."[82] This level of detail demonstrated Jackson's capacity to synthesize sources, but his adherence to the details of biblical history made his remarks on these topics highly influential.

RATIONAL ARGUMENTS

In addition to the work of historians, contributions to eighteenth-century alphabet studies arose in the emerging field of diplomatics. Established by the foundational study of the French scholar Jean Mabillon in his 1681 publication, *De re diplomatica* (Diplomatic matters), the field was largely concerned with the authentication of documents. Two key figures, the French scholar Charles Toustain and the British writer Thomas Astle (Keeper of the Records of the Tower of London), bear mention because each was concerned to locate alphabetic writing within a larger context of historical development. Both struggled to establish a historical chronology for the alphabet.

In his 1750 work *Nouveau traité de diplomatique* (New treatise on diplomatics), Toustain posed the familiar conundrum of the biblical texts quite bluntly: "What use could one have of the written Law if letters had not existed already?"[83] Did God give Moses an understanding of the characters which he then taught to the Israelites? How could this be reconciled with the writing of the Babylonians, which, by the mid-eighteenth century, Toustain asserted, was older than that of Moses. In a mistaken comparison, Toustain suggested Chinese characters had an even older history. He reiterated the explanation of differences between modern and ancient Hebrew through reference to Babylonian captivity and struggled to place Assyrian and Samaritan writing into the historical sequence in which the Phoenicians, whom he identified as Hebrews, were ultimately given credit for the original invention. Toustain drew on all known authorities and attempted to reconcile their opinions with a coherent narrative.[84] He finally gave up trying to resolve disagreements over the question of whether Noah, Abraham, Moses, or God was responsible for the invention.[85] His contemporary, Astle, had no doubts about the fact that "the letters were first communicated to Moses by God himself; whilst others have contended, that the Decalogue was the first alphabetic writing."[86]

However, Astle believed that even the stories of Moses must be subjected to scrutiny, to see "if it shall appear that they are warranted neither by *reason* or by *scripture*."[87] Though he made clear that "it is incumbent on us to have recourse to the Holy Scriptures themselves," he had invoked reason as an aid to scholarship.[88]

He went on, noting that the first mention of writing recorded in Scripture will be found in Exodus xvii, volume 14: "And the Lord said unto Moses, Write this for a memorial, in a book, and rehearse it in the ears of Joshua."[89] He commented that there was "not the least hint to induce us to believe that writing was then newly invented; on the contrary, we may conclude, that Moses understood what was meant by *writing in a book*; otherwise, God would have instructed him, as he had done Noah in building the ark."[90] The discussion was prolonged, with Astle reiterating that Moses expressed "no difficulty of comprehension," and that, in fact, the first twenty-one chapters of Exodus are written by Moses *before* "the tables of stone were even so much as *promised*."[91] Moses "nowhere mentions that the alphabet was a *new thing* in his time, much less that he was the inventor of it; on the contrary, he speaks of the art of writing, as a thing well known, and in familiar use."[92] Astle even suggested that had Moses been the inventor of writing, he would, in directing workmen to engrave "names and sentences on stones and gold," have said "in these engravings you shall use the alphabetic characters which God hath communicated to me, or which I have now invented, and taught you the use of."[93] But Moses did not.

Astle dismissed the story of divine invention by Thoth, Theuth, or Mercury more summarily, citing Plato in his defense, "that some, when they could not unravel a difficulty, brought down a god, as in a machine, to cut the knot."[94] He paraphrased Bishop Warburton's *The Divine Legation of Moses*, saying that the "learned bishop of Gloucester observes, that the ancients gave nothing to the gods of whose original they had any records: but where the memory of the invention was lost, as of feed corn, wine, writing, civil society etc. the gods seized the property."[95] He concluded this discussion thus: "The holy scriptures having left this subject open to investigation, and the prophane writers having given us nothing satisfactory upon it, we are at liberty to pursue our *inquiry into the origin of letters*."[96] To do so, he took a systematic approach to the contemplation of their nature, and of their *powers*, or sounds.

Through this analysis he determined that neither Divine nor mythic intervention had been involved. Astle concluded by saying that the alphabet was based on the analysis of the sounds of language and that "symbols were in general use among mankind, before they knew the use of letters; and therefore the invention of the latter was nothing more than the transferring of the former method of representation, to the elements of sound."[97] By the end of the eighteenth century, Astle had arrived at an analysis that would later be supported by archaeological evidence.

The story could be left here, with its clearheaded analytic understanding, except that the quest for verification of biblical texts and their use as points of reference did not disappear simply because the understanding of alphabetic writing shifted to a rational plane. More than a century would elapse before mainstream scholarship caught up with Astle's reasoned insights.

CONCLUSION

The search for evidence of the account of Moses's reception of the Tablets on Mount Sinai prompted many travelers and archaeologists to create detailed accounts of the possible route of the Exodus. Richard Pococke, in *A*

Description of the East (1743), was among the earliest scholars to publish copies of the inscriptions in the Sinai. His well-documented travels in Egypt, Arabia, and other parts of the Near East included a detailed attempt to follow clues in the biblical text.[98] Searching for the site of Moses's reception of the Tablets would remain a motivation for travelers, cartographers, and photographers trying to match biblical descriptions with geological features. Pococke's book set a frame for later work by stating that he was following "the journey of the children of Israel" through the Sinai. His trip included a visit to St. Catherine's monastery and he notes the appearance of many inscriptions "on the large rocks that lay about the valley leading to Mt. Sinai."[99] Though he could not read the inscriptions, and would have had little way of knowing how to date them or even identify their language, Pococke rendered them accurately enough that they were able to be studied by other scholars. As some of the first images produced from copying the Sinai markings, they remained an important milestone and resource for modern paleography.

Moses did not appear in these inscriptions and neither did the square Hebrew letters or their "Chaldean" counterparts. Recent quarrels over the language of the Sinai inscriptions—whether they are Hebrew or Canaanite and whether they contain evidence of biblical figures—remain highly charged.[100] The desire to reconcile core beliefs with modern-day discoveries continues to provide motivation for finding kernels of truth in biblical texts. After several millennia, the classical texts and the biblical ones still offer major frameworks for the study of the alphabet's origins and identity. If, as it turns out, the "original of letters" was in fact created sometime in the fourteenth or thirteenth century BCE, then the historical timeline for the mythic figure of Moses is not impossible to reconcile with evidence. Missing from such a story, however, would be the Tablets, the finger of God, and any need for Divine intervention as a primary cause.

Attention to biblical sources persists, travel narratives expand the firsthand knowledge and documentation of inscriptions, and the combination of mounting evidence and ongoing scholarship proliferates the details and particulars on which historical arguments are developed. No one has resolved the logical question of how Moses could read the Laws if he could not write or already know the alphabet. But historians from antiquity, through to the early modern historians, gradually shifted from a literal reading of biblical passages to a rational reassessment of their interpretation. Their elaborate lineages of textual citation slowly shifted to the background as other modes of knowledge transmission came into play. Another mode of transmission—graphic copying—also played a role in keeping mythic traditions alive and in imbuing the letters with magical powers.

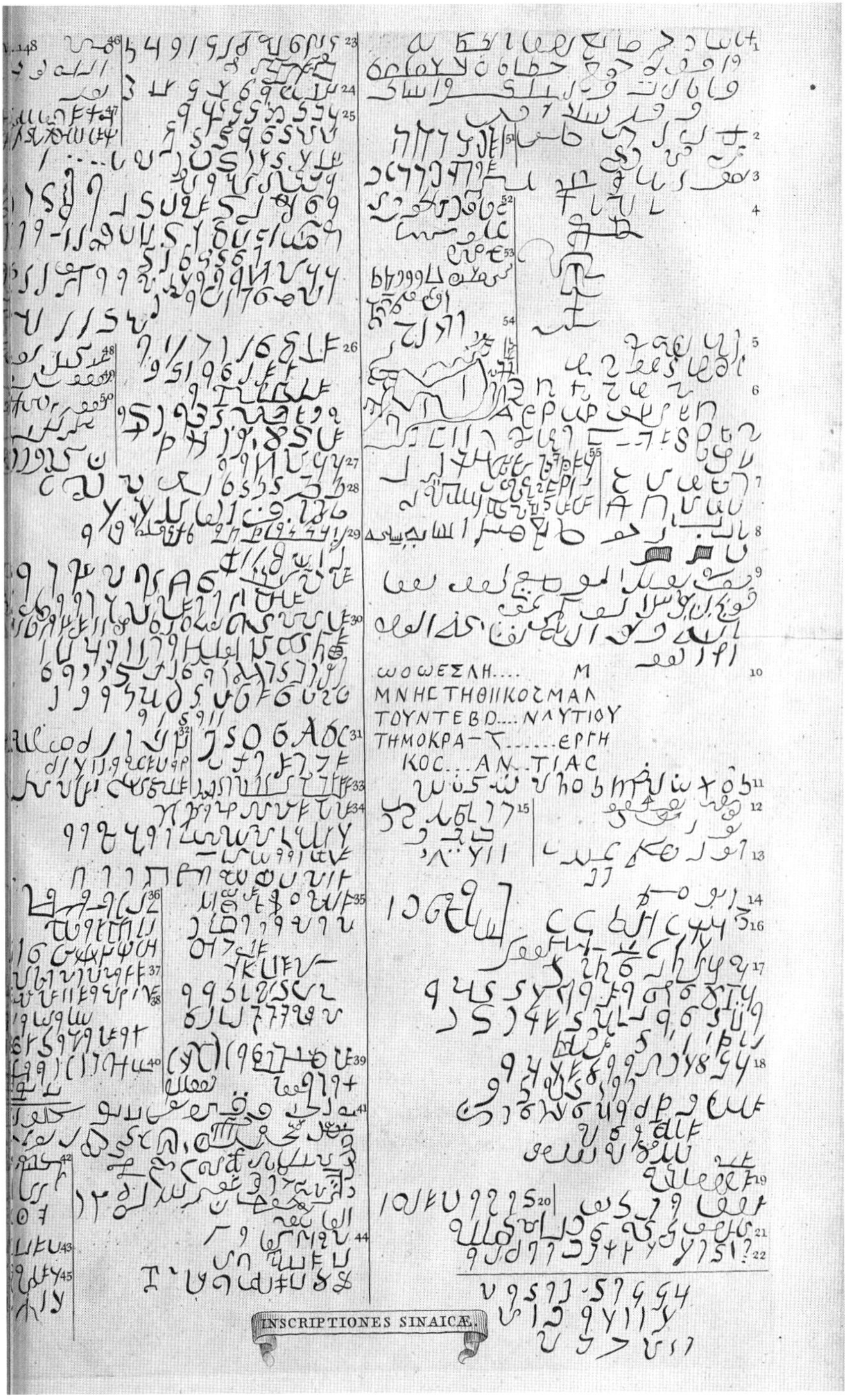

INSCRIPTIONES SINAICÆ.

FIGURE 2.2 Richard Pococke, "Inscriptiones Sinaicae." From *A Description of the East* (London, 1743). Public domain.

THREE

Medieval Copyists

Magical Letters, Mythic Scripts, and Exotic Alphabets

The tradition of copying adds a graphic dimension to alphabet studies. Classical and biblical texts *referenced* alphabetic scripts, but they did not *show* them. The Greeks conceived of the alphabet as a *notation system* that circulated through cultural exchange, and the biblical and Kabbalistic traditions conceived of the alphabet as a *Divine gift* with powers to bring the world into being. But graphic transmission demonstrates an understanding of the alphabet as made up of specific visual forms, which have potent *symbolic power* or *historical identities*. The mix of scripts copied and passed forward from antiquity included actual alphabets used for writing documents as well as magical, mythic, and exotic ones copied intact from exemplars that were never used for composing a text. Well into the modern era, mythic and actual scripts were not fully differentiated from each other, and compendia contained examples of both in their collections.

GRAPHIC TRANSMISSION

For centuries, all reproduction of images or texts was achieved through hand copying, and each copy was individual. A visual *script* had to be seen to be replicated even if a *text* could be transmitted orally and written down. No amount of verbal description provides enough information for a scribe to produce letters they have never seen. Someone trying to create a copy of an unfamiliar script without a visual exemplar—Hebrew, Arabic, Coptic, or Syriac, let alone one attributed to Noah or an angel—would find the task impossible. Alphabets that were in constant use became part of scribal knowledge and were learned as stroke patterns, or manual exercises. But copying an unfamiliar graphic form involves replicating its features as specific pictorial shapes, not strokes.

Fanciful inventions in particular had to be copied one character at a time. Several varieties of such scripts exist, each with their own lineages: magical, celestial, mythic, and exotic alphabets. All are reproduced with remarkable accuracy across centuries, though few were ever used to write a language. These scripts are first transmitted across manuscripts and, eventually, print, but in most cases, trying to find a single original prototype results in an infinite regress into obscurity. That early history often belongs to a period for which the evidence is lost.[1] For instance, at some moment, in some manuscript or inscription, the first celestial letters with lunettes terminating their strokes appeared—but where and when? Similarly, an original version of the alphabet attributed to a mythic traveler, Aethicus Ister, must have been penned by some graphically gifted scribe.

Among the artificial scripts, the *magical* alphabets have the longest history, originating in the traditions of Graeco-Egyptian magic and Babylonian incantation. The association of letters with angels is of long standing, reaching at least to the early centuries of the Common Era. *Celestial* scripts originate within Jewish mysticism and early Christian Gnosticism, and, like the magical alphabets, they are variants of Hebrew letters.[2] A handful of *mythic* alphabets that are associated by name with historical, biblical figures—Abraham, Adam, Noah, and King Solomon—are related to actual Hebrew and Aramaic scripts. Some *exotic* alphabets were complete fabrications, but renderings of Hebrew, runes, and other scripts were also *exoticized* to serve cultural agendas.

THE LINGUISTIC CONTEXT

Readers in Europe and England throughout the Middle Ages, and into the early era of print, would (with varying degrees of accuracy) have associated unfamiliar alphabets with various cultural contexts, geographic locations, and time periods. A limited number of languages were known and studied between the dissolution of the Roman Empire and the gradual emergence of urban centers, universities, and established communications in the later Middles Ages. Latin was the written language of the empire and the Church used in theological commentary, canon law, religious history, and the writings of the Christian Fathers. These texts occupied clerics and other scholars of the early Middle Ages in Europe and constituted the bulk of literate productions in scholarly communities, along with herbals, histories, and a small corpus of classical works. In the millennium after the dissolution of the Roman Empire, the gradual emergence of vernacular languages began to result in written materials (such as charters, administrative documents, and literary works) in Old English, French, Italian, Germanic, Slavic, and Scandinavian tongues. At the same time, many local and nationalistic *hands* (local stylistic variants of the Latin alphabet)—such as Old English, Carolingian, German black letter, Italian rotunda, chancery, and charter hands—proliferated.

Certain linguistic communities gradually developed their own variant alphabetic *scripts*—Cyrillic, Slavonic, Armenian—modifying letters to represent the sounds of their language. (For instance, the Latin *script* does not include the *thorn* or *yod* used to write Old English.) Some, like runes (an alphabetic script invented early in the Common Era for Germanic and Nordic languages), seemed mysterious in origin and appearance since, at first, knowledge about them was not grounded in historical information. But all these alphabetic inventions have clear and identifiable histories. Many scripts in current use achieved their modern form in the Middle Ages. In fact, it is the last period in which major modifications in alphabets occurred in the West (such as additions of letters in Cyrillic script), though stylistic inventions in type and letter design continue into the present.

The number of languages that would have been known by a European or English scholar in the Middle Ages was extremely limited. Besides knowing their local tongue (e.g., Anglo-Saxon or Celtic dialects), a scribe might have been familiar with written forms of Greek, the Latin alphabet, and possibly some runic scripts. However, the awkward rendering of Greek, or in rare cases, Hebrew, often gives stark evidence of unfamiliarity.

Greek, where spoken or preserved within a community, provided access to untranslated texts, the Septuagint, and crucial theological and classical writings. The schism of the Eastern and Western Church in the eleventh century further divided language communities. The fall of Constantinople to the Ottomans in 1453 resulted in a significant migration of Greek scholars into Europe, fostering renewed exchange, but within the Western Church, with its Latin service and study, St. Jerome's translation of the Bible had rendered knowledge of Greek unnecessary for anyone but scholars. The context for language learning was limited outside the cosmopolitan centers of the old Roman Empire and major cities of the ancient Near East.

The study of ancient languages did not become part of the European context until well after the establishment of the first universities in the eleventh and twelfth centuries (Lisbon, Paris, Cambridge, Oxford, Naples, Toulouse).[3] Knowledge of Hebrew, for instance, was utterly absent from Britain before the Norman Conquest in 1066. Even by the fifteenth century, when Johannes Reuchlin was urging establishment of university positions for this purpose, fewer than a thousand, and possibly half that many, scholars in Europe could read Hebrew, "the Holy Tongue."[4]

Within the Caliphate centers of learning in Baghdad and other erudite communities of the Islamic empire, Arabic translations of classical texts were produced alongside publications of advances in medicine, astronomy, and the sciences beginning in the eighth century. But the linguistic isolation as well as cultural divisions kept these communities separate from those in Europe until later. Only in North Africa, Sicily, and southern Spain did cross-cultural exchange foster substantial linguistic knowledge, and that occurred in limited contexts until the tenth and eleventh centuries. Trade routes and military campaigns brought Arabic, Hellenistic, and other influences into Europe (and gradually, the British Isles). The mix of cultures, languages, and beliefs that existed in Mozarabic Spain and southern Italy spawned a massive translation industry from Arabic into Latin, but this development, also, was not until the eleventh and twelfth centuries. Knowledge of Arabic and its alphabetic script, as well as its magical traditions, continuous in the Near East and throughout the Islamic courts of the empire, only came to Europe in the late Middle Ages. The twelfth-century translator Gerard de Cremona produced editions of scientific and medical texts that brought centuries of learning, as well as classical expertise, into the European context. But the first university chair in Arabic was not established in England until 1636, when William Laud provided for its creation at Oxford.[5]

In Europe, the Semitic languages of the Near East such as Samaritan, Syriac, and Chaldean (Aramaic) were virtually unknown in the Middle Ages, as evidenced in the ways that travel narratives recorded "exotic" languages from the territories of Egypt through Arabia, Asia Minor, and beyond. Following the Crusades, and the establishment of modern trade routes, these languages gradually entered the European context. One sign of the interest in these Semitic languages was their presence in the print publication of polyglot Bibles, the earliest of which, the Complutensian Bible, published in 1501, contained texts in Greek, Latin, and Hebrew. Polyglot texts became more and more complex in terms of the number of languages, layouts, and printing challenges. The Bible edited by Brian Walton and published in London in six volumes between 1655 and 1657, contained nine languages (Syriac, Hebrew, Greek, Latin, Aramaic, Ethiopic, Armenian, Samaritan, and Persian) displayed simultaneously.[6] Such publications required the cutting and casting of fonts in these scripts. By the seventeenth century, the scholarly interest in unlocking "early Christian knowledge" and its underlying tenets spurred enthusiasm for the study of Greek, Syriac, Aramaic, and Hebrew.[7] Once-exotic scripts became common. The quest for the "original" letters was ongoing.

Many spurious texts were also produced in the medieval period, claiming ancient origins to legitimate their contents. Grimoires with magical spells invoked "lost" texts of great antiquity, such as the magical work (falsely) attributed to the biblical king, the *Key of Solomon*. The work of alchemist Roger Bacon contained scraps of cited, reworked, copied, and invented text as well as graphic signs in a hybrid that blurred scholarly accuracy with fantasy.[8] Bacon attempted to put together a Hebrew grammar in the mid-thirteenth century, and though flawed, it provided a picture of the materials available for such a project at the time.[9]

In this context, magical scripts and exotic alphabets became available through exemplars in manuscript grimoires and occult texts as well as travel narratives and mystical writings. Several of the alphabets were assiduously copied and circulated intact. Others went through various modifications or corruptions as they were reproduced. Some were only characters, individual letters or signs, and sigils (string letters) used in magic practices. But it is the remarkable consistency with which certain of these artificial alphabets come forward into the present that speaks to the circulation of examples.

MAGICAL SCRIPTS AND CELESTIAL LETTERS

Celestial letters associated with angels and magic occasionally appear in manuscripts and print editions, sometimes as just a few individual characters. These characters have had a sustained and successful history owing to the belief in the power of graphic signs.[10] Some had their origins in magical texts that can be traced from Babylonian-Egyptian and Greek sources in late antiquity, and their association with "remote" origins adds an aura of mysterious authority to them. Arabic scholars provided one conduit for these letters into the West, as did Jewish magical traditions. Evidence from antiquity suggests that some of these practices originated with Aramaic inscriptions and incantations, but their earlier history is unclear.[11] Recent work on Jewish magic examines the complexities of their origin and transmission, suggesting they may have been modified during adaptation, though their shape as Hebrew letters is a conspicuous aspect of their identity.[12]

The letters that appeared in magical contexts are referred to as "brillenbuchstaben" "ring letters," or "charaktêres" (Karaqtiraya or Kalaqtiraya in Arabic).[13] They have ringlets (or lunettes) on their tips, and they appeared frequently in Hebrew prayer books. The Greek term *charaktêre* is used to call attention to the fact that these letters have magical properties. The same *charaktêres* appear in Arabic, Graeco-Egyptian, and Jewish texts, and they are always versions of Hebrew letters "transmitted smoothly from Late Antiquity to medieval Cairo" without visual alteration.[14] These letters also appeared in incantations in Greek papyri as well as in manuscripts found in the Cairo Genizah.[15] Of the two hundred thousand fragments in the Genizah, more than a thousand are magic related, and many contain these "ring letters."

In occult literature, the magical letters were also associated with complex sigils or signs. Sigils contain strokes combined in ligatures—joined letters—to produce elaborate symbols that seem charged with power. Many instances are found in manuscripts of the *Key of Solomon*, a magical text that is probably from the thirteenth or fourteenth century. Not strictly alphabetic, these composite signs were often found in the same texts as the magical characters. They were generally associated with angels

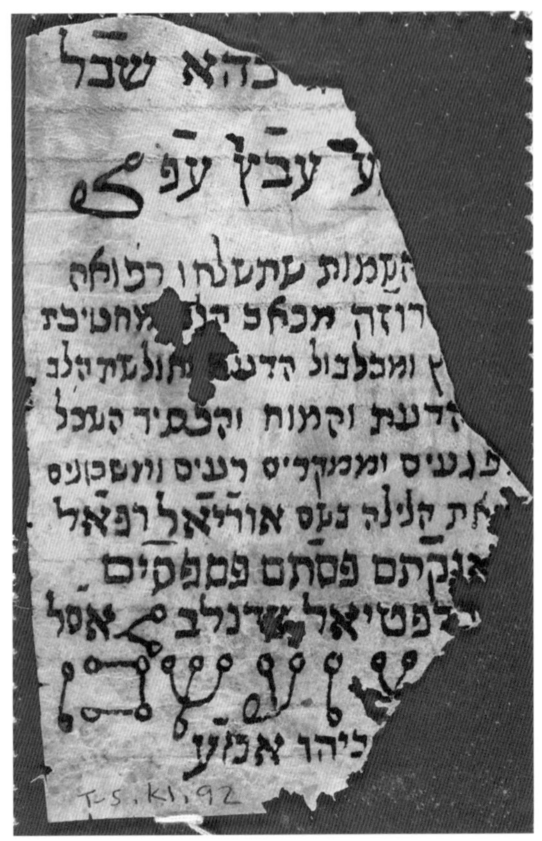

FIGURE 3.1 An example from the Cairo Genizah, date uncertain, showing the magical "ring letters" at bottom, from T-S. K1 92 (dated sixth–nineteenth century). Reproduced by kind permission of the Syndics of Cambridge University Library.

and frequently constructed from some combination of the letters in their names. Sigils were sometimes referred to as "string letters" because of their continuous strokes. Interest in alphabets associated with angels appeared in the Ashkenazi communities of the Middle Ages, where there were, to cite recent scholarship by Gideon Bohak, "an almost endless variety of the alphabets of angels, often copied one after another and making one wonder exactly what their users made of all these supposedly secret scripts, which seem to have been of no use whatsoever in deciphering the actual *charaktêres* found in dozens of magical recipes within the very same manuscripts."[16] Only peripherally related to alphabet study, these symbols played a role in grimoires and other texts concerned with demons, magic, and angelology.[17]

The notion that letters possess magical properties is an old concept. Graeco-Egyptian and Babylonian magical texts from classical antiquity were inscribed in manuscripts and on physical objects as part of ritual practices. Jewish Aramaic incantation bowls from the early centuries of the Common Era often contained angel names and references. Some of these were first identified by the nineteenth-century archaeologist Austen Henry

Layard, who uncovered them in the ruins of Nineveh and other sites in ancient Babylonia.[18] One bowl, an image of which was published in 1853 in Layard's *Discoveries of the Ruins of Nineveh and Babylon*, contained this sentence listing angels by name: "Thy petition shall be in the name of Barakiel, Ramiel, Raamiel, Nahabiel, and Sharmiel."[19] The same names appear in medieval texts and later magical publications. Many of these ancient incantation bowls were used in prayers asking for intervention for relief from pain or assistance in life circumstances.

As the medieval grimoires proliferated, with their elaborate spells and recipes for magical potions alongside alchemical texts, they reinforced the idea of the powers of letters. The *Libro de dichas maravillas* (Book of amazing tales), an Arabic manuscript dated to about 1601, contains examples of these *letras anteojadas* ("already seen letters"), but earlier instances can be cited.[20] Magical scripts were often linked to an earlier corpus of Hermetic texts from the first centuries of the Common Era. Some of these works were part of a resistance literature termed *aljamiado*, created in Arabic script after the use of the spoken language was banned by Phillip II in Spain in 1567.

These alphabets and *charaktêres* are intimately associated with the Cabalistic practices that emerged in Spain in the thirteenth centuries where the highly influential *The Book of Raziel* first appeared. *The Book of Raziel* is considered a grimoire, or practical magic book, and was composed in the Middle Ages in Hebrew and Aramaic. It was translated into Latin as the *Liber*

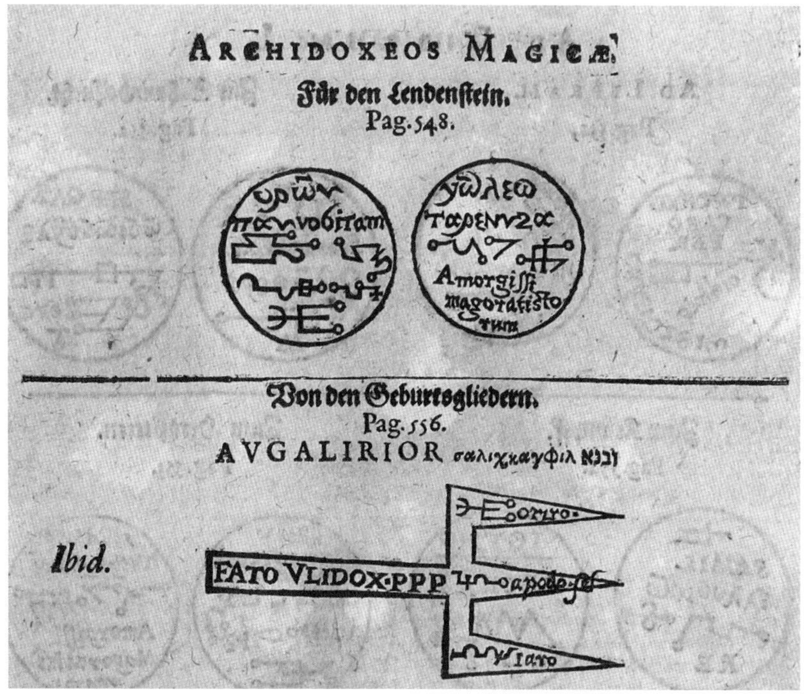

FIGURE 3.2 Sigils in Iohan Huser, *Archidoxis magicae* (1590). From *Aureoli Philippi Theophrasti Bombasts Von Hohenheim Paracelsi* (Strassburg, 1616). Public domain.

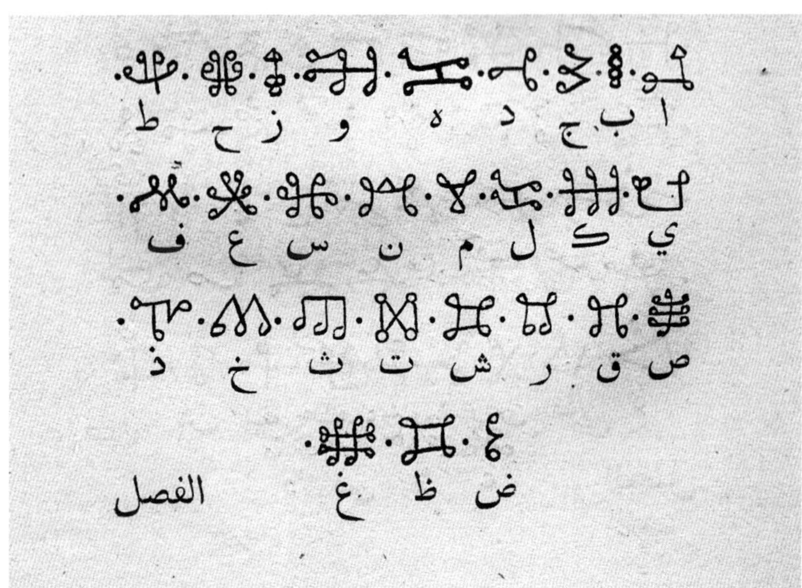

FIGURE 3.3 Example of magical script attributed to Colphoterios, in *aljamiadas* text, as shown in Ibn Wahshiyyah's text. Public domain.

Razielis archangeli (Raziel becomes Raphael once Latinized), a place and period in which Jewish mystical beliefs were being codified. No evidence of the book exists before this date, but it is mentioned in *The Sword of Moses: An Ancient Book of Magic*, itself a work with an unclear origin.[21] Some of this obscurity is deliberate, some incidental, but Jewish Kabbalah is dated to the Middle Ages, not antiquity. A version of *The Sword of Moses* was edited in 1896 by Moses Gaster, who used a thirteenth-to-fourteenth-century manuscript in his own possession to translate and publish its spells and formulas, which included mention of the powers of letters borrowed from the *Sefir Yetzirah* and other texts. The magical alphabets became a standard part of medieval and later publications, offering visual authenticity by their odd appearance. The recently digitized magical manuscripts in the Leipzig library provide a particularly rich inventory of such works.[22] Among them the "seventeenth-century (primarily) Hebrew magical manuscripts" contain "techniques identical to ones discovered in the Cairo Geniza as well as in Heikhalot [esoteric and mystical] literature."[23] Knowledge of these scripts circulated through networks concerned with esoteric knowledge. One example is the scholarly work of a sixteenth-century scholar from Salonika, Joseph ben Elijah Tirshom, who traveled widely to locate magical works in Damascus, Jerusalem, Egypt, and throughout the Levant in order to copy them.[24]

Ultimately these angel alphabets proliferated so promiscuously that they became an unregulated graphic currency whose conspicuous lunette characteristics simply invoked magic by association. Pages from different editions of *The Book of Raziel* show how perfectly the passages and the magical elements are copied. The editions vary graphically; some are delicately printed, with magic letters cut in elegant lines. Another used a woodcut block to imitate those forms, and the result is much cruder and more medieval looking, perhaps by design, to indicate greater age and mystery, or perhaps merely for expediency of production since the letters could have been more easily cut on a block than cast in metal.

A major treatise for transmission of Arabic magic, the *Picatrix* (*Ghayat al-hakim; The Goal of the Wise*), is usually dated to the eleventh century. The *Picatrix* contained many samples of these magical alphabets, revealing its association with Jewish mysticism and later Christian Cabala. The manuscripts pictured many of these lunette scripts to spell fragments and short phrases. The angels, it seemed, were only capable of brief communications.

The *Picatrix* influenced Hebrew writings in the fourteenth and fifteenth centuries and became a crucial source for Cornelius Agrippa, whose much-cited 1533 *Philosophia occulta*, was a comprehensive reference text of occult philosophy. Many signs appeared in the manuscripts of the *Picatrix*, but none of the complete magical alphabets that appeared in Agrippa are there. Agrippa's work was widely translated and circulated and itself became a much-cited source for these celestial alphabets (as well as several associated with angels and other figures).

Like the magic characters, the so-called celestial scripts were drawn with their lines terminating in open circles, to show they were copied from constellations in the heavens. This tradition had been codified by the sixteenth-century Cabalist Guillaume Postel and then extended by the seventeenth-century French Cabbalist Jacques Gaffarel.[25]

Gaffarel saw letters in everything: plants, flowers, the skin of fishes, cranes in their flight, and finally the arrangement of the letters in the Heavens. He gave credit to Postel for having tried to introduce this knowledge into Europe and cited the usual lineage of occult writers—Christian Cabalists, Johannes Reuchlin, Pico della Mirandola, Cornelius Agrippa, Heinrich Khunrath, Robert Fludd, and many Jewish rabbis—in support of his theory.[26] Gaffarel reproduced a version of Postel's chart of the celestial script, showing the distribution of letters in the heavens and their derivation from it, noting that the forms of the letters in the stars were clearly Hebrew, not Samaritan or Arabic.[27] He interpreted the first verse of the Bible as "In the Beginning, God created the Letter or Character of the Heavens."[28] The "Writing of the Angels," clearly meant celestial writing, Gaffarel noted, as per Rabbi Simeon Ben-Yochay in *The Zohar* and others. Rabbi Moses (likely Moses Kimchi), a learned Jew, was referenced to support the notion of the letters as Blessed Intelligences, animate, endowed with souls.

Aside from the grimoires and books of magic already cited, a handful of other texts played a role in this transmission history. Among these is an unusual ninth-century text attributed to Ibn Wahshiyyah.

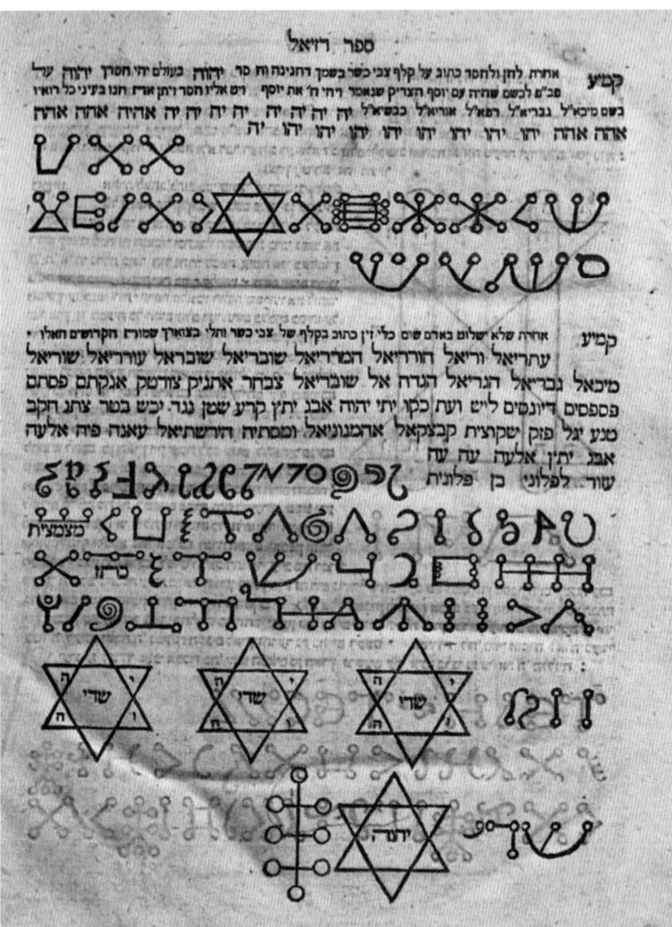

FIGURE 3.4 *Sefer Raziel Ha-Malakh Liber Razielis Archangeli*, 1st ed., (Amsterdam, 1701).

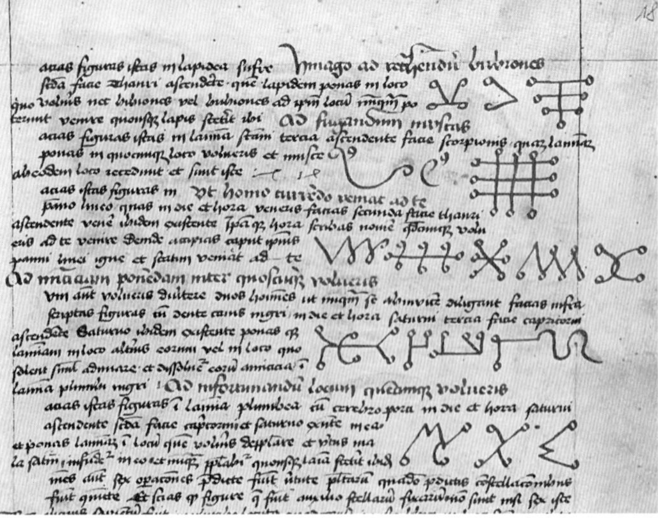

FIGURE 3.5 Excerpt of page of Latin version of *Ghayat al-hakim*, known in Latin as the *Picatrix* manuscript. Public domain.

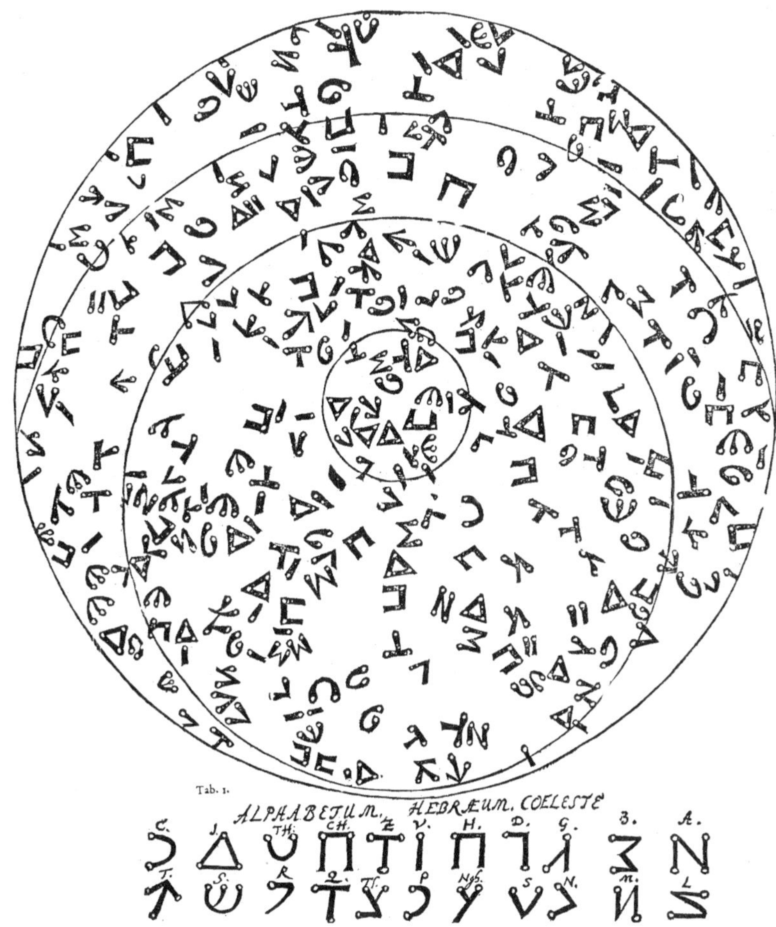

FIGURE 3.6 From Jacques Gaffarel, *Unheard-of Curiosities* (1632), which he copied almost exactly from Guillaume Postel. Public domain.

IBN WAHSHIYYAH

Ibn Wahshiyyah is the purported author of an unusual Arabic manuscript from the ninth century that contained multiple examples of magical and "ancient" scripts. The text, dated to year 241 of the Hegirah, or 863 of the Common Era, was translated into English in 1806 by Joseph Hammer von Purgstall with the title *Ancient Alphabets and Hieroglyphic Characters Explained*. Venetia Porter, in her recent work on Arabic magic, translated the title more vividly as *The Frenzied Devotee's Desire to Learn about the Riddles of Ancient Scripts*.[29] The authenticity of the text is not proved, and its plethora of magical alphabets may be as much the result of invention as copying. Many of its examples appear to be mere fabrications by a creative scribe, and only a few of the alphabets it contains have recognizable identities that connect it to the longer tradition.

Ibn Wahshiyyah (or Washiah) was, however, an actual historical figure.

Works associated with his name are listed in various Arabic encyclopedias, but whether he wrote this text on ancient alphabets is dubious. Hammer, his nineteenth-century translator, was an Orientalist and diplomat who spent more than a decade in Istanbul and claimed that the text of *Ancient Alphabets* was deposited in the treasury of the calif Abbd-ul-malik bin Marwan in the 241st year of the Hegirah.[30] The actual Wahshiyyah was best known for his work *Nabathaean Agriculture*, but the other titles associated with his name—*Pearls of Scientific Instruction*, *Natural Magic*, and *Tree of Paradise*—give some idea of his study of traditional knowledge in combination with magical practices. Recent scholarship suggests that *Ancient Alphabets* was a compendium of sorts, aggregated by a number of authors and then attributed to Wahshiyyah to give it credibility.[31] The writings of Wahshiyyah were likely a "result of successive rewritings, revisions etc. of materials from antiquity" that were "preserved, amplified and modified by Syrian and Alexandrian Hellenism" during a period of much transmission of knowledge and cultures of the ancient world.[32] The very fact that the manuscript invokes hieroglyphics and mixes the Egyptian signs into the alphabetic compendium indicates a connection to North Africa and Syria that distinguishes it from that of the European grimoires and Cabalistic manuscripts.

Wahshiyyah's text contained a proliferation of scripts, about eighty in total, each of which was given some kind of description and supposed identity and origin. Some were actual scripts, such as Cufic, Maghrabin, and a numeral script from India. Alongside these examples from the Indian context were alphabets of the ancient Near East: Hebrew, Syrian, Greek, Nabathaean, Masnad (Indian?), or Himyaritic (associated with the ancient Yemeni king). The associations were not always clear, and these identifiable alphabets were followed by a host of scripts associated with planets, constellations, philosophers, and kings—all of which could have been known in a learned ninth-century Islamic community. The names of the philosophers included the Greeks—Plato, Pythagoras, and Aristotle—but many Arabic, Jewish (Zozimus), and Eastern figures as well.[33] Wahshiyyah mentioned scripts associated with Hermes, and an antediluvian one with the name Mimshim that resembled the angel alphabets described above. The variety of names and spellings was an indication of the syncretic character of the book's text, and each cluster of scripts offered an opportunity to track its references into one of many Near Eastern traditions. To go through each of these many examples would fill a tome on its own, since *Ancient Characters* is an exhaustive collection. Some scripts are found in other works, but many have never been cited elsewhere and constitute an anomalous graphic corpus.

Even Hammer, in his introduction, was cautious about the authenticity of the scripts while he tried to make a case for their possible role as codes or secret writing: "Although it is difficult to say how many of the eighty alphabets herein deciphered may have been really used by nations, or how many letters in every one alphabet may have been disfigured and misrepresented either by the want of sufficient information in our author himself, or by the ignorance and blunders of copyists; yet it is not presumption to assert, that real truth lies at the bottom of most of them, and that those which were not alphabets for common writing, were used as ciphers amongst different Oriental nations."[34] Oriental, in this context, refers to the countries of the Near East, and Wahshiyyah reinforced this perception through his own statements: "The original alphabets, from which all other ancient and modern ones have been derived, are no more than three. The old Syrian alphabet, or the first original divine alphabet, taught by God the Almighty to Adam. The Celestial alphabet, or the alphabet in which the books which Seth (health be with him) received from Heaven were written. The alphabet of Enoch brought down by the angel Gabriel."[35]

Each of the examples noted in this cluster of scripts in the Wahshiyyah manuscript had some resemblance to Syriac (a version of Aramaic related to other Semitic scripts in the region). Wahshiyyah identified Chaldean as the most ancient among these original alphabets, though the examples presented in the printed edition bore only a faint resemblance to any Aramaic originals on which they could have been based.[36] Wahshiyyah, or whoever composed the work, would have needed to have access to the kinds of materials most likely to be found in the libraries of Baghdad and Cairo, an argument for the location of its production.

While the history of the book is hard to pin down definitively, Hammer's copy does not seem to have been unique, and the manuscript from which he translated in 1806 seems likely to have been at least several hundred years older.[37] The seventeenth-century scholar Athanasius Kircher is reputed to have possessed a copy of Wahshiyyah, which he referred to as a very old "Arabico codice" written by "Aben Vaschia" and which he claimed to have obtained in Malta among the Turks.[38] Hammer obtained his in Cairo among the Arabs, 150 years after Kircher's claim. A note at the end of Hammer's version says that this particular manuscript was already a copy, taken "in 413 of Hegirah" (around 1040 CE) and then recopied into the one from which this is printed in 1166 (1790). In addition, according to one source, the book is mentioned in the *Kitab al-fihristi* (The book catalogue), composed in the tenth century by the Islamic scholar Ibn al-Nadim.[39] This copying accounts for the consistency of the alphabets in this edition (in each case they were copied by a single hand) but could also explain their lack of resemblance to other magical scripts if the manuscript was composed without influence from Western grimoires or magical texts.

One of the alphabets, the Mimshim, identified as an antediluvian script, displayed its connection to other "lunette" or "ringlet" scripts. The treatment was the same—small circles at the end of the arms. The actual characters were not consistent with any other standard scripts, but the lunette provided the important graphic reference. Many of the other alphabets in Wahshiyyah, however, were clearly inventions and appeared nowhere else. It is possible, of course, that these all have a place in Arabic manuscript

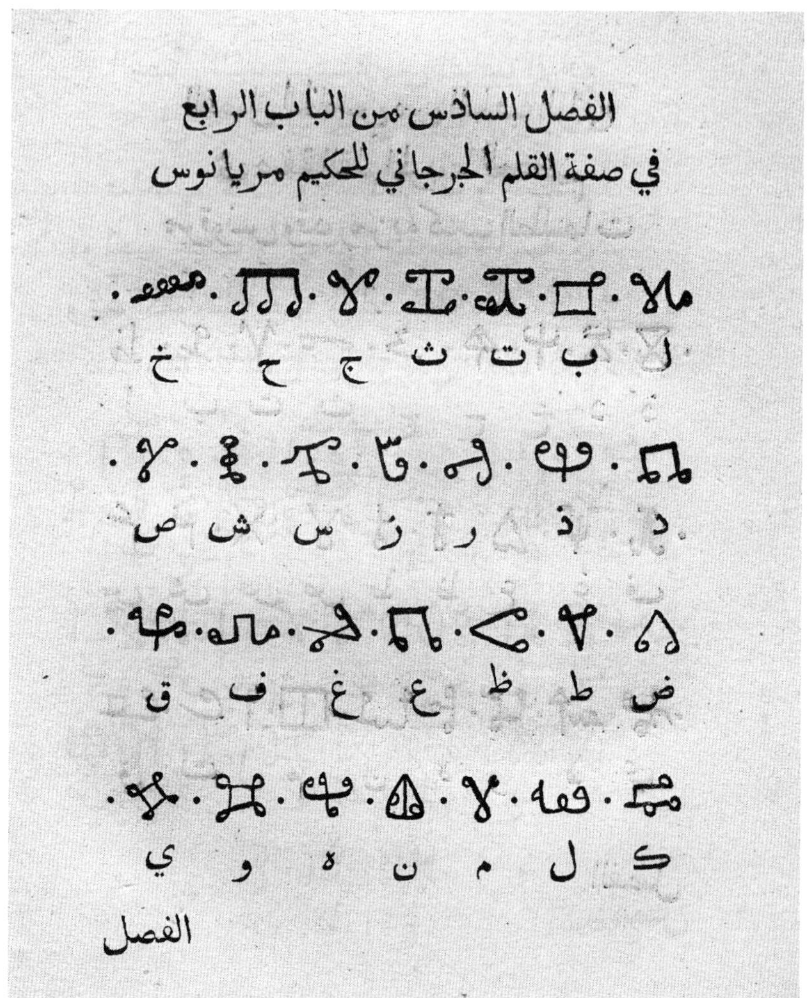

FIGURE 3.7 Mimshim alphabet, from Ibn Wahshiyyah, *Ancient Alphabets and Hieroglyphic Characters Explained*, trans. Joseph Hammer von Purgstall (1806). Note the Arabic alphabet right to left below the characters of the Mimshim. Public domain.

traditions, where they would have provided source material for Wahshiyyah.[40] But the consistent style of drawing in the Hammer version strongly suggested an artist's imaginings applied to make the multiple script forms.

Wahshiyyah's text is unique. No other compendium of such extent showing such variety is known from the period or within Arabic literature. Its exhaustiveness is not equaled until the compendium efforts of Angelo Rocca and James Bonaventure Hepburn were published at the beginning of the seventeenth century. Each of them had access to the Vatican library holdings, but neither showed any knowledge of Wahshiyyah's manuscript. If a copy was present in that collection, it did not surface to their attention, and their tables did not contain most of the scripts that appeared in Wahshiyyah, many of which have never been identified outside his presentation.

MYTHIC ALPHABETS: CROSSING THE RIVER, SOLOMON, HONORIUS OF THEBES, ADAM, ABRAHAM, NOAH

If the scripts that appeared in Ibn Wahshiyyah's work were unusual to the point of appearing to be fabrications, other scripts were remarkably standardized across centuries of manuscript and print publications. Several of these scripts were identified by name and have a sustained and repeated presence. Among these are Crossing the River, the Theban Script of Honorius, the Celestial, and Malachim. Another is identified as Adam's alphabet, one is linked to Solomon, and one occasionally to Noah. Other regularly used designations are *antediluvian* alphabets, those attributed to Esdra (Ezra) the scribe, and those attributed to Enoch. These scripts were always presented as complete alphabet specimens. The attribution of a script to a biblical or historical figure obviously lends authenticity, as in the dubious attributions of grimoires and magical texts. For instance, the *Sepher ha-Razim*, or *Book of Secrets*, dated to the third century, is supposed to have been given to Noah by the archangel Raziel and passed to King Solomon. This would make it earlier than the fictive Talmudic-period dates of the foundational Kabbalistic work, *The Zohar*, which, like the other Jewish mystical texts discussed above, was probably composed in the thirteenth century.[41]

These named alphabets may have been part of magical manuscripts, but they make a crucial appearance in the work of the scholar Johannes Trithemius, whose name echoes through occult and cryptographic literature. One, the Theban alphabet, has its earliest instantiation in his 1518 *Polygraphia*. Trithemius, a scholar and monk responsible for building a considerable library in the abbey at Sponheim, brought a great breadth of knowledge to this task. His earlier book, *Steganographia*, though finished by 1499, was only published posthumously in 1608 because of fears about its magical (possibly occult) practices.[42] Trithemius's focus was on encrypted communication, but his elaborate cipher codes prompted suspicion of conjuring with spirits.

In *Polygraphia*, Trithemius attributed the "Theban" alphabet to Honorius, whose *Liber juratus honorii* (*Sworn Book*) is a medieval grimoire. No trace of this script seems to exist in manuscript form, but the reasons for this may have more to do with the systematic destruction of magical materials by monks and clerics than with the alphabet's original author or actual source. Trithemius's example was copied many times. For instance, it appeared in Agrippa's 1533 *De occulta philosophia* (Occult philosophy), attributed to the thirteenth-century figure Petrus de Abano, whose *Heptameron* was a well-known book of rituals for the days of the week and the angels governing each. While Agrippa gave no citation, his version was close enough to Trithemius's to have been copied from it. The overlap in contents of d'Abano's *Heptameron* and the *Sworn Book*, both medieval grimoires,

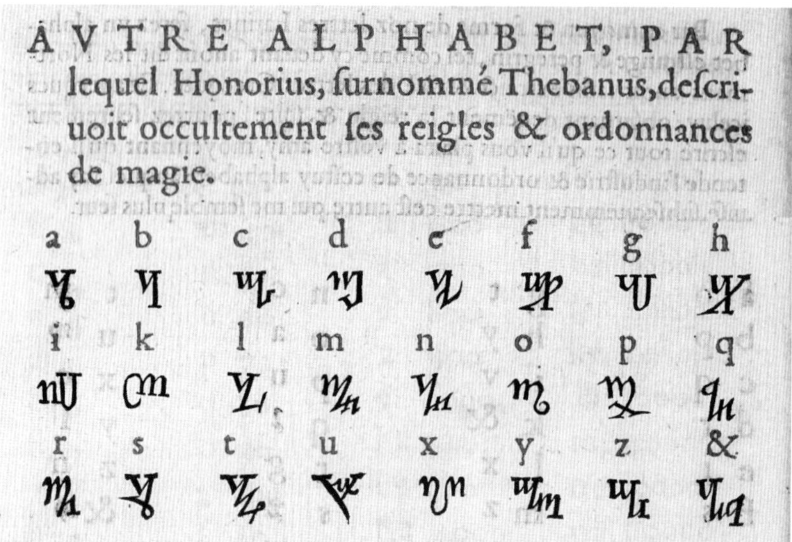
AVTRE ALPHABET, PAR lequel Honorius, surnommé Thebanus, descriuoit occultement ses reigles & ordonnances de magie.

a b c d e f g h

i k l m n o p q

r s t u x y z &

FIGURE 3.8 Johannes Trithemius, Theban alphabet (above), from *Polygraphia* (1518). Library of Congress, Rare Book and Special Collections Division.

could have prompted confusion.[43] Obscurity of authorship and attribution was common for medieval magical texts, as were copying practices without source citations.

Agrippa's printed text was copied and translated widely, and his work has remained a source for these alphabets into the present. While much consistency exists in this transmission tradition, variation occurs at the level of individual characters or in the names attached. The rendering of the "Theban" in Trithemius was entirely redrawn for the Agrippa edition, with the "key" letters carved on the same block and in the same style as the Theban ones. By contrast, Trithemius's printer set the key letters in metal type and printed them in red to contrast with the carved Theban characters, printed in black. Though Agrippa's engraver did a careful job of studying the shapes of each character, the letters as a whole were more crude, less regular in the execution of the vertical strokes, and each pitched at slightly different angles, giving the whole a less stable quality. Agrippa's version was a *picture* of the first, and the fact that the letters were carved on a single block emphasized the alphabet as a single thing, not a set of elements to be used.

Even more frequently reproduced, the alphabet known as Transitus Fluvii, or Crossing the River, was traditionally associated with Abraham's departure from Chaldea, hence its name. The script appeared in the work by the alchemist Johannes Pantheus, *Voarchadumia*, published in 1530, where the letters were crudely carved in wood. They had a strong graphic power to them in this rendering, seeming almost primal, a graphic argument for their being the "original" letters. They are mainly lunette characters, but not exclusively, with the *alef* close to the square Hebrew letter. In Agrippa's version, 1533, the letters appeared to be cast in metal, since they were more

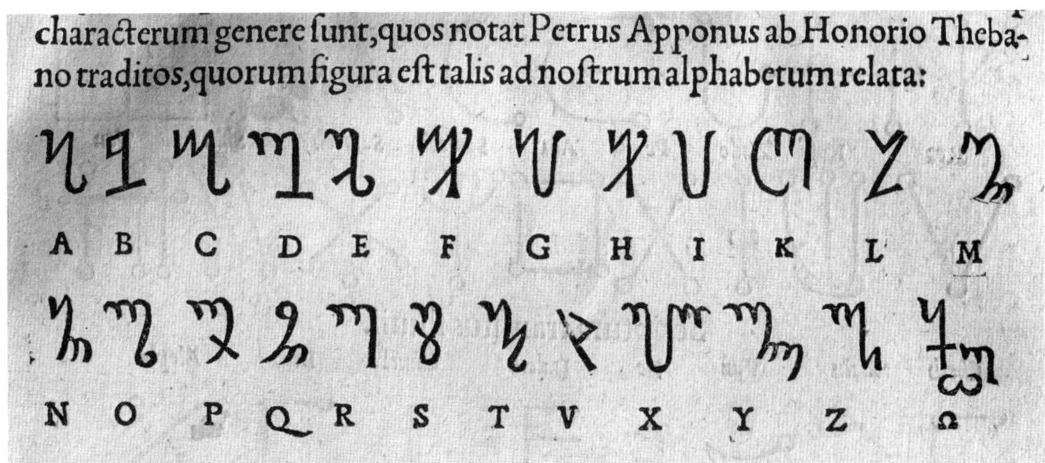
characterum genere ſunt, quos notat Petrus Apponus ab Honorio Theba-
no traditos, quorum figura eſt talis ad noſtrum alphabetum relata:
A B C D E F G H I K L M
N O P Q R S T V X Y Z Ω

FIGURE 3.9 Cornelius Agrippa, Theban alphabet, with the attribution to Petrus de Abano. From *De occulta philosophia* (1533). Library of Congress, Rare Book and Special Collections Division.

delicate, and included more curves. The "flying" *alef* was often the first element in this script, but variations appear, as was evident in the image of Claude Duret's 1613 version in *Le thrésor*. Crossing the River was repeated in one compendium after another, with only minor alterations in a few characters.[44] The basic lunette form suggested the same medieval origins as the celestial scripts, and the name gave the alphabet its affiliation with biblical antiquity. Variants of this script, sometimes titled Celestial, and sometimes with a square *alef* or a *beth* with an inward pointed spine, were, again, copied consistently.

Among other widely copied scripts, one was frequently associated with Adam (sometimes identified as a gift from the angel Raphael, or Raziel). A version of Adam's alphabet also appeared in Wahshiyyah, evidence that this author had access to similar traditional sources.[45] The "Adam's alphabet" in Wahshiyyah was much closer to Syriac script, however, while another version in a vast compendium edited by Teseo Ambrogio in 1538 was described as coming from Raphael through the (unidentified) *Book of Fire* to Adam and his children.

The alphabet usually attributed to Adam had several distinct glyphic forms that were not close to the lunettes, nor to the Paleo-Hebrew and early Samaritan associated with Moses. In Adam's alphabet, other graphic influences, perhaps shapes borrowed from Egyptian Coptic, were evident in the rounded strokes and lyre-like forms. Like Crossing the River, it was copied intact and repeatedly until the habit of including artificial alphabets in script compendia ceased at the end of the eighteenth century.

The other named alphabet among these artificial scripts was the Malachim. The unusual *alef* and *beth*, the many-branched *samech*, and the square *cheth* were quite distinct, and these features were also copied repeatedly and more or less faithfully in graphic transmission.

The alphabet attributed to Noah (or sometimes to Moses) was actually

FIGURE 3.10 Johannes Pantheus, Crossing the River (Transitus Fluvii), *Voarchadumia* (1530). Note the woodcut quality of the letters by contrast with the metal key letters. Public domain.

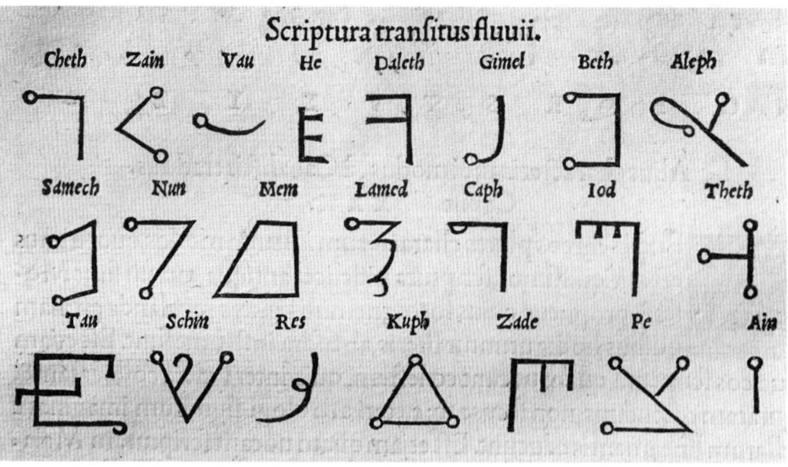

FIGURE 3.11 Cornelius Agrippa, Crossing the River, *De occulta philosophia* (1533). Note the fluid curves of the metal version. Library of Congress, Rare Book and Special Collections Division.

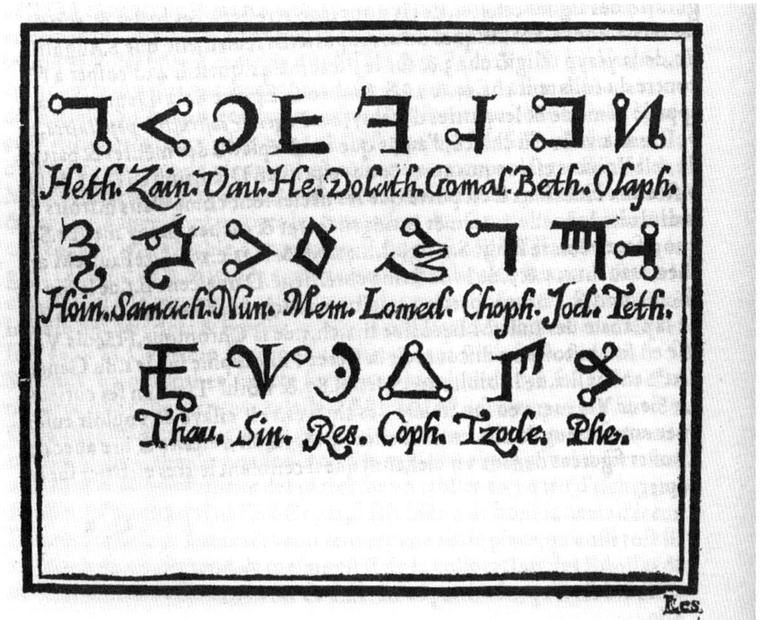

FIGURE 3.12 Claude Duret, Crossing the River, *Le thrésor* (1613). Public domain.

a form of Paleo-Hebrew. This script had a less robust career than Transitus Fluvii or Malachim, and was sometimes present, sometimes not, in the occult compendia. Though each individual script was copied with a fair amount of consistency, these alphabets did not travel as a group but individually. As compendium makers such as the de Bry brothers exercised their encyclopedic impulses, many of these scripts would reappear, carefully redrawn or recut, and faithfully described and attributed. The fact that they were alphabets mattered, sustaining their identity as elemental symbols. The characters were the components of the world, and each magical or celestial script aspired to be the building blocks of the cosmos, imbued with Divine power, a persistent echo of Kabbalistic beliefs and other mystical traditions.

ENOCH

One of the few alphabets in this magical tradition to actually have been used, the Enochian, played a role in the conjuring activity of John Dee and Edward Kelley.

The Book of Enoch was referenced by a few early Christian authors, who appeared to have some knowledge of its contents. Fragments of the work, perhaps by a "Jewish or Samaritan Hellenist," were passed through Alexander Polyhistor (a Greek historian, first century BCE) and Eusebius, common conduits.[46] No early manuscript provides a text for this book, though

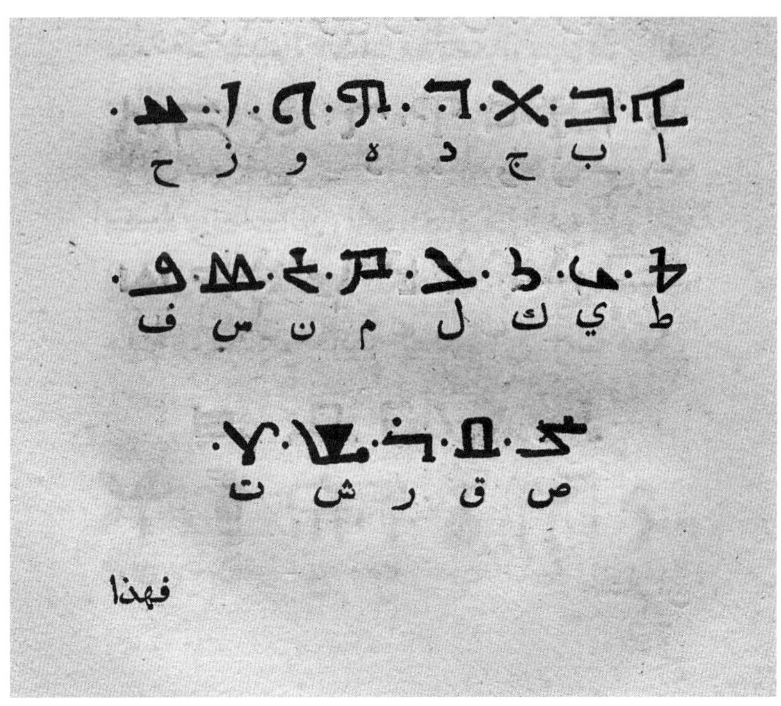

FIGURE 3.13 Ibn Wahshiyyah, Adam's alphabet. Ninth century. Public domain.

DIVERSARVMQ. LITERARVM. 203
inuentas. Angelũ Raphiel, in libro qui dicitur liber ignis, illas Adæ Protoplaſto dediſſe ſcriptas aſſeuerat, & ob id filios Adam eas recuſare non poſſe. Quarum quidem literarum figuræ, & nomina ſunt infraſcripta, videlicet.

Hhet. Zain. Vau. He. Daleth. Gimel. Beth. Aleph.

Ain. Samech. Nun. Mem. Lamed. Caph. Iod. Teth.

Thau. Sin. Res. Coph. Zadai. Phe.

Poſuit autem ibidem Raziel, dictarum literarum inter=

FIGURE 3.14 Teseo Ambrogio, Adam's alphabet, from *Introductio in Chaldaicum linguam* [. . .] (1538). This alphabet has very little in common graphically with Wahshiyyah's version. Public domain.

some scholars have argued for the presence of fragments of the text among the Dead Sea Scrolls.[47] Apparently Origen, the biblical scholar of the third century, and Augustine in the fourth, both dismissed the existing Enoch materials as inauthentic, but various other authors have referenced them since the early centuries of the Common Era. The oldest manuscripts are in Ge'ez, an ancient South Semitic language that emerged around the fifth century BCE, which is consistent with the claims made for its antiquity. In the East, the Book of Enoch dropped from discussion after the ninth century (in the West, a little earlier), until it was mentioned by the medieval scholars Alexander Neckham (twelfth century) and Vincent of Beauvais (thirteenth).[48] More recent scholarship suggests that the book may have been composed in Aramaic originally and, as common, been the work of several authors. The text was considered lost until copies were brought from Abyssinia to Europe in the late eighteenth century and then translated into English in the early nineteenth.[49] A script designated as Enochian appeared in Pantheus's 1530 *Voarchadumia*, in company with the Transitus Fluvii discussed above. Like the other magical scripts, it was copied, sometimes with variations, by many others afterward.

FIGURE 3.15 Theodor de Bry and Israel de Bry, *Alphabeta et charactères* (1596). The script assigned to Moses is, appropriately, Paleo-Hebrew. The modern square letters appear below. Source: gallica.bnf.fr / Bibliothèque nationale de France.

FIGURE 3.16 Enochian script in Johannes Pantheus, *Voarchadumia* (1530), possibly the earliest print version. Public domain.

The Enochian adopted by Dee and Kelley had an equally obscure pedigree, though the pair of conjurers supposedly possessed a copy of the apocryphal book in manuscript.[50] Dee's records of his work indicated that an alphabet was "revealed" on March 26, 1583.[51] This angelic alphabet appeared to be "an alternate Roman of only 21 characters" that omitted the *K* and *Y*.[52] The Enochian scripts recorded by Dee or Kelley appeared in various of their manuscripts.[53] Dee's Enochian only partly matched that of Pantheus, so it was probably not copied from that source.[54] Dee had gone to great lengths to obtain a copy of Trithemius's *Steganographia*, the banned book on cryptography containing magical spells as well as cipher codes. Discussion of Dee's sources has occupied scholars since the seventeenth century, when Meric Casaubon, writing about Dee's angelic letters, suggested that they were from Teseo Ambrogio, who had taken them "out of Magical books, as himself professeth."[55] Dee owned a copy of Ambrogio's 1538 *Introductio in Chaldaicum linguam* (Introduction to the Chaldean tongue), which drew on Pantheus (1530) and Agrippa (1533), but no Enochian script appeared in either Ambrogio or Agrippa's work, only in Pantheus. Agrippa had relied heavily on Book 6 of Trithemius's *Polygraphia* of 1518, demonstrating, yet again, that graphic transmission history was central to the spread of these scripts.[56] The precise source of Dee and Kelley's script remained unclear, even if the characters are copied afterward and codified as Enochian.

FIGURE 3.17 Sloan mss. 3188, "John Dee's conferences with angels," f. 104, showing Enochian taken from Dee's notes, around 1583. Image © The British Library Board. By permission.

HRABANUS MAURUS AND AETHICUS ISTER

Copies of a remarkable alphabet, attributed to a fictive seventh-to-eighth-century writer, Aethicus Ister, appeared with striking consistency in several medieval manuscripts whose production was separated by time and place. The alphabet was mythic in origin, like its author, and never used to write a textual document. But it was reproduced repeatedly with a fair amount of accuracy—a feat that could only have been accomplished through direct copying from one exemplar to another. In each rendering, the letters have the same forms, names, and sequence as any other alphabet, thus preserving a structural correspondence to standard scripts as well as an identical relation with each other.

Copies of the Aethicus alphabet appeared in at least two manuscripts of *Cosmographia*, one from the end of the eighth century (currently at the Bodleian) and one from the end of the tenth (now in Leiden), where the script was appended to the text as part of the story.[57] Aethicus claimed to be a Scythian and nomad from an area of modern Iran. But the alphabet associated with his name is not to be found among any of the scripts of that region. In *Cosmographia* he features as one of two fictive characters in this anonymous seventh-to-eighth-century travelogue, staged as a conversation between the protagonist and St. Jerome. Sometimes termed a "forgery" because it is anachronistic in its claims and references, the work contains a great deal of humor and irreverence as well as "information" about various exotic areas of the world. The same unusual alphabet shows up in multiple manuscripts from the ninth through twelfth centuries, including the very famous compendium of runic scripts produced by an Anglo-Saxon monk, Byrhtferth. Finally, virtually unchanged, the Aethicus alphabet finds its way into print where it is produced, often in company with German or Scandinavian runes with which it is only peripherally related.

The unsurpassed scholar of runic scripts, René Derolez, linked this transmission history to a text by the ninth-century bishop in the Germanic monastery

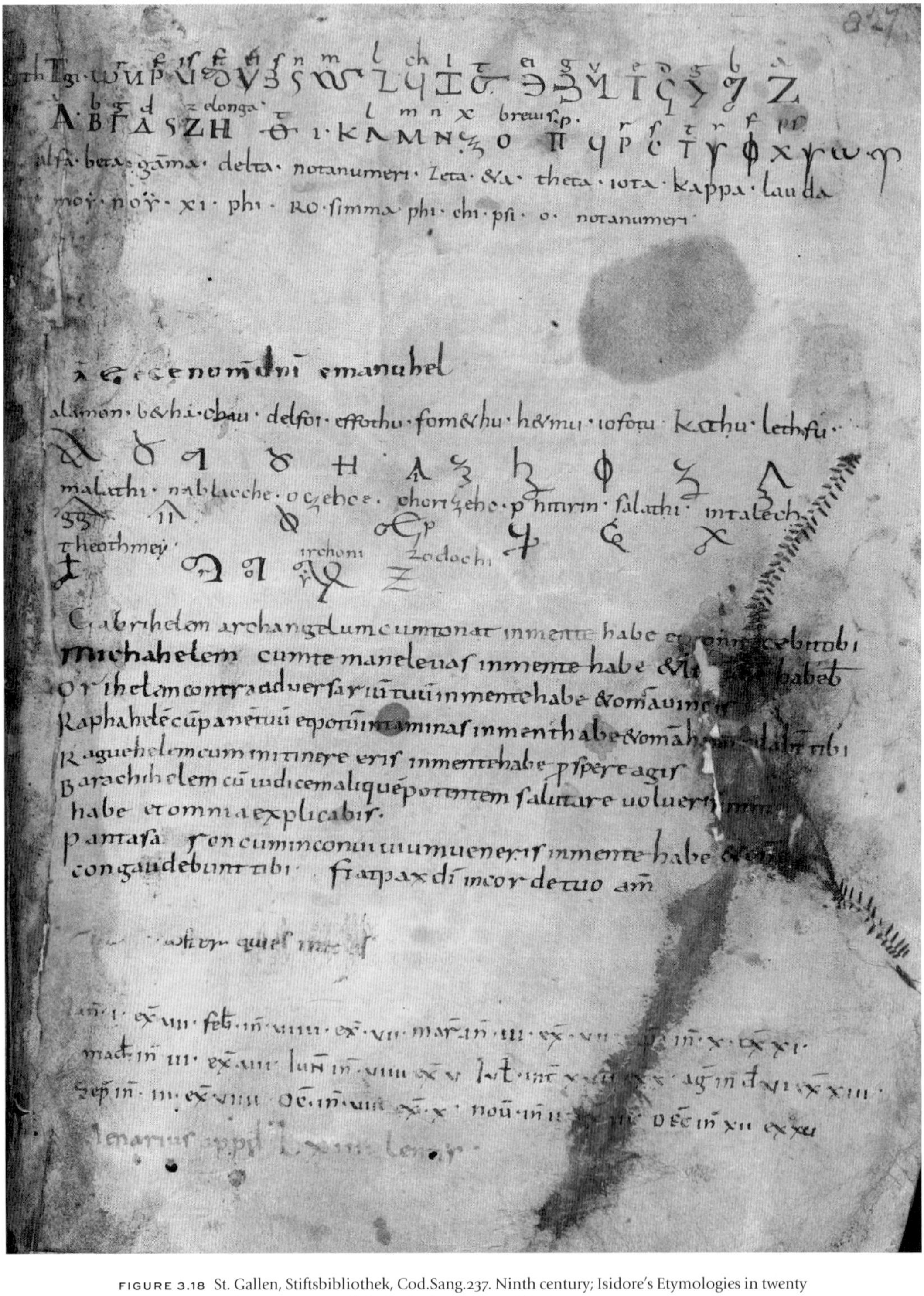

FIGURE 3.18 St. Gallen, Stiftsbibliothek, Cod.Sang.237. Ninth century; Isidore's Etymologies in twenty books. Showing the Aethicus Ister alphabet in the center. Public domain.

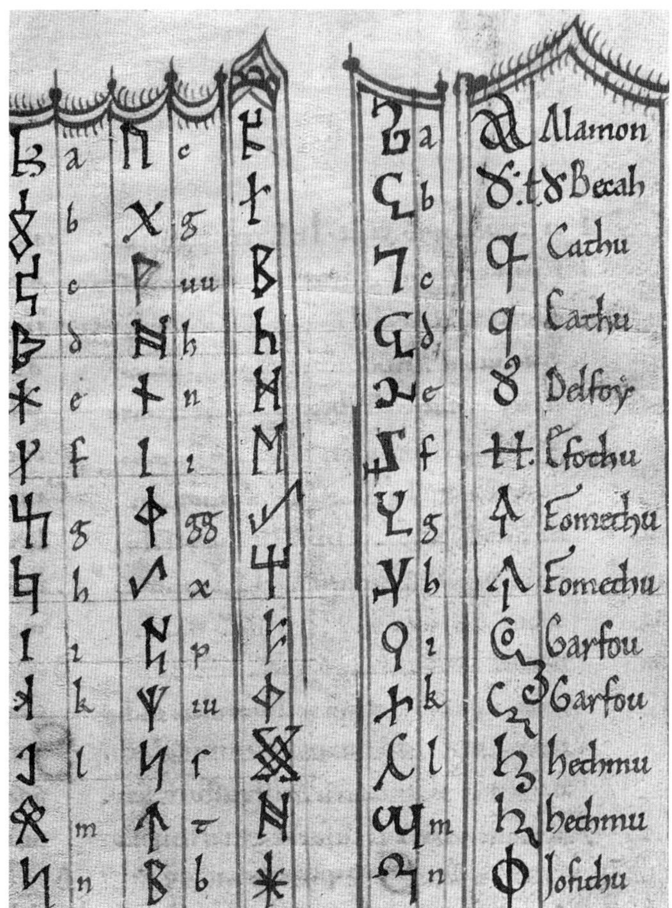

FIGURE 3.19 Thorney Computus, St. John's MS 17 folio 5v. Twelfth century (approx. 1110–11). Detail showing first part of Ister alphabet, farthest right, from Byrhtferth. By permission of the president and fellows of St John's College Oxford.

at Fulda, Hrabanus Maurus.[58] In *De inventione litterarum* (The invention of letters), the Aethicus alphabet appears in company with Greek, Latin, Hebrew, and, depending on the version, various runic scripts. Derolez tracked the manuscript lineage of the short text by Maurus, noting the presence and absence of the Aethicus script in every example. In some instances, only the names of the letters (*alamon*, *becha*, etc.) were preserved, not the forms (for which variations of Greek or Latin were inserted). Maurus was known for his religious writings and also his remarkable visual poems, and this small text on letters did not figure prominently in his work. But a handful of manuscripts of Hrabanus's text contained similar alphabets. The Codex Sangallensis 878, for instance, an early ninth-century manuscript from Fulda, contained Greek, Hebrew, Anglo-Saxon runes, alongside a Scandinavian runic alphabet and a Furthark.[59] These were all living scripts, and the engagement with runes could be attributed in part to geographic location and availability of language as well as examples. Runes were an invention of the Common Era, and their occult associations came much later. Originally

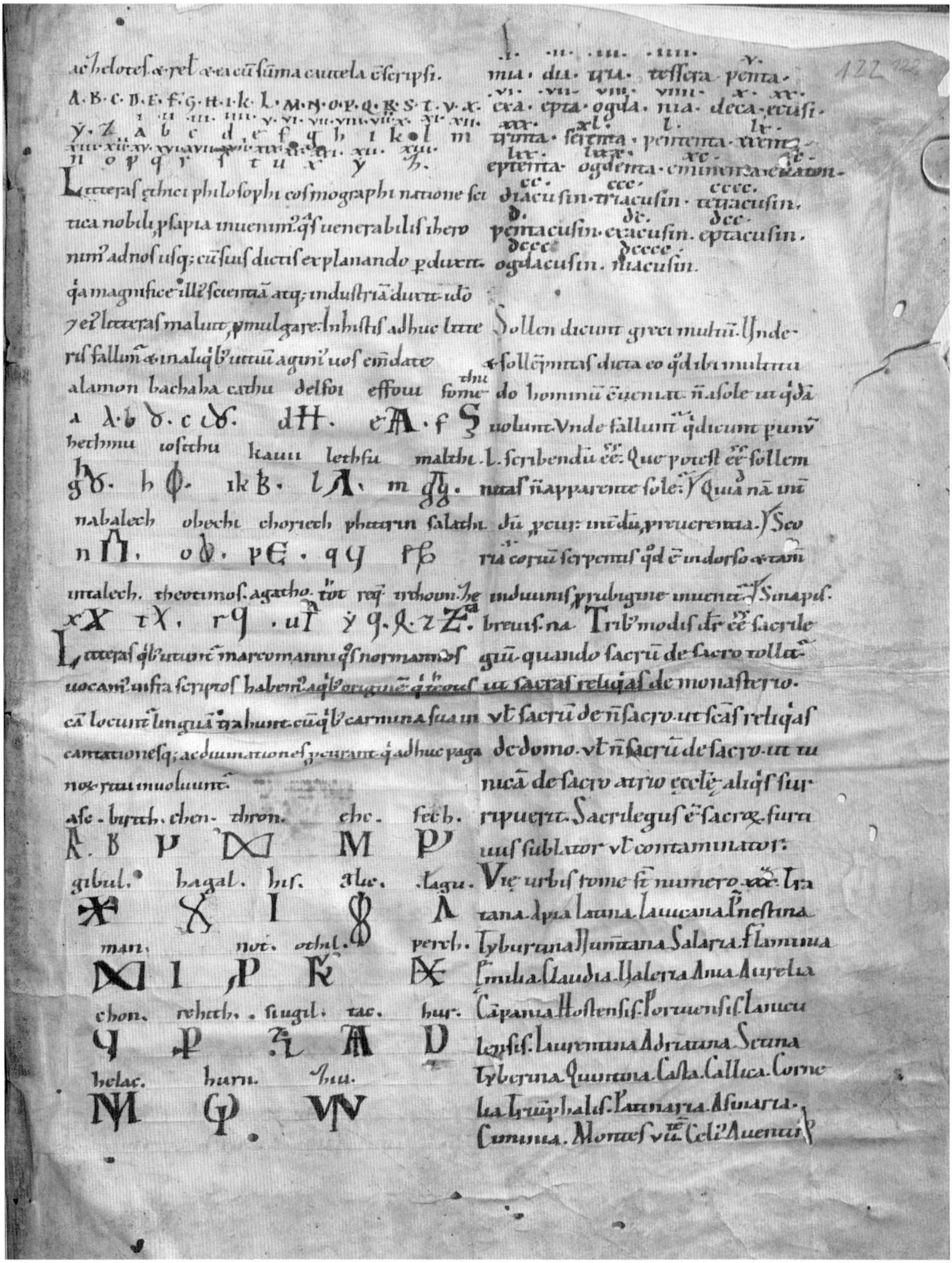

FIGURE 3.20 Twelfth-century manuscript of Hrabanus Maurus showing the Aethicus alphabet in the middle of the left-hand column. Mss. 1966, fp; 121v–122r; second half of twelfth century, Nuremberg. © Germanische Nationalmuseum.

Litteras etiam Æthici philosophi cosmographi natione Scythica, nobili prosapia, invenimus, quas venerabilis Hieronymus presbyter ad nos usque cum suis dictis explanando perduxit, quia magnifice ipsius scientiam atque industriam duxit; ideo et ejus litteras maluit promulgare. Si in istis adhuc litteris fallimur, et in aliquibus vitium agemus, vos emendate.

alamon. becha. chatu. delfoi. effothu. fonethu. garfou. hetmu

a b c d e f g h

iofitu. kaitu. lehtfu. malathi. nabalech. ozechi. chorizech. phitirin. salathi. intalech.

i k l m n o p q f x

theotimos. agathot. req. yrchoim. zeta.

t r u y z

FIGURE 3.21 Melchior Goldast, *Alamannicarum antiquitatum* (1606), showing the Aethicus alphabet second from top in this reproduction of Maurus's text. Public domain.

they were used as a variation of the Latin alphabet, and the signs were made with short, straight lines that were easy to carve in stone and wood. Putting the Aethicus alphabet in their company indicated more about Maurus's location than the origin of the fictive script, though Derolez also noted the scholarly tradition that suggested a lineage of runic scripts from the Venerable Bede, to the Continent by way of Alcuin of York, the monk responsible for the Carolingian script, and then into the work of Maurus. The argument was that the Aethicus script traveled with them.[60]

Maurus defended the Ister alphabet, claiming that Jerome had called for greater knowledge of it. This was likely a result of Maurus's having taken the dialogues in the *Cosmographia* as genuine. *Cosmographia* featured St. Jerome as a character in dialogue with Aethicus, with their conversation propelling the narrative. Therefore the Jerome that ninth-century Maurus was referencing here was not the fourth-century editor and translator but the fictional character from the eighth-century imaginative *Cosmographia*.[61] Other instances of the same alphabet appeared in an early twelfth-century manuscript of Maurus's work, now in the German National Museum, another in the Austrian National Library, and a handful of others.[62] The Aethicus alphabet was also present in the famous twelfth-century (1130) Anglo-Saxon Byrhtferth manuscript, a major compilation of medieval scientific knowledge, where it was placed alongside several variations of runes. Clearly the script had traveled intact from the Continent through such copying.[63] Melchior Goldast, in *Alamannicarum antiquitatum* (Ancient Germans) (1606), also put the Aethicus alphabet in proximity to runes.[64]

Though the Aethicus script had some vaguely runic features in its angular strokes, it was an artificial script (Derolez called it "spurious") that would not have been extracted from texts, only copied like the other artificial alphabets already discussed. The script was repeated almost exactly in other manuscripts of *Cosmographia*, while further indication of the connection between runes and the Aethicus script is demonstrated by various instantiations in Derolez's definitive twentieth-century study, *Runica manuscripta* (Runic manuscripts).[65] Once in place, and with a false pedigree established, the Aethicus script seemed to carry authenticity. Its graphic specificity, that it was unlike anything else and yet clearly alphabetic in sequence and number of characters, made it seem genuine, especially in the company of exotic-seeming runes.

MANDEVILLE, HIS SCRIPTS, AND PENTEXTOIRE

Hebrew was also treated as an "exotic" script in the manuscripts of another fictive traveler, the twelfth-century John Mandeville. Supposedly an English knight who went to Jerusalem, the narrator "Mandeville" described the "marvelous East" and the wonders of India and the biblical lands. The book was a best seller, translated into more than ten languages, and influenced Christine de Pisan, Christopher Columbus, Sir Walter Raleigh, and Gerhardus Mercator, among the more famous of its readers.[66] Slightly later, the accounts of an actual pilgrim, Bernard Breydenbach, contained images of a handful of Hebrew, Saracen, Coptic, and other actual alphabets as evidence of his travels, adding authenticity to his tales by their presence. The exotic and the artificial were not always clearly distinguished in these contexts, nor were fictive and fanciful accounts.

Debates about John Mandeville's identity are less easy to resolve than those of the clearly fictive Aethicus. Mandeville may have been an actual person, though possessed of a different name, but it seems he never visited the places he described in his famous *Travels*. His use of scripts, "an enigmatical alphabet for each of the countries described" was a gesture of authenticity, making his faked experience more real as a result.[67]

The scholar Malcolm Letts inventoried the alphabets in all Mandeville manuscripts and determined that the following scripts were named in the tale: Greek, Hebrew, Egyptian (Coptic), Saracen, Persian/Chaldean, Tartar-Russ, and Cathayan/Pentextoire. Except for the first three, the designations of these are not stable, and determining the sources for their graphic forms leads into a minefield of possibilities. For instance, Derolez, the scholar of runes mentioned in connection with Aethicus, compared the "Cathayan" script in Mandeville's work to a Gothic one ascribed to a specific "Ratisbon scribe who studied in France about A.D. 1000" and came to the conclusion that "these two alphabets go back to a common prototype."[68] He also pointed out that Mandeville's Chaldean contained the letters of the Scythian alphabet appended to Aethicus's *Cosmographia*. However, the Scythian alphabet resembled runes (straight lines, branches, and treelike forms), and the Aethicus alphabet was closer to Coptic (round and fluid).[69] By contrast to the actual scripts, this Cathayan "Pentextoire" appeared to be a fully "fantastic alphabet . . . spoken in the fabulous kingdom of Prester John" (the legendary Christian ruler).[70]

The idea that the letters might simply be fabrications, "introduced in order to increase the atmosphere of wonder and mystery which surrounds the whole book" seems credible.[71] Making use of some resemblance to known scripts would be sufficient, in this case. Some alphabets seem to have been added by the scribes, not copied from a source manuscript, since they showed considerable variation in whether, as well as how, they are presented. Various copyists took the liberty of adding more at will, and one version from 1430 has seventeen alphabets. Another included a script named for the "Old Man of the Mountain," while one adventurous scribe added a Chinese script.[72] So while the Aethicus alphabet was copied correctly in its transmission, the scribes adorning Mandeville's text seemed to feel freer to introduce other inventions and scripts, an interesting act of deference for Aethicus and its perceived authenticity as a specific, not generic, script.

The ideology of scripts, their use for a cultural agenda, was also evident in Mandeville, particularly with the way the Hebrew script was mapped onto geography. In her careful study, the medievalist Marcia Kupfer showed that the scribes who interpolated the letterforms into the Mandeville manuscripts drew on compendia that went back into the Middle Ages and used them to create mangled and approximate images of letterforms with which they were not familiar—"invented characters and runes for Egyptian, Chaldean, and Saracen" for instance.[73] Her argument was that by making connections between alphabets (or languages) and national borders, the author could suggest that Jews, in particular, were contained within specific regions rather than participating in diverse communities.[74] The geography of alphabet distribution was thus inflected with racial overtones.

Continuing her discussion, Kupfer described one manuscript (in a corpus of more than 250) in which a scribe created a "perfect iteration of a single alphabet—Hebrew." This image was rendered by "a calligrapher emulating a model with studied, archaeological accuracy." Kupfer commented on the copying technique, calling it "mimicry" used in the "representation of ethnic identity." This particular manuscript was commissioned by Charles V, and the Hebrew was not written by someone accustomed to the scribal stroke patterns, but was made by "carefully copying unfamiliar forms."[75] Kupfer contrasted this with another "fully calligraphic" example of Hebrew.[76] The presence of the expert rendering in the commissioned manuscript was to support the image of Charles V as an "erudite ruler, conversant in the archetypal sacred language . . . the original language spoken between God and man."[77] This occurred even as Charles was putting anti-Semitic policies in place (an Expulsion had been ordered in 1394 from all of the regions of France governed by the crown).[78] Her discussion made a striking case for the way the graphic renderings of the alphabet served ideological purposes by making them more or less exotic and legitimating their association with specific peoples.

The sources on which scribes of the Mandeville manuscripts might have drawn included Isidore of Seville's *Etymologies*, the medieval encyclopedia whose discussion of the origins of scripts dates to the late eighth century and whose manuscript renderings may have included script compendia.[79]

The scholar Elmar Seebold has identified several manuscripts with alphabet compendia, containing at least Chaldean (Aramaic), Egyptian (Coptic), Greek, and Hebrew, the scripts that would have been best known in the period.[80] Authentic sources for copying existed, so not all travelers' accounts made use of fanciful or fictional alphabets.

EXOTIC SCRIPTS: RUNES, SYRIAC, SAMARITAN

While many magical and mythic scripts were preserved in traditions of travel narratives, some genuine alphabetic forms were also exoticized in works that used images of scripts to portray their own authenticity—as well as to engage in the culture politics of "othering" that is part of cross-cultural encounters (as per Kupfer's discussion of Hebrew). In the early 1480s, Bernard Breydenbach, a wealthy German cleric, decided that his life had been sufficiently wicked that he needed to make some demonstration of humility and faith. He organized a journey to the Near East with a small group of friends. An account of this pilgrimage, *Travels to the Holy Land*, was first published in 1486.[81] In addition to pictorial and remarkably precise cartographic images, the edition included printed versions of several unusual looking scripts.[82] These alphabets were exotic to the European readers for whom even Hebrew, Arabic, and Greek were unfamiliar, and for whom scripts like Coptic, Syrian, and Ethiopic were, as they might be to readers of the Latin alphabet today, unknown. All were alphabets accurately copied from examples of texts in living languages. None were fanciful or artificial. But they were presented as specimens from exotic lands, the graphic embodiment of languages still largely outside the experience of European and English readers. They were engraved on relief blocks (probably by Erhard Reuwich, the illustrator who provided the rest of the renowned woodcuts in the work) from original drawings possibly supplied "by Paul Walther of Guglingen . . . a Franciscan friar who joined Breydenbach and his tour in Jerusalem in the summer of 1483, having previously spent a year there studying the languages of the Holy Land."[83] These details suggest direct observation and documentation.

Much care and expertise went into the production of these graphic examples. Whoever had made the originals from which the blocks were cut had extracted the letters from texts. They were presented as specimens, in the form of abecedaria—where each letter accompanied by its name (*alef/aleph, beth/beta*, etc.) presented in the conventional order. The presentation of alphabet specimens this way was already an established convention in medieval manuscripts, but in Breydenbach the travelogue provided a context that assured these letters would be read with a particular inflection.

The visual character of the scripts was meant to communicate several things to the readers of the narrative. Their exotic quality lent Breydenbach's text authenticity, while casting the Holy Land as a place of otherness. Travels into and out of that region had been limited for centuries and though contact with the Near East, the Holy Land, and Arabia had been renewed with the Crusades and trade through the Mediterranean had never ceased, it was managed mainly through a Venetian monopoly. With the exception of Greek, knowledge of the languages of these scripts was limited or nonexistent in the European and British contexts, and so the appearance of these exotic, but highly organized, sets of letters on the page was a provocation to scholarly engagement as well as popular fancy. Unlike some of the images of imaginary and legendary creatures (humans with feet big enough to use as umbrellas, unicorns, and so on that had also appeared in Mandeville's *Travels*), the scripts in Breydenbach's work were excerpted from the careful study of living alphabets, scripts used for actual languages. Within the mode of graphic transmission, Breydenbach's accounts stand out for their rigorous commitment to factual reality.

CONCLUSION

Graphic transmission of knowledge and the reproduction of visual forms of information are quite distinct from those of textual production. For where a paraphrase or restatement of textual information may alter it slightly, graphic errors can easily corrupt visual information past all usefulness. A graphic copy depends on an exemplar, a prototype, that must be seen, looked at, studied, and replicated—not described but instantiated.

A copy can either replicate stroke sequences and gestural patterns or be a picture, redrawn, of letters treated as images. In the refined regularity of medieval hands, stroke sequence and gesture are highly disciplined, and the skill of making letterforms is embodied. The scribe does not stop to think about each stroke of the pen but enacts the writing in a physical gesture trained by long habit. Drawing a letter is not the same as writing it, an important distinction. Drawing a letter requires studying each visual graphic form as a shape and making a picture of it, rather than following the stroke patterns of habit. This distinction in copying will mark certain examples of scripts as exotic when their rendering embodies the act of copying an unfamiliar visual exemplar. A copy is a marked remediation. Until the advent of mechanical means in the nineteenth century, all copying involved a human eye and hand as part of that remediation.

The virtuosity of writing masters in later centuries was evident in their capacity to copy—hands, styles, scripts, and even printed letters—with exquisite accuracy. Some of these copies were done through skilled hand movement, but others also fall into the category of drawn pictures of letters. Interestingly, almost none of the magical alphabets appeared in the work of Renaissance writing masters, with the exception of a lunette script in Giovanni Battista Palatino's 1540 *Libro nuovo d'imparare a scrivere* (New book for learning to write), and in Urbanus Wyss's *Das Schreibbuch* (Writing book; 1549).[84] These manuals were demonstrations of skill, promotional materials for engaging clients, and the appeal of magical alphabets may have been limited.

Exotic alphabets have their own lineage, and the fanciful and imaginary ones can be tracked, at least partially. In the case of imaginary or "spurious" alphabets, such as the one attributed to Aethicus, copying was the only way such graphic forms could have been transmitted with integrity. Likewise, the "artificial" alphabets, such as magical, celestial, and angelic scripts, were passed forward through imitation.

By the end of the eighteenth century, these imagined and exotic scripts were largely marginalized, excluded from "serious" studies of the history of writing and scripts. Though they did not disappear entirely, they were almost never included among the compendia of scripts that composed the writing systems of the world. Edmund Fry's 1799 publication, *Pantographia*, was the chief exception.

FOUR

The Confusion of Tongues and Compendia of Scripts

In an early sixteenth-century vogue for compendia, a number of printed volumes containing specimens of alphabetic scripts appeared in rapid succession.[1] These were fueled by various impulses: a drive to collect occult or esoteric knowledge, curiosity about exotic and ancient scripts, and a desire for an encyclopedic grasp of information across spans of history and geography. The analysis of the diversity of languages as evidence of the Confusion of Tongues at Babel, an event considered historical fact, sustained a long-standing quest to discover the "original" alphabet of humankind.

Questions about the identity of that "original" alphabet occupied scholars throughout the sixteenth and seventeenth centuries (and after, but in different form). As knowledge of scripts expanded, it brought a growing recognition that Hebrew might not have been the "first" language, and the modern square letters, invented between the seventh and first centuries BCE, not the original script. This forced a reassessment of what had happened before and after Babel. The drive to resolve this question, fraught as it was with theological implications for the authenticity of Scripture, created interest in collecting examples from ancient languages and diverse scripts.

Compendia gradually played another role as well. By serving as sites for the collection of specimens from the widening world of global expansion, in combination with those representing the equally exotic history of ancient and mythic alphabets, they provided a site in which to unify this diversity. Scholars sought specimens of writing the same way they captured insects, shells, or plants, and alphabet compendia participated in the organized representation and ordering of global and historical knowledge.[2] Compendia documented the unfamiliar writing of "others," while simultaneously offering a unifying narrative about the existence of an original language, thus marking and erasing cultural difference simultaneously.

One example of this encyclopedic impulse is Conrad Gessner's *Mithridates* (1555), whose title invokes the second-century BCE Anatolian emperor renowned for his knowledge of languages.[3] Gessner began his work with this statement: "The story of the Confusion of Tongues, handed down in the sacred texts, does not need to be told to us again."[4] His *Mithridates* was a "catalogue of the then known ancient and modern languages of the world" that gave "condensed information about 16th century knowledge of individual languages and theories concerning their history and their genetic relationship."[5] Gessner was not focused on visual specimens. Instead, his enumeration of languages created a lexicon through which to link them to geographic locations, thus providing a foundation for future language atlases and gazetteers. Between 1545 and 1549, Gessner had created an even more massive reference, the *Bibliotheca universalis* (Universal library), intended to be a bibliography of all the authors who had ever lived and the total of their works, along with an equally complete listing of the animals, plants, and insects of the world.[6] Most of the compendium makers agreed with Gessner that the story of the Confusion of Tongues did need not to be stated anew in every instance. They took it as a given historical precondition for understanding the differences among languages—and scripts. Gessner's models of history were descriptive rather than analytic, but he recognized that common features and marked distinctions among language communities in various locations were not arbitrary or random.

Other fundamental questions about biblical history contributed to the intellectual frameworks on which sixteenth- and seventeenth-century scholars approached language. Some wondered what language Adam had used when he followed God's command to name all things—and whether he had writing. The story of Seth continued to be cited in scholarly literature but without debate. The pillars of stone and brick were also described as historical fact. Another question was whether Noah spoke Hebrew and instructed his sons and their descendants in the tongue, and if so, how long was it from the Deluge to the days of Moses (writing and the Law) and Babel (Confusion)? These questions are germane to alphabet studies because the desire to recover the oldest, original, most "holy" language of the scriptures persisted.[7] Prime contenders were various versions of Hebrew, Chaldean, Syrian, or the "rediscovered" Samaritan, and other Semitic and Aramaic scripts. As late as the 1850s, Nabataean was put forth as the "oldest" alphabet, even though it was derived from Aramaic in the second century

BCE.[8] Each was assessed against the background of biblical history guided by the question of whether they descended from a single tongue.

Compendia had existed in manuscripts, but printed works circulated in a culture of bibliographical citation.[9] The compendium makers were the last scholars who relied exclusively on textual authorities and graphic exemplars for their work. Artifacts and physical evidence became increasingly available in the seventeenth and eighteenth centuries, shifting investigation into modern frames of historical reference. Not every compendium contained occult or angelic scripts, and by no means was every alphabet in these collections an esoteric one. But these authors did not make clear distinctions between esoteric and natural languages, nor between scripts used within occult practice and those that were used to record living speech. Magical alphabets retained the allure of esoteric keys to systematic knowledge associated with multiple traditions—Greek Hermeticism, ancient magic with Babylonian roots, Christian Gnosticism, and both Jewish Kabbalah and Christian Cabala. The erudite works of the compendium makers created a chain of citations on which later scholars of the alphabet depended to track these many traditions and filiations.

THE TRADITION OF COMPENDIA

With two exceptions, the focus in this chapter will be on works from the sixteenth and seventeenth centuries. One exception is Edmund Fry's remarkable *Pantographia*, published in London in 1799, which provides an important endpoint to this several-centuries long citational history.[10] Fry's work occurs at a transitional moment between the eclectic, inclusive compendia that begin with the early sixteenth-century work of Johannes Trithemius, rooted in biblical timeframes, and works that subscribe to a modern concept of history and knowledge in the later eighteenth century. Fry's collection was eclectic as well as comprehensive, and his bibliographic citations identified the source for every specimen—even to the page number of the works on which he drew. Published in the last year of the eighteenth century, Fry's book appeared just as discoveries in geology and archaeology transformed chronological understanding from biblical to long timescales. His work provides an overview of the state of linguistic knowledge in the British Empire in the period and marks the termination of the eclectic tradition—after which professional specializations took over. Compendia continue to be produced even now, but their assumptions are different, as per the discussion of the other exception at the end of this chapter, Peter Daniels and Timothy Bright's *The World's Writing Systems* (1996).[11]

Compendia are not, strictly speaking, a genre. Unlike grammars, dictionaries, or encyclopedias, they are not an identified type of reference work. Some are embedded in grammars for modern or ancient languages along with discussion of the "forms and powers" (shapes and sounds) of letters. Compendia always contain specimens, but except for the display works created by writing masters, they are not *simply* specimens. The examples are presented with scholarly arguments for understanding diverse languages. Longer historical understanding of the evolution of languages was not available until the nineteenth century.

The emerging technology of print production in the West also factors into compendium production. The mechanical reproduction of print editions supported the codification and stabilization of unfamiliar letterforms. Beginning in the mid-fifteenth century, printing methods called attention to written language in reproductions (woodblocks and copper engravings) as well as through production of standard fonts for Latin, Greek, Hebrew, and gradually other scripts. The labor of font production had to be warranted, as in the printing of polyglot Bibles, for instance, or the creation of materials for specific communities of readers. The work of punch cutting and casting new letterforms was demanding, and making metal type that had no commercial or practical value would have been pointless. The prolific development of fonts for use by the Propaganda Fide (Congregation for the Propagation of Faith) of the Catholic Church, beginning in 1626, is evidence of their essential role in spreading religious doctrine.[12] Knowledge of foreign and ancient languages was essential for the publication, translation, and dissemination of sacred texts and expansion of the Church's constituencies.

Concepts of history framed in mythic or biblical terms gradually changed as the classical and biblical sources (Herodotus, Pliny, Diodorus, the Old Testament, Josephus, and so on) expanded to a pantheon of early modern authors whose works became a canonical reference base.[13] The works of these authors formed a tightly linked chain within alphabet studies. Thus, Trithemius was cited after a few decades by his influential protegé, Cornelius Agrippa, and soon after by a host of others. This particular line of citation ends with Fry, as the conceptual foundations of historical study shifted. By the eighteenth century, antiquarians began to distinguish between artificial and actual alphabets, as documentation of historical events, such as coins from the time of the Maccabees, the Romans, and evidence linked to specific historical periods became available. Earlier sources started to be put aside if they suggested the angel Raphael was a fully believable agent of alphabet transmission.

Several clusters of compendia can be distinguished by intellectual affinity and period. The first is composed of early sixteenth-century scholars: Trithemius (*Polygraphia*, 1518), Johannes Pantheus (*Voarchadumia*, 1530), Cornelius Agrippa (*De occulta philosophia*, 1531), Guillaume Postel (*Linguarum duodecim characteribus differentium alphabetum introductio* [Introduction to twelve different languages and characters]; 1538), and Teseo Ambrogio (*Introductio in Chaldaicum linguam*, 1538).[14] These are closely connected by their publication dates as well as their engagement with cabbalistic and occult practices.

A second group includes the influential writing masters: Giovanni Battista Palatino (*Libro nuovo*, 1540), Urbanus Wyss (*Das Schreibbuch*, 1549), and Theodor and Israel de Bry (*Alphabeta et charactères*, 1596).[15] The range of their samples and inclusion of exotic scripts among the actual alphabets makes them worthy of commentary.

The third "group" contains a single work, the monumental achievement of Claude Duret *Le thrésor de l'histoire des langues de cest univers* (1613), which stands above all the rest of these volumes for its extension and depth.[16] Over a thousand pages long and divided into ninety-nine chapters, it is an almost inexhaustible source of information about the state of knowledge of language in the period.

The fourth group exemplifies direct borrowing, beginning with a publication by Joannes Baptista Gramaye (*Specimen litterarum & linguarum universi Orbis* [Specimens of language and letters of the entire world]; 1622) and its role as a source for scripts included by Samuel Purchas in his famous collection of travel narratives (*Hakluytus Posthumus, or Purchas His Pilgrimes*, 1624).[17] Many other compendia exist, but two, one by Blaise de Vigenère (*Traicté de chiffres*, 1586) that was entirely appropriated by François Colletet (*Traittez des langues estrangères, de leurs alphabets, et des chiffres* [. . .] [Treatise on foreign languages and their letters and numbers . . .]; 1660) will be touched on, in part because of their unique connection.[18] Many more compendia exist, but their arguments become repetitive, with endless citation and paraphrase.

Fry's culminating collection references many of these texts of the past, but the comprehensive twentieth-century work by Bright and Daniels exemplifies the recent scholarly framing of contemporary compendia.

THE FIRST COMPENDIA, EARLY SIXTEENTH CENTURY

The first significant printed compendium, Trithemius's aptly named *Polygraphia*, was published in 1518. The book created a crucial bridge between manuscript sources and printed publications and was cited by scholars for centuries.[19] Most of Trithemius's own citations were vague references or attributions not linked to specific bibliographic sources or individual manuscripts.

The first four books of *Polygraphia* were taken up with the presentation of one cipher script after another—Trithemius's passion.[20] These included many devices for encoding, including tables of transformation and volvelles whose rotating discs created a visual aid for substitution scripts (essentially keys for swapping letter and number values).[21] Other codes in Trithemius's text were Tetragrammatic and Ennagrammatic ciphers, which use a minimal number of components in combinations of four and nine elements respectively to represent letters.[22] Whether Trithemius ever used any of these ciphers is dubious. The complex character of the glyphs, and the effort that would have been involved in trying to replicate them in a passage of code, argues against their practicality.

Cryptography was associated with secrecy in diplomatic communications, but Trithemius's elaborate codes were also linked to occult knowledge systems. For instance, he assigned different codes or ciphers to individual angels for each day of the week, drawing on Christian Cabalistic practices that were synthesizing older Hermetic and Neoplatonist hierarchies and symbolism. He aligned everything—astrology, mythology, alchemy, and elements. These formal structures were ways of making the organization of the world legible in all its dimensions—material and spiritual—in keeping with overall perfection of Divine plans and a medieval approach to knowledge as based in signs. No record suggests that Trithemius was involved in practices of conjuring or black magic, and, like his renowned follower and acolyte Agrippa, he defined "occult" philosophy simply as knowledge that went beyond natural science.

Trithemius's mythic concept of history becomes clear in the opening of Book 5, where he presented his script specimens. Discussing the origin of the world, life before writing, and the roles of Saturn, Venus, Jupiter and Mercury in the affairs of humankind, he suggested that in the formative period the world was governed by planetary intelligences assisted by angels (Anael, Sachariel, Orfiel, and others). Trithemius aligned elements with gods and planets, including the letters. As elements of the natural world of the heavens and earth, these were linked through multiple associations. He integrated highly formalized structures into a single system of wisdom on a plane of (occult) knowledge. Within these practices, the alphabet and the esoteric (rare and unfamiliar) scripts seemed to provide keys to higher planes or dimensions. To a Renaissance reader, the references that drew on Hermetic and Neoplatonic concepts from the second and third centuries would have been familiar from fifteenth-century revivals of interest in the writings of Plotinus and others.

Trithemius expanded his discussion of the languages of symbols to define different historical epochs.[23] Under the influence of Mercury, he stated, writing was developed. Then, in a telescoped timeframe, Trithemius suggested that the story of Cadmus's gift to the Greeks followed quickly after events in Plato's account of writing among the Egyptians.[24] He positioned the ciphers within that history by suggesting that the proliferation and variety of scripts provoked individuals to their own inventions of secret writing to manage their private affairs.[25] He said, "Various tyrants and princes of antiquity did not hesitate to have and use among themselves certain specific means and characters of writing, totally different from the common and universal order of letters." He justified his decision to reproduce these obscure scripts for future use, lest they be lost and perish from view, a prescient impulse, and attributed them to "very ancient authors, who write occult sciences and magic in these letters."[26]

In Book 5, Trithemius presented fourteen script specimens that were not ciphers, probably from the sources he had collected through one of his major professional activities, the transformation of the Abbey of Sponheim into a center for learning and study.[27] He was said to have increased the size of the library from forty items to two thousand volumes, a considerable number for the period. Trithemius claimed the library contained "books on all the learned disciplines which ever have been known in Christendom."[28] Quite of few of these are believed to have been manuscript texts (his essay "In Praise of Scribes" remains a much-referenced essay to this day).[29] The compilation of information in his own writings argues for direct access to a significant inventory of references, though his habits of citation were minimal—*Polygraphia* is often the vanishing point for tracking the sources for his alphabets any further, even though his versions of them became the source for multiple authors.[30]

The influence of Trithemius's work justifies detailed attention to the antique and esoteric specimens it contained. These scripts represented a mix of older European letterforms, some real and some mythic, and a few of more obscure origin. The first was attributed to "Septentrionaux & Nortmans," or people from the North (in the French edition, they are identified as Allemans and Germains), who, he claimed, adapted it from the Greek but made it their own, as per the advice of Bede, for secret communications.[31] Like the three alphabets that follow, it resembled runes. These are attributed in turn to ancient Germans, to a figure named Doracus, and to Charlemagne, according to one Ottride.[32] These were hybrid scripts, borrowing features from extant letterforms, but not reproducing any individual script directly.[33] Another, described as "hardly beautiful" was also attributed to Charlemagne. One was described as composed of "antique characters." Yet another was attributed to the ancient diviner, Hichus, and two more were supposedly extracted from work by the Venerable Bede.[34] Attempts to match these with specific runic scripts proves largely futile in spite of partial similarities, and indeed, Trithemius seemed most interested the capacity of these letters to be used to conceal information and work as ciphers.[35]

Of all the scripts in Trithemius's publication the one he attributed to Honorius of Thebes was the most copied, perhaps because of its association with ancient magic. This is its first known appearance in print. Replicating the script a few years later, Agrippa attributed its source to Petrus de Abano, a medieval scholar. Trithemius advocated chaste and moral uses of alchemical processes, and his magical inclinations were circumscribed throughout by adherence to political and religious rules of decorum. Among the last examples he included several sets of signs culled from Cicero's shorthand (also known as Tironian notes after Cicero's slave and scribe).[36] Finally, he added a script reputed to be that of Iamiel [*sic*], ancient king of the Artic, a man who was "very sage and knowledgeable, who in his time, made use of this alphabet for his secret and mystic affairs."[37] The obscurity of their history cloaked the origins of these scripts in mystery and antiquity—and added to their authority.

The influence of Trithemius was enormous, but his was not the only sixteenth-century publication to contain images of esoteric scripts and

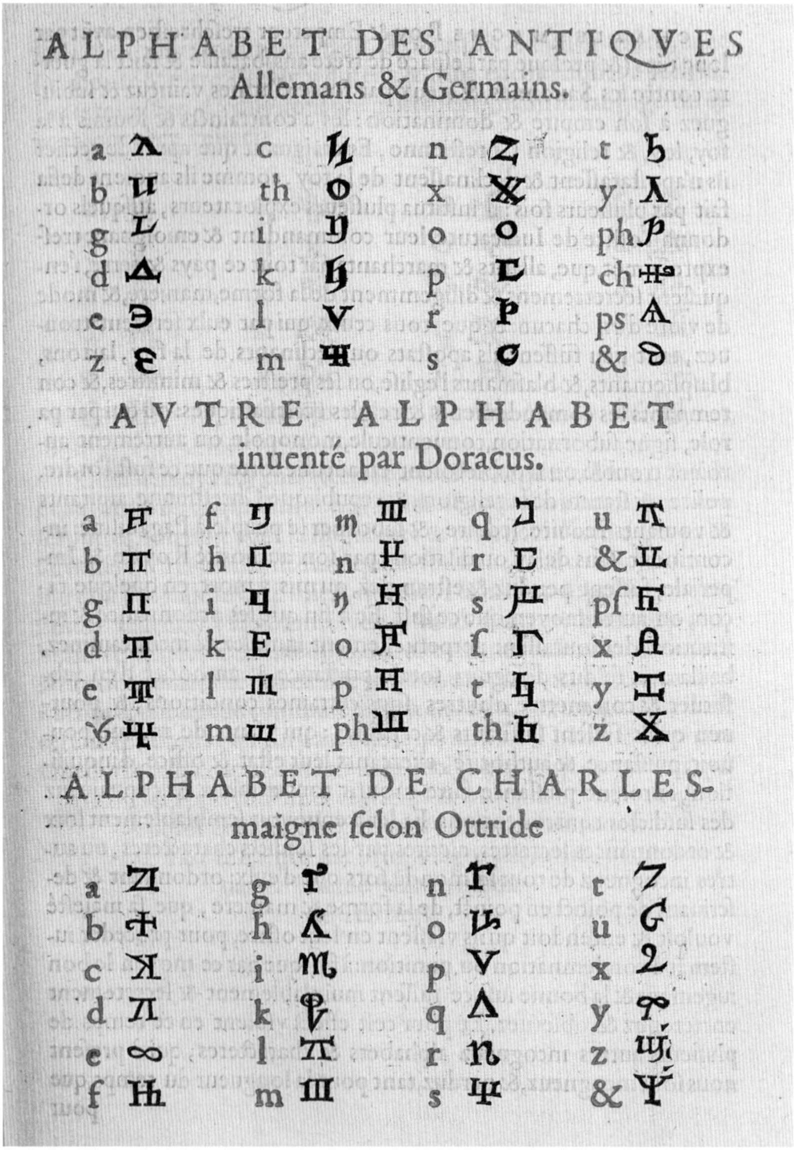

FIGURE 4.1 Page from Johannes Trithemius's *De polygraphie* (French edition of *Polygraphia*) with three sample scripts of vaguely Runic type. Public domain.

alphabets linked to occult traditions. Ambrogio's rigorous *Introductio in Chaldaicum linguam* (1539), a substantive grammar of Chaldean, Syriac, and Armenian languages, contained an appendix with scripts attributed to Raziel, Raphiel, Solomon, and others. Pantheus's unusual *Voarchadumia contra alchemia* (1530), an alchemical treatise, contained only three scripts, but they are important as part of a chain of citations: Hebrew (attributed to Moses), Crossing the River (linked to Abraham), and an alphabet attributed to Enoch. The *Voarchadumia* was focused on alchemical transformation, which Pantheus described as "a liberal art" premised on occult wisdom. In presenting the Hebrew letters, he described them as components, like the other elements—fire, air, water, earth—that also had power to be transformed, just as gold was created from other matter. This was Cabalistic teaching, embodying the belief that the letters were assistants of the Creator, who helped shape the cosmos.[38] Pantheus gave no source for his specimens, which were clearly cut from wood and given highly defined characteristics. Pantheus and Trithemius provided later scholars (and their printers) sources from which to copy scripts and attributions.

CORNELIUS AGRIPPA

As a young scholar, Cornelius Agrippa had studied with Johannes Trithemius. At the end of that period of study (around 1510), he decided to dedicate his book, *De occulta philosophia*, to his mentor. The book was not published until 1531, but it contained an acknowledgment to Trithemius and a reference to a meeting that took place between them. Trithemius had died in 1516, when Agrippa was thirty years old, but the direct connection between the two men was reflected in the contents of their work. Agrippa's philosophical view was broader than that of his mentor, and his influence was greater and longer lasting, no doubt because *De occulta* was a far-ranging work, examining many aspects of the material world to try to understand its metaphysical dimensions. Agrippa divided the world into the Elemental, Celestial, and Intellectual realms. His approach to occult knowledge can be grasped from an example in which he discussed the nature of "fascination" between human beings, describing the forces that bond individuals together. By contrast, his work on the alphabets was bibliographic rather than philosophical. The four specimens were only briefly noted, and he comments that they are "nothing else than certain unknowable letters and writings, preserving the secrets of the Gods."[39] On the topic of Hebrew, his comments are strictly in line with standard Cabalistic thinking: "There are therefore two and twenty Letters, which are the foundation of the world, and of creatures that are, and are named in it, and every saying, and every creatures are of them, and by their revolutions receive their Name, Being, and Vertue."[40]

The four script specimens that appeared in Agrippa's work were cited so frequently in the centuries afterward that they have an outsized presence in the literature. They appeared in Book 3 of *De occulta*, closely packed onto several pages.[41] For the first, the Theban alphabet, he acknowledged Trithemius as his source. But he had added another attribution to the script, saying that it first appeared in a work by Petrus de Abano, an Italian philosopher and astrologer who lived between the thirteenth and fourteenth centuries.[42] Agrippa followed this with three other scripts whose pedigrees were traced to unspecified medieval sources: Celestial, Malachim, and Transfluvial (Crossing the River) scripts.

Versions of Agrippa's specimens of occult scripts found their way into

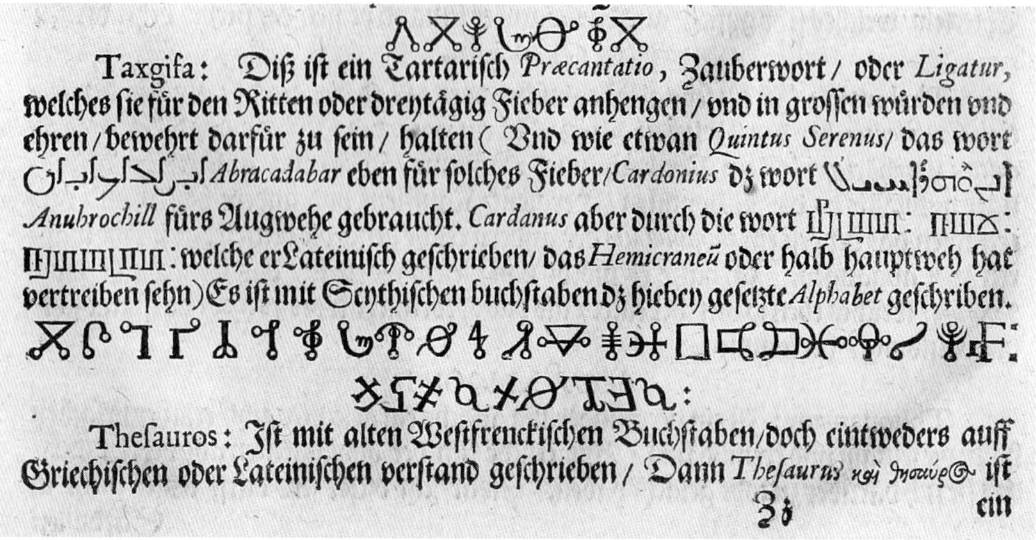

Taxgifa: Diß iſt ein Tartariſch *Præcantatio*, Zauberwort / oder *Ligatur*, welches ſie für den Ritten oder dreytägig Fieber anhengen / vnd in groſſen würden vnd ehren / bewehrt darfür zu ſein / halten (Vnd wie etwan *Quintus Serenus*/ das wort *Abracadabar* eben für ſolches Fieber/*Cardonius* dz wort *Anubrochill* fürs Augwehe gebraucht. *Cardanus* aber durch die wort : : welche er Lateiniſch geſchrieben/ das *Hemicraneū* oder halb hauptweh hat vertreiben ſehn) Es iſt mit Scythiſchen buchſtaben dz hiebey geſetzte *Alphabet* geſchriben.

Theſauros: Iſt mit alten Weſtfrenckiſchen Buchſtaben/doch eintweders auff Griechiſchen oder Lateiniſchen verſtand geſchrieben / Dann *Theſaurus* καὶ θησαυρὸς iſt

Z z ein

FIGURE 4.2 Leonhard Thurneysser, *Melitsat ka hermeneia: Das ist Onomasticum und Interpretatio* (Berlin: Noclaum Voltzen, 1583). Public domain.

multiple publications. It may have been one source for the Celestial script in the alchemical work of Leonhard Thurneysser, *Onomasticum*, from 1583, where it appears in the company of a handful of Gothic, runic, and Ostro-Frankish scripts.[43] Over the centuries, Agrippa's name became synonymous with occult traditions, often with much misunderstanding of how he meant the term and what it meant in context. Like his mentor Trithemius, Agrippa sought to synthesize knowledge systems to show a single Divine pattern behind all things. This necessarily included letters: "The position of the Stars being first made in the seat of God, which is heaven, after the figure of them (as masters of the Hebrews testify) are the most fully formed letters of the Celestial mysteries, as by their figure, form, and signification so by the numbers signified by them, as also by the various harmonies of conjunction."[44] He divided the twenty-two Hebrew letters, as per Jewish Kabbalistic mystical tradition, into the twelve simple, seven double, and three mothers—numbers that correspond to the twelve signs, seven planets, and three elements (fire, water, earth). He took the Hebrew letters, of course, as the originals, though "the true character of the heavens is in the writing of the angels, called Malachim."[45] Within Agrippa's occult framework, the properties of things were to be understood in terms of essences rather than appearances, with the power of things including letters revealed by more than superficial affinities. Agrippa recognized that the most ancient script, originally used by "Moses, and the Prophets," was lost. It had had a form "which is not rashly to be discovered to any; for those letters which they use at this day, were instituted by Esdras."[46] Again, this was the common account of a shift from the lost ancient Hebrew to its modern form following Babylonian captivity.

POSTEL AND SAMARITAN SCRIPT

Guillaume Postel, Agrippa's contemporary, was a French Cabalist and scholar of "oriental" languages. His compendium, *Linguarum duodecim* (Twelve languages), published in 1538, was a study of twelve languages.[47] Postel's motivations were very different from those of the cipher maker Trithemius and the occult philosopher Agrippa. His scripts represented languages with which he had come into contact in travels from Paris through Italy to Bosnia, Dalmatia, Armenia, Russia, and Arabia. Along with the classical and ancient tongues, they reflected experience of the political geography of European-Ottoman relations suffused with Christian faith and a belief in cultural connections. Collected in the service of a belief in a universal tongue, primordial and potentially unifying, the examples in his compendium were recorded during his work to advance French interests in the Ottoman Empire. Postel believed a religious war would set the stage for the return of Christ.[48] Alphabets and history were blended in a Messianic narrative.

The twelve languages in Postel's book are from the region around the Levant and Near East. Every section was dedicated to an actual script: Hebrew, Chaldean, Samaritan, Punic, Arabic, Indian, Greek, Georgian, Tzervian, Dalmation. Armenian, and Latin. Postel did not simply present specimens. He included a guide to each of the twelve languages represented, including pronunciation, a description of its cultural location and relation to the other languages represented, and a sample of the script transcribing the Lord's Prayer. The book is meant to provide instruction, an introduction to the languages of the region.

While the Hebrew, Arabic, Greek, and Latin specimens were printed from metal type, the samples of the other scripts (Chaldean, Samaritan, Indian/Ethiopic, Georgian/Jacobite, Hieronymian/Dalmation, Armenian, and the Celestial/Crossing the River) were all cut (rather crudely) in wood, evidence that they were rare, unfamiliar, and not necessarily considered worthy of being cast in metal fonts. (The specimen of a Slavic script, Tzervianorum, appears to be metal type.) His Chaldean was a version of Syriac, but on the page, he placed its characters next to a celestial Hebrew lunette script, the now-familiar Crossing the River, which was the only mystical script in his collection of living alphabets. Though heavier and cruder than the sample in Agrippa, with the exception of the *alef*, Postel's specimen was composed of the same graphic characters. The tradition of copying so important to the medieval period continued in the assiduous production of print exemplars.

Postel asserted unequivocally that Hebrew was the parent of all other "oriental" tongues—by which he meant all the oldest extant alphabetic scripts as well as languages. He believed—along with many of his contemporaries—that the differences among languages could be traced to the dispersal of the sons of Noah after the Flood, and the Confusion of

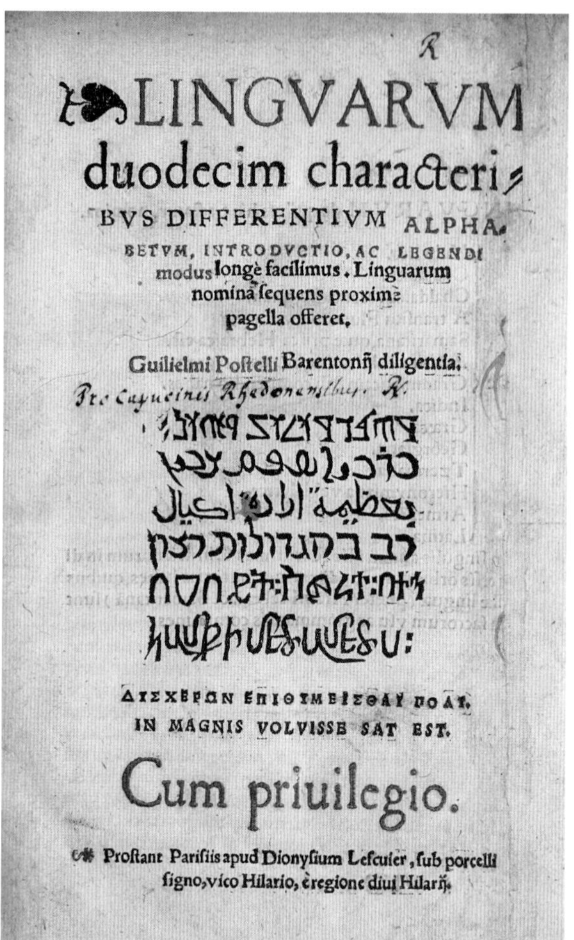

LINGVARVM
duodecim characteri-
BVS DIFFERENTIVM ALPHA-
BETVM, INTRODVCTIO, AC LEGENDI
modus longè facilimus. Linguarum
nomina ſequens proximè
pagella offeret.

Guilielmi Poſtelli Barentonij diligentia.

ΔΥΣΧΕΡΩΝ ΕΠΙΘΥΜΕΙΣΘΑΙ ΠΟΛΛΑ.
IN MAGNIS VOLVISSE SAT EST.

Cum priuilegio.

Proſtant Pariſiis apud Dionyſium Leſcuier, ſub porcelli ſigno, vico Hilario, è regione diui Hilarij.

FIGURE 4.3 The title page to Guillaume Postel's *Linguarum duodecim characteribus differentium* (Paris, 1538). Scripts on this page appear to be woodcut specimens. The top line is Samaritan, the third is Arabic, the fourth is Hebrew, the fifth is "Indica" (Ethiopic), and the second and sixth are difficult to match with his specimens. Public domain.

Tongues approximately a hundred years later.[49] Postel wanted to find a single true religion and, in his quest, studied Judaism and Islam to figure out how a unified belief system could emerge. His interest in languages of the Near East was directly related to reading the Koran, Hebrew sacred texts, and Kabbalistic literature, since he believed these texts "provided the key to uncover and reconstruct the primordial human language."[50] Postel, who was French, also suggested that the Celtic language came from Noah, another harbinger of attitudes to come in which national groups sought their "original" language and script outside Semitic traditions and even without reference to classical ones.[51]

Among the other noteworthy accomplishments of Postel's publication was its inclusion of a specimen of the characters of the Samaritan script. This was the first such appearance of the script in print. This specimen alone would have caused a sensation, but it was also accompanied by drawings of two coins with Hebrew inscriptions, the first known reproduction

Alphabetũm Hebraicum antiquũ, nũc Samaritanorum.
Prima figura typographica eſt altera chirographica.

aleph a,e,i,o,v.
beth b.vel v.cõſonans
gimel. g
daleth d
he h aſpiratio leuis.
vau v conſonans & vocale.
zain z
Heth hh aſpiratio fortis:
teth t
iod i vocale & conſonum.
chaph ch k hebr.
lamed l Hebræorum eſt inuerſum.
mem m
nun n cõuenit hebræ.
ſamech s
hain a,e,i,o,u. aſpirata.
phe ph,vel p.
tzadic tz,vel zz,Italorum.
coph k
res r
ſin ss hebr.conuenit.
thau th

ירושלים הקדושה Ieruſalaim halzedoſſah.
Ieruſalem ſancta.
שקל ישראל Selzel Iſraël
Pondus ſeu numiſma Iſraël:

Grammatica ipſa nil differt ab Hebraica, ideo vbi characteres differentes habes, omnia habes.

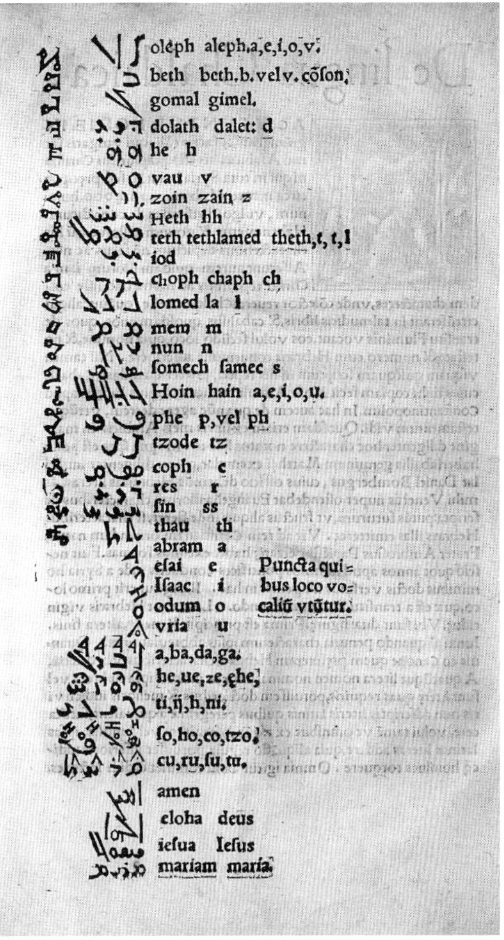
oleph aleph,a,e,i,o,v.
beth beth.b.vel v.cõſon.
gomal gimel.
dolath dalet: d
he h
vau v
zoin zain z
Heth hh
teth tethlamed theth,t,t,l
iod
choph chaph ch
lomed la l
mem m
nun n
ſomech ſamec s
Hoin hain a,e,i,o,u.
phe p,vel ph
tzode tz
coph c
res r
ſin ss
thau th
abram a
eſai e
Iſaac i
odum o
vria u
Puncta quibus loco vocaliũ vtũtur.
a,ba,da,ga.
he,ue,ze,ehe,
ti,ij,h,ni.
ſo,ho,co,tzo.
cu,ru,ſu,tu.
amen
eloha deus
ieſua Ieſus
mariam maria.

FIGURE 4.4 (*left*) Guillaume Postel, *Linguarum* (1538). Typographic Samaritan copied from handwritten models. Public domain.

FIGURE 4.5 (*right*) Guillaume Postel, *Linguarum* (1538). Chaldean compared with celestial. Public domain.

of actual inscriptions in ancient Semitic script. Postel had actively sought a Samaritan manuscript on his travels to Constantinople in 1536.[52] He finally acquired one from a lawyer named Fabius Spoletanus, who was an expert in Greek and Hebrew and who worked in the literary circles around the Venetian printer Daniel Bomberg.[53] Postel was apparently so excited by being shown a copy of a manuscript that contained genuine Samaritan letters that he immediately asked for it to be copied. When he got to Rome, he showed it to "that polyglot, Flaminius, most learned among the scholars of his day. He declared it most certainly Samaritan, and he did not disdain to copy the alphabet in his own hand."[54] This reliance on hand methods of reproduction was essential, and what is remarkable is how accurate the letterforms in Postel's publication are. Both scribe and letter cutter were doing their work scrupulously.[55]

The Samaritans were (and still are) a small ethnographic community who believed they were left behind in Chaldea when Abraham crossed to

Canaan (though today they live in and around the West Bank). The Samaritans had dispersed in the Hellenistic period, and though they preserved their language and script, their population was small, and the community was scattered throughout Cairo, Damascus, Aleppo, and areas of modern Lebanon.[56] The Samaritans and their version of the Torah had been "rediscovered" in the sixteenth century, though the Samaritan Pentateuch was not available in Western Europe until the seventeenth century when Jean Morin published a bilingual version of it in Paris in 1631.[57] Many believed that this Samaritan version of the Old Testament was the original, uncorrupted one and that their alphabet might be an older script than modern Hebrew.[58] Passages in the Talmud that described Samaritan as the original writing of the Law were well known in the rabbinic tradition that kept knowledge of Samaritan alive as a reference, even without examples or direct knowledge of visual script. A thirteenth-century Jewish scholar, Moses ben Nahman, supposedly wrote in Paleo-Hebrew and claimed the Samaritans could read it. In fact, Samaritan is an offshoot of Paleo-Hebrew, older than the square modern Hebrew letters. Debates about whether Samaritan was the original alphabet, or was invented by Adam or by Moses, continued. Some explanation was needed for the obvious distinction between modern square Hebrew and its antecedents. In Postel's period, this discussion was part of an ongoing discussion about which was the oldest and "most holy alphabet."[59]

Had Hebrew been the same alphabet since Creation and did it predate Babel? The question was tangled in debates within the Christian and Jewish Kabbalistic communities, both of whom drew on biblical sources and also commentaries. St. Jerome, for instance, noted that Samaritan and Hebrew had the same number of letters (as did the Syriac and Chaldean, which have the same sounds). Jerome espoused the conventional explanation for the difference between the ancient and modern letterforms: after Babylonian exile, Ezra the scribe had "found other letters we now use, for up to that time the Samaritan and Hebrew characters were the same."[60] Not everyone agreed with this much-cited account. The celebrated fifteenth-century philosopher Pico della Mirandola suggested that this change had never taken place and that Moses and the patriarchs used the same Hebrew letters still in use. In support of this argument, he said that Moses had hidden Divine secrets in the texts that would not be able to be discerned (using Kabbalah) if they were in different or changed characters.[61] These debates drew on commentaries by Abraham Abulafia, the prominent thirteenth-century Kabbalist who, among others, suggested that a *metacharakterismos* (a method of copying one character at a time) had been invented to write Hebrew.

Pico played another role in alphabet studies, since his library was sold at his death in 1494 to a collector, Domenico Grimani. These materials were consulted by many scholars, including Teseo Ambrogio, as a source for esoteric scripts. Grimani's library was eventually sent to the convent of the Augustinians of Sant'Antonio in Castello, where much of it was destroyed by

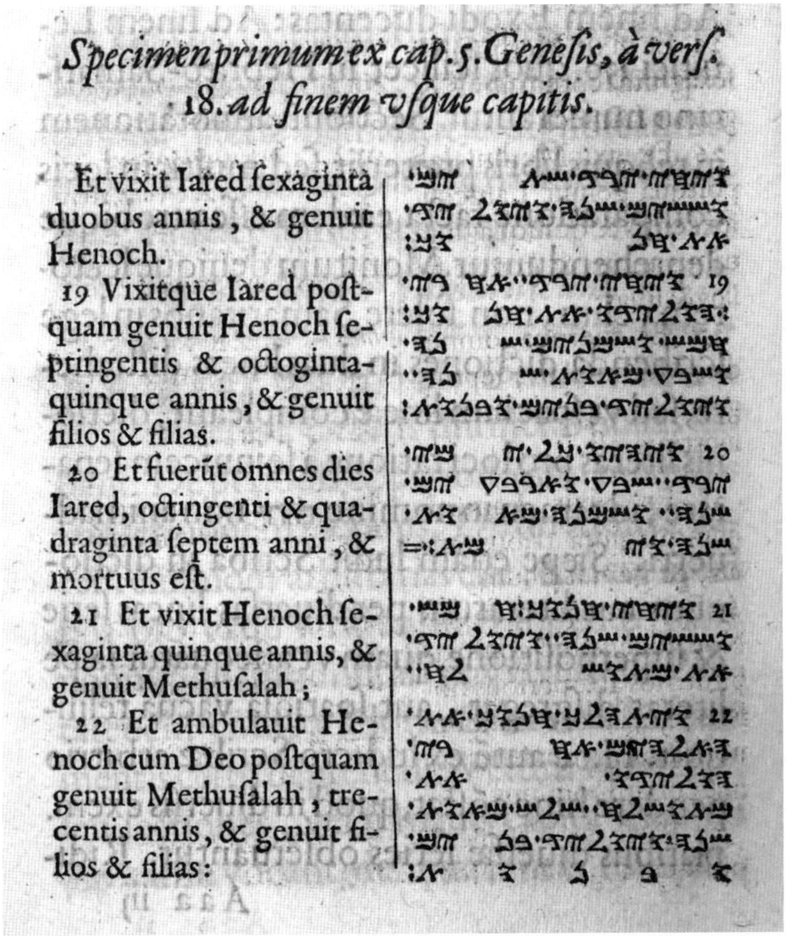

Specimen primum ex cap. 5. Geneſis, à verſ. 18. ad finem vſque capitis.

Et vixit Iared ſexaginta duobus annis, & genuit Henoch.

19 Vixitque Iared poſtquam genuit Henoch ſeptingentis & octoginta-quinque annis, & genuit filios & filias.

20 Et fuerũt omnes dies Iared, octingenti & quadraginta ſeptem anni, & mortuus eſt.

21 Et vixit Henoch ſexaginta quinque annis, & genuit Methuſalah;

22 Et ambulauit Henoch cum Deo poſtquam genuit Methuſalah, trecentis annis, & genuit filios & filias:

FIGURE 4.6 Page of the bilingual Samaritan and Latin Pentateuch edited by Jean Morin, published 1631. Public domain.

fire in 1687 when the monastery was used as an ammunition depot during conflicts with the Turks.[62] Even before that, many of the occult and magical alphabets had been purged by the monks as suspicious.[63] These libraries played a crucial part in the transmission of graphic exemplars, many of which are now preserved only in these printed texts. For instance, in 1523, Abraham de Balmes, an Italian savant who was physician to Grimani, published his grammar book *Mikneh Avram: Peculium Abrae; Grammatica Hebraea una cum Latino* (The gifts of Abraham: Hebrew and Latin grammar) in Venice.[64] In it he included a copy of the Transitus Fluvii (Crossing the River), which he mentioned had been found in a very old book. Balmes imagined the Transitus Fluvii might be the Samaritan alphabet, since samples of that script had not yet circulated, but he also designated the sample as the "true Assyrian script" used to write the Aramaic language, again linking it to the biblical geography of Canaan.[65] Balmes's book was followed two years later by a publication of Sigismondo Fanti, which also contained

מספר האותיות וצורתן

Numerus lraꝝ & eaꝝ forma.

[1]non sint nisi in litteris capituli audi scripti in deutronomii cap. vi.[2] & alii dicunt ꝙ hoc fit in oĩbus locis: & si in his sit pͤceptum de præceptis[3] Dei: & in reliquis locis sit libertas: & hoc est conuenientius: & hæ sunt super lris[4] scin: hayn: teth: nun: zayn: cghimel: czade: tres zayn sup singulis lris & tres super mem clausa: & super lra[5] he vltra duas coronas: quas scripsimus superius quinq; zayn: & in lra kof in quibusdã[6] locis duas: & alicubi tres zayn vltra coronã quam scripsimus: [7] & sup ipsas teth: totaphot: aliqui dicunt ꝙ non sufficiãt eis tres: sed indigẽt[8] quatuor zayn: & hoc est cõplementũ oĩum lrarum ad ipsas faciendum perfectas ẽm ipsarum species. [9] Hucusq; scripsimus formã lrarum in scriptura assyria ẽm ueritatẽ: [10] sed post hoc inuenies ꝙ scriptores ad ornãdum [11] suã scripturã mutauerũt suas formas ẽm populos suos ẽm ydiomata sua mutatione de qua non est dignum curæ: [12] sed post hæc in reliquis scripturis uulgi cecidit mutatio nimia in litteris: & non[13] fuit seruata scriptura assyria nisi in Biblia: & ob amorem breuitatis non scribam[14] hic minutias illarũ: sed scribã vnã illaꝝ vsitatiorẽ uulgo: & tu[15] intelliges illarũ minutias ex illis quæ scripsimus superius in assyria. Et en tibi suum exemplum. [16] Scriptura hispanorum.

[18] Hęc ẽ scriptura trãsitus fluuii, put iueni in lib. uetustissimo.

[23] Et in hoc ponemus finẽ verbis formæ lrarũ quã pmisimus explicare[24] in caplo hoc laudeẽ adiuuans amen. [25] Verũtamen ipsarũ platio in pnunciatione sic partiẽ ẽm instrumẽta pnũciationis[26] quæ est lingua in suo sono in locis quibus pnũciat[27] hõ ex ore qñ pnũciat illas: sicq; ẽm auctorẽ libri

FIGURE 4.7 Abraham Meir de Balmes, *Mikneh Avram: Peculiam Abrae; Grammatica Hebraea una cum Latino* (Venice: Bomberg, 1523). The same version of the mystical script inserted in the Hebrew and Latin texts. The cutting of Transitus Fluvii is expert and contrasts with earlier woodcut versions by the clean evenness of strokes. Public domain.

the Transitus Fluvii. This was in turn copied by the type designer Geoffroy Tory in 1529 as "Lettres Chaldaiques," from whom Giovanni Battista Palatino copied it in 1540 as the "Alphabetum Hebraicum ante Esdram."[66] The idea that this was the Hebrew alphabet before Ezra became common, thus setting aside the question of Samaritan, direct knowledge of which was supplied for the first time by Postel. All the scripts in Postel's publication also reappeared in Claude Duret's exhaustive 1613 publication, *Le thrésor*, and in the work of the writing master Urbanus Wyss, whose hand-drawn samples were meant for a very different audience. Postel's and Duret's works were scholarly while Wyss's samples were for display and demonstration.

AMBROSEUS: GRAMMAR AND LANGUAGE

One curious episode in this scholarly tradition concerns the rivalry between Postel and a colleague, Teseo Ambrogio (Theseus Ambroseus). Ambrogio's *Introductio in Chaldaicum linguam, Syriaca*, published in 1538, was a grammar book. It contained several Aramaic scripts as well as a section called "Appendix Multarum Diversarum Literarum" (Appendix of many di-

illi, & inter doctos ſui tēporis viros doctiſſimō Flaminio oſtēdiſſem, Samaritanū omnino eſſe aſſeruit, nec dedigna= tus eſt, ſua manu ſcriptum alphabetum, ad exſcribēdum & cum alio conformandum concedere, quod qdē tale eſt.

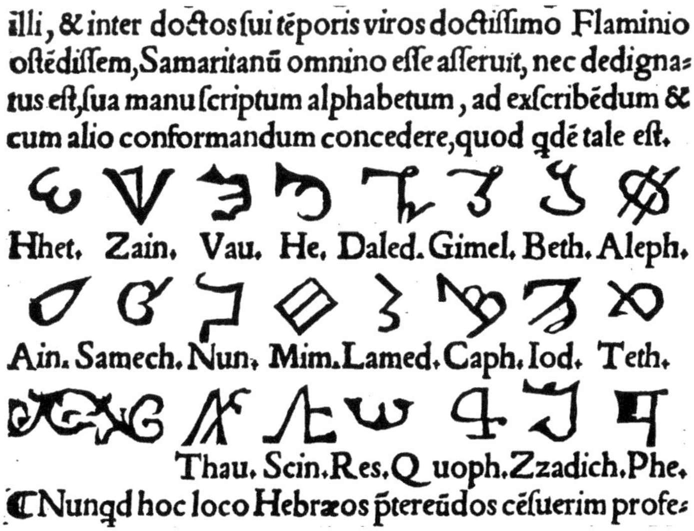

Hhet. Zain. Vau. He. Daled. Gimel. Beth. Aleph.

Ain. Samech. Nun. Mim. Lamed. Caph. Iod. Teth.

Thau. Scin. Res. Quoph. Zzadich. Phe.

Nunqd hoc loco Hebræos ptereūdos cēſuerim profe=

FIGURE 4.8 Samaritan script in Teseo Ambrogio, *Introductio in Chaldaicum linguam, Syriaca* (1538). Public domain.

verse languages) of about thirty-six different specimens and explanations of their vocalization. Ambrogio's efforts were in the service of linguistic knowledge but were also evidence of the collecting impulse that motivated all compendia. In the main part of the book, he focused on Syriac, Chaldean, and Aramaic (not Hebrew); commented on Postel's alphabets; and reproduced a version of Samaritan that he claimed he had obtained from Ludovico (Fabius?) Spoletano, the same person who had supplied Postel his sample characters. In addition, he drew on the library of one Antonio de Fanti, a philosopher in Treviso.[67]

Ambrogio's sample of Samaritan did not resemble the script, though he noted his source for the specimen as, again, the Grimani Library.[68] The alphabet of Adam, with its conspicuous aleph, the one attributed to Solomon, and then the celestial scripts—were all reproduced alongside others identified as Egyptian, Etruscan, and Gothoruum. He cited many of his sources (e.g., Pantheus's *Voarchadumia*) and proceeded to assign the original to Adam or the angel Raphael without too much attention to the details.

But the most curious specimen in Ambrogio's book was in a passage purported to have been composed by the devil. Ambrogio suggested that Spoletano, source of the Samaritan specimen, had summoned the devil to respond to a question. Once he had posed it, a mysterious power took hold of his pen and wrote what was recorded on the page. This may have been a joke at Postel's expense for getting the edge on Ambrogio in publishing the Samaritan script. The text has never been deciphered. In addition to having features of various Armenian and Ethiopic alphabets, it was distinguished by the graphic pitchfork characters that wrap around letters across several lines, bedeviling the rest of text.

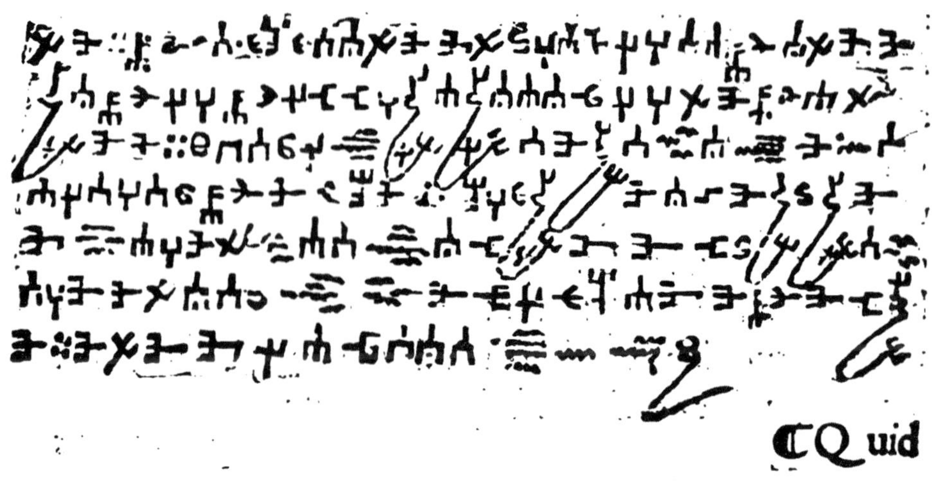

FIGURE 4.9 Devil writing in Teseo Ambrogio, *Introductio in Chaldaicum linguam, Syriaca* (1538). Public domain.

WRITING SAMPLE BOOKS: PALATINO, WYSS, DE BRY

While scholars worried over the history of languages and scripts, writing masters of the Renaissance outdid themselves in producing sample books that demonstrated their capacity to provide calligraphic samples to compete with the metal letterforms available for printing. These works contained no commentary, but the way they identified their samples, such as "Ante Esdram," pointed to alphabet scholarship. They familiarized the exotic scripts by including them among others in daily use and simultaneously exoticized them by associating them with newly discovered lands.

The renowned calligrapher Giovanni Battista Palatino included several exotic scripts in his specimen book, *Libro nuovo d'imparare a scrivere*, published in 1540.[69] Two were cipher scripts, or Lettre Cifrate, composed of formal parts in logical combinations. These were followed by Greek, Hebrew, Hebrew before Ezra, Antique Chaldean, Arabic, Egyptiorum, Indicum, Siriorum, Saracen, Hieronymi (Illyric or Sclavonic), and Cyrillic. Also included were several pages with a rebus text, reflecting the fashion for hieroglyphics and visual signs. The specimens showed the same lack of distinction between actual and mythic scripts as other compendia, and the writing master evidently saw a value in including these specimens even if they would never be used in composition.

In 1549, another expert penman, Urbanus Wyss of Zurich, published a work titled *Das Schreibbuch* with an almost identical collection of exotic scripts.[70] Wyss's elegantly written pages showcased his virtuosic handwriting a hundred years after the invention of moveable type. Each of the more than 120 full-page images was produced from a carved woodblock that depicted a specimen surrounded by an individually designed frame. Most of the samples were specific styles of handwriting for different purposes and circumstances—charters, formal invitations, polite communication, and so forth, the niche role of calligraphy.

Most of his specimens were of the Latin alphabet in its Roman, longhand, and variant forms (black letter, textura, and so on), but Wyss included the nearly identical collection of ten non-Latin alphabets that Palatino had reproduced: Hebrew, Greek, Hebrew before Ezra, Indian, Arabic, Siriorum, Saracen, Illyrian, Egyptian, and Antique Chaldean. Again, the specimen of Hebrew before Ezra is a version of the Celestial script, reinforcing an accepted version of that scribe's invention of modern Hebrew.

Israel and Theodor de Bry's masterful 1596 publication, *Alphabeta et charactères, jam inde creato mundi* (Alphabets and characters from the entire world), also contained a compendium of scripts.[71] The de Bry brothers published several ethnographic studies of voyages to America, including the much-cited illustrated edition of Thomas Harriot's *A Briefe and True Report of the New Found Land of Virginia* (1590).[72] Theodor was responsible for the engravings for Harriot, including scenes of cannibalism and other activities that never took place but provided a lurid image of New World cultures. The European bias in Theodor's depiction of Native Americans was evident, but he also produced graphic depictions of the Spanish atrocities recorded by Bartolomé de las Casas in *Narratio Regionum indicarum per Hispanos Quosdam devastatarum verissimai* (Account of the Indian region truly devastated by the Spanish) in the 1614 edition.[73] These illustrated travel narratives provided a model for *Alphabeta*, which provided a similar travelogue of the written world.

In the introduction, the de Brys suggested that the first letters were Chaldean, invented by Abraham. The engraved title page depicts Abraham holding a table inscribed in Syraic (Aramaic), with Cadmus standing opposite and the finger of God writing on the Tablets in the vignette above. This combination of figures mixed biblical and historical references. But the text kept to the standard account: "These letters were delivered to Moses and the Jews, but not in exactly the same letters, which were supposedly invented by Ezra, who turned them into an instrument for writing books."[74] Their inventory of different scripts began with the apparently oldest, that invented by Abraham and the Antique Chaldean (identical to that in Palatino), then noted the other ancient scripts—the Celestial, Malachim, and the alphabet of Moses followed by the Aegyptian, Arabic, Samaritan, and Greek.[75] The sequence was vaguely, but not strictly, chronological. Publication of these scripts in the context of the De Bry collection linked the presentation with their other books—and reinforced their exoticization in the same way as their works had done with other aspects of foreign culture.

Writing masters continued to create showpieces of their skills well into the eighteenth century. But their commitment to esoteric and historical scripts diminished, no doubt because business using ancient Phoenician, Chaldean, and the scripts of the angels was replaced by service to tradesmen and commercial clients whose eyes were not cast to the heavens in search of letters among the stars.

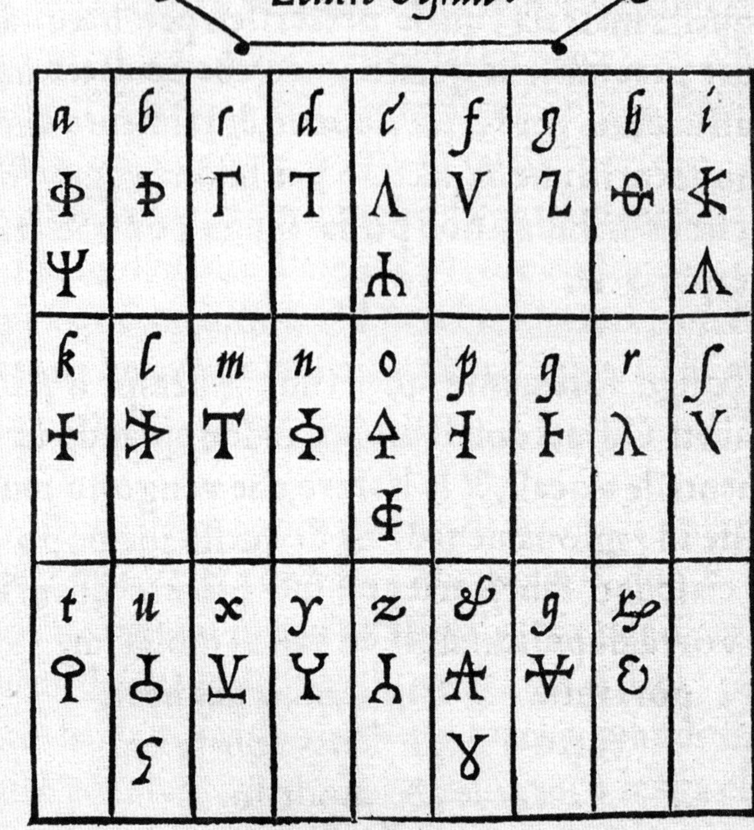

FIGURE 4.10 Giovanni Battista Palatino, *Libro*. These images are from the 1568 edition, but the blocks are the same as those in the 1540 original; *from left:* cipher script, Antique Chaldean, and Hebrew before Ezra (which is formally almost identical to Transitus Fluvii in Agrippa where the *alef* is the "flying" form of the letter). Public domain.

Alphabetum Hebraicum Ante Esdram.
a Aleph
b Beth
g Ghimel
d Daleth
h He
u Vau
z Zain
h Heth
t Teth
i Iod
c Caph
l Lamed
m Mem
n Nun
s Sámech
h Hain
p Pe
z Zzadi
c Cof
r Reß
sc Scin
t Tau

Alphab. Chaldaicum antiquum.
ABRAHAM
Syras, & Chaldaicas literas inuenit.

FIGURE 4.11 Theodor de Bry and Israel de Bry, *Alphabeta et charactères, jam inde creato mundi* (1596). Engraved samples of ancient Chaldean, above, and Syriac attributed to Abraham, below. Public domain.

LE THRÉSOR: CLAUDE DURET AND THE LANGUAGES OF THE UNIVERSE

The publications of sixteenth-century writing masters can be taken as evidence of a popular interest in exotic scripts among a general literate population. But they were specimen books, not scholarly publications. One of the first—and still one of the most comprehensive—texts to address the history of language and scripts, was *Le thrésor de l'histoire des langues de cest univers* (1613) by Claude Duret.[76] As a "history of the languages of this universe," Duret's subject was all of the "origins, beauties, perfections, decadences, mutations, changes, conversions, and ruins."[77] Duret gathered everything that could be known about language and synthesized it into his monumental tome. The work was based on the conviction, shared by his contemporaries and predecessors, that the people of the world had originally been speakers of one language. The biblical story in Genesis provided a clear account of the relation between human hubris, God's punishment, and the diversification of languages after Babel.

Duret started his exhaustive study by discussing the origin of language according to the pagan philosophers and then the Hebrew, Greek, and Latin theologians. Chapter 2 began: "The great and admirable Hebrew Prophet Moses in Chapter 2 of his book of Genesis, and the historian Josephus, in . . . the Antiquities of the Jews, have demonstrated clearly that the Hebrew language, the first and oldest of this universe, was introduced during the construction and building of the tower of Babel."[78] He went on at length to defend this version against the counterargument of Philo the Jew suggesting the metaphoric nature of Moses's account. Then he summarized the opinions of various authors in a citation chain from Alexander Polyhistor and the Sybil through Eusebius, the *Seder olam* of Rabbi Abraham (a second-century chronology of the Jewish people), and assertions by Berosus (a Chaldean priest), Aban Ezra, a host of Jewish rabbis, Gilbert Génébrard, and other authorities of Jewish history to figure out how many years elapsed between the Deluge and the adaptation of Hebrew. He arrived at the conclusion that it was perhaps 340 years, or 301, or maybe just 150—depending on the works consulted.[79]

Duret described the dispersal of the sons of Noah—Shem, Ham, and Japhet—as they divided the world (Near East, Africa, Europe) into linguistic categories that later became the basis of racial characterizations. The antiquity of the alphabet was becoming a basis for modern political identities. Duret struggled with the place-names in biblical history even as he tracked the proliferating offspring of Noah and his children across generations. He invoked Druids, Bretons, and ancient Hebrew Kabbalists to support the belief in the powers of the twenty-two Hebrew letters, suggesting that "below our secrete notes, our ciphers, is hidden the True Writing."[80]

For Duret, the most ancient language of the world, without question, was Hebrew:

> As Moses says, in Chapter 2 of Genesis, several years after the deluge and in the period when the descendants of Cham divined the quadrants of the orient, and came to live in the land of Sennar, all of the earth was of one language and speech, which is to say, the Patriarch Noah, his sons, and all the familiars that issue from them, even if they do not all live together, speak the same language, which was Hebrew, the same that had been taught and given by the Eternal to our first father Adam in terrestrial paradise at the beginning of the world for him and his successors.[81]

In a later chapter he detailed the history of Hebrew as a revelation to Adam, used to carry out the command given to him to name the objects in the world, and his task of passing the language to posterity.[82] The first world lasted 1,656 years, and Adam lived 930 years, and he and "his successors conserved the Hebrew language."[83] His elaborate arguments were all proofs of the same point, that there was only one language before the Deluge, and it was Hebrew, and Noah, the true son of Adam, also spoke and retained this language and taught his sons. Sixty-four years after the Deluge corruptions began to appear—though the people all spoke the same language on the plain of Sennar, where they gathered to build the Tower of Babel. The only ones who did not suffer from the confusion were the children and descendants of Shem (Sem) among whom the original Hebrew language remained (hence the term Semitic applied to these languages).[84]

Duret's table of contents gives an idea of his historical and geographic range as he fulfills the compendium makers' dreams of comprehensive knowledge and global collecting. After the initial discussion of the invention of language, the original Hebrew, and the confusion following the Tower of Babel, he included an elaborate discussion of the Cabala, drawing heavily on the work of a Christian Cabalist, Petrus Galatin. This was followed by a summary of the Talmud (its topics and sections), and the history of Jewish sects, groups, rabbis, and communities. A hundred pages into this history, the first script was presented—that given to Adam by the angel Raphael (which Duret copied from the version in Ambrogio).[85] Next he presented the Celestial alphabet, copied from Guillaume Postel, as the one given to Abraham as he left Chaldea to go to Canaan (though he also included the familiar Crossing the River). He mentioned the Malachim script as well, noting that according to Eusebius and Isidore, Moses was the inventor of these letters. He presented square Hebrew letters with an assertion that their forms had been extracted from engraved monuments. The Enochian, taken from Ambrogio and Pantheus, also made an appearance among the other Hebrew scripts. Two scripts of Solomon, one attributed to Ezra, one to Apollonius Thianeen, and two cursive scripts of German and Spanish Jews, finished the presentation of Hebrew and related scripts.

The legitimacy of these scripts was guaranteed by a citation history with a clear lineage: Pantheus, Postel, and Ambrogio. Each script was carefully explained and linked to biblical histories. A long discussion of the etymology of the letters, mystical practices, gematria, combinatorics, other letter-based practices from the Cabalistic tradition, and even older associations—with letter symbolism and light, planets, numbers, and angels—were presented in text and table form. The songs of the angels in heaven, in Hebrew, and composition of the songs of Solomon as well as the role of celestial intelligences—all attested to the sacredness of the Hebrew language. This was just the beginning, an inventory of early scripts. Even in schematic form, Duret's impressive collection is overwhelming.[86]

A third of the way through his massive book, Duret described the proliferation of languages after Babel into seventy different tongues.[87] Of these he had listed about sixty on his title page, mainly the languages of the ancient world, Western and Eastern Europe, Africa, the Balkans, India, China, Japan, New Guinea, and the Indians of the New World. His chapters followed these topics in a scheme that combined chronology and geography—Jerusalem, the miseries and calamities of the Jews, and the decadence of Hebrew. He tracked the language of Canaan, the Samaritans, Chaldeans, Syrians, Egyptians (and discussion of their magical practices), of Carthage, and the Punic tongue.[88] He added Judaic, Chaldean, and Maronite inside a long discussion of the Chaldean language citing Pico della Mirandola and Marcelino Ficino. Then he included Arabic, the religion and beliefs of Mohammed, the wisdom of Averroes and Avicenna. He moved into discussion of the Saracens (the non-Islamic Arabs), the Persians, Tartars, and even their Kabbalah, followed by Africa, Ethiopia, Nubia, and a discussion of the fictive Presbyr John. He described the Christian Greeks, the Albanians, and the invention of characters among the Armenians, Latins, Georgians, Goths, and many other individual language groups and families. He even included a discussion of Aethicus but no specimen of his alphabet.[89] Armenian, Tzervianorum (an odd Illyrian script), Dalmation and Cyrillic, Georgian and Jacobite, echoed the work of Postel, but Duret also added Cophtite, Etruscan, and then samples of Chinese, before he concluded with the Indians of the New World. His final chapters dealt with technologies of production, including the invention of print, and comments on the causes of decadence and changes in language. His final short chapter focused, amazingly, on the language of animals and that of birds.

Duret's vision was global, his concept of history was geographic, and his range demonstrated acquaintance with all modern tongues—within which the questions of the original alphabet could be framed as the source for all others. Duret asserted that Samaritan had no "letters or characters of its own, they are all Hebrew, but very ancient, as is well known among those who are acquainted with the Hebrew, Syriac, and other ancient languages."[90] His Samaritan specimen was a genuine Paleo-Hebrew.[91] Ultimately, Duret implied that the various alphabets should be understood as multiple remakings of one graphic system. Beneath the "transformation and mutations" of his subtitle was a single template of "the" original alphabet—merely reworked in each iteration—showing that the many languages of the earth shared a common history.

STOLEN SCRIPTS: VIGENÈRE AND COLLETET

Duret's book was tightly connected to two other publications, one which precedes and one which followed. In 1586, Blaise de Vigenère published *Traicté des chiffres* (Treatise on numbers), and in 1660, almost a century later, François Colletet published *Traittez des languages estrangères, de leurs alphabets and des chiffres* (Treatise on foreign languages, their alphabets and numbers).[92] While these appear in different moments in the history of language and alphabets, both are intimately related to Duret's 1613 *Le thrésor*. The scripts in Vigenère (and their sources) repeat the range of specimens in precedents and sources, but a few particular cases should be mentioned. Vigenère reproduced the Enochian alphabet from Pantheus's *Voarchadumia* (duly cited), followed by Crossing the River, other Chaldeans, and a Samaritan from Ambrogio, as well as scripts that had been reproduced by Postel—those of the Near East—Syriac, Phoenician, Greek, Armenian, Georgian, and then Egyptian, and Ethiopian. Vigenère also cited the Grimani Library as a source for several exotic scripts and included the Theban attributed to Petrus de Abano, as well as the scripts credited to Salomon [*sic*] and the angel Raphael cited by earlier authors. The compendium lineage was intact and the citation history codified by these repetitions.

Vigenère was eclectic in his selection of historical accounts. He recounted that Enoch was the secretary of Adam (improbable given the amount of time between Creation and the Babylonian captivity, but Vigenère did not perform the kinds of calculations that often accompanied such accounts). He confused matters by suggesting the Enochian alphabet was the one used by Seth for the pillars. He calculated there were three hundred years between the Deluge (dated to 1656) and the birth of Abraham (1996), according to biblical calendars. He noted that Enoch was revered in Aethiopia even to the present, which conformed to the association of the Book of Enoch with that geographic region. He discussed *The Zohar*, or *Book of Creation*, and other Kabbalistic beliefs in a grab bag of miscellaneous knowledge about the alphabets and their history and sources.

His statements reflected prevailing beliefs—that because they had "kept the ancient characters, Esdras and the Jews kept the true religion and true and only God and had nothing to do with those who wanted to use other letters and writing; and the Samaritans also preserved the ancient writing."[93] These beliefs would eventually be weighed by modern paleographers and Semitic epigraphers against available physical evidence. Already in Vigenère the cultural stakes of authenticity were being raised. Adherence to the idea of "ancient characters" was taken as a sign of a sacred covenant as well as a claim to historical priority. Vigenère also mentioned that in addition to the usual authors and texts, his sources included diverse medals, marbles, and antique bronzes. This was also a harbinger of techniques to come. He acknowledged that Postel's publication of the two coins in the *Linguarum* fifty years earlier in 1539 had been the first such presentation of antiquarian evidence. The final group of alphabets in Vigenère's book was lifted directly from Trithemius, whom he acknowledges.[94]

Vigenère's scripts were absorbed wholesale by François Colletet in *Traittez des languages estrangères, de leurs alphabets et des chiffres* (1660).[95] Colletet was completely unapologetic about his massive act of appropriation and even wrote in his "Advice to the reader" that

> I do not doubt that many who are going to see these Alphabetical Tables, knowing that they are in Vigenère, are going to believe, first, that this work is only a transcription, & that I took the discourse of that Author, as well as the illustrations; but I beg them to only leaf through it, & they will have a totally different judgment. It is indeed true that I have followed this great man's footsteps in some places; however, I did not take many things from it, and I followed more closely what was written about it by Sir Fulvio Montaury, born in Sienna Italy, the glory of whose work I do not wish to steal. It will be known therefore that he composed a Book entitled *Raccolta di diversi Antichi Alphabeti con l'annotationi in linguia Italiana* and obtained the Privilege of the King to print it in the year 1643 & this manuscript having fallen into the hands of my Printer, I was forced to accompany each illustration with a short discourse which explains it.[96]

Colletet made many excuses, noting that he was using the library of his late father and was under pressure from the printer to finish the writing. He had been given, he claimed, three weeks to do a year's work and, rather like an undergraduate with a deadline, seemed to have been content to "borrow" most of the substance of his publication from existing sources.[97]

Colletet commented that Moses had used vulgar characters in the Decalogue, known mainly to himself, but that God did not want him to write only for himself but for others who would live after. This version of the story seems to be unique to Colletet, who went on to avoid the hard questions by saying he had no idea if the Hebrew letters now in use were the same as those of Moses, or if they were the ones invented by Esdras, or used by the Masorites. A strain of anti-Semitism began to arise here as Colletet suggested the Jews changed their letters out of malice, to take away the letter that looked like a cross because it was the sign of Redemption. While citation and paraphrase were common, Colletet's wholesale appropriation was notable.[98]

THE PILGRIMS AND THEIR SCRIPTS: GRAMAYE AND PURCHAS

In another massive act of appropriation, Samuel Purchas absorbed an entire corpus of scripts—and even, it seems, the woodblocks on which they were carved—from a 1622 publication by Joannes Baptista Gramaye, into the four-volume 1625 edition of *Hakluytus Posthumus, or Purchas His Pilgrimes*.[99] Gramaye's small book had been gathered from specimens in his travels and thus worked perfectly to illustrate the accounts of Purchas's wandering authors. Presented in equal terms with other trophies and records of peregrinations, the scripts served as authentic presentation of the writings of "others."

Gramaye's book was simply a set of specimens, as per his title, *Specimen litterarum et linguarum universi orbis in quo centum fere alphabeta diversa sunt adumbrata and totidem quam; super sunt annotate operisque maiores ration et aucctores institutum aperitur* (Specimens of the many letters and languages of the world in which a hundred alphabets are presented and defined [. . .]; 1622).[100] Gramaye began his presentation with Hebrew, in recognition of its priority, and assigned its origin to Adam. Then he recounted the story of Seth, and then Moses, drawing in passing on sources of rabbinic literature. Greek and Latin got full discussion, and, notably, these specimens were presented using metal type. Following this were two pages of tables that showed parallels between ancient Hebrew, modern Hebrew, Aethiopic, Syriac, Arabic, Armenian, and Dalmation on one page and Rustic, Jacobitic, Aegyptian, Indian, Persian, Turkish, and Syriac on the next. These tables combined the individual letters with the vowel *a* to illustrate their sound values alongside the visual properties of the scripts. The usual scripts appeared—Celestial, Malachim, and ancient Hebrew,

Runes, Punic, Chaldean, and Saxon in no particular order or sequence. The sources noted included the familiar Trithemius, Duret, and Postel, as well as Thomas More (his Utopian script made a frequent appearance), Angelo Rocca, and Hermannus Hugo. The canonical lineage was now well established, as was the geography of collecting from Europe through the ancient Levant.

The scripts added an extra dimension of "truthiness" to the accounts of his pilgrims and their many texts: "Intending to present the World to the World in the most certaine view, I thought a world of Authors fitter for that purpose than any One Author writing of the World."[101] Purchas had gathered travel accounts from many sources, and his book swelled to multiple volumes. Among his sources was the posthumous publication of the manuscripts of Richard Hakluyt (d. 1616), a writer who passionately promoted colonization of the New World. The encyclopedic collection was meant to fulfill the promise of its title: *Hakluytus Posthumus, or Purchas His Pilgrimes Containing a History of the World, Sea Voyages, & Lande Travelles, by Englishmen & Others; Wherein Gods, Wonders in Nature & Providence, the Acts, Arts, Varieties & Vanities of Men, with a World of the World's Rarities Are by a World of Eyewitness Authors Related to the World.*[102]

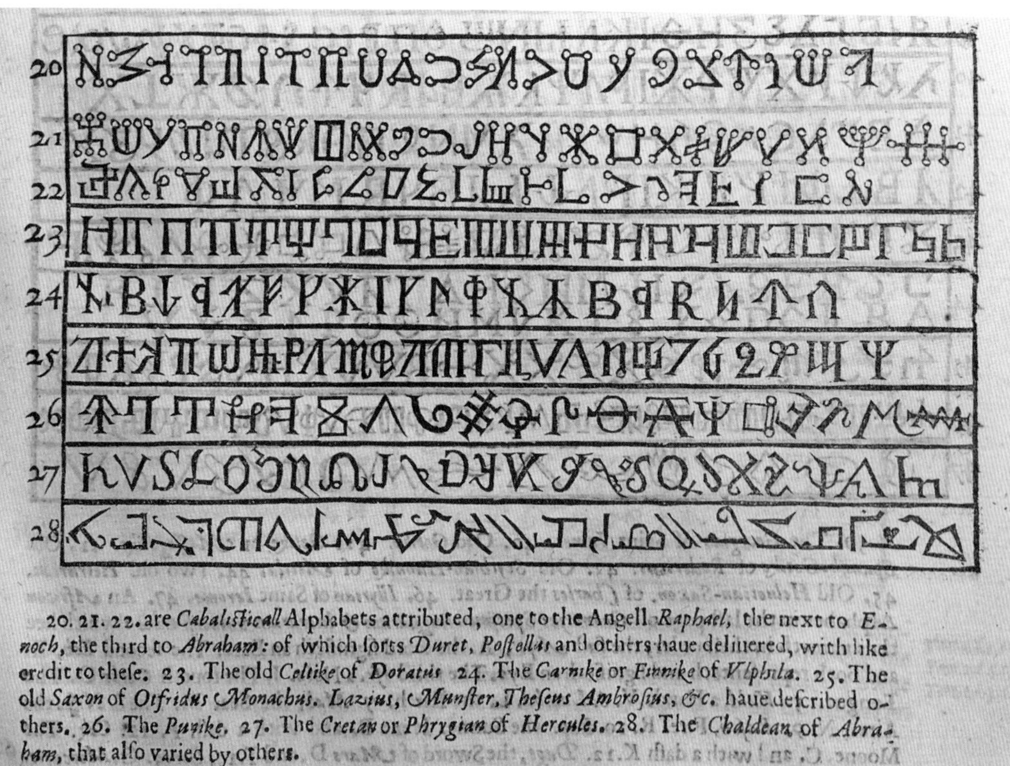

20. 21. 22. are *Cabalisticall* Alphabets attributed, one to the Angell *Raphael,* the next to *Enoch*, the third to *Abraham:* of which sorts *Duret, Postellus* and others haue deliuered, with like credit to these. 23. The old *Celtike* of *Doratus* 24. The *Carnike* or *Finnike* of *Vlphila*. 25. The old *Saxon* of *Otfridus Monachus. Lazius, Munster, Thesens Ambrosius, &c.* haue described others. 26. The *Punike.* 27. The *Cretan* or *Phrygian* of *Hercules.* 28. The *Chaldean* of *Abraham,* that also varied by others.

FIGURE 4.12 Samuel Purchas, *Hakluytus Posthumus, or Purchas His Pilgrimes* (1625). A detail showing nine of the many scripts borrowed directly from Gramaye. Public domain.

Purchas made no claim to originality in thought or composition. He cited and paraphrased, edited and published, the words and authority of others. His versions of the history of the alphabet were standard, taken from Josephus, Pliny, and the Bible. His knowledge of languages, of "Mother Tongues and Orientall Languages I will here out of Scaliger (our European Mithradates) relate."[103] He did not adjudicate among varying opinions, merely reporting that Postell [*sic*] and Scaliger believed the "ancientist kind of Letters" to be Phoenician, or "as now they are called, the Samaritan, first used by the Canaanites (of which the Phoenicians were a part) and Hebrews."[104] He got things partly right by not specifying the actual identity of Samaritan letters, or the differences, which he would not have known, among the many variants of ancient Semitic scripts. He followed Scaliger's suggestion that the "Chaldees fashioned their letters from the Phoenicians now used by the Nestorians and the Maronites," and yet the Hebrew and Phoenician were both "Mother-letters to the rest of the World."[105] Purchas used the scripts to signal authenticity and historicity, cultural identity, and the reality of those foreign lands to which he, himself, had not gone. These pilgrimage travelers sought more than knowledge of exotic letters on their journeys, but the script specimens reinforced a mythic origin tale for Hebrew mapped from the ancient region.

THE QUERULOUS THOMAS BANG

Thomas Bang's *Caelum orientis et prisco mundi yriade exercitationum literarium repraesentatum curisque* (The oriental sky . . . ; 1657) provides a final example of these cycles of repetitive citation.[106] Bang listed no less than thirty-three "inventors" of letters.[107] He also reproduced what he called *The Book of Enoch* and prefaced it with a long discussion of evidence for whether Enoch had an alphabet. Bang's sources comprised what was at that time the full list of authorities in the field, including contributions by Lorenz Schrader (1592), Theodor and Israel de Bry (1596), James Bonaventure Hepburn (1616), and others already discussed. He devoted an entire chapter to the question of whether Adam invented the alphabet, struggling as others had before him with the conundrum of how Adam could name everything unless he had language. If he did, then what language could it have been?

Bang examined each authority to determine whether there was evidence for a celestial origin of the letters or credibility to the notion of Adam's having invented an antediluvian script. He reproduced the two scripts attributed to Adam from Hepburn's table and shored up the analysis with supporting evidence from Rocca, Duret, and Ambrogio.[108] He quibbled with Pantheus's version of the Enochian and introduced another, as well as one attributed to Noah, also from Duret and Ambrogio.[109] Can Hepburn be correct? he asked. Was his evidence valid?[110] He analyzed five Egyptian scripts in detail, and then he presented the Samaritan script–based specimens from Morin's printed typefaces for the bilingual Bible.[111] He finished with Etruscan, and then several standard Cabalistic scripts—Celestial, the "double" script (rendered as parallel lines connecting lunettes), and then Malachim. In questioning the historical origins and pedigree of these scripts, he cited Agrippa, Rabbi Abraham, Athanasius Kircher, and Leonhard Thurneysser.

The compendia came full circle with Bang, validating their own evidence through the processes of citation and reproduction in these collections. The scripts were so codified that they were taken on their own terms, as graphic forms whose use within a living tradition was not questioned. Some, like Samaritan and Hebrew, were in fact living scripts, but the investigations of the alphabets of Adam, Noah, Abraham, and Enoch were treated with the same degree of scholarly attention. Bang questioned the specifics of these arguments, never the authority of the evidence.

FRY'S *PANTOGRAPHIA*: 1799

The compendium mode began to decline after the seventeenth century, in particular because antiquarian methods that emerged were not based simply on mining the textual inventory for sample specimens. But the last work in this particular tradition—a book that still preserved the blend of actual and mythical scripts side by side without distinction—was Edmund Fry's 1799 publication, *Pantographia*.[112] Remarkable for many reasons, and sixteen years in the making, it was, first and foremost, a specimen book.[113] Fry, a punch cutter and type founder, created all the specimens himself. The claims of the volume were that it contained: *Accurate Copies of All the Known Alphabets in the World; Together with an English Explanation of the Peculiar Force or Power of Each Letter; to Which Are Added, Specimens of All Well-Authenticated Oral Languages; Forming a Comprehensive Digest of Phonology*. This typically elaborate eighteenth-century title expressed an intellectual hubris aligned with the political and cultural reach of the British Empire at the time but also asserted that this was a unique work in its range and scope—which it was.

Fry published his compendium of specimens just as new archaeological approaches were beginning to reshape historical understanding. His bibliographic citations provided a snapshot of late eighteenth-century opinions about the chronological structures of the past. His notes on the subject gathered the many threads of biblical, mystical, cosmological, and historical understanding into a single collection. But alongside these varied frameworks, a clear attention to the history of the alphabet emerged.

Fry conscientiously cited his sources, works, and pages, and this made his compendium singularly useful as a reference text for alphabet historiography. Some of the scripts he described are not alphabetic (e.g., Japanese and Chinese), and many of the phonological transcriptions in Roman characters are of indigenous languages for which a written form did not exist ("Virginian" and "Esquimaux").

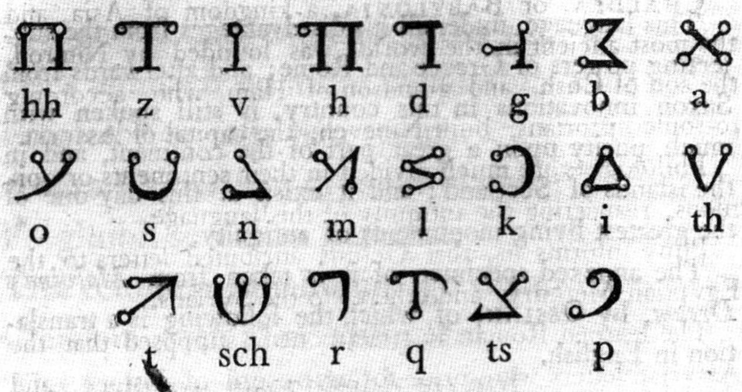

FIGURE 4.13 Edmund Fry, *Pantographia* (1799). Three of the Chaldean scripts, whose attributions stated that the first was "called Coelestial" from the figures of the stars (Gaffarel); the second, according to Teseo Ambrogio, was brought by the angel Raphael from heaven to Adam (Duret); the third was also "said to have been used by Adam." Public domain.

Among the scripts that Fry included in his compendium were twenty versions of the Chaldean script. These were those same scripts that had never served a language, had never been used to write a document, and had their origin among occult practitioners and mystics, transmitted through the grimoires and alchemical texts. Fry believed, as did most of his contemporaries, that language and writing had to be of Divine origin. The invention was too remarkable to have been the work of human beings, whose role would have been to tweak and modify the gift according to their needs and local habits. Fry's model of history was grounded in a biblical chronology but included a larger cosmological timescale alongside dates that belong to known events or periods of human history.

All of the twenty scripts Fry included under the rubric Chaldean are versions of the magical, celestial, and angelic alphabets that can be tracked to the usual European and English sources.[114] Missing from his Chaldeans are the Honorarius script and any alphabet attributed to the fictive figure Aethicus Ister. Fry was as interested in Britain's imperial reach as in the myths of the past. His specimens of living languages had global range, truly a reflection of empire.

Understanding of the formation of the alphabet within other cultural exchanges, locations, and processes would change dramatically in the course of the nineteenth century. Fry provided a report on the end of the era of textual knowledge and graphic transmission, when belief in the Divine origin of language and writing still prevailed. Fry was willing to entertain the idea of angels, celestial patterns, and other imaginative sources for the letters, signs so powerful that only such an origin seemed to make sense. The concept of Chaldea, the ancient kingdom, would also change with archaeological evidence, as the understanding of the alphabet would be reconfigured along with other features of the historical past. But the compendium makers had forged a bridge between textual and graphic accounts of letters that had begun in a medieval notion of knowledge as signs to the larger global framework for historical understanding of the alphabet within colonial explorations and geographies.

CONCLUSION

Compendia served the dual purpose of unifying knowledge about the alphabet and pluralizing it by collecting the variety of scripts associated with distinct languages, historical periods, and geographies. While *the* alphabet was reified in the identification of the *original* script, with Hebrew as the prime candidate, the concept of *alphabets* produced as variants became increasingly evident. Compendia laid the foundation for a progressive history of the development and diffusion of alphabetic scripts but also their submission to a single narrative.

By the middle of the eighteenth century, the distinctions between artificial and actual alphabets were well marked and knowledge of ancient languages had been codified into grammars and lexicons within university curricula and scholarly practices in England and Europe. Knowledge of ancient languages had been seen as crucial to reading the Scriptures in the original, though the question of the earliest—and holiest—alphabet was not resolved, since that expertise engaged with the study of the historical evidence of the past.

Twentieth-century scholars rarely attempt a comprehensive approach to the study of alphabetic scripts in all their variants. When they do, as in the case of Timothy Bright and Peter Daniels's edited volume, *The World's Writing Systems* (1996), they make use of rational approaches that consider scripts largely as a way *to write spoken language* rather than as autonomous *graphic systems*.[115] Such solid scholarship leaves little room for imaginative fancies and engages its objects of study on very different premises from those of the compendium makers of earlier centuries. This contemporary attitude privileges speech as the primary method of human communication. But it divorces the study of the alphabet from the rich cultural agendas in which more was at stake than the mechanics of notation. The Celestial script may not have been able to be used to write texts, but its power as a symbol of the Divine presence in alphabetic forms cannot be dismissed, especially given the hundreds of years in which this belief persisted. In Bright and Daniels, the history of knowledge about the alphabet within older concepts of history and origins is eliminated. Much of the intellectual discourse from earlier centuries is marginalized as inaccurate or incomplete. But writings of the earlier compendium makers provide valuable insight into the ways the alphabet was imagined. Understanding the contributions of these early scholars is essential to an intellectual history now forgotten or eclipsed but which provided its own full explanation of phenomena. The compendium makers' attempts at ordering and organizing a comprehensive view of knowledge provided a transition to modern scholarly modes. They did not have the tools for understanding origins and development, but they collected and preserved both actual and mythical information on which that understanding could emerge. In the next phase of intellectual work, mythical constructs were put aside as investigation of material evidence ascended.

FIVE

Antiquity Explained

The Origin and Progress of Letters

Until the seventeenth and eighteenth centuries, the main sources of information on the origins of the alphabet had been bibliographic. Textual citations and images had passed through long lineages of copying but were rarely supplemented with observation of material objects. Physical evidence was still scarce. A few known inscriptions in Greece, southern Italy, and other sites around the Mediterranean demonstrated the diffusion of alphabetic scripts but not their origins, despite growing interest in determining the age of these remains. Knowledge of hieroglyphics; character-based scripts in China, Japan, and Korea; and New World writing systems all offered their own conundrums but were mainly explained by mythic tales of Divine gifts or inspiration from nature.

Slowly, attention to ancient objects began to produce a shift in historical understanding of the development of written forms, even if only a few artifacts linked to the early sources of the alphabet in the Near East could be identified. By the eighteenth century, two complementary lines of intellectual inquiry matured. One arose among collectors of antiquities fascinated with rare objects and their link to the historical past. Reading these objects required knowledge of ancient languages as well as skill in studying the visual formats and material features of inscriptions. The other was fostered in the practice of diplomatics, the field concerned with authentication of documents, where systematic forensic methods attended to physical features such as wax seals, parchment, paper, and, above all, handwriting. The antiquarians and the diplomaticists shared an affinity for empirical approaches to research and description, even if the former were intent on expanding the narrative of the past and the latter were focused on historical warrant for the function of documents in the present. Perhaps more profoundly, their approach supported an understanding of the alphabet as a human invention, not a mythic gift from a Divine source, miraculous though it remained in their perception.

The search for the "origins" of the alphabet continued but with an increased interest in the gradual transformation of written forms—or the "progress of letters." Though textual accounts were not abandoned, they were no longer considered sufficient, and techniques borrowed from the natural sciences began to inform historical analysis. This fostered a nascent concept of developmental history, rather than of a single moment of invention for "the" alphabet as something intact and unchanging. This work was informed by the recovery of inscriptions in the form of coins, statuary, pottery, monuments, and other "antiquities" assembled in cabinets and private collections or copied in situ and reproduced in lavish volumes. While the line between amateur and professional was not distinct in this era, scholarly networks became more established, largely through the founding of the National Academies, particularly in Europe and the United Kingdom. Interestingly, among the five units that formed the first learned society, the Institute de France, founded in 1667, one was designated the Académie des Inscriptions et Belles-Lettres, signaling the importance of documents for scholarly study.

THE VALUE OF ARTIFACTS

Throughout the seventeenth and eighteenth centuries in Britain and Western Europe, it seemed nearly every gentleman (and occasionally a woman) with a little means and spare time took up antiquarian pursuits. The first meeting of a group whose existence was indicative of this trend, the British Society of Antiquaries, took place in London on December 5, 1707.[1] Attending were Humfrey Wanley, John Talman, and John Bagford, who in subsequent gatherings examined objects collaboratively as well as discussing theories of history. While these are hardly commonly known figures three hundred years later, they were prominent members of British scholarly circles in their time, and their presence as a founding group set antiquarianism on a prestigious footing. In 1751 the (by then much larger) society received a Royal Charter officially charging it with focus on historical antiquities.

While ancient Britain provided one source of fascination, the longer history of humankind provoked acquisition of materials from far afield. Such collecting habits had precedents frequently justified by dubious practices. For instance, in the 1620s, the Earl of Arundel and the Duke of Buckingham had attempted to acquire an entire gate from the ancient wall of Constantinople (they failed when the effort raised a public outcry in the ancient city).[2] While such grandiose gestures were rare, many collectors assembled cabinets of smaller objects from exotic and remote lands.[3] Global exploration expanded the range of sources from which these materials could be acquired, and even egregious acts of cultural appropriation were understood differently than they are now. Many European and British collectors felt no hesitation at removing ancient artifacts from their sites.

The rise in use of the term *antiquities* signaled the new scholarly focus on *objects*. It appeared in the title of a major contribution by the founding figure Bernard de Montfaucon, a Benedictine monk, whose *Antiquité expliquée et representée en figures* (Antiquity explained and represented in figures) appeared in multivolume folio format in 1719.[4] The theme was still present half a century later, in Comte de Caylus's 1752–57 *Recueil d'antiquités égyptiennes, étrusques, grecques et romaines* (Collection of Egyptian, Etruscan, Greek, and Roman antiquities), an equally encyclopedic publication of carefully studied, drawn, and engraved plates of ancient objects. Caylus's introductory remarks included this statement of justification: "Antique monuments are essential for knowledge. They explain specific uses, clarify obscure or badly detailed facts among authors, and they put the progress of art in front of our eyes, and serve as models for those who cultivate them. But it is important to note that Antiquities were not always regarded this way: they were seen simply as supplements and proofs of history, as isolated texts, liable to long commentaries."[5]

The focus on objects embodied in this remark was echoed by many other antiquarian scholars. For instance, when the historian William Massey cited the familiar passages about the inscribed pillars of Seth from Josephus in his 1763 work, *The Origin and Progress of Letters*, he concluded that "unless some instances of antediluvian writing" can be found, this remained a specious tale.[6] No manuscripts or inscriptions using Adam's alphabet (or that of his sons) had ever been identified, though the specimen script that bore his name had been constantly reproduced in many compendia. Such "spurious" scripts largely disappeared from the antiquarians' inventories and analyses. A line had been drawn between real and imagined histories. The insistence on evidence—physical artifacts—to shore up the biblical account distanced Massey from his predecessors. He was not content simply to cite the texts of antiquity, no matter how authoritative.

As methods of assessing evidence became more systematic, the antiquarians derived their understanding of the history of writing *from* evidence, but they also saw the remains of the alphabet *as* evidence to be looked at and assessed in increasingly empirical terms. The antiquarians wanted to take their information from *objects* and to examine for themselves the physical evidence of the past. This empirical bent distinguished the antiquarian sensibility.

While legions of individual scholars actively sorted, identified, collected, and classified artifacts of history, the detailed examinations of objects in the publications of Montfaucon, Caylus, and others were just that—isolated objects, stripped of context. They might be identified as "Greek" or "Etruscan" and surrounded with commentary, but their provenance was often lost, incomplete, or vaguely specified, and some were difficult to date. An additional dilemma for these antiquarians was to fit evidence into existing chronological frameworks still grounded in biblical timescales.

Of the two strains of intellectual development that bear directly on alphabet studies, antiquarianism was an intellectual, cultural engagement with historical study and diplomatics a professional field that announced itself from the outset as a "science" established on empirical methods. Diplomatics formed the foundations of modern archival study and practice. Antiquarianism had no set rules, and its tenets of belief were never put into a formal document or manual. Both approaches were evidence based and relied on empirical observation and formal description. But while diplomatics attended to the trail of custodianship as part of its assessment, it was, by contrast, often convenient for antiquarians to forget or overlook this aspect of an artifact.

Antiquarians anticipated modern scientific history even as they situated new evidence in older paradigms of chronology. But they were also motivated by intellectual fashions such as a belief in independent, culturally distinct origins of national identities for Europeans rooted in mythical pasts: Teutons, Celts, Britons, or Anglo-Saxons, for example. The discovery and analysis of runic alphabets had a special role to play in these imaginings, but claims for authentic Celtic, Belgian, and Spanish originals were also put forth.

Crucial to antiquarian pursuits were expertise in languages and understanding of historical chronologies. The first provided the necessary means to read and interpret inscriptions; the second supplied the temporal framework to evaluate antiquities.

ANCIENT LANGUAGES

Knowledge of ancient and exotic languages continued to expand in Western scholarship in the seventeenth century. For one exceptional example, consider Thomas Comber, master of Trinity College between 1631 and 1645, who, in addition to the modern languages (French, Spanish, Italian) and classical ones (Latin and Greek), knew the Semitic tongues (Hebrew, Arabic, Coptic, Samaritan, Syriac, Chaldean, and Persian).[7] A growing conviction that Christ had spoken Aramaic (linked to early Syriac), along with the notion that Arabic was essential for understanding the Hebrew Bible, fostered scholarly interest for competence in these languages. Lectureships in Hebrew and Arabic were established at both Oxford and Cambridge in the early seventeenth century. In addition, as European travel, trade, and missionary work went further afield, travelers' phrase books for the languages of Africa, the New World, and Asia appeared along with dictionaries and grammars.[8] Brian Walton's renowned polyglot Bible, published between 1654 and 1657, included texts in Hebrew, Samaritan, Greek, Chaldean, Syriac, Arabic, Aethiopic, Persian, and Latin, an indication of the state of linguistic erudition (and typographic design skill) in the latter half of the seventeenth century.[9]

Comparative linguistics would not mature until the nineteenth-century work of German philologists, but inquiries were well underway when Christian Ravis, writing in *The Discourse of the Oriental Tongues* in 1649, listed the "Ebrew, Calde, Samaritan, Syriac-Arabic, and Ethiopic" as all one language.[10] Indeed, they are all parts of the Afro-Asiatic language group of which the Semitic languages are a large subset: "The Antiquity of them is granted by all to be before any of the European Tongues whatsoever."[11] That "Ebrew" has "no comparison for antiquity" was a given, as was the fact that all humans originally had one and the same language, the one given to Adam.[12] Ravis believed the original unity of all languages could be tracked by looking at their scripts. Only twenty-two letters (reducible to twenty in some circumstances) were used by all people from David and the Prophets until the present day. There was not only one language but also one orthography. Ravis's notions were part of common understanding, just as his sources were composed from the usual list of modern and ancient authors from Herodotus onward. In the seventeenth century, the general belief about the antiquity of the Samaritan script and its connection with ancient Hebrew prevailed along with the systematic rediscovery of Samaritan texts.

Knowledge of Samaritan was virtually absent in Christian Europe until the sixteenth century. Jews, who referred to the Samaritans as Cuthites, were curious about the connection between their own Hebrew language and that of these people.[13] Direct contact with Samaritan came in the early sixteenth century with the previously noted work by Guillaume Postel and then Jean Morin's 1631 bilingual Samaritan Pentateuch. Seventeenth-century systematic European scholarship of Samaritan texts prompted many to suggest that the script was the ancient Hebrew alphabet.[14] Knowledge of the script had come from studying letters on ancient coins, shekels in particular, inscribed in actual Samaritan, comparing those with a form of ancient Hebrew on them that the Samaritan priests could read.[15] Such work was scrupulously rooted in observation rather than based on imagined histories.

CHRONOLOGICAL FRAMEWORKS

While the language context provided one framework within which the alphabet and its history could be understood, the calculation of time, or *comptus*, was another crucial aspect of antiquarian scholarship. Joseph Scaliger's highly influential *De emendatione temporum* (1583) had broadened understanding of historical time beyond classical frameworks to include that of other ancient cultures, such as the Babylonians, Egyptians, and various populations of the Near East.[16] He continued his work by reconstructing the foundational *Chronologies* of the third-to-fourth-century historian Eusebius. Debates about particulars in these chronologies would inflame tempers and incite publications in response, but Scaliger's belief that Christian truth would and could be confirmed by pagan sources motivated his desire for a complete and accurate account of human events. His work shaped Western chronological study for centuries.

Highly detailed and influential chronologies were part of every historical work. Sir Walter Raleigh's multiple-volume *Historie of the World*, written in prison and published in 1614, included a minute analysis of the days of Creation, discussion of God's labors, and evaluation of the proper day for the Sabbath—Saturday or Sunday.[17] Raleigh included a detailed account of the invention of letters according to the usual biblical tales beginning with Seth and continuing to Enoch, Noah, and Methuselah until arriving at Moses who taught the use of letters to the Jews "of whom the Phoenicians their neighbors received them; and the Greeks of the Phoenicians by Cadmus."[18] Raleigh was not an antiquarian, and his source materials were textual, but his authority guaranteed that his chronological outline was frequently referenced.

A more significant chronological authority was Bishop James Ussher. The *Annales veteris testamenti, a prima mundi origine deducti* (Annals of the Oldest Testament . . .), computed by Ussher, was first published in Latin in 1650.[19] Notes from the English version of 1658 were regarded as so authoritative that his timeline dating Creation to October 23, 4004 BC, was used to annotate events in editions of the King James Bible well into the nineteenth century.[20] Even Sir Isaac Newton, the astronomer and physicist, meddled in these matters. His *Chronology of Antient* [sic] *Kingdomes Amended*, published in 1728, arrived at a slightly different calculation and challenged Ussher's timeline by a few years, making a considerable uproar when he placed Creation at 4000 BC.[21] The influence of these chronologies during the seventeenth and eighteenth centuries required reconciliation between physical evidence and their accounting systems, and alphabetic scripts had to be positioned in their schema.

THE ELABORATIONS OF JOHN JACKSON

The work of the already-noted eighteenth-century English antiquarian John Jackson provides an example of the ways chronologies and antiquarian studies were entangled and connected to alphabet studies. In *Chronological Antiquities, or The Antiquities and Chronology of the Most Ancient Kingdoms, from the Creation of the World, for the Space of Five Thousand Years, in Three Volumes* (1752), Jackson opined on biblical chronologies, first by disparaging the Jews and their historians.[22] Citing St. Augustine, he suggested "that the Jews were suspected of having corrupted their copies (as to the antediluvians) out of envy to the Christians, and to diminish the authority of the Greek Scripture used by the Christian Church—and to confound the time of Christ's coming. This was easy to be done through their Sanhedrim, who controlled all Jews."[23] Jackson stated that "to reconcile the Chronology of the Scripture, whether we follow the Hebrew or Greek computations, with that of other Nations in the early Times, especially the Egyptian, Chaldean, and Chinese, has been thought impossible and therefore was never attempted."[24] Jackson noted that the present Hebrew Bible and the Septuagint differed by nearly fourteen hundred years in the calculation of the interval from Creation to the Birth of Adam. These were material concerns, not theoretical abstractions, within eighteenth-century understanding.

In describing ancient languages, Jackson reiterated the prevailing view: "That Samaritan is the ancient or original character of the Jewish scriptures is owned by the most ancient and most learned Jews and Christians."[25] Jackson suggested that the third-century scholar Origen and the fourth-century Church father Jerome had believed the original Hebrew letter was Phoenician or Samaritan and that they had been aware of ancient shekels inscribed with Samaritan.[26] Jackson repeated the standard tales with great conviction: that Assyrian or Chaldean characters had been adopted during Babylonian captivity (as per the familiar story of Ezra the scribe) when the Jews abandoned their original letters.

Jackson added other details about the Egyptians being descended from the race of Ham and the source of their writing ascribed to Hermes, Thoth, or Taaut. By virtue of this they made what he considered false claims about being able to have "Letters and written Records . . . before the universal Deluge."[27] Still, he thought it was reasonable to think that "some sort of Letters or Characters were used in the first Ages of the World" from the time that the "History of Creation was revealed to Adam until the Flood."[28] Jackson made elaborate chronological calculations. Thoth, he said, was living at the time of the dispersion of the descendants of Noah, 531 years after the Flood. If Thoth was born about 150 years after the Flood and lived 460 years, then at about 610 years after the Flood and 79 years after dispersion he would have stayed in Phoenicia before he came to Egypt bringing the letters. This kind of calculation lent alphabet studies an air of authority.

The date of the Flood was crucial for Jackson's arguments about the invention of writing. While he simply dismissed as groundless the Jewish tradition in which Seth invented Hebrew letters, and cited Pliny's assertion that the Phoenicians believed the Assyrians always had letters, he noted that no mention was made of letters during the antediluvian ages in the five books of Moses. Further, he argued that "he [Moses] could not have failed making mention . . . of so wonderful and useful an invention" since he told us about the invention of more trivial things such as a tent and a harp.[29] Ultimately, then, Jackson placed the invention of letters "after the Dispersion of Mankind into different countries" though the Phoenicians, Syrians, Egyptians, and Chaldeans all pretended they were the inventors of letters and that these had been in use in the "first Ages of the World" long before the Flood.[30] Finally, despite his prejudices, he conceded that the Semitic-speaking Chaldeans had greatest claim to antiquity, since they have "written Records to show, that Letters had been known and used among them at least 2234 Years before the Christian Era."[31]

Without evidence on which these arguments about the biblical past could be supported, difficulties remained. In fact, the oldest objects Jackson could cite as physical evidence were the Iguvine tables, a set of seven bronze tablets that had been found in 1444 near ancient Iguvium in Italy. They dated to between the first and second centuries and were written in an early version of the Latin alphabet. Jackson gave a scrupulously detailed analysis of the antiquity of each of the letters, tracing their history, noting which modern letters were missing.[32] But even the most shortsighted antiquarian knew the Latin letters were a much-later formation than the Hebrew.

Meanwhile, detailed study of classical inscriptions and their dates continued on its own track, as the account of the Sigean inscription demonstrates.

THE SIGEAN INSCRIPTION

When the Sigean inscription was "discovered" on the western coast of Anatolia in the first decade of the eighteenth century, it became a sensation, and its reception reveals some of the growing tensions between textual and historical methods. Credit for identifying the inscription goes to William Sherard, a botanist who had become consul at Smyrna in 1703 and developed a passion for finding and copying ancient inscriptions.[33] The "discovery" was much celebrated, and the antiquity of the letterforms made it a focal point for discussion of the development of the Greek alphabet. For the inhabitants of Sigeum, in western Turkey, where the pillar was in place at the entry to the Church of St. George and had long been used for ritual cures and practices, the stone hardly needed European eyes for its "discovery." The tablet was worn and had suffered from having been used as a seat before being placed outside the church where it remained accessible after Sherard called it to attention. The ongoing damage to the inscription was already considerable—but the text was almost entirely effaced before Lord Elgin included it among objects he so infamously removed to the British Museum around 1801.[34]

Travel to the Near East was still considered difficult and dangerous in the seventeenth, and even eighteenth, century and was not undertaken lightly or casually. Often the collections were assembled by figures associated with diplomatic posts or commercial business, like Sherard, or his colleague, Edmund Chishull, who served in the capacity of chaplain to the Levant Company at Smyrna. Chishull's initial publication of the inscription in 1721 in his *Inscriptio Sigea antiquissima Boustrophedon exarata* (Sigean inscription, the oldest sample of boustrophedon) brought it to the attention of the renowned classicist Richard Bentley.[35]

The inscription was almost immediately identified as the oldest known

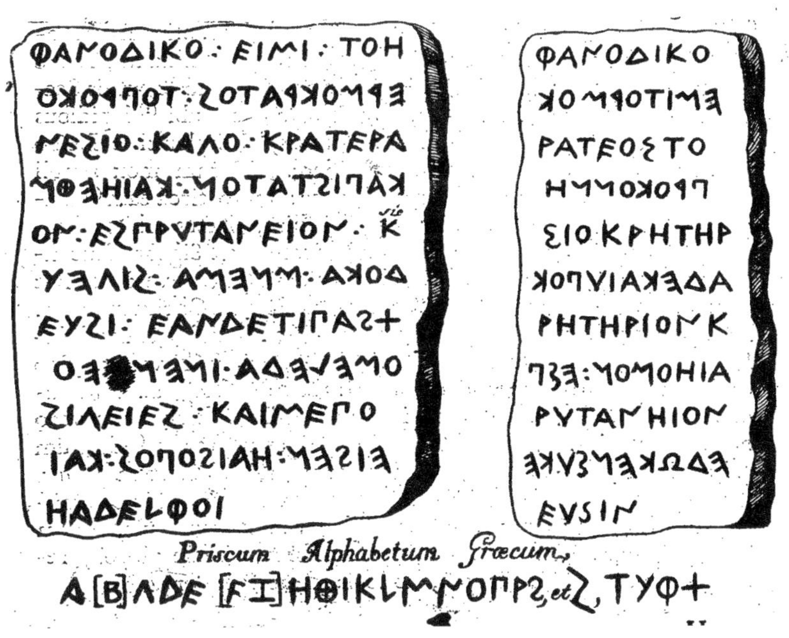

Greek writing that had been found to date, and its letterforms were perceived as close to Phoenician originals by virtue of their linearity and similarity to known examples on medals or coins.[36] The text was written in boustrophedon, the antique form in which the direction of letters and their sequence reverses line to line, rarely found in Ionic inscriptions. According to Bentley, the city of Sigeum where it was found, near the Dardanelles, was built "out of the materials of ancient Troy" and thus this stone "being nine feet in height, might be fancied to have once held the place of a portal in the palace of King Priam."[37] The pillar might have a pedigree linking it to the proposed date of the Trojan War (the twelfth century BCE), but the two inscriptions it bore were of much later vintage, raising the question of when they had been written.

FIGURE 5.1 Edmund Chishull, *Inscriptio Sigea antiquissima Boustrophedon exarata* (1721). Note that carelessness of copying, even in later versions, would make reproductions useless for studying the letterforms. Public domain.

Chishull's interpretation relied on historical information as well as his reading of the texts, which he identified as variants of each other. The longer, lower one was in the dialect of Attic (mainland) Greek used in Athens, and the upper, in larger letters, was in Ionic, used locally. The text celebrated the gift of a ceremonial bowl by one Phanodikos to the city of Sigeum but did not reference other historic events.[38] However, the presence of the two dialects suggested that the inscription be dated to the period of the early sixth century BCE when Athenians had invaded the colony of Mytilene and been given the city of Sigeum in a negotiation with the ruler of Corinth, Periander, who died in 585 BCE. Though the Mytilenaens managed to free themselves from Athenian rule, they were again subject to it sometime between 535 and 524 BCE. Establishing this historical framework allowed Chishull to date the inscription to the early sixth century, particularly since the inventory and shape of the letterforms suggested they were close to the "Cadmean" letters (the Phoenician originals). Chishull introduced other details into his interpretation, and some of these included construing the Greek in ways that Bentley considered inaccurate. For instance, Chishull read the statement "Aesop and his brothers made me" on the pillar to suggest that this referred to the author of the famous fables. This, among other details, caught Bentley's attention.

Bentley received a copy of Chishull's publication from a friend, Dr. Richard Mead, and claims he read it the exact same night before going to bed.[39] Bentley then penned a letter to Mead in which he expressed considerable respect for Chishull's erudition but still took issue with aspects of his work. Bentley believed that the Aesop mentioned was merely a local craftsman, not the famous author, and that the inscriptions had been copied from the ceremonial bowl onto the pillar, which had served as a base for its public use. Bentley's analysis of every detail of the Greek in both texts was virtuosic, including discussion of the historical usage of the case of the nouns and the verb forms.[40] Philology, and expert knowledge of the ancient language, rather than geography and historical events, guided his approach.

The question of the date of the inscription raised several points on which Chishull and Bentley agreed. The forms in the inscription suggested to Bentley that it was written before "the four letters of Simonides" used for noting vowels had been introduced. In fact, Bentley notes that the first inscription (the Ionic) contained two letters that were not among the "Cadmean" while the second (the Attic, below) was written entirely in "Cadmean" letters.[41]

In his comprehensive volume *Antiquitates Asiaticæ* (Asian Antiquities; 1728), Chishull reproduced a more detailed engraving of the monument. This included three other drawings of the inscription by Homerus (a Turkish guide who had produced the earliest copy), Samuel Lisle (who traveled with Sherard), and a third copyist, B. Mould, thus calling attention to the variants introduced even with direct observation. Chishull did not dismiss the linguistic or textual evidence, but he extended the methods to include historical and formal analysis.

The dating controversy was still considered sufficiently relevant at the end of the century that it provoked a discussion in the *Gentleman's Magazine* in January 1799.[42] An article about an inscription copied from the pillars of Herodes Atticus in the Farnese palace in Rome, compared its Greek characters with those of the Sigean inscription.[43] The comparison included a tally of all the letters present, noting that with the exception of a single one, the two inscriptions made use of the same characters. At stake in these debates was a struggle between modern approaches to history and commitments to textual traditions, which, increasingly, were being combined.[44] While Bentley's prestigious classical erudition triumphed, Chishull's methods were the harbinger of the future.

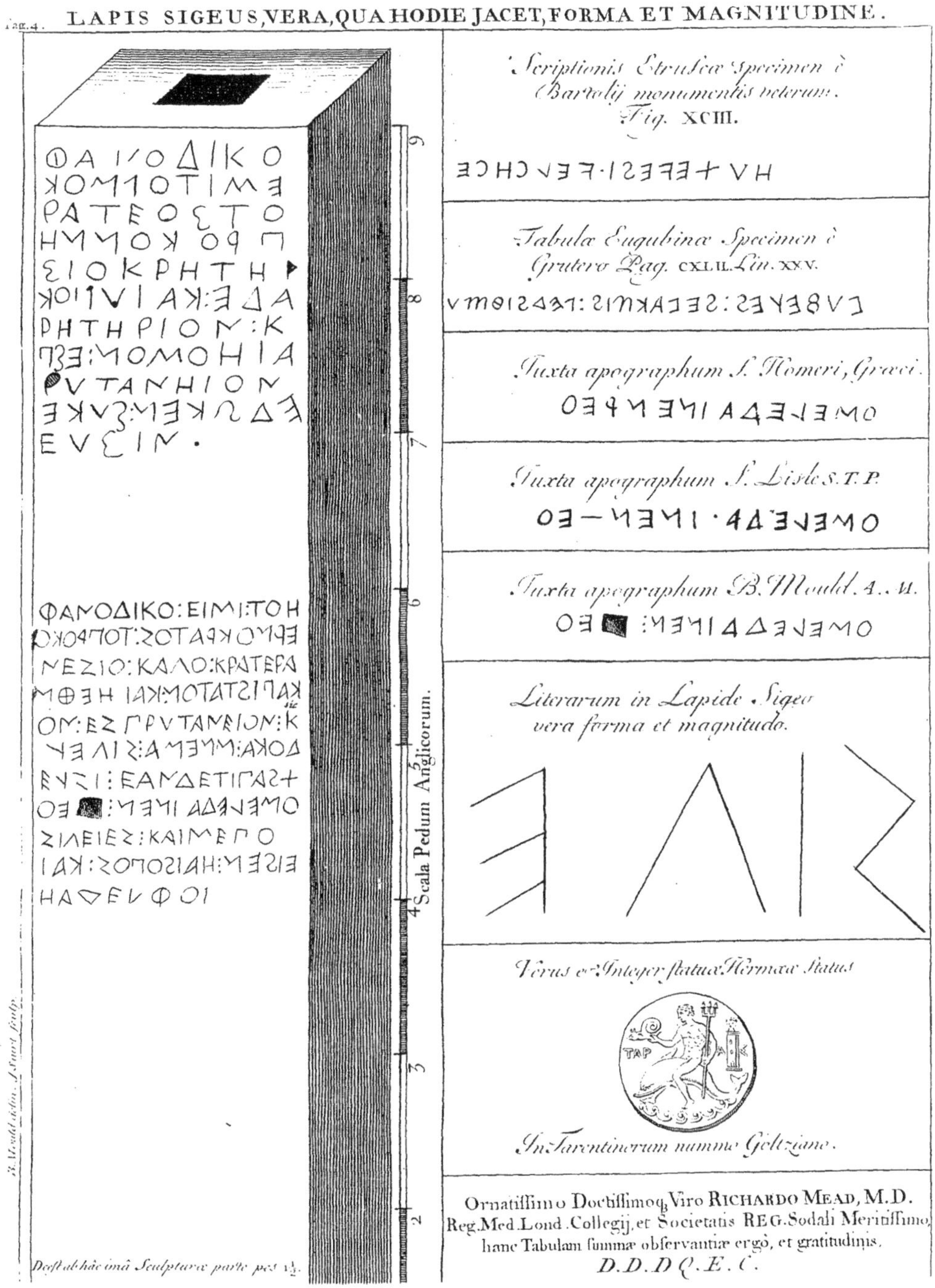

LAPIS SIGEUS, VERA, QUA HODIE JACET, FORMA ET MAGNITUDINE.

Scriptionis Etruscæ Specimen è Bartolij monumentis veterum. Fig. XCIII.

Tabulæ Eugubinæ Specimen è Grutero Pag. CXLII. Lin. XXV.

Juxta apographum S. Homeri, Græci.

Juxta apographum S. Lisle S.T.P.

Juxta apographum B. Mould. A.M.

Literarum in Lapide Sigeo vera forma et magnitudo.

Verus et Integer statuæ Hermææ Status

In Tarentinorum nummo Goltziano.

Ornatissimo Doctissimoque Viro RICHARDO MEAD, M.D. Reg. Med. Lond. Collegij, et Societatis REG. Sodali Meritissimo, hanc Tabulam summæ observantiæ ergò, et gratitudinis, D.D.D.Q.E.C.

Scala Pedum Anglicorum.

Deest ab hâc imâ Sculpturæ parte pes 1½.

B. Mould delin. J. Stuart sculp.

FIGURE 5.2 Edmund Chishull, *Antiquitates Asiaticæ* (1728). On the right, specimens of Etruscan inscription (top two on right) and variant copies of the Sigean from Homerus, Lisle, and Mould, four characters rendered in "true" size and form, and on the left, Mould's full image of the stone. At bottom right, an expression of gratitude to Richard Mead for his observations on the stone. Public domain.

ANTIQUITY EXPLAINED: MONTFAUCON'S FOUNDATIONAL WORK

Several obstacles prevented the study of the alphabet's origin. Not only were materials from the ancient Near East scarce, but they were inconspicuous and difficult to recognize by contrast to a dramatic object like the Sigean inscription or Iguvine tablets. Inconsequential scratchings on stone surfaces or a handful of unskilled glyphs on a potsherd could not compete for visual attention with the elegant monumental remains from classical antiquity. For eyes trained on the remains of Rome, the crude glyphs of Proto-Canaanite scribes would not have been impressive. Remarkably, a handful of eighteenth-century travelers, notably Richard Pococke, would in fact not only take note but also make rubbings and devote considerable energy to obtaining accurate copies of the carvings found in rock faces of the Sinai. Even today, artifactual evidence for alphabet origins is visually modest by contrast to that of major archaeological monuments or collections of documents in archival custody.

For antiquarian studies, the importance and influence of the Benedictine monk Bernard de Montfaucon cannot be overstated. His name is practically synonymous with the founding of the field. Beginning with his comprehensive study of inscriptions, *Palaeographia Graeca* (*Greek Paleography*), published in 1708, and then solidified in the monumental *Antiquity Explained* (first English edition 1721–22), his work became the foundation of antiquarian study.[45] In the preface to the first, he described all the materials of inscription (papyrus, lead, ink, stone, and the writing implements for each), provided a detailed description of the history of Greek libraries, and added an inventory of the number of Greek manuscripts in all London libraries.

His attitude toward material artifacts was stated explicitly in the preface to the second, "A Verbal Description, however exact and particular it may be, can never give us such a clear Idea of some things, as the Image and Picture of those things themselves, drawn from the Life."[46] The experience of seeing original objects "surpasses vastly the Idea we form'd from the Description of the Writer or Picture of the Designer who only drew them from Conjecture."[47]

The history of the Greek alphabet stretched back only to Cadmus. Montfaucon added a discussion of the Samaritan script. He supported arguments for its antiquity with research from the previous century that understood Hebrew as the language of Canaan, and Samaritan as the older original language and script. He saw evidence for this in the residual manner of always writing the Tetragrammaton in Hebrew, while the Transfluvial alphabet, mentioned here as a historical rather than mythical script, was that acquired by the Jews in Canaan (after crossing the river from Chaldea). While he cited various authorities such as Moses Maimonides and Rabbi Azarias, his discussion of Samaritan was linked to coins in museums and samples in European libraries. The sources of his elaborate drawings were carefully identified (e.g., "on p. 304 the specimen was taken from Codice Regio nu. 2498").[48] He even provided a very elaborate pedigree for each letter of the Samaritan alphabet—from Walton, the Vatican, various coins, and so on.[49] His presentation of Greek, Phoenician, and Samaritan (copied from examples in Scaliger) was spare and elegant, a comparative image unencumbered by mythical or magical letters.[50]

In *Antiquity Explained*, Montfaucon reinforced the emphasis on observation, first listing the classical authors (and moderns) he had read and adding, "Not contenting myself with their Explanations of Mythology and History, [I] began to make a Collection of Drawings and antique Pieces about six and twenty years ago."[51] He traveled to Italy to "see the ancient Monuments and Cabinets." Because he refused to work from any but physical sources, he opted not to describe any Jewish antiquities—because they only existed in descriptions in texts. He objected to the fact that the "Form of the Temple of Jerusalem, of the Vestments of the Priests, the Ark, the Tabernacle, the Candlestick" and other objects have been presented as the result of "mere guess-work. . . . I had rather reckon the Form and Image of these Antiquities among the things that are unknown, than take any side in a doubtful Matter."[52] Making such distinctions into assessment criteria was a distinguishing characteristic of his method. He included long sections on Abraxas gems from Egypt, details of funeral processions, elaborate drawings of tunics, togas, buckles, and clasps. And he mentioned Ba'al, whose name would play a part in the twentieth-century analysis of the Serabit el-Khadim inscriptions, as one who "was worshipped by the greater part of the Eastern Nations . . . particularly by the Babylonians and Assyrians."[53]

The massive *Antiquity Explained*, produced in fifteen folio volumes between 1719 and 1724, was a testament to the passion for antique objects that had captured scholarly and popular imagination. Montfaucon's approach to careful drawing and expert reproduction set a standard for research into antiquity. But drawing by hand, even from observation, remediated the objects. Many renderings of foreign objects became inflected with Europeanism in the process; eighteenth-century graphic translations of often unfamiliar ancient motifs were rendered in a contemporary idiom. The images communicated eloquently but without the physical site or cultural context of their production. Lacking this information, the artifacts were, in an important sense, only partial objects.

Throughout, Montfaucon had been motivated by a desire to locate evidence of the biblical past. Though he found classical antiquities and Egyptian artifacts in abundance, he was disappointed in his search and mentioned the absence of biblical materials specifically.

THE FIELD OF ANTIQUARIANS

Antiquarian scholarship flourished in the seventeenth and eighteenth centuries with a pantheon of frequently cited authors whose works show the gradual shift from textual to empirical methods. Among these, several have importance for alphabet studies.

Ezechiel Spanheim's much-cited *Dissertationes de præstantia et usu numismatum antiquorum* (Dissertation on the remarkable use of ancient coins; 1671) was nearly a thousand pages long and filled with engraved images of coins from Greek and Roman history before the Caesars.[54] Organized by region and theme, Spanheim's *Dissertationes* remained a standard reference for studying inscriptions and classical history—and provided Edward Gibbon with a wealth of detailed information for *The History of the Decline and Fall of the Roman Empire*. The abbreviation "Span. *Diss.*" Appeared with great regularity in antiquarian literature, but the text had little information about alphabet origins.

Thomas Godwin's *Romanae historiae anthologia recognita et aucta: An English Exposition of the Roman Antiquities, Wherein Many Roman and English Offices Are Parallel'd, and Divers Obscure Phrases Explained* (first published in 1623) was also very closely linked to classical sources.[55] He gleaned what he could from their texts: "Writing in no nation came to its perfection on a sudden, but by degrees. The opinions of the ancients concerning the Authors and inventors of the letters are different."[56] He summarized the usual account of Cadmus, the Phoenicians, the Egyptians, and the Assyrians. But Godwin was also attentive to the Hebrew alphabet: "It is much controversed, whether the Jews did from the beginning write with vowels or accents or whether they were added by the Masorites, for the understanding of which it will be needful, first, to enquire who the Masorites were; secondly, what their work was, and then to deliver in a proposition what may be probably thought in this point."[57]

In 1662, Edward Stillingfleet made similar arguments in *Origines sacrae, or A Rational Account of the Grounds of Christian Faithd*.[58] These repetitions of citations continued in Samuel Shuckford's *The Sacred and Prophane History of the World Connected, from the Creation of the World to the Dissolution of the Assyrian Empire at the Death of Sardanapalus, and to the Declension of the Kingdoms of Judah and Israel, under the Reigns of Ahaz and Pekah* (1731).[59] He began with the usual questions about the earliest language being Hebrew, Syrian, or Chaldean.[60] He added that the "use of letters was certainly very early, for else we could not have had the short Memoirs we have of the First Ages of the World."[61] By these he means the biblical accounts. His antiquarian sensibility began to show as he considered the Tripods described by Herodotus. He took Scaliger to task for saying he had a copy of these inscriptions in old Ionian letters, certain that Scaliger had merely copied an inscription on the Triopium column of Herodes "which stood formerly in the Via Appia," confounding the names and terms. Herodotus's original tripods were not to be found, of course.

Shuckford also became interested in the controversy about the age of the letters in the Farnese inscription, or Herodes, saying: "The Letters on this Pillar do not seem to be the old Ionian, as may be seen by comparing them with Chishull's Sigean Inscription, or with the Letters on the Pedestal of the Colossus at Delos, of which Montfaucon gives a Copy ; but they are either (as Dr. Chishull imagines) such an Imitation of the Ionian, as Herod, a good Antiquary knew how to make; or are they the character which the Ionian letters were in a little time changed to, for they do not differ very much from them."[62] As reproduced in the engraving of the *Gentleman's Magazine* in 1799, the letters are mannered in ways that are strikingly different from the spare linear forms in the Sigean inscription. These specific antiquities had sufficient visibility from reproductions to serve as common points of reference in discussion. The way an inscription *looked* began to factor into the way it was discussed and assessed.

Shuckford was more precise than earlier writers about how the alphabet dispersed and modified among the Greeks, Arcadians, and Italians. He refuted Athanasius Kircher's claims that the Phoenicians learned their letters from the Egyptians by pointing out that the names of the Greek letters were not consistent with this view, and he then proceeded to review the full sum of existing literature—Scaliger, Casaubon, Hugo Grotius, Vossius, Bochart, Morin, Walton, etc.—for their opinions. But only one among these had irrefutable evidence, "Bishop Walton has provided it beyond contradiction from some ancient Jerusalem coins, called Shekels."[63] The physical evidence mattered.

Published years later, Charles Davy's *Conjectural Observations on the Origin and Progress of Alphabetic Writing* (1772), repeated almost the exact same accounts, starting with the statement that the Hebrew, Samaritan, Syriac, and Greek were all seen to have had one author.[64] Then he made a remarkable observation that the objects for which the letters are named, at least in the opinion of a "late learned antiquary," were all items in an Arab's tent—and that those of the Israelites had the same furnishings.[65] This novel anthropological view of the origins of the letters tied it to cultural contexts that were more complex than simple faith or a relation with God. Nonetheless, he quickly added another powerful statement that the principle of derivation was far less important than that of the capacity of letters to represent sound. While the "powers" of the letters—their sound values—had been discussed in grammars and dictionaries, the principles of sound analysis would become more important in the emerging study of language based on comparative principles.

Davy reviewed the standard literature on the history of writing, including canonical authors from Dionysius of Halicarnassus to his own contemporaries—including Chishull. Newton was a particularly important source for him, and he followed that author's chronologies quite strictly, giving 1039 BCE as the date of the transmission of the letters to Greece by the Phoenicians.[66] Davy also made a notable attempt to match the shapes of the letters to the mouth, in another of the "natural" explanations of the alphabet that persisted into the nineteenth century as the concept called "visible speech."[67] This somatic reference provided its own authority, even

FIGURE 5.3 Reproduction of the Farnese inscription from the *Gentleman's Magazine* (January 1799). Note that most of the letters are not Greek, though the language is. Public domain.

if it lacked historical grounding. Gone were the mystical scripts, but the convergence of citations reinforced their authority and the continuing belief that the "original of letters" had been given to the Hebrews, in the First Age, when all people were of one language. While these retellings did little to advance evidence-based arguments, they were useful references as attention to artifacts continued to progress.

DIPLOMATICS: METHOD AND TECHNIQUES, MABILLON AND TOUSTAIN

The modern field of diplomatics arose from protocols designed by the French Benedictine Dom Jean Mabillon. He established methods for authentication of documents, particularly Merovingian charters on which ownership of Church property was being contested. Discussions of the authenticity based on physical characteristics and also custodianship had been part of Roman law, in particular, a section of the Codex of Justinian.[68] But legal customs for the handling of documents had changed in the Middle Ages, and modern practices emerged in recognition of the need for standardized protocols of analysis. Attention to the properties of handwriting were among these, and that led to studying the emergence of varied scripts and letterforms.

Mabillon's founding text, *De re diplomatica* (On diplomatic matters), was published in 1681, and it is still referenced in archival studies.[69] His principles were meant to provide a set of empirical rules for examining documents based on observation and rigorous assessment. He also attended scrupulously to the issues of provenance or custodianship. Mabillon had less interest in the ancient past for which evidence was scarce, but he was interested in the complete history of writing. He exercised considerable influence on Thomas Astle, Charles Toustain, and others for whom the present could not be considered without some acknowledgment of this longer history.

Mabillon organized the specific hands used in clerical writing into four families—Roman, Gothic, Anglo-Saxon, and Longobardic. This classification was based on stylistic features, as well as the geographic distribution of their development. He mentioned the Egyptian Thoth as well as the Phoenicians, their wanderings, and their gift to the Greeks. He cited Ole Worm on the topic of runes and Hrabanus Maurus on the invention of letters. But it was his methods that broke new ground. He advocated for "prudence and moderation" in examining the evidence of antiquity.[70] The embodiment in the material, the seals, the glosses, and signatures—all were to be examined because many factors came into making an accurate assessment of authenticity. Since a hand might be written (and imitated) at any time, if the historical information and the physical testimony disagreed, then no matter how authentic something appeared to be, it might be liable to error. He described the already mentioned families of scripts in their development from Roman forms. Though not a historian of the alphabet, Mabillon paid attention to the specifics of evidence that led him to establish paleographic standards that remained relevant in later works.

Among those relevant here was *Nouveau traité diplomatique* (New treatise on diplomatics; 1750), by Charles François Toustain. It was a direct application of Mabillon's methods to the history of writing and the alphabet.[71] He suggested at the outset that writing "formed when an unlettered peasant put marks on the walls of his room to remember something."[72] This was a novel theory, but oddly modern in its association of invention and functionality. He detoured through the familiar biblical territory discussed earlier, using the usual logical arguments—how could Moses have written the Law "if letters had not existed already?"[73] He revisited the usual questions of attribution (Phoenicians, Chaldeans, Syrians, etc.) and Kircher's theory of Egyptian hieroglyphic origins of the letters. He suggested that perhaps alphabetic and hieroglyphic writing were both "original" since one was "a writing for sounds and one for thought."[74] Toustain mustered all the requisite ancient and modern authors in his arguments about the sources of the Greek letters. He criticized Scaliger's presentation of the three inscriptions described by Herodotus and was more generous toward the version attributed to Samuel Shuckford.

His paleographic orientation showed in his engagement with the Sigean letters controversy, and he lauded Shuckford's efforts to present better versions of the inscriptions.[75] He noted that an image in Shuckford was very badly served by the engravers, signaling an increased attention to material properties—of the original sources and of the reproductions: "Only with great difficulty can the Sigean inscription . . . be recognized. Aside from the fact that the writing is badly observed, many characters are altered, and even entirely corrupted."[76] No other author had ever commented on the quality of an image before or noted its role in the transmission of knowledge. Though allowing that over time the Cadmean letters might have changed considerably, Toustain was not content with the evidence presented to him. He devoted the final sections of his work to studying individual characters across alphabets to find evidence of resemblance and shared origins. In this way, the alphabet was subjected to a process of careful, comparative paleographic analysis.

He returned to the central issue of the day in discussion of alphabet origins: "If you judge the antiquity of letters by the testimonial of authors and the most ancient monuments, everything argues in favor of the Samaritan Pentateuch."[77] What ancient monuments? The answer was those reproduced in the publications of other authorities, including the work of Edmund Chishull and Pere Etienne Souciet, whose 1715 *Dissert: Sur les medailles Hebr.* [*sic*] (Dissertation on Hebrew medals) he presumably consulted for its images of inscribed medals. Ultimately, he lined up his experts around the question. One group asserted that the Samaritan letters were the oldest. Another, equally robust and esteemed, advocated for the Hebrew (Chaldean), and he reminded the reader that the Hebrew and Samaritan were the same before Babylonian captivity. Despite his insistence on attention to physical evidence, he still drew heavily on this canonical survey of experts. The scientific examination of documents had not separated into an empirical field, but manuals of diplomatics anticipated the fuller development of paleography.

COMMITMENT TO OBSERVATION

Where was actual evidence of the early alphabet to come from? The antiquarians scoured their collections of medals and inscribed objects. For instance, Kaspar Waser's 1605 publication, *De antiquis Numis Hebraeorum, chaldaeorum, et Syrorum S. Biblioa et Rabbinorum scripta meminerunt* (Ancient Hebrew, Chaldean, Syrian coins . . .), contained elaborate drawings of coins.[78] The trouble was that many of the materials were forgeries, as not many authentic Jewish coins were available in Europe in the sixteenth and seventeenth centuries. One that many considered authentic is written in

Paleo-Hebrew and stamped to show it was minted in the first year of the Jewish war against Rome.[79] While these coins were important, they were late examples, mostly from the early decades of the Common Era or just prior.

Jewish scholars had also searched for evidence of biblical history and of the original alphabet. The renowned medieval rabbi Moses ben Nahman had gone to Jerusalem late in his life (around 1270) to look for the tomb of Rachel.[80] He sought examples of the "sacred shekel" described in the Torah, half of which was to be given in tithe for the census. When he went to Akko (near modern Haifa), he found "a silver coin with engravings, on one side resembling the branch of an almond tree, on the other some sort of dish, and on both sides, around the edges, clearly engraved writing."[81] This he purportedly showed to the Samaritans and found that they could read the text, proving that it was written in the script of their language. These were also coins minted in the Great Revolt (around 66 CE to 70 CE) against the Romans and that bore inscriptions in the ancient Paleo-Hebrew script. Nahman's story was used as a way to support the assertion that Samaritan *was* the ancient Hebrew.

The Comte de Caylus was one of the first antiquarians to voice an appreciation of the beauty of the objects with which he was concerned. The publication of his *Recueil d'antiquités* between 1756 and 1767 included many Egyptian, Etruscan, Greek and Roman artifacts.[82] In his preface, he notes that "when I began engraving these objects, I had in view men of Letters, who look to these monuments only for proof of the testimony of the Ancients."[83] But then he became interested in those who cared about these monuments for their artistic qualities as well. Caylus argued for the need to use drawings in combination with the art of looking and comparing and

men alterâ parte diversâ inscriptione: שלישית השקל ישראל
schelischith hasschékel Israël: TRIENS SICLI ISRAELIS,
Sicli videlicet sacri, sive ecclesiastici:

8

De Sicli Quadrante.

SEQVITVR Quadrans Sicli. *Is Hebræis* רבע rébah, *et Græcis* τέταρτον, a numero quaternario *dictus, numus ille*

FIGURE 5.4 Drawings of ancient shekels from Kaspar Waser, *De antiquis Numis* (1605), with Paleo-Hebrew writing dating to the first centuries of the Common Era. Public domain.

explicitly stressed visual skills over textual knowledge.[84] He stated, "I have reported the material and proportions of each fragment with great care. I don't think this exactitude is insignificant."[85] He noted the way the properties of objects could indicate features of their use, attending to their volume and scale, proportions, and details in a groundbreaking manner.

In the 1770s, Caylus brought into his discussion the monuments in the Sinai that had been copied by Richard Pococke a few decades earlier. Caylus's observations were prescient, and he anticipated findings about those inscriptions that would only become accepted in the late twentieth century. He wondered, as others had, whether the Phoenician letters might have arisen from the Egyptian: "This question is especially difficult to resolve because Phoenician monuments are even more rare than those of the Egyptians; we only know of one of their inscriptions which was not even found in Phoenicia. We have some medals stamped at Tyre, at Sidon, in Sicily, in Carthage, and Malta and with characters that have had some alteration in different places. But in general they have a strong affinity with the Egyptians."[86] Ultimately, he admitted to the difficulty of finding enough monuments in Phoenician to pursue this research and other impediments: "To recover the alphabet of a language one does not speak, it is necessary at least to know that it has some connection with those which one does know—how else will it be possible to compare and analyze them?"[87]

Another monumental contribution, Poinsenet de Sivry's 1778 *Nouvelles recherches sur la science des medailles* (New research on the science of medals; 1778), also focused on what could be extracted from looking at physical objects.[88] He divided the medals into three groups: tokens, proper medals, and coins. In nuancing these categories, he expended considerable energy debating whether or not medals might bear the image of the emperor or only coins. Then he focused on two particular medals, one written in Samaritan letters, which he said could be easily translated into Hebrew values. The other he claimed had Greek characters on one side but unknown writing on the other. His analysis of the visual evidence was systematic. First, he described the direction of the script, and the strange layout of the text, and culled as much of the meaning as he could make out. The Greek letters could not, he believed, be ancient because of their direction (left to right, not right to left as in the oldest inscriptions). He read the inscription as "Didon Achem, Sidonii Fratre"—the designation of a subsidy given to Jews in Judea by their brothers, Jews in Sidon. This, he said, placed the coin in the first year of the liberation of Israel. The iconography of the Sidon coin showed a sterile tree—while the one on the Samaritan coin had borne fruit. To read the letters on the coin from Sidon he turned them sideways and then had to justify why a "Jewish medal" would have Greek writing on one side and Samaritan on the other, and why Greek writing was being used for a Syriac phrase. The explanation he provided was that Jews of Sidon were merchants, and these characters would have been useful for commercial transactions. He was not completely mistaken.

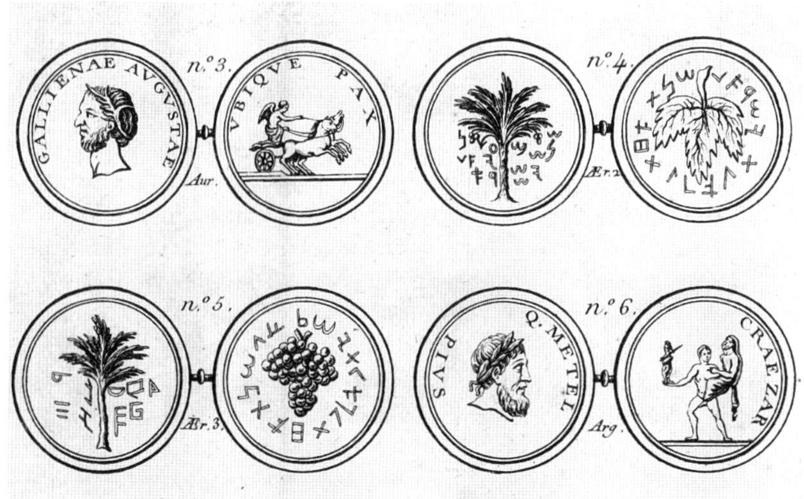

FIGURE 5.5 Coins with Paleo-Hebrew (upper right, lower left) reproduced in Poinsenet de Sivry, *Nouvelles recherches sur la science des medailles* (1778). Public domain.

ECCENTRIC HISTORY

To a very real extent, the elaborate publications of Caylus, Montfaucon, de Sivry and others served as circulating display cabinets in their own right, providing much broader access than the collections themselves. But their authoritative research did not inhibit eccentric use of their work as sources. In his 1752 *Ensayo sobre los alphabetos de las letres desconocidas* (Essay on alphabets of unknown letters), the Spanish scholar Velásquez de Velasco drew extensively on published images by Bernard de Montfaucon and also medals from a work by Fulvio Ursino, *Familia Romana* (Roman families), published in 1577.[89] He borrowed runic inscriptions from Oloa Wormio (Ole Worm), from a book published in Amsterdam in 1636, and others from Spanheim's constantly cited study of coins, *De praestantia et usu numismatum* (1671).

Velasco created a systematic comparison of scripts through production of a set of tables of individual letters pulled from the inscriptions, including Phoenician and Samaritans, stretching his range beyond the classical history into the ancient Near East. His particular focus was on ancient Spanish letters and their sources, which meant tracking early Phoenician characters on the Iberian Peninsula where he perceived the connections among these and the other alphabets of Phoenician origin. He embedded his observations in the usual narratives—the dates of the Flood, the confusion of tongues, and the history of the "letras primitivos de los antiguos Espanoles" ("the primitive letters of the ancient Spaniards") to date the arrival of writing into Spain.[90] The oldest inscriptions to which he had access were from about 500 BCE. He knew there must be a longer history, but none of his venerable sources could provide older physical material.

However, Velasco also saw relations between ancient Spanish letters and runes, convinced that the ancient Iberian inscriptions were of Gothic origin.

He immersed himself in the work of the Danish authority Ole Worm, whose comprehensive study, *Danica literatura antiquissima* (Oldest Danish letters), had been published in 1651. Velasco tried to find a lineage independent of the Phoenicians, who were too "Asiatic" for his purposes (a theme that will recur ahead). Velasco was steeped in the literature of ancient history; he drew on standard authors like those just mentioned, but he depended most on the eighteenth-century historian of "primitive Spain," Francisco de la Huerta y Vega, who had argued that "these characters are not Latin, not Greek, not Syriac, not Hebrew, nor any other Nation of which we have a memory," but that they are "native Spanish characters."[91] Furthermore, according to Huerta, "these Spanish letters are older than the time of Moses and Abraham and thus are not Phenician nor Carthaginian, nor any other people's."[92] Antiquity and priority guaranteed the autonomous purity of Spanish culture for Velasco.

In spite of his citation of the usual classical and modern references for support, Velasco's real focus was on paleographic evidence.[93] He compared examples of each letter of the alphabet taken from medals and artifacts. He connected these with Greek, Phoenician, and Runic by observing their formal qualities. He created detailed comparisons: "Kappa: The first K is in common Greek. The second is different from the first just in the fact that its lower line is elevated. This makes it resemble the Digamma of the Etruscan and Runic. The third is part of the Etruscan alphabet, as per a medal from Emporia etc."[94] Using paleography as a fundamental tool, Velasco considered the formal features of letters as irrefutable in his argument about a non-Asiatic origin for the Spanish alphabet. He was neither the first nor the last scholar to engage paleographic and epigraphic evidence for such idiosyncratic arguments.

THE EXEMPLARY THOMAS ASTLE

Among the many (and there were many, as should be evident even in the small sampling presented here) British antiquarians, Thomas Astle stands out for his work *The Origin and Progress of Writing, as well Hieroglyphic as Elementary* (1784).[95] Keeper of the Records of the Tower of London, Astle was a consummate scholar of diplomatics, absorbing the lessons of Mabillon and Toustain. The dual emphases in Astle's approach—on the visual properties of the letters and on their development within historical frameworks—made his high-profile contributions particularly important in moving alphabet studies towards a modern mode.

He acknowledged his debt to Mabillon in his introduction when he wrote, "One of the principle objects of the following work is the illustration of what has for near two centuries been called, the Diplomatic Science: the knowledge of which, will enable us to form a proper judgment of the age and authenticity of manuscripts, charters, records, and other monuments of antiquity."[96] He went on, "The divine and the lawyer labour to little purpose, unless they can shew that the testimonies which they adduce, are accompanied by all the necessary marks of authenticity."[97] Astle's approach reinforced his concern for the authenticity of "original instruments" in the face of possible (frequent) forgery.

Astle reproduced hundreds of specimens in facsimile images copied with expert care. In a demonstration of his respect for custodianship, he identified all the sources in detail. For instance, the first inscription on the top of Table 2 was identified as "that most ancient inscription, found at Amyclea, in Laconia (2), which is supposed to have been written about one hundred and sixty years before the siege of Troy, and one thousand three hundred and forty-four before CHRIST (3). It is now preserved in the French king's collection at Paris, with some other pieces discovered in the same city by the Abbé Fourmont."[98] Another manuscript specimen of the Book of Genesis, he noted, was "brought from Phillipi by two Greek bishops, presented to Henry VIII, telling him it had been 'Origen's own book.' Queen Elizabeth gave it to St. John Fortescue, her Greek preceptor, who put it in the Cottonian Library. Specimen here made while the writing was in the original state."[99]

Astle pointed out that the letters had been considered as "nothing more than marks for sounds," which meant that "their FORMS, hath not as yet been a necessary object of our attention"; however, he suggested "a competent knowledge . . . is absolutely necessary for ascertaining the age and authenticity of inscriptions, manuscripts, charters, and ancient records."[100] Astle was eclectic and comprehensive. For instance, he cited Baron van Helmont's conviction that the letters were based on the organs of speech, a position supported by Charles Davy as well as the French president de Brosses. He also described the work of L. D. Nelme, who analyzed all letters as combinations of two components, line and circle, and noted Antoine Court de Gébelin's suggestion that the characters have hieroglyphic origins. He qualified these attitudes by asserting instead that the letters "may be considered as mere arbitrary marks."[101] The presence of these scholars was symptomatic of the exhaustiveness of his approach.

Astle held the view that all alphabets are not derived from one, though he believed that most of those in use in Europe, Asia, and Africa "are derived from the Phenician."[102] Astle's chronologies were still biblical, so in referencing an inscription at Oxford, he situated it historically by trying to date it to "the deluge, recorded by Moses, . . . two thousand three hundred and forty-nine years" before the birth of Christ.[103] His commitment to physical evidence continued in discussion of the Pelasgian characters of which the "most ancient inscriptions . . . I have seen, are those found at Eugubium, a city in Ubrian in the Apennines, [found] in the year 1456. Seven tables of brass were discovered, five of which were in Pelasgic or Etruscan characters, and two in Latin."[104] These were the Eugubine (aka Iguvine) tablets already mentioned, and Astle was aware that the variation in their script forms was significant.[105]

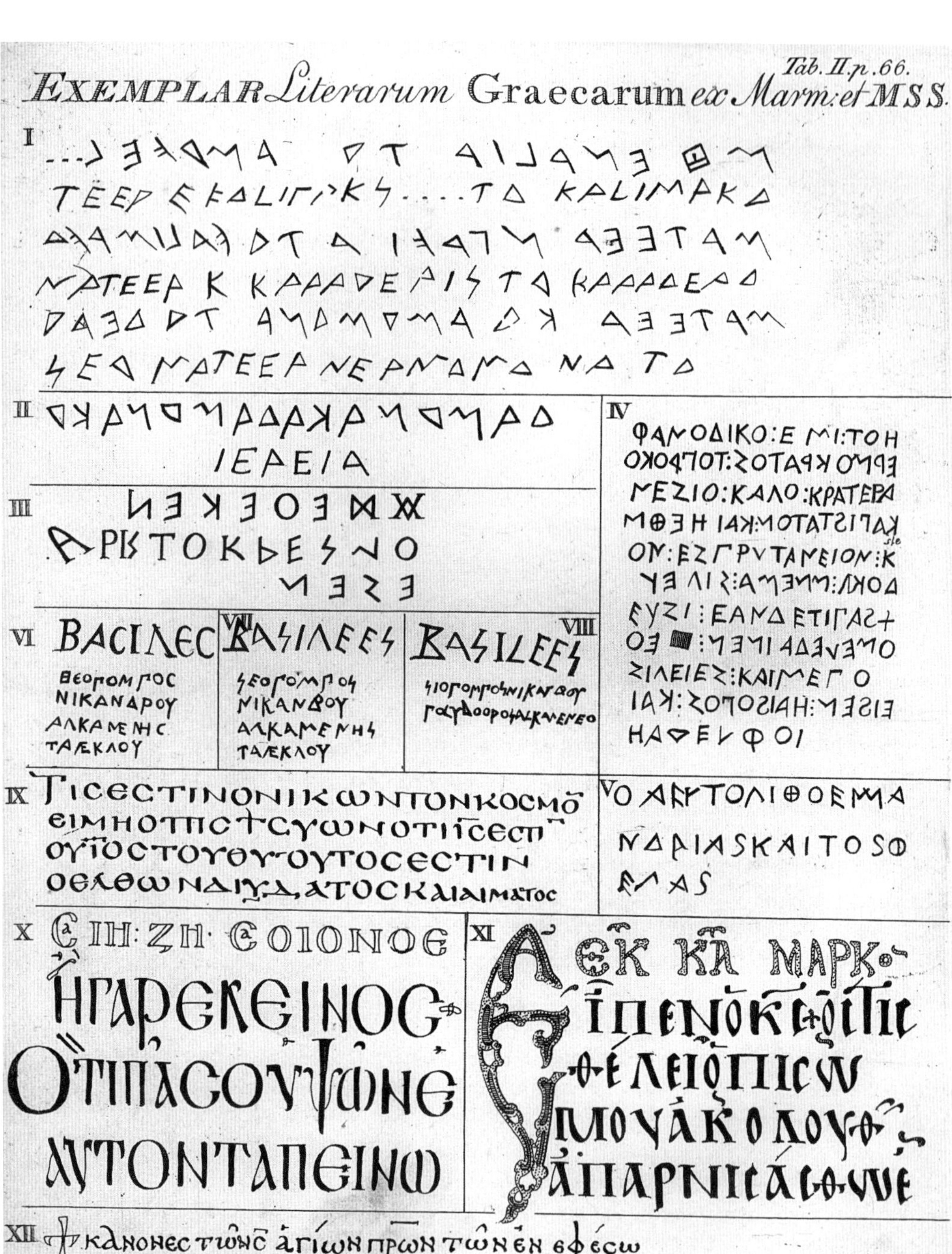

Tab. II. p. 66.
EXEMPLAR Literarum Graecarum ex Marm: et MSS.

FIGURE 5.6 Thomas Astle, *The Origin and Progress of Writing* [. . .] (1784). Table 2. Note the top inscription in ancient Greek, quite close to Phoenician in form. Public domain.

Astle's concern for the material aspects of history showed in his inventory of the losses of libraries of the past, the destruction of material objects, temples, and collections through political actions and accidental circumstances.[106] He detailed the successive waves of destruction (Alexandria, Constantinople, the monasteries and the Cottonian Library, to list a few of those he named) and concluded with an inventory of the percentage of classical books lost in the process. For instance, of the twenty books of Roman antiquities produced by Dionysius of Halicarnassus, Astle stated, only eleven remained. His detailed lists of such facts were extensive.

In defense of his methods, Astle argued: "It has long been the fashion to laugh at the study of Antiquities, and to consider it as the idle amusement of a few humdrum, plodding fellows, who, wanting genius for nobler studies, busied themselves in heaping up illegible Manuscripts, mutilated Statues, obliterated Coins, and broken Objects."[107] He insisted that Antiquarian studies were essential for knowledge of "the Divine," otherwise "how show the harmony between the sacred and profane writers, without a thorough knowledge in History and Chronology? And how are those to be acquired but by study of Ancient Monuments, Statues, Coins, Manuscripts, and Customs?"[108]

Astle's work was in good company in eighteenth-century Britain. William Massey, cited earlier, had been more skeptical than Astle. In his earlier, similarly titled work, *Origin and Progress of Letters* (1763), he criticized the Moses hypothesis for "substituting a miracle where natural means would answer the purpose."[109] Again, he called attention to the absence of evidence, "We have no records in writing from Adam's time, nothing in characters for the first thousand years after creation of the world."[110] Noah's flood, by his calculations, took place in the 1,656th year of the world, and there was no recorded use of letters until the wanderings in the Sinai. Nor was there any trace of a written covenant before Abraham was in Egypt. Massey described the cultural contexts of biblical history, the blend of Babylonian and Egyptian science in astronomy and the role of writing, and the conditions in which Moses and Abraham would have functioned. He concluded with a thesis that argued against the very idea of a Divine gift, stating that "let the art of writing however begin, when it will, without doubt the first essays were rude and irregular."[111] Another contemporary of Massey's, Anselm Bayly, was similarly skeptical. In his 1758 publication, *An Introduction to Languages, Literary and Philosophical: Especially to the English, Latin, Greek, and Hebrew; Exhibiting at One View Their Grammar, Rational, Analogy, and Idiom in Three Pars,* he stated: "But as to the early Use of Writing there seem to be no sure Proofs either from Facts, Tradition, or the History of Moses."[112] Still, Bayly considered the invention of writing so powerful an achievement that he could not imagine it was done by human beings:

> First, reason may shew us how near to an Impossibility it was, that a just and proper Number of convenient Characters for the Sounds in Language

should naturally be hit upon by any Man, for whom it was easy to imitate and vary, but not to invent; and therefore Livy justly ascribeth the Discovery of Letters miraculo & divinitati. Secondly, from Evidence of the Mosaic History it appeareth that the Introduction of Writing among the Hebrews was not from Man, but God; Thirdly, there are no evident Vestiges of Letters subsisting among other Nations till after the delivery of the Law at Mount Sinai, nor then among some till very late.[113]

However, Bayly was too much of a modern scholar to ignore evidence and argument and so he duly noted the Assyrian and Babylonian inventions, claims supported by Brian Walton, and the statements of Diodorus Siculus in favor of the Syrians who are "opposed to the Phoenicians" (who must be the Hebrews).[114] He tried to sort out the relationships of languages—the language called Chaldean was elsewhere known as Aramaic but rendered in Syriac and different from what was spoken in Judea. He knew that some claimed the Aramaic character was the same as the Samaritan but that Ezra had rejected the Samaritan letters because they were not the originals. As to the change from an original script to a modified one, "God writ the Law, called the Ten Commandments with his own Finger; that is, he was sole Author of that Writing."[115] The mixture of erudition and skepticism characterized the state of knowledge of the alphabet in the late eighteenth century.

NATIONALISMS AND WEIRD LINGUISTICS

No discussion of seventeenth- and eighteenth-century European alphabet scholarship would be complete without at least some mention of the interest in runes and claims about their origins. The most frequently cited early works were those of Ole Worm (*Runica Danica*, 1636) and Johann Georg von Eckhart (*De origine Germanorum eorumque vetustissimis coloniis etc* [The origin of the Germans and their oldest colonies etc.]; 1750).[116] Worm used all the textual evidence he could muster—about 150 sources from the ancients (Tacitus, Strabo, Virgil, Cicero, Dionysius of Halicarnassus, Eusebius, Josephus, Plutarch, and numerous others) through the moderns (the De Bry brothers, Cornelius Agrippa, James Bonaventure Hepburn, Philip Melancthon, Joseph Scaliger, Polydorus Virgil, and Johannes Trithemius)—to argue for the derivation of the runes from the Hebrew alphabet. His work was the foundation for Eckhart's visually documented arguments published a century later.

Like Velasco, these authors participated in the rise of linguistic nationalisms rooted in fantastic origin stories for Western languages and cultures. The idea of distinct roots for individual peoples, and with them, the invention of a writing or language unique to their cultural identity, became a scholarly vogue of the eighteenth century. Celts, Teutons, Anglo-Saxons, Aryans—even Belgians—were each given their turn as inventors of the

PAX VOBISCVM ET SALVS PAX

supersunt istae.

Alphabeta Septem in Codice Ratisbonensi membranaceo seculi Undecimi repertae

1. HEBRAICE: a aleph, b beth, b beth, g gimel, g gemel, d doleht, e he, e he, u uau, u uau, z zai, z zai, t the, t the, i ioht, c chaph, h chi, l lame, m mem, m mem, n nun, s samet, c ain, f fe, s sad, c cof, r ref, s sen, t tau.

2. SIRIACE: a ac, b berg, c con, d dorn, e car, f feb, g gebo, h hagal, i is, i cale, k ker, k xi, l lago, m man, n nod, o odil, p perd, q qur, r rat, s sigo, t tac, u uur, x elux, y ine.

3. ARABICE: a ase, a caar, b bica, b berih, c caon, d doro, e cor, f feu, g geur, h hed, i ios, k keir, l lin, m men, n naut, n net, o os, p peru, q quor, r tir, s sol, t tau, u ur, x elx.

4. ÆGYPTIACE: a atahe, b binrchin, c cinoht, d dmain, e eni, f fin, g gomor, h heletha, i iamin, k kattha, l luzamnus, m mihe, n naim, o oldath, p pilon, q quin, r iron, s sicen, t tola, u ur, x xiron, y yph, z zain, thu.

5. GOTHICE: a atahe, b binrchin, c cinoht, d dmain, e eni, f fin, g gomor, h helotha, i iamin, k kattha, l luzamnus, m mihe, n naim, o oldath, p pilon, q quin, r iron, s sicen, t tela, u ur, x xiron, y yph, z zain.

6. CHALDAICE: a alm, b bem, c cem, d dem, e ethrin, f fethim, g gyth, h hiht, i itohim, k kam, l lathim, m moin, n nithoim, o olaph, p pisas, q quimit, r ir, s seith, t tiot trot, x xith, y yn, z ziph, r rosi.

7. ALANICE: a alm, b bem, c cem, d dem, e ethrin, f fethim, g gyth, h, i, k, l, m, n, o, p, q, r, s, t.

FIGURE 5.7 Johann Georg von Eckhart, *De origine Germanorum eorumque vetustissimis coloniis etc.* (1750). Source: gallica.bnf.fr / Bibliothèque nationale de France.

alphabet or the original language. L. D. Nelme, in *An Essay Towards an Investigation of the Origin and Elements of Language and Letters*, imagined an entire history of the settlement of the earth by the sons of Noah in the symbolism of the *I* and *O*, the elemental graphic components of the letters.[117] Nelme championed the Celts as the original people, but his position had competition.

For instance, Johannes Goropius Becanus's *Origines Antwerpianae sive Cimmeriorum* (Antwerpian and Cimmerian origins; 1569) argued that the oldest language should be simplest.[118] He followed this observation with fantasies, suggesting that therefore, the "Antwerpian Brabantic, spoken in the region between the Scheldt and the Meuses Rivers, was the original language spoken in Paradise."[119] On the basis of this theory and its author, Leibniz coined the term *goropism* to designate absurd etymological theories. "Never have I read greater nonsense," wrote Scaliger of Goropius's etymologies.[120]

Eighteenth-century language study was more sophisticated. Though still in pursuit of the "original" language, Albert Schultens, for instance, noted that Hebrew, at least in the modern form in which it could be studied, was not the parent of all Semitic languages.[121] His observations were comparative and based on his knowledge of Arabic. The realization that languages belonged to families, intuited in the older notion of the "confusion of tongues," shifted analysis from a biblical foundation to scientific one.[122] Nonetheless, one scholar, Henri de Bukentop, argued for the Belgian letters as the oldest, on the basis of a complete confusion between the identities of scripts and languages.[123]

Rowland Jones argued in 1764, in *A Postscript to the Origin of Language and Nations*, that the Ancient Britons were "originally possessed of the Celtic or Tuscan letters."[124] He saw these as the same letters that Cadmus had offered to the Greeks and that the Romans had borrowed from the Tuscans (by which he meant Etruscans). But he then went on to refute this because of the radical differences in the shapes of the letters and sounds they represented, presenting instead an argument for Celtic as the original tongue. This was part of a general Celtic nationalism.[125] The notion of the Celtic/Gaelic identity of the original British people had a longer history (George Buchanan began to explore this in the sixteenth century), but in the eighteenth it was linked to political agendas and a strain of philology combining national identity and language. Finding Celtic roots for English words and an alternative source for the alphabet in a set of very basic combinations of *O* and *I* (as the "OI" of all things) became a popular distraction. Edward Lhuyd, in *Archaeological Britannica* (1707), spelled out his goal of "tracing the Original Language" of Gaelic.[126] He drew on earlier work, Richard Verstegan's *A Restitution of Decayed Intelligence in Antiquities concerning the Most Noble and Renowned English Nation*, published in 1605.[127] This remarkably titled work asserted without any equivocation that the English descended from the Germans—that is, the Saxons—whose language he somehow conflated with the "Irish" tongue. This, he argued, was originally German and spoken by Adam and Eve, the etymology of whose names he teased out in imaginative fashion to show that they were one person—"even"—meaning "the same as" because "Eve" was Adam's wife.[128]

These arguments usually involved some version of the sons of Noah and dispersion. The more exotic of these stories accounted for Native Americans as lost tribes or original ones, such as the nineteenth-century account by George Jones, *The History of Ancient America prior to the Time of Columbus Proving the Identity of the Aborigines with the Tyrians and Israelites* (1843).[129]

CONCLUSION

Though a shift toward examination of evidence and development of observational and empirical methods was a crucial aspect of antiquarian approaches to alphabet studies, the persistence of textual traditions and their interlocked citational histories continued to exert a strong influence on the field.

The explanations of antiquarians have a completeness to them that is supported by conscientious scholarly examination of graphic and linguistic forms. This completeness makes their contributions particularly useful for understanding how a historically modern concept of alphabet development emerged through the analysis of artifacts. As chronological frameworks were rethought, alphabet history was also reinvented. By the end of the eighteenth century, various scholars, including the towering William Warburton, had introduced the idea that writing *evolved* from pictographs to alphabets. The notion that the alphabet was the result of a complex, long, and culturally rich process would become central to understanding its identity and origins.[130]

Antiquarianism was a broad popular phenomenon, fueled by interests in local history and incipient nationalism as well as ambitious historical projects. Diplomatics was bound up with professional and political use of documents according to their purported authenticity. Both fields emphasized empirical approaches. Through their observational methods, these scholars laid the foundation for the modern study of archaeology and anticipated the systematic examination of ancient inscriptions in paleography and epigraphy. One of the chief hazards of antiquarian collections was that they deracinated their artifacts, separating them from contexts or provenance histories essential to their accurate interpretation and dating. This approach changed as archaeological methods emerged.

SIX

The Rhetoric of Tables and the Harmony of Alphabets

In 1700, a Dutch scholar named Willem Goeree published a pictorial engraving of a scene from biblical antiquity that contained a table of ancient alphabets.[1] Embedded in a landscape whose iconography linked it to the deserts of the Near East and biblical history, the table was copied almost without alteration from the work of the Jesuit polymath, Athanasius Kircher, in whose *Turris Babel* (Tower of Babel) it had originally appeared in 1679.[2] This recycling of visual information not only put the table into a new context to inflect its reading but also reified the format. Tables were not just the tools for scientists performing calculations or accountants managing their books but part of the popular imagination about knowledge. Goeree's image was not meant for specialists but designed to engage a broad audience in a narrative of history. The table was a useful prop, and an authoritative one. As tables became increasingly familiar, even banal in their habitual use and pedestrian in their design, these intellectually powerful instruments served an array of purposes for comparative study of the letters of the alphabet across timelines of progress and geographic distribution of scripts.

Tables are an efficient, graphically legible means for presenting information in a way that calls attention to similarity and difference—though

FIGURE 6.1 Facsimile of an engraving originally published by Willem Goeree, *Voor-Bereidselen tot de bybelsche Wysheid, en Gebruik der heilige en kerklijke Historien: uit de alder-oudste Gedenkkenissen der Hebreen, Chaldeen, Babyloniers, Egiptenaars, Syriers, Grieken en Romeinen* (Utrecht, 1700). The labels of the columns read from left to right as follows: *The Value of the Letters; Mysterious double letters given by the Angels; Characters from the time of Crossing the River, from Abraham Balmis* [*sic*]; *Ancient Samaritan letters extracted from coins and various authors; The "floridus" letters extracted from coins; The Mosaic character in which the Law was written and taken from various monuments; The true Hebrew or Assyrian letters.* From *La galerie agréable du monde*, ed. Pieter Boudewyn Van Der Aa (1729). Source: gallica.bnf.fr / Bibliothèque nationale de France.

at the cost of sacrificing context. Letters lifted out of their original inscriptions and into tabular form lose much of the information essential to understanding their site and circumstances of production, but they are readily engaged at the formal level for comparison. Though tables are an ancient graphic form, the format, now so familiar as to be almost invisible to a contemporary reader, was first put into use for the study of the origins and development of the alphabet when Cornelius Agrippa published his small example in the 1530s. Then the use of tables for rationalized comparison of historical information began to proliferate in the seventeenth century. Tables create various arguments about knowledge—despite their similar format, they do not all perform the same intellectual work.

THE TABLE FORMAT

The authors of compendia presented their scripts as specimens, which made comparison across examples—keeping a Greek *alpha* in mind while looking at a Hebrew *alef* and a Roman *A*—difficult. A different format was required for comparative work, and that format was the table.

From earliest antiquity, the Babylonians used table forms for arithmetic, accounting, and even presentation of synonyms and other categories. Tables and graphic formats are essential to mathematics—even to the business of adding and subtracting numbers. But the tables that organize the presentation of script forms for comparison in the history of writing required a conceptual shift. The question of *what* was being compared and *how* would vary depending on available historical and epigraphical evidence, and whether the letterforms were being identified by language, location, source, or date.

The rational format of the grid worked graphically, showing that letters in any single line were versions of the same thing to be compared by using similarity as a way to call attention to differences (*alef, alpha,* etc.). The structure was a graphic typology—each row and column showed one type of thing, with exemplars frequently presented in horizontal rows. This orientation allowed size, stroke direction, and other formal features to be compared through proximity and took full advantage of visual methods. But making such a table—like that pictured in Goeree's illustration—relied on a graphic remediation. Each sign or letterform was copied individually, raising questions about accuracy. The variations in the original sources—worn coins, faded inscriptions, handwritten and many-times recopied documents—were eliminated in the perfected examples in the tables.

Every new copy is also its own original. Size standardization was produced by the engraver and did not record the dimensions of the sources. Other features of the graphic forms might or might not be authoritative. Every detail of stroke, orientation, direction, and proportion becomes a significant clue in the piecing together of the early formation of the alphabet. Tables continue to be used into the twenty-first century, with ever-more meticulous attention to the sources and forms of individual characters. The table form did not emerge suddenly in mature form but developed in fits and starts.

To reiterate, specimen charts and graphic tables present a great deal of visual information efficiently. But each of the several formats involved has its own rhetoric—and its outstanding examples. Those formats can be divided into *specimen charts* (sorted by script or language), *comparative tables* (from evidence, linked to geography, or monuments), and *progressive tables* (linked to time period, location, and even specific artifacts). Some were compiled directly from evidence (with Guillaume Postel's 1538 comparison as an early printed example), some from printed sources, borrowed and reordered (Bernard, *Orbis Eruditi*, 1689; Caylus, *Recueil d'Antiquités*, 1722; Morton, *Tables*, 1734; Astle, *Origin and Progress*, 1784), and, as more physical evidence was available and greater knowledge of the distribution of languages in the geography in ancient Canaan, Lebanon, Sinai, and Phoenicia, the tables were linked to specific objects or archaeological sites (Forster, *One Primeval Language*, 1854; Lidzbarski, *Handbuch*, 1898; Taylor, *Alphabet*, 1899; and Sass, *Genesis of the Alphabet*, 1988).

THE EARLIEST SCRIPT TABLES: AGRIPPA

Cornelius Agrippa's rudimentary script tables were published in 1531, in the first book of *De occulta philosophia*.[3] Ordered in five columns, they aligned astronomical symbols with letters from the Greek, Latin, Hebrew, and Chaldean scripts. The individual letters of each script were large and distinct, and where visual correlation existed (as between Greek and Latin for instance, or Chaldean and Hebrew) it could be clearly seen. This correlation of *values* was reinforced by the grid structure, which suggested equiv-

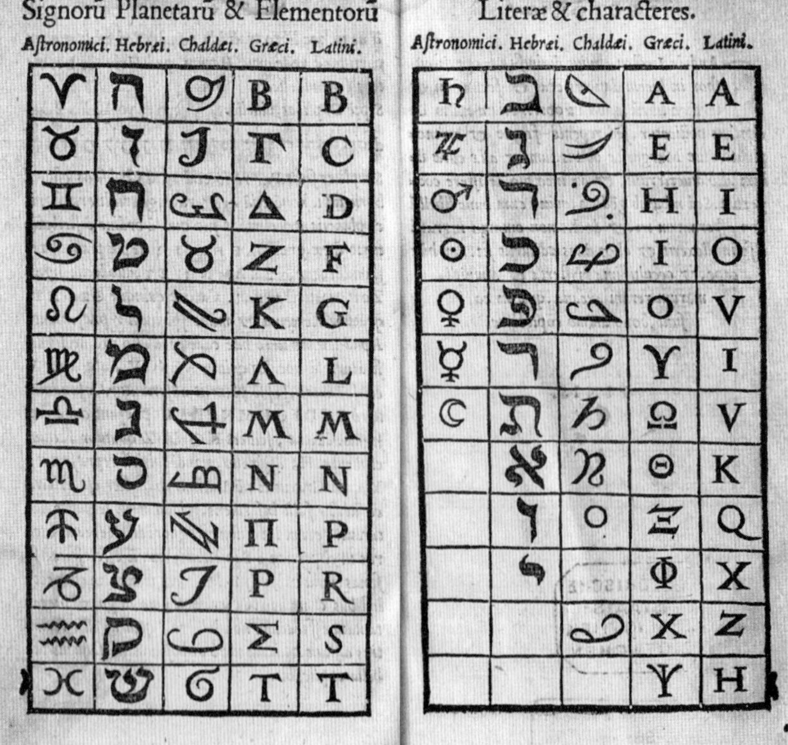

FIGURE 6.2 Cornelius Agrippa, excerpt from *De occulta philosophia*, book 1 (Paris, 1531). Source: Bayerische Staatsbibliothek, CC BY-NC-SA 4.0

LIBER PRIMVS. XCVII.

♈	Β	B
♉	Γ	C
♊	Δ	D
♋	Ζ	F
♌	Κ	G
♍	Λ	L
♎	Μ	M
♏	Ν	N
♐	Π	P
♑	Ρ	R
♒	Σ	S
♓	Τ	T
♄	Α	A
♃	Ε	E
♂	Η	I
☉	Ι	O
♀	Ο	V
☿	Υ	I cõſo.
☽	Ω	V cõſo.
Terra	Θ	K
Aqua	Ξ	Q
Aër	Φ	X
Ignis	Χ	Z
Spiritus	Ψ	H

FIGURE 6.3 Agrippa, 1533 edition. Note the difference between the versions where the second makes use of metal type except for the Chaldean and Hebrew while the middle row woodblocks of Chaldean letters have been imposed on the grid in a not-quite-perfect fit. Source: Library of Congress, Rare Book and Special Collections Division.

alence among elements in aligned positions. Drawing on Hermetic, Neoplatonic, and occult traditions—the works of Marcelino Ficino, Pico della Mirandola, Johannes Reuchlin, and Johannes Trithemius—Agrippa had plenty of support for his planetary associations. His graphic source for the Chaldean characters was not noted, and the woodcut renderings in two different editions were not identical.[4] Agrippa's tables established a precedent, but they were modest in scale by contrast to the charts assembled by Angelo Rocca and James Bonaventure Hepburn.

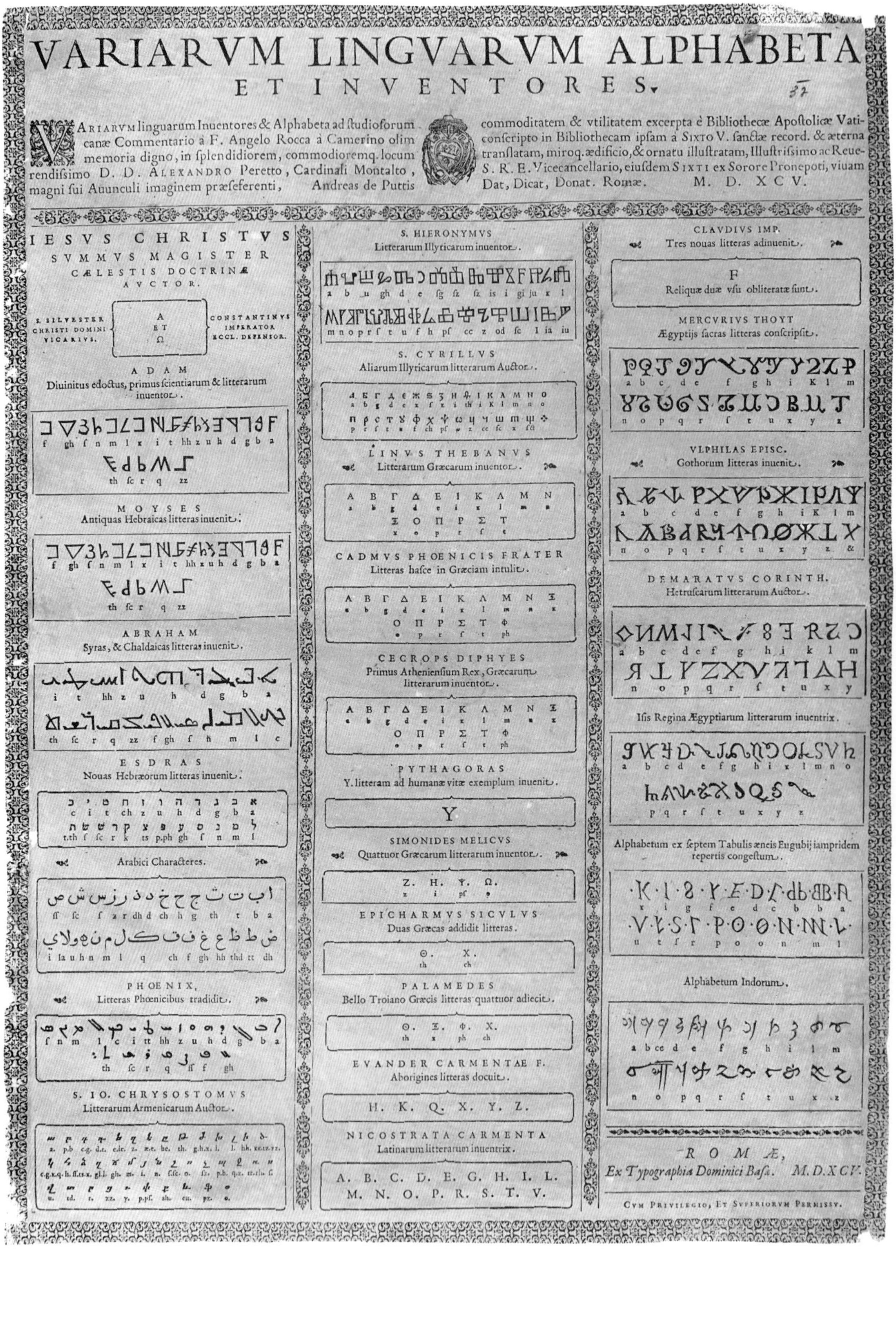

VARIARVM LINGVARVM ALPHABETA ET INVENTORES.

37

VARIARVM linguarum Inuentores & Alphabeta ad studiosorum commoditatem & vtilitatem excerpta è Bibliothecæ Apostolicæ Vaticanæ Commentario à F. Angelo Rocca à Camerino olim conscripto in Bibliothecam ipsam à SIXTO V. sanctæ record. & æterna memoria digno, in splendidiorem, commodioremq. locum translatam, miroq. ædificio, & ornatu illustratam, Illustrissimo ac Reuerendissimo D. D. ALEXANDRO Peretto, Cardinali Montalto, S. R. E. Vicecancellario, eiusdem SIXTI ex Sorore Pronepoti, viuam magni sui Auunculi imaginem præseferenti, Andreas de Puttis Dat, Dicat, Donat. Romæ. M. D. XCV.

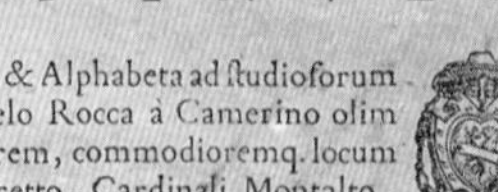

IESVS CHRISTVS
SVMMVS MAGISTER
CÆLESTIS DOCTRINÆ
AVCTOR.

S. SILVESTER CHRISTI DOMINI VICARIVS. — A ET Ω — CONSTANTINVS IMPERATOR ECCL. DEFENSOR.

ADAM
Diuinitus edoctus, primus scientiarum & litterarum inuentor.

f gh ſ n m l x i t hh z u h d g b a
th ſc r q zz

MOYSES
Antiquas Hebraicas litteras inuenit.

f gh ſ n m l x i t hh z u h d g b a
th ſc r q zz

ABRAHAM
Syras, & Chaldaicas litteras inuenit.

i t hh z u h d g b a
th ſc r q zz f gh ſ ñ m l c

ESDRAS
Nouas Hebræorum litteras inuenit.

כ י ט ח ז ו ה ד ג ב א
c i t ch z u h d g b a
ת ש ר ק צ פ ע ס נ מ ל
t.th ſ ſc r k ts p.ph gh ſ n m l

Arabici Characteres.

ص ش س ز ر ذ د خ ح ج ث ت ب ا
ſſ ſc ſ z r dh d ch h g th t b a
ي لا و ه ن م ل ك ق ف غ ع ظ ط ض
i la u h n m l q ch f gh hh thd tt dh

PHOENIX,
Litteras Phœnicibus tradidit.

ſ n m l c i tt hh z u h d g b a
th ſc r q ſſ f gh

S. IO. CHRYSOSTOMVS
Litterarum Armenicarum Auctor.

a. p.b c.g. d.t. e.dc. z. æ.e. be. th. g.h.x. i. l. hk. zz.tz.tz.
c.g.x.q. h. ſſ.ts.x. gl.l. gh. m. i. n. ſ.ſc. o. ſz. p.b. q.z. tt.tl.s. ſ.
u. td. r. zz. y. p.pſ. ah. eu. pz. o.

S. HIERONYMVS
Litterarum Illyricarum inuentor.

a b u gh d e ſg ſz ſz is i gi ju x l
m n o p r ſ t u f h pſ cc z od ſc I ia iu

S. CYRILLVS
Aliarum Illyricarum litterarum Auctor.

a b g d e x ſ z i th i K l m n o
p r ſ t u f ch pſ o cc ſc x ſct

LINVS THEBANVS
Litterarum Græcarum inuentor.

Α Β Γ Δ Ε Ι Κ Λ Μ Ν
a b g d e i x l m n
Ξ Ο Π Ρ Σ Τ
x o p r ſ t

CADMVS PHOENICIS FRATER
Litteras hasce in Græciam intulit.

Α Β Γ Δ Ε Ι Κ Λ Μ Ν Ξ
a b g d e i x l m n x
Ο Π Ρ Σ Τ Φ
o p r ſ t ph

CECROPS DIPHYES
Primus Athenienſium Rex, Græcarum litterarum inuentor.

Α Β Γ Δ Ε Ι Κ Λ Μ Ν Ξ
a b g d e i x l m n x
Ο Π Ρ Σ Τ Φ
o p r ſ t ph

PYTHAGORAS
Y. litteram ad humanæ vitæ exemplum inuenit.

Y

SIMONIDES MELICVS
Quattuor Græcarum litterarum inuentor.

Ζ. Η. Ψ. Ω.
z i pſ o

EPICHARMVS SICVLVS
Duas Græcas addidit litteras.

Θ. Χ.
th ch

PALAMEDES
Bello Troiano Græcis litteras quattuor adiecit.

Θ. Ξ. Φ. Χ.
th x ph ch

EVANDER CARMENTAE F.
Aborigines litteras docuit.

H. K. Q. X. Y. Z.

NICOSTRATA CARMENTA
Latinarum litterarum inuentrix.

A. B. C. D. E. G. H. I. L.
M. N. O. P. R. S. T. V.

CLAVDIVS IMP.
Tres nouas litteras adinuenit.

F
Reliquæ duæ vsu obliteratæ sunt.

MERCVRIVS THOYT
Ægyptijs sacras litteras conscripsit.

a b c d e f g h i K l m
n o p q r ſ t u x y z

VLPHILAS EPISC.
Gothorum litteras inuenit.

a b c d e f g h i K l m
n o p q r ſ t u x y z &

DEMARATVS CORINTH.
Hetruscarum litterarum Auctor.

a b c d e f g h i k l m
n o p q r ſ t u x y

Isis Regina Ægyptiarum litterarum inuentrix.

a b c d e f g h i x l m n o
p q r ſ t u x y z

Alphabetum ex septem Tabulis æneis Eugubij iampridem repertis congestum.

x i g f e d c b b a
u t ſ r p o o n m l

Alphabetum Indorum.

a b c d e f g h i l m
n o p q r ſ t u x z

ROMÆ,
Ex Typographia Dominici Basæ. M.D.XCV.

CVM PRIVILEGIO, ET SVPERIORVM PERMISSV.

SPECIMEN CHARTS: ANGELO ROCCA AND JAMES BONAVENTURE HEPBURN

Two truly remarkable specimen charts, one assembled by Angelo Rocca and the other by James Bonaventure Hepburn, occupied the intellectual and rhetorical space between compendia and tables. They showed scripts out of context, and their formal arrangements and presentations used the alphabets as graphic exemplars, rather than comparing them systematically. They did not link the scripts to languages or history and did not propose a progressive or comparative reading of the letters. But both were referenced frequently, and each presented specific information about the state of alphabet historiography, hence their significance.[5]

Rocca and Bonaventure's charts displayed a considerable number of graphic examples in a compressed space, presenting exhaustive knowledge of existing script forms. The sheer size and scope of their formats created a dramatic graphic impact.

Rocca's broadsheet, *Variarum linguarum alphabeta et inventores* (Alphabets of many languages and inventions), printed in Rome in 1595, presented eighteen full scripts.[6] In addition, it contained information about the Greek letters invented by Simonides, other additions by Palamedes, and various other bits of alphabet lore.[7] Rocca had been appointed head of the Vatican Printing Office (Typographia Vaticana, established in 1587) and compiled a thorough bibliography of holdings in the Vatican Library, *Bibliotheca apostolica Vaticana a Sixto V*, published in 1591. Four years later he produced this sheet of specimens.[8] In this broadsheet Rocca reproduced the specimens published in *Bibliotheca*, with a new borders and textual commentary. Though his attributions followed the familiar mythical and textual references (Adam, Abraham, or Thoth), each of the specimens in Rocca's sheet

Mercurius Thoyt Aegyptijs ſacras litteras conſcripſit.

Alphabetum Aegyptiacum alterum.

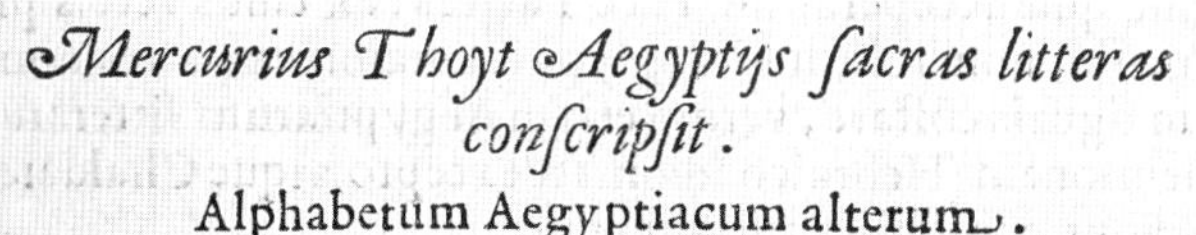

MERCVRIVM ſacrarum litterarum inuentorem fuiſſe fere omnes fatentur: cuiuſmodi autem eſſent litterarum characteres apud Aegyptios, dictum eſt paulo ſuperius, necnon in ſexto Emblemate

Plutarch. & Strabo lib.7. Diodor. Sic. li.1. & 4. in princip. Cic. lib.3. de Nat. Euſeb. de

FIGURE 6.4 (*facing*) Angelo Rocca, detail of specimen sheet (1595), with exemplars extracted from the Vatican library. Public domain.

FIGURE 6.5 Alphabet shown in upper-right column of specimen, printed in Rocca's *Bibliotheca* (1591). Public domain.

was a verifiable script. Rocca's striking specimen, and his authoritative bibliography, became standard references for later scholars, but the original broadsheet has survived only in a few copies.[9]

The specimen he attributed to both Adam and Moses was actually Paleo-Hebrew, the one attributed to Abraham is a version of Syriac, those attributed to Esdras (Ezra) were modern Hebrew, and the Phoenix, or Phoenician, was a version of Western Syriac. Arabic, Armenian, Illyric, Indic, as well as Cyrillic, and then Runic were all verifiable scripts. The script attributed to Thoth (second from the top on the right) as a sample of sacred letters of the Egyptians was the only one difficult to identify, though it might be linked to medieval alchemical texts. The Typographia Vaticana had been established by Pope Sixtus V to assist in propagation of the faith, including publication of sacred texts in multiple languages under supervision of the Vatican. The frescoes painted in Sixtus's new Vatican Library also contained multiple "exotic" and other alphabetic script samples and may have been borrowed from a specimen sheet from 1587, by Simone Verovio, *Essemplare di XIIII lingue principalissime* (Examples of fourteen principal languages) (Rome: Nicolas van Aelst).[10] A separate publication documented the fresco scripts, Luca Orfei's extensive *De caracterum et litterarum inventoribus ex picturis Bibliothecae Vaticanae liber* (Invented letters and characters pictured in the books of the Vatican library; 1589).[11] All the scripts in these works are identifiable with the exception of the "Aegyptian," which, as in Rocca's sheet, seems to be a hybrid of various Coptic, Syriac, and invented forms.

Rocca's compendium sheet looks modest when contrasted to that of James Bonaventure Hepburn, a Scottish scholar of Hebrew who became the Keeper of Oriental Books and Manuscripts at the Vatican in the early seventeenth century.[12] In that capacity, he would have been well positioned to study the various primary sources needed to create his ambitious and graphically stunning chart.[13] The *Virga Aurea, the Heavenly Golden Rod of the Blessed Virgin Mary in Seventy-Two Praises*, was published in 1616.[14] The incredible range of seventy-two scripts (the number has many significances, including a biblical reference to the number of languages confused at Babel, one for each descendant of Noah) represented a truly virtuosic work of culling and copying from existing sources. Even if he had used Rocca's work to guide him, Hepburn would have had to exert considerable scholarly effort to locate and identify these additional individual scripts and have them carefully redrawn on this single sheet.

The *Virga Aurea* combined mystical and actual scripts without discrimination. The sheer scope of Hepburn's collection was staggering, as is the accuracy of copies on the elaborate plate. His is the summa of specimen sheets, a massively erudite collection of real and esoteric information.[15] Many of the familiar celestial scripts were present, at the top right-hand side of the sheet. Alphabets associated with Enoch (actually Hebrew), Adam, Solomon, and Noah also made their appearance. An unusual, geometricized script, identified as Arcanum, and a version of celestial labeled Brachmanian, along with a square Hebrew broken into flame-like strokes and labeled Mysticum, completed the list of exotic scripts. The rest were exemplars of the known Western and Eastern branches of the alphabet, among which a few dubious attributions can be detected (such as the Phoenicum, Galilaeum, and Mercuraniam), along with Judeo-Samaritanum, a Paleo-Hebrew variant. The Vatican Printing Office included printing fonts for multiple languages, but the fact that this specimen sheet was made as an engraved plate speaks to the esoteric character of its collections. No fonts were cut for Enochian or Adamic alphabets, which were reproduced in woodblocks, engravings, or calligraphic copies. In this engraving, each script was rendered with care and detail, and also shown in use in a small circular vignette located next to the box in which it was contained. These vignettes resembled coins, as if to suggest that each of these scripts had a legitimate historical past.

Magnificent though the *Virga Aurea* is, however, it was a specimen sheet and not a table in the formal, fully rationalized sense that was hinted at in Agrippa's earlier format.

COMPARATIVE CHARTS AND PICTORIAL NARRATIVE

The table in Athanasius Kircher's *Turris Babel* (1679), created almost 150 years after Agrippa's first efforts, was a fully developed intellectual instrument for comparison of scripts.[16] The letters had been drawn to resemble each other in size and scale. Their original modes of production were effaced—leaving no information about whether they were originally scratched in stone, written in ink, cast on coins, or produced by other means. In fact, the table was deliberately designed to remove the letters from these conditions so they could be studied in relation to each other.

Following his arrival in Rome in the 1630s, Kircher had access to the library of the Collegio Romano, but though the specimens in his table were clearly identified, their sources were not. From left to right, the eight columns (containing a total of ten scripts) were labeled: The Value of the Letter (indicated by a Roman majuscule), the mystical character of the Angels (celestial script and letters of flame), Crossing the River (source given as Abraham de Balmes), the oldest Samaritan letters (noted as extracted from various authors), Samaritan taken from coins, the Mosaic character in which the Tablets of the Law had been written, Syriac, and Hebrew. The elegantly engraved table, with its mythic creatures in the headpiece, became a model for organized comparison. The letterforms were aligned—by position in the alphabet, by graphic resemblance (showing variations in each letter across scripts and connections among scripts across characters), and by association with the "value" given in the first column. The importance of this structure should not be underestimated. In later paleographic and linguistic study,

VIRGA AVREA septuaginta duobus Encomijs B·V·MARIAE cælata
Aue superum Regina, Rosa pura sine spina
Salus, uirtus, medicina, fouens DEI filium
Aue Templum Trinitatis, Speculum humilitatis,
Mollis flamma Charitatis, Castitatis Lilium.
Aue stellis coronata, Luce Solis obuallata,
Sub qua Luna est locata, Virum cingens Fœmina
Aue Virgo quam amauit Pater, flamen obumbrauit,
Verbum DEI fœcundauit, Fidei ferens semina.
Tota pulcra es Amica mea, et macula non est in te. Cant. 4.
כלך יפה רעיתי ומום אין בך
ΟΛΗ ΚΑΛ
ΣΗΜΕΙΟΝ
ΜΕΓΑ
BEATISSIMO PATRI, ET DOMINO NOSTRO PA
Delusa Cacodæmonis fuco, doloq; antiquitas, pacē petituros Lauri ramo armare consueuerat; depulsis tenebris erroꝝ gentilitatis, exortu Solis Iustitię, liceat nunc ueniā, saluteq; rogaturis Iessæam preferre virgam, aureū
floribusq; circūtextā, et varijs concinnisq; numeroꝝ symbolis, ceu lemniscis ornatā humillime ad Bnis Vrę pedes uotiuā tabulam depono, figoq; animi mei scīz pignus, enixissime noctu, diuq; optantis, et anhelantis longa
q oia potest DEVS. Et quidni Virga munitus audeā Bnē Vrā compellare. Quā DEVS ut Moysen Virgā, et sceptro illustrem, augustūq; fecit. Hoc tamen Moyse maiorē, et celsiorem; quod ille Rector partis, et delibati
Bdo Vrā veritatis; Ille Xpi antecessor, Bdo Vrā Successor uterq; duplici Virga, seu ptāte donatus Regia, et Sacerdotali; Sed ille Virgā suā serpentes necuit, mare secuit, aquā ex petra elicuit. Vrā Bdo sua ex pane Pet
interimit; Moysis illa portentis, Bnis Vrę veris inclyta miraculis; vtraq; Iessææ Virgæ typus, at Bnis Vrę expressior Dignare itaq; Bme Pr. tenue istud munusculū deuotionis erga Beatiss. Virginem, et mei erga S. Vrā obseq
VIRGÆ AVREÆ Dilucidatio
AQVÆDVCTVS PARADISI Eccl. 24.
ALΦABETVM BABILONICVM
GRATIA PLENA Luc. 1. 28
GOTHICVM
SPECVLVM SINE macula Sap. 7.
HIEROGLYΦICVM
EVA mr uniuersoꝝ uiuentium Ge. 3.
GETICVM
APOLLONIANVM
SCYTHICVM
princeps Ge. 37.
PAVLVS V BVRGHESIVS PONTIFEX OPTIMVS MAX
Dat MINIMVS minimum munus Tibi MAXIME Mundi; Cerne ANIMVM DANTIS, MATEHEMO DATI

FIGURE 6.6 James Bonaventure Hepburn, top part of the *Virga Aurea* (1616) showing sixteen of the seventy-two scripts. Public domain.

FIGURE 6.7 Detail of upper-right column of Hepburn's sheet showing angel, celestial, Chaldean (Syriac), and other scripts. Public domain.

the relation of scripts whose appearances were dissimilar would be based in part on precisely these properties—letter value and position.

Two decades after Kircher's publication, when Goeree borrowed the table almost in its entirety for his 1700 publication, *Voor-Bereidselen tot de bybelsche Wysheid* (Preparations for biblical wisdom), he situated it within the pictorial frame shown at the beginning of this chapter.[17] By putting it into a vivid scene, Goeree turned the table into a piece of historical theater, surrounding it with props and figures in dramatic poses. The information was copied precisely, except that one column of the original, which contained Syriac letters, was eliminated, and a row was added at the far right, just at the edge of the columns, in which the names of the Hebrew letters are spelled out. No justification was given for the elimination of the Syriac, but the visual difference from the Paleo-Hebrew and Samaritan might have made it seem like an outlier.

In Goeree's plate, the background glimpsed through the archway behind the woman contained an obelisk and a domed structure as well as a series of ruins leading into a hilly background, clearly referencing the ancient Near East. The motifs suggested a generic Old Testament context that was not specifically Jerusalem, Alexandria, or Sidon. Of the three figures, the muscular male, nude to the waist except for a strip of toga over his far shoulder, embodied the strength of tradition as he shifted a heavy block inscribed with a caption for the table. Paraphrased from Dutch, the text

FIGURE 6.8 Athanasius Kircher, *Turris Babel* (1679). Public domain.

described the table as follows: "Wherein the old letters derived from Godly principles are reproduced and compared and shown to be descended from one model."[18] The inscribed face of the block was cast in shadow and thus served as a foil for the carefully cut slab lying at an oblique angle to the frame. On this was written, "The unspeakable name of god," accompanied by the Tetragrammaton rendered in the Samaritan characters identified in the table as the "Old Hebrew Letters." This slab was propped on the edge of a large platter holding shekels inscribed with a variant of Hebrew. (The *lamed, mem, and samech* on the surfaces of the coins did not match the Samaritan script.) The references to the story of the half shekel (the required annual tribute of Jews to the Temple) as well as to antiquarian collections of coins (as sources for early scripts) were both clear. The most active figure in the image was the man on the right explaining the table. His fez, soft shoes, and robes all called forth associations with the ancient Near East, while the ermine edging on his robe connoted authority. The modest woman stood in for the reader or viewer, to whom all is being made clear through the combination of presentation and commentary.

The other engravings in Goeree's publication depicted individual scripts in similarly dramatic historical scenes.[19] In Plate 1, Abraham's alphabet appeared on a wall behind a river god while Abraham pointed across the river he was crossing on a raft, accompanied by camels, sheep, and other people—a portrayal of the Transfluvial script. In Plate 2 Enoch appeared in discussion with an angel, and the version of his script was taken from Pantheus but with the letters copied out of order.[20] In Plate 3 Ezdra [*sic*] sat among scribes, all writing assiduously. Plate 4 contained two Samaritan alphabets (the second of which was Paleo-Hebrew and usually associated with Hebrew on tables and charts, as per Rocca) accompanied by the image of Christ with the Good Samaritan. Plate 5 depicted King Salomon [*sic*] in a splendid turban crown and robes instructing a scribe, while in the background a grand edifice (the Temple, no doubt) was under construction. (The script was copied from Ambrogio.) In Plate 6 a Chaldean stirred a pot of coals while sacrifices were offered by priests and accompanied by men at prayer. In Plates 7, 8, and 9, Syrian, Phoenician, and then two Egyptian scripts (including "hieroglyphic") were similarly situated. Plate 10 showed Coptic (with another graphic motif taken from Kircher), 11 contained Armenian, and 12 exhibited Chinese characters. A final, fanciful plate indulged in a pastiche of Christian Egyptomania in which birds, snakes, mummies, rams, oxen, flowing water jugs, and an adoring female holding an ancient multibreasted fertility figure all surrounded a glowing Christ whose proximity to a row of Tau crosses was underscored by an inscribed plaque in his hand reading "I am the Alpha and the Omega." The alphabetic letters behind him were redrawn from Kircher's *Oedipus Aegyptiacus*.[21] These scenes of alphabet specimens were not tables, but taken in relation to Goeree's rework of Kircher's table, they made these scripts come alive in connection to unprecedented pictorial presentations of biblical history.

With Goeree and Kircher, the mélange of mystical and actual scripts comes to an end, as do theatrical narratives of explanation. Though the continuing quest for understanding the history of letters—and recovering the "original" alphabet—remained a driving force, the combination of new evidence and emerging empirical methods resulted in the elimination of celestial and magical alphabets from all but occult and esoteric literature. Many other instances of compendia, partial tables, and scholarship could be cited from the sixteenth and seventeenth centuries, but in the eighteenth century a rational approach to comparative study was put into table form.[22]

TWO ENGLISH TABLE MAKERS: EDWARD BERNARD AND CHARLES MORTON

Like Rocca and Hepburn, the British scholar Edward Bernard was a librarian with access to a considerable range of manuscript and print materials, in his case, in British and Irish libraries. In 1689, Bernard assembled the materials for a large, engraved plate that contained about three dozen scripts. In 1759, Charles Morton absorbed Bernard's collection into a larger plate, adding notes and updated information of his own (giving Bernard full credit). The title of Bernard's table described it as a study, guided by God, of the Samaritan letters presented in a manner that was "useful, and not unpleasant" (his characterization).[23] Bernard's structure was, as he claimed, both functional and attractive (if cluttered and overwhelming), since he managed to align the letters from his dozens of scripts so they could be compared across columns, even without hard grid lines. The plate is clearly a scholarly instrument, not an illustration or amusement for amateurs.

By the eighteenth century, knowledge of runes, Coptic, Punic, Syriac, and Samaritan, as well as multiple variants of the Latin and Greek scripts, was sufficiently well codified that Bernard could date his graphic evidence to specific points in historical time. Because of his reliance on chronologies we would now question, Bernard's dating of scripts is more useful for the insight it provides into then-current concepts of history than for the actual dating of the specimens. In Column 8, for instance, he suggested that the Greek letters he called "Cadmean," in accord with the established account, were from about 1500 BCE while the Samaritan letters in Column 1 he traced to Noah, Adam, and Abraham and dated to five millennia before the Common Era. While no celestial scripts appeared among the Samaritan characters, these attributions to biblical figures were residual holdovers from long-standing textual traditions. Closer to the present, his dates were, understandably, more accurate, with the Greek, Latin, Saxon, and Gothic (runes), Russian, Slavic, and other scripts dated to the first centuries of the Common Era. Bernard's inventories allowed Charles Morton to build on his work. Morton held the position of principal librarian of the British Museum, with responsibility for the large, rare manuscript collection

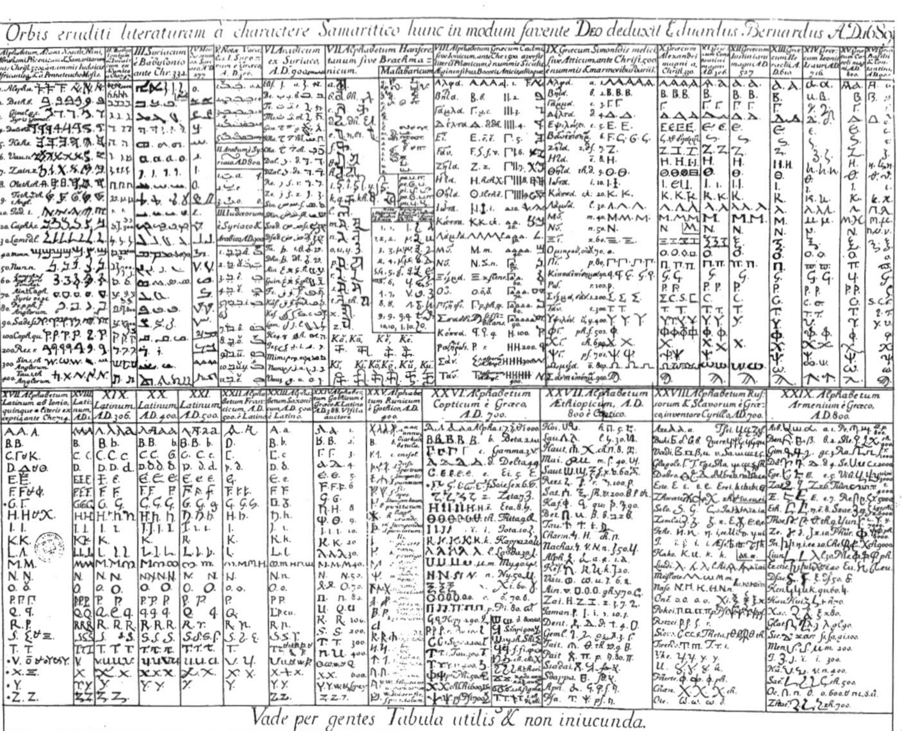
Orbis eruditi literaturam à charactere Samaritico hunc in modum favente Deo deduxit Eduardus Bernardus
Vade per gentes Tabula utilis & non iniucunda.

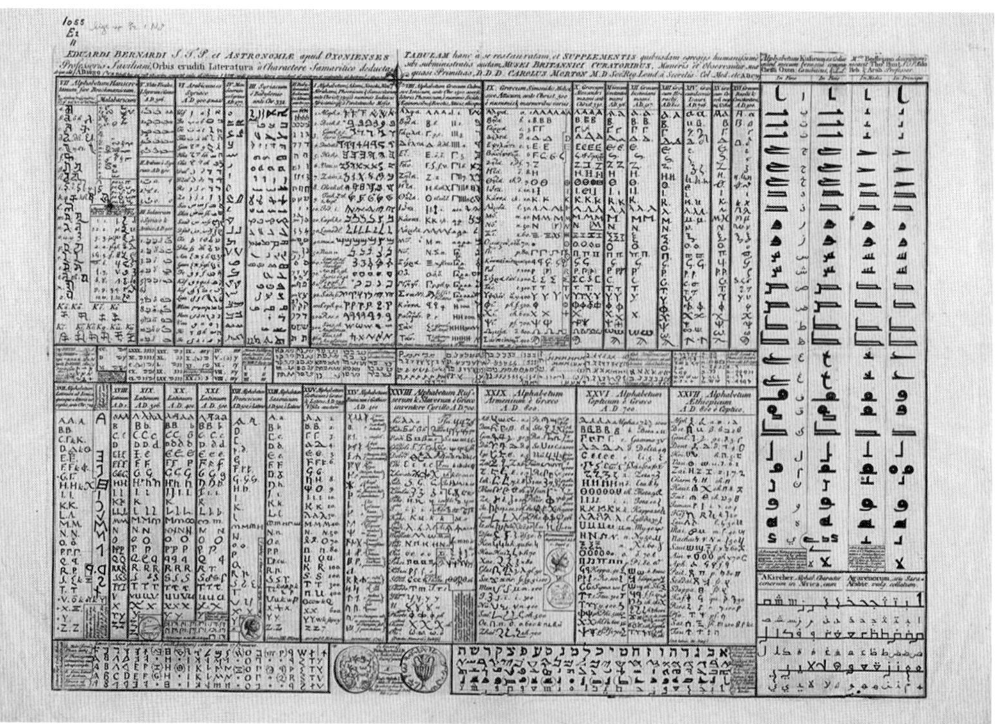
EDUARDI BERNARDI S.T.P. et ASTRONOMIÆ apud OXONIENSES
Professoris Saviliani, Orbis eruditi Literatura à Charactere Samaritico deducta

assembled by Robert Harley (and his son Edward), which supplied other valuable primary resources.

Morton added considerable annotation of sources to Bernard's chart. He added tables of the Kufic script and various early Hebrew originals, including a coin with Paleo-Hebrew, copied from the museum of one Philip Barton, that was also reproduced in the much-cited *Chronological Antiquities*, by John Jackson.[24] Morton's references added value to Bernard's original, and the names inscribed (e.g., Velásquez de Velasco, George Hickes, and Bernard de Montfaucon) were known within the transmission lineage. He also drew on the earlier work of the librarian and paleographer Humfrey Wanley, another founding figure in antiquarian studies, who had been the cataloguer of Robert and Edward Harley's collection before it was sold to the nation as part of the founding materials of the British Museum.[25] Wanley, who had also worked with Bernard, and was employed at the Bodleian Library, was known for his paleographic skills as well as for cataloguing of English and Irish manuscripts. His efforts as a paleographer and antiquarian were part of the foundation on which Bernard's and Morton's plates were established.

FIGURE 6.9 (*facing, top*) Detail of Edward Bernard, *Orbis eruditi literarum* [. . .] (1689). Public domain.

FIGURE 6.10 (*facing, bottom*) Detail of Charles Morton's "Table of Engraved Alphabets" (1759). Much of this was copied directly from Bernard's table, with some of Morton's additions shown at bottom. Public domain.

THE ANTIQUARIANS AND DIPLOMATICISTS

The evidence-based antiquarian trend, described in Chapter 5, is exemplified in the table published in 1728 in Edmund Chishull's *Antiquitates Asiaticæ Christianam æram antecedents* (Asian Antiquities . . .), which also contained a discussion of the Sigean inscriptions.[26] Chishull's table was lean and spare by contrast to the massive display in the Bernard-Morton plates and organized by a different logic to emphasize a developmental approach. The first two lines, labeled together as #1, compared modern Hebrew with the oldest Phoenician forms of these letters. The implication was clear—that the later (above) was derived from the former (below) despite formal variations. Then Phoenician and Cadmean Greek forms were compared in the second pairing, with Latin and Etruscan in the third. Notes on a few Samaritan letters and the additional Greek letters occupied the final lines. The passage toward the modern Roman alphabet was emphasized within a chronology of development. The coins at the bottom, providing material evidence, were taken from Brian Walton, the figure responsible for the major Polyglot Bible publication of 1657. No mystical scripts were present, and Chishull's scholarly intentions were a clear presentation of empirical evidence in the service of historical analysis of the origins and development of the alphabet.

Similar clarity of organization was present in the 1708 work of Bernard de Montfaucon, and echoed in that of Giovanni Bianconi in 1763, which showed how established the format had become.[27] Bianconi argued in *De antiquis litteris Hebraeorum et Graecorum* (The oldest Hebrew and Greek letters) that the earliest Hebrew letters were never abolished, just transformed over time, with the modern square letters adopted after captivity

Post Pag. 24.

NATURÆ ATQUE ORBIS ALPHABETUM,

SIVE

Primariarum Literarum Tabula, cui adjuncta est et altera Secundariarum.

(48)

1 *Primariæ Septendecim Hebraicæ, Assyriacâ novâ formâ, & Phœniciâ Antiquâ.* (a)

2 *Ex Phœniciis, eodem ordine ac potestate, totidem Cadmeæ Græcæ, modo utroque Scriptæ.*

3 *Ex Græcis Latinæ ad dextram, Etruscæ ad lævam, versæ.*

A B C D E F * H * I K L M N * O P * * R S T V

1 *Quinque Secundariæ Hebraicæ, Assyriacâ formâ, & Samaritanâ Biblicâ.*

2 *Ex iis, eodem ordine ac potestate, quinque Secundariæ Græcæ; Latinæ duæ.*

3 *Etrusca Series sine Secundariis pura, ut Cadmea, mansit; et priscam Cadmearum formam persæpe propias expressit; ut in Tuscis Deûm nominibus,* ... *cum Æolico digammu, Latinè* Minerva, ... Hercules, ... Castor. (b)

Sextæ literæ, vocalis factæ, repetitio.

Literæ Hebræo-Phœniciæ *in Siclo ante Capt. Babyl. è Waltoni introd. P. 31.*

Literæ Hebræo-Assyriacæ *in Siclo post reditum, è Waltoni introd. P. 33.*

Literæ Etruscæ *è ponderibus duobus inter Fabretti Inscript. P. 528.*

(a) *Hierosolymis Babyloniâ expugnatione deletis, omne instrumentum Judaicæ literaturæ per Esdram constat restauratum.* Tertull. de cultu fœm. l.1.c.3. (b) *v. Etruriæ Regalis Tabb. 5,2,7.*

J. Sturt sculp.

FIGURE 6.11 Edmund Chishull, *Antiquitates Asiaticæ Christianam æram antecedents* (London, 1728). Public domain.

and the older letters preserved in Samaritan, and his table supports the argument. The lineages of his scholarship were clear—Josephus, Vossius, Johannes Buxtorf—but the mentions of Adam, Abraham, Noah, and Enoch were gone.

Many eighteenth-century scholars in paleography, antiquarian studies, and diplomatics published works supporting what Thomas Astle had termed "the origin and progress of letters." Already discussed in the context of antiquarianism in the previous chapter, Astle and the French diplomatist Charles Toustain published outstanding examples of rational charts. Their precise attention to the specific properties of the glyphs in the tables was exemplary.

By the middle of the eighteenth century, alphabet scholars generally put Samaritan into competition with Paleo-Hebrew for priority while recognizing that modern square Hebrew was not the ancient biblical script. Toustain titled his table "Hebrew, Phoenician, or Samaritan," eliding the three distinct scripts.[28] Paleo-Hebrew was an offshoot of Phoenician, and emerged around 800–700 BCE, while Samaritan was a somewhat later modification from around 600 BCE, and Toustain, rightfully, saw that these characters were all related. He did not address the various temporal and geographic distributions that distinguished them but limited his approach to formal analysis.[29]

The curious figure Antoine Court de Gébelin was among the many sources on whom Astle drew for his work. Court de Gébelin was the first

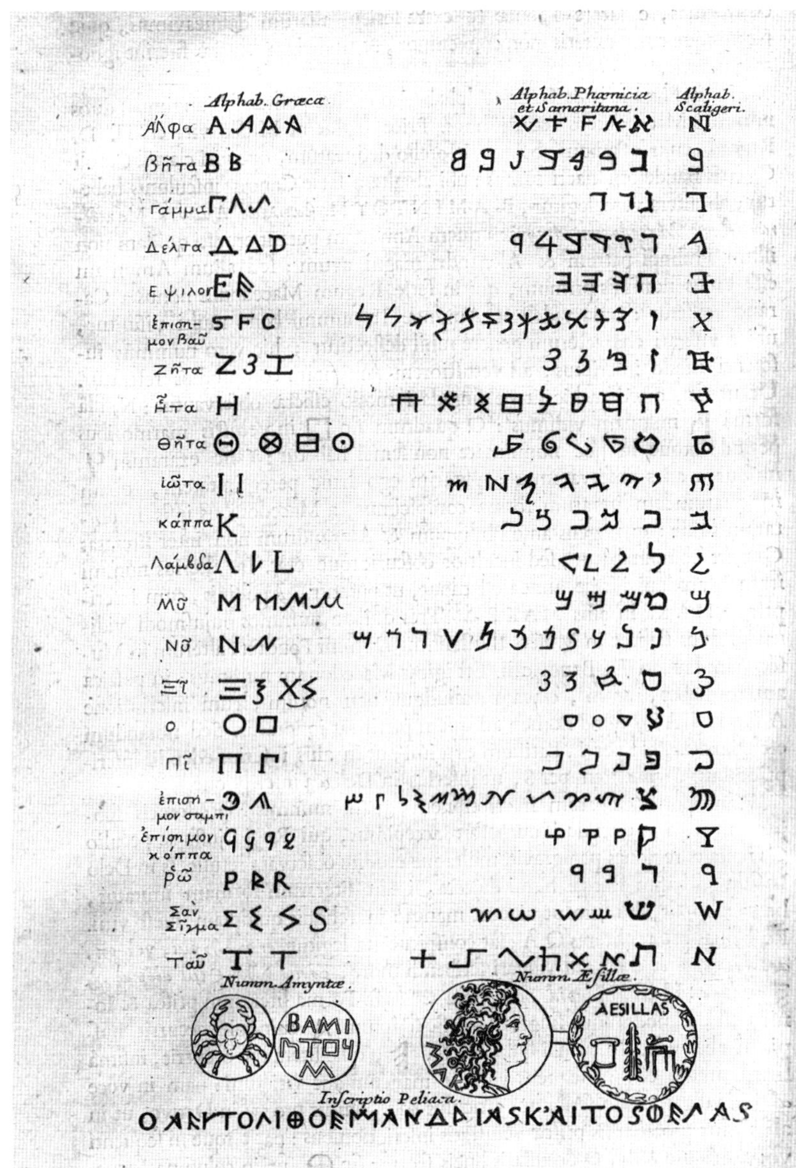

FIGURE 6.12 Bernard de Montfaucon, *Paleographia Graeca* (1708). Public domain.

proponent of tarot readings in modern Western Europe, a student of hermetic and esoteric thought, and a patient of Franz Mesmer (who may have been responsible for his death by a "treatment" in 1784).[30] Gébelin's romantic language of the "primitive world" suited the eighteenth-century Enlightenment scholars' concept that human beings had existed in a natural condition before the emergence of modern civilization. Deeply engaged with symbolism, Gébelin had a facility for seeing the figurative

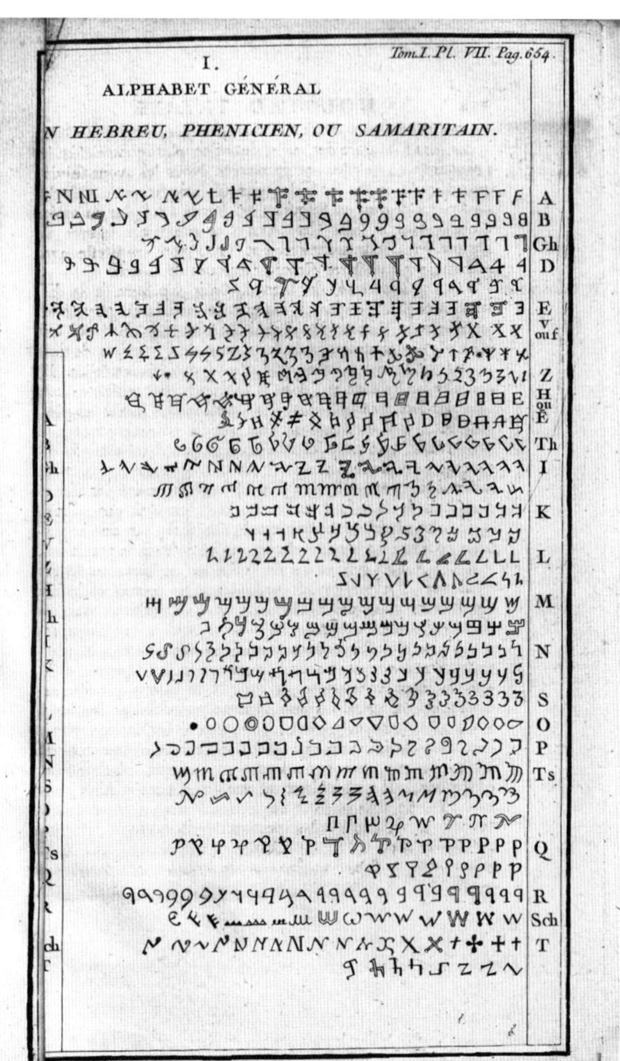

FIGURE 6.13 Charles Toustain, *Nouveau traité de diplomatique* (1750). In general, the Samaritan forms occur at the far-left end of the lines. Note the absence of the ox-head form of *A* in the first line and the range of variants for *K* and *L*, as well as others. Public domain.

motifs in schematic forms—like alphabetic letters—and linking them to speculative values. Gébelin used the term "hieroglyphic" in the title of his table of sixteen letters, but he was not drawing directly on Egyptian sources. Gébelin relied on the rational structure of the table to suggest correspondences among Roman letters, words, images, and Chinese as well as Spanish, Hebrew, Phoenician, and Greek letterforms and to shore up a theory of a single source for all written language.

Gébelin also had a concept of "natural" language in which words were supposed to have originally had a direct connection with things. In *Le monde primitif*, published beginning in 1773, he put forth a theory that the letters were formed from "nature," by which he meant the visual representa-

ALPHABET HIÉROGLYPHIQUE ET PRIMITIF DE XVI. LETTRES

Lettres	Sens qu'elles designent	Objets qu'elles peignent	Les mêmes au Simple trait	Caracteres CHINOIS Correspondans	Alphabets Espagnols	Hébreu des Medailles	Inscription Phénicienne de Malte	Samaritain	Hébreu carré	Grec ancien	Etrusque	Nombre
A 1°.	MAITRE Celui qui A			Lui Homme								I
2°.	BOEUF			Boeuf								
H	CHAMP 2e Source de la Vie			Champ								II
E	EXISTENCE VIE			Etre Vie						Inscript. d'Heraclée		
I	MAIN en Oriental ID d'où AIDE			Main								III
O	OEIL			Oeil								IV
OU	OUIE Oreille			Oui Oreille un Clou			Phénicien					V.
P	LE PALAIS			Bouche								VI
B	BOETE Maison			Boete tout ce qui contient								VII
M	ARBRE Etre productif			Plante Montagne								VIII
				Clés Chinoises de MM. Bayer et Fourmont	Alphabets Espagnols de Don Velasquez	Medailles Hebraiq. par Souciet &c.	Inscript. de Malte Expliq. par M. l'Abbé Barthelemi	Alphabets Samarit.	Bibles Hebraiq. et Diction..	Memoir. de l'Acad.. des Inscript.	Alphabets Etrusques de Maffei, Swinton &c.	

FIGURE 6.14 Antoine Court de Gébelin, *Monde primitif analysé et comparé avec le monde moderne considéré dans son génie allégorique et dans les allégories auxquelles conduisit ce genie* (1777). A completed different view of the alphabet, putting its letterform into a pictorial history of hieroglyphics. Note the "Chinese" column fifth from the left. Public domain.

tion of things apprehended immediately by the eye. Gébelin's table showed "hieroglyphic" precursors as graphic evidence of this history, and his analysis of sound was couched in Romantic terms, suggesting each vocalization was destined to express a different sentiment, an idea shared by philosophers like Jean-Jacques Rousseau. His idea was that in a "primitive" alphabet in which each letter specified an object, its pronunciation would "give rise to its idea whenever it was heard."[31] These ideas had a longer history in philosophical discussions of universal language.[32] Gébelin believed that the invention of all writing had been hieroglyphic, based on principles of depiction, thus embracing the popular idea that writing "progresses" from pictorial to syllabic to schematic forms.[33] That abstract, schematic alphabetic forms could be invented without some reference in the world of actual things seemed impossible. Objects were painted by the voice and rendered in writing to represent *things* to the mind—that was the purpose of language, according to Gébelin, but this was a philosophical position, not a historical one, and his analysis did not draw on paleographic methods.

As evidence of a universal process of development, Gébelin included Chinese characters to show shared origins based on formal resemblance, a common fallacy. But it was the hieroglyphics on which he based his strongest convictions: "We assert that alphabetic characters are themselves hieroglyphic and that they reach into the highest antiquity; they are themselves much older than the time in which they were believed to be born and when Egyptian hieroglyphics were abandoned."[34] Every letter was originally a character, in his view, though not all characters invented by Thoth (Mercury) had become letters.

This mash-up of mythology and fantasy was based on a history of Egyptian writing that did not include hieratic script but saw the alphabet as a direct derivative of hieroglyphics. This is evident in Gébelin's tables, which show a process of schematic simplification of pictorial images into letterforms. The truth of Egyptian influence was both simpler and more complicated, though not entirely unrelated to Gébelin's thesis.

By contrast, Astle, though he drew on Gébelin as one among a multitude of sources, was rational and realistic. He mustered his evidence carefully and followed Toustain's careful copying of glyphs accompanied by information that linked them to locations. Astle carefully separated the Punic (found in Carthage) from the Pelasgian (found in Greece), Oscan (Southern Italian) from Arcadian (Peloponnesian), and ancient Gallic (from Gaul). He followed Toustain, however, in the final broad column of his plate of ancient scripts where the oldest letters are grouped under the single rubric of Phoenician, ancient Hebrew, and Samaritan.

Astle's table contained two main sections, "Alphabeta Antiquissima" and "Alphaeta Antiqua," with three additional bottom strips displaying "Alphabetum Phoenicium," "Alphabetum General Etruscorum," and "Alphabetum Palymyrenian." The first ten of the "oldest" (antiquissima) alphabets were "so familiar in their general outlines, that we apprehend it will be easily admitted that they are all derived from the same source."[35]

The eighteenth-century mania for comprehensive collecting and antiquarian study resulted in the creation of many such comparative tables of scripts as powerful intellectual and rhetoric instruments. They were *intellectual* because they created highly efficient visual methods of comparing enormous amounts of information in a legible graphic presentation and *rhetorical* because the column-row structure of the grid implied a similarity across scripts that might or might not be linked to strict evolution or derivation of one from another. The grid arrangement implied that Greek was directly derived from Phoenician and Latin from Greek and so forth in strict linear processes. In addition, the Hebrew letters were almost always presented as a point of reference, but in their square, modern, form. This sometimes created a false impression of the historical priority of this modern version of the Hebrew script. Actual diffusion and modification were generally more complicated.

The liability of the table structure was that it reinforced a highly mechanical and in some cases overdetermined reading of the evidence. Though apparently rational in their form, tables obscured some of the decisions

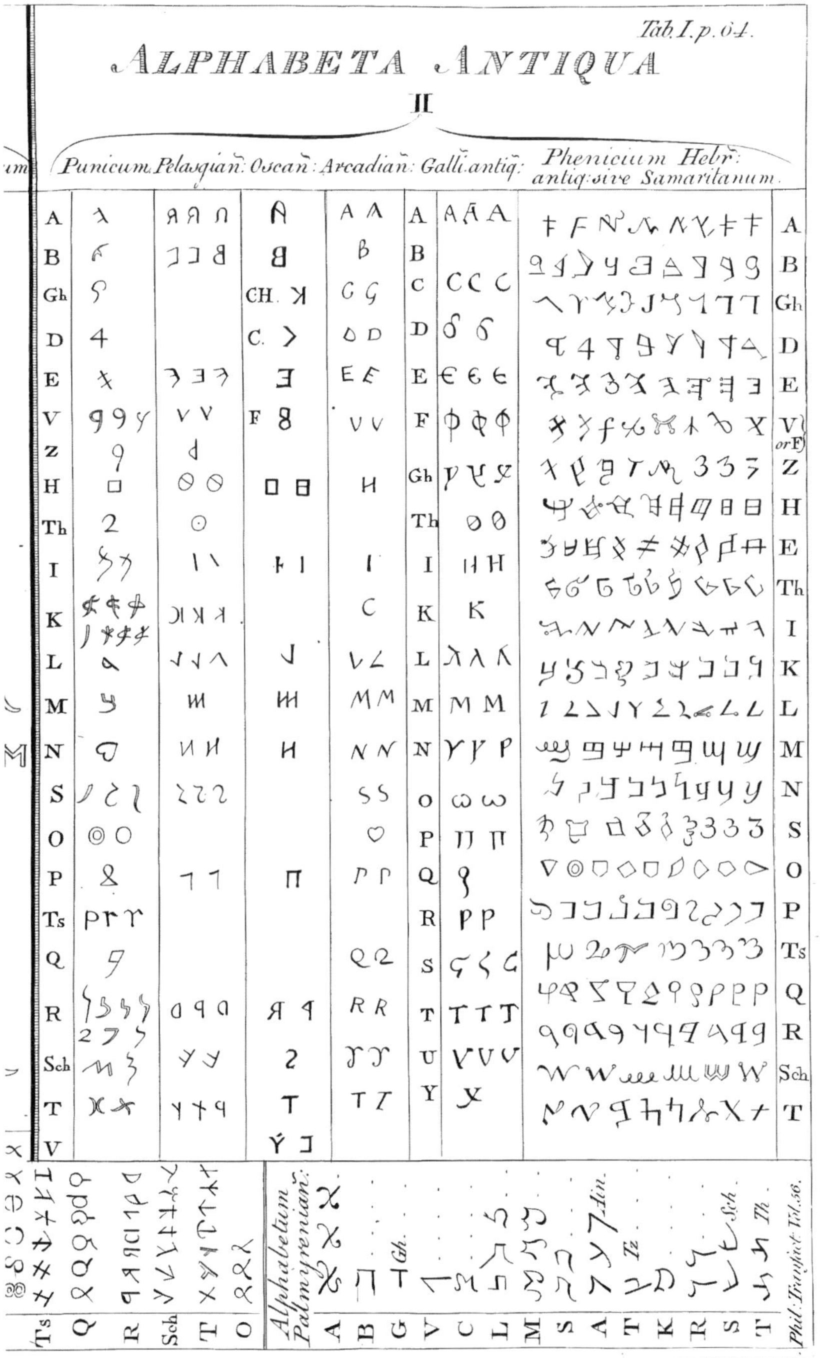

Tab. I. p. 64.

ALPHABETA ANTIQUA

II

Punicum. Pelasgian: Oscan: Arcadian: Galli antiq: Phenicium Hebr: antiq: sive Samaritanum.

A B Gh D E V Z H Th I K L M N S O P Ts Q R Sch T V

A B C D E F Gh Th I K L M N O P Q R S T U Y

A B Gh D E V (or F) Z H E Th I K L M N S O P Ts Q R Sch T

Ts Q R Sch T O

Alphabetum Palmyrenian: A B G V C L M S A T K R S T

Gh. Ain. Tz. Sch. Th.

Phil: Transact: Vol. 56.

FIGURE 6.15 Thomas Astle, *The Origin and Progress of Writing* [. . .] (1784). Note that the letterforms in Astle's far-right column bear more similarity to each other than the widely varying ones in Toustain's, perhaps to make a stronger case for the relatedness of the three scripts: Phoenician, Hebrew, and Samaritan. Public domain.

through which they presented information. They depended heavily on formal comparisons among script forms despite the cautions issued by paleographers who noted that mere coincidence of letter shapes was not necessarily a sign of a familial relation among scripts. They lifted their graphic characters out of context, giving all signs the same orientation, scale, and size. Irregularities in form and position were erased, and a single example was made to stand for a whole set of possible variants of any individual character. Once Semitic epigraphy was firmly established, attention to these unique—sometimes minute—variations would become an integral part of scholarship.

By the nineteenth century, these comparative tables were used by historical linguists and paleographers to compare samples of inscriptions from specific monuments and their geographic locations, as well as time periods, to support highly granular analyses of their relationships. A few idiosyncratic figures and one authoritative author deserve notice in this lineage.

A HARMONY OF PRIMEVAL ALPHABETS

A passionate scholar, Reverend Charles Forster struggled for years to synthesize a comprehensive view of the origin of the alphabet guided by rational principles, in combination with faith in the accuracy of biblical texts. This was not an anomalous position in the mid-nineteenth century, even as biblical chronologies became situated within frameworks of deep time. Forster's magnificent table, produced lithographically, presented his argument explicitly.[36]

Forster, who apparently never traveled to the Sinai or other areas of the ancient Near East, worked from published evidence to produce this extensive chart, distinguished by a few interesting features. The title combines the concepts of "harmony" and "primeval," pointing to the possibility of repairing the confusion of Babel while identifying the alphabet of the earliest ages of humankind. Forster's study stretched to several volumes. Like his previous work, *The Historical Geography of Arabia* (1844), this drew on current research by the foremost scholars and travelers of the day for reference on biblical place-names.[37] Forster's columns are identified geographically: Ethiopia, Sinai, Hisn Ghoreb, Mareb, and other place-names were conspicuous. Only a handful of specimens were merely identified by language (e.g., "Arabic"). He included cuneiform characters from the inscription at Behistun, as well as from Nimroud and Babylon, and letterforms from southern Arabia, Tyre and Sidon, Carthage and Malta, as well as Petra. Hieroglyphics were present, and the hieratic script was identified as "enchorial," linked to the Rosetta stone, among other artifacts. The geographic information about inscriptions had gained in specificity.

Forster relied heavily on the accounts of a Mr. G. F. Grey, whose 177 published plates of the Sinai inscriptions provided much of the visual material for Forster's study and those of others.[38] The habit of using published sources to compile tables of scripts was well established. Forster's somewhat idiosyncratic readings of this material gave his work an anachronistic quality, but the convictions of faith remained an active aspect of interpretation of alphabet origins. In the text of the volumes of which this table was a part, Forster developed highly detailed analyses of individual inscriptions, convinced that what he referred to as the "voice of Israel from the rocks of Sinai" would confirm biblical history.[39]

IGNATIUS DONNELLY, THE ANTEDILUVIAN WORLD, 1882

Intellectual structures and graphic formats are agnostic with respect to contents. The most rigorous rational structures can be used to contain completely irrational or nonsensical arguments. The table provided by Ignatius Donnelly in *The Antediluvian World*, published in 1882, is a perfect example. In his quest to describe the lost continent of Atlantis and the world in a pre-Flood stage of civilization, Donnelly established connections between New World writing scripts and those of the ancient Near East. Mayan glyphs and their supposed "intermediate forms" are all placed in line with the Phoenician, Old Hebrew, and Greek signs to which they are meant to correspond. Donnelly shared with Forster a desire to identify a single common origin for writing. But he imagined it described by Plato and others commenting on the Flood. No evidence for a common origin of writing existed to link Old and New World scripts. Olmec scripts are considered the oldest of these and are conventionally dated to the sixth or fifth century BCE with Mayan as the most sustained and long-lived.[40] However, Donnelly's theories found a wide audience, and even if they had no impact on alphabet studies, they made the image of the island of Atlantis a permanent feature of popular imagination.

By contrast, Isaac Taylor's two-volume study, *The Alphabet*, published in 1883, was a factual authoritative text.[41] Taylor attended to the emerging scholarship on the earliest development of the alphabet, and the table titled "The Phoenician Alphabets" was only one among many well-designed presentations in his publication. Like Forster, he noted the specific geographic source for each of the scripts he extracted. In addition, he appended the date of each inscription by century, thus allowing the visual signs to be seen as evidence of a geographic distribution across time. The conceptual and organizational clarity of his table embodied the increased sophistication of scholarship in his sources as well as Taylor's own clarity of mind.

Taylor made a point of stating that the images of some of the scripts in his table had been reproduced using a photographic process, thus assuring authenticity of their graphic forms. These were in the inscription on the Mesha Stele (also known as the Moabite Stone) discovered in 1864. The inscription is dated to the ninth century BCE, and its letters were a fully mature

A HARMONY OF PRI

	Hebrew Alphat & characters from Ethiopic.	Arabic Alphabet.	Sinai Alphabet.	Rosetta Enchorial Alphabet.	Hisn Ghôreb Alphabet.	Mâreb Alphabet.	Hamâm or Dis Alphat S.A.	Nakhb el Hajar Alphabet.	Etruscan Alphabet.	Alphabet from "Sepulchres of Ancient Etruria."	Phoenician Alphabet from Ruins of Citium, Cyprus.	Alphabet from Ruins of Palmyra.	Double letter Mâreb Alphabet.	Double Bactrian
A	א													
B	ב													
G	ג													
D	ד													
	ה													
V	ו													
Z	ז													
H	ח													
	ט													
I	י													
C	כ ך													
L	ל													
M	מ ם													
N	נ													
Š	ס													
Ã	ע													
F	פ													
Ts	צ													
K	ק													
R	ר													
Sh	ש													
T	ת													

	Hebrew Alphabet & characters from Ethiopic.	Arabic Alphabet.	Egypt. Alphabet of the Hieroglyphic Inscriptions.	Rosetta Stone, Alphabet of its Hieroglyphic Inscriptions.	Alphabet from Monuments of Central America.	Hieroglyphic Alphabet from Lon rock Hamum, Southern Arabia.	Chaldean characters from bricks of Al Hadhr.	Celtiberian Alphabet.	Characters from Abyssinian Inscripns.	Double letter Alphabet, from Coins of Tyre & Sidon.	Punic Alphabet from Site of Carthage.	Punic Characters from Malta.	Alphabet of the Chozar Tartars, A.D. 600 ... 950. From Collection of Dr. Meade on Copper.
A	א												
B	ב												
G	ג												
D	ד												
	ה												
V	ו												
Z	ז												
H	ח												
	ט												
I	י												
C	כ ך												
L	ל												
M	מ ם												
N	נ												
Š	ס												
Ã	ע												
F	פ												
Ts	צ												
K	ק												
R	ר												
Sh	ש												
T	ת												

FIGURE 6.16 Detail from Charles Forster, *The One Primeval Language* (1851). Public domain.

MEVAL ALPHABETS.

…letter Alphat	Arrowhead Alpt. Behistan.	Arrowhead Alpt. Persepolis.	Enchorial Alphabet Persepolis.	Brickformed characters Nimroud.	Enchorial characters Nimroud.	Egyptian characters Nimroud.	Arrowhead Alphabet Nimroud.	Arrowhead Alphabet Babylon.	Arrow-head Alphabet Babylon.	Mixed Alphabet Nimroud.	Alphabet of Obelisk Nimroud.

Alphabet from Saba & the Great Dyke.	Axum Alphabet.	Abraxas Alphabet.	Tartaro Siberian Alphabet.	Double-letter Punic Alphabet from Site of Carthage.	Etruscan Alphabet on blocks embedded in walls of Paestum.	Nabathean Alphabet. Um-Amdan Petra.

Day & Son, Lithrs to the Queen.

The Alphabet.

FIGURE 6.17 Ignatius Donnelly, *The Antediluvian World* (1882). Chart showing Mayan glyphs at the far left as a component of a theory of a unified origin of writing. Even the formal features do not bear out Donnelly's claims. Public domain.

form of the Moabite alphabet (a variant of Paleo-Hebrew and Phoenician) used in a text that was considered the earliest mention of Yahweh. Far from primitive, these letterforms showed considerable maturity.

Taylor still believed a connection existed between Egyptian hieratic cursive forms and the Phoenician schematic and that their differences could be explained by a gap in time. He noted that the derivation of Roman letters from Greek had occurred in an even shorter period.[42] The archaeological evidence was minimal—Taylor noted that until discovery of the Moabite Stone (found east of the Dead Sea), the extant inscriptions of early alphabetic prototypes had been from Malta and Sardinia.[43] Taylor's table showing the Phoenician alphabets identified their variants by geographic region: Tyre, Nineveh, Abu Simbel, Sidon, Marseille, Carthage, Spain, Moab, Judea, the Maccabean, and Nablus (for Samaritan). Taylor's thorough knowledge of the state of scholarship in the field, and his careful weighing of evidence

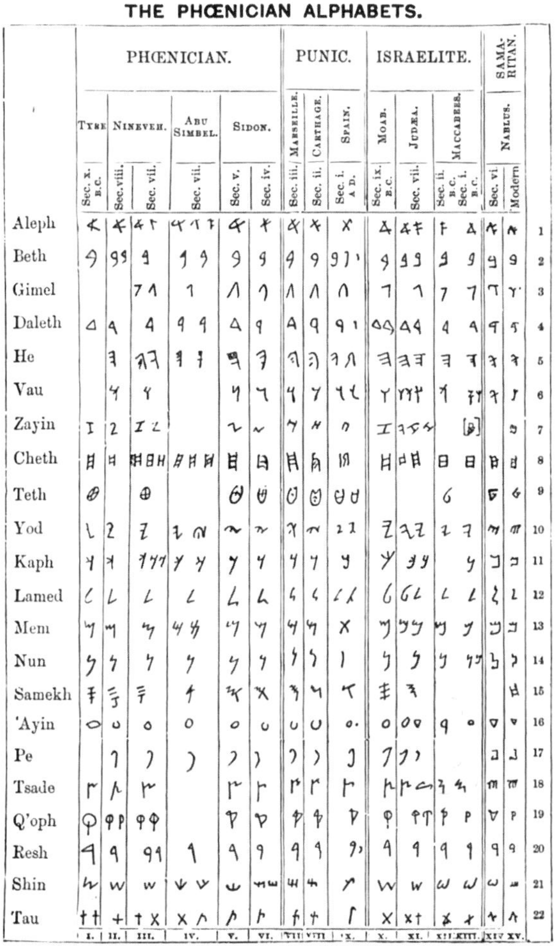

THE PHŒNICIAN ALPHABETS.

	PHŒNICIAN. Tyre Sec. x. B.C.	Nineveh Sec. viii.	Nineveh Sec. vii.	Abu Simbel Sec. vii.	Sidon Sec. v.	Sidon Sec. iv.	PUNIC. Marseille Sec. iii.	Carthage Sec. ii.	Spain Sec. i. A.D.	ISRAELITE. Moab Sec. ix. B.C.	Judæa Sec. vii.	Maccabees Sec. ii. B.C. Sec. i. B.C.	SAMARITAN. Nablus Sec. vi.	Modern	
Aleph															1
Beth															2
Gimel															3
Daleth															4
He															5
Vau															6
Zayin															7
Cheth															8
Teth															9
Yod															10
Kaph															11
Lamed															12
Mem															13
Nun															14
Samekh															15
'Ayin															16
Pe															17
Tsade															18
Q'oph															19
Resh															20
Shin															21
Tau															22
	I.	II.	III.	IV.	V.	VI.	VII.	VIII.	IX.	X.	XI.	XII. XIII.	XIV.	XV.	

FIGURE 6.18 Isaac Taylor, *The Alphabet* (1883). Table of Phoenician alphabets. Public domain

for origins and development, made his texts a valuable resource for understanding the historiographical context.

NINETEENTH-CENTURY LINGUISTS AND MODERN PALEOGRAPHERS

The definitive *Hebrew Grammar* of the nineteenth-century German linguist Wilhelm Gesenius was republished, translated, and used as an authoritative reference into the twentieth century. The English-language edition from 1910 contained a table assembled by the highly respected Polish Semiticist Mark Lidzbarski. Its crucial features were similar to those of Taylor—the combination of dates and places in the headers of the columns. Evidence had become more abundant, particularly that of excavations and findings in Syria, Lebanon, Jordan, Palestine-Israel, and the Sinai, along with the

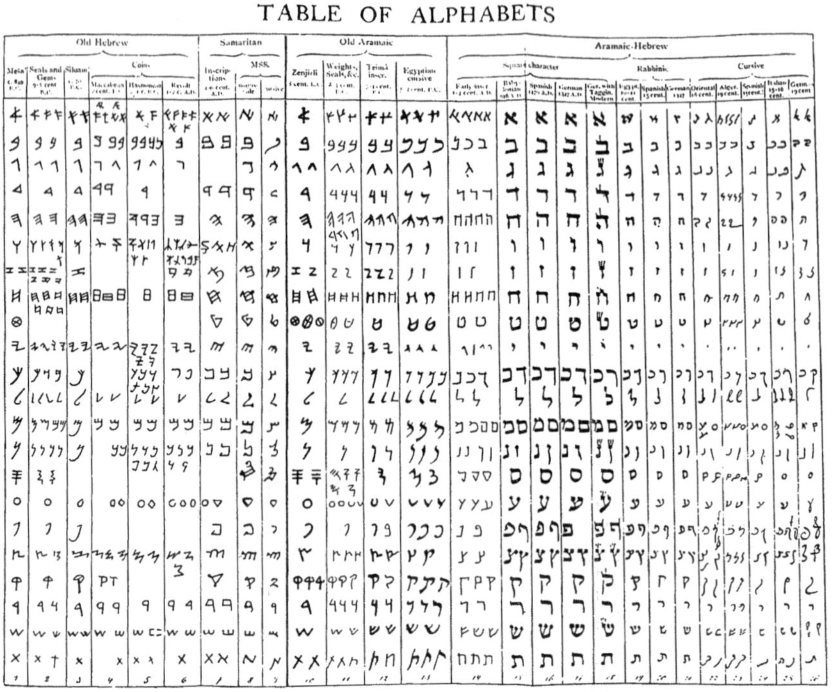

TABLE OF ALPHABETS

FIGURE 6.19 "Table of Alphabets" by Mark Lidzbarski, in Wilhelm Gesenius, *Hebrew Grammar*, 2nd English ed. (1910). Public domain.

recognition that linking evidence to sites was an important feature of its value for research. Lidzbarski's table for Gesenius, like the charts in his own publications, presented a mature model of scholarship. The comparative structure of the table had been augmented by more precise correlation of graphic, temporal, and geographic information.

Lidzbarski's 1898 tables exhibited graphic refinement (e.g., highly effective use of line weight to structure the division among categories: Aramaic, Palmyrenic, and Nabataean). The technique directed the reader's attention, breaking with the usual overall evenness of tone in the tables. Lidzbarski also identified the specific source artifact for each of his samples—not just the site. Not only did this add considerably to the amount of information in the table, but it assured that the information could be checked by future researchers. The glyphs in each row were from a specific inscription. This detail countered the tendency of tables to generalize signs, lift them from context, and erase their provenance. The importance of this cannot be overstated, since it signaled a far more rigorous scholarly practice than heretofore. Given the emphasis in twentieth- and twenty-first-century epigraphy on geographic and temporal information as a feature of analysis in mapping the emergence of the alphabet, Lidzbarski's approach embodied a shift in the intellectual framework of understanding. The integration of geography and epigraphy was not new. The work of Adolf Kirchhoff, published a decade earlier, had mapped early Greek script forms quite deliberately. But the attribution to specific inscriptions was a marked improvement.

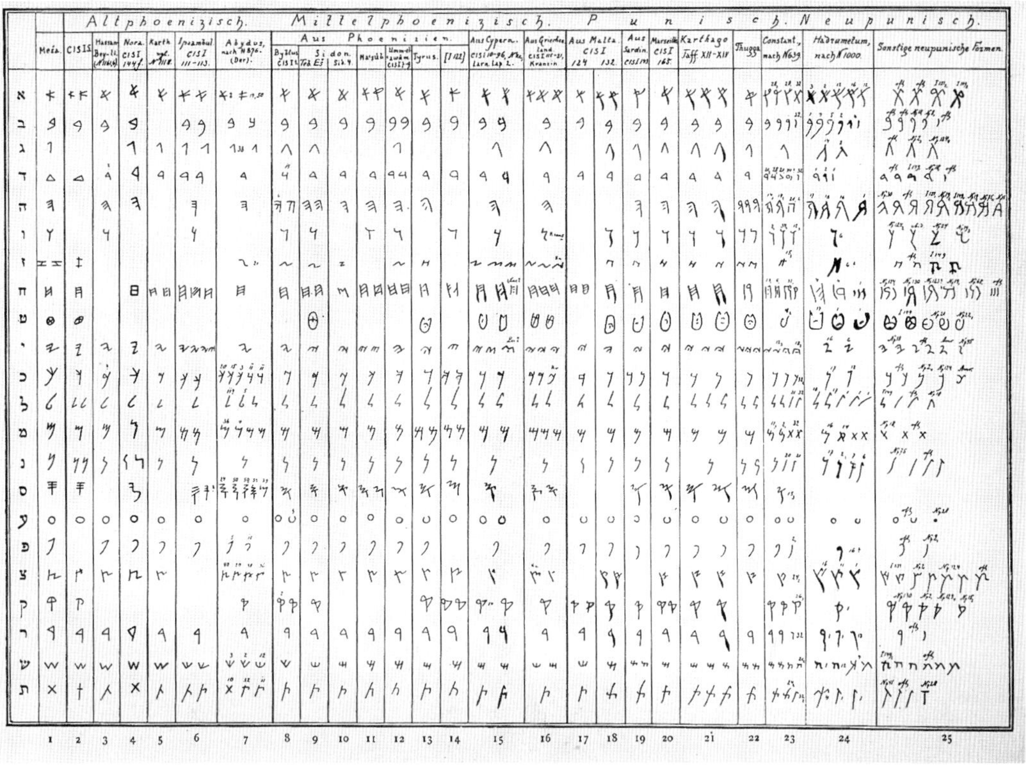

FIGURE 6.20 Detail from Mark Lidzbarski, *Handbuch der Nord-semitischen Epigraphik* (1898). Public domain.

A look at the charts by Lidzbarski (and others) make graphically clear the ways the modern letterforms in Roman, Greek, and Hebrew emerged from Phoenician prototypes. The visual information is organized to show how the recognizable letters slowly took shape. Formal similarity in itself, though important as a basis for analysis, is never sufficient. The contexts of language, culture, and time period have to support the visual evidence. By the end of the nineteenth century, the basic history of the alphabet from about a millennium before the Common Era was known and mapped, but to piece together the earlier history, other methods, notably archaeology and paleography, were required.

The standardization of size, weight, and general appearance in Lidzbarski's expert presentations implied uniformity of scale and production technique. But Lidzbarski's scrupulous approach established the model for twentieth-century scholarship of Semitic epigraphy. In his 1948 *Semitic Writing: From Pictograph to Alphabet*, the esteemed Godfrey Driver provided information about whether his copies were taken from photographic reproductions or from hand-drawn copies of originals.[44] His book contained nearly one hundred figures and almost sixty photographic plates, evidence of the massive increase in specific information available since Taylor had pointed to its scarcity sixty years earlier. More will be said about Driver's contribution ahead, but in the context of tables, what is significant is that

Hieroglyph	Egyptian: Word	Egyptian: Meaning	Egyptian: Value	Semitic: Phoenician[1] Signs	Semitic: Arabian[2] Signs	Semitic: Name Meaning	Semitic: Value
	id	'hand'	*d*			*yôd* 'hand'	*y*
	rı, ri	'mouth'	*r*			*pê'* 'mouth'	*p*
	zḫn·t	'prop'	—			*wâw* 'peg'	*w*
	n·t	'water'	*n*			*mêm* 'water'	*m*
	(?)	(?)	—			*tâw* 'mark'	*t*
	ḳms	'throw-stick'	—			*gîmel* 'throw-stick'	*g*
	zwn, zin	'arrow'	—				
	?	'bolt'	*z*			*zayin* 'weapon (?)'	*z*
	?	'folded cloth'	*s*				
	tp	'head'	—			*rêš* 'head'	*r*
	ir·t	'eye'	—			*'ayin* 'eye'	'(ע)
	cı	'door'	—			*dâleṯ* 'door'	*d*
	kı	'ox'	—			*'âlep̱* 'ox'	'(א)
	ḥnt	'rush'	—			*kap* 'hand; bough'	*k*
	ḫs·t	'hill-country'	—			*šin* 'tooth; peak'	*š*
	cw·t	'peasant's crook'	—				
	ḥqı	'crooked staff'	—			*lâmeḏ* 'goad'	*l*
	wıs	'sceptre'	—				
	h	'courtyard'	*h*			*bêṯ* 'house'	*b*
	in·t	'*bulti*-fish'	—			*sâmeḵ* 'fish (?)'	*s*
	wıḏ·t	'cobra'	—			{Aram. *nûn* 'fish' / Eth. *nahâš* 'serpent'}	*n*
	qıı	'high'	—				
	ḥrı	'rejoiced'	—			*hê'* 'lo!'	*h*
	ḥc	'mourner'	—				
	ḥ	'twisted hank'	*ḥ*			*ḥêṯ* —	*ḥ*
		———	—			*ṭêṯ* —	*ṭ*
		'grasshopper'	—			*ṣâḏê* 'cricket'	*ṣ*
		'monkey'	—			*qôp̱* 'monkey (?)'	*q*

[1] Taken only from inscriptions dated *c.* 1300–900 B.C.
[2] Chosen from the South-Arabian alphabets without regard to dialect with a view to comparison with the corresponding Phoenician letters.

FIG. 92. Comparison of Egyptian and Semitic letters.

FIGURE 6.21 Godfrey Driver, *Semitic Writing: From Pictograph to Alphabet* (1948). Table of Phoenician inscriptions. © The British Academy 1948. Material reproduced with permission.

he noted the specific sources and media—objects, fragments, monuments, drawings—for his evidence. His tables identified variants within individual sources, giving a palpable sense of scribal practices as well as script evolution. Driver cited (and agreed with) Lidzbarski's refutation of claims for a Sumerian pictographic origin but drew on discussions in support of Egyptian influences and the Sinai as a site of cultural formation of the alphabetic scripts.

With such meticulous scholarship in place, future scholars had much on which to build, including new discoveries which could—and would—be analyzed in every detail of stroke, orientation, and form.

Coming to the end of the discussion of tables requires mentioning Benjamin Sass, the consummate epigrapher. Designed to serve a disciplined scholarly purpose in organizing and presenting information at a minute

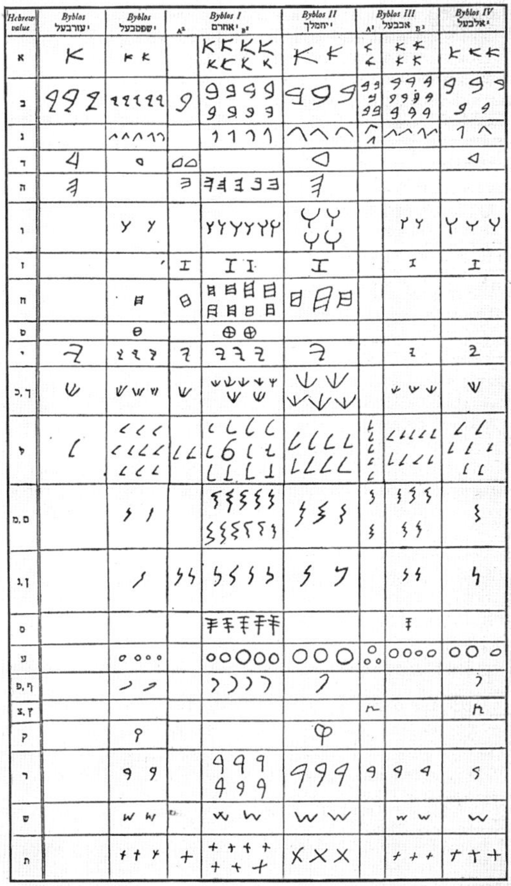

¹ Taken from photographic reproductions. ² Taken from hand-drawn copies.

FIG. 96. Byblo-Phoenician alphabet*.

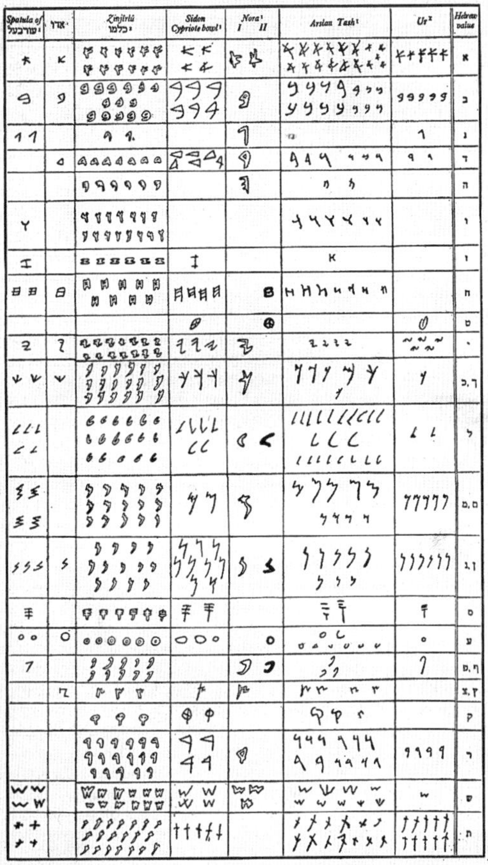

¹ Taken from photographic reproductions. ² Taken from hand-drawn copies.

FIG. 97. Phoenician alphabet*.

scale of attention, Sass's tables lack superfluous aesthetic properties. The tables are closer to spreadsheets than they are to pictorial representations—hard to imagine any contemporary Goeree embedding these in a pictorial rendering or narrativized account. Sass tabulated information from specific bits of physical evidence, each identified by a unique numerical form. Sass counted the number of instances of each glyph in each inscription, noted the variations in shape and orientation, and drew the signs in the conditions in which they appear—worn, broken, fragmented. The sheer comprehensiveness of the undertaking is evident in the presentation, and the rhetorical force of Sass's tables is at once methodological, embodying a fully empirical approach, and substantive in attending to the sites and physical remains through which the emergence of the remarkable system we call the alphabet can be tracked.

	345	346	347	347A	348	349	350	351	352	353	35
ʾ											
b											
g ?											
d											
h											
w											
ḏ											
ḥ											
ḫ											
y											
k											
l											
m											
n											
ʿ											
p?											
ṣ?											
q?											
r											
š?											
ṯ											
t											
Unidentified											
Unclear	1?				1?						
Total	14–16	29–30	3	2	9–10	27	13	17	26	34	:

FIGURE 6.22 Benjamin Sass, *The Genesis of the Alphabet* [. . .] (1988). Detail of table showing numbers of the Sinai inscriptions and redrawn glyphs for research study. Material reproduced with permission of the author.

CONCLUSION

Graphic tables became major instruments for creation and presentation of arguments about the origin and development of the alphabet. The basic grid format of rows and columns has had a long history within this field of study (and even longer outside it). The format functions effectively to convince a viewer of relationships through a structure that presumes similarity across a body of signs extracted from their contexts and presented in a uniform size, scale, and order. These rational methods can be appropriated to fanciful ends, but such is the case with any and all forms of knowledge production. But the rigorous disciplines of paleography and archaeology can be appropriated for bizarre arguments, even as they are used to expand understanding. The contemporary knowledge of the origin and development of the alphabet is based on these disciplines, even though the complete story may remain elusive, owing to the relative scarcity of evidence. But sufficient materials for solid speculation exist now more than at any point in the past. Curiously, with some modification of dates and timescales, the empirical evidence supports ancient traditions and historical accounts from classical antiquity.

SEVEN

Modern Archaeology

Putting the Evidence of the Alphabet in Place

MODERN HISTORY OF THE PAST

Greek, Roman, Etruscan, and other inscriptions on monuments and coins provided some insight into writing in European antiquity after Phoenician transmission. But before the nineteenth century, physical evidence on which to construct the early development of the alphabet in the Levant remained almost nonexistent. Even in the twenty-first century, the total number of relevant artifacts dating to the crucial period of the second millennium BCE is small, several hundred, in contrast to hundreds of thousands of cuneiform tablets and hieroglyphic carvings from the same era.[1] Those found in verifiable archaeological contexts is even smaller. The excitement and thrill of each discovery often provokes excruciatingly detailed analysis. In the twenty-first century, new finds are codified within a well-established scholarly framework, but that too had to be created through a painstaking process.[2] Current research builds on the techniques of modern archaeology as it emerged step by step from an amateur undertaking to a professional field.

From the nineteenth through twenty-first centuries, the discovery of inscriptions in the geographic region from Egypt through the Levant created an emerging map and timeline of the alphabet's early development. These preliminary discoveries were unearthed as the concept of "deep time," introduced in part by the eighteenth-century geologist James Hutton, was changing Western concepts of historical chronology. Though this did not immediately or uniformly transform attitudes in all fields, it altered the understanding of the origins of the alphabet, gradually placing it within archaeological rather than biblical periods. The vague story linked to the territory of "the holy land" was replaced by a scientifically organized history.

We can now describe the origin of the alphabet chronologically and geographically with some degree of reliability. The basic outlines are these: The alphabet was formed in the context of cultural exchanges between Semitic-speaking people from the Levant and communities in Egypt after or around 1800 BCE. The earliest evidence is dated to Wadi el-Hol, a site in Egypt just west of the Nile, north of Luxor. Later inscriptions in the Sinai and throughout the Fertile Crescent show the gradual distribution and evolution of alphabetic writing, with most evidence dating from the fourteenth century BCE and after. Late in the second millennium BCE, a relatively standardized version of this alphabetic script—known as linear Phoenician—became part of the culture of the coastal cities of Tyre, Byblos, and Sidon. Variations of the early alphabet, designated as Proto-Canaanite, were used in inland settlements of Lachish, Gezer, Tel El-Hesi, and other sites that lie in the coastal plain between the Mediterranean to the west and the Judaean mountains to the east. This activity took place in the tenth through ninth centuries in periods of technological and social development designated Iron I and II by archaeologists.[3] A wider distribution of alphabetic writing occurred after 1000 BCE as maritime trade from these coastal cities spread the linear Phoenician script throughout the Mediterranean—even as variants such as Paleo-Hebrew emerged in the homeland. The arrival of alphabetic characters into Spain, Italy, Greece, Turkey, and various islands, through overland trade routes and coastal ports, can be tracked by comparing inscriptions and artifacts. Local modifications of these scripts developed into Greek, Etruscan, Italic, Iberian, and other variants in the West in the final centuries before the Common Era. Ethiopic, Arabic, modern Hebrew, and then Indian scripts also emerged from this common source and became defined in the East and throughout Asia, many in the last centuries before the Common Era. The process of development took about two thousand years from original impulse to the foundations for the alphabetic scripts used in every continent of the world today.

For this historical narrative to be established and verified, modern archaeology was required. Its emergence was fueled, in part, by the quest of many American, British, and European scholars seeking evidence to prove the historical authenticity of the Old Testament—a motivation that weaves through alphabet studies at every era. The search for places named in the Bible was one of the motivating impulses for mapping the Sinai and Levant—and had been for centuries. Though the concept of "biblical archaeology" no longer dominates the research in the region, it played a major role in initial exploration. Archaeological work was also linked to colonialism, imperialism, and territorial disputes—the political dimensions are always present in the region—as well as cultural appropriation. This legacy also endures. Many ancient artifacts remain in British and European museum collections, even though control of antiquities gradually moved to regional authorities. Discussions of historical national identities are also fraught with ongoing political agendas. Does the "voice of Israel" cry out "from the rocks of Sinai" as many authors have suggested?[4] Myths of national origins have to be treated carefully, particularly in assessing archaeological evidence. The Proto-Sinaitic inscriptions were made by Semitic speakers working in an Egyptian context—but long before a national identity for "Israel" existed.[5]

Another challenge for archaeologists working in sites of ancient Phoenicia, Philistia, Canaan, the Sinai, or other parts of this region was that the evidence recovered there was different in scale and appearance from that of the monumental temples and palaces of earlier Egyptian culture and the later classical world. Excavations on monumental sites whose ruined past was visibly evident were begun as early as the seventeenth century, with attention to Pompeii and Herculaneum in Italy, or the pyramid tombs of Egypt in the eighteenth and early nineteenth centuries. The large structures from ancient Babylonia and Assyria needed to be unearthed from the desert in the nineteenth century. The sands literally had to be stripped away to reveal the ancient palace of Sargon, Library of Ashurbanipal, or the ruins of the Hanging Gardens of Babylon. But these mythic sites had a long historical pedigree to project onto their ruins.

Nothing like the pyramids at Giza or the palaces at Knossos and Nineveh had been built by the communities who developed the alphabet. For instance, the imposing Giza pyramids were constructed in the middle of the third millennium BCE, but the crude characters scratched into rocks in the Sinai desert were made about a thousand years *later*. The early alphabetic "monumental" inscriptions of the first millennium BCE are modest, appearing on sarcophagi or plaques—not pyramids or palaces. Some of the most important evidence, like inscriptions drawn on bricks or ostraca—or in valley walls—at first seemed too insignificant to warrant notice.

Archaeological discoveries related to the alphabet are concentrated in a few geographic locations whose ancient populations belonged to distinct cultural groups. The area known as Phoenicia in the northern coastal area of the Levant, modern-day Lebanon, provided the Byblian royal inscriptions and many other smaller artifacts made by Semitic-speaking inhabitants of the ancient land of Canaan. Ancient Philistia, further south on the coast, was occupied by people who had arrived from the Aegean in the second millennium following the Mycenaean collapse. They took up the Phoenician or Canaanite scripts for use with the Philistine language. To their north was ancient Israel stretching across the Jordan River, whose inhabitants also spoke a Semitic language, as did those of other municipalities of ancient Judah, Moab, Ammon, and Edom. Variations in alphabetic script form are associated by name with these regions, their cultures, and their languages (Moabite, Ammonite, etc.). All provide evidence of pockets of scribal culture in existence throughout the region by about 1000 BCE making use of a shared alphabetic system derived from Proto-Canaanite roots.

The older inscriptions in the rocks of the Sinai to the south offer insight into the earlier development of alphabetic script in a complex cultural exchange of graphic forms and conceptual influences between Egypt and its neighbors to the north and east. Discoveries in 1994–95 of early alphabetic writing in Wadi el-Hol raised new speculations about the range and sites of origin. Creating a coherent timeline of this development depends, in part, on providing an explanation of long periods for which little evidence exists. The alphabet was created across a several-hundred-year period in a region where cultural exchange was active and in which scribal practices were distributed but sufficiently coordinated to bring about standardization in the forms of early writing.

The most crucial effect of archaeological exploration in the region of the ancient Levant was that it *spatialized* historical understanding within evermore specific *chronologies*. The lateral dimension of landscape was mapped with scientific methods, and the horizontal layers of stratification were measured and read. Using modern empirical methods, archaeologists recovered the history of the alphabet on the site of its original development. In the process, the alphabet changed status. It was no longer perceived as a *given* but instead as a human system that had been *made* in a particular time and place by people who could be identified and situated within specific historical circumstances. This understanding emerged from discoveries in several key locations beginning in the mid-nineteenth century as, in a tangible sense, modern archaeology reinvented the alphabet.

Though they share a common origin, Proto-Sinaitic Semitic inscriptions are distinguished from the Sinaitic writings carved in later centuries in the same locations, as well as from the Proto-Canaanite ones found in the wide region of ancient Canaan (often referred to as Northwestern Semitic scripts), by geographic and temporal designations. Early Semitic inscriptions have also been found in southern Asia Minor, and throughout the Levant, a term used to identify ancient Syria-Palestine and the modern countries of Lebanon, Jordan, Israel, Syria, and western Iraq.

ACCESS TO THE LEVANT

As political changes in the control of Ottoman territory occurred in the mid-nineteenth century, the region that stretched north to Aleppo and south to the Sinai peninsula and Egypt became more accessible to travelers. Nearly a century later, control would pass to France and Britain following World War I in a League of Nations mandate through which the British governed modern-day Iraq, Palestine, and the Transjordan while the French controlled Syria, Lebanon, and other regions into Turkey. The complex political history of this region is an ever-present aspect of archaeological work.

Western knowledge of the geography of the region had its own history. Samuel Bochart's compilation of a complete list of place-names and their relation to the biblical references, *Geographia sacra* (Sacred geography) (1646), provided a starting point for travelers well into the nineteenth century.[6] Bochart's goal had been to track the distribution of the sons of Noah after the Flood and before the Confusion of Tongues through an inventory of place-names.[7] Bochart also had his own idiosyncratic agendas and used pseudo-philological explanations of the origins of Hebrew and Chaldean to show they were derived *from* Teutonic and Celtic. Bochart's fancies were savagely pilloried by the French philosopher Voltaire: "Astonishing with what confidence these men of genius have proved that expressions used on the banks of the Tiber were borrowed from the patois of the savages of Biscay."[8] Still Bochart was frequently cited as an authority by later writers, and it would not be inaccurate to suggest that even the most "modern" nineteenth-century travelers to the Holy Land carried some of Bochart's views into their researches. A more reliable and comprehensive source of geographic knowledge was compiled by Hadriano Relando (Adriaan Reelant). His *Antiquitates sacrae veterum Hebraeorum* (Ancient and sacred Hebrew antiquities), first published in 1715, was an illustrated geography of ancient Palestine, and his detailed nomenclature of the landscape set the stage for the work of antiquarians.[9] The first complete modern surveys of this region did not get produced until the mid-nineteenth century, when the Palestine Exploration Fund, a British organization, sent missions to the area.

THE COMING OF MODERN ARCHAEOLOGY

In 1907, Frederick Jones Bliss published a comprehensive historical study, *The Development of Palestine Exploration*.[10] After summarizing classical texts, pilgrimage narratives, and travelers' tales from earlier centuries, he stated that in the nineteenth century, "the time had come for a scholar . . . to enter this tempting field with thermometer, telescope, compass, and measuring tape."[11] In his opinion, this scholar was Edward Robinson, considered one of the founding figures of modern archaeology. The list of tools Bliss described emphasized Robinson's shift to empirical methods, even as textual foundations remained an important impetus to new discoveries. Robinson relied on well-known prior authorities on the geography of the region, such as Adrian Reeland and others like Karl von Raumer, John Lewis Burckhardt, and Léon Marquis de Laborde, all of whom would have been common references at the time.[12] Like these predecessors, he sought to identify biblical sites within the physical geography of the Holy Land.[13]

Into this intellectual context, modern archaeological approaches introduced two transformative methods–spatialization and stratification–

both of which conceived of physical space as a legible index to history. They linked objects to places and (sometimes) datable layers of an excavated site, making them part of historically specific cultural development and social practices.

THE DISCOVERY OF THE SIDON INSCRIPTION

The first major Phoenician monument discovered on native soil was found near the ancient coastal city of Sidon, and it caused a popular and scholarly sensation. Before this, the only identifiable Phoenician inscriptions (besides a pair of inscribed pillars from Malta) were those on coins, the earliest of which might date to the fifth century BCE.[14] But on February 22, 1855, Aimé Peretié, a diplomat attached to the French consulate to Beirut, was walking southeast of the site of the ancient coastal city of Sidon, apparently looking for signs of treasure in what he believed to be an ancient cemetery. Peretié's attention was drawn to a disturbed area of rubble and debris. Investigation led him, and the workmen he had hired, through a series of shafts to underground chambers. Here they discovered royal tombs.[15] While they did not come across gold or other treasure hoards, what they found was, arguably, infinitely more valuable. In what was later labeled Tomb V, they unearthed an intact sarcophagus carved in Egyptian style bearing a magnificent Canaanite (Semitic) language inscription written in the Phoenician script, now known to date to the fifth century BCE.[16]

News spread that for the first time, a monument had been found in situ in the lands associated with the history to which the inscription would attest. This discovery provided evidence for a wide range of scholarly investigations—historical, philological, paleographic, and biblical. Accounts of the discovery spread quickly, and their details provide a picture of technologies of knowledge distribution in the mid-nineteenth century, as well as information the artifact provided about the alphabet.

American missionaries made hand-drawn copies of the inscription and sarcophagus on site. According to a contemporary account, one of these drawings was made by Dr. C. V. A. Van Dyck, a member of the Albany Institute (among the oldest museums in America), who was in Syria at the time. He immediately sent the drawing back to his colleagues in upstate New York.[17] Another copy went to a scholar in London (M. le chevalier Bunsen) who passed it to a M. Dietrich, a scholar in Marburg with knowledge of Semitic languages. Other copies of the drawings were produced, and attempts at decipherment or translation followed immediately. However, since the inscriptions had been copied by hand by persons who had no familiarity with the unknown script, they proved to be flawed, hampering attempts at accurate analysis (some of the characters were illegible).[18]

In April 1855, just a few months after the discovery, Van Dyck's drawing was presented to the Albany Institute's Society, and in May 1855, a transla-

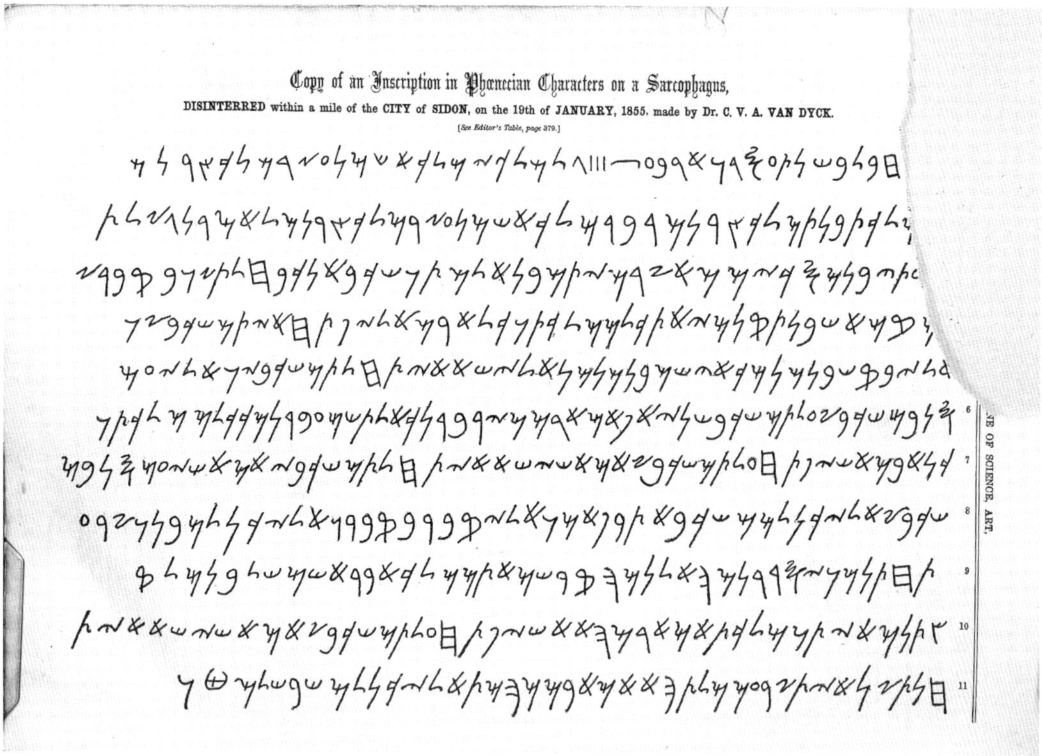

Copy of an Inscription in Phœnician Characters on a Sarcophagus,

DISINTERRED within a mile of the CITY of SIDON, on the 19th of JANUARY, 1855, made by Dr. C. V. A. VAN DYCK.

[See Editor's Table, page 379.]

FIGURE 7.1 Copy of the Sidon inscription made by a Dr. C. V. A. Van Dyke on January 19, 1855, from a recently disinterred monument found in Sidon that was reproduced in full in the *United States Magazine* in April of that same year to considerable acclaim. Public domain.

tion of the inscription by Messrs. Salisbury and Gibbs was published in the *New Haven Daily Palladium*, one of many to follow.[19]

Meanwhile, after quarrels with the English consul about ownership rights were resolved, the object was removed from the subterranean tomb near Sidon by the French. A contemporary witness described a ceremonial procession: a team of oxen pulled a cart bearing the weighty sarcophagus trimmed with flowers and palm leaves along a rocky route to a French vessel, *La Sérieuse*. The entire population of the city turned out to watch and cheer its progress. When the oxen failed in their efforts to keep the cart moving along a sandy track, the stalwart sailors of the French navy lent their physical strength and spirit to the undertaking.[20] The object, carefully swaddled and protected, was loaded onto the ship, which set sail for France. Attributing a "Phoenician" identity to the artifact was (and arguably still is) an act of colonial appropriation. The term is anachronistic, "an heirloom of Western reception" from classical antiquity, since there is no record of any entity ("ethnic, political, or 'national'") "that understood or labelled itself Phoenicia."[21] However, the term has become ubiquitous in the literature to identify the region, the people, and the script. It will be used here—though it should be remembered that like all nomenclature for geographical regions, peoples, and languages, it has a complex history.

In August 1855 came the announcement that the noble and very wealthy French antiquarian Monsieur le Duc de Luynes had acquired the object and was donating it to the Louvre. Luynes created squeezes from the inscription and published the results, along with a translation of the text transcribed in Hebrew letters. This technique provided more accurate images than the drawings of the American missionaries, and on the basis of these improved facsimiles, new translations were produced. The sarcophagus and its inscription spawned a rapid flurry of publications. In an 1856 account, published barely a year after the discovery, the Abbé J. J. L. Bargès summarized the many responses the inscription had provoked.[22] They are telling for their desire to situate the object within biblical historical periods rather than the modern ones then emerging:

> The discovery of the Phoenician inscription made in Sidon, in the heart of ancient Phoenicia, had already caused a great sensation in the scholarly world; everyone was impatient for the decipherment of the epigraph, which contained around a thousand characters. Some believed it was contemporary with Moses; others dated it to the time of Abraham; yet others, braver still, assigned it to an era before the universal Flood, certain that it had been the threat of the cataclysm threatening to swallow the globe and all of its inhabitants that had caused the king mentioned in the inscription to have this sarcophagus carved in basalt, an extremely hard stone, before he died and to place it in a tomb cut from the living rock two meters below the surface of the earth.[23]

By 1859, nearly a dozen different translations had been produced and circulated widely enough that a scholar named William Turner could inventory each author's reading of every glyph and sign in the inscription.[24] In his inventory, Turner noted 324 individual variants of the twenty-two letters in the Phoenician inscription, pointing out where the reading of the text depended on careful (and debatable) understanding of the glyphs.[25] The text furnished precious information on the language spoken by the Phoenicians about 500 BCE, and no inscription of any length in this tongue had ever been found before. Turner stated that the writing was "traced by a firm hand, trained and skilled" except for the first few lines which "showed some inexperience of the engraver with the tool."[26] Indeed, the inscription shows a mature state of the letterforms, highly standardized, their right-to-left direction and regular angles, size, and orientation expertly executed. The text was a funerary inscription for King Eshmunazar II warning ordinary and royal persons alike not to disturb the coffin of the dead king and threatening misfortune should they do so.

Turner made an attempt to date the inscription through a combination of historical and paleographic evidence, comparing the state of the writing with other inscriptions, particularly some recorded by Richard Pococke in Cyprus in 1743 and inscriptions found at "Marseilles, Carthage, Citium, Malta, Athens, and most of the coins of Phoenicia and the neighboring

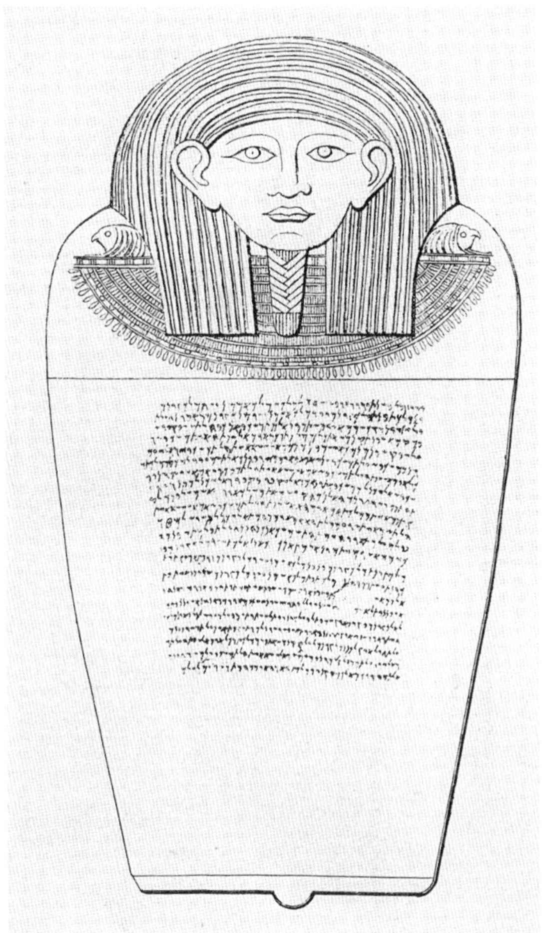

FIGURE 7.2 (*left*) Drawing of Eshmunazar sarcophagus, from L'Abbé Bargès. His source was Albert de Luynes, who owned the object at the time and also published a description of the monument, *Mémoire sur le sarcophage et l'inscription funéraire d'Esmunazar, roi de Sidon* (1856). Public domain.

FIGURE 7.3 (*right*) Photograph of Eshmunazar sarcophagus. Differences between the inscription and the hand-drawn copy are evident. Photo: Franck Raux. © RMN-Grand Palais / Art Resource, NY.

regions to the north."[27] The chief point of this discussion was to emphasize the significance of the inscription's having been found in "Phoenicia proper."[28]

Turner characterized the Phoenician language as close to biblical Hebrew and therefore useful as "a direct contribution towards elucidating the language of the Hebrew Scriptures."[29] The term *biblical Hebrew* designates an archaic branch of the Canaanite Semitic language in use by the tenth century BCE.[30] He noted the absence of the *matres lectionis* ("mothers of reading") and other details in the inscription's orthography. Like the other scholars involved in these translations, Turner had not seen the original artifact, only the various reproductions of its inscription. But his work showed how rapidly epigraphic methods and historical analysis could advance given such a rich piece of evidence.

This first discovery of a Phoenician inscription in situ merits considerable attention because it profoundly changed historical knowledge and inquiry. Successive discoveries built a more complete picture of the history of the kings of Sidon, and with each new inscription, the inventory of letterforms increased along with the capacity of scholars to identify even the smallest variations among them. Meanwhile, other major discoveries shifted the geographic focus in exciting ways—to the ancient kingdom of Moab and to that most significant city, Jerusalem.

MORE DISCOVERIES: THE MESHA STELE

Following the crucial discovery of the Sidon inscription, the number of newly identified artifacts related to the early stages of the alphabet's development grew steadily. Some objects were found accidentally, but many emerged through the systematic investigations of sites by increasingly professional archaeologists.

Two objects deserve particular attention for the dramatic circumstances surrounding their discovery: the Mesha Stele (also known as the Moabite Stone), found in 1868, and the Siloam inscription in Jerusalem, found in 1880. Like the Sidon sarcophagus, these items were found in what are termed "secure" archaeological contexts and were monuments whose extensive inscriptions provided historical and linguistic information as well as material for epigraphic analysis. As noted above, the text of the Sidon inscription of King Eshmunazar was self-referential, a warning about not disturbing the sarcophagus. But the text of the Mesha Stele directly referenced historical events, thus giving it additional resonance.

In August 1868, Reverend F. A. Klein, a Prussian who was part of an Anglican missionary group in Jerusalem, reportedly became the first European to be shown the Mesha Stele. Klein was traveling for his own amusement in the company of a local chief named Zattan who offered to show him a curious stone in the ruins of Dhibân (ancient Dibon, in modern Jordan, east of the Dead Sea).[31] The stele was simply lying on the ground. Since it was late in the day at the time they viewed the object, Klein copied only a few words so he could consult experts when he returned to Jerusalem. By Klein's account the stone was "in a most perfect state of preservation."[32] Unfortunately, because of the way events unfolded, Klein was not only the first—but also the last—European to see the monument in one piece.

The beautiful black polished-basalt stone (a little more than three feet high and half as wide) contained an elegantly carved inscription in the Moabite language. It was written in an expertly executed linear Phoenician script later dated to the mid-ninth century BCE. On his return to Jerusalem, Klein showed his sketches of the inscription to a Dr. Petermann, the Prussian consul, who happened to be an amateur paleographer. Petermann recognized the characters as Phoenician and contacted the Royal Museum in Berlin about the prospect of acquiring the object. By September 15, a few weeks later, he received approval for purchase in what at first seemed like what would be a simple transaction.[33] But negotiations for purchase of the stone took about a year and involved exchanges among many parties, including "the Prussian government and various Arabs and Turkish pashas."[34] Finally, all agreed that the stone would be handed over for a sum of £80.[35] Meanwhile, Captain Charles Warren, a British employee of the Palestine Exploration Fund, became alerted to the existence of the object. At first, finding that negotiations were already underway to remove it, he let the matter drop, and through the winter of 1868–69, the stone remained in place. As negotiations continued the Arabs began to understand the value of the stone and increased the asking price. This prompted the Prussian consul to enlist assistance in negotiating with the Turkish government for its sale.

During these protracted negotiations, Charles Clermont-Ganneau, a French diplomat in Jerusalem, also heard of the existence of the stone and also began to bid for its acquisition. Now the Germans, British, and French were all competing to acquire the object. Meanwhile, Clermont-Ganneau apparently hired a young Arab named Yâqoub Caravacca to make a squeeze of the inscription. These efforts created considerable excitement, and squabbles ensued among the Bedouin groups during the process. When Caravacca went to take an impression from the stone, he ended up with a lance wound in his leg. Luckily, a horseman "named Djemîl had the presence of mind to seize the squeeze paper, still damp" that Caravacca had been handling and take it from the stone in fragments.[36] Meanwhile the unfortunate Caravacca escaped. The existence of this squeeze proved extremely important. Though Clermont-Ganneau had offered £375 to acquire the stone from the local Arabs, the governor of Nablus demanded the stele for himself through a subordinate, the modir of Salt. But since the local Bedouins had suffered in a conflict with the Ottoman government the year before, they determined that rather than give up the piece to the Turkish authorities, they would destroy it.[37] The local Arabs, who claimed descent from Moab, built a fire under the stone and then poured cold water on its heated surface, breaking the basalt stele into many pieces. These they distributed and placed in granaries to "act as blessings upon the corn," fearing that otherwise "a blight would fall upon their crops."[38]

Warren and Clermont-Ganneau gathered these remains, some of which went to Paris and others of which were sent to England. Tracings were sent to a Mr. Deutsch, a renowned Semiticist, employed by the British Museum in the 1870s.[39] In combination with the information from the squeezes, the monument was restored with cast parts patched among the remnants. The restored object resides in the Louvre.

Dated to about 860 BCE, the Mesha Stele is considered a major source of information about the Moabite language, an extinct offshoot of Canaanite and part of the Northwest Semitic languages of the region. The account of historic events in the inscription matches those in the Bible in which King Mesha leads the Moabite people to victory against Israel. The name Israel is explicitly present, as is the term Yahweh and hence the resonance of the text. The script is variously described as Phoenician and Paleo-Hebrew.

FIGURE 7.4 Mesha Stele, or Moabite Stone (860 BCE), showing patched fragments. Photo: Mathieu Rabeau.

FIGURE 7.5 Siloam inscription. Uploaded by user Wikikati. Public domain, via Wikimedia Commons.

More round, less compressed and elongated than the later (fifth-century BCE) Sidon inscription, the letterforms in the carving show the consistency and skill of an already practiced scribe.

Like the Sidon inscription, the Mesha Stele occasioned considerable popular interest, and a report of its discovery and the many complications around its history were widely published. An account by George Grove of the Palestine Exploration Fund appeared in the *New York Times* in February 1870, followed by Clermont-Ganneau's version in the French *Revue d'instruction publique*, and another by Frederick Klein soon after in the *Pall Mall Gazette*.[40] Moab was about 250 miles to the southeast of Sidon, and the inscriptions were also separated by a four-hundred-year time period, but scholars recognized they were part of a single process of diffusion and development. Observable differences in the elongation of strokes and orientation of the rendering suggested that the writing on the Stele was at an earlier stage of development than the inscription from Sidon. But they shared a recognizable set of characters, and both contained highly standardized individual glyphs. The Moabite stone was evidence that as early as the ninth century BCE, the linear alphabetic script was being used to write official accounts of historical events throughout the region, not just in the powerful cities of the coast where access to the sea and available timber had fostered a thriving maritime trade.

ON SITE IN JERUSALEM: THE SILOAM INSCRIPTION

The next major discovery was sensational in part because it was found in Jerusalem. During his travels in 1838, Edward Robinson, mentioned above, had explored the Siloam tunnel, a water channel whose existence, known in modern times since 1625, was associated with the figure of Hezekiah in the Bible. This channel had been carved in antiquity, probably between the eighth and seventh centuries BCE, to bring water into Jerusalem from the Gihon Spring outside its walls, a pool below the Temple Mount. Robinson had not pushed his exploration of the channel further than an initial encounter. Discovery of the inscription took place more than four decades later, in 1880, when a local pupil of a German architect named Dr. Schick was playing in the subterranean channel. The young man, Jacob Eliahu, slipped and fell in the water and on "rising to the surface, he noticed, in spite of the darkness, what looked like letters on the rock which formed the southern wall of the channel."[41] Dr. Schick returned to the spot and tried to copy the inscription, but the light was bad and conditions difficult. According to another scholar, Archibald H. Sayce, who visited the site a few years later, Schick faithfully copied "every crack and flaw in the stone." In his attempt to get an accurate copy, Sayce noted he "had to sit for hours in the mud and water, working by the dim light of a candle."[42] As a consequence, his "copy required correction in several points, and it was not until the arrival of a Dr. Guthe six weeks later that an exact facsimile was obtained. Guthe removed the deposit of lime by the application of an acid and so revealed the original appearance of the tablet. A cast of it was taken, and squeezes made from the cast. The squeezes could then be studied at leisure and in a good light."[43]

Dated to about 700 BCE, the Siloam inscription was the first monumental early alphabetic text found in Jerusalem. For this reason alone, it would have had a celebrity beyond that of the Sidon inscriptions. The inscription tells the story of the tunnel's construction to bring water into the city in case of siege. The specific references, as well as the fully authenticated site, meant that the inscription's script could be dated with considerable accuracy. The language is ancient Hebrew, and the script belongs to one of the southern branches of Paleo-Hebrew that derived from old Phoenician. Artifacts of such profound importance were—and are—studied character by character. Some of the individual letters appeared to be older in form than those of the Moabite stone, though that monument is dated to about 850 BCE. Such inconsistencies have been studied to explain the way writing was embedded in the social structure of scribal culture in the distributed municipalities of the region in the period.[44] Local changes in scripts did not always advance synchronously.

These three monuments alone would have made the final decades of the late nineteenth century a turning point in the archaeology of the alphabet. Sidon was a stratified site and the Siloam tunnel a legible one. The Moabite stone had a geographic location attached to its discovery even though it lacked an archaeological context. Multiple new finds added quickly to the sum of available evidence for study of the development of the alphabet, and their geographic range continued to expand. For instance, another ninth-century BCE stone monument bearing a Phoenician inscription, the

Kilamuwa Stele, was found by a group of German scholars in Sam'al, in southern Turkey, on an expedition between 1888 and 1902.[45] Unlike the incised inscriptions of Sidon, this stele had raised characters carved in relief. Also dated to the ninth century BCE, it was written in a variation of the Phoenician script identified as Old Aramaic. The style of the carvings on this stele is much closer to that of Assyrian motifs, linking alphabetic writing to a wide range of cultural influences in the northeastern area of the region. Cuneiform was the oldest writing system in the ancient Near East and raised questions about connections between these wedge-shaped signs, so different in their appearance, and the early alphabet. Some clay tablets found in 1928 in the coastal area of Ugarit prompted more discussion.

The Kilamuwa Stele is also now known as KAI 24, a designation within the established catalogue of *Kanaanaische und aramaische Inschriften* (Aramaic and Canaanite inscriptions), an inventory first published in 1960 to standardize references to these artifacts. The *KAI* catalogue is organized by script form (Phoenician, Punic, neo-Punic, Moabite and Ammonite, Hebrew, and Aramaic) subdivided by region (Syria and Asia Minor, Egypt, Africa, Sardinia, Greece, and Europe, etc.). The *KAI* remains the standard reference for Canaanite and Aramaic inscriptions. The sum total of entries is scarcely more than three hundred items, and each of these has been studied extensively with regard to language, letterforms, location, and the contents of their texts. The existence of the *KAI* is itself a testimony to the scholarly attention to and codification of these discoveries. The Ahiram sarcophagus described below holds the privileged designation, KAI 1, followed by the other major Byblian inscriptions, signaling their priority of discovery and importance.

ASSYRIAN AND UGARITIC CONNECTIONS

The Assyrian connection attested by the style of carvings on the Kilamuwa Stele confirmed the earlier finds of Austen Henry Layard in his systematic excavations of the ancient Assyrian capital of Nineveh, begun in the 1840s.[46] Layard discovered several lion weights with both cuneiform inscriptions and Phoenician-Semitic lettering dating to about the eighth century BCE.[47] A brief discussion of the contributions of Layard will suffice here, since his chief focus was on the Assyrian ruins of Nineveh and Babylon.[48] But he also reported finding three Phoenician seals, which he had not expected. In a footnote Layard suggested that the "characters may belong to some other Semitic nation, as a cursive alphabet, having a close resemblance to the Phoenician."[49] He found other intriguing remnants, such as terracotta pieces with "ancient Chaldean characters" (the term Chaldean was still being used for Aramaic scripts in the nineteenth century) that he thought dated to the third century BCE.[50] The letters were a mix of Syriac and Palmyrene, resembling Phoenician. In other words, they are a blend of later Northwestern Semitic scripts, as per the inscriptions found on the Lion

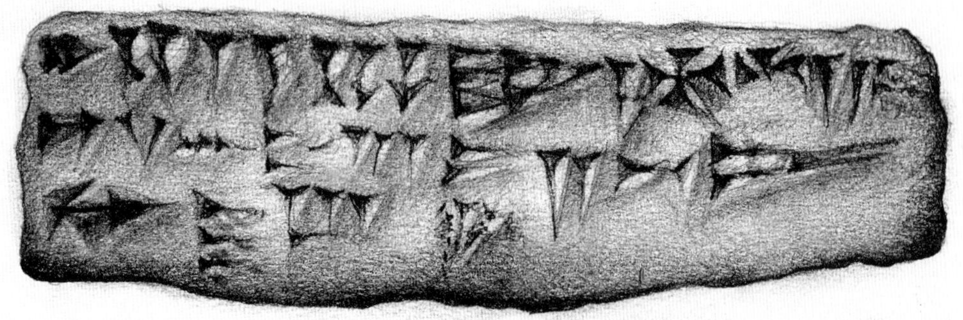

FIGURE 7.6 Ras Shamra alphabet tablet; drawing by J. Drucker.

weights. Such bilingual inscriptions were important, but a more revolutionary connection between alphabetic principles and a cuneiform script soon became evident.

In 1928 a group of intriguing clay inscriptions, known as the Ras Shamra tablets, was found at the site of the ancient city of Ugarit on the northern coast of Syria. Eight years of careful digging at Ugarit, under supervision of an archaeologist from Strasbourg, Claude F. Schaeffer, unearthed a large collection of cuneiform clay tablets dated to the fourteenth–thirteenth centuries BCE. These Ugaritic inscriptions were clear evidence that a cuneiform script had been used for a Semitic language. The script contained thirty different signs, which suggested that the twenty-two-character scripts consolidated around 1000 BCE might be reductions of this earlier system.[51] The symbols were distinct from those of Akkadian cuneiform, and the letter sequences found on abecedaries (inscriptions of the letters of the alphabet, often created for pedagogical purposes as exemplars or ordered word lists) followed those of both North and South Semitic alphabets. In other words, these inscriptions used a unique set of cuneiform signs to represent the sounds of the Semitic language. At first, the discovery of the Ras Shamra tablets gave rise to the theory that the Phoenician alphabet had been derived from these cuneiform characters.[52] Ultimately, this theory did not hold up.

However, the fact that Semitic speakers had distilled the components of their language into sound components represented in the Ras Shamra cuneiform signs showed that the foundational principles of alphabetic writing existed in multiple communities. The wedge-shaped forms of the Ugaritic cuneiform are not part of any Proto-Canaanite forms, which are linear (whether carved or painted). Ugarit was a port and thus a site of major cultural exchange between Egypt, Cyprus, the Hittites (in Asia Minor

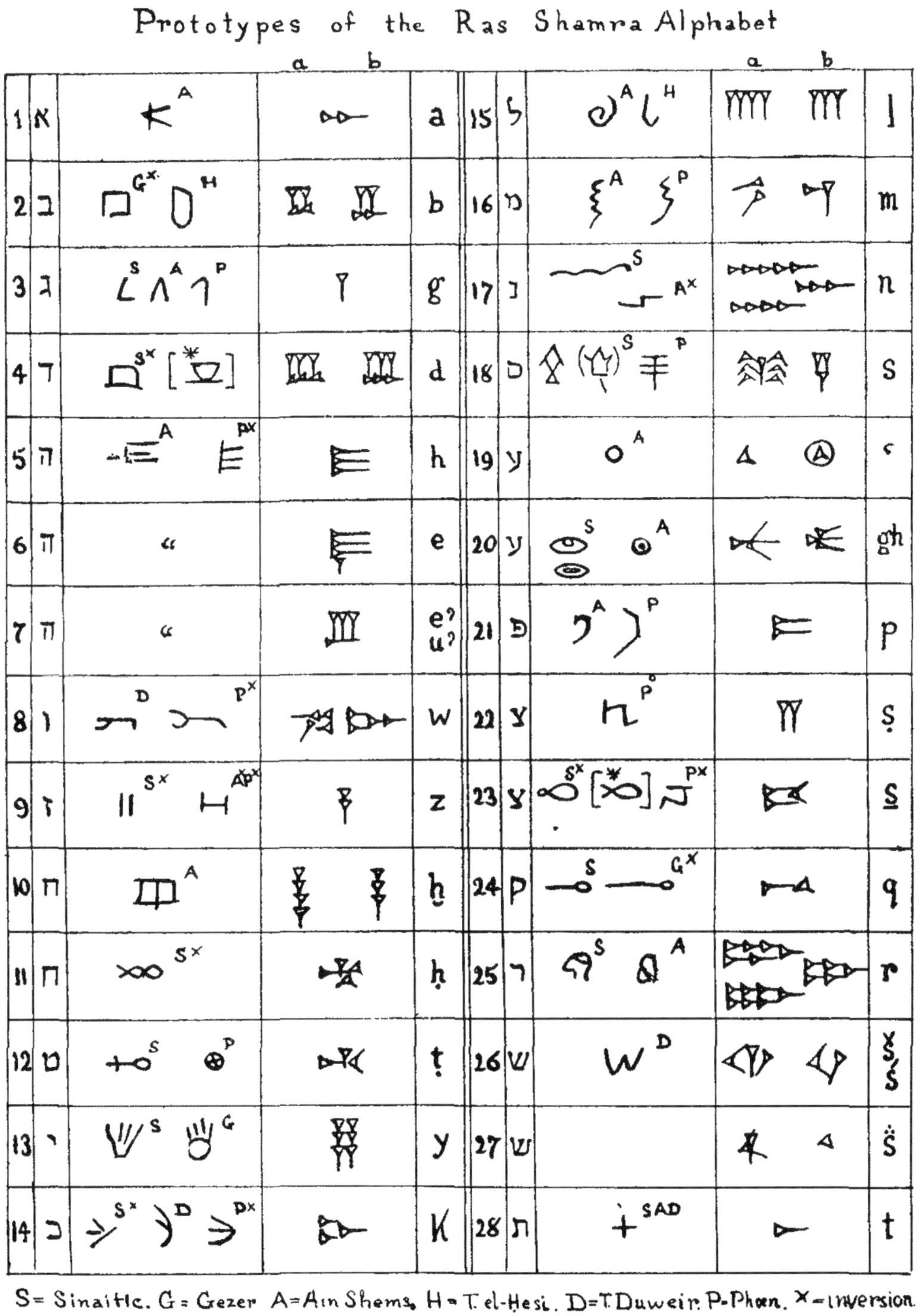

Prototypes of the Ras Shamra Alphabet

No.	Hebrew	Prototypes	a	b	Value	No.	Hebrew	Prototypes	a	b	Value
1	א	A			a	15	ל	A H			l
2	ב	Gx H			b	16	מ	A P			m
3	ג	S A P			g	17	נ	S Ax			n
4	ד	Sx [*]			d	18	ס	S P			s
5	ה	A Px			h	19	ע	A			ʿ
6	ה	„			e	20	ע	S A			gh
7	ה	„			e? u?	21	פ	A P			p
8	ו	D Px			w	22	צ	P			ṣ
9	ז	Sx ApX			z	23	צ	Sx [*] Px			s̱
10	ח	A			ḫ	24	ק	S Gx			q
11	ח	Sx			ḥ	25	ר	S A			r
12	ט	S P			ṭ	26	ש	D			š ś
13	י	S G			y	27	ש				s̈
14	כ	Sx D Px			k	28	ת	SAD			t

S= Sinaitic. G= Gezer A=Ain Shems, H= T. el-Hesi. D=T. Duweir. P-Phœn. X-inversion.

FIGURE 7.7 Eric Burrows, "Prototypes of the Ras Shamra Alphabet" (1936). Table provides comparison of Ras Shamra with other extant alphabetic forms; the comparison shows little formal connection between the cuneiform signs and the schematic letters.

to the north), and possibly Mycenaean Greece.[53] The discovery had made clear that the *concept* of the alphabet circulated in this world, as well as its graphic forms.

The capacity for linguistic analysis is a prerequisite for representing the sound elements of a language. These cuneiform signs had been created expressly for this purpose, not borrowed from other Ugaritic systems. Though Ras Shamra inscriptions turned out to be an anomaly, rather than a part of continuous development, their importance remains undiminished in understanding the larger process through which the alphabet came about.

ROYAL BYBLIAN INSCRIPTIONS

The corpus of Royal Byblian inscriptions, whose discovery had begun in Sidon in 1854 with the sarcophagus of Eshmunazar, became systematically codified and studied with each new find. In 1881, an inscribed bust was found by a German archaeologist in Byblos. On it was carved a cartouche identifying the tenth-century BCE Egyptian ruler Osorkon, whose territory was known to have extended throughout the Levant in the period.[54] This was accompanied by somewhat cruder, alphabetic inscription that provides evidence of a bilingual and multicultural Egyptian-Semitic environment. Political and economic ties between Egypt and the coastal cities was well known, but precise links among their writing systems were unclear. The hieroglyphics were evidently pictorial and iconic, and the alphabet inscriptions were linear and schematic.

Aware of the potential richness of the royal tombs in the region, archaeologists persisted in searching for new artifacts. In 1887, the sarcophagus belonging to Eshmunazar's father, Tabnit, was also found in Sidon. Other discoveries followed, such as the Abiba'l inscription found in 1895 by Clermont-Ganneau. The highly significant Ahiram sarcophagus was discovered in 1923, the Yehimilk inscription first published in 1930, the Safatba'al inscription was found in 1936, and the Shipitba'al inscription (KAI 7) was discovered in 1936 (though only published in 1945 after the end of World War II). This group of artifacts forms the corpus known as the Royal Byblian inscriptions and exhibits a well-established and fully standardized script linked to specific sites in tenth-to-ninth-century BCE Byblos and Sidon.

In this group of remarkable finds, the discovery of the Ahiram sarcophagus in 1923 stands out because its script marked a mature stage of development of the linear Phoenician alphabet. It was found on the site of the ancient city of Byblos during an excavation led by Pierre Montet.[55] Dating of the artifact has raised various problems. Scholars have argued for as early as 1200 BCE, on the basis of the tomb site, or as late as 900 BCE, depending on consideration of historical information in the text (stating it was made by Itobaal, the son of Ahiram, the king of Byblos) and the state of development of the script.[56] The inscription was crucial to understanding the state of Phoenician script at the time it began to circulate through the Mediterranean since its forms are considered to be those that found their way along the maritime trade routes. An earlier date (e.g., 1200 BCE) would suggest a considerable time lag between a mature Phoenician script and its distribution. Adding to complications, the earliest inscriptions on Thera, in Greece, are more crude than the sarcophagus lettering, suggesting an earlier phase of development, but they are dated later.[57] Did script forms deteriorate in the hands of widespread adopters? Or were the people picking up the script and trying to use it simply less skilled? The accomplishments of a scribe creating a princely commission might be expected to be different in quality from those of a Phoenician sailor, but the forms in alphabetic inscriptions should reflect the state of evolution of the script at the moment of their creation.

By the time the Ahiram sarcophagus was found by Montet, the discovery was no longer acclaimed as miraculous. It still attracted international attention but was received within an established scholarly framework. The Harvard University scholar Charles C. Torrey, describing the Ahiram inscription in an article in the *Journal of the American Oriental Society* in 1925, two years after the inscription's discovery, could systematically analyze the text, character, and contexts of the inscription within an established literature.[58] Torrey assigned the sarcophagus to the thirteenth century BCE, a date no longer accepted (850 BCE is the current consensus), but he cited work by prominent scholars, René Dussaud and Mark Lidzbarski, using their translations and commentary from 1924 as his point of departure. Guesswork and amateur decipherment had been replaced by professional scholarship.

As the corpus of Royal Byblian inscriptions grew, the combination of historical information in sites and in the texts themselves supported greater precision—and more debates—about the dates. While the succession of the monarchs could be established in part through the use of patronymics—Eshmunazar identified as "son of" Tabnit—the external framework for historical dating had to be established through other materials in the site as well as the increasingly careful observation of strata. An artifact might be older than the other items in an archaeological layer, present in a site as an heirloom or significant gift.[59] William Albright, one of the major figures in twentieth-century biblical archaeology, emphasized that knowledge about "grammar, lexicography, and spelling" should be factored into dating as well.[60]

All the Byblian inscriptions—including Ahiram, Yehimilk, Eliba'l, and Abiba'l—are considered homogenous linear Iron Age Northwest inscriptions. That is, they are part of a single, related body of inscriptions with common characteristics. The Mesha Stele and other artifacts associated with the kingdom of Moab and other communities inland from the coast are considered distinct modifications that have differentiated from the Phoenician exemplars.

Art historical analysis of the Ahiram sarcophagus also contributes to the dating debates but with the recognition that the inscription could have

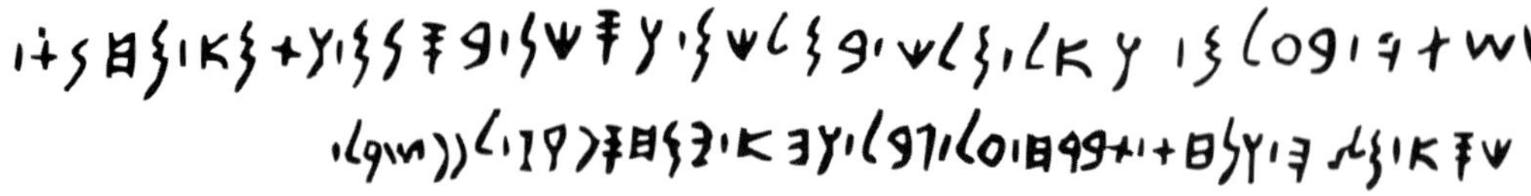

FIGURE 7.8 Inscription on Ahiram sarcophagus showing a mature form of the linear Phoenician script, around 850 BCE. Uploaded by unknown user. Public domain, via Wikimedia Commons.

been added at a later date.[61] The carvings on the sarcophagus are elaborate and show a dead father holding a drooping flower in a poignant gesture as he raises his other hand in benediction of his surviving son. The style shows strong Egyptian influence, and the cultural contacts that support this are well documented.[62] This art historical analysis places the sarcophagus in the early first millennium, just around 1000 BCE. At stake in these analyses is the detailed understanding of how script forms standardized and changed in the cultural diffusion that spread them through the Levant.

Ongoing twentieth-century work by Montet, Dussaud, Maurice Dunand, and other French archaeologists in the area near ancient Sidon and Tyre continued to add to the Byblian inscriptions, but it was discoveries in the areas farther east that complicated the narrative.

DISTRIBUTED DISCOVERIES

Sites in the broad region of ancient Canaan revealed artifacts that suggested "widespread use, in early and mid-second-millennium, of one or more alphabetic writing systems."[63] These artifacts are exciting for their geographic range as well as for the variation they exhibit in degree of standardization. Together they argue, as Ben Mazar, Christopher Rollston, and other scholars have asserted, for distributed communities of localized, scribal culture in the late second millennium in the various municipalities of the Levant.

These multiple pieces of physical evidence did not supply an immediately coherent historical narrative. The Ras Shamra tablets suggested Ugaritic understanding of the structure of the alphabet while the Byblian inscriptions document the maturation of the linear script. Each new discovery altered the big picture of how these inscriptions were bound into a single line of development, particularly as early stages of such processes were often missing. The excavation of a site at Tell el-Hesi provides a vivid example of the challenges posed by this archaeological research.

W. M. Flinders Petrie, a renowned British archaeologist, selected the site for excavation in March 1890. Petrie, already famous for his work in Egypt, had applied to the Turkish government for permission to look for a site to dig in Syria. After his arrival in the region, he began looking at multiple locations. These included ones at Umm Lakis and Khurbet Ajlan. These modern names, he believed, were variants of the ancient biblical Lachish and Eglon respectively. His initial examination of each spot proved disappointing. He found only surface layers to investigate, and these were filled with Roman artifacts. But his initial impression of the Tell el-Hesi site was that "from its height and the pre-Greek style of its pottery" it might yield a richer reward. Petrie assessed the archaeological potential of the site by taking its measure, literally and conceptually. One of Petrie's foundational contributions to archaeology had been his 1877 publication titled *Inductive Metrology*, in which he outlined an approach to deriving ancient systems of measure from archaeological observation.[64]

Located sixteen miles east of Gaza, the site was approximately sixty feet high and might well contain successive layers. Petrie obtained permission to dig and was assigned a Turkish official to monitor any antiquities unearthed and to facilitate communications with local people hired to work on the site.[65] Petrie's description of the strata at Tell el-Hesi provided a record of his careful technique as well as of his findings. The earliest dwellings in the lowest layer of the site he dated to about 1670 BCE, a stratum of rounded stones without regular brickwork where construction had been achieved mainly by piling. Later walls had been built in successive restorations of the fortification. The earliest Phoenician pottery seemed as old as 1350 BCE, the latest was dated to 850 BCE, and he found no Egyptian objects in the site at all.[66] The study of pottery forms, shapes, and stylistic evolution provided another useful metric. But in all this work, and its carefully documented evidence, he found only a *single* inscription on a fragment of pottery.[67] The inscription contained three signs but generated considerable attention.[68] Initially perceived as combining Sinaitic and Phoenician scripts, the inscription was later interpreted as evidence that the scribes at Tell el-Hesi "employed a pre-Phoenician, or, at any rate, a non-Phoenician system of the Semitic alphabet."[69] This raised questions about whether or not linear Phoenician had been the common source for Semitic scripts, as had long been believed, especially in these varied locations.

EVIDENCE ACCUMULATES

Other sites in Syria and Palestine continued to yield discoveries that ranged from highly significant to minute—but crucial—inscriptions. In 1908, Stewart Macalister, an Irish archaeologist working with the Palestine Exploration Fund, discovered a limestone tablet in Gezer, twenty miles west of Jerusalem. Referred to as a calendar because it describes a yearly cycle of agricultural activities, it is dated to the tenth century BCE.[70] The object was not found in a stratified site, and the inscription still generated debate about the identity of its language (Hebrew or Phoenician) and script (Canaanite or Paleo-Hebrew). The style of the characters and their organization on the stone is far less expert than in the Byblian inscriptions. A potsherd from Gezer and a dagger from Lachish show related letters at an even earlier phase of development than the calendar stone. These are characterized as Proto-Canaanite and dated to after 1500 BCE, but the corpus is not extensive.[71] Though the dagger from Lachish was considered by some scholars to be the oldest alphabetic artifact from the ancient Near East, possibly as early as 1750–1659 BCE, it is now considered more likely from the thirteenth century.[72] A bowl fragment from the same area has been dated to the thirteenth or twelfth century BCE, but marks on pots from Gezer in the seventeenth or sixteenth century BCE have been dismissed as nonalphabetic.[73] In other words, a handful of inscriptions from these regions are dated to the centuries before the Phoenician script matured. Their early dates and physical location suggested geographic distribution of alphabetic writing before adoption of the Phoenician linear script.

In 1935, another important find of ostraca, or pottery sherds, was discovered by the British archaeologist James Leslie Starkey. These contained a group of letters exchanged between the city of Lachish and the administration in Jerusalem at the time of Nebuchadnezzar's attack (605–587 BCE).[74] Historical context along with identifiable events and persons fixed their date, and they provided a wealth of information for the study of paleography and language—including grammar and the niceties of rhetoric in epistolary communication in classical Hebrew.[75] Monumental as they are in importance, however, these bits and pieces of ceramic remains can only be made sense of within highly specialized arguments in which a few letterforms are read in great detail. Other small remnants accumulated gradually, each discovery creating scholarly excitement, but very few could catch popular imagination until the discovery of the Dead Sea Scrolls. However, the Scrolls provided only a few examples of late Paleo-Hebrew. Evidence for understanding early alphabet history continued to emerge from more modest materials.

For instance, in 1954, at El-Khadr, a site near Bethlehem, on the west bank of the Jordan river, a group of inscribed arrowheads written in early Canaanite was found that could be dated to about 1100–1050 BCE. Their letterforms are not standardized in stance or direction. These were cited by Frank Moore Cross, the formidable epigrapher, as one of the transformative pieces of evidence in building the historical understanding of the early development of the Proto-Canaanite script. Many more such archaeological instances of materially modest but significant finds could be cited and detailed, from this region and from sites around the Mediterranean—the Honeyan inscription from Cyprus, a bowl from Tekke in Crete, the Nora Stone from Sardinia, all dated to the ninth century BCE. Each piece of physical evidence discovered allowed for yet more granular analysis of the development, modification, and distribution of the many scripts that contribute to the formation of the alphabet.

But while the picture of the alphabet's development in the region from the coast of the Mediterranean to multiple sites across the Levant continued to expand, other transformative discoveries occurred in the Sinai. There, among inscriptions that had been known to travelers since antiquity, new attention from archaeologists in the first years of the twentieth century tilted the place of alphabet origins earlier and to the south, far from the land of Canaan.

PREMODERN ENCOUNTERS WITH THE SINAI INSCRIPTIONS

The earliest description of the Sinai inscriptions is attributed to a first-century Greek historian, Diodorus Siculus. His description of the experience is cited here in a nineteenth-century account: "And according to Diodorus Siculus . . . , there was in his day and earlier a spot of the like kind in the peninsula of Sinai, a luxuriant palm grove with fountains and streams, an oasis in the midst of a desert region, otherwise without water or shade, and with a southern exposure."[76] And from Siculus directly: "Moreover, an altar is there built of hard stone and very old in years, bearing an inscription in ancient letters of an unknown tongue."[77] Siculus's engagement with the inscriptions stops there, but the mention serves as a touchstone for later inquiry for travelers who saw it as part of the path of the Israelites from Egypt.

A sixth-century Greek merchant, Cosmas, also recorded seeing inscriptions in the Sinai. His account was barely noted in the centuries between its composition and the beginning of the modern period, according to the nineteenth-century scholar Charles Forster, who provided considerable detail:

> It is now somewhat more than thirteen hundred years since a merchant of Alexandria, Cosmas by name, from his voyages to India surnamed Indicopleustes, visited on foot the peninsula of Sinai; and was the first to discover or at least make known to the world the extraordinary fact of the existence, upon all the rocks at the various resting stations throughout that uninhabitable wilderness, of numerous inscriptions in a then, as now, unknown character and language. By certain Jews, who formed part of his company, and who professed to understand and interpret their meaning, these inscriptions, Cosmas further relates, were assigned to the age of Moses and the Exode, and ascribed to their own ancestors, the ancient Israelites, during their wanderings in the desert of Sin [*sic*].[78]

Forster goes on to observe that Cosmas was writing in the era of Justinian when "the world and the Church were occupied with other matters than researches into the far distant past."[79] So "the curious report of the Egyptian merchant lay, accordingly, unnoticed, in his work titled *Christian Topography* (*Topographia Christiana*). Nor was its repose disturbed from the sixth, until the commencement of the eighteenth century of our era, when the geographical treatise in which it occurs (Cosmas's only extant work) was published for the first time, with a Latin version and notes, in the year 1706, by the celebrated Montfaucon."[80]

Traces of ancient accounts such as these served as inspiration for the frequently mentioned *A Description of the East and Some Other Countries*, by Richard Pococke, published in 1743.[81] The book is a monumental tribute to the perseverance—and privilege—required for gathering evidence of ancient inscriptions in the eighteenth century. Pococke traveled into what were then considered dangerous as well as remote regions to make copies of antiquities and rock carvings on site. Pococke was not an archaeologist. He did not dig into or disturb the surface of the earth. But he took assiduous notes and also created an entire set of what he called "squeezes," or cast paper molds, of existing monuments. These records, along with exquisitely measured and careful drawings, formed the core of his contribution to our knowledge of inscriptions in the Near East and set a precedent for serious empirical study of evidence in situ.

Pococke considered his travels to be an imitation of the journey of the children of Israel, an approach repeated by many others before and after. The search for evidence of the biblical past remained a common theme in the eighteenth century, but Pococke was the first European traveler who went to the Sinai with the express purpose of getting copies of the inscriptions. While much of Pococke's *A Description of the East* was consumed with the study of Greek inscriptions found in Egypt (which would have been legible as well as conspicuous), he also devoted several chapters to Mount Sinai and the journey of the "children of Israel." The casts he made involved less mediation than drawing, and he also conscientiously recorded the locations of the sites in which he took his examples. He also noted that there were inscriptions on the large rocks that lay about the valley leading to what he identified as Mount Sinai, and more on the mountain itself. Location was important, not only because it provided authenticity but because it allowed the historical record to be linked to biblical geography.

THE SINAI EXPLORED

Even into the nineteenth century, travel narratives to this region were framed as "journeys into the inhospitable countries of the mysteries of our ancient faith."[82] This characterization from Lottin de Laval's *Voyage dans le peninsule arabique du Sinai et l'Egypte moyenne, histoire, geographie, epigraphie* (Voyage in the Arabic peninsula of Sinai and middle Egypt . . . ; 1855–59) was accompanied by recapitulations of earlier pilgrimage narratives. Laval drew on other travelers' experiences (he cited the eighteenth-century accounts by Pococke and the Danish explorer Carsten Niebuhr among others) of viewing numerous inscriptions on the rocks along the track he was convinced had been followed by the Hebrews fleeing Egypt.[83] This familiar narrative is supported with elaborate descriptions of each stage of his four-to-five-month journey obtaining rubbings so that he could return to Paris with a voluminous collection of archaeological materials.

Pococke had wondered about the alphabet in which these inscriptions were written and so did Laval. The characters were unknown to him but also, to his surprise, to the local people. If the script had been an invention of the Arabs in the region, why couldn't they read it? Where was the memory of this script and language? Laval calculated the precise time of the Flight and Moses's path, using landmarks described in Exodus (for instance, he objected to the idea that Memphis was the point of departure since it was not named in the biblical text). But he was mostly concerned with the riches of the Wadi Mokatteb ("written valley"). Laval came to the surprising realization, looking at the many engraved characters, that the "twenty-two letters of the demotic Egyptian alphabet can be found constantly in the Sinaitic inscriptions."[84] From this he concluded that the "Sinaites borrowed their writing from Egypt as did the Phoenicians and later the Palmyriennes."[85] The alphabet in use, he went on to say, was "popular in and little modified in Ancient Egypt" and used to write the Arabic or Aramaic language.[86] If it was not the Israelites who wrote these, then he thought it had to have been the Nabataeans. In actuality, the Nabataean alphabet is an offshoot of the Aramaic script that emerged from Phoenician and came into being about 200 BCE, much later than the Proto-Sinaitic. The juxtaposition of inscriptions in these two different scripts in the Sinai caused confusion about dates and origins.

EXODUS PILGRIMAGES: ARTHUR STANLEY AND SAMUEL SHARPE

Similar pilgrimages to recover the authenticity of biblical history motivated Arthur Stanley, Samuel Sharpe, Eli Smith, and Edward Robinson, to single out just a few of many mid-nineteenth-century individuals.[87] Smith and Robinson's work, *Biblical Researches in Palestine*, published in 1841, was based on travels in which they mapped and described ancient places.[88] In 1857, Stanley tracked the "Route of the Israelites" from Egypt to the Red Sea and beyond in *Sinai and Palestine in Connection with Their History*. His map of the area was drawn in part to discuss which mountain was the original Sinai—Jebel Musa or Jebel Serbal. Stanley was certain that the Sinai inscriptions must be older than the St. Catherine monastery, founded by Justinian in the mid-sixth century. He used Josephus's description of Mount Sinai and the Rock of Moses as working documents, testing sight lines and other physical features of the landscape against biblical accounts. He cited Diodorus and Cosmas, as well as a 1753 published account by Bishop Clayton of Sinai inscriptions and those (much referenced) by Mr. Grey in 1820. The inscriptions on which he focused are those in Wadi Mokatteb, the same area identified by earlier and visited by later scholars.

From Stanley's perspective, the inscriptions had been made by a "traveler"—an assessment that was not far wrong.

Samuel Sharpe's account, *Hebrew Inscriptions; from the Valleys between Egypt and Mount Sinai* (1875), drew on the same contemporary authorities, Professor Eduard F. F. Beer of Leipsic, whose *Studia Asiatica* appeared in 1840, and Charles Forster's several publications.[89] Sharpe's work contained drawings recorded on site, as well as drawings published by Grey in his *Sinai Inscriptions*.[90] Beer correctly supposed these inscriptions were "neither Hebrew nor Jewish, but written by Nabataeans, the inhabitants of the neighborhood, mostly in the fourth century of our era."[91] Forster, mainly by conviction, suggested on the contrary that they were "ascribed to the ancient Israelites" during their wanderings under Moses.[92]

Furthermore, Sharpe went on, a "Professor E.H. Palmer of Cambridge has had the advantage of examining the living rocks, and he is of opinion, as stated in his 'Desert of the Exodus, 1871,' that the Sinaitic inscriptions are in an Aramaean or Semitic dialect akin to Arabic; that while a few are Christian, a large portion are Pagan; that they are the work of traders and carriers, are of little worth, and have nothing to do with the children of Israel."[93] He continued citing Palmer "that inscriptions are abundant on the road from Wady Feiran to the top of Serbal."[94] Sharpe objected to the work of his predecessors, as he believed none of them had "satisfied the conditions required for us to accept their opinions as final."[95] Beer had visual transcripts but no translations, Forster had translations but no graphic transcripts, and Palmer had neither—merely observations anecdotally reported. Sharpe proceeded to provide copies of the inscriptions, transcriptions into Hebrew, and translations as well as a table of letterforms.

Sharpe analyzed the letters on the Sinai inscriptions. Like Pococke, he observed they were "often on lofty rocks," up high, not easy to reach.[96] Sharpe believed the forms had been pen-made first, then carved. Sharpe estimated that the story of Exodus had been written about 1030 BCE and augmented in around 870 BCE.[97] Sharpe saw the inscriptions as embedded in cultural practices. The alphabet was as much evidence of biblical truth as it was the means of inscribing it. The rich harvest of inscriptions waited for further investigation, even as he observed that there were few inscriptions in the "centuries of quiet which the Jews enjoyed under their Persian and then their Greek masters," which would have stretched from the conquest by Cyrus the Great in 539 BCE to the arrival of Alexander about two hundred years later.[98]

Sharpe relied in part on the frequently cited drawings produced by G. F. Grey published in the *Transactions of the Royal Academy* in 1820.[99] Sharpe transcribed the inscriptions into Hebrew, letter by letter, glyph by glyph. He wrote: "It is unnecessary to remark that writings which may at first have been badly chiseled into the rock, and then after two thousand years badly copied, may now be wrongly transcribed into Hebrew letters and wrongly translated into English."[100] Nonetheless, Sharpe proceeded, fully aware that "our Sinaitic inscriptions look very unlike the Hebrew of the MSS. Which

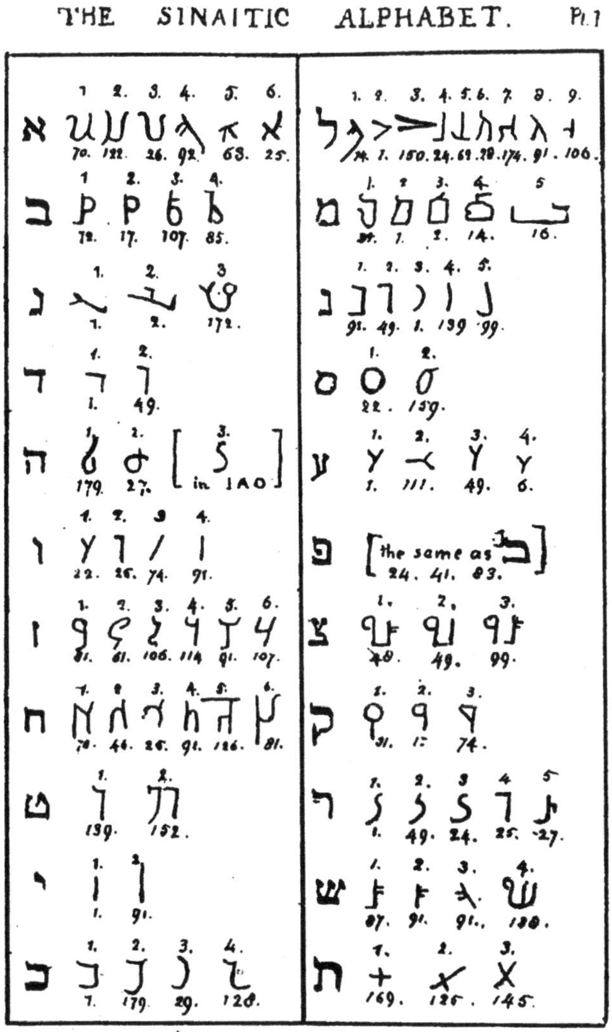

THE SINAITIC ALPHABET. Pl. I

FIGURE 7.9 Samuel Sharpe, *Hebrew Inscriptions* (1875). Public domain.

we have adopted for printed books, yet they show our present Hebrew letters in their earlier forms."[101]

Sharpe linked the inscriptions to historical events, including the Flight of Jews into Egypt following Assyrian invasion of Judea in about 714 BC.[102] He saw Mount Serbal and the surrounding valleys, including Wadi Mokatteb, as part of a pilgrimage site for Jews living in Egypt to visit the place where Moses had received the Law. By his estimation, the inscriptions were done over a long period, more than a thousand years, up through the reign of Constantine, but the texts in the "Unknown Character" contained "a pious prayer to Jehovah for the welfare of the nation."[103] He noted a linguistic distinction between Jews who were natives of Judea and used the name "Jehovah" by contrast to those of the north, the Israelites, who used the name "Elohim."[104] The inscriptions "have not the regularity of those cut by the Greeks, Romans, Assyrians, and Babylonians, people who had been used to carve on stone. They have often the easy and careless flow of penmanship."[105] These were not graffiti, like markings on the statues at Thebes, but inscriptions that fulfilled the whole purpose of the pilgrimage, made with tools brought expressly for this purpose. Sharpe's careful copies and studies of the individual glyphs in the inscriptions were meticulously done. He knew the Wadi Mokatteb had been a major transit route for successive waves of exiles who had fled the Babylonians, gone to Egypt, settled, and made pilgrimages.[106] The beginning of a fuller understanding of alphabet origins had begun. But modern concepts of history were still pitted against deeply held beliefs.

THE ONE PRIMEVAL ALPHABET: PERSISTENCE OF BELIEF

Publications of the Sinai inscriptions incorporated this material into Sunday school texts and works for general readers, as well as for specialists. One prolific contributor to this public discourse was Charles Forster. Unlike the more general texts that addressed biblical history, as per his book's title, his work focused entirely on the alphabet of "the one primeval language."[107] Forster's "primeval" alphabet is not the same as Gébelin's "primitive" one. The term *primitive* identified the category of "natural" signs, like those imagined by Court de Gébelin, that were assumed to communicate directly through a one-to-one relation between words and ideas or things. "Primeval" characters presumably gained authority from their place of historical priority, as the original letters whose age shrouded them in biblical or mystical pasts. These debates had only small kernels of historical accuracy within them and would be replaced with an understanding grounded in evidence rather than belief. Forster's was a historical paradigm even if his theories tended toward imaginative rather than rigorous methods, as per the full title of his work: *The One Primeval Language Traced Experimentally through Ancient Inscriptions in Alphabetic Characters of Lost Powers from the Four Continents Including the Voice of Israel from the Rocks of Sinai: And the Vestiges of Patriarchal Tradition from the Monuments of Egypt, Etruria, and Southern Arabia* (1852).[108] A preacher in the Cathedral of Canterbury, he was determined to demonstrate the "truths of Revelation" including the reality of a "Single language before the Flood."[109] Such an attitude harkened back to earlier paradigms such as the Confusion of Tongues and other biblical narratives, and Forster even struggled to reconcile cuneiform inscriptions with those of the "Rocks of Sinai."[110] He had immersed himself in the extant literature and was conversant with the texts of Carsten Niebuhr, Georg Friedrich Grotefend, Austen Henry Layard, and other scholars. Still, he suggested that Assyria, Babylonia, and Persia were interesting only as the biblical Land of Captivity.

Forster dismissed many of the linguistic premises on which other scholars were working to study and decipher ancient inscriptions. He thought that Henry Rawlinson's use of Sanskrit and Zend to translate ancient Persian was a waste of time.[111] He was also convinced that if the Sinaitic inscriptions were the work of the Israelites, they must contain records of the Exodus. Armed with these two principles, Forster freely invented decipherments to suit his purposes. For him, the alphabet was almost oracular, a means through which to access Divine truths. This put him into conflict with figures like Eduard F. F. Beer and others whose knowledge of ancient languages exceeded his own. They had a more astute sense of the broad historical period in which these inscriptions—cuneiform from Behistun and others from Arabia, the Sinai, and elsewhere in the region—had been produced, while Forster wanted them to be read as the work of a single generation, to be the "autograph records of Israel in the wilderness."[112]

One detail that provoked the greatest contention was whether the use of the sign of the *t* in the form of a cross indicated Christian authorship of ancient inscriptions. Beer argued this position, while Forster refused to allow that the *t* was exclusively Christian in its meaning or its use. Forster's tracing of the "one primeval alphabet" was driven by belief first and evidence after. His use of archaeological research was channeled into preexisting arguments. For instance, in looking at the inscriptions, he saw an image of an animal that might be a horse, a goat, or an ass. This led him to discussion of the ass as a symbol of rebellious Israel, and he cited a passage in Jeremiah 2:23–24 to prove it: The "Lord, that brought us up out of the Land of Egypt, that led us through the wilderness, through a land of deserts and through a land of drought and of the shadow of death, through a land that no man passeth through, and where no man dwelt? Thou art a swift dromedary traversing her ways, a wild ass used to the wilderness."[113] Thus, by a series of associations, from a drawing of a nonspecific animal to his interpretation to a passage of the Bible, he arrived at what he called a "demonstrable decipherment." He was surprised to find "not a single text of the Old Testament," "contrary to every natural anticipation," which suggested to him the inscriptions were written before the Pentateuch.[114] But the majority of inscriptions had, at their outside, a combination of characters that invoked "the people," a phrase identified with the concept of Israel (a notion that others returned to later).[115] Because he believed that the alphabet had to be the letters of Moses, their existence in engraved rocks must confirm scripture.

As it turned out, Forster was interpreting Nabataean inscriptions that were much later than the period to which he wished them to be attributed, carved closer to the beginning of the Common Era. Their crude informality is now interpreted as showing their authors were "the 'country cousins' of the Nabataeans of Petra," who were writing in the second and third centuries.[116] It was half a century before the Proto-Sinaitic inscriptions could be definitively sorted from the Nabataean ones and the locations in which each was found also given more detailed analysis within the context of other archaeological evidence. For this, Flinders Petrie played a crucial role.

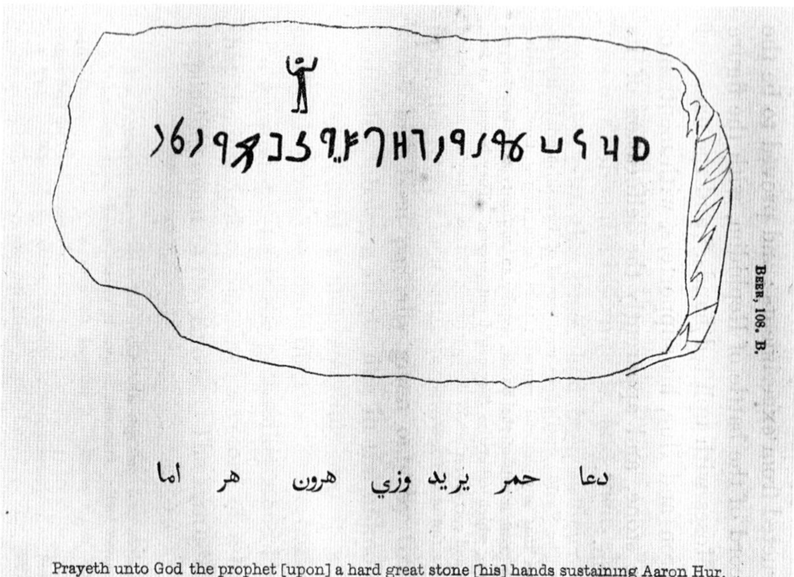

دعا حمر يريد وزي هرون هر اما
Prayeth unto God the prophet [upon] a hard great stone [his] hands sustaining Aaron Hur.
BEER, 108. B.

FIGURE 7.10 Charles Forster, reproducing Eduard F. F. Beer, in *The One Primeval Language* (1851). Public domain.

PETRIE'S WORK AT SERABIT EL-KHADIM

In the winter of 1904–5, Flinders Petrie spent four months in the area of Serabit el-Khadim in the southwest Sinai peninsula where turquoise had been mined during several crucial periods—from 1910 to 1764 BCE and again from the sixteenth century BCE to 1139 BCE.[117] Work in the mines was carried out in part by Semitic speakers who had been hired, captured, or brought as slaves from the North, or, as the area was termed, "southwest Asia." Petrie's *Researches in the Sinai* was published in 1906 and contained exhaustive photo-documentation, site information, and a detailed analysis of the culture whose remains he had engaged.[118] Petrie's discovery of inscriptions at Serabit el-Khadim provided a crucial foundation for epigraphic and paleographic study.

Researches detailed every aspect of the expedition as carefully as the account at Tell el-Hesi had recorded the excavation of that site more than a decade earlier. The preface contained pragmatic advice about the costs of renting camels, securing guides and protection, the benefits of shipping flour from England, and other matters. Petrie acknowledged his reliance on the geographic surveys completed with support from the Palestine Exploration Fund, though he noted that having exhausted its funds for his work, he had gone to the Sinai in part seeking a sight where "copying" rather than excavating would drive the work. Petrie's colonial biases were evident throughout in his disparaging remarks about the character of the local people—even though without them none of the work could have proceeded.

The existence of a temple at Serabit el-Khadim had first been noted by Carsten Niebuhr in the mid-eighteenth century, and after Petrie's excavations, the site was visited by expeditions from Harvard, Tel Aviv University, and others into the present, resulting in numerous publications of the inscriptions.[119] But among the many discoveries was a small red sandstone sphinx with an early alphabetic inscription. This find made the Sinai expedition crucial to alphabet historiography because it contained "writing peculiar to the region some centuries earlier than the Exodus."[120] Petrie's wife, to whom he gives credit, seems to have been the first to notice certain rock inscriptions in a previously unrecognized script. These were the same as those on the sphinx.

Much has been made of the sphinx inscription, and Petrie connected it with other inscriptions found on the site, concluding that "it is a definite system, and not merely a scribbling made in ignorant imitation of Egyptian writing by men who knew no better. The repetition of the same five signs in the same order on the figure and on the sphinx from the temple, as well as on three of the tables over the mines a mile and a half distinct, shows that mere fancy is not the source of this writing."[121] The text is a Semitic prayer to Ba'al, and the writing is often characterized as graffiti because of its crude quality. Petrie dated the inscription to about 1500 BCE through association with a piece of pottery found on the site (mine L) and by the use of the red sandstone, associated exclusively, according to Petrie, with Tahutmes III. Petrie had his own framework for reading the evidence: "I am disposed to see this as one of the many alphabets which were in use in Mediterranean lands long before the fixed alphabet selected by the Phoenicians. A mass of signs was used continuously from 6,000 or 7,000 B.C.

FIGURE 7.11 Sphinx from the Serabit el-Khadim, discovered by Hilda and W. M. Flinders Petrie (1904–5). © The Trustees of the British Museum. Material reproduced with permission.

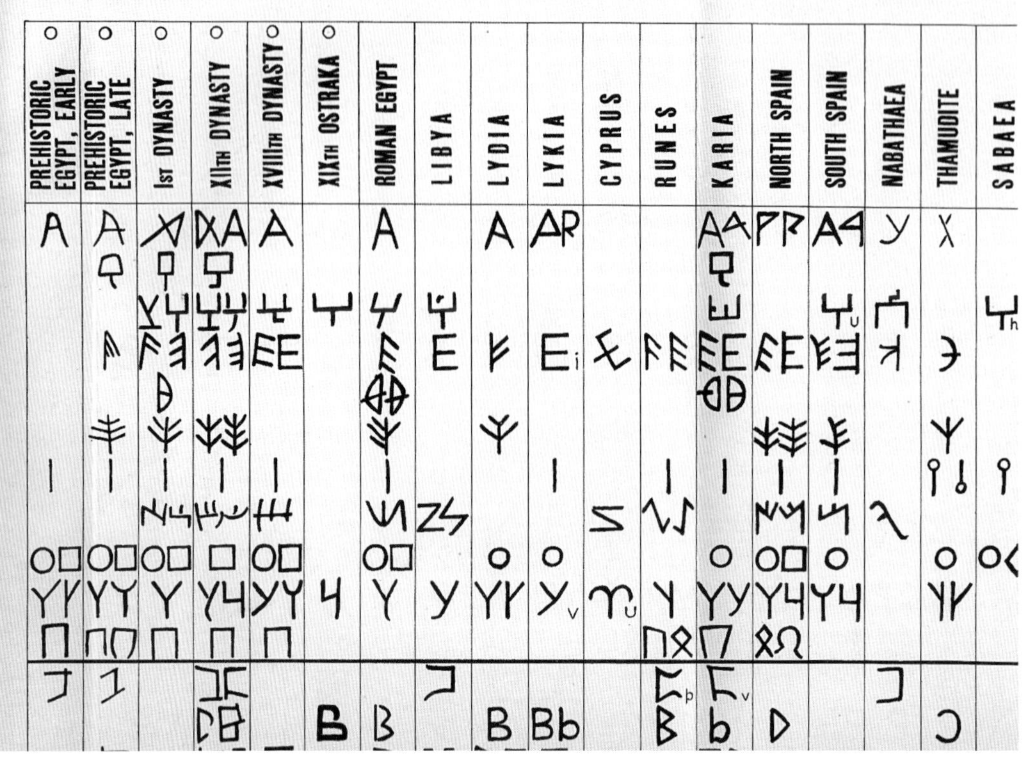

PREHISTORIC EGYPT, EARLY
PREHISTORIC EGYPT, LATE
Ist DYNASTY
XIIth DYNASTY
XVIIIth DYNASTY
XIXth OSTRAKA
ROMAN EGYPT
LIBYA
LYDIA
LYKIA
CYPRUS
RUNES
KARIA
NORTH SPAIN
SOUTH SPAIN
NABATHAEA
THAMUDITE
SABAEA

FIGURE 7.12 W. M. Flinders Petrie, *The Formation of the Alphabet* (1912), detail from table. Public domain.

until out of it was crystallized the alphabets of the Mediterranean—the Karians and the Celtiberians preserving the greatest number of signs, the Semites and Phoenicians keeping fewer."[122] Petrie's dates were off. The sphinx is now assumed to have been made closer to 1800 BCE and the assignment of an early diffuse set of signs, Petrie's personal theory, did not find acceptance—nor is there evidence for any such early set of writing or systems. But he made one final important observation, "that common Syrian workmen, who could not command the skill of an Egyptian sculptor, were familiar with writing at 1500 B.C., and this is writing independent of hieroglyphics and cuneiform."[123]

THE FORMATION OF THE ALPHABET

After the Sinai expedition in 1904, Petrie conceived a unique theory of alphabet formation. Prevailing scholarly opinion still held that the alphabet had emerged in Canaan, consolidated into linear Phoenician in the northern coastal cities, and then then spread. He admitted that the "traditional view of the derivation of the Western alphabets from the Phoenician fitted well enough to most of the facts then known" a generation earlier.[124] Published in 1912, his *Formation of the Alphabet* suggested a model

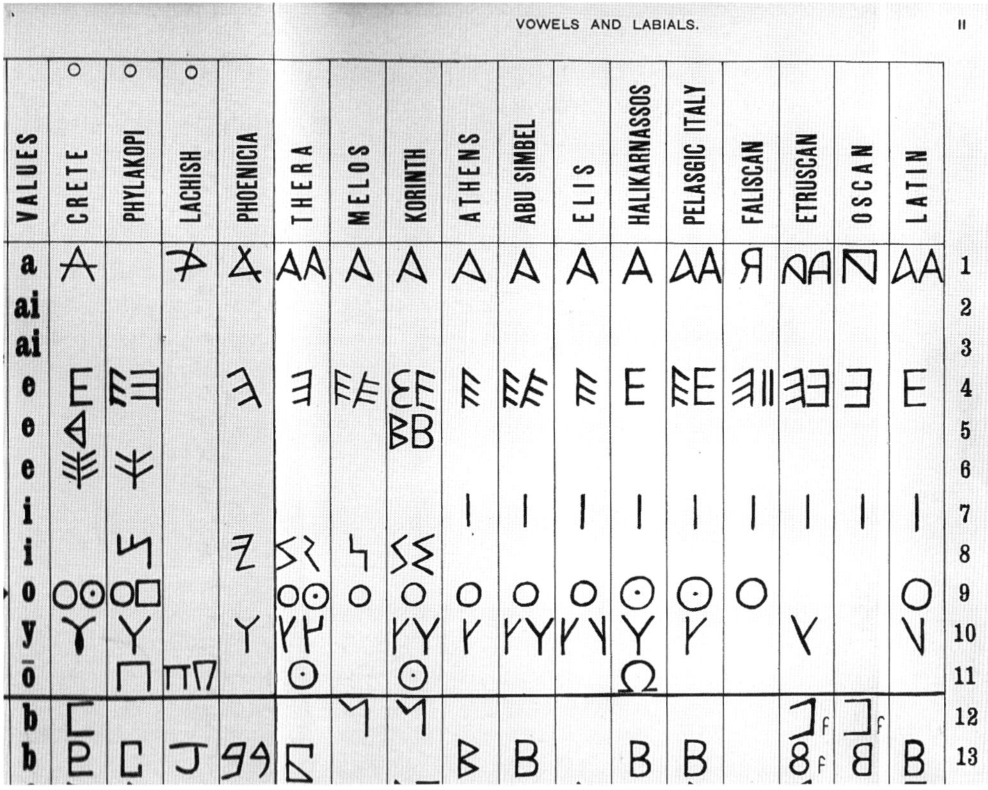

of cultural exchange and circulation as the basis of the alphabet's origins and development.

The tables in Petrie's publication made his argument clear. Geographic distribution of early forms of the letters was, for him, evidence for multiple sites of evolution into mature forms. He believed that the alphabet had emerged, coalesced, from a set of signs in sites around the Mediterranean through processes of cultural exchange and contact: "The point of view here presented is not that of a systematic alphabet, invented by some single tribe or individual in a developed civilization."[125] Petrie believed this early signary was: "On the contrary, it appears that a wide body of signs had been gradually brought into use in primitive times for various purposes."[126] Petrie observed that the signs used in many locations exhibited different degrees of sophistication and developmental distance from each other. For him this meant that if there were a common source, it had to have been encountered at different moments and modified along a whole variety of different lines of change. These had gradually become a set of standard signs. Intriguing as the notion was for its concept of an emergent system, rather than the cultural diffusion of an already fixed set of signs, it did not match the empirical evidence—which clearly tracked inscriptions to a Phoenician source. What Petrie's work did show was that the process of distribution and standardization took time, and took place in successive waves and points of contact, so that the scripts that arrived in the Iberian Peninsula, in the Italian one, in the islands of Greece, and in Asia Minor shared common ancestry but had their own careers in reaching mature form.

He suggested that "it must always be possible that the Phoenician alphabet is descended from some utterly lost, non-Egyptian system of writing, traces of which may someday turn up."[127] He thought more attention should be paid to the relations of one alphabetic script to another. He took Philippe Berger's study of the Iberian alphabet as his example, noting that the borrowing had to have happened early, since the forms of the characters resembled ancient Phoenician quite clearly. But within the Iberian alphabet other signs appeared that resembled those of the Greek alphabet. The compound nature of the evidence worked against a single line of simple derivation from the Phoenician in his opinion. He believed he had found material that was "older and far more widespread than that of the Graeco-Phoenician world" that required a rethinking of the entire field. All this speculation depended on notably unreliable dating.[128]

Petrie proposed that there had been about sixty signs in the original signary and that about forty-four of these could be found in Egypt in a pre-alphabetic and pre-hieroglyphic condition. Other letters displayed distinct provenance. He knew the Phoenician *tzade* had no precedent in prehistoric Egypt, but he saw a direct connection with a Cretan hieroglyph he believed was probably added to the signary between 1500 and 1000 BCE. This dating was consistent with the specific time period he imagined was necessary for this sign system to form.

Petrie believed that the earliest signs were from "when drawing was of the rudest" and simple marks served to "satisfy the mind" before "more exact copies of forms were thought needful."[129] More evidence was mustered by the fact that though Eastern forms in Arabia and Western forms in the Mediterranean had much in common, their features were not part of the Phoenician signs from which they were supposedly derived. For evidence he showed ten signs shared by a geographically distributed range of scripts, none of which were in the Phoenician. They even appeared, he believed, in the Greek alphabets, which argued against a single source.

In summarizing his work, Petrie organized a signary for each area in which alphabetic writing was found and compared them formally. He took into account the distinctions between media of production, noting that some differences among signs were the result of tendencies toward rounder forms in pen and brush writing, such as long tails and strokes in brushwork. Clay marks tended to be short straight lines, and chisel cutting resulted mainly in square forms and also straight lines. In the final analysis, he arrived at northern Syria as the source point for the "first arrangement" of the signary that remained "embedded in our own alphabet."[130] Thus, despite his Egyptian investigations, Petrie did not fully grasp the importance of the Sinai inscriptions.

MID-TWENTIETH CENTURY

Throughout the 1920s and 1930s, various European, British, and American excavation teams turned up many new inscriptions. David Diringer was able to draw on this growing substantial corpus for his highly regarded 1948 publication, *The Alphabet: Key to the History of Mankind*. He organized the archaeological evidence into three groups following a periodization scheme he had outlined in 1943, in his article "The Palestinian Inscriptions and the Origin of the Alphabet," acknowledging the recent contributions to knowledge.[131] Though noting the value of the Proto-Sinaitic inscriptions in creating a link to the later Iron Age developments, Diringer was particularly keen on addressing the "ten known Canaanite" inscriptions. The drawings give a sense of how obscure the signs were, the challenges they posed to decipherment, and the attention that each of these objects garnered. The image illustrating these objects contains a key showing the ways each glyph had been interpreted by six different scholars. The first three items included the Gezer potsherd found in 1929, Shechem stone plaque found in 1934, and the Lachish IV dagger, found in 1934, published between 1936 and 1937. These he assigned to the Middle Bronze Age: sixteenth–fifteenth centuries BCE.

He dated the second group to the fourteenth century BCE: the Tell el-Hesi potsherd, found in 1891 by Petrie; the Tell el Ajjul pot, found in 1932; and the Beth Shemesh ostracon, discovered in 1930. These were presented with the same amount of detail, drawing on the authority of multiple scholars. The third group from the second half of the thirteenth century consisted of the Lachish ewer, found in 1934, for which eleven readings by individual scholars were registered. The Lachish II bowl, Lachish III censer-li, and a final Lachish bowl had all been found between 1934 and 1936.[132] All of these had been found in Palestine, to use Diringer's language, and the thorough examination of the signs was essential to assessing whether they were linked to the Sinai inscriptions. Diringer did not feel the evidence supported a "missing link" theory—the signs on these Proto-Canaanite artifacts were not themselves sufficiently unified to show a single line of derivation, nor did they exhibit clear resemblance to the Proto-Sinaitic inscriptions.[133] Through these modest but expertly studied objects, Diringer weighed the evidence for the development of variations of alphabetic script in Bronze Age Canaan between the sixteenth and thirteenth centuries—the crucial time gap in development.

RECENT DISCOVERIES

Discoveries relevant to the origins and development of the alphabet are not finished. In the last four decades, major finds have contributed to changed understanding. These include the Ketef Hinnom amulets of inscribed silver, found in a tomb in 1979, and the Tel Dan Stele, found in 1993 or 1994 in northern Israel, among other objects and fragments.[134] Dated to the ninth–

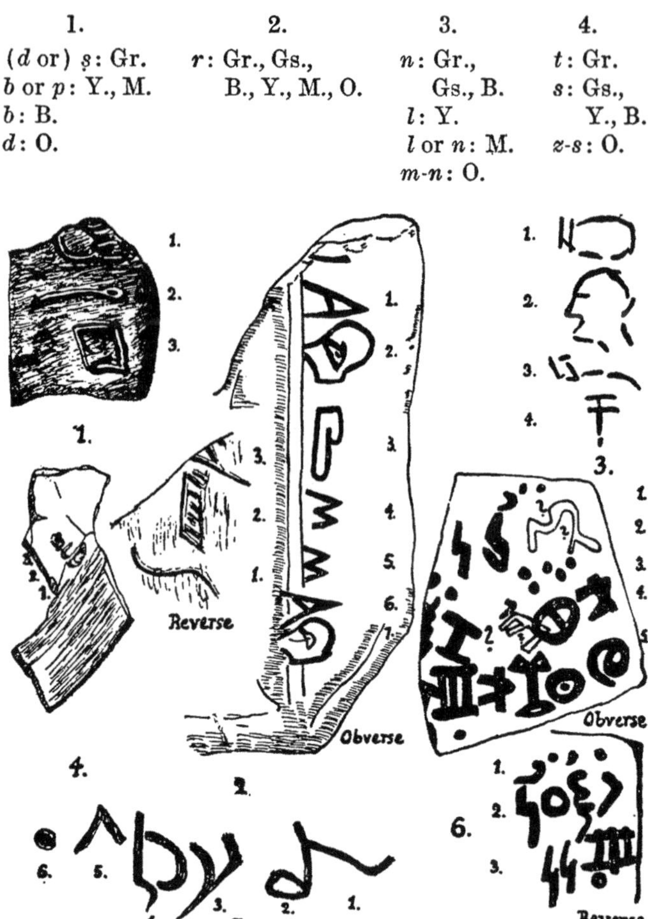

FIG. 1. 1. Gezer Potsherd (c. XVIII-XVII cent. B. C.). 2. Shechem Stone Plaque (c. XVII-XVI cent. B. C.). 3. Inscription Lachish IV (Dagger) (c. 1700-1600 B. C.). 4. Tell el-Hesy Potsherd (c. XIV cent. B. C.). 5. Tell el-ʻAjjûl Inscription (c. XIV cent. B. C.). 6. Beth Shemesh Ostracon (c. XIV cent. B. C.?), according to Yeivin and Maisler.

FIGURE 7.13 David Diringer, "The Palestinian Inscriptions and the Origin of the Alphabet" (1943). © 1943 American Oriental Society. Material reproduced with permission.

eighth century BCE, the stele is incised in a well-executed Aramaic script and language. The inscription exhibits clear evidence of a practiced hand and a regular script produced by a professional scribe. The letters have an evenness to them that shows they are made by someone well versed in their production. This is an inscription by someone using writing, not inventing it.

The Zayit stone, found in 2005, dated to the tenth century BCE, is a limestone boulder with a Paleo-Hebrew abecedary. The alphabet appears to be complete, but the characters appear in a nonstandard order.[135] It was found in the Guvrin Valley some thirty miles southwest of Jerusalem in the lowlands area of ancient Judah and is considered by scholars to be part of the transitional scripts that may have developed from Phoenician in central

FIGURE 7.14 Tel Dan Stele, dated to 800 BCE. Oren Rozen, CC BY-SA 4.0, via Wikimedia Commons.

and southern Canaan. The stone is evidence of broader literacy in the administrative centers of this region at the beginning of the first millennium BCE. But determining the specific identity of the inscription within the multiple variants of scripts in the region raises questions about whether it is the earliest example of Paleo-Hebrew, a form of Phoenician, or a version of South Canaanite.[136] These questions will remain unresolved unless more evidence surfaces on which to make definitive conclusions.

In October 2008, at Khirbet Qeiyafa, in the Elah Valley, west of Jerusalem, an object bearing the name Ishba'al (Eshball) was discovered and dated to between 1020 and 980 BCE on the basis of context and references in the inscription. The name Ishba'al was connected to the history of King Saul in the Book of Chronicles, where, as Saul's son, he appears as David's rival for the throne.[137] Study of such objects raises questions about how much argument a single fragment can support.

In 2012 an inscription was discovered by the archaeologist Eliat Mazar in the south wall of the Temple Mount. Known as the Ophel Pithos, the fragment of a ceramic jar contains five complete and several fragmentary letters that were clearly inscribed before the object was fired and dated to the eleventh–tenth century BCE.[138] The type and shape of the pot, the source of the clay, and the location of the find all factor into how the inscriptions are read and dated.[139] Such finds ignite immediate sparks and provoke lively exchanges among scholars keen to position the object within its possible histories.

CONCLUSION

Tracking the alphabet to its origins, if such a task could even be accomplished, meant finding multiple sites of inscription and trying to piece them together into a coherent narrative. This is a very different task from trying to discover Troy or any other site that is fixed in a particular location.

Once a framework of archaeological recognition and chronology was established, objects that were found in Egypt, throughout the Levant, into Syria, on Cyprus, and around the Mediterranean could be classified in a unifying scheme. One eighth-century BCE Phoenician seal was unearthed in Ireland, for instance, and a Punic inscription was identified in Malta in the nineteenth century.[140] All these finds displayed versions of the alphabet after it had stabilized into the form spread by the Phoenicians along their far-flung trade routes after about 1000 BCE. Regional differences and contributions were varied. By the 1920s, archaeological discoveries in Syria, Lebanon, Jordan, and other parts of the region dramatically altered the number of sites and materials available for study. This work continues into the present, and each discovery has potential to rework the basic models of the emergence of alphabetic writing in the Levant in the second millennium BCE.

Archaeological methods have changed since the "modern" period to which the breakthrough discoveries described here belong. Stratigraphic reading has been modified in recognition of palimpsest-like conditions in which layers interpenetrate each other rather than remaining discrete. These conditions are brought about through successive reuse in the course of historical development as well as through disturbance to sites—few sites have survived fully undisturbed across millennia. Innovations in digital imaging introduce noninvasive techniques for study of materials, as well as for reconstruction into legible form.[141]

Archaeological methods and discoveries shifted the concept of the alphabet into that of a concrete historical object that had come into being through a diffuse geographic and cultural process of exchange. The alphabet ceased to be a *given* and became a thing *made* by human beings within specific cultural circumstances located in particular geographic places and times. Old concepts persisted, and paradigms only slowly lose their force. Throughout the nineteenth century, and even into the present, scholars with a deep investment in the Old Testament as literal history persist in interpreting the archaeological evidence within that particular frame. In many cases, it seems easier to shape evidence to serve belief than to change belief in response to evidence.

EIGHT

Reading the Early Alphabet

Epigraphy and Paleography

RECENT EVENTS

In 2014, a tiny fragment of ancient pottery was found in a site at Megiddo, in northern Israel. On it were two letters that appeared to have been painted with a brush about three thousand years ago. In archaeological terms, the site was associated with "an Iron IIA context," thus dating it to somewhere between 1000 and 925 BCE.[1] The discovery of this small bit of evidence prompted two prominent scholars in the field of Semitic epigraphy, Benjamin Sass and Israel Finkelstein, to publish a paper updating their previous work on early alphabetic inscriptions.[2] Just two letters were enough to justify the portentous suggestions of their title, "The Swan Song of Proto-Canaanite in the Ninth Century BCE [. . .]."[3] Sass and Finkelstein argued that the script on the fragment provided a significant clue to the "transition from Proto-Canaanite to cursive writing"—in other words, the point at which early script forms became mature within a variety of communities and practices.[4] The level of detail in their assessments gives an idea of the maturity of alphabet studies.

The two experts, Sass and Finkelstein, demonstrated dramatically that a single small scrap of paleographic evidence, read at a fine-grained and detailed level, could alter the historical picture. Just two letters, one only partly visible, provided the full extent of the inscription on the jug fragment. The particulars are highly technical, but the gist is that a combination of archaeological techniques (dating of the strata, identification of materials, knowledge of ceramic production techniques of the period including metallurgy) and paleographic ones (discernment of the stroke weights and sequence, analysis of the orientation of the inscription, ability to identify writing materials such as brush and paint) allowed the letters to be declared "diagnostic." In other words, the tiny sample is indicative of a crucial stage of development that connects scripts in the Sinai to the south with adaptation and differentiation of alphabetic letters in Canaan in the northwest. Geography, as well as chronology, factors into the significance of such inscriptions.

Sass and Finkelstein contrasted the two Proto-Canaanite characters, identified as *beth* and *he*, to what they believed to be contemporary and earlier instances of the same letters—all of which had been carefully classified by date, site, shape, orientation, and stroke weight by Semitic epigraphers (including Sass).[5] This led them to adjust the date at which Proto-Canaanite script spread geographically in the first half of the ninth century BCE and became the distinct emerging West Semitic form.[6] The bit of pottery, with barely two letters, changed the chronological model of alphabet transmission and modification in municipalities of the early Iron Age in ancient Canaan.

How did Semitic epigraphy and paleography evolve to the point of such nuanced complexity that a minute scrap of evidence could be of dramatic importance in analyzing the historical record? The highly specialized work of these disciplines began in the eighteenth century as distinctions among Proto-Canaanite, linear Phoenician, and Proto-Sinaitic scripts gradually became established through paleographic analysis.

MODERN PALEOGRAPHY AND EPIGRAPHY

The work of paleographers and epigraphers is responsible for taking the generalized idea of the "origin of the alphabet" and linking it to specific pieces of explicit and concrete evidence. Almost four thousand years after it occurred, the early development of the alphabet is finally verifiable, countering mythic, legendary, biblical, vague, or imagined tales with empirical science and scholarly investigation. Paleography and epigraphy began as decipherment, attempts to read signs and make sense of ancient texts. This developed into a systematic study and organized inventory of the signs themselves using typological sequencing methods borrowed from archaeology combined with the study of the cultural conditions of the production of written forms.

Reading the actual inscriptions posed—and still poses—many challenges. The physical signs were often obscure, partially worn away after thousands of years. Individual characters could often be identified only with difficulty and uncertainty. Before scripts were standardized around 1000 BCE, characters sometimes faced one direction, sometimes another, or were arranged in a vertical order rather than a horizontal one, making their sequence unclear. To be read as texts, the inscriptions must be linked to ancient languages. These languages, also, had their own stages of development and differentiation within national territories or cultural groups—for example, ancient Moabite needed to be distinguished from Elamite or Canaanite through gradual alteration from common linguistic roots.

Paleography is the study of handwritten marks made with brush or pen. Epigraphy is the study of inscriptions in hard surfaces like stone or clay. The two are related in their careful attention to the specific shape, stance, and stroke patterns of characters. Modern paleography, as noted in the discussion of antiquarians, was inaugurated by Jean Mabillon. Many of the same formal techniques used to study characters in potentially fraudulent documents became useful for the study of historical inscriptions. Formal evidence alone is not sufficient to positively situate an inscription in a historical context, but historical arguments without evidence are mere speculation.

By contrast, epigraphy had its roots in the curiosity of intrepid travelers to foreign lands trying to read and decipher inscriptions on ruins, rocks, monuments, and other objects of antiquity. The study of classical *texts* in manuscript and print had continued unbroken from antiquity, but the formal, typological study of Greek and Latin *inscriptions*—which were plentiful—was only codified after the seventeenth century.[7] Semitic epigraphy was largely a product of the nineteenth century, prompted by archaeological discoveries. While the paleographer's work mainly deals with documents and the epigrapher's with artifacts, a sharp distinction cannot be made between their methods. The epigrapher sometimes has the advantage of archaeological context to assist in establishing the language of a text, its cultural milieu, period, and meaning, while the paleographer relies heavily on typological analysis and provenance of a document.

Both disciplines share a reliance on an "eye for form" celebrated by one of the towering twentieth-century figures in the field, Frank Moore Cross.[8] While historical knowledge, biblical archaeology, and linguistic expertise are crucial to these disciplines, before any text can be read its signs have to be identified and distinguished, one from another. Given the partial and damaged nature of evidence, like that of the Megiddo potsherd, this is not a simple task. Visual reading of the actual signs remains the foundation of paleographic and epigraphic work.

Epigraphic and paleographic methods *concretized* the alphabet, studying each inscription within a *systematized typology* of characters. The epigraphers are the forensic experts of alphabet history, and their contribution renders the history concrete as a more complex, distributed process of adoption and local modification of scripts.

Eighteenth-century scholars, such as Charles Toustain and the Abbé

Barthélemy, made the first steps toward Phoenician and Semitic paleography.[9] Gradually, the discovery of multiple developments in the history of writing in the West—cuneiform, Cypriot syllabaries, Linear A and B, and Egyptian hieroglyphic and hieratic scripts—began to expand knowledge of the processes by which the alphabet had come into being. In the nineteenth century, pioneering work was done by Georg Grotefend, in deciphering cuneiform, important as background, and by Wilhelm Gesenius, in studying Phoenician inscriptions.[10]

Successive generations of scholars have pieced together a several-thousand-year history across the broad geographic swath of the ancient Levant with a smattering of evidence. Only about fifty Proto-Sinaitic inscriptions have been identified, many consisting of only a few characters. A more replete corpus of about three hundred Proto-Canaanite and early Phoenician linear inscriptions constitutes the evidence of the Northwestern Semitic scripts. This is why the Megiddo inscription noted above was so significant. The slow, careful inventory of glyphs on each known inscription was the contribution of the nineteenth- and twentieth-century paleographers and is still ongoing.[11] In the twenty-first-century context, this erudite examination of objects sometimes gains an assist from digital techniques capable of extracting features from evidence so faded, eroded, or damaged that it would not reward the efforts of even the most expert scholar without the aid of computational processing.

Though we now have considerable historical evidence, discussion of *what it is evidence of* often depends on who is making an argument. The study of alphabet history did not proceed without partisan issues and politics. Into the present, the reading of ancient inscriptions is framed within points of view that adhere to beliefs as well as methods, and the drive to reconcile empirical evidence with traditional—particularly biblical—narratives continues to cause controversy and division among scholars.

EARLIEST ATTEMPTS AT PHOENICIAN STUDIES

Questions about the identity of the Phoenician language began to occupy scholars in the sixteenth and the seventeenth centuries, including Joseph Scaliger and Samuel Bochart. At the time, they had little evidence with which to work. The first authentic Phoenician text to be found on what was the original homeland was the Eshmunazar sarcophagus, discovered in 1855.[12] But inscriptions around the Mediterranean that provided evidence of early script forms began to be noted and analyzed, even though many were of much later date than the tenth-to-ninth-century BCE letterforms spread by the Phoenician traders.

As had been the case with "ancient" or "original" scripts, the search for "Phoenician" had its mythic dimensions. A famous example is an inscription purported to be Phoenician described and pictured in various seventeenth-century publications of the so-called Emerald Tablet, also known as the Tabula Smaragdina, of Hermetic Wisdom. This tablet's text was of appropriately obscure origin and had appeared in Arabic and Latin works in the Middle Ages associated with esoteric traditions. Isaac Newton produced a translation of the work and it remained celebrated as a source of ancient knowledge.[13] However, this textual transmission was not linked to any specific physical original. When rendered in illustrations, the tablet took on various forms. An engraving from a 1606 rendering by Heinrich Khunrath depicted it as a giant rock crowned by fire inscribed in Latin and German with references to Hermes Trismegistus.[14] But when rendered in a 1667 publication, by the German alchemist Wilhelm Christoph Kriegsmann, it bore an inscription in characters meant to suggest Phoenician or Paleo-Hebrew letters. The engraved plate and title page of Kriegsmann's *Hermetis Trismegisti Phoenicum Aegyptiorum sed et aliarum Gentium Monarchae Conditoris sive Tabula Smaragdina* identified Hermes Trismegistus as the founding monarch of the Phoenicians, Egyptians, and other ancient

HERMETIS
TRISMEGISTI
PHOENICUM ÆGYPTIORUM
Sed et aliarum Gentium
MONARCHÆ CONDITORIS
ſive
TABULA SMARAGDINA
à ſitu temerariiſq;
nunc demum priſtino Genio
Vindicata per
WILHELMUM CHRISTOPHORUM
KRIEGSMANNUM.
DEUTER: XXXIII. vers: 13.14.16.
Benedictum eſt à DOMINO terræ ejus pretioſo
Coeli fructu, Rore; et ex abyſso cubante infer-
ne: pretioſo fructu proventuum Solis; et
pretioſo fructu influentiæ Lunæ: pre-
tioſo deniq; fructu terræ, ubertate-
q; ejus.
Adjectum eſt
Teſtamentum Arnoldi de Villa Nova

FIGURE 8.1 Wilhelm Christoph Kriegsmann's 1667 publication of the *Tabula Smaragdina*. Note the sigil-type letters with their open circles, referencing a mystical tradition, and the square, more linear ones. The forms of the letters are a variant of Paleo-Hebrew. Public domain.

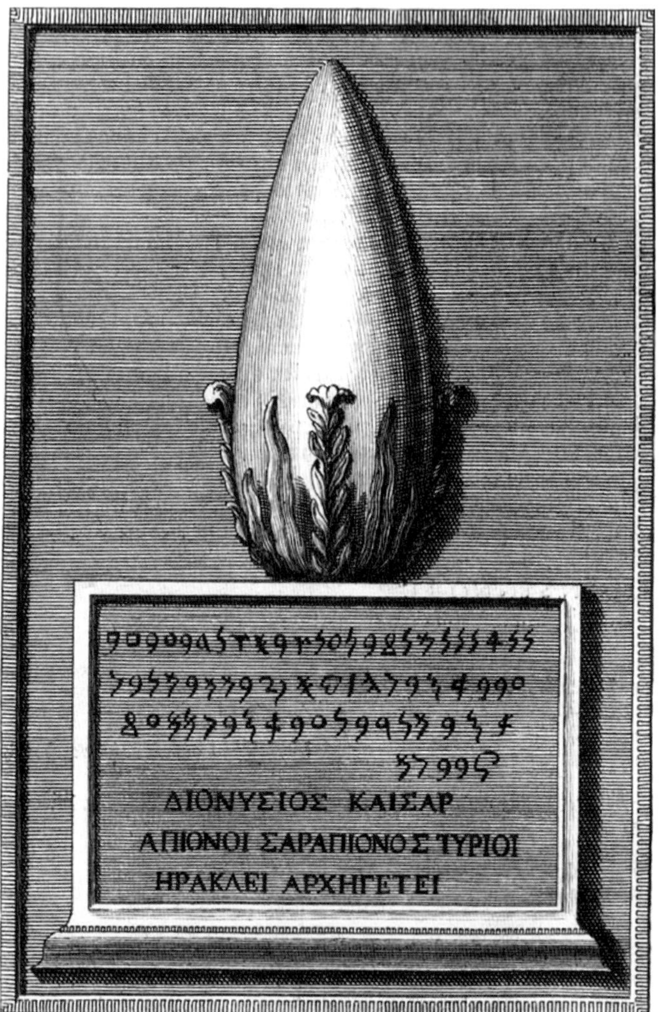

FIGURE 8.2 *Inscriptio Melitensis prima*, according to Guyot de Marne (1735), from Lehmann, "Wilhelm Gesenius" (2013). Public domain.

people.[15] Kriegsmann claimed to have restored the original of the tablet, and his glyphic versions of alphabetic letterforms lent authenticity to his claim. The writing is not Phoenician, but Kriegsmann likely drew on various Paleo-Hebrew inscriptions from coins and exemplars in compendia of scripts, to lend an air of authenticity to his image.[16]

FIRST DECIPHERMENT: THE ABBÉ BARTHÉLEMY

The first authentic Phoenician inscriptions identified were on two marble objects found in Malta in 1694. Known as the Cippi of Melqart, or Inscriptio Melitensis Prima Bilinguis, they were first noticed (though details of the discovery were not documented) by Ignazio de Costanzo and published in an engraving made by Guyot de Marne several decades later, in 1735.[17] The

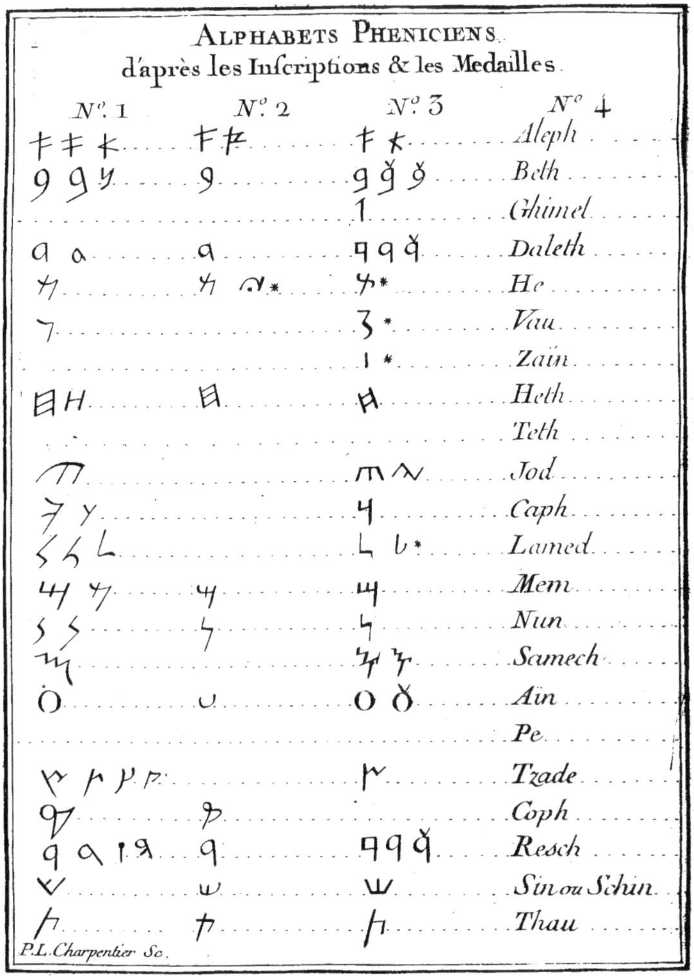

ALPHABETS PHENICIENS
d'après les Inſcriptions & les Medailles.

N.° 1 N.° 2 N.° 3 N.° 4

Aleph
Beth
Ghimel
Daleth
He
Vau
Zaïn
Heth
Teth
Jod
Caph
Lamed
Mem
Nun
Samech
Aïn
Pe
Tzade
Coph
Resch
Sin ou Schin
Thau

P.L. Charpentier Sc.

FIGURE 8.3 L'Abbé Barthélemy, "Reflexions sur quelques monumens phéniciens et sur les alphabets qui en résultent" (1758). Source: gallica.bnf.fr / Bibliothèque nationale de France.

bilingual inscriptions in Greek and Phoenician letters are now dated to the second century BCE.

Attempts at their translation came slowly. Confusion about the unfamiliar individual characters persisted, as did absence of knowledge of the Phoenician language.[18] But in 1758, the Abbé Barthélemy presented a paper on the Cippi to the French Royal Academy of Inscriptions titled "Reflections on some Phoenician Monuments and on Their Alphabets," which included a careful paleographic analysis of the letterforms.[19]

Barthélemy began his paper by reviewing the state of Phoenician epigraphy. He noted that Scaliger and Bochart had given the same name to the Phoenician and Samaritan alphabets, which he (rightly) considered a mistake. (Samaritan, derived from Paleo-Hebrew, had emerged around the sixth century BCE and was thus a later development than Phoenician.) In the eighteenth century, Edward Bernard and Bernard de Montfaucon had associated the Samaritan letters with those found on Punic (North African) and Phoenician medals. This Barthélemy also found problematic, in part because the readings these scholars had produced were not based on observation of actual monuments but on reproductions. In addition to the Maltese inscriptions, Barthélemy cited those identified by his contemporary Richard Pococke found in Cyprus (some dating from the eighth century BCE and later). Finally, he fixed his attention on the Maltese plaques, first describing several unfaithful copies of the inscription and mistranslations by Charles Toustain and others. Noting discrepancies among the various published images, Barthélemy decided to go and see the plaques himself, writing to the French antiquarian Comte de Caylus in advance for permission to take impressions of the inscriptions.

With this evidence, Barthélemy was able to read the inscriptions as texts by Phoenicians who had been thrown off course in their travels, landing at Malta, where they made a dedication to Herakles. While his decipherment of the text has been superseded, and though his use of biblical references introduced questionable vocabulary, Barthélemy correctly identified sixteen of the seventeen Phoenician characters present, aligning the letters, sounds, and names in his table.[20] Interestingly, in the text of his publication, Hebrew fonts were used to represent the Phoenician letters. This substitution was in part occasioned by the fact that Phoenician printing fonts did not exist—who would have cut them and for what purpose? But it reinforced the idea that modern square Hebrew, though a much later invention, was close enough to the ancient Phoenician to serve for transcription of the text. Barthélemy's efforts put Phoenician epigraphy on a solid footing.

THE PIONEERING SYSTEMATIZER: WILHELM GESENIUS

In the introduction to his publication *The Antiquity of the Greek Alphabet* (1975), P. Kyle McCarter traced the development of Phoenician epigraphy in parallel to that of Greek and Latin. McCarter began by noting the work of German scholars who initiated the publication of the complete record of existing classical inscriptions. The *Corpus inscriptionum Graecum* was organized initially by August Böckh and appeared in sequential volumes beginning in 1828. Such large-scale scholarly undertakings would be the model for comprehensive scholarship and provided the foundation on which systematic script comparison could take place. Before this publication, the evidence was scattered in sites, collections, and miscellaneous locations.

The publication of the first handbook on Greek epigraphy followed a little more than a decade after, authored by Johannes Franz in 1840, *Elementa epigraphices Graecae*.[21] (Greek grammars had of course been in existence since antiquity.) But study of the ancient Greek inscriptions, important though it was, could not address the origin and early development of the alphabet.

The term Phoenicians (*foinikes*) was actively revived in the eighteenth century. The word is linked to Cadmus in the bibliographic tradition that cites Herodotus as well as the excerpts of an ancient historian, Sanconiatho, preserved in Eusebius. In the Bible, Canaanite was the inclusive term. John McClintock, author of the 1891 *Cyclopedia*, noted that the name Phoenician did not occur in the Old Testament and was present only in three passages in the New.[22] The term was never one of self-identification by the people in the region (who called themselves "Kana'anim," or Canaanites). The idea of the Phoenicians provided a convenient identity for the creators of Western writing. Located in the right place, they were ambiguous regarding religious affiliation. Semitic speakers but not Jews, they were entrepreneurial and settled, not nomadic or tribal, with developed urban centers. They were adventurous rather than agricultural, could be portrayed as intrepid, embodying the values of a developed ancient culture able to sell purple dye, wood (cedars from Lebanon), glass, textiles, and wine. They imported metal, slaves, spices, gems, and animals. Their trade routes were considerable, and they connected Arabia and India with trading centers around the Mediterranean and even as far, perhaps, as Britain.[23] They moved goods, many of which they did not produce themselves, through systems of exchange. That included the alphabet, which though only partly a Phoenician invention, could still be associated with these maritime adventurers instead of with nomadic tribes or desert settlers.

Archaeology in the regions around the major cities of Tyre, Byblos, and Sidon only matured in the late nineteenth and early twentieth centuries. And, to reiterate, almost no new physical evidence had appeared between Barthélemy's meticulous mid-eighteenth-century study and the work half a century later of Wilhelm Gesenius, whose name became synonymous with Phoenician epigraphic studies. Gesenius's monumental *Scripturae linguaeque Phoeniciae monumenta quotquot supersunt*, published in 1837 in Leipzig, is all the more remarkable and important for this reason.[24] McCarter credits the work with having "inaugurated the science of Semitic epigraphy."[25]

Gesenius had published a Hebrew grammar in 1813 that remained a major reference in the field for generations.[26] Turning his formidable intellect to what were to be the founding studies in Phoenician, Gesenius brought the same techniques of morphological and formal analysis that informed philology, with its careful study of sound change and word forms, to the study of inscriptions. He knew that analysis of formal features could never be divorced from an understanding of languages and their history, but that an essential element of the expertise required was to read inscriptions and codify their signs. When and where these letters had originated was not a question he was in a position to answer, but drawing on his expertise as a Semiticist, he could analyze the structure of the language and the conventions for its inscription.

Gesenius's volume was over five hundred pages. In his first chapter,

Gesenius provided a history of Phoenician writing so far as it was known. He was not given to speculation. His history began with Punic inscriptions in northwest Africa and others found around the Mediterranean and included bibliographic sources for its study (a useful profile of the state of scholarship at the time). An examination of these sources reflected the up-swelling of interest in ancient inscriptions that had been part of late eighteenth-century antiquarian study. Works by the Abbé Barthélemy and John Swinton, beginning from about 1750, were core references, with Jacob Rhenferd's 1706 work cited as one of the earliest to identify examples of Phoenician scripts. Gesenius had scoured the pages of every extant antiquarian publication to locate evidence, and in his second chapter, he detailed all the regions and time periods in which Phoenician inscriptions had been found. His inventory referenced monuments and collections in Athens, Carthage, Sardinia, Britain, Sicily, Italy, and other sites. Through this effort, he distilled descriptions of each letter of the Phoenician alphabet. His final volume contained engraved images of sherds and ostraca as well as careful drawings of the letters from these sources. The work is encyclopedic, and it established a systematic approach to the inventory of letterforms.[27]

McCarter noted that Gesenius had had to rely on his expert knowledge of Hebrew to decipher the Semitic language of the Phoenician script, so his methods were largely formal and bibliographic.[28] Gesenius argued that Phoenician was its own language, not a blend of Hebrew, Chaldean (Syriac), and Arabic—all later variants of the older shared root in the Canaanite language. To advance his understanding of the script, Gesenius inventoried each letter in each instance in inscriptions. This approach was criticized by some later paleographers who felt the development of the alphabet could not be studied piecemeal, letter by letter, but needed to proceed from the study of whole systems and attention to the total number and variants of characters. This was not possible given the early state of Phoenician epigraphy, and later scholars all built on Gesenius's monumental efforts.

Epigraphy continued to advance as a discipline, and the designation "Semitic" signaled a shift from identification with a single people to one associated with a language group.[29] In 1833, E. F .F. Beer, a German Semiticist who was a contemporary of Gesenius, published another comprehensive volume, *Inscriptiones et papyri veteres Semitici* (The oldest Semitic inscriptions and papyri).[30] This was followed in 1840 by his work focused on Sinai inscriptions, *Inscriptiones veteres litteris et lingua hucusque incognitis ad Montem Sinai*.[31] Beer drew heavily on earlier publications and translations of Sinai inscriptions, which provided the most comprehensive and authoritative visual source material at the time. These included those of the ubiquitously cited Grey, whose numbering system, location information, and translations into Hebrew appeared in Beer's text. Beer also relied on Barthélemy and speculated on the extent to which letters were used to represent monosyllables, which he considered the basic sound elements of language.[32] This phonetic analysis would be extended by other Semiticists even as it built on earlier work by Pococke, Niebuhr, and Grey.[33]

Meanwhile, a detour in historical understanding of alphabet origins appeared when a French scholar revived an older theory of Egyptian influences through the lens of apparently modern methods.

THE EGYPTIAN HYPOTHESIS: A DETOUR BY WAY OF THE HIERATIC SCRIPT

Hieroglyphics had been known in the West since earliest antiquity. They had never disappeared from view and exercised fascination on European imagination for centuries.[34] The seventeenth-century Jesuit scholar Athanasius Kircher's extensive and synthetic research into language and its origins combined mystical and historical approaches to foster the idea that the alphabet had been invented by the Egyptians.[35] Kircher had become fascinated with Coptic, the Greek lettering that came into use in the second century BCE to write the Egyptian language. But Kircher's chief passion was for hieroglyphics. He viewed Egyptian civilization as a source for all ancient wisdom by virtue of its age and sophistication.[36] The link between Coptic and Egyptian allowed him to imagine—albeit incorrectly—a longer history of pictorial (hieroglyphic) origins for alphabetic letters. Kircher's interpretations of the hieroglyphics were speculative at best, and fanciful at worst, and he was hardly the disciplined paleographer required for this work.

Knowledge of the Egyptian language and scripts increased with the decipherment of the famous multilingual Rosetta stone, a task that took more than twenty years after the object's discovery in 1799. The successful efforts of the British scholar Thomas Young and the French philologist Jean-François Champollion made them into celebrities. Three scripts and two languages were inscribed on the massive second century BCE stone, and though the text was a quite banal administrative decree by a council of Egyptian priests, it provided the means to correlate the Greek and hieroglyphic inscriptions and to relate these to the third, a hieratic inscription. Prior to this, hieratic, the cursive shorthand form for writing Egyptian language, and demotic, derived from it, had garnered little attention. This cursive script would be misconstrued for several generations as a form of alphabetic writing. The lineage of Egyptian scripts from pictorial hieroglyphic to schematic, cursive hieratic and the more easily written demotic had no direct connection to the origin or development of the alphabet, but the discovery of a unique ancient papyrus became the basis of a sustained misconception.

In 1846, a French archaeologist, Émile Prisse d'Avennes, purchased from a local source in Egyptian Thebes a papyrus, which he published in facsimile in 1847. The hieratic script of the papyrus was interpreted as evidence of a crucial link to alphabetic notation.[37] Now dated to sometime around 1800 BCE, it was believed to be the oldest papyrus document that had ever been found.[38] Its elegant execution in a highly developed brush lettering written across eighteen surviving pages caused the Prisse Papyrus to be described by the authoritative historian of the alphabet, Isaac Taylor, writing in 1883, as the "most perfect specimen of the Hieratic writing of the early period."[39] Taylor presented the evidence for the alphabetic link from existing scholarship but also visual analysis, suggesting that the old hieratic form presented the "tails which are possessed by several of the Semitic letters."[40] The textual content of the manuscript appeared to be older than the writing, and Prisse believed that it could be dated to a period of Egyptian history before an event known as the Hyksos invasion. The Hyksos were Semitic speakers from the East who had conquered and occupied areas of northern Egypt and the Nile delta for about a hundred years beginning in about 1630 BCE. Like various Canaanite groups who had mingled earlier with Egyptian populations, they brought their language with them. The letterforms in the hieratic script were those in ordinary use for literary and commercial purposes at the time of the Semitic conquest; in other words, they were a well-established form of writing that served many purposes that the more elaborate, labor-intensive, and ceremonial hieroglyphics could not. The Hyksos were known for having preserved older Egyptian documents through copying, such as a famous mathematical treatise known as the Rhind Papyrus. The argument for hieratic adoption was that the rapidly produced ink and brush or pen strokes could be put to use to represent the newcomers' language.[41] Taylor also noted that the French scholar Emmanuel de Rougé had seen these characters "as the prototypes of the letters of the Semitic alphabet."[42]

A British scholar, Reverend I. D. Heath, was credited with first calling attention to the contents of the papyrus "in an essay published in the *Monthly Review*, 1856."[43] But it was de Rougé, the renowned Egyptologist, whose extensive study resulted in the "mémoire sur l'origine égyptienne de l'alphabet phénicien," in the *Comptes rendus des séances de l'Académie des Inscriptions et Belles-Lettres* (Accounts of the meetings of the Academy of Letters and Inscriptions; 1859).[44] A summary of his text began, "Science has preserved no doubt whatsoever about the original unity of diverse alphabets employed by Semitic people from which the derivations have extended through all of Europe and into parts of Asia. Many archaeologists have struggled to discover the prototype of the alphabet in Egypt, but have not arrived at any satisfying results. M. de Rougé believes he has found a solution to these difficulties in a study based on documents that are much older than those used by his predecessors."[45]

De Rougé was encouraged by his mentor, the archaeologist François Lenormant, who supported the hypothesis. Lenormant believed that "the Phoenicians had chosen, from the mass of hieroglyphics, a certain number of figures, such that each object presented, in the first initial of its name, contained one of the essential elements of the Phoenician language."[46] So, for instance, from the Egyptian monuments they picked an image of the head of an ox, with no concern for what it signified as a hieroglyphic, just because the word for ox, *alouph*, began with an *aleph*. This practice is known as the principle of acrophony (the name assigned to the letter begins with that letter), which gives rise to association with an image of the object named. In fact, acrophony is largely used for *mnemonic* purposes and is not evidence that the schematic shape was *derived* from a pictorial prototype. But as de Rougé built his analysis, he selected hieratic forms that represented sounds that could be matched to those of the alphabet, ignoring others. In this, he followed Lenormant's suggestion that the Phoenicians borrowed the bulk of their hieratic prototypes from the Egyptians according to their sound values, not what they had represented as schematic versions of hieroglyphics.[47] Thus the thesis, supported by another scholar, the Abbé Van Drival, was that the Phoenician letters were derived from Egyptian signs that stood for the sounds to which they corresponded, the conclusion shared by de Rougé.[48]

De Rougé formulated basic rules for his paleographic analysis: "Pick the oldest Phoenician archetype of a letter; 2) relate this to the Egyptian cursive form as old as the original Semitic alphabet; 3) the characters for comparison should be chosen from among the alphabetic ones; 4) the comparison should be established sign by sign and conform to the correspondence of sounds between the two languages; the resemblances among the letters should be approached to explain the differences in studying the circumstances that governed their respective modifications."[49] Such a systematic approach produced results that gave the visual appearance of accuracy, and his table attests to its rhetorical effectiveness—even though the premise was incorrect.

De Rougé had available to him certain new archaeological artifacts that could not have been known by his predecessors. This included the remarkable 1855 discovery of the Sidon inscription on the sarcophagus of Eshmunazar. This inscription contained a complete alphabet of well-formed Phoenician letters. De Rougé demonstrated what he believed was a correspondence between these signs and the hieratic cursive from Papyrus Prisse. But his seemingly irrefutable link was based on formal correspondence, not historical lineage or connections.

De Rougé's table made a vivid graphic argument. It suggested hieratic was the script source for the later Phoenician and then later Greek. He even went so far as to coin the term "Egypto-Phénicien" to title his tables and to state directly that the Egyptian hieratic had served as the prototype of Phoenician letters.[50] He was not alone. Friedrich Ballhorn's *Grammatography: A Manual of Reference of the Alphabets of Ancient and Modern Languages*, published in London in 1861, contained a table in which hieroglyphic, hieratic, and demotic signs, each correlated with a letter of the Hebrew alphabet, were given a place in the columns of "Oldest Characters."[51] In the absence of ancient alphabetic inscriptions, these hypotheses took hold, driven by

Alphabet Egypto Phénicien

Egyptien	Phenicien	Phénicien Archaïque	grec Ancien	Valeur	Egyptien	Phenicien	Phénicien Archaïque	grec Ancien	Valeur
				א					ל
				ב					מ
				ג					נ
				ד					ס
				ה					ע
				ו					פ
				ז					צ
				ח					ק
				ט					ר
				י					ש
				כ					ת

*N. B. Les trois signes marqués d'un * sont tirés de papyrus moins anciens.*

FIGURE 8.4 De Rougé's table showing ancient Greek, Phoenician, hieratic, Hebrew, and modern Greek letters. The graphic argument is convincing in this presentation because of the careful selection of specific schematic hieratic forms. Public domain.

a desire to identify alphabet origins with artifacts of antiquity. Other theories of alternative origins included a cuneiform syllabary, from Ras Shamra noted earlier; Cypriot syllabaries; and the Minoan scripts, Linear A and B.

CUNEIFORM REVISITED

The discussion of cuneiform is largely tangential to alphabet history, except for the Ugaritic tablets. Summarizing archaeological discoveries of the previous century in his milestone publication *The Archaeology of Cuneiform Inscriptions* (1908), the British Assyriologist Archibald H. Sayce registered the "ever-growing revelation" of the role of Babylonian culture in the Near East, stressing that there was "quite as much intercommunication" then as in the present.[52] He encouraged others to "revise our old ideas about an absence of intercourse between different parts of the ancient Oriental world."[53] Sayce also noted the remarkable recent increase in the size of cuneiform artifact collections (the massive British Museum materials had once been housed in a single small case). Sayce gave credit for first knowledge of cuneiform inscriptions to the Italian Renaissance composer and traveler Pietro della Valle, who had produced copies of a few inscriptions from Persepolis's ruined palaces.[54] He also noted that few cuneiform inscriptions had yet been published in England by the start of the twentieth century, even though the eighteenth-century Danish explorer Carsten Niebuhr had made several volumes of published materials available.[55] Niebuhr performed his own analyses in the course of trying to decipher the inscriptions, saying that in some "systems of cuneiform writing . . . only forty-two characters were employed, and he therefore concluded that the system was alphabetic."[56] Around 1802, Georg Grotefend, the German philologist central to cuneiform studies, recognized that these texts represented three different languages.[57] (Over its history, cuneiform was used for about fifteen different languages.) Sayce tracked the painstaking work by which cuneiform decipherment had advanced.[58] He documented the slow process of distinguishing syllabic from alphabetic cuneiform until it became "clear that Assyrian was a Semitic language," a point "proved to demonstration by the French scholar, de Saulcy in 1849."[59] He believed that linking the Semitic language to a set of cuneiform signs clinched the argument about the identity of the Ras Shamra signs as alphabetic. Such scholarship was still laying foundations for the understanding of cuneiform scripts and ancient languages in the nineteenth century.

At the beginning of his chapter "The Archaeological Materials," Sayce made a strong argument for archaeology as "an inductive science; its conclusions . . . drawn from the comparison and co-ordination of objects which can be seen and handled, as well as tested by all competent observers."[60] It was built on "what our German friends would call objective facts, and the method it employs is that carefully-disciplined and experimentally-guarded application of the ordinary logic of life which can alone give us scientific results."[61] He went on to put this approach in opposition to the "purely literary" methods practiced by those who seem to be incapable of even understanding what "is meant by scientific evidence."[62]

Ultimately, however, the Ugaritic cuneiform abecedary is not part of a larger continuous alphabet history. Cypriot and Minoan theses were also false leads, and their evidence was either too geographically circumscribed or else too historically removed to provide a foundation for origins of the writing in the Bronze Age Levant. The origin of the alphabet lay elsewhere. But the awareness that Egyptian hieratic scripts and Ras Shamra cuneiform had been used phonetically offered suggestive evidence of the intellectual processes in which the alphabetic notation also derived from an understanding of the sounds that composed the Canaanite and other Semitic languages.

PALEOGRAPHY AND EPIGRAPHY PROFESSIONALIZED

Paleographic work continued to advance in technical studies but also in publications with broader audiences, such as Philippe Berger's comprehensive *L'histoire de l'écriture dans l'antiquité* (The history of writing in antiquity; 1891).[63] Berger dedicated the book to his former teacher, Ernest Renan, the distinguished epigrapher, saying that it was owing to his efforts that Phoenician epigraphy, at the "heart of the history of the alphabet," can now be considered a science of the same stature as that of Greek and Latin epigraphy.[64] Indeed, Renan's important account of archaeological discoveries from the *Mission de Phénicie*, published in his 1864, added to the corpus of artifacts from Lebanon whose paucity had been noted by Gesenius.[65]

Like Isaac Taylor's 1883 two-volume publication, *The Alphabet*, Berger's work mapped the development of scripts through a summary of archaeological and paleographic efforts. Unlike their colleagues a century earlier, both Taylor and Berger eschewed the references from antiquarians (with their lineage of classical references) and instead drew extensively on the scientific publications and academic journals of professional scholars. Berger's use of photographic reproduction reinforced the tone of objectivity he brought to the presentation of evidence.

Berger treated paleography and epigraphy, not as esoteric disciplines, but as approaches that interpreted archaeological evidence through comprehensible formal methods. Berger's photographic images, carefully excised from their background, rendered artifacts with mechanical accuracy, accompanied by carefully redrawn versions of the inscriptions and expertly designed tables that called attention to particular features and comparative examples. Berger's work was and remained, like that of Taylor, a major reference work on the history of writing and scripts.

Berger began his introduction by saying, "We are now far from the time when anyone believes that the Hebrew alphabet was the most ancient form of writing and that it was given to the first man at the same time as language."[66] Myth had been replaced by science. Berger included discussion of New World writing and Chinese as independent developments and made clear that connections among the Semitic alphabet and Egyptian hieroglyphics, as well as Babylonian and Akkadian cuneiform, had not been proved.

He tracked the work of Semitic epigraphy through major efforts of German and French scholars. His starting point for Phoenician epigraphy was the Abbé Barthélemy and the Greek-Phoenician bilingual Maltese Cippi inscriptions. The text had been translated by Barthélemy "thanks to a severe method, based on minute comparison of different characters."[67] As a

FIGURE 8.5 This page from Philippe Berger, *L'histoire de l'écriture dans l'antiquité* (1891), gives an idea of the thoughtful presentation of material. The object, a near-complete text of the Ten Commandments in Samaritan, has been beautifully photographed with raking light to display the inscription. Its image has been trimmed out from the background so that it appears as a dimensional object. The transcription has been copied as carefully as possible to show the glyphs. This is followed a few pages later by a table of the Samaritan characters in contrast with other Semitic scripts. Public domain.

consequence, the Abbé "was able to disengage the study of Phoenicia from the insanities which accumulated under this rubric."[68] That phrase "minute comparison of different characters" was key for describing epigraphic methods.

Berger gave Gesenius full credit for a new comparative approach, citing his 1837 *Monuments of Writing in Phoenician Language*, but also noted that throughout the nineteenth century, more evidence had appeared to supplement the eighty-five inscriptions so meticulously studied by Gesenius. Berger also acknowledged other scholarly initiatives in the field of Semitic epigraphy, such as one in France led by the Duc de Luynes, who had given the sarcophagus of Eshmunazar to the Louvre.

After surveying the history of his field, Berger turned to more recent developments and noted that one benefit of the increased number of inscriptions was that it had made it possible "to distinguish the diverse families" of Semitic alphabets and to begin to determine their chronology.[69] His teacher, Renan, had been crucial to institutionalizing the study of Phoenician epigraphy in the decade after his initial publications in 1864 (as had courses offered at the Collège de France).[70] The decision to unite all of the

Phoenician inscriptions resulted in an international project, with contributions by Renan, de Rougé, and others. The *Corpus inscriptionum semiticarum* (Corpus of Semitic inscriptions) (modeled on the corpus of Greek inscriptions), the first volume of which was published in Paris in 1881, fully consolidated the field.[71] This collection was divided into multiple parts, each of which took up one of the major families of Semitic alphabets: Phoenician, Aramaean, Hebrew, and Himyaritic (the latter includes the southern Semitic, used in Arabia, Yemen, and other late offshoots).

Berger recognized the importance of geography and mapped these script families onto locations. He began with the fundamental recognition that Phoenician script had appeared in native soil near Tyre and Sidon and spread to multiple sites around the Mediterranean from Cyprus to Carthage and farther west. He showed that in the South of Phoenicia, the alphabet gave rise to two forms of Hebrew, one from the period of the Kingdom of Israel (after 1050 BCE), the other that of the Maccabees in the second century BCE. He also noted that the local territorial scripts such as the Aramaean had appeared in Syria beginning around the eighth century BCE, with a branch that reached south as far as Egypt in the Persian era. Palmyrene, close to square Hebrew, and Nabataean, the writing of the Aramaean nomads, Syriac, and eventually Arabic, penetrated the Sinai and the center of Arabia in the final centuries before the beginning of the Common Era. In the lower meridians, Himyaritic and Ethiopian were used before the spread of Islam introduced Arabic in the seventh century. Given the late nineteenth-century context of Berger's text, this was a complete account.

Berger knew that epigraphic methods had allowed scholars to assign dates on the basis of modifications that could be tracked in the changing shapes of the scripts. He also imagined that the alphabet had transformed more rapidly and radically than other writing. While Egyptian hieroglyphics had preserved their forms over many centuries, in part on account of their sacred quality, Phoenician writing, which was secular and common, had changed quickly in the work of scribes who valued efficiency—they wanted to lift their hands as infrequently as possible.[72] When he turned to the Eshmunazar inscription, he noted that the writing was almost entirely mature: "The letters have lost their angular and steep appearance, which they had in the archaic alphabet; they are more slanted and lean forward in line; at the same time, their tails are more elongated and adopt a uniform and regular angle; the entire alphabet starts to have a tendency towards cursive forms of writing. Archaic Phoenician letters were made of separate traits, but over time, it became the habit to make a single stroke and little by little, a curved line. This is the case for the *mem* and the *sin*."[73]

Berger called attention to minute changes in characters as indexical traces of time and place, tying his detailed and careful investigation to individual monuments and inscriptions. His language stressed the dynamic processes in which traits *disappear* or *develop* in the physical evidence. For instance, in discussing the differences between Punic and neo-Punic in-

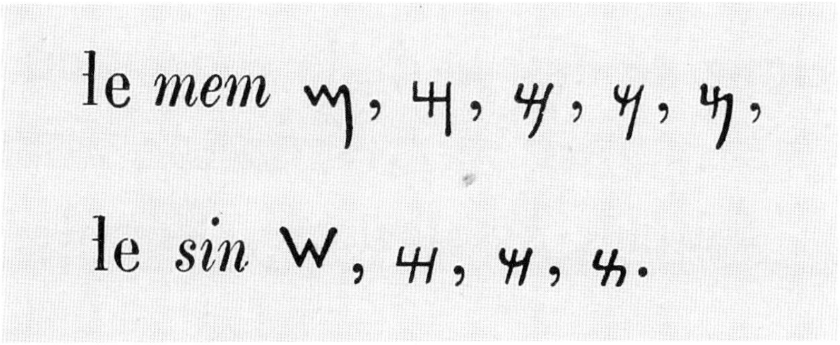

FIGURE 8.6 Detail from Philippe Berger, *L'histoire de l'écriture dans l'antiquité* (1891). Note the development of the glyphs from those with short parallel lines, like those of the *samech* on the bottom line, follows from left to right. Public domain.

scriptions, he noted details that suggested the cursive script had returned to a more lapidary state. The Neo-Punique is more angular and reduced than the Punique, though it is a later development. He also qualified this by saying that the observation might be the result of the fact that the evidence available for study was inscriptions, rather than manuscripts, and an effect of the writing medium.

When he shifted his attention to the Hebrew alphabet, Berger suggested its history could be reduced to "a very small thing" as so little evidence existed. Simply stated: "We possess almost no monuments of ancient Hebrew writing."[74] The reason was not that the Hebrews did not write—ancient accounts of conquests at the time of David and Solomon included many descriptions of steles. As early as 800 BCE, Berger suggested, a written Hebrew literature existed because of which the Jews were known as the people of the book. But the Moabite stone, discovered in 1869, remained the only significant monument of Semitic epigraphy whose script was closely related to ancient Hebrew. Again, Berger supported his arguments with paleographic detail, calling attention to certain characters in the inscription (the *hé* and the *vau*) that were particularly close to Hebrew versions and used in places where Phoenician used *alef* and *yod*.[75] On the basis of the sophistication of the Moabite stone script, Berger was convinced that there had been Hebrew writing for at least as long as Phoenician, and that by about 1000 BCE, it was well developed. His paleographic and epigraphic methods atomized the alphabet into minutiae while at the same time systematizing all existing evidence into geographically, chronologically, and linguistically integrated analysis.

SYSTEMATIC ORDER: MARK LIDZBARSKI

As a practitioner and historian, Berger had demonstrated the value of epigraphic techniques. But it was a Polish philologist, Mark Lidzbarski, whose 1898 *Handbuch der nordsemitischen Epigraphik* (Handbook of North Semitic epigraphy) provided the culminating reference work for the nineteenth century.[76] In an obituary written in 1928, Lidzbarski was described as having

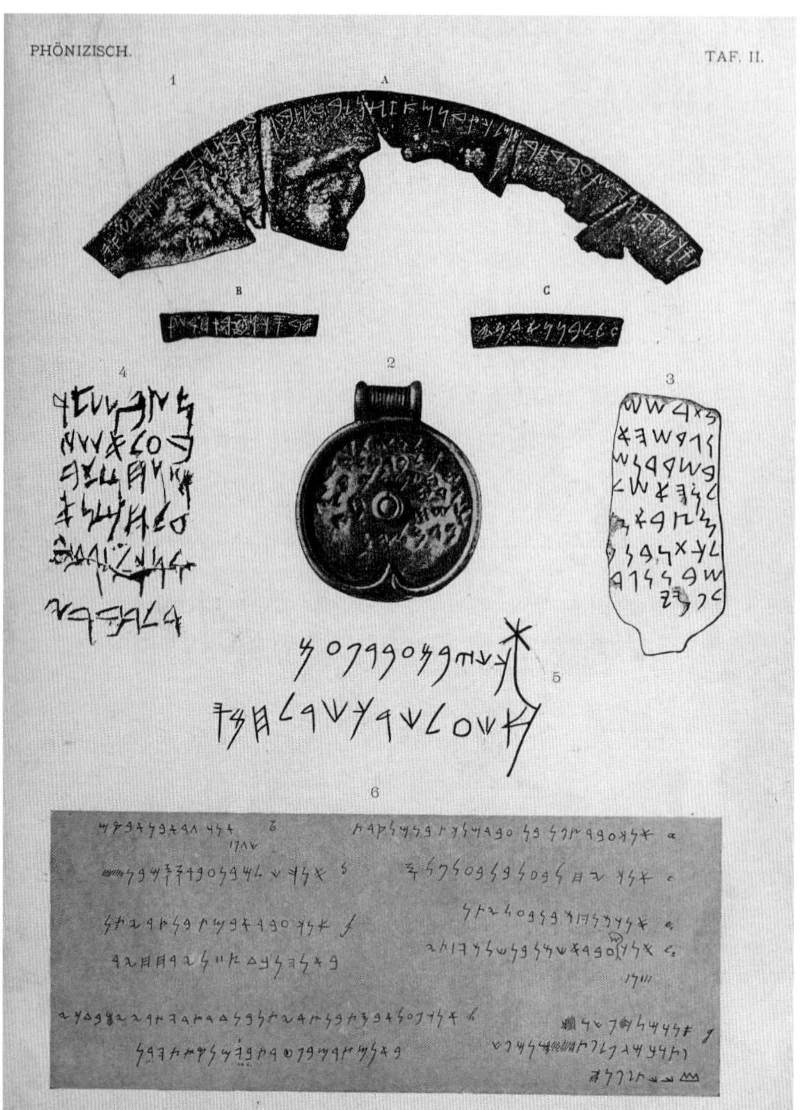

FIGURE 8.7 Mark Lidzbarski, *Handbuch der nordsemitischen Epigraphik* (1898). Images and script studies. Public domain.

put order into the mass of Phoenician inscriptions.[77] Lidzbarski's work was aimed at specialists. His presentation supported comparison among different renderings of the evidence as each group of artifacts progressed, script by script from the Mesha Stele (the Moabite inscription), to Phoenicia, Punic, old Hebrew, Samaritan, and so on.[78] Lidzbarski's comprehensive tables identified the individual sources of their scripts, making these groups clear, along with their relative age and relation to each other—and to the geographies of the ancient Near East. Nothing was generalized, every observation was particular, and the specificity of each specimen was preserved in the plates. The distance between this work and that

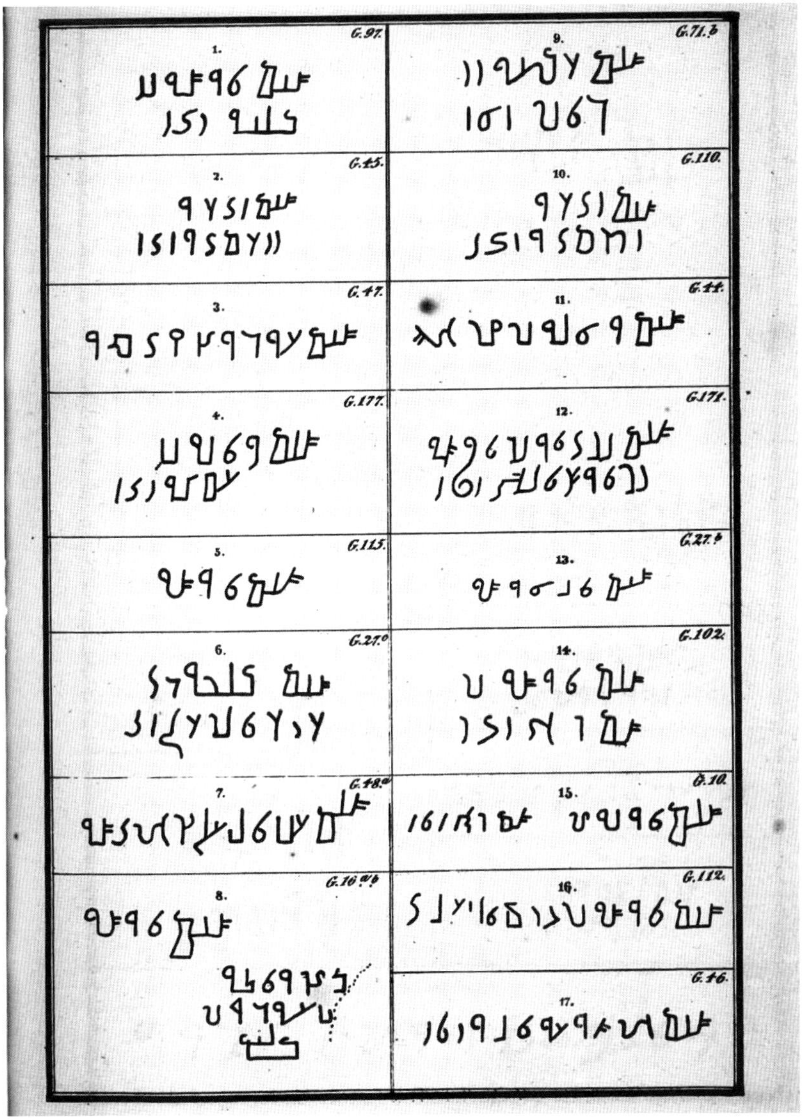

FIGURE 8.8 Eduard F. F. Beer, *Inscriptiones et papyri veteres semitici* [. . .] (1833). Copied from Grey's drawings. Public domain.

of Beer, published sixty years earlier, was dramatic. Beer had been a careful observer, and his inventory identified each inscription with a particular site and carving. But Lidzbarski, like Berger, offered accurate facsimile evidence in a highly structured format.

A NEW EGYPTIAN HYPOTHESIS: ALAN GARDINER'S CRUCIAL ESSAY

By the beginning of the twentieth century, alphabet studies seemed to have stabilized in the terms embodied in Lidzbarski's work. Clearly, an alphabet suited to notation of Semitic languages had been consolidated by the Phoenicians by about 1000 BCE and then spread by trade around the Mediterranean. The alphabet was conceived as a more or less intact entity, transmitted, adopted, and modified locally. This fit the historical understanding that Greek, Latin, Arabic, and other scripts throughout the ancient Near East were all descendants of this original set of characters. The Mesha Stele had been dated to the ninth century BCE, and the other Byblian inscriptions, particularly the crucial Eshmunazar sarcophagus, fit into this narrative. The Ahiram sarcophagus served to fix 1000 BCE as the date after which little modification of the Phoenician script occurred in the homeland, even though the alphabet changed when it was taken up by people in Arabia, Asia Minor, Greece, Italy, Spain, and North Africa. This account still did not describe the stages by which the Phoenician script or its immediate predecessors had come into being.

The inscriptions discovered by Petrie near Serabit el-Khadim, designated Proto-Sinaitic for their location and age, raised the possibility of a new thesis of Egyptian origins. The earlier Egyptian hypothesis was troubled by a number of factors, including a time gap between the sophisticated hieratic, already well formed by 2000–1800 BCE, and the appearance of a polished Phoenician script. What had happened in the intervening near millennium? And if hieratic was not the precursor of the Phoenician, then examples of early forms of emerging alphabetic writing must exist.

In 1916, the British Egyptologist Alan Gardiner published a milestone article titled "The Egyptian Origin of the Semitic Alphabet," in the *Journal of Egyptian Archaeology*.[79] He began by summarizing current research, stating that among the "unsolved problems" in the study of Semitic scripts was the original source of "the alphabet of twenty-two linear signs" that "appears upon Syrian soil" about "the tenth century B.C."[80]

Gardiner suggested that the Phoenician script was "so simple, and therefore so perfect, an instrument" that "more primitive methods of writing must have preceded it."[81] Gardiner believed that this writing had to have been modeled on the script of older civilizations in the region. A number of candidates had been put forward: Egyptian hieroglyphics (as per Kircher, Lenormant, and his pupil de Rougé) or hieratic (argued by de Rougé himself), Babylonian cuneiform (highly inconclusive given the lack of paleographic evidence that could connect its visual forms to alphabetic script), Cypriot (an early syllabary but without geographical distribution), or Cretan writing systems (the argument put forth by Sir Arthur Evans, who unearthed the various Minoan scripts, Linear A and B, which also had no geographic range). Gardiner also cited Petrie's "crystallization" argument—that the alphabet had formed from an array of signs in circulation in the Mediterranean.[82]

Gardiner took a broad view, shifting from exclusive focus on the origin of the "Phoenician" script to the wider category that preceded it, the "Proto-Semitic." He noted that in 1901, Lidzbarski had not distinguished the Phoenician from Proto-Semitic but considered it to be the common ancestor of various later scripts like Sabaean (which came into use around 500 BCE). The biggest fault Gardiner found with Lidzbarski was his assumption that because the Phoenician alphabet had not changed much after the earliest known Byblian inscriptions, it must not have altered much in the centuries leading up to that point.[83] Gardiner thought the earlier development of the alphabet had to have gone through gradual stages.

Gardiner placed considerable importance on the meaning of the letter names to establish transmission histories and focused on the question of whether these were primary (original) or secondary (adopted).[84] In seventeen cases, the names and the image from which the letters might be derived were clear—*'alf* meant an ox, *bet* meant house, etc.[85] But five of the letter names had no meaning or were highly contested even in Hebrew. He, and others, knew that the names for the Greek letters belonged to the fourth–fifth century BCE and that they were simply nonmeaningful translations of the Hebrew names. In other words, as per Eusebius (third–fourth CE), he knew they were Hebrew names "in Greek garb."[86] He was aware that the Greek letter names had allowed them to be dated to about 700 BCE and that most scholars believed that the names pointed "to the pictorial character of proto-Semitic letters" because the assumption was that if the name for *'alef* was the word for ox, the original sign must have been an ox head. This suspicion was confirmed by the fact that "the forms of certain early Semitic letters are roughly in agreement with the shapes indicated by the names."[87]

Lidzbarski, he noted, had dismissed the names and interpreted the visual features of the letters according to his own scheme—asserting that the Phoenician *delt* could have been a female breast, not a door, and so on. Gardiner remained skeptical about putting too much emphasis on the resemblance of schematic signs and pictorial images.[88] However, he still assumed that the early, primitive precursor of the alphabet had to have been pictorial or hieroglyphic—in part because of the names. In his opinion, this eliminated early cuneiform as a source since it had lost its pictorial features by 2000 BCE, leaving Minoan scripts, Hittite forms, and Egyptian. Egyptian hieroglyphics and Proto-Semitic writing shared important structural features—they did not note vowels explicitly, only consonantal values. By contrast, Babylonian and Mediterranean scripts like the Cypriot were syllabic (vowel-consonant combinations). On the basis of this phonetic similarity, Gardiner argued for connections between early alphabetic notation and Egyptian writing systems, pointing out that the geographic position of Egypt made it the most likely "school where Semites learned to write."[89] He posited Lebanon and the Sinai peninsula as the most probable sites of contact but noted that no evidence of trade with Egyptian's pharaonic culture had been found in the former. More evidence of the trade exchanges surfaced in the twentieth century, but after Gardiner's 1916 publication. In the Sinai, however, he knew that many traces of contact existed from the third through first millennium BCE.

Guided by Petrie's discoveries, Gardiner cited ten inscriptions that were not hieroglyphs that were published by the archaeologist in his *Egypt Exploration Fund* expedition (1905). These inscriptions in an "unknown script" contained signs that were not part of any Egyptian system even though they had some pictorial feature. Petrie had dated these inscriptions to about 1500 BCE. Gardiner imagined they might be as early as 1700 BCE and was convinced they were made by foreign workers who had come with the Egyptians on temporary campaigns in the Sinai. Archaeological evidence of the presence of these "Asiatics"—as people from the Levant were known to their contemporaries—was an important part of this story, since without it the difficulty of proving actual contact and opportunities for exchange was insurmountable. Semitic speakers had to have been present in Egypt, to have borrowed its writing.

Gardiner's argument proceeded on epigraphic grounds as he discerned "signs foreign to the Egyptian hieroglyphs, but answering well to the names or forms of proto-Semitic letters."[90] He continued: "In comparing the forms of some of the individual picture-signs with their earliest Semitic equivalents we can hardly fail to be struck with the ease with which the transition from the one to the other could be effected."[91] He noted repetition of certain sequences of signs that could be matched with the Semitic alphabet to spell the word "Ba'alat"—the Semitic name for the goddess called Hathor in Egyptian. The eleven inscriptions Gardiner investigated contained 150 individual signs, reducible to thirty-two different types. He could match six of these with the seventeen letters in the Semitic alphabet that had intelligible names (ox, house, water, eye, head, cross) though there were also a number of signs that had no resemblance to living Semitic letters.

From this, he concluded that "not later than 1500 BC, there existed in Sinai—that is, on Semitic soil—a form of writing almost certainly alphabetic in character and clearly modeled on the Egyptian hieroglyphs."[92] This was a crucial argument and quite distinct from the argument for hieratic. The connections between these Proto-Sinaitic signs and those of the scripts to the north in Syria, Lebanon, and ancient Canaan were still not clear, but Gardiner had firmly established the site and general date of the alphabet's origins.

FROM SYSTEMATIZATION TO TYPOLOGY

Gardiner's evidence for Egyptian influence on the early development of the alphabet was provocative, but the research was not yet complete. The time gap between Proto-Sinaitic signs and the mature, elegant linear Phoenician script remained—a period of several hundred years for which not much evidence existed.

The Minoan expert Arthur Evans had held that Linear B and A might have been the predecessors to the alphabet rather than Egyptian writing.[93]

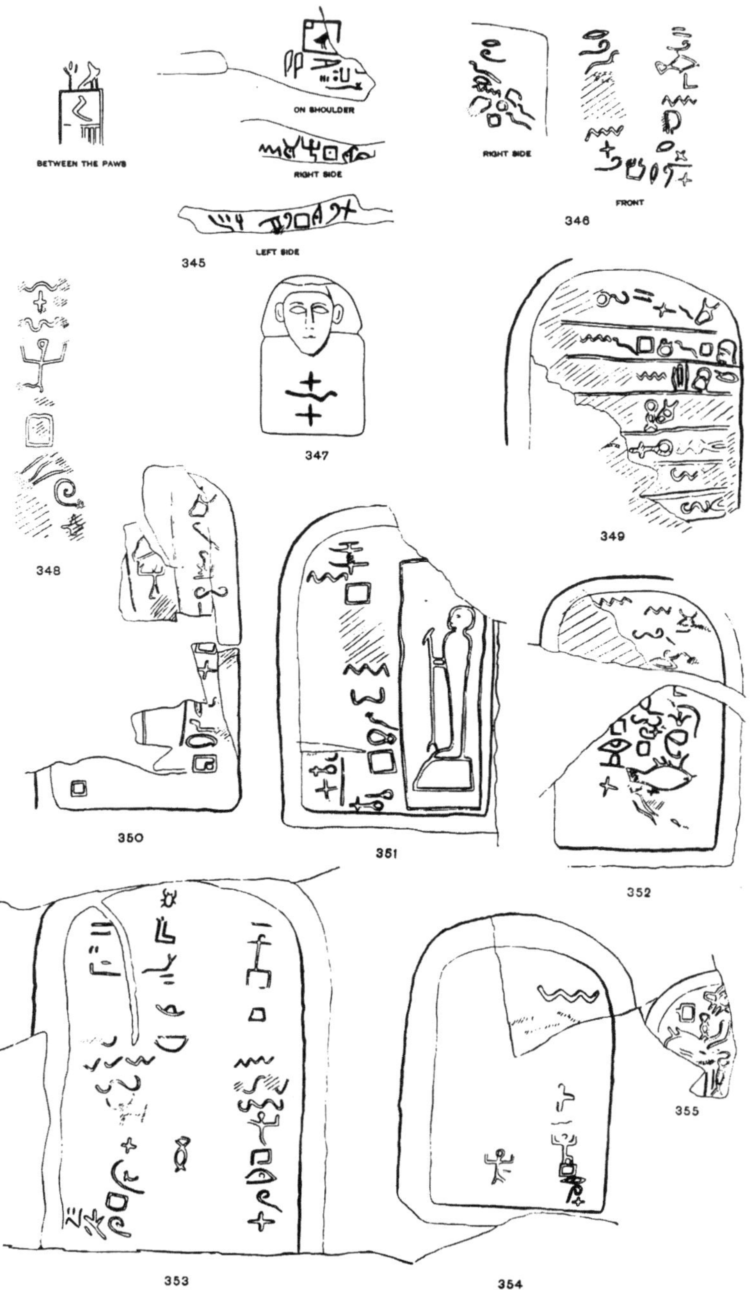

FIGURE 8.9 Alan Gardiner, "The Egyptian Origin of the Semitic Alphabet" (1916). Citing Petrie, Sinaitic inscriptions (note the head, arm, etc., in upper left) and from the Sphinx, on right. Public domain.

He saw continuity between these scripts of Mycenaean Greece and those of a later period and believed that the borrowing could have taken place as early as 1600 BCE before the so-called Mycenaean collapse around 1200 BCE. Evans saw strong formal relations between the symbols in the Phoenician alphabet and those of the scripts from Crete, but no archaeological evidence testified to distribution of the Cretan scripts beyond their home region. Petrie, writing later, saw the Cretan scripts as part of that larger signary from which he felt the alphabet had formed. But once it became clear that Linear B was actually a script form used for the *Greek* language, the argument fell apart since the earlier Phoenician script created for Semitic languages could not possibly have been derived from a later development.

Discoveries in the region of the ancient Levant slowly built the composite picture. This linked the Proto-Sinaitic scripts from the early second millennium BCE (that had been Petrie's discovery and Gardiner's focus) to the Proto-Canaanite that is the tap root of western Semitic scripts. Two crucial figures in this research were William Fox Albright, the biblical archaeologist, and his student, Frank Moore Cross, who solidified the foundations of Semitic epigraphy and paleography in the twentieth century. Both were influential teachers as well as distinguished scholars.[94]

Mark Lidzbarski died in 1928 just as Albright came of age as a scholar. Cross was a generation younger. Albright's archaeological training stressed the importance of location and dating in sites and using the formal (typological) classification of potsherds.[95] Albright went to Egypt in 1948 and, as a result, reassessed his judgment about the Sinai inscriptions, shifting the date of these to about 1500 BCE, several hundred years later than Gardiner. This narrowed the crucial gap between these early scripts and the Phoenician. Albright identified twenty-seven distinct signs for consonants in the Sinai scripts. His granular analysis of inscriptions that were partial and damaged, in which signs are often difficult to identify, was meticulous. To an untrained eye, the work of the epigrapher seems almost impossible, so unclear and worn are the marks under investigation.

Cross advanced Albright's research of the Proto-Canaanite alphabet in crucial ways, in his own work and then that of his students, among them Benjamin Sass, so that the fuller picture of origins and development became solidified.[96] Sass described Cross's importance, saying that his "far-reaching work, especially his pioneering papers of 1954 and 1967, . . . put Proto-Canaanite paleography on firm foundations."[97] In the same text, Sass repeated the observation about "the paucity of texts and their fragmentary nature" among the Proto-Sinaitic and early Proto-Canaanite inscriptions.[98] Given the distance of time and deterioration of the historical evidence, this remains the limiting factor for Semitic epigraphy.

The two crucial papers by Cross that Sass referenced were "The Evolution of the Proto-Canaanite Alphabet" (1954) and "The Origin and Early Evolution of the Alphabet" (1967). The first opened with a survey of recent finds and developments, justifying the recent revision of the dates of the Sinai inscriptions to 1500 BCE.[99] Cross noted that little had changed since Gardiner had argued in his 1916 paper that Semitic scripts had been derived on acrophonic principles from Egyptian sources. But by the 1950s important discoveries had been made in Byblos as well as ancient Palestine, Syria, and Jordan on which the development of the Proto-Canaanite script could be analyzed. Cross listed these various artifacts, which included some monumental objects, like the Ahiram sarcophagus, but also numerous modest objects—a bronze spatula, arrowheads, ostraca, and other items. Significantly, these were not monumental. Instead, these small fragments became the crucial evidence on which the development of alphabet scripts could be tracked for the period between the Sinai inscriptions and the Byblian ones from around 1050 BCE. The many modifications were distributed across the municipalities and geographies of the region and could be used to map the dissemination and transformation of alphabet script.[100] The objects cited by Cross bore great weight in establishing a clear chronology and were referenced by proper names—"the Lachish Ewer" or "the Beth-shemesh Ostracon"—because of their importance. Thus, even by 1954, Cross could confidently "discuss the general lines upon which the evolution of the script moved."[101]

The importance of these finds, modest though they were in size and number, was that they provided crucial evidence of the period between Proto-Sinaitic Egyptian origins in the second millennium and the polished scripts of the Byblian monuments around 1000 BCE, such as the Ahiram sarcophagus (specifically dated to 850 BCE). Potsherds, ewers, arrowheads, and other objects were marked with signs showing the evolution from the earliest Proto-Sinaitic through the Proto-Canaanite alphabet. These were widespread throughout the ancient Levant. By 1000 BCE this had led to the refined linear Phoenician from which, in turn, Paleo-Hebrew, Moabite, Elamite, and other Semitic scripts emerged. Marked changes in direction of scripts and orientation of letterforms, as well as features such as stroke and shape, helped date the span of development to a period between the seventeenth and the twelfth century BCE.[102] These fragments provided the crucial evidence of gradual stages of development.

In a later publication, "Early Alphabets and Pots: Reflections on Typological Method in the Dating of Human Artifacts" (1982), Cross described his methodological approach explicitly. He referenced his teacher, Albright, and the way his work had built on that of Flinders Petrie to establish a typological framework modeled on archaeological techniques that correlated formal properties and dating systems. The typological method assumes that the forms of artifacts, including scripts, change developmentally over time. This concept of "sequence dating" reveals continuity and continues to prevail in epigraphic studies, qualified by the realization that individual scribes, local communities of practice, and other factors modify any strictly linear chronology of "progress."[103] Cross stressed the need for attention to both "linguistic change and orthographic development," but he did not address cultural contexts or conditions.[104] Cross firmly established methods of formal analysis, but the questions of the specific site and moment of origins could not be answered without addressing historical circumstances. Many details remained unclear about when, where, and under what circumstances Semitic speakers had adopted a version of Egyptian writing and how long it had taken for the alphabet to spread and mature.

A DETOUR: "PHOENICIANS" IN BRAZIL

Enthusiasm for the antiquity of the Phoenicians extended estimates of their historical priority into millennia and also geographic regions that defied probability. In 1826, a stone with a "Phoenician" inscription was found by a priest, Don Joseph Galea, in Malta and interpreted by the Marquis de Fortia d'Urban as containing references to Atlantis.[105] The stone was a hoax; d'Urban's translation was based on a trail of concocted evidence and quickly discredited. But another faked inscription linked the intrepid traders to Brazil and enjoyed rather more enduring celebrity.[106] Translations of the text based on a drawing commanded a brief spurt of attention, even that of prominent paleographers at the time.[107]

A century later, Cross had an encounter with this forgery.[108] The stone inscription was supposedly found in 1872 in Parahyba, Brazil, but the stone itself was never located. However, a copy of the "Phoenician" inscription was sent to the president of the prestigious Instituto Historico e Geographico Brasiliero in 1873.[109] He, in turn, passed it to the director of the Museu Nacional in Rio de Janeiro, Dr. Ladislau de Souza Mello Neto, who published it.[110] Attempts at the time, and later, to locate the provenance of the original reached one dead end after another. The purported source, a person named Antonio Alves da Costa, proved as elusive as the original artifact. Therefore, all subsequent "translations" were based on the "copy" of the inscription. The translated text gave an account of Sidonians blown off course from Africa landing in Brazil. This gave Cross plenty of material for wry wit: "We note . . . the singular set of circumstances, that three women were aboard for more than two years with the twelve-man crew and yet there are no infants mentioned."[111] Human sacrifice, however, does appear in the text. Cross's characterization of the forgery was grounded in his specific expertise of the letterforms: "One of the striking and suspicious aspects of the inscription is its clarity."[112] The characters had somehow been perfectly preserved at the point where Neto copied them (thus suggesting that the intact inscription had survived for at least a millennium and a half without any wear or damage). Well-versed in the historiography of Phoenician inscriptions, Cross also pointed out that "every letter form is known either in inscriptions extant in 1870 or in standard charts of the Phoenician script in mid-nineteenth-century publications."[113] In other words, Cross knew the exemplars for the letters were well documented in the existing scholarship while deviations from these would have been more likely in an original inscription.

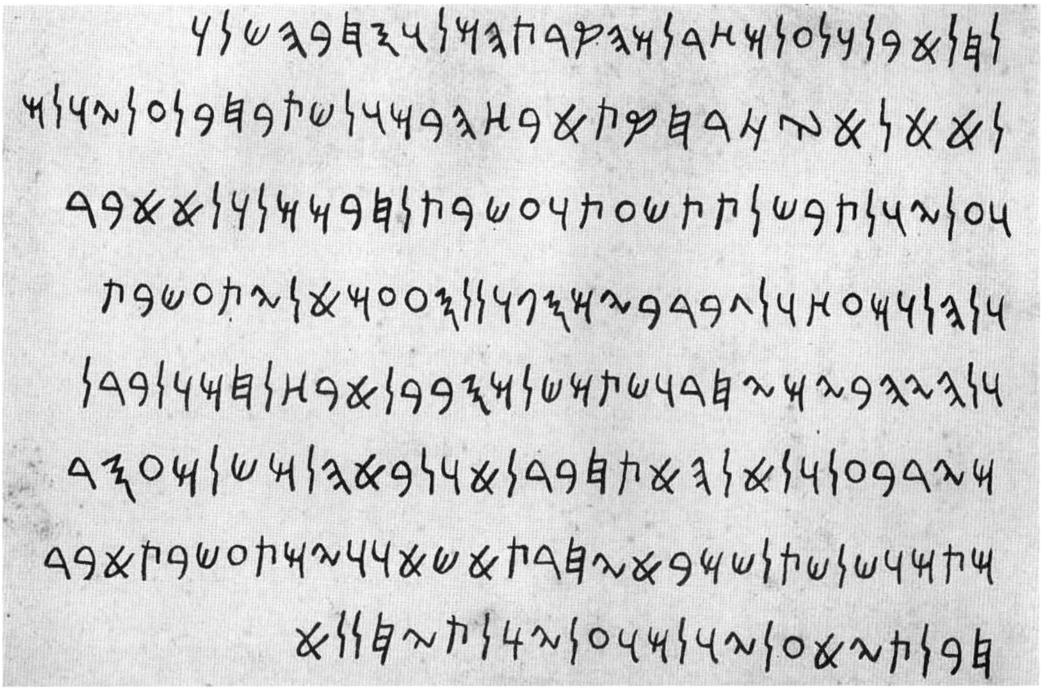

The artifact had long been discredited, and the only reason that Cross was drawn into this discussion was that in 1968 the esteemed biblical scholar Cyrus Gordon took up the cause of the inscription, arguing that he had translated it successfully.[114] Gordon's justification for the authenticity of the document came from his having received a facsimile of Neto's original. Prior to this he had only see a "garbled copy" published in 1899 (by which time the inscription had been declared a forgery by Mark Lidzbarski as well).[115] Gordon dated the script to about the sixth century BCE, a little earlier than the inscription on the well-known Eshmunazar sarcophagus. Gordon went further in his support, noting that all the linguistic "errors" in the text could be found in other early examples that would *not* have been available to a nineteenth-century forger. (For instance, the word for "man" that appears in the inscription was not attested to by any extant evidence until a 1933 discovery.) Gordon supported his enthusiasm for the thesis that America had been visited and colonized by Phoenicians by citing the highly respected New World archaeologist Zelia Nuttall, who had argued this point in 1901, though without citing the Parahyba inscription.[116] Whoever had created the inscription was clever enough to circulate it only through a copy, thus obviating any chance of testing materials, site, and archaeological and physical evidence. The epigrapher thus became the expert witness in the case.

FIGURE 8.10 The Parahyba "Phoenician" inscription from 1872. Museu Nacional. Public domain, via Wikimedia Commons.

MIDCENTURY ASSESSMENTS: IGNACE GELB, DAVID DIRINGER, GODFREY DRIVER, AND OTHERS

As the field of scholarship in Semitic epigraphy expanded, specialists, generalists, and popularizers each played roles in the production and dissemination of knowledge about the alphabet.

When Godfrey Driver composed *Semitic Writing*, based on lectures given in the early 1940s, his sources included many standard references and other inventories of the known corpus.[117] The specialization of the discipline had grown exponentially and included nearly a hundred academic journals devoted to scholarship in the field. By the time Joseph Naveh published *The Early History of the Alphabet* in 1997, fifty years later, he had yet more professional expertise on which to draw.[118] Every artifact, bit, and piece of inscribed pottery, arrowhead, bowl, or plaque had its own specialized bibliography.

In addition to the scholarly literature, two significant contributions to a broader public understanding were provided by Ignace Gelb and David Diringer. Gelb was an Assyriologist, and in *A Study of Writing* he argued for a general paradigm in which writing moved from pictographic to logographic then syllabic and finally alphabetic stages of development.[119] This linear and overdetermined sequence privileged alphabetic writing over that of other scripts and has been subject to considerable revision since its original publication in 1952.[120] Diringer, a skilled Semiticist and the editor of major reference works in Semitic inscriptions, published his classic, *The Alphabet: A Key to the History of Mankind*, in 1948.[121] Gelb and Diringer were almost exact contemporaries and came of age within a humanistic tradition of historical study that included an imperative to communicate expert knowledge to a general audience.

Driver and Diringer both struggled to reconcile the dating of the early Sinaitic inscriptions with those from Palestine.[122] Using the evidence from the Sinai dated as early as 1800 BCE as a starting point, Driver asserted that objects from Gebal (on the coast north of the Phoenician city of Sidon) also belonged to this first period 1800–1650 BCE, and he put other evidence from Gezer and Shechem (inland cities west of the Jordan River) in the same time frame. The second period in his chronology, 1700–1550 BCE, included other artifacts (the Lachish dagger and the Tell-el-Hesi pottery), "in a layer dated archaeologically before 1600 BCE," and continued with "the next period . . . approximately from 1400 BCE to 1100 BCE comprised of more artifacts from these sites."[123] This periodization corresponded with Diringer's, but the two scholars reached opposite opinions about the continuity between Proto-Sinaitic and Proto-Canaanite scripts. Driver argued for a single narrative of development in which the new evidence demonstrated that the early alphabetic forms had spread north and been modified. Diringer was not convinced. He thought this was too simplistic and reductive. In a detailed analysis published in 1943, he summarized the epi-

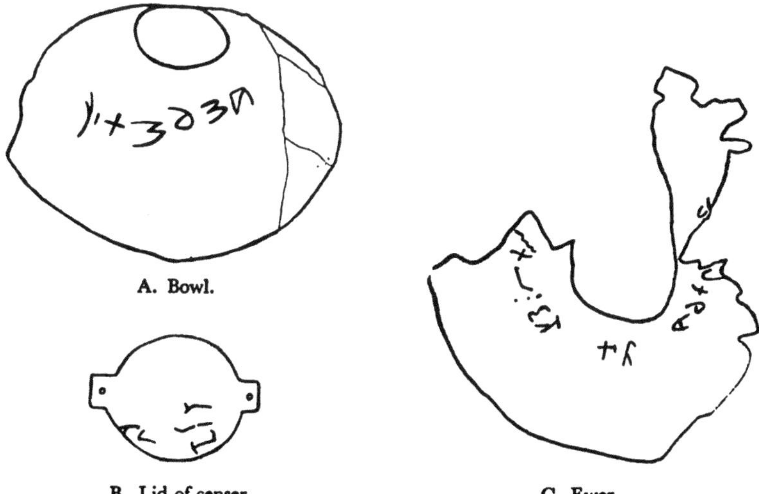

FIGURE 8.11 Godfrey Driver, *Semitic Writing from Pictograph to Alphabet* (1948). Detail drawing of Lachish potsherd. © The British Academy 1948. Material reproduced with permission.

graphic scholarship on each existing fragment, its glyphs, and texts—for which there was considerable variation of interpretation even of the letters. He concluded the evidence did not supply a clear "missing link" between the Proto-Sinaitic and Canaanite inscriptions.[124]

Driver accounted for the combination of formal continuity and difference through analysis of writing materials and their distribution. Papyrus remains had rarely been found in Phoenicia even though its import into the region from Egypt had been well known. Clay, not found in abundance in Syria or Palestine, was not used in that region. He believed the change in writing materials explained changes in the forms of the letters—more cursive pen and brush forms—an approach that has been taken up recently by scholars describing the development of cursive Phoenician scripts from forms in stone inscriptions.[125]

If the Egyptian origins and influences were clear, the advanced condition of the standardized Byblian scripts still posed a problem—no transitional stages were recorded. Even if the Sinai inscriptions were dated as late as 1500 BCE, a gap of evidence existed to 1000 BCE. Therefore, finds like the Lachish ewer dated to the mid-thirteenth century BCE (discovered in 1934 by J. L. Starkey), though modest in scale, were profound in importance. Along with other significant artifacts, they were carefully marshaled to support a single narrative of development. Driver pointed out that Albright had argued for the Phoenician alphabet to have been developed after the reduction of North Semitic sounds to twenty-two meaningful ones (the earlier Ugaritic cuneiform systems represent about twenty-nine sounds). The signs should correspond to the structure of the language since it was unlikely that language would change to match the signs.[126] The transformation of a syllabary to an alphabetic notation had no precedent and was considered highly unlikely because the structural dissimilarities were too great.

These considerations among others led Driver to the origin theory still favored today, that "the obvious place would be a district in the immediate neighborhood of Egypt occupied by a Semitic people preferably of Canaanite stock."[127] Then, this "completed alphabet passed to all the nations of the western hemisphere—one, and only one, of the gifts of the Semites to mankind."[128] The question remained of who those Semitic people were and when they had been in Egypt. They seem to have been distinct from the Hyksos and were less established and without a permanent settlement.

BENJAMIN SASS AND THE GENESIS OF THE ALPHABET

In *The Genesis of the Alphabet and Its Development in the Second Millennium B.C.* (1988), Benjamin Sass also began his study with a summary of the state of research.[129] By the time Sass was writing, major evidence, unavailable to earlier scholars, had been discovered and analyzed. In addition, as he freely acknowledged, he had the work of Cross and Albright to draw on. Sass's updated inventory consisted of thirty Proto-Sinaitic inscriptions along with about thirty Proto-Canaanite and early Phoenician ones that could be ordered chronologically with varying degrees of certainty. As Sass stated, only three methods of dating were reliable: stratigraphy and typology from a secure archaeological site, the mention of a known historic event or person, and radiometric dating.[130] The Proto-Sinaitic inscriptions he ordered by date of discovery "since no line of internal development can be discerned."[131] Sass was scrupulous in noting the shortfalls and idiosyncrasies (as well as achievements) of his predecessors. Commenting, for instance, on the earlier twentieth-century scholarship of the renowned Semiticist Hubert Grimme, he said, "He identified all sorts of things—scratches on rock, differences in the colour of the stone and shadows seen in the photographs of the inscriptions—as letters and in his system of decipherment dragged in Moses, Hatshepsut, Yahweh and Sinai."[132] Sass was more discerning.

By 2005, in *The Alphabet at the Turn of the Millennium: The West Semitic Alphabet, ca. 1150–850*, Sass had rethought the chronology of the emergence of Proto-Canaanite and its divergence into Phoenician and then Aramaic (by about 750 BCE).[133] Sass posited the significance of each formal variation according to what makes the letterforms "diagnostic." Taking for example the modification of the character for *bet* across the Byblian inscriptions, he showed how careful observation supported the dating and identification of the scripts. His methods of direct collation included the study of individual glyphs on each inscription. Sass provided details of the geographic location of these, noted where artifacts resided if they had been removed, described the specific surface or object on which they were inscribed (on a wall, a rock, an object, a plaque) and the place found (in a mine dump or on a temple path). His observations were fine grained and detailed. For instance, in one case where Albright saw a "bet," he saw a possible "resh," suggesting that to insist on "bet" "involves ignoring the line(s) to the right."[134]

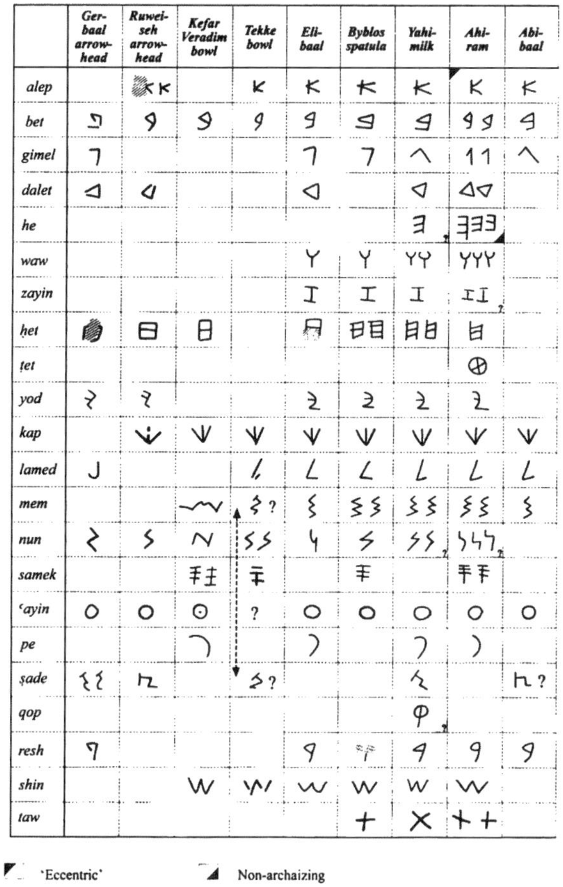

'Eccentric' Non-archaizing

FIGURE 8.12 The "diagnostic" letters from Byblian inscriptions, from Benjamin Sass, *The Alphabet at the Turn of the Millennium: The West Semitic Alphabet, ca. 1150–850* (2005). Material reproduced with permission.

This level of detail is essential in reading the physical evidence. He carefully distinguished Proto-Canaanite examples (Northwest Semitic scripts) from Proto-Sinaitic (southern) ones.[135] He still felt plagued by the "paucity of texts" which made it impossible to fully decipher or describe the progress of these scripts.[136]

Key among the objects Sass considered were Petrie's finds at Serabit el-Khadim, those referred to as "Proto-Sinaitic" scripts. Sass noted that Petrie had *not* imagined these could be part of the history of Phoenician scripts—the semipictographic signs seemed too remote geographically and formally from the linear alphabet used on the Levantine coast to the north. Gardiner, as per the discussion above, had dated those Proto-Sinaitic inscriptions to about the nineteenth or eighteenth century BCE. Cross had revised them, to about 1500 BCE or later. Sass determined that the context of this invention depended on the presence of Semites—as military mercenaries or in some other temporary capacity—in the Sinai. Noting that no evidence of permanent settlements existed in the terrain near the turquoise mines, Sass correlated three attested periods of known contact and determined that the cultural borrowing that resulted in the alphabet must have occurred during one of these.[137] According to Sass, the Sinai inscriptions "float" in the period from 2000 to 1300 BCE. If assigned the earliest date of cultural contact, the period of the Egyptian twelfth dynasty (1991–1783 BCE), then the "paleographic standstill" of several hundred years before the appearance of Proto-Canaanite derivatives of the script would have to be explained.[138] No evidence of intermediate development or continuous use of the alphabet was found in the Sinai after its initial invention. Five hundred years of "silence" seemed improbable.

Sorting through the evidence, Sass reached the conclusion that the only way to overcome the "severe stumbling blocks for all previous attempts to date the genesis of the alphabet" was to recognize that it was "born shortly before the gradual loss in Palestine in the 13th–12th centuries of the 'Proto-Sinaitic' look and transition to linear shapes of the letters."[139] Because no inscriptions in Palestine "can be dated with confidence before the 14th century," he believed that the most likely scenario was that "Asiatic [*sic*] mercenaries in the Egyptian army were exposed to Egyptian writing practiced by the scribes of their units" deployed in the deserts and working in quarries and mines in the fourteenth century BCE.[140] The Egyptian scribes "took literate Egypt with them" and thus the conditions for the origin of the alphabet "existed beyond the urban, lettered centers" in the cultural exchanges among these groups.[141]

Sass integrated the existing evidence into a systematic timeline that included historical events. The dates of the Byblian inscriptions were adjusted. By shifting the Ahiram sarcophagus closer to 1000 BCE, for instance, the amount of time between Proto-Sinaitic and mature Phoenician by way of Proto-Canaanite shrank. As one of the earliest inscriptions in a fully developed Phoenician script, it is considered the terminus ad quem for standardization of that script.[142]

Sass drew on the same materials as his predecessors—a "minute Gezer sherd discovered in 1929, which showed three letters that resemble the proto-Sinaitic script" which "aroused interest in inverse proportion to its size."[143] Ostraca found at Beth Shemesh (dated to about 1150–1100 BCE), and a dagger, ewer, and bowl found in Lachish, all found in the 1930s, "laid the foundation of Proto-Canaanite paleographic research."[144] But he had additional objects as well, such as the arrowheads found at El-Khadr (near Bethlehem), first published in 1954, which exhibited a clear transitional stage between Proto-Canaanite and Phoenician and dated to the thirteenth–twelfth century BCE.[145] Cross had suggested that "the brief texts of the arrowheads provided secure readings of alphabetic signs at precisely the period of transition from the older pictographic (Proto-Canaanite or Old Canaanite) script to the Early Linear (Phoenician) alphabet."[146] Sass continued to revise his earlier work in the light of ongoing discoveries. Of these, none had as much dramatic impact as the Wadi el-Hol inscriptions in the mid-1990s.

WADI EL-HOL—HISTORICAL CIRCUMSTANCES

The Wadi el-Hol, a valley in the Egyptian desert, was once a major area of activity and trade. The discovery of the inscriptions there in the 1990s was the single most dramatic recent discovery in alphabet studies.[147] The discovery was made by John and Deborah Darnell who in 1993–94 noticed graffiti-like inscriptions on the rock walls of an old caravan route. No signs of this kind had been located in Egypt before, except in the Sinai. Wadi el-Hol is near Luxor, on the continent of Africa, and in the Valley of the Kings. The Wadi was a major caravan route, and much traffic went through the entire region for thousands of years, so it contains extensive archaeological remains, according to John Darnell, including many inscriptions that "range in date from the early Predynastic through the Ptolemaic and Roman Periods."[148] The site had considerable strategic importance in earlier millennia, and its rocks were heavily marked with inscriptions dated to a period between 2050 BCE and 1350 BCE.[149] Many are in Egyptian hieratic script, but "also present in the Wadi el-Hol are two short Early Alphabetic inscriptions."[150] Because of their "derivation from lapidary hieratic" these are different in form from the Sinaitic inscriptions. Darnell characterized them as "roughly drawn and hieroglyphicizing." He noted that this is a script particularly well suited to "carving rock inscriptions."[151] Moreover, these alphabetic inscriptions can be linked paleographically to the Proto-Sinaitic ones from Serabit el-Khadim.[152]

The Darnells returned to the site in 1999 with the Semiticist Bruce Zuckerman and a team with highly sophisticated photographic equipment to record the inscriptions. Their initial publication had a seismic impact on the scholarly world—and made headlines in the *New York Times* and other mainstream venues.[153] Frank Moore Cross, reached for comment in his status as emeritus professor at Harvard, said these were "clearly the oldest of alphabetic writing and very important." Enough of the signs were similar to later Semitic, he said, that "this belongs to a single evolution of the alphabet."[154] Their location in *Egypt* rather than in the Sinai or in the Syria-Palestine area of ancient Canaan was without precedent. Along with other contextual information (an inscription on the site in nonalphabetic Egyptian writing), the inscriptions argued strongly for the presence of Semitic speakers who had adopted the Egyptian models for their own purposes. Dating them posed challenges.

Darnell based his dating on the way the sign showing a head is made to point and the orientation of sign for water is in a vertical rather than the horizontal position associated with later developments. On the basis of these observations, he dated the inscriptions to 2000 BCE. Others have suggested 1800 BCE or even later.[155] The writing is indisputably of a Semitic language, and the find pushed the dates of alphabet origins back about three hundred years from that assigned to the Sinai inscriptions (1600 BCE).[156] Assigning such early dates is dramatic, but it may not be accurate.

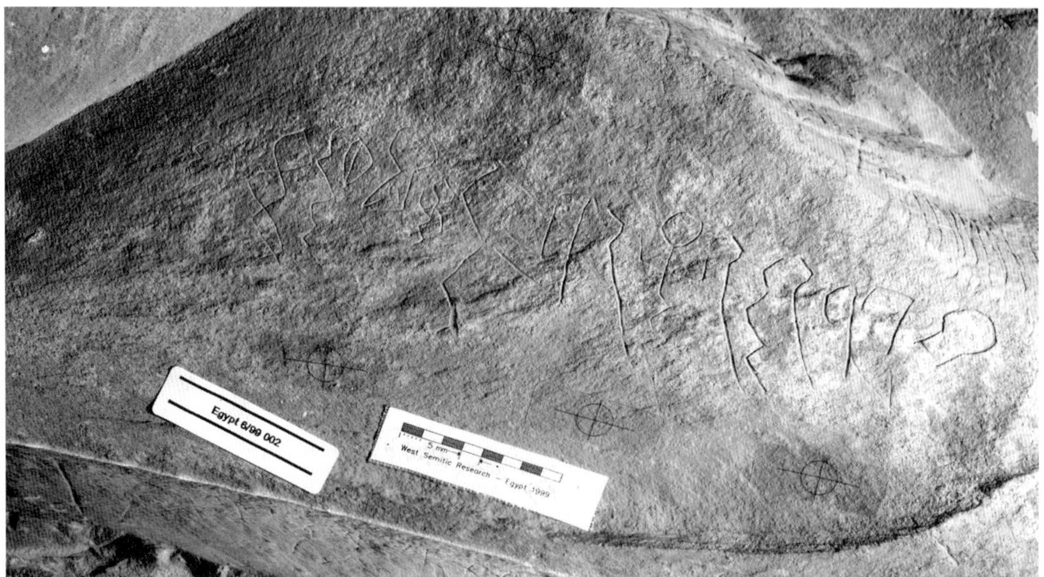

FIGURE 8.13 Photograph of scratched alphabetic signs from the Wadi el-Hol site. Photograph by Bruce Zuckerman and Marilyn J. Lundberg, West Semitic Research. Courtesy Department of Antiquities, Egypt.

Darnell also made a historical argument about the social situation in the Middle Kingdom (2050–1550 BCE) in which "Western Asiatics armed as auxiliaries" accompanied "Egyptian mining expeditions in the Sinai," the same argument that Gardiner, Sass, and others had put forth.[157] But Darnell extended this interaction to the site of the Wadi el-Hol and described it as a "melting pot of Egyptian expeditionary forces" that "gave rise to the alphabet during the Middle Kingdom."[158] Furthermore, he linked the alphabetic inscription to mercenaries under a general named "Bebi" who had been put in charge of "the Asiatics" (again, the term used by Egyptians to describe people from anywhere to the east of Egypt). Darnell continued: "Rather than being the random creation of unlettered 'barbarians' confronted with hieroglyphic inscriptions they could not comprehend," these inscriptions were the outcome of interactions in border areas of cultural contact.[159]

The Wadi el-Hol inscriptions, which consist in total of about thirty glyphs, have been analyzed for every aspect of their orientation, shape, direction, and order. Even information about how each glyph was carved has been compiled from detailed study of their production—through analysis of the depth, direction, and width of the incised lines. This study led to statements like these: "the horizontal arms are a separate element, each made with one continuous line" or "the upper loop is a continuous curve."[160] Dating and decipherment remain subject to discussion, as do questions of whether hieroglyphic and or hieratic scripts had provided the graphic prototypes. So "the ox head, twisted flax, coil of rope" suggest hieroglyphic prototypes while "the serpent, seated man, head, eye," etc., suggest hieratic sources.[161] Along with stylistic features, "the 'zigzag' represen-

FIGURE 8.14 Drawing of the same Wadi el-Hol inscription by Marilyn Lundberg, West Semitic Research Project. Public domain, via Wikimedia Commons.

tation of the legs and feet of the seated figures," these graphic elements are used for dating.[162]

Questions remain about who actually created these inscriptions. Were they made by people already literate, familiar with writing either as a concept or practice, who were visiting the region when they produced these signs? Or were they created by illiterate people who got the concept of writing from the Egyptians and decided to create a script appropriate to their Semitic language?[163] The impact of this discovery remains profound, but the "likelihood that alphabetic writing began geographically in Egypt" is now a strongly supported thesis.[164] While some scholars continue to push the dating of the Wadi el-Hol inscriptions back as early as 1900–1800 BCE, Sass's arguments seem definitive in making the best account of the timeline and circumstances for the invention and development of the alphabet. That does not stop controversy from arising within the scholarship.

TWENTY-FIRST-CENTURY DEBATES ABOUT HISTORY AND CONTEXT

Douglas Petrovich began his 2016 study, *The World's Oldest Alphabet*, by referring to Daniel Defoe's account of Moses receiving the Tablets from God at Mount Sinai.[165] Petrovich's agenda was clear—though he wanted to demonstrate that Defoe's version is "a romanticizing of the biblical text" and "has no basis in reality," he believed there was evidence to support the assertion that "the other alphabets of the ancient world did derive from the PCH [proto-consonantal Hebrew] script that is attested as early as 1842 BCE."[166] Petrovich, trained as a biblical historian, archaeologist, and paleographer skilled in ancient languages, is fully aware of the multiple conditions required for describing the original formation of the alphabet.[167] Petrovich's argument was that Hebrew speakers who grew up in the Egyptian court would have learned Middle Egyptian in their youth and been able to choose twenty-two words from the Egyptian sign list, using the principle of acrophony to construct an alphabet for the Hebrew language.[168]

This is actually similar to the argument made much earlier by de Rougé for hieratic, and Petrovich's dating is close to that of the Prisse Papyrus. But the crucial question is whether the language of second millennium BCE inscriptions is Hebrew or another Semitic variant. But despite objections from other scholars, Petrovich tracked what he believes are the origin and development of all twenty-two letters "from their Egyptian hieroglyphic roots until their derived forms at the time of the Israelite monarchy."[169]

Addressing the issues of the derivation and differentiation in the regions and time periods concerned, the late Joseph Naveh stated that around 1000 BCE (the beginning of the Iron Age in Syria-Palestine) three alphabetic scripts developed—Phoenician, Hebrew and Aramaic—from a common Proto-Canaanite ancestor.[170] At this time, with the development of the linear forms, the stabilization of the right-to-left direction, and the reduction of the number of letters to twenty-two consonants, the Proto-Canaanite developed into the Phoenician script."[171] The "Hebrews" had adopted the "script together with other cultural values" from the Canaanites in the two prior centuries, but they "followed the current Phoenician as they developed "their own national script."[172] Aramaic developed soon after, also borrowing the Phoenician. The upshot, Naveh concluded, was that determining the language and identity of scripts from this period depended on contents and historical information.

Given this background, Christopher Rollston, the renowned biblical scholar and Semiticist, argued that "the Proto-Sinaitic Inscriptions from Serabit el-Khadim and Wadi el-Hol" were not in the Hebrew language.[173] Rollston pointed to their date as one factor. Wadi el-Hol inscriptions might be dated to the eighteenth century BCE but the earliest "written in the distinctive Old Hebrew script" cannot be dated earlier than the ninth century BCE, and these scripts are formally distinct.[174] Rollston cites Joseph Naveh's arguments that associating the Sinai script with Israelites after Exodus constituted "romantic views no longer accepted."[175] But above all, Rollston relied on linguistic evidence in support of his argument that the language of the inscriptions is a second millennium BCE Northwest Semitic dialectic. He noted that "Canaanite" is the generic term for any of a number of Semitic languages—many of which share words to such a degree that distinguishing among them is particularly difficult.[176] The Sinai inscriptions contain, in sum, twenty-seven letters, while the later, Old Hebrew, was distilled to twenty-two. Furthermore, Rollston noted that the script used in the Sinai inscriptions was not "one of the distinctive national scripts" but an "early ancestor of all of these scripts." While accepting the term "Proto-Sinaitic," Rollston proposed "early alphabetic" for historical reasons.[177] The age of the Sinai inscriptions places them in the ancestral role to the other alphabetic scripts.[178] On the basis of Sass's arguments, and those of others, the dates of that ancestral role have been brought closer to the thirteenth-century period, after which the alphabet seems to have been transmitted to ancient Palestine and consolidated as Proto-Canaanite.

The beginnings of paleography were formal studies of individual glyphs and signs that gradually led to a highly sophisticated inventory. Formal analysis is only one dimension of current epigraphy. Rollston, one of the most prominent figures in Western Semitic epigraphy working today, outlined its methods in his work *Writing and Literacy in the World of Ancient Israel.*[179] Published in 2010, the volume demonstrates the intellectual synthesis possible when the various kinds of expertise essential for translation, typological observation and sorting of letterforms, archaeological context, and historical knowledge are combined. The outcome is that epigraphic work, important in its own right, becomes a foundation for understanding the culture of a period that is referred to as the early Iron Age, beginning about 1200 BCE. The origins of the alphabet are somewhat older, but it is the stage of culture in which writing and literacy play a role that is the focus of Rollston's study.

Epigraphic evidence provides highly legible foundations in Rollston's work. The emergence of various regional differences in script indicates distinctions in local dialects, shedding light on the ways distinct communities and municipalities began to be identified. For such work to be authoritative, the epigraphic evidence has to have a secure relationship to its location—and here the techniques of stratified excavation and documentation play a part to identify when a particular potsherd was inscribed and within what conditions it was used. Analysis of the contents of the text allows cross-referencing with other historical documents or information. The degree of specificity of which Rollston and others working with this evidence are capable is clear in a statement like this one at the beginning of his introduction: "The Lachish II ostraca contain information about the troop movements (e.g. of the Judean army commander Conyahu to Egypt), rations, and prophetic warnings that were reported to officials (e.g. Ya'ush) at the fortified royal bastion of Lachish during the period immediately preceding this strategic Judean city's destruction in the early sixth century B.C.E."[180] The correlations among historical facts and attested events supports the dating.

Rollston describes the many educational and administrative activities within which writing is used, taught, and standardized in the twelfth and eleventh centuries BCE. We learn of intrigues and political plots in the royal houses of Syria and the nascent Israel. We read of victories and deaths, are introduced to cultic and prestige items, and prayers to Yahweh but also multiple goddesses and gods. Epigraphic evidence alone would not be sufficient. The ostraca and arrowheads and other inscribed objects are essential witnesses to the particular conditions of culture and language in these various places and periods. The reading of this evidence permits an entire narrative of cultural history of the emergent nations and religions to be constructed.

Among the more curious features of epigraphic evidence are artifacts that are not merely archaic—that is, belonging to an early stage of development—but also a small subset of objects that may exhibit characteristics of *archaizing*. This is the act of creating an inscription with the intention of making it look older than it is, giving it the graphic character of writing done in an earlier age. The concept requires considerable imagination, and the execution demands a high level of sophistication. Scribes would need to have thought about the desire to artificially age an artifact—give it a "ye olde" treatment—and also have the ability to locate specific script forms and imitate their characteristics. Rollston describes the complexities in trying to sort out whether such a possible practice can be seen on an artifact known as the Tell Fakhariyeh inscription written in a version of Phoenician script. The debate is highly technical. First, it involves assessing whether older forms of scripts might have persisted in peripheral communities and thus simply have been used without much alteration for a century or more after they had stabilized, while during this same period, the script evolved in more central locations or population centers. The date of the artifact is much later than the style of the script, and both Sass and Rollston concur "archaizing is a recognized phenomenon, and Fakhariyeh is a textbook case."[181] Rollston persists in detailed analysis of the elements "within the script itself" to demonstrate that it "does not date to the eleventh or tenth centuries." By examining "vertical downstrokes" or "bottom horizontals," he arrives at the conclusion that the inscription should be dated to the ninth century BCE but made to look older. These stylistic features speak of a complex scribal culture with highly differentiated features in specific locations across a broad region of cultural exchange and shared scripts and languages.

Epigraphy matured from its first identification of individual signs and glyphs, and yet, the typological techniques that are used for this identification remain crucial to the method on which the alphabet, as a concrete, physical, actual system, is understood. We may never know if a scribe in the ninth century BCE had in mind to imitate an antique style or was merely copying the exemplars available in a provincial setting, but it is owing to the skill of modern epigraphers that these questions can even be asked.

The use of computational methods has also contributed to advancements in the field. Bruce Zuckerman and his colleagues at the West Semitic Research Project created an innovative application of imaging technologies.[182] Using techniques that extract different features of an artifact through several methods of lighting, scanning, and photographing, they are able to computationally merge the information gathered to optimize the legibility of ancient inscriptions. The techniques of multispectra, reflectance transformation and photography are merged. The result is a noninterventionist approach that augments the capacities of human observation—the computational output is literally something that could not be perceived directly by the eye. Their imaging techniques, along with expertise in Semitic languages and epigraphy, have been the foundation of *InscriptiFact*, a digital library of inscriptions curated by Zuckerman with Marilyn Lundberg and Leta Hunt.[183] Epigraphy has come a long way since the conscientious attempts at direct copying by hand.

CONCLUSION

Semitic epigraphy began as the study of a handful of Phoenician inscriptions. Curiosity about the Sinai rock carvings was of long standing. Making a connection between the elegant linear script of the monuments from Sidon and Byblos and the crude quasi-pictorial marks in the Sinai required persistent study of slowly accumulating evidence to prove they were part of a single alphabetic development. Between the work of the eighteenth-century Abbé Barthélemy and the meticulously systematic and synthetic methods of current scholarship, the history of epigraphy has evolved from decipherment, systematic ordering, and identification of early alphabetic signs to an understanding of the origins and development of the alphabet as a culturally and historically situated process.

The Semitic epigraphers combine an empirical study of script signs with a knowledge of language, historical context, and cultural history. They systematically examine the written evidence from archaeological sites to build a coherent picture of the emergence of the alphabet in sites from Egypt in the south to ancient Lebanon and Syria-Palestine to the north. Formal analysis of physical evidence still undergirds the field. The meticulous study of every piece of evidence, and the careful inventorying of each and every extant sign from the second millennium forward, relies on a highly trained group of specialists.

This chapter has attempted to describe and summarize the considerable and admirable achievements in this field, as well as some of the still (and perhaps always to be) unanswered questions about the history of the alphabet. But as a historiographic topic, epigraphy has clear lineages and legacies. The alphabet is a concrete development that emerged in a specific historical context as a result of cultural conditions and exchanges that began in the early second millennium BCE. This was the outcome of a highly refined intellectual process in which the tools of stratification, periodization, historical and linguistic knowledge, and expertise in graphic analysis have combined. The number of outstanding scholars in the field is now too large to allow a single list of their names, and the individuals singled out for discussion above are not the only significant figures in the field, merely some of those whose work has been definitive.[184]

As a historical object, the "alphabet" continues to be read through frameworks that sometimes drive the narrative to fit the artifacts, and sometimes fits the evidence into a particular frame—and the politics of alphabet historiography remain a feature of a field in which much emotional weight attaches to every discovery and piece of evidence.

S ʃ Σ

ش

S S

S ש S ʃ

NINE

Alphabet Effects and the Politics of Script

A COHERENT NARRATIVE

By the late nineteenth century, scholarly methods for interpretation in areas of paleography, epigraphy, archaeology, ancient languages, and history became increasingly sophisticated and disciplined as empirical evidence had accumulated. The result was—and continues to be—a more and more fine-grained understanding of precisely where, when, and by whom the alphabet was invented. The scholarly consensus is now sufficient to present the basic history.

LESSONS IN HISTORY

The concept of writing had been part of the ancient Near East since the early Sumerians developed their first proto-writing and a conventionalized accounting system using tokens beginning by about 7500 BCE and then in pictographic and cuneiform notation around 3000 BCE. Whether the Sumerian script had any connection with Egyptian hieroglyphics is an unresolved question. But in the second millennium BCE, alphabetic script emerged in a process of cultural exchange in the region stretching from Egypt and the Sinai, north and east along the shore of the Mediterranean

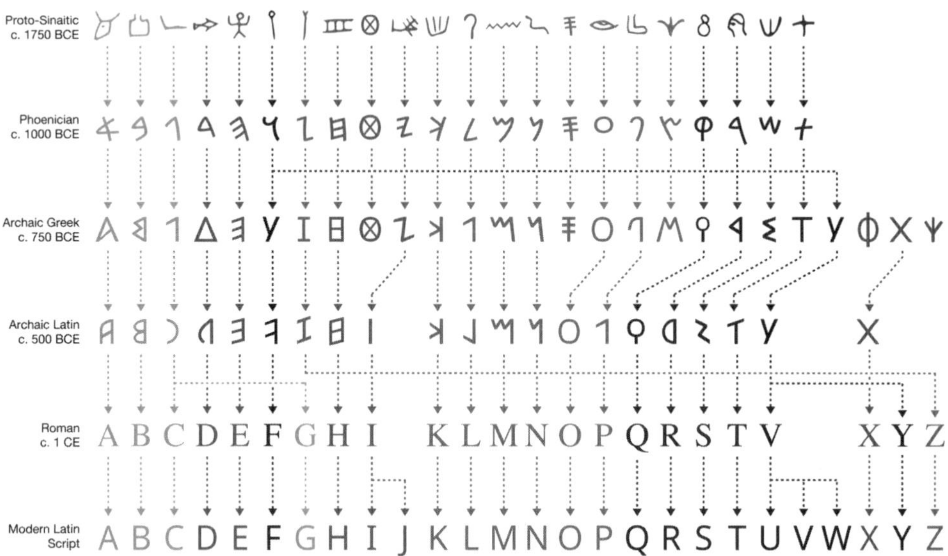

FIGURE 9.1 Matt Baker, "Evolution of the Alphabet." This chart focuses on the lineage of Western European alphabets and shows, graphically, the connections of Greek, Roman, and Latin to the Proto-Sinaitic and Phoenician sources. From UsefulCharts.com. Creative Commons BY-SA-NC.

into modern Israel, Lebanon, Jordan, and Syria. Two fundamental conditions were essential for the phonetic alphabet to emerge: (1) language speakers had to have a sufficient understanding of the basic sound components of speech to break it into essential, significant, units and (2) cultural conditions had to support the consensual use of a defined set of standardized signs. These two conditions were met in various places in the ancient world in the second millennium BCE. It appears that Linear B and the Cypriot syllabary met these conditions in Mycenaean Greece, as did the Ugaritic cuneiform syllabary in what is now western Syria and Egyptian hieratic used for syllabic writing. These late Bronze Age developments occurred sometime between 1500 and 1300 BCE.

The signs that became the alphabet might have appeared as early as 1800 BCE, though some scholars still believe the date may be later, 1400–1350 BCE. The earliest alphabetic inscriptions are located in Egypt in a once much-trafficked valley, Wadi el-Hol, and the assumption is that they were made by Semitic-speaking visitors to the region. They display the graphic features of an emerging, rather than established, writing system (rough design, unskilled execution, imperfect repetition). There were no sustained Semitic settlements in the area around Wadi el-Hol, though the geographic distribution of developing alphabetic inscriptions stretched broadly, from Egypt through the Sinai and across multiple regions of the Levant.[1] Many specific details about the precise place at which the alphabet was stabilized before it was spread by Phoenician traders throughout the Mediterranean may never be known, owing to lack of physical evidence, but the general outlines follow the course just sketched. The names and sequence of the letters became fixed by the time the alphabet spread, as the evidence of abecedaries from 1400–1200 BCE makes clear.[2]

The scholarship of the late Joseph Naveh and ongoing work by Christopher Rollston, Benjamin Sass, Israel Finkelstein, and many others provide a solid foundation for this account. Fieldwork and microanalyses are aided by digital technology and other advances for dating, imaging, and classifying glyphs.[3] Each new piece of evidence can subtly shift the dates of the contributions of one geographic location or another, but this does not change the basic fact that during the second millennium BCE, a fully coherent and consistent "alphabet" emerged from a gradual but steady process.

Perhaps that is the right stopping place for a historiographic study of the alphabet—with the research of realistic and rational scholars. But this final section addresses the politics of script in order to return to the larger thesis of this project—that the alphabet is not *discovered* but *invented* through the modes of knowledge production that constitute it as an object. The multiple biases that are reported in this chapter are more conspicuous than those of empirically based observation. But even empirical work is based on beliefs and values. The expert eye is trained to see, to discern one form and not another, aided by the technologies of the period. The field of alphabet studies is not without its fractures and rifts, and controversies continue to arise owing to beliefs that inform interpretation of evidence.

Ending with these studies of impassioned, if sometimes disputed, or even troubling, assessments demonstrates that intellectual trends have their fashions and that what appear in the present to be value-free techniques may reveal their own limiting assumptions with the passage of time. The expertise of the archaeologists, paleographers, and Semiticists is undisputed. But blind spots of presentism remain. The ways the alphabet will be imagined by generations ahead is impossible to predict from within the current historical position.

One of the conspicuous paradoxes in alphabet historiography is that as evidence mounted in the nineteenth century, interpretations that introduced cultural biases and misperceptions increased as well. From the time of Herodotus and of Old Testament biblical histories, the origin of the alphabet had been associated with Semitic-speaking peoples in the East. Various waves of intellectual bias entered into the discussion, first in a late nineteenth-century skepticism of the antiquity of the Phoenicians and Indo-Europeans and then through claims built on analysis of Greek classical poetry and language. Historical narratives polarized along political lines. A binary distinction between Semitic and Greek versions of the alphabet hardened into a story of cultural differences weighted with value judgments. Highly divisive notions of literacy were used to create distinctions between "superior" and "primitive" cultures—and writing systems. Alphabet studies provided a vivid example of the principle that scholarship is framed—and legitimated—within systems of belief.

Modern scholarship on the origin of the alphabet intersects with wider historical debates about the relative antiquity of individual cultures. Claims for the priority of the invention of literature, philosophy, technology, and expressions of administrative structure such as laws and accounting systems juggle historical facts with partisan beliefs. The Phoenicians, Sumerians, Chinese, Indus valley cultures, Celts, and others took turns enjoying popular status as the "oldest" civilizations with the same regularity that extraterrestrials are now invoked on certain current television channels to explain the creation of ancient monuments. Mainstream scholarship eschews extreme or unverifiable interpretations, but empirical evidence can be put to the service of every possible point of view.

THE ARYANS APPEAR

One politicizing concept that affected alphabet studies was the attempt to create a non-Semitic history of the Phoenicians. Beginning in the mid-nineteenth century, the notion of an Aryan race was promoted in Arthur de Gobineau's massive, fourteen-hundred-page *Essai sur l'inégalité des races humaines* (*An Essay on the Inequality of the Human Races*; 1853–55).[4] The Sanskrit term for Aryan had appeared in Indo-Iranian in the Vedic period (about the middle of the second millennium BCE). But in the nineteenth century, the date for these texts was stretched back several millennia to suggest that they had been composed around 6000–7000 BCE (now considered impossible). The term Aryan applied to a broad group of Indo-European language users and only became a racialized word when Gobineau, along with the German linguist Friedrich Max Müller, used it to identify an imagined master race of blond, blue-eyed people from a vaguely defined period of prehistory. A French aristocrat, Gobineau produced writings that supported elitist and racist biases that had arisen in the aftermath of the French Revolution and were used in support of slavery in the United States. His work had little direct discussion of the alphabet, but his vocabulary and concept of racial identity were absorbed by scholars working in the field.

Among them was Isaac Taylor, who in addition to his authoritative work on the alphabet, published a book in 1889 called *The Aryan Controversy* to provide scholarly clarity in the discussion. Unlike Gobineau, Taylor was well versed in knowledge of history and language and familiar with groundbreaking work among the eighteenth-century philologists. Their understanding of the structural relationships among languages posited Sanskrit as the common ancestor of the Indo-European tongues (it is now considered a derivative of an older Indo-Aryan root). As Taylor noted, the old nomenclatures, such as Semitic and Hamitic, that associated the geographies occupied by the sons of Noah with languages and peoples in these regions, the Levant and Africa, should have meant that the label "Japhetic" would have had to be applied to European languages in that tradition. (According to biblical accounts, Japhet was the son of Noah, to whom the European lands had been allocated in division of the earth after the Flood.) The difficulty was that the word Aryan was used to signal more than a geographically associated group of languages.

Taylor identified the term as the invention of the German linguist Friedrich Max Müller. He further observed that a series of lectures delivered by Müller in 1865, in which he spoke of an "Aryan race" that included "the Indians, the Persians, the Greeks, the Romans, the Slavs, the Celts, and the Germans," contained "more mischievous words" than "have seldom been uttered by a great scholar."[5] As a refutation, Taylor gathered anthropological and linguistic evidence to demonstrate that race and language are neither identical nor overlapping. He dismissed the claims for promoting the superiority of the former merely on the basis of describing the history of the latter. But the idea of racial inequity, and all the justifications it allowed, had potency. Taylor himself could not entirely resist a narrative considered independent of Greek sources. He brought in a discussion of the Cypriot syllabary, which he identified as an advanced form of writing, to show "that if the Greeks had not obtained their alphabet from the Phoenicians they would before long have succeeded in developing from a wholly different source an alphabet of nearly equal excellence."[6] However, the comment was pure speculation. The Cypriot syllabic script may have emerged around 1100 BCE, possibly from the Minoan Linear B (itself dated at the earliest to 1600 BCE), or both might have had a common ancestor from older writing systems in Egypt and Mesopotamia. Trade and contact with Cyprus in the Mycenaean period was considerable, and the model of a script developed for Semitic languages or other Afro-Asiatic tongues might have sparked the development of Cypriot writing. But Taylor knew no archaeological evidence supported the theory.

Taylor's otherwise judicious discussion of the Cypriot syllabary contains an unfortunate passage: "The radical nature of the vowel sounds, together with the delicate inflexional machinery of the Aryan languages, must be reckoned among the chief reasons why the final stages of alphabetic development should in so many cases have been effected by Aryan nations." The result was that the various developments in Semitic scripts, he said, "passing into the possession of the Aryan races of Northern India, became the parent of the most perfect scientific alphabet which has ever been invented."[7] The identity "Indo-Aryan" was being attached to the language group in South India whose historical roots were traced to the second millennium BCE (the origins of Indo-European languages are somewhat earlier).[8] In Taylor's usage, it bore no racial association, only a cultural one. If the Aryan language could be identified as Indo-European, and if it was the source for modern European languages and could be claimed to be the oldest original language, then the status of Semitic sources could be subordinated to the larger process, if not ignored or debased entirely. The Semitic proto-language source was Afro-Asiatic, dated to perhaps 16,000 BCE.[9] Praise for the "perfection" of one alphabetic variant over another embodies a bias that discounts the specific needs of individual languages for notation systems matched to their sound structure.

DISPELLING THE "MIRAGE"

In 1893, Salomon Reinach published a two-part essay, "Le mirage orientale," in the Paris-based journal *L'anthropologie*, expressing a desire to dispel what he considered to be the myth of the "Asian" origins of Western culture.[10] The reference was to the culture of Semitic peoples in the Levant, considered "Asiatics" from ancient times. Reinach's attack included the Phoenicians as a source for Western culture, but even more broadly, the Indo-European languages as the foundation of modern European ones. His work was part of a backlash provoked by a nineteenth-century passion for these "oriental" origins of Western civilization and language.

For generations, scholars had sought verification for Hebrew as the "original" language. But modern scientific analysis had begun to track word forms, sound changes, and other structural features as part of empirical study of the emergence of different language groups. In the nineteenth century, the fields of historical linguistics and comparative philology had moved language scholarship onto a scientific footing. Technical studies of language change and derivation focused attention on Sanskrit. The German philologist Franz Bopp had advanced claims for Sanskrit's primacy as the earliest Indo-European language because it preserved the oldest forms of word roots and syntax shared by modern European languages. Later research has demonstrated that Sanskrit is itself a derivative of that earlier Indo-Aryan source and appeared around 2000 BCE, but popular as well as scholarly imagination was stimulated by the discoveries. For instance, enthusiasm for this mythic history had even prompted a clever forger to add a few letters from the Devanagari script (the major modern branch of the ancient Brahmi alphabet used in India) into a Stone Age cave inscription to support an imaginary past for the text.

Though Sanskrit was not the source for Indo-European languages, this linguistic theory had had repercussions within a nineteenth-century culture accustomed to thinking of the source of Western civilization as classical, mainly Greek. The idea of an older Proto-European ancestor for Western culture and language offered an alternative to Semitic sources located in the ancient Near East. Reinach noted that the idea of Hebrew as the oldest language had lost ground in the eighteenth and nineteenth centuries with increased recognition that European culture had been influenced through contact with Egypt. The discovery of the Papyrus Prisse in 1847 had even provided the suggestive misperception that alphabetic scripts had been derived from Egyptian hieratic. The history of the Hebrew language and its script, as well as the alphabet's development within Semitic language communities around the eleventh–tenth centuries BCE, were based on facts to which nineteenth-century linguists had limited access.

Reinach drew on models of history that pitted nonhierarchical and antiracialist values against those asserting the superiority of "advanced" cultures over others. He did not engage directly with alphabet studies, but his work attempted to recast relations among Indo-Aryan, Phoenician, and European influences in the two millennia of alphabet development and dissemination leading up to the Common Era. Reinach began his essay by suggesting that the identification of Phoenician remains, place-names, and influences around the Mediterranean had created an improbable version of the historical past, making them seem much earlier and more extensive than was likely. By the late nineteenth century, the Phoenicians had been given credit for every known early site of settlement from Anatolia and Cyprus to the British Isles. Spurious inscriptions attributed to their visits or sustained presence were "found" as far away as Peru and the New World. No wonder Reinach was skeptical.[11]

Reinach wanted to address what he perceived to be nationalist tendencies within the assertions about the Indo-Aryan and Phoenician sources of European culture. Reinach's original anthropological research had focused on ancient peoples and a systematic examination of multiple features of Neolithic cultures to establish a chronology of cultural exchange. He discussed the domestication of animals, arrival of tin, use of bronze and iron, and other aspects of human development in various geographic regions of the ancient world. In one part of his paper, he asked how the Mycenaeans, who pictured lions on a gate erected in southern Greece around 1250 BCE, would have known about these animals. Though vanished from the region by Reinach's time, the lions pictured in cave paintings in France and their presence in Greece had been noted by ancient writers, including Herodotus. In fact, these animals had been present in parts of southern Europe until the beginning of the Common Era.

However, Reinach argued vehemently against the "anteriority" of the Eastern civilizations. He suggested that graphic motifs and decorative stylistic elements found in Greek art did not need to be explained by the influence of Egyptian and Babylonian sources but could be found in the indigenous imagination of the Greeks themselves. Reinach went so far as to engineer the history of influence in reverse. By the end of the first part of his article, he made the statement that Mycenaean civilization was "entirely European in origin" even though it became "Orientalized" through later contact with Syria and Egypt. He cited the archaeologist Arthur Milchhöfer, who argued that the visual motifs found in these artifacts had been introduced *into* Egypt by the Phoenicians who had picked them up *from* the Mycenaeans.[12] The idea of Greek culture as the *source* for Egyptian art strained credibility.

But the implications of Reinach's argument were clear. European culture had to be understood as distinct from that of the ancient Near East but also distinct from any source in Aryan (Indo-Aryan in particular) roots. Reinach was Jewish and publicly committed to intellectual life associated with Jewish causes.[13] The idea of positing Indo-Aryan origins of Greek myths to justify an Aryan origin of Western culture, put forth by the linguist Max Müller, had become increasingly aligned with anti-Semitic and racialized discourses in France and elsewhere in Europe in the nineteenth century. So Reinach distanced himself from the notion of an "Aryan" race and its influence and instead asserted the indigenous European origins of Western culture. In his major contributions to comparative religion, he argued vigorously that they all shared the characteristics of mythic belief systems. None could be considered superior to another. Rejecting religious faith in favor of secular reason, Reinach claimed to be opposed to "blood-based racial hierarchies as well as religious ones," but his arguments suggested otherwise.[14] His comparative and universalist beliefs generated increasing criticism in the first decades of the twentieth century and met with resistance from both rising Jewish nationalist Zionist movements and anti-Semitic ones.

Though rarely cited in alphabet literature, Reinach's work was discussed by P. Kyle McCarter in his 1975 publication on beliefs about the antiquity of the Greek alphabet.[15] Beneath the "mirage" of orientalism, McCarter argued, Reinach had attempted to identify a European identity without influence from an overmythologized Aryan and Phoenician past. In the process, he helped make an opening into which racialized theories of cultural difference would appear, particularly those in which Greek culture would be characterized as "superior" and its modified alphabet would take on a distinctly autonomous identity.

THE "SUMER-ARYANS"

In 1927, Laurence A. Waddell published a work in support of the Aryan myth based on even greater distortions of the historical record. A British army officer, explorer, and amateur archaeologist fascinated by the Sumerians, Waddell offered his interpretation in *The Aryan Origin of the Alphabet*.[16] His book began with the statement that the "origin of our Alphabet . . . and its authors have remained unknown. . . . Nevertheless, its authors have been assumed to be Semites by all modern writers."[17] This, Waddell explained, was because the Greeks ascribed it to Cadmus, king of the Phoenicians, who were "wrongly" regarded as Semites.

Waddell's thesis asserted an Aryo-Sumerian ancestor for the West with a direct link to early Britain. He attributed the origin of the alphabet to a "Sumerian or Aryan race outside Mesopotamia," which he placed in the Indus valley but connected to the Hittites in Cappadocia and Cilicia-Syria (Asia Minor).[18] Furthermore, he said "these Hittites, or properly *Khatti* or 'Catti'" also bore "the clan-title of the Ancient Briton kings."[19] Through this geographic distortion, he crafted a lineage for Cadmus the "great inventor."[20]

FIGURE 9.2 Glozel "inscription." These are rectilinear, modern letterforms and have none of the elegance, grace, or scribal style of Phoenician script. © Antiquity Publications Ltd 1930. Material reproduced with permission.

As he presented his evidence for the "Aryan racial nature of the Phoenicians," a number of issues arose.[21] For instance, he cited the 1924 discovery of a "Phoenicoid" script on some of the tablets found in an underground chamber on a farm at Glozel in the Loire section of France. These materials have been universally condemned as forgeries, and even as early as 1927, a commission appointed by the International Institute of Anthropology declared the Glozel artifacts to be fakes.[22] Recent research has dated these clay artifacts to the first centuries of the Common Era, possibly as late as 700 CE, but Waddell also claimed to have found inscriptions by the "Brito-Phoenician kings" dated before 1050 BCE, or the date at which the Phoenician alphabet was assumed to have stabilized.[23]

Waddell argued unequivocally that attempts to link the origins of the alphabet to Egyptian or Babylonian sources had failed.[24] Citing the renowned Egyptologist Flinders Petrie, whose *Formation of the Alphabet* had been published in 1912, Waddell misappropriated his theories of a nonmonogenic origin of the alphabet. Petrie had proposed the "formation" was a gradual process across diffuse populations and locations, now understood as the result of the Phoenician transmission and dispersion of the script. But Waddell misused Petrie's arguments to reject a Semitic origin while distorting most of the paleographic evidence. Using inscriptions Petrie had collected from Spain and Thera, he made a corrupt reading, claiming Aryan origins for them. He even went so far as to include the late Common Era inventions, oghams and runes, to assert a distinction between Semitic and Aryan letters, ignoring the time gap of one to two thousand years. Waddell

1 SUMER	2 AKKAD	3 EGYPTIAN Early Alphabetic	Hiero.	4 PHŒNICIAN THERA c. 900 B.C.	5 MOAB c. 900 B.C.	6 PHRYG. MIDAS c. 900 B.C.	7 CARIA c. 900 B.C. - 650 B.C.	8 SIMBEL c. 900 B.C.	9 LYDIA c. 900 B.C.	10 PERSIA DARIUS 500 B.C.	11 INDO-ASOKA 250 B.C.	12 HINDI Modern	13 GREEK ATHENS 409 B.C.
O, U, O, 365, 337.				(ō)									(ō)
Pa 77.										(P) (Pa)	(?)		
Qa, Qi 63, 316, 419.			(Qy)			(X?)				(Qu)	(Gh)	(C)	
Ra, Ri 207.										(Ra)	(Ru)		
Si(g) 527.			(S)							(S)			
Si(b) 94.			(S)							(Sh)	(Sh)		
Sa (Śa) 300.			(Ś)								(Ś)		
Ta(r) 12.										(Tr?)	(Th)		
Ti(b) 70.										(T)			
U, V 365.							(F?)			(V)			
Wa 383.										(V)	(V)	(V)	Ph
Xa, Xi 160.										(Kh)	(C) (Ch) (Khi)	(Ksh) (Ch)	
Za(g) 249										(Z)	(J) (Jh)	(J)	

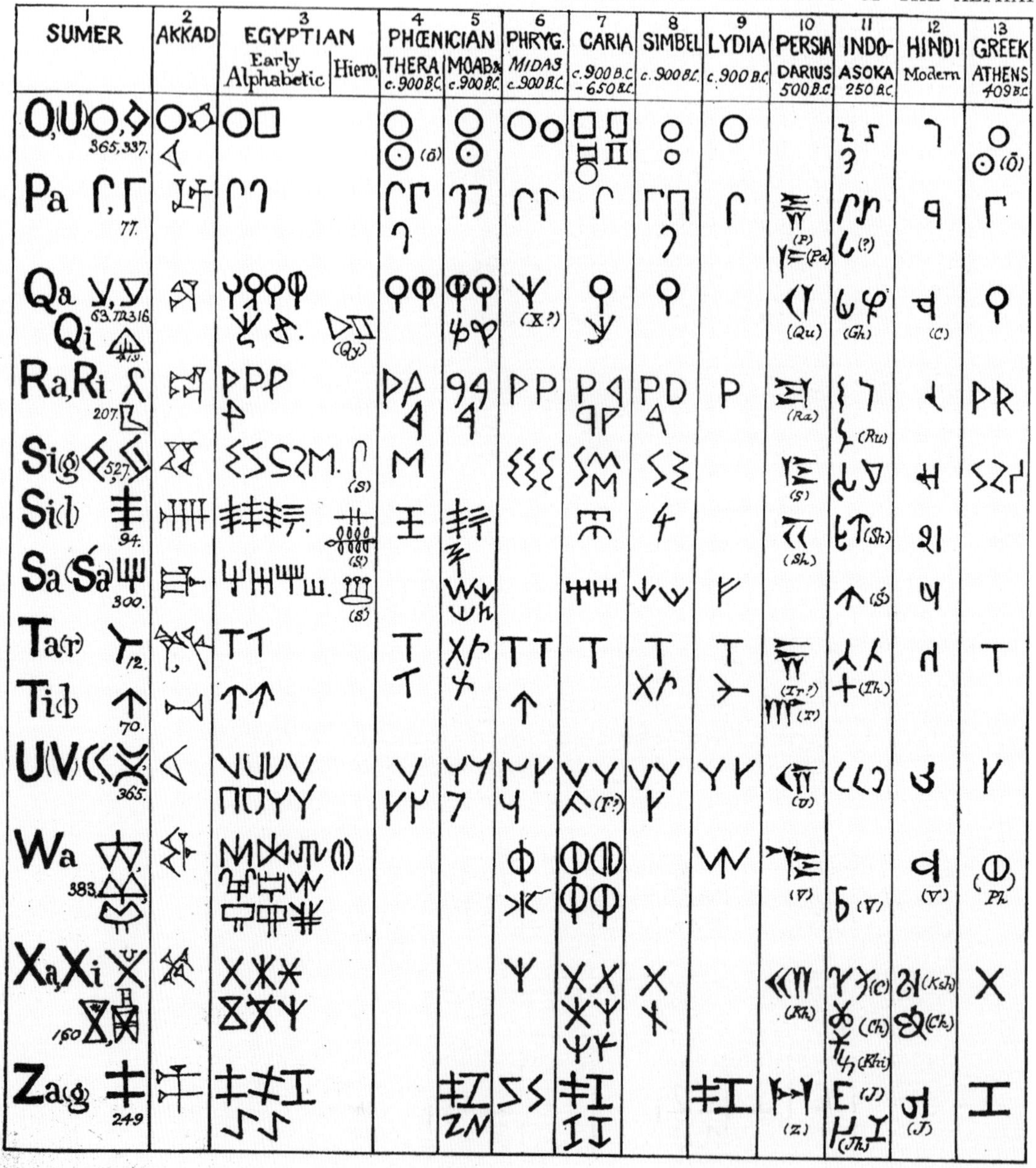

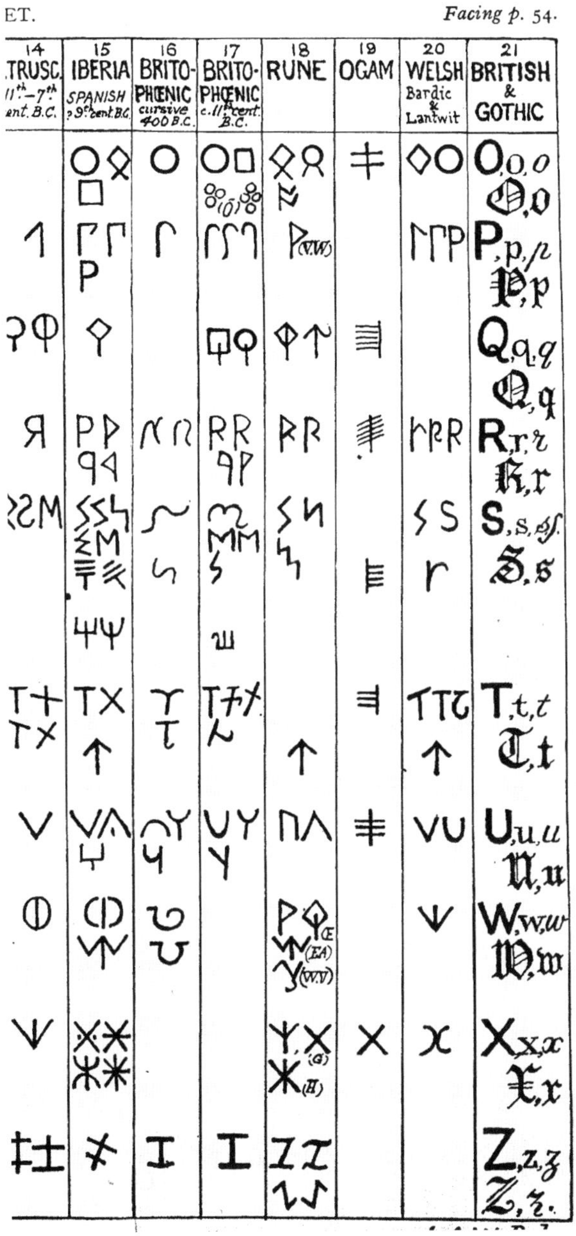

ET. *Facing p.* 54.

14 .TRUSC. 11th–7th ent. B.C.
15 IBERIA SPANISH ? 9th cent. B.C.
16 BRITO-PHŒNIC cursive 400 B.C.
17 BRITO-PHŒNIC c. 11th cent. B.C.
18 RUNE
19 OGAM
20 WELSH Bardic & Lantwit
21 BRITISH & GOTHIC

O, o, o
P, p, p
Q, q, q
R, r, r
S, s, s
T, t, t
U, u, u
W, w, w
X, x, x
Z, z, z

FIGURE 9.3 Chart from Laurence A. Waddell, *The Aryan Origin of the Alphabet* (1927). The signs are mainly a combination of linear Phoenician and early Greek. Public domain.

invented a vocabulary of terms like "Brito-Phoenician," "Indian-Aryan," and then finally "Sumer-Aryan" to make his case.[25] The neologisms had no grounding in historical reality but served his purpose, as if the key to history lay in discerning connections hidden within language roots, even if the words had been translated across multiple linguistic boundaries.

Waddell concluded that the alphabet was not originated by Phoenicians on the coast of the Levant but instead in North Syria, in Sumer. Though the Sumerian language is actually a "language isolate" unrelated to Indo-European, Waddell asserted it was "radically Aryan in its vocabulary and structure."[26] He also identified Sumerian as the parent of English and connected to Aryan languages he believed had demonstrable links to the third-century BCE Indo-Aryan emperor Ashoka. Finally, he suggested that Sumerian had been used in Britain before the founding of Rome.[27]

Waddell assembled a table in support of these contortions. With vague dates and locations, it presented evidence of diffusion of a script he attributed to Sumer.[28] He included detailed description of each letter and its Sumerian parentage, associated with the Semitic language, Akkadian, which he conveniently characterized as an Aryan language. Waddell spun his fantasy history through bogus orthography and citations of, for instance, Professor Bedrich Hrozny, a Czech linguist, who asserted correctly that the Hittites spoke an Indo-European language and used a monoconsonantal writing system. Waddell distorted Hrozny's research to his own ends.

Waddell denied that any Semitic language was the basis for alphabetic writing, which he characterized as the supreme accomplishment of a "rare genius" who had figured out that "all the necessary sounds for spelling words numbered no more than about 24 or so, and that the existing Sumerian linear pictograms of those sounds in their most diagrammatic forms then current for domestic purposes were all that were needed."[29] This inventor "was presumably a Hittite or Hitto-Phoenician, and thus an Aryan in race."[30] Waddell stressed that King Cadmus was contemporary with the Trojan War, about 1200 BCE, and thus part of the original Aryan civilization in Greece.[31] Waddell's agenda was clear in his conclusion: "It is seen that the Semites (including the Hebrew) and the Hamites borrowed their alphabetic letters from their Aryan overlords, along with the leading elements of the Aryan civilization. . . . It thus affords further evidence for the conclusions set forth in my previous works that Civilization is mainly a matter of Race, and that the Higher Civilization is broadly Aryanization, through the culture evolved by our especially gifted and scientific Aryan ancestors of the Northern fair long-headed race."[32] He finished by noting the racial deficiency of Africans and Bushmen, the strength of the Gothic tradition, and the many contributions of the Aryans/Sumer-Aryans including their legends, written under King Heria, Thor, or Ar-Thur.[33] Having thus created a racial divide that put northern Europeans and early Britons into contrast with the people of Africa, he had even managed to make King Arthur a Sumer-Aryan.[34]

Waddell's was perhaps the most overt expression of anti-Semitism, but it was not the only work on alphabet origins that reflected distorted intellectual judgment in the 1920s and 1930s. The idea that the Greek alphabet was somehow "other" than the Phoenician, and that the Phoenician could be divorced from its Semitic identity, was persistent. A half century after Waddell's publication, Martin Bernal stated: "Consciously or unconsciously, almost every educated European of the late nineteenth and early twentieth centuries saw Greece as the quintessence of Europe and the Aryan race, and the Phoenicians were seen as resembling their Semitic kinsmen, the Jews."[35] Bernal defended the linguist Max Müller, who wrote in 1888 that "an ethnologist who speaks of Aryan race, Aryan blood, Aryan eyes and hair, is as great a sinner as a linguist who speaks of a dolichocephalic dictionary or a brachycephalic grammar."[36] But Müller himself, on occasion, used the phrase "Aryan race," reinforcing racial bias.[37]

Bernal, already noted in chapter 1, documented the way these attempts to prove the Aryan origin of the alphabet came to the fore between 1925 and 1940 and linked these to anti-Semitic trends in scholarship.[38] The idea that the Greeks were part of an invasion of people from the North who had been involved in the Aryan conquest of India (thus solving the evident problem of race in its association with pigmentation) allowed for a new term, Caucasian, to be put into play. This built on the terminology and concepts invented by Johan Friedrich Blumenbach, among others, in the early nineteenth century, to classify human races by type. In the 1920s, the concept of the "pre-Hellenes," early Greeks who were "racially Caucasian," built on theories of migration that invoked both an "Asian steppe" and an Anatolian origin for some Europeans.[39] DNA research continues to build better understanding of these migration histories but does not support an alternative history of the origin or diffusion of the alphabet.[40]

THE "GREEK" ALPHABET

"Of the many splendid achievements of the ancient Greeks, the alphabet was perhaps the most marvelous and certainly the most influential."[41] This statement, written in 1997 by Roger Woodard, is typical of assertions about the "Greek" alphabet.[42] In this version, instead of being an adaptation and modification, the alphabet becomes a unique invention, even if, as Woodard goes on to say, "it stands on the shoulders of the consonantal script of the Phoenicians."[43] Its influence—and that of Greek culture generally—is celebrated uncritically, lauded for superiority in terms of cultural advances, intellectual innovations, changes to the very concept of self and other, and, even, changes to the physiological bases of cognition. This political interpretation of alphabet historiography achieved unprecedented acceptance in the twentieth century. How did a statement like Woodard's—which embodies a common misperception—come to displace the tales of the Phoenician Cadmus told by the Greeks and of Moses recorded in the Old Testament, let alone the work of archaeologists? While Cadmus and Moses may challenge historical facts, they are still more likely in substance than Woodard's assertion, which is based on assumptions about the nature of alphabetic scripts and judgmental claims for literacy. Whether or not one accepts his premises—notions that logic, reason, and Greek democracy represent unquestionable "genius" and are the foundation of major accomplishments and progress in Western culture—his hard distinction between Eastern/Semitic and Western/Indo-European writing systems cannot be justified.

Along with this distinction between the Greek and Semitic alphabets, a pernicious concept known as the "alphabet effect" became established. Closely associated with the Canadian group of media theorists known as the "Toronto School," which included Marshall McLuhan, Harold Innis, and Walter Ong, the "alphabet effect" was a phrase coined by Robert Logan, who used it as the title of a book published in 1987.[44] Building on the work of his predecessors, Logan took the concept further, though some of the earlier proponents of the idea, notably Jack Goody, were already modifying their own earlier theses by the time Logan's book appeared.

At stake in the argument was an assertion that Greek culture was superior to the Semitic cultures of the ancient Near East, as well as to those of China and India, by virtue of its achievements in the areas of the arts, philosophy, politics, and science. The claim was that rational thought, democracy, ideas of the individual, and empirical science were unique achievements of Greek civilization and that the so-called Greek alphabet, on account of its capacity for phonetic notation, had a major role in fostering these developments. In other words, the alphabet was being cast as a *cause* as well as a part of these superior advancements.

The roots of this bias are clear in Western European classicism. The erasure of African-Egyptian cultural influence on the Greeks—another aspect of history well known to the Greeks themselves—added a tinge of racial prejudice that permeated classical scholarship. Bernal was the first and most thorough critic of the racist tone of these approaches. While the focus on dating the transmission of the Greek alphabet provided part of that story, the fuller politics of script included a more developed set of presumptions about orality and literacy, even extending to neurological and physiological effects of the alphabet, and to "gendered" characterization of different societies.

Study of these biases begins with the work of classical scholars focused on the Homeric epics and extended to research on the brain, alphabet, and literacy.

THE CASE OF HOMERIC POETRY

The scholars who built on the work of Milman Parry, published in the 1930s (discussed in chapter 1), notably Alfred Lord and Eric Havelock, conceived a hard break between the oral culture of Homer and the written language forms of Plato.[45] They used this as the basis of many assertions that would become amplified, accepted, and then subject to critical analysis in the later twentieth century.

For instance, Havelock developed a concept of the "Western mind" formed by "Greek thought," and suggested a major rupture with earlier traditions and a sharp distinction from Semitic roots of writing, the alphabet, and other cultural influences.[46] He stressed that the relationship between alphabetic writing and rational thought had provided the Greek foundation of Western culture. Neither Parry nor Havelock was proposing overtly racist viewpoints, but their dismissal of the Asiatic roots of Western culture amounted to advocacy for the superiority, and "racial purity," of the Greeks.

Havelock, along with other faculty members at the University of Toronto, was concerned with definitions of literacy. Extending Parry's view, he stressed the binary distinction between oral and written literacy in poetic composition. In *Preface to Plato*, published in 1963, he first stated these theories directly, though its arguments have much in common with those of his influential predecessors.[47] He stated that a break in compositional (and intellectual) approaches appeared in Greek literature with the adoption of the alphabet, the date of which continued to trouble him.[48] Havelock believed that the "intellect of man" was "discovered" at the end of the fifth century BCE, an event he characterizes as "linguistic," with the result that notions of "selfhood and soul lacking in the Old Testament" were discovered by Socrates and "textualized" by Plato.[49] But the eighth- or seventh-century BCE date of alphabetic transmission was earlier than the "break" linked to Plato in the fifth century, thus the difficulty.

Havelock pursued this theme throughout his career. *Prologue to Greek Literacy*, published in 1971, continued to draw directly on Parry's work.[50] Havelock noted that Homer made no mention of alphabetic writing.[51] But even without epigraphic evidence or any inscriptions from Homer's time, Havelock suggested that "it is not credible that Greeks preceding or contemporary with Homer were illiterate."[52] Again, he invoked the Mycenaean Greeks who had been literate centuries earlier, though their writing and even its memory had apparently disappeared from use or mention.

Havelock struggled constantly with the dating and other issues, but the more extreme statements in his work had nothing to do with dates, rather with cultural politics. Before the existence of writing, Havelock said, the Greeks could not be "democratized." The invention of a concept of democracy may be an accomplishment of Greek city-states, but other practices central to civic organization, such as laws, record keeping, and administration, had long precedents. Havelock made dramatic contrasts between Old Testament texts and those of Homer's epics and the Greek dramas, suggesting that the "basic complexity of human experience" was not present in the Hebrew Bible since it was a text whose power was to appeal "to simple people."[53]

Havelock invoked the racial superiority of the Greek people explicitly:

"The Greek genes conferred upon adults a better equipment with which to achieve creative effort in art and intellect."[54] Though he qualified these statements by saying that the Greeks exercised a "technological" rather than racial superiority in their reworking of the alphabet, his invocation of "genes" suggests otherwise. Havelock focused on the invention of discrete consonants rather than vowels (which he recognized had already been present in Linear B, the Mycenaean script). The technicality here is interesting, since the Semitic languages for which the alphabet had been developed used tri-consonant roots, which were sufficient for writing these languages unambiguously. Havelock called the consonants "objects of intelligence," emphasizing a process of atomization in which spoken language is understood as a combination of units (of voiced and unvoiced sound). He made a contrast between earlier systems "which were content to symbolize actual sounds which any mouth makes when it speaks, and a system like the Greek which analyzed such sound into abstract components."[55] Elsewhere, Havelock had criticized syllabaries for being "redundant," since each sign contained a vowel.[56] He believed that the Greeks, with their "atomic theory of matter" had been able to understand the alphabet as a set of primary elements whose value could be disambiguated without regard for context.[57] Sound analysis and abstraction had been shown to exist in Egyptian script forms in the seventeenth–fifteenth centuries BCE through Alan Gardiner's analysis. Havelock's distinction did not hold up under linguistic scrutiny.

Havelock believed that the capacity of Greek oral culture was unique and allowed the analysis of sound into abstract components.[58] Since the Greek alphabet could not have been "invented" earlier than the last half of the eighth century, Havelock built on work by Rhys Carpenter to suggest that this later date only reinforced the great achievement of Greek poetry, which could be seen as fully formed before the arrival of writing. Havelock made the point that alphabetic writing was easier to learn than earlier forms and thus allowed greater participation by a larger portion of the population than earlier forms. This argument ignored fundamental aspects of Jewish culture, such as the requirement that all male children be schooled in the Torah to prepare for a Bar Mitzvah ritual that is a demonstration of literacy, and also dismissed Babylonian and Egyptian scribal schools and traditions.[59]

Havelock's monolithic concept of literacy was not nuanced in any way or put into discussion of larger patterns of cultural development; he simply believed that the specific form of literacy in Greece was the sine qua non of superior civilization. The designations of the "primitive" Semitic and the "noble" Greek and Roman alphabets, which had been made by Isaac Taylor in 1883, became part of the legacy of the classicists' approach.[60] In 1986, in *The Muse Learns to Write*, Havelock expanded his claims yet again: Greek philosophy came about *because* of the alphabet;[61] the *self* is a Socratic discovery, textualized by Plato.[62] What was *known* became separate from the *knower* within Greek philosophical traditions.[63] Whether or not these statements can be supported within an analysis of Greek texts is less relevant than the fact that Havelock attributed a deterministic role to the alphabet. He accorded a philosophical concept—the distinction between the subject and object of knowledge—an uncritical positive value.

Havelock concluded, mistakenly, that "Greek literate revolution" simply was not available to pre-Greek civilizations, reiterating his long-term association of literacy with civilization.[64] Such value-laden constructs were developed by other scholars in the Toronto circle and influenced by their ideas. In many standard references on the alphabet, this version of the "Greek origin" continues to be repeated.[65]

THE LITERACY ARGUMENT: ONG, GOODY, MCLUHAN

In the twentieth century, the flourishing field of communications brought attention to writing as a system of political power, not just a mode of transcription. In 1950, the Canadian historian Harold Innis published *Empire and Communication*.[66] A landmark work, this book was quickly followed by *The Bias of Communication* (1951).[67] Innis's emphasis was on infrastructure—roads, rail, publishing networks, and the complexities of systems through which extensions of culture were produced. His work was a shift from earlier, more deterministic work on the technology of media that had been produced in response to propaganda and its effects in the early twentieth century.[68] Innis wrote about the specific properties of media when few precedents for such analysis existed. While the study of the history of writing, its material substrates, and formal qualities had formed the foundation of diplomatics and its methods, the construction of a theoretical argument about the distinctions between, for instance, stone and papyrus in Egyptian culture, or writing and printing, was new.[69]

Innis pointed out that writing had spatial extension—it allowed empires to stretch their boundaries beyond the limits of face-to-face administration (a fact that contributed to the downfall of Rome, since the empire stretched way beyond its capacity to maintain control on its overtaxed, remote populations). The alphabet, whose development Innis placed squarely in the ancient Near East, was intimately bound to commerce and served the entrepreneurial activities of the Phoenicians, who were not, he noted, particularly concerned with knowledge.[70] By contrast, the use of the alphabet among the Hebrews, to use Innis's vocabulary, resulted in a privileging of language and the word (over images) and promoted a reverence for Scripture. He recognized the richness of Hebrew literature, the creation of monotheism, and the role of the alphabet in creating political organization for a nascent state.[71]

Though Innis was committed to a nondeterministic approach, one in which technological systems and media were not isolated from the broader cultural conditions in which they worked, other Toronto School scholars veered toward more hard-edged binarisms. Marshall McLuhan, whose 1964 publication, *Understanding Media*, became a popular phenomenon, began his study of media with a stark discussion of the Cadmus myth.[72] McLuhan emphasized the part of the story in which Cadmus sows dragon's teeth—the letters—from which soldiers spring up, thus stressing the link between military management, power, and writing. McLuhan characterized the phonetic alphabet as a set of "semantically meaningless letters used to correspond to semantically meaningless sounds." An arbitrary code, void of essential meaning or value, the alphabet was nonetheless the most "pervasive technology" of human culture. The notion of atomistic components became the foundation of a theory of technological efficacy: "only alphabetic cultures have ever mastered connected linear sequences as pervasive forms of psychic and social organization. The breaking up of every kind of experience into uniform units in order to produce faster action and change of form (applied to knowledge) has been the secret of Western power over man and nature alike."[73]

A subset of this discussion expanded the politics of literacy.[74] In *The Bias of Communication* (1951), Innis had argued that literacy could not be understood in a "frontier" mode in which media bring a culture into being.[75] He pondered whether literacy caused or followed particular stages of cultural development. For instance, scholars of the ancient Near East, Jean Bottero and his collaborators, in *Ancestor of the West* (2000), noted that writing did not appear *everywhere* that there are states and societies but *only* where these exist.[76] Reflections on the conditions that require or benefit from writing make clear that business, accounting, communications, and other social infrastructure are important. Poetry can exist orally, but a receipt or deed needs material instantiation.

Two other influential figures, Jack Goody and Ian Watt, were early proponents of the binarism of orality and literacy. Their essay "The Consequences of Literacy," published in 1963, was already informed by critiques of the older models of "primitive" and "advanced" societies that had featured in pioneering anthropology work in the early twentieth century.[77] This included Lucien Levy-Bruhl's *How "Natives" Think* (1910), which had elaborated a theory of the "primitive" mind.[78] Goody and Watt were clear that the opposition of "literate/non-literate" did not map onto these outmoded concepts, although the distinction between two states of culture was still operative. Their characterization of writing systems in ancient civilizations, including China, suggested that the difficulty of acquiring literacy meant that only specialists could become adept.[79] Even Hebrew culture "continued to be transmitted orally long after the Old Testament had begun to be written down."[80] These scholars did not examine the codependence of orality and literacy.

Goody and Watt linked Greek literacy to a period of economic boom when trade with Egypt brought papyrus into circulation. They characterized the Greek alphabet as "modified Semitic" and dated its adoption to the late eighth century BCE, the recognized date, also noting that the custom of ostracization, which required that a name be written on a sherd of pottery, was an indication that broad literacy existed in the time of Solon (539–534 BCE).[81] Though registering an objection to the idea of "the Greek mind," they remained committed to the belief that the development of the alphabet was in part responsible for the creation of an "immutable impersonal logic" and other analytic trends within Greek culture.[82] In support of their positions, they drew on the work of the linguist Benjamin Whorf as well as the sociologist Max Weber, for whom modes of rational Western thought were directly linked to the specific qualities of its language. Among these rational properties were a capacity for taxonomic classification that was considered one of the hallmarks of Greek philosophy and systematic knowledge formation. Objections to such positions came from comparatists, and by 1977 Goody had modified his positions with respect to the alphabet, rethinking his literacy/nonliteracy classifications.

One development of Goody's later work was attention to the "cognitive" features of Greek literacy. In a 1977 publication, *Domestication of the Savage Mind*, he tried to identify the psychological effects of literacy—not just of the alphabet, and he called "for brain-related studies to begin to explore more deeply the cognitive differences between western cultures and others like the Arabic, the Indic, the Japanese, or the Chinese, which use different writing systems."[83] (Actually, Arabic and Indic scripts are derivatives of the Semitic).[84] Goody's language focused on "causal relationships between cultural and biological phenomena" and "gene-culture coevolution theory."[85] He was looking for evidence in support of neurological modification, changes that participated in natural selection and thus found their way into the genotype. If the human "brain and nervous system organize themselves selectively according to the kinds of tasks to which the organism is exposed," then what modifications might have been wrought by the alphabet?[86]

The answer to this question, and a fuller extension into generalizations about culture and the connection to neurological features, became central to the work of Robert Logan, Derrick de Kerckhove, and Ivan Illich, among others.

THE ALPHABET EFFECT: LOGAN AND DE KERCKHOVE

Marshall McLuhan did not assert any direct casual relations between the alphabet and the creation of codified law, monotheism, science, logic, or individualism.[87] But another Toronto scholar, Derrick de Kerckhove, believed the alphabet had neurological and social impacts. In "A Theory of Greek Tragedy," published in 1980 (the year of McLuhan's death), he proposed that the development of theater had allowed the effects of the alphabet to reach a nonliterate population. These effects included increased attention span, a capacity to break experience into sequences, and the ability to train visual skills, do phonetic code, analyze sequences, and follow linear modes of thought.[88] As a result (and the causal connection was explicit in this work), "the nature of memory must have changed: you did not memorize sounds and images, you memorized a code."[89] Greek theater, by its spatialization and organization, he suggested, provided an "apprenticeship of literacy" and "assimilation to new modes of learning."[90] The theater provided a "stage for exteriorization for the new visual synthesis fostered by the phonetic alphabet."[91] In de Kerckhove's assessment, the "combined effects of the alphabet and the theater isolated, redefined, verticalized, centralized, and lateralized the human body," and "the practice of the phonetic alphabet could promote the neurological activities of the left hemisphere of the brain."[92]

Directionality of writing played a key role in de Kerckhove's theories. He tracked this shift in the seventh century BCE from the Semitic systems' right to left orientation, to boustrophedon's back-and-forth around the sixth, through a phase of *stoichedon*, where letters were evenly spaced along vertical lines like soldiers in formation. Finally, at the end of the fifth century BCE, with the official adoption of the Ionian alphabet in 403 BCE, came the standardization of the left to right direction. This decision, de Kerckhove insisted, reinforced left-hemisphere dominance, which he considered a "specific characteristic of the Western mind."[93] In keeping with Havelock's theories, de Kerckhove attributed other distinctions—such as the separation of "knower" and "known" to the phonetic alphabet—accelerated, in his opinion, by the invention of the theater. He was convinced "that the relationship between reading and the brain was changed when the Greeks introduced fixed characters to represent the sound of vowels in the Phoenician system." In part this was a result of the shift from "feature" recognition to "sequence" detection in the forced "re-lateralization of the script."[94]

In a later work, de Kerckhove formulated the question directly: "Did the fully phonetic alphabet developed by the Greeks and still used today in Greece (and in the rest of the West in its Latin and Cyrillic variations) have a conditioning impact on the biases of specialized brain processes?"[95] The core of his thesis was that because Semitic consonantal systems required context for accurate comprehension; they were radically different from the sequence-based reading practices supported by the Greek alphabet. These changes in reading, he argued, reorganized the brain with far-reaching consequences on the biases of Western cognition.[96] De Kerckhove was convinced there were "causal connections" between processes in the brain and features of script.[97]

Coincidence and causality are hard to separate. Robert Logan's succinct and well-informed study was evidence of the way the contemporaneous appearance of the phonetic alphabet and other elements of culture presented a dilemma for assessing causality. His straightforward observation was that codified law, monotheism, and the alphabet appeared at the same period of the second millennium BCE in the ancient Near East. Logan's book, *The Alphabet Effect*, began with a clear acknowledgment of the influence of his colleagues in Toronto. The initial formulation of his ideas, described in "Alphabet, the Mother of Invention," was coauthored with McLuhan in 1977.[98] Innis was also cited as an important influence on the concept of media as an "active force in creating new social patterns."[99] Logan's synthesis of the historical development of the alphabet tracked its origins in the Sinai and Canaan, grouped, as per Joseph Naveh's scheme, under the shared rubric "Proto-Canaanite."[100]

Logan, citing Havelock, stated that the Greek alphabet was the invention which "cannot be improved upon," and noted that Ignace Gelb, another comprehensive historian of writing, insisted that the Semitic alphabet was a syllabary, not a "proper" alphabet (the position taken in current scholarship by Peter Daniels, who coined the term "abjad" to mark the distinction).[101] Logan's discussions of causality, however, were entirely focused on the Greeks and what he termed "subliminal effects" and "by-products" of alphabetization.[102] These efforts included the ability to code and decode, to convert auditory signals into signs, to think deductively, to classify information, and to order words through alphabetization.[103] The "by-products" were the capacity for abstraction, analyses, rationality, and classification.[104] These claims invited debate and refutation by other scholars, particularly those working with Chinese character scripts. Logan asserted various medium-specific theses that were novel and exciting within the field. He made striking statements suggesting that Eastern and Western thought patterns are as polarized as their respective writing systems.[105] Such generalizations tend to impose their intellectual scheme on complex phenomena and reduce it to fit the binarism. He composed a list of oppositional terms to this end and then described the innovations in Chinese science as mere "technological progress" rather than "abstract science."[106] His characterization of Taoist, Confucianist, and Logical Chinese philosophies as subservient to political interests ignored the parallel history of Western science in relation to the Church and other institutions of power. When he cited Joseph Needham, a well-respected twentieth-century historian of China, as support, he suggested that Needham's analysis of cultural conditions left out the key element—the difference in writing and the inadequacy of Chinese to provide flexible and efficient classification systems.

Logan's work was subjected to systematic criticism by Dominic Yu, whose "Thoughts on Logan's *The Alphabet Effect*" was published in 2003.[107] He stated bluntly: "Logan's basic premise, that Chinese characters are inherently less abstract than alphabetic characters, is incorrect." While some characters have pictographic origins, functionally, characters represent sounds. In stating that the Chinese law system had nothing to do with writing, Yu continued, Logan was similarly mistaken. Furthermore, Logan had no evidence to support his claim that "the Chinese script has subliminal or hidden effects which are adverse to abstract or scientific thinking."[108] Logan's suggestion that the pictographic origins kept Chinese thought literal rather than abstract, and that the alphabet is a "natural tool for classification," missed the more profound point that classification is not the key to modern science. Classification, Yu said, is a cognitive process, connected to the sorting and decision-making essential for daily life and cultural management. Modern science is about method, observation, hypotheses, testing, Yu noted, not about classification. Elsewhere in his text, Logan qualified these views, noting that "elements of universality, abstraction, and classification . . . became part and parcel of Babylonian thinking under the influence of phonetic writing."[109]

Yu went on with his criticism: "Logan's most ridiculous claim is that the development of monotheism was encouraged by alphabetic writing."[110] Seth Sanders, another distinguished historian of ancient culture, theorized that Hebrew was invented by Jews in parallel with their national identity and monotheistic beliefs.[111] Logan and Sanders both believed this shift in concept had an impact on political organization (though Sanders emphasized the linguistic structure of Jewish prayer as well). In his initial discussion of the Mosaic tradition, Logan recognized that monotheism was not merely a matter of having fewer "gods" but a matter of a different concept of a deity—abstract, not embodied or visible. Giving the Greeks credit for monotheism stretched credibility. The Greeks who adopted the alphabet were far from monotheistic—and the gods of Greek religion are embodied, anthropomorphic, irrational, and flawed. Logan rationalized his analysis of Greek religion by saying that it took about five hundred years for "literacy to take hold of Greek mind."[112] This statement is hard to reconcile with historical evidence.[113] In one of his final passages on the impacts on Greek thought, Logan stressed the extent to which the alphabet effected a separation of the visual from the multisensorial experience of "preliterate man" (*sic*).[114] Without ways of testing such hypotheses, they simply remain assertions.

PUSHBACK AGAINST THE ALPHABET EFFECT

The most systematic criticism of Logan's argument was published in 2004 by Paul Grosswiler in an essay titled "Dispelling the Alphabet Effect."[115] The core premise of the "alphabet effect," Grosswiler stated, was the idea that the alphabet uniquely advantaged Western civilization by providing the foundation for intellectual achievements unavailable to nonalphabetic cultures.[116] He cited Harold Innis, Marshall McLuhan, Walter Ong, and Jack Goody, among others, as figures who participated in this thesis, noting that Goody had eased his support for the position in his later work. Grosswiler's argument included references to scholars in comparative linguistics who noted the presence of abstract thought and advancement in other cultural contexts. He mentioned work on the Vai language, for example, where the effects of schooling were even more significant than those of literacy in changing socialization patterns.[117]

Still, Grosswiler pointed out the persistence of the basic beliefs: "Canadian communication theory has accepted as one of its major tenets the superiority of Western civilization brought about by the phonetic alphabet."[118] Grosswiler argued instead for a "writing effect" and for more careful study of the conditions of literacy within a social and cultural matrix.[119] He noted that Innis thought the combination of paper plus alphabet "checked" oral tradition and helped produce secular works and administration. Attention to this single substrate ignored the impact of clay, papyrus, parchment, and stone. In China, paper, Confucianism, and a communication empire of reports and newsletters were in existence by the second century CE.[120] McLuhan's opposition between a visual Western culture and an acoustic Eastern one did not hold. McLuhan had believed Havelock was the first to suggest that the alphabet disturbed the balance of the ancient world. Like Havelock, McLuhan imagined that the alphabet created civilization differently than in China where there was, supposedly, no linear rationality and no individual or separate citizen.[121]

The main object of Grosswiler's critical focus was Logan's assertion that alphabetic letters are abstract and Chinese script is not. He also noted that Goody, an early proponent of the "alphabet effect" concept, had retracted his support on grounds of ethnocentrism. In a 1996 book titled *The East in the West*, Goody criticized his own exaggerated view.[122] Revising his earlier position, he argued for a "writing effect" rather than an alphabetic one: "It is a gross ethnocentric error of Europe to attribute too much to the alphabet and too much to the West."[123] Goody had also realized the bias of classical education against the Semitic parent script of Greek and had come to understand that the Greek alphabet was a less dramatic development than he had earlier thought. In *The East in the West*, he suggested that the promotion of the alphabet was a form of ethnocentrism, acknowledging that, in fact, the Bronze Age cultures in the ancient world had many developments in common.

Denise Schmandt-Besserat's groundbreaking scholarship in the history of writing was also cited by Grosswiler, because of her account of the development of a form of proto-writing in cuneiform from accounting tokens, clay objects used to make impression. This account offered an alternative to the standard history of script. More contrasts with Chinese writing and literacy brought up the longevity and universal use of characters, essentially unchanged for centuries, and used by populations to write different languages but in forms legible to all their users. This character-based system contrasts radically with alphabet systems, whose letters can be read if they are within a certain script family (alphabets with Roman letterform roots, for instance, in contrast to Greek or Cyrillic), but which provide no access to the meaning of the language for which they are used. In other words, Grosswiler pointed out, alphabetic writing is harder to read across languages than are character-based scripts.

THE MOST SEVERE CRITIC

Martin Bernal formulated the strongest critique of the presumed superiority of the Greek alphabet.[124] Bernal tracked the racial biases he perceived in the work of classicists who had asserted fundamental differences between the Greek and Semitic alphabets. He argued, convincingly, that the terms on which the Greek alphabet was distinguished from that of its root source in Semitic scripts from the ancient Near East were designed to make it seem like a unique development. He asserted that the motive for discrediting the idea of Phoenician settlements was simply to preserve Greek racial identity. Efforts to isolate the borrowing and place it far from the mainland in places like Crete, Rhodes, and Cyprus meant that the mainland Greeks could be remote from the contact.[125]

The supposed superiority of the Greek alphabet was based on the idea that it contained a fuller notation system—including vowels—than the Semitic scripts. Their use of notation based on consonants—in particular, the tri-consonant word roots that are endemic to Semitic languages—was not suited to Indo-European languages, of which Greek is one. The linguistic distinction was often blurred to make it seem that the Semitic script was "primitive" and the Greek modification "advanced"—or that one, the Greek, is a "true" alphabet. These arguments justified an ideology on misused linguistic principles. One might as easily suggest that the binary system of 1/0 notation is primitive because it does not contain the other eight numerals.

As a crucial part of his argument, Bernal also dismantled the "tree" theory of alphabet derivation in which each form of the alphabet sprang directly from previous ones.[126] Criticizing it as too literal and reductive, he mustered considerable evidence to show that the many versions of an early Semitic alphabet arose and modified, then spread, even as their forms and shapes continued to evolve in multiple sites. Bernal focused on the Proto-Canaanite scripts in the ancient Near East that developed long before this diffusion, noting the variety of modifications that occurred in southern Italy, Spain, and around the Mediterranean that attested to this process.

Bernal's discussion, though three decades old (*Cadmean Letters* was published in 1990), is still compelling. While his points have their partisans and detractors, other equally controversial conversations have arisen that build on earlier notions of the "alphabet effect," often with slim evidence. One example is that of Ivan Illich and Barry Sanders.[127] They began their 1998 book (*The Alphabetization of the Popular Mind*) with the following statement: "The alphabet does exactly the opposite of what most hieroglyphics and ideograms, and, most importantly, what Semitic letters were created to do."[128] The ideogram is silent and reading it was like solving a rebus. The authors further noted, "Quite suddenly, around 1400 B.C., an entirely new kind of script made its appearance on the border between the Egyptian hieroglyphic tradition and the cuneiform of Mesopotamia."[129] Noting that this North Semitic Byblos alphabet does not have vowels, they discounted this script as "the" alphabet, stating: "It is astounding with what audacity a clutch of pastoral tribes in Canaan claimed the invention as their own."[130] But claims to invention—Semitic, Greek, Ugaritic, Egyptian—were all the work of later scholars, not the early scribes. Bernal's critical approach would have found ample material for extension.

Bernal was pointed in his discussion of the anti-Semitism, anti-orientalism, and anti-Africanism of scholarship in the 1920s and 1930s that made the "Greek alphabet" into a distinct writing system. Bernal criticized the progress of writing model in which pictograph-syllabary-alphabet are envisioned as stages of gradual improvement, each superseding the last.[131] A similar criticism was leveled by Robert Fraser in 2008, in *Book History through Post-colonial Eyes*, in which he demonstrated that oral societies might go directly to print or digital technology without first adopting writing.[132] In addition, a considerable literature on the problematic characterization of literacy as an automatic benefit has shifted the basis on which assertions of alphabetic superiority can be made. Critical interventions in decolonization of knowledge and rethinking of assumptions about Western tradition have reframed the values asserted by Havelock and others. The politics of script cannot be separated from other cultural struggles and questions, and the history of the alphabet continues to be debated within systems of belief.

OTHER BINARISMS AND INTERPRETATIONS

Various authors have continued to read the historical record according to their own more or less idiosyncratic interpretations. They have used historical evidence to demonstrate that the alphabet was inferior or superior to a specific cultural transformation or development, or indicative of it. For example, Leonard Shlain argued in his 1998 book, *The Alphabet versus the Goddess*, that the arrival of the alphabet was accompanied by a debasing of feminine principles in ancient culture.[133] The outcome was a demise of "goddess" worship in favor of an increase in masculinist and patriarchal values. Shlain's research into ancient Near Eastern cultures stressed the presence of goddess figures in Mesopotamia—Inanna, Isis, Asherah, and Astarte.[134] He pointed out that each of these had a younger, weaker male consort whose utility was mainly linked to procreation. In some of these cultures, writing was associated with a goddess figure. The Sumerians, for instance, understood cuneiform as a gift from Nisaba, the goddess of grain. Shlain took up the theme of neurological effects touched on above, agreeing with his predecessors that the alphabet is associated with (if not explicitly the cause of) abstract thinking and systematized knowledge.[135] While he explicitly denied essentializing gendered traits, and from the outset made clear that "masculine" and "feminine" were descriptive terms rather than characteristics associated with gendered individuals, he used traditional oppositions in his description: "As more and more people could read and write, the dominant pen wielding right hand played an increasingly critical role in communication, masculinizing culture."[136]

Other aspects of Shlain's argument included the discussion of a shift from idols to logos, points made by Logan about the role of the alphabet in Jewish culture. But this argument falters when transmission to the classical world is taken into account. The Greeks and Romans, despite their development of abstract logic, had a highly developed culture of idolatry in which goddesses abounded. Shlain's arguments found many enthusiastic adherents for the thesis that "the thug who mugged the Goddess was alphabet literacy."[137] The issue whether the alphabet was an instrument for transformation has to be situated within the rest of the cultural conditions in which its adoption and use occur—was the alphabet *responsible* for a shift away from "goddess" culture? The ancient Near East and the classical world offer contrasting evidence.

Seth Sanders, in his 2009 text, *The Invention of Hebrew*, made a different argument for the role of the alphabet among the ancient Jews.[138] Drawing on a combination of historical and bibliographic evidence, he described the development of the alphabet as a nonlinear process, distributed among various localized groups. The earliest alphabetic writing was not standardized, and Hebrew could not serve as an official language until about 1000 BCE. In the tenth–ninth centuries, three vernacular languages were written—Ammonite, Moabite, and Aramaic. The texts included first-person conquest narratives but also, and most important for Sanders, the biblical texts, which included the frequent use of *you* as a way to invoke the people of a nation, Israel. In this construction, the "people" become an agent and are instructed to follow laws that are encoded in the narrative of the Old Testament, as well as in the Mosaic code. For Sanders, the crucial role of the alphabet arises in its connection to political beliefs that imagine and call forth a people—rather than a state—in a collective identity. Sanders considered the role of the biblical text, and alphabetic writing, to be generative of the public, which is constantly addressed, directly, in its passages—but also witnessed in its Bronze Age inscriptions.

CONCLUSION

The material evidence on which a history of the origin and development of the alphabet can be pieced together has increased considerably in the last century. Curiously, so have interpretative frameworks with inherent and conspicuous biases. But the current conception of the alphabet is built on enough historical materials and empirical findings to create a verifiable study of its origins and early development. The alphabet, a cultural artifact, was created through a now well-known process of exchange of visual signs, inscriptional writing practices, linguistic analysis, and communication concepts. Within the long-extant empires of the ancient Near East—Egypt,

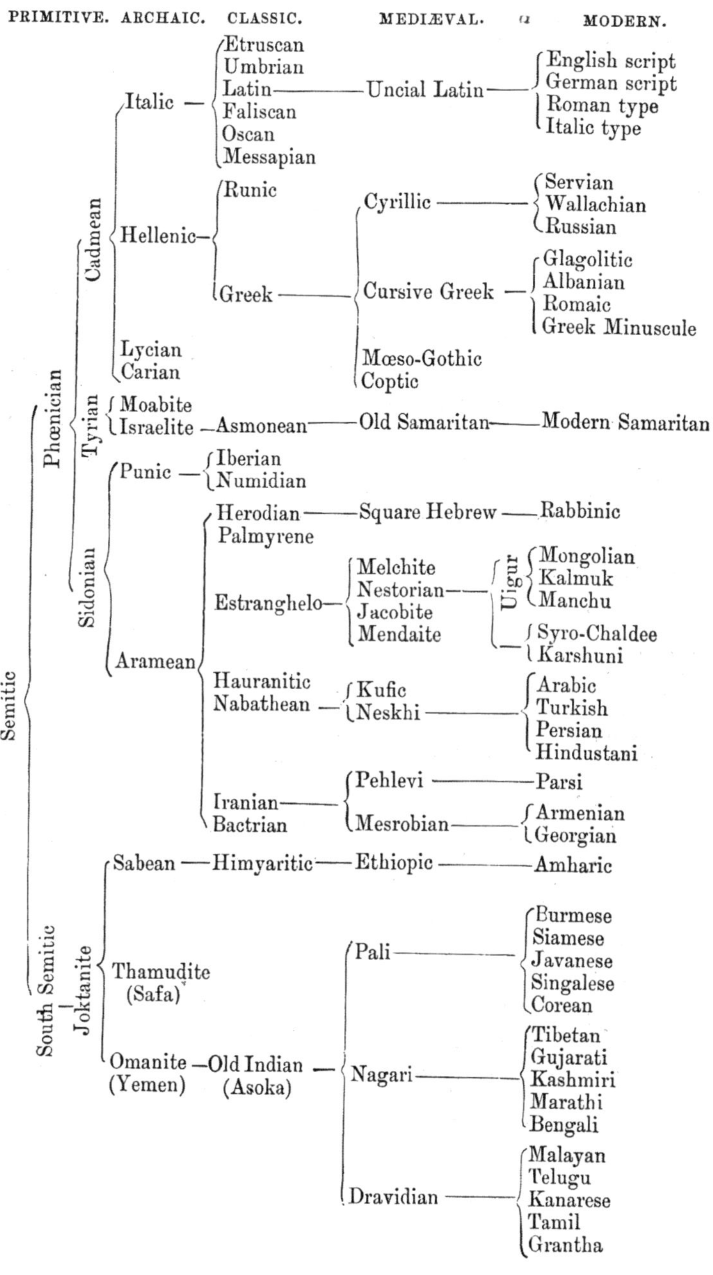

FIGURE 9.4 Chart from Isaac Taylor, *The Alphabet* (1889), showing the derivation of alphabetic scripts from the Semitic taproot. This tree model has been qualified in recent scholarship as overdetermined and reductive but still makes clear the connections to common sources. Public domain.

Akkadia, Babylonia—the alphabet emerged and became consolidated among a scattered population of tribes, Semitic speakers, who created a stable set of signs from precedents and then distilled it into a stable system. The alphabet was not created to do the administrative work of a king, to take care of accounting, or to enable monumental inscriptions. It emerged from marginal, modest, small-scale marks and signs. That it came to serve emerging nations in the ancient world, including many population groups around the Mediterranean, demonstrated its versatility and flexibility. As it spread, its forms modified, and sometimes, the number of letters as well, to accommodate the needs of different language speakers. The graphic variety became so developed that it might be difficult to see the connection among scripts in current use, though they all derive from the same source.

As a construct, an object constituted by intellectual inquiry, the alphabet continues to intrigue writers across a range of theoretical beliefs. Even as new evidence comes to light, the alphabet will continue its existence as an integral element of past and present global culture.

Postcolonial theories and cultural studies of writing, literacy, and scripts have provoked pointed discussion of the racial prejudices and cultural biases that form part of alphabetic studies. Critical engagement with digital media offers opportunities to rethink the identity of the alphabet as a form of code. Questions of hegemony and cultural imperialism remain, explicit or not, in the ways alphanumeric notation functions in digital media and the programming languages of the World Wide Web. The extent to which the alphabet participates in global hegemony provides the topic for the brief coda to this study.

CODA

Alphabetic Agency and Global Hegemony

The widespread adoption of the alphabet across geographies and time spans makes it one of the most important innovations in human history. But it is also one of the most pernicious in terms of its relation to forces of colonization and normalization. Literacy is essential to power—and to abuse—as well as to liberation. The alphabet is a way of organizing information and knowledge within standards that become so naturalized their assumptions disappear.[1] But the endurance and versatility of alphabetic writing are also conspicuous features of its identity.

Computational media and digital networks of communication are intimately connected with alphanumeric systems at a level just above the binary code of machine digits and bits. This ancient code is integrated into global systems. But features of this technical infrastructure also encode cultural biases that produce ongoing inequities and disenfranchisement at a significant scale. The persistent system of alphabetic signs asserts its agency within contemporary global networks—even across languages that do not use this script.

Ideas about the *origin* of the alphabet form a bibliographic chain from antiquity to the present. The theoretical discussion of what constitutes the *identity* of the alphabet—as well as its ongoing instrumental agency—draws on a related bibliographic corpus but also touches on the politics of alphabetic literacy in contemporary life. Except for Japanese, Korean, and Chinese (character-based scripts), alphabetic scripts compose the world's writing systems—and all were derived from the same Proto-Semitic origin, then spread throughout Europe, Arabia, Africa, Southeast Asia, and beyond, becoming as differentiated visually as Greek, Cyrillic, Tamil, Burmese, Balinese, Roman, and Thai, among many others.

In current scholarship, where decolonization of knowledge is a familiar theme within scholarly conversations, thinking about the alphabet as a neutral technology is no longer tenable. Clearly, the alphabet is itself a complex cultural system, one whose agency is partly instrumental, partly incidental, sometimes deliberately used with positive or negative impacts. Standard systems participate in a political asymmetry that asserts the power of those who create standards over those on whom it is imposed. Any mode of literacy enfranchises and disenfranchises simultaneously. But the reality is that the legacy of the alphabet will likely persist for as long as there are cultures engaged with memory and communication, and that much that is precious, unique, and essentially human is preserved because of its existence. Its historical status and role in the production and transmission of knowledge and imagination cannot be undone without doing violence to much of what constitutes our humanity. The alphabet is an artifact of long historical standing with a presence in multiple global systems. A few topics will be touched on briefly to conclude: the notion of the alphabet as an active agent, an open set (in mathematical terms), a logical structure, a collection of graphic elements, an agent of literacy, and a hegemonic global system baked into the infrastructure of communication.

ALPHABETIC ANIMISM AND AGENCY: THE VISION OF LUTHER MARSH

The starting point here for the discussion of the alphabet as an active agent is an unlikely and obscure reference. In 1885, a figure named Luther Marsh presented a talk to the New York Historical Society in which he described the alphabet as the "Alpha and Omega of all thought and expression."[2] While this was not an original formulation, Marsh had his own unique twist. He began by invoking the figure of Cadmus and import of his act: "How faintly could Cadmus have dreamed, as, twelve hundred years before Christ, he trudged through the sands, bearing the letters from Phoenicia to Greece, with what unknown powers he was laden."[3]

Marsh expanded his unusual argument with a slightly mystical orientation, based in a theory of animism. Feeling, as had Cabalists and pre-Socratics, that the letters had agency as elements of the universe, he said, "A sleeping force lies within them which revolutionizes the world."[4] He referenced the discovery of the Papyrus Prisse in 1846, calling it "a strange papyrian waif" that is "older than Moses, older perhaps than Abraham, pre-dating the Moabite stone."[5] The combination of biblical and archaeological evidence was typical of the period. But then his paper took a curious turn. He invoked the evolutionary history of humankind, asking how long it might have taken to "have developed Abraham and Moses and the author of Job from Quadrapedal or Saurian forms; or, yet, beyond this strange pedigree, from a vegetable ancestry."[6]

The hold of evolutionary theory on the popular imagination was clear, though extension to the vegetable kingdom and even simpler life forms was an unusual insight: "From what protoplasm such ancestral vegetables were evolved these sage deponents say not. Nothing but the alphabet could have brought that mighty secret of creation from the antecedent entities." He called these antecedents "protoplasmic progenitors" and urged his contemporaries to "read" the world of letters within a trope of natural history, as part of a single, unfolding, evolutionary chain. "If some old Cadmus of a trilobite or a toad-stool, a radiate, a beetle, or a mollusk, had invented the alphabet aeons before the Phoenician arose, then, perhaps, man, as now developed, might have known when, as he passes the field or wood, to lift his hat with filial respect, to his vegetable forefather—a mullein or a thistle."[7] His closing remarks were salient and poignant, as he indicated that he did not believe evolution would end with human beings. His extended forecast suggested that "in life's lengthened Alphabet what used to be to our sires X,Y,Z is to us A,B,C." His optimism prevailed, as he celebrated the combinatoric inexhaustibility of the letters, saying there is no "combination but they can instantly assume, no manoeuvre they cannot perform." He finished with the imaginative statement "We find them in a new position every morning, after the night's activities."[8]

Marsh's language had an irresistibly poetic quality to it. His atomistic and animist approach had predecessors, to be sure, but it was the agency of things—in this case, the letters of the alphabet—within our contemporary environment, that is compelling to consider in the light of Marsh's thoughts. Letters do have agency, though perhaps not in the particular way Marsh imagined. They also have identity, and the advent of computing introduced new frameworks for understanding the fundamental definition of the alphabet. In addition, in a globally networked communications environment, the alphabet becomes an integral part of far-reaching hegemonic systems whose dependence on standards puts Western biases into multiple levels of infrastructure. The signs and glyphs from Semitic-speaking desert communities have come to be the symbol set on which digital systems operate at certain levels of encoded information exchange. Amazingly, the letterforms found in the Sinai, at Wadi el-Hol, on a Phoenician sarcophagus in Byblos, a potsherd from Gezer, a dagger from Lachish and other remnants of Bronze and Iron Age civilization are a vital part of our daily lives at multiple scales of communication.

THE GRAPHIC IDENTITY OF LETTERS AND THE "OPEN" SET

The advent of computing brought new possibilities for conceptualizing the identity of letters. Though far from the histories of origins, these ideas add an interesting dimension to the notion of the alphabet. Are the letters a set of differentiated signs whose form could be swapped out, as in Morse code or other ciphers, replaced by any useful set of distinct marks or images? Or is there an essence to the letters, some cosmological identity to their forms, magic quality to the formal properties of these images, that makes each unique and significant?

Donald Knuth, the mathematician responsible for creating TeX and Metafont, two programs for drawing letters and layouts, came up against the issue of the identity of letters in a surprising way.[9] He set out to design a program that he thought could render letters in any font by encoding their "essential" forms in a discrete algorithmic description. Knuth struggled for some time with this project, imagining a design platform that would begin with sans serif fonts at one end of a design spectrum and perhaps something like black letter on the other—with all kinds of variations in between. It turned out that the concept was mathematically flawed. The letters did not have individual formal identities that could be specified in a single algorithm. Their legibility and distinction depended on their difference from other letters in the same font or script. The number of possibilities for describing even a single letter turned out to be unlimited. The descriptions were part of what Douglas Hofstadter characterized as an open set.[10] The phrase applies to sets in which each instance extends a category. For instance, the things that belong to the set "chairs" cannot be strictly described through formal requirements (four legs, a seat, and a back). Instead, the set expands with each new instantiation that meets the somewhat elusive criteria of "chair-ness." The identity of letters, Knuth discovered, was similar. A completely innovative font might create broken, distorted, or elaborately decorated letters that are still legible. This theoretical realization has implications for tasks like identifying letters in computational environments on operational bases such as optical character recognition.

THE LOGICAL IDENTITY OF LETTERS: UNICODE

Digital character codes, in particular the standard known as Unicode, are the alphanumeric standards that allow the letters, glyphs, signs, and characters of the world's writing systems (or most of them) to be translated and represented in computational displays and accurately identified in various protocols. The standards for this encoding were originally created around 1980 and are constantly updated. New standards are reissued on a regular basis to keep pace with innovations and changes. The original research that became Unicode, now overseen by the International Standards Organization, was developed at Xerox as the need for industry standards was recognized.[11] Unicode is based on the assignation of values to bits in an overall "codespace" that allows each character to have its own identity. This is indexed to representations (libraries of fonts and glyphs) for storage and display. Struggles over how it identifies each unique individual script pertain directly to the question of the identity of the alphabet.[12] Current debates are surprisingly close to topics that have been present throughout this study.[13] Phoenician letterforms have their unique Unicode character IDs. But does the discovery of Paleo-Hebrew require that a new set of character spaces be developed for its signs? Are these the same or different scripts? Here we are right back to fundamental questions: What is the "original" alphabet and how is its identity defined? To display the alphabet used at Lachish, a different set of characters is required than for those of the Royal Byblian inscriptions. But is the script itself distinct, structurally speaking? Does it contain a different number or sequence of signs? Does this apply as well to the Proto-Sinaitic scripts?

Unicode is technically complex. The work of creating standards that can cross linguistic and cultural boundaries is not trivial. The goal of text encoding was to define an unambiguous way to create a computationally defined character set.[14] A "character" in this definition is the smallest unit of communication, not to be confused with a specific font or image of a letter (which is a rendering of a character). The conceptual definition of characters is determined by how many unique entities exist in any given set. So, for writing English in the Latin alphabet, twenty-six upper- and lowercase characters, numbers, and punctuation are needed (128 code points).[15] For writing European languages that use a variant of the Latin alphabet, additional characters with accents and inflections were needed. A character has a *unique* identity, but its representations can be many. Unicode assigns *every character in every language a unique number*. The "numbers" are encoded in bytes. The first Unicode system only had 256 distinct entities, then a 2-byte system was introduced which allowed for something like 65,536 unique characters. When the number of characters in world languages (Chinese, Japanese, Korean) is taken into account and all the different variations of the alphabetic scripts of the world (Cyrillic, Greek, and so on) this quickly becomes inadequate. Current Unicode standards include over a million "code points" or unique entities.

Unicode does not store renderings of characters; it merely preserves the unique identifiers. The way a character looks, or how it is drawn, depends on the library of renderings and fonts in the protocols of the screen display, printer, browser, or output device. Unicode is based on the concept of discrete uniqueness, not form, and depends on how many different entities have to be identified individually. But Unicode identities—and this is the crucial point of relevance to alphabet studies—are written in alphanumeric code (known as Unicode "spelling"). So, to give an example, the "plus" sign has a "representative glyph" that looks like "+" but also has a number 2B, written 002B, which can be turned into hexadecimal notation for

10900 **Phoenician** **1091F**

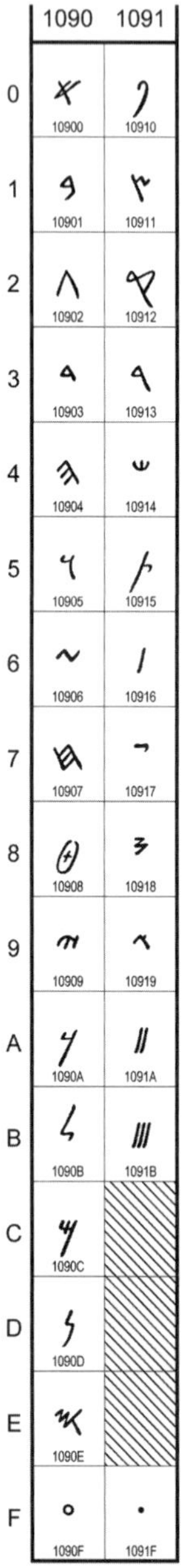

	1090	1091
0	𐤀 10900	𐤐 10910
1	𐤁 10901	𐤑 10911
2	𐤂 10902	𐤒 10912
3	𐤃 10903	𐤓 10913
4	𐤄 10904	𐤔 10914
5	𐤅 10905	𐤕 10915
6	𐤆 10906	𐤖 10916
7	𐤇 10907	𐤗 10917
8	𐤈 10908	𐤘 10918
9	𐤉 10909	𐤙 10919
A	𐤊 1090A	𐤚 1091A
B	𐤋 1090B	𐤛 1091B
C	𐤌 1090C	
D	𐤍 1090D	
E	𐤎 1090E	
F	𐤏 1090F	𐤟 1091F

Letters

10900 𐤀 PHOENICIAN LETTER ALF
→ 05D0 א hebrew letter alef
10901 𐤁 PHOENICIAN LETTER BET
→ 05D1 ב hebrew letter bet
10902 𐤂 PHOENICIAN LETTER GAML
→ 05D2 ג hebrew letter gimel
10903 𐤃 PHOENICIAN LETTER DELT
→ 05D3 ד hebrew letter dalet
10904 𐤄 PHOENICIAN LETTER HE
→ 05D4 ה hebrew letter he
10905 𐤅 PHOENICIAN LETTER WAU
→ 05D5 ו hebrew letter vav
10906 𐤆 PHOENICIAN LETTER ZAI
→ 05D6 ז hebrew letter zayin
10907 𐤇 PHOENICIAN LETTER HET
→ 05D7 ח hebrew letter het
10908 𐤈 PHOENICIAN LETTER TET
→ 05D8 ט hebrew letter tet
10909 𐤉 PHOENICIAN LETTER YOD
→ 05D9 י hebrew letter yod
1090A 𐤊 PHOENICIAN LETTER KAF
→ 05DB כ hebrew letter kaf
1090B 𐤋 PHOENICIAN LETTER LAMD
→ 05DC ל hebrew letter lamed
1090C 𐤌 PHOENICIAN LETTER MEM
→ 05DE מ hebrew letter mem
1090D 𐤍 PHOENICIAN LETTER NUN
→ 05E0 נ hebrew letter nun
1090E 𐤎 PHOENICIAN LETTER SEMK
→ 05E1 ס hebrew letter samekh
1090F 𐤏 PHOENICIAN LETTER AIN
→ 05E2 ע hebrew letter ayin
10910 𐤐 PHOENICIAN LETTER PE
→ 05E4 פ hebrew letter pe
10911 𐤑 PHOENICIAN LETTER SADE
→ 05E6 צ hebrew letter tsadi
10912 𐤒 PHOENICIAN LETTER QOF
→ 05E7 ק hebrew letter qof
10913 𐤓 PHOENICIAN LETTER ROSH
→ 05E8 ר hebrew letter resh
10914 𐤔 PHOENICIAN LETTER SHIN
→ 05E9 ש hebrew letter shin
10915 𐤕 PHOENICIAN LETTER TAU
→ 05EA ת hebrew letter tav

Numbers

10916 𐤖 PHOENICIAN NUMBER ONE
10917 𐤗 PHOENICIAN NUMBER TEN
10918 𐤘 PHOENICIAN NUMBER TWENTY
10919 𐤙 PHOENICIAN NUMBER ONE HUNDRED
1091A 𐤚 PHOENICIAN NUMBER TWO
1091B 𐤛 PHOENICIAN NUMBER THREE

Punctuation

1091F 𐤟 PHOENICIAN WORD SEPARATOR
• sometimes shown with a glyph for a short vertical bar
→ 002E . full stop
→ 00B7 · middle dot
→ 2E31 ⸱ word separator middle dot

FIGURE C.1 A part of the Unicode standard for Phoenician. As indicated in the standard, the representative glyphs are not to be considered "prescriptive." Note that the Unicode specification in the right-hand column is being cross-walked to match modern square Hebrew letters. Antonsusi, from the German Wikipedia site. Creative Commons BY 3.0 DE, via Wikimedia Commons.

computability. It also has a standard name, "PLUS SIGN," and other properties (e.g., "line breaking is permitted after the character").[16] As the technical literature stresses repeatedly, the "definitions of characters in Unicode are logical," and the "representative glyph" is used to make the identity of the character legible to human readers. A computer needs only to know that it is a unique entity whose specific presentations—whether in digital form or other displays already noted—will be invoked.

The glyphs on which Unicode Phoenician are based have many points of similarity with late versions of Paleo-Hebrew but differ from those of earlier periods that stretch back another eight or nine hundred years. The question of identity revolves around whether the differences between the two scripts simply rely on different glyphs (for representation and display) or whether they contain distinct logical categories. An argument for the distinctiveness of the older script forms can be readily supported on visual evidence—but so can the difference between an *a* in Palatino and in Comic Sans, though they are logically the same (they have the same position, role, identity, and "power" within the Roman alphabet). Phoenician and Paleo-Hebrew currently use the same Unicode keyboard.

GRAPHIC ELEMENTS

Optical character recognition (OCR) treats the visual forms of alphabetic notation quite differently from Unicode. The invention of OCR was motivated by the desire to produce a reading apparatus for the blind, but its value for remediation of print documents to digital files quickly became evident.[17] By the 1970s, OCR systems were being developed by major technology companies, and in the twenty-first century, OCR processing can even be enabled through a phone as well as on high-quality scanners and other sophisticated devices.

OCR works on a single character at a time, though handwriting and word-recognition programs have also been developed that can deal with compound units. OCR programs treat text as image, particularly in the first stages of preprocessing, which removes noise and background color, reduces the visual information to black and white, checks for skew and other distortions, and then does "zoning" to isolate paragraphs and format elements. Finally, the program isolates the characters through segmentation protocols. Matching, feature extraction, and "crossing point" approaches are used to identify the individual letters. The transcribed text is often processed through a dictionary or lexicon to clean up the words and spelling and improve accuracy. In the programs that use "matching," the task is based on pattern recognition, and the letters in the text subjected to OCR are compared with a set of glyphs. These can be font specific, or even handwriting specific, and "training" an OCR program can also involve generating the set of glyphs from an original source document—not unlike traditional training in paleography. In this circumstance, the alphabetic characters (or other glyphs, for that matter) are treated as atomized images.

Feature recognition and processing is more complicated since it involves specifying the components of letters—strokes, loops, intersecting lines. In other words, in the feature-recognition model, letters are understood as combinations of smaller components whose presence or absence determines their identity. Handwriting usually requires this kind of processing because letterforms are more complex when rendered in script than in fonts (whose standard forms are more readily patterned and matched). A variant on feature detection uses crossing point approaches. These track what is present or absent in any particular zone of a grid that is artificially imposed on each letter and then demarcated for processing purposes. The protocols then search to see if there is a stroke that reaches to this corner or that, is present in this quadrant, in the center, and so forth. This technique also identifies the letter against a list of features, but these are more schematic and reductive than in handwriting recognition.[18] In all instances, a letter is a graphic form whose individual identity is being determined in relation to models or within a set. More sophisticated processing methods are constantly being developed, and the scale, range, and scope of OCR continues to expand. But whether the methods are statistical, heuristic, or based in neural networks and other protocols, they all conceive of the alphabet as a set of graphically discrete elements whose identity resides in their capacity to be differentiated one from another.[19]

AN AGENT OF LITERACY

The identity of letters operates within digital networks, but the hegemony of the alphabet functions in human systems as well. The very notion of literacy is often associated with practices of coercion and domination (tied to larger political and social patterns) but also practices of liberation and empowerment.

The acquisition of literacy is often identified in Western culture as a process of learning "the ABCs."[20] Analyzing the means by which such learning is encoded in texts and graphics offers a striking portrait of the ways instruction in literacy includes moral, ethical, political, religious, and other values. Some of the earliest primers, published from about the middle of the sixteenth century, opened with the verse "In Adam's Fall, we sinned all" as the mnemonic text for learning the letter *A*.[21] This cheering bit of moral instruction was reprinted for centuries as the introduction to letters. Other rhymes and themes incorporated information about farm life, manners and decorum, animals and birds, then railroads and ships, particularly in the nineteenth century, as the children's book industry expanded and campaigns for universal literacy increased young readership. The proliferation of ABC books brought with it an unabashed program of indoctrination into cultural values—and prejudices. One particularly striking example is *An ABC for Baby Patriots* published by the renowned British company Dean

B, b.
PENINSULA
WATERLOO
CRIMEA
INDIA
CHINA
EGYPT
KHARTOUM
C, c.
B b
B stands for Battles
By which England's name
Has for ever been covered
With glory and fame.
C c
C is for Colonies.
Rightly we boast,
That of all the great nations
Great Britain has most.

FIGURE C.2 From Mrs. Ernest Ames, *An ABC for Baby Patriots* (London: Dean and Son Publications, 1899). Public domain.

and Sons.[22] Written by one Mrs. Ernest Ames (a pseudonym?), the book is a prime example of the kind of ideologically driven presentation that normalizes behaviors and values in the course of literacy instruction. Racism, gender bias, speciesism, ableism, classism, imperialism—pretty much every form of unacknowledged (or deliberate) bias appears in these works. Alphabetic literacy became a ubiquitous instrument of social engineering, normalizing points of view and integrating them into educational systems of reward and advancement.

Nearly every alphabet book for children serves these double purposes—to introduce the elements of literacy and to inculcate values of a dominant or mainstream culture. The relationship between cultural hegemony and alphabetization, the phenomenon by which literacy is introduced or imposed using an alphanumeric notation system, is an entire area of study in which the alphabet is conceived as a positive instrument of administration, education, and advancement. The global spread of the alphabet follows trade, as we have seen from the history of Phoenician transmission. But it also follows industry—into the mines of Sinai and military expeditions (inscriptions in Wadi el-Hol and throughout the Greek islands)—as well as exploration and colonization. The alphabet was imported by missionaries as well as provincial governments where the conduct of religion and administration depended on the use of standard codes.

It would be simplistic to suggest that the adoption and modification of alphabetic writing throughout Africa, Arabia, India, and throughout Europe, the New World, and Asia was always a matter of aggression of one nation or people against or over another. But it would be naïve to suggest that the imposition of dominant modes of alphabetic literacy did not have profound implications. The alphabet is an efficient and flexible system of communication and notation. Its adoption was often voluntary, independent, and motivated by the drive toward writing from within cultural contexts. The alphabet has agency and is a tool of ideology. Its presence is, de facto, necessarily an agent of control.

In one study of this phenomenon, Craig Brandist wrote about the alphabet in revolutionary Russia. He carefully charted the ways attitudes toward Cyrillic were "tainted by associations with Tsarist Russian policies" but how the invention and introduction of a modified Latin alphabet into areas of the new Soviet Union, meant to circumvent these legacies, created problems.[23]

Multiple instances of this process could be cited. A considerable literature exists on the oppressive aspects of the politics of orthography and the imposition of literacy on indigenous populations. These are not, strictly speaking, part of the historiography of "origins" of the alphabet. Brief mention of them here is meant to signal the recognition that no discussion of these histories can ignore the realities and implications of the alphabet as an instrument of cultural force.

GLOBAL HEGEMONY

For cultures whose writing is character based, the extent to which alphabetic systems are "baked into" the infrastructure of communication systems poses particular challenges that cannot be resolved with simple crosswalks of letter to character equivalence or substitution. In his groundbreaking 2017 study, *The Chinese Typewriter*, Tom Mullaney studied the ways assumptions of universalism are part of information infrastructure.[24] Looking, for instance, at Morse code, Mullaney showed how the alphanumeric underpinnings of the system made its use almost impossible for Chinese characters. The number of dot-dash symbols could not proliferate to the extent necessary for even the most meager and basic set of characters to be sent telegraphically. The solution was a double mediation in which a code of codes was created so that every character had to be translated into an alphanumeric code before it was transmitted.[25] The number of pulses required for this work was far greater than for alphabetic letters, and each message had to be translated again using the decoding book—so that the sequence of alphanumeric characters could be matched against a Chinese lexicon of characters. The disadvantages in speed, efficiency, and intellectual effort are substantial. Where alphabetic Morse code requires one set of translations, the Chinese code required several in sequence, increasing labor and also chance of errors.

Efforts to create a "typewriter" for the Chinese language required a reengineering of the fundamental Western design and only met with success in the twentieth century.[26] As Mullaney detailed, when computer-based communications using QWERTY keyboards appeared, the need for a character-based system required an elaborately engineered solution.[27] The result was, again, a multipart mediation in which an initial stroke introduced an initial criterion for a selection decision in a multistep selection process. Likely candidates that met that criterion appeared on the screen and then were subject to selection of a numbered or sequenced character suited to the writer's need. The system relied on sequential mediations through an "Input method editor," or IME.[28] The selection process is a multistep activity, not a one-to-one correlation of keystroke and character.

As Mullaney made clear, technologies that were "viewed by many as language agnostic, neutral, 'universal'" could be adapted for almost all writing systems in the world—except Chinese. From the telegraph code to the present, his argument outlined the ways in which Chinese script was placed "in a position of structurally embedded 'inequality.'"[29] These structural issues exist at nearly every scale of information technology, as per this quote from Mullaney: "Early in the history of computing, Western engineers determined that a 5 x 7 dot matrix grid offered sufficient resolution to print legible Latin alphabetic letters. To do the same for Chinese—a writing system with no alphabet, and whose graphemes present greater structural nuance, variation, and complexity—required engineers to expand this grid to no less than 18 x 22." This graphic calculation became more complicated yet when translated into what is known as "bit-coding" for digital operations. Mullaney noted that "128 addresses offered sufficient space for all of the letters of the Latin alphabet, along with numerals and key analphabetic symbols and functions" but that "Chinese characters, by comparison, in theory demanded no less than 16-bit architecture to handle its more than 70,000 characters."[30]

The full hegemony of the alphabet is present in the extensive, subtle, even insidious reach of computational infrastructure. Even if no deliberate agency motivated this design, the incidental effect has real consequences. The "letters" do not act, nor does the alphabet, but the integration of alphabetic and alphanumeric systems into the structure of global communication makes the alphabet a hegemonic force millennia after its emergence in a very different set of conditions and circumstances.

CONCLUSION

The elements used to create the unique identifiers for the digital environment are alphanumeric. The Arabic numerals and the zero, part of basic Unicode, were not part of the writing system of ancient Semites or even Phoenicians. Whatever the life of letters has been, in their role in international, global, networked environments, they continue to be vital and potent. We rely, more than we realize, on ancient inventions created almost four thousand years ago by Semitic-speaking people in a desert environment in the ancient Levant. No other communication system or code has integrated itself so persistently, so pervasively, or so successfully. The alphabet remains a major component of human systems, and the capacity of the letters to serve as discrete but related elements of a set of signs has only increased in power. The origin stories and history of the alphabet remain areas of attention in scholarly investigation and popular imagination. If we were to remove the alphabet from the current environment, and all traces of its past, the history of human culture and development would largely vanish. Even in those areas of the globe where alphabetic writing is not the primary mode of communication, in our current networked world, the infrastructure of communication systems depends on its existence. More to the point, given the complexities of emerging standards and character codes in the contemporary moment, our shifting concepts of historical evidence, and the changing paradigms of human knowledge, we are still, it seems, in the process of inventing the alphabet.

Notes

INTRODUCTION

1 A long list could be compiled of recent works on the history of writing and the alphabet. In addition to the authors noted in the text, consider work by Albertine Gaur, *A History of Writing* (London: British Library, 1984); Steven R. Fischer, *A History of Writing* (London: Reaktion, 2001); Geoffrey Sampson, *Writing Systems* (Stanford: Stanford University Press, 1985); and Peter Daniels and William Bright, *The World's Writing Systems* (New York: Oxford University Press, 1996).

2 John F. Healey, *The Early Alphabet* (Berkeley: University of California Press, 1990); Joseph Naveh, *The Early History of the* Alphabet (Jerusalem: Hebrew University; Magnes Press, 1982); Andrew Robinson, *The Story of Writing* (London: Thames and Hudson, 2007); and Anne-Marie Christin, *L'histoire de l'écriture* (Paris: Flammarion, 2001).

CHAPTER ONE

1 Herodotus, *Histories*, book V, trans. A. D. Godley, Loeb Classical Library (Cambridge, MA: Harvard University Press, 1920–25), http://penelope.uchicago.edu/Thayer/E/Roman/Texts/Herodotus/5C*.html.

2 Isaac Taylor, *The Alphabet* (London: Kegan Paul, Trench, 1883).

3 See the definition of the two Greek words in the WordHippo dictionary: https://www.wordhippo.com/.

4 Lilian Jeffery, *Local Scripts of Archaic Greece* (Oxford: Clarendon Press, 1961).

5 Herodotus, *Histories*. For a slightly different translation, see Ancient History Source, Fordham University, excerpt from Herodotus, *The History*, trans. George Rawlinson (New York: Dutton, 1862), https://sourcebooks.fordham.edu/ancient/430phoenicia.asp.

6 Herodotus, William Thayer, "Herodotus," Loeb Classical Library Edition, http://penelope.uchicago.edu/Thayer/E/Roman/Texts/Herodotus/5C*.html.

7 The "witnesses," or existing manuscripts of the *Histories*, actually differ little from each other, suggesting that what comes forward are texts with a common source considered reliable A tenth-century manuscript, known as Laurentianus 70.3, is considered "our oldest and best witness to the text." See R. A. McNeal, "On Editing Herodotus," *L'antiquité classique* 52 (1983): 110–29. See also Jesica Jayd Lewis, "A *History of the Histories*: From Papyrus to Codex, From Codex to Today," *A&P: Antiquorum et praesentis*, December 20, 2014, www.antiquorumetpraesentis.com. For a slightly different translation, see Rawlinson excerpt on Ancient History Source, Fordham University, https://sourcebooks.fordham.edu/ancient/430phoenicia.asp.

8 John K. Papadopoulos, "The Early History of the Greek Alphabet: New Evidence from Eretria and Methone," *Antiquity* 90, no. 353 (October 2016): 1238–54. Inscriptions from Eretria include texts in the Phrygian language using the Phoenician alphabet. The Phyrgians came from Asia Minor, and their language is not Semitic, suggesting they had already modified the alphabet for their own purposes before contact with the Greeks. This kind of complexity is typical of the cultural exchanges through which the alphabet takes hold locally as it spreads, and it demonstrates the difficulty of tracking a single path of transmission.

9 Mycenaean Greek developed from Proto-Greek and both are Indo-European languages.

10 Roger Woodard, *Greek Writing from Knossos to Homer* (New York: Oxford University Press, 1977), 218–19.

11 Very little discussion of writing or its history exists between late antiquity and early modern scholarship except for Isidore of Seville's seventh-century *Etymologies*.

12 Godfrey Driver, *Semitic Writing from Pictograph to Alphabet* (Oxford: Oxford University Press, 1954), 128–29.

13 Bill Thayer, *The Annals of Tacitus*, accessed June 9, 2021, http://penelope.uchicago.edu/Thayer/E/Roman/Texts/Tacitus/Annals/11A*.html.

14 Adolf Kirchhoff, *Studien zur Geschichte des griechischen Alphabets* (Berlin: F. Dümmler, 1877).

15 Driver, *Semitic Writing*, 129.

16 Driver, 129.

17 Driver, 129; n.b. Agenor is Cadmus's father.

18 Driver, 128–29.

19 Claude Duret, *Le thrésor des langues de cest univers* [. . .] (Cologne: Matt. Berjon, pour la Société caldoriene, 1613).

20 Duret, 644. Unless otherwise noted, translations are my own.

21 Duret, 644.

22 Hermannus Hugo, *De prima scribendi origine* [. . .] (Antwerp: Officina Plantiniana, 1617), 26.

23 Thomas Godwin, *Romanae historiae anthologia recognita et aucta* (London: Printed for Henry Cripps, 1661–62), 248.

24 Godwin, 248.

25 Lucan's Latin text begins: "Phoenices primi (famae si credimus) ausi / Mansuram rudibus vocem signare figuris."

26 Lucan, *Pharsalia*, book 3, Massilia, trans. Sir Edward Ridley (London: Longmans, Green, 1905), 69.

27 The many authors who cited the classical authors and then cited each other citing the classical texts included Edward Stillingfleet, *Origines sacrae* (London: Printed by R. W. for Henry Mortlock, 1662); John Marsham, *Chronicus canon* (London: T. Roycroft, 1672); Anselm Bayly, *An Introduction Literary and Philosophical to Languages* (London: John Rivington, 1756); Thomas Astle, *The Origin and Progress of Writing, as well Hieroglyphic as Elementary* (London: T. Payne and Son, 1784); and Henry Noel Humphreys, *The Origin and Progress of the Art of Writing* (London: Ingraham, Cooke, 1854). Many more could be added to this list.

28 Guillaume Postel, *Linguarum duodecim characteribus differentium alphabetum, introductio, ac legendi modus longè facilimus* (Parisiis: Apud Dionysium Lescuier, 1538).

29 John Jackson, *Chronological Antiquities, or The Antiquities and Chronology of the Most Ancient Kingdoms, from the Creation of the World, for the Space of Five Thousand Years: In Three Volumes* [. . .] (London: Printed for the author, 1752).

30 Jackson, 5–6.

31 Citation conventions are still minimal, even in someone as erudite as Edward Stillingfleet, who notes his sources in the margins but has no bibliography. Ability to decode the references assumes familiarity with most of the sources.

32 McNeal, "On Editing Herodotus."

33 Stillingfleet, *Origines sacrae*, 18.

34 Stillingfleet, 18.

35 Stillingfleet, 19.

36 Stillingfleet, 20.

37 Stillingfleet, 22.

38 Stillingfleet, 21.

39 Stillingfleet, 24.

40 Stillingfleet does not include any of the writers in the Cabalistic tradition, such as Postel, Reuchlin, Trithemius, Agrippa, and others. This separation, between rational historians and mystical ones, becomes marked in the citation histories.

41 Astle, *The Origin*.

42 Astle, 33–34.

43 Astle, 36.

44 Astle, 33.

45 Astle, 33.

46 Astle, 32.

47 P. Austin Nuttall, *A Classical and Archaeological Dictionary* [. . .] (London: Whittaker; Oxford: J. H Parker, 1840).

48 Nuttall, viii.

49 Edward Pococke, *India in Greece* (London: John Griffin, 1852), 23–24.

50 Pococke, 15.

51 This distinguished them from the northern Dorians, western Aeoloians, and Achaeans in Asia Minor.

52 Taylor, *The Alphabet*, 2, citing Hugh James Rose, *Inscriptiones Graecae vetustissimae* (London: John Murray, 1825).

53 Taylor, 2.

54 Taylor, 3.

55 Taylor, 19–22.

56 Elena Martin Gonzalez, "The Drawings on the Rock Inscriptions of Archaic Thera," *Inscriptiones Graecae* (*IG* XII3, 536–601; *IG* XII3 Suppl. 1410–93), Society for Classical Studies. Gonzalez cites Jeffery as her authority.

57 A.W. Johnston, "The Alphabet," in *Sea Routes from Sidon to Huelva: Interconnections in the Mediterranean*, ed. N. Stampolidis and V. Karageorghis (Athens: Museum of Cycladic Art,, 2003), 263–76.

58 Taylor, *The Alphabet*, 8.

59 Kirchhoff, *Studien*.

60 Taylor, *The Alphabet*, 22–27.

61 Taylor, 58–59.

62 He described many variations among the Ionian, Aegean, Corinthian, Argive, Attic, and Peloponnesian, among which he considered the Euboean the most different.

63 Taylor, *The Alphabet*, 61.

64 Jeffery, *Local Scripts*, 1.

65 Jeffery, 2.

66 Jeffery, 7.

67 Jeffery, 9, citing Diodorus, vol. 58.

68 Jeffery, 17.

69 Jeffery, 17.

70 Cited by Humphreys, *The Origin and Progress*, 11.

71 Ingrid Rowland, "Athanasius Kircher and the Egyptian Oedipus," in *The Ecstatic Journey: Athanasius Kircher in Baroque Rome* (Chicago: University of Chicago Press, 2000) 1–20, excerpted in Fathom Archive, accessed June 9, 2021, http://fathom.lib.uchicago.edu/1/777777122590/; Athanasius Kircher, *Prodromus Coptus sive Aegyptiacus* (Rome: Typis S. Cong. De Propag. Fide, 1636).

72 Yale Peabody Museum of Natural History, "Echoes of Egypt," accessed June 9, 2021, https://echoesofegypt.peabody.yale.edu/egyptosophy/sphinx-mystagogaturris-babel.

73 Adam Parry, *The Making of Homeric Verse: The Collected Papers of Milman Parry* (Oxford: Clarendon Press, 1971).

74 Rhys Carpenter, "Letters of Cadmus," *American Journal of Philology* 56, no.1 (1935): 5.

75 Carpenter, 7.

76 Carpenter, 6.

77 Carpenter, 10.

78 Carpenter, 8.

79 Carpenter, 10.

80 Carpenter, 9.

81 Carpenter, 9.

82 Carpenter, 10.

83 Carpenter, 10.

84 Martin Bernal, *Cadmean Letters* (Winona Lake, IN: Eisenbrauns, 1990), 1.

85 A more recent reassessment of linguistic, archaeological, and epigraphic evidence by Willemijn Waal offers a careful review that argues for a transmission period that begins later than Bernal's suggestion but earlier than that of traditional classicists. Willemijn Waal, "On the 'Phoenician Letters': The Case for an Early Transmission of the Greek Alphabet from an Archaeological, Epigraphic, and Linguistic Perspective," *Aegean Studies* 1, no. 4 (December 2018): 83–125.

86 Woodard, *Greek Writing*, 3–4.

87 Lukasz Niesiolowski-Spano, "Early Alphabetic Scripts and the Origin of Greek Letters," in *Haec mihi in animis vestris templa: Studia Classica in Memory of Professor Lesław Morawiecki*, ed. Piotr Berdowski and Beata Blahaczek (Rzeszów: Institute of History, University of Rzeszów, 2007), 47–63.

88 Woodard, *Greek Writing*, 5.

89 Niesiolowski-Spano, "Early Alphabetic Scripts."

90 Niesiolowski-Spano, 184, citing Christos G. Doumas, "Aegeans in the Levant: Myth and Reality," in *Mediterranean People in Transition: Thirteenth to Early Tenth Century* BCE, ed. S. Gitin, A. Mazar, and E. Stern (Jerusalem: Israel Exploration Society, 1998), 129–37.

91 Waal, "On the 'Phoenician Letters,'" 89. "Semitist" is Waal's spelling.

92 Waal, 89. By contrast, Waal continues, Carpenter saw more similarity with the Phoenician of the ninth to eighth centuries BCE.

93 Cited by Waal, 97.

94 Waal, 100.

95 Laurence DeLooze, *The Letters and the Cosmos* (Toronto: University of Toronto Press, 2016), 5.

96 Godwin, *Romanae historiae*, citing *Euseb. Praepar. Evang. Lib.*, 18.

CHAPTER TWO

1 See Thomas W. Davis, *Shifting Sands: The Rise and Fall of Biblical Archaeology* (Oxford: Oxford University Press, 2004), for a discussion of the history of biblical archaeology as a field.

2 The King James version of this final passage is almost exactly the same: "[12] And the LORD said unto Moses, Come up to me into the mount, and be there: and I will give thee tables of stone, and a law, and commandments which I have written; that thou mayest teach them." "The Book of Shemot (Exodus): Chap. 24," Jewish Virtual Library, JPS Electronic Edition, based on the 1917 JPS translation, copyright © 1998 by Larry Nelson, American-Israeli Cooperative Enterprise, 1998–2021, https://www.jewishvirtuallibrary.org/shemot-exodus-chapter-24.

3 For a hint of the kind of discussion this finds in popular culture, see lostinspace, "The Columns of Seth and Their Possible Existence," AboveTopSecret.com, Above Network, November 22, 2004, http://www.abovetopsecret.com/forum/thread99782/pg1.

4 Jewish Virtual Library (American-Israeli Cooperative Enterprise), accessed June 9, 2021, https://www.jewishvirtuallibrary.org/hebrew-in-ancient-jewish-scriptures.

5 See Jewish Virtual Library, accessed June 10, 2021, https://www.jewishvirtuallibrary.org/decalogue.

6 Peter Kirby, "Clement of Alexandria, The Stromata, or Miscellanies," Early Christian writings, 2001–21, http://www.earlychristianwritings.com/text/clement-stromata-book1.html. A twentieth-century translation of Eusebius's third-century *Praeparatio Evangelica* (Preparation for the Gospel), contains a version that barely differs: "But Eupolemus says that the first wise man was Moses, and that he was the first to teach the Jews letters, and from the Jews the Phoenicians received them, and from the Phoenicians the Greeks, and that Moses was the first to give written laws to the Jews." Jewish Virtual Library, accessed June 10, 2021, https://www.jewishvirtuallibrary.org/eupolemus.

7 Quite possibly the translation here uses the term "grammar" to translate the Greek *grammata*, which is the word for "letters." Peter Kirby, Early Christian Writings, http://www.earlychristianwritings.com/text/clement-stromata-book1.html.

8 Stephen A. Barney et al., *The Etymologies of Isidore of Seville* (Cambridge: Cambridge University Press, 2006), 39, https://sfponline.org/Uploads/2002/st%20isidore%20in%20english.pdf.

9 See Tim Denecker, "The Origin and Nature of Language," in *Ideas on Language in Early Latin Christianity from Tertullian to Isidore of Seville*, Vigiliae Christianae, Supplements, vol. 142 (Boston: Brill, 2017), 25–56, https://brill.com/abstract/book/9789004276659/B9789004276659_003.xml.

10 Editors, "Joseph Justus Scaliger," *Encyclopedia Britannica*, accessed June 10, 2021, https://www.britannica.com/biography/Joseph-Justus-Scaliger.

11 Joseph Scaliger, *Opus novum de emendatione temporum* (Lutèce: Mamert Pattison for Sebastien Nivelle, 1583).

12 If we can believe the alphabetically sorted entries of the *Secunda Scaligerana*, a candid

collection of table talk originally recorded during the years 1604–06, these are the words of praise that Joseph Justus Scaliger—Huguenot philologist extraordinaire and Europe's first research professor (at Leiden, from 1593 to his death in 1609)—used in speaking to his students about Flavius Josephus. C. P. E. Nothaft, "Josephus and New Testament Chronology in the Work of Joseph Scaliger," *International Journal of the Classical Tradition* 23, no. 3 (2016): 246–51, https://link.springer.com/article/10.1007%2Fs12138-016-0403-9.

13 *The Works of Flavius Josephus, Jewish Historian*, trans. William Whiston (London,1737), accessed June 10, 2021, https://penelope.uchicago.edu/josephus/ant-1.html.

14 Flavius Josephus, *Of the Antiquities of the Jews, Book I, Containing the Interval of 3833 Years from the Creation to the Death of Isaac* (London, 1737), chap. 2, http://penelope.uchicago.edu/josephus/ant-1.html. This passage changes very little across time, as can be seen by a citation from Henry Christmas, *Universal Mythology* (London: J. W. Parker, 1838): "The Patriarch Seth . . . knowing that Adam had foretold how everything on earth should perish, either by fire or by a general deluge, and fearing lest philosophy and astronomy should be effaced from the remembrance of men, and be buried in oblivion, engraved his knowledge on two columns, the one of brick, the other of stone, that if the waters should destroy the former, the later might remain and instruct the human race in astronomical knowledge. This column is still to be seen in the Siridiac land" (54).

15 For a long discussion see Alexander Winslow, "The Pillars in the Land of Siriad," Squires Publishing, accessed June 10, 2021, http://www.squirespublishing.co.uk/files/syriad.htm.

16 The Sefiria site dates the text to somewhere between 200 BCE and 200 CE, while acknowledging that some scholars place it in a medieval period, even though it absorbed some earlier texts and traditions: A Living Library of Jewish Texts, Sefaria, accessed June 10, 2021, https://www.sefaria.org.

17 "Sefir Yetzirah," Sefiria, accessed June 10, 2021, https://www.sefaria.org/Sefer_Yetzirah?lang=bi.

18 "Sefir Yetzirah," Sefaria Community Translation, accessed June 10, 2021, https://www.sefaria.org/Sefer_Yetzirah.1?ven=Sefaria_Community_Translation&lang=bi.

19 *Sefer Yetzirah*, trans. Isidor Kalisch (New York: L. H. Frank, 1877), 15, https://archive.org/details/sketchoftalmudwo02kali.

20 Guillaume Postel, *De originibus seu de Hebraicae linguae & gentis antiquitate, deque variarum linguarum affinitate liber* (Paris: Apud Dionysium Lescuier, 1538) and Jacques Gaffarel, *Curiositez inouyes hoc est curiositates inauditae de figuris Persarum talismannicis, horoscopo patriarcharum et characteribus coelestibus* (Paris: Hervé du Mesnil, 1629).

21 JF Ptak Science Books, "Blog Post 1166," accessed June 10, 2021, https://longstreet.typepad.com/thesciencebookstore/2010/10/catechizing-the-sky-writing-on-the-stars.html.

22 It might be more correct to say that mystical thought became separated from mainstream scholarship; interest in its pursuit never wanes.

23 Rob Barrett, "Johann Reuchlin, Philologist and Mystic: The Christian Recovery of Hebrew" (Vancouver: Regent College, 2001), 1, https://www.academia.edu/333690/Johann_Reuchlin_Philologist_and_Mystic_The_Christian_Rediscovery_of_Hebrew. Some scholars have ascribed the nearly one-thousand-year history of ignorance of Hebrew in European scholarly communities to anti-Semitism; see Barrett's discussion for details.

24 Grammars and dictionaries proliferated. Barrett, 6.

25 Barrett, 15.

26 Cited in Barrett, 6; Johannes Reuchlin, *Recommendation Whether to Confiscate, Destroy, and Burn All Jewish Books*, trans. Peter Wortsman (New York: Paulist Press, 2000).

27 Jé Wilson, "Francis van Helmont and the Alphabet of Nature," *Public Domain Review*, June 1, 2016, https://publicdomainreview.org/2016/06/01/francis-van-helmont-and-the-alphabet-of-nature/.

28 Allison Courdert, *The Impact of the Kabbalah in the Seventeenth Century: The Life and Thought of Francis Mercury van Helmont (1614–1698)* (Leiden: Brill, 1999).

29 Courdert, *The Impact.*

30 Pico della Mirandola, *Heptaplus* (Venice: Bernardinus Venetus, 1489); Abraham de Balmes, *Mikneh Avram: Peculium Abrae; Grammatica Hebraea* (Venice: Daniel Bomberg, 1523); and Hermannus Hugo, *De prima scribendi* (Antwerp: Officina Plantiniana, 1617). On Pico, see Chaim Wirszubski, *Pico della Mirandola's Encounter with Jewish Mysticism* (Cambridge, MA: Harvard University Press, 1989).

31 Brian Copenhaver, "Giovanni Pico della Mirandola," in *Stanford Encyclopedia of Philosophy*, accessed June 10, 2021, https://plato.stanford.edu/entries/pico-della-mirandola/#WorkRepu.

32 Saverio Campanini, "The Quest for the Holiest Alphabet in the Renaissance," in *A Universal Art: Hebrew Grammar across Disciplines and Faiths*, ed. Nadia Vidro, Irene E. Zwiep, and Judith Olszowy-Schlanger (Boston: Brill, 2014), 211.

33 Alexander Top, *The Olive Leafe* (London: W. White for George Vincent, 1603), n.p.

34 Top, n.p.

35 Top. n.p.

36 Hugo, *De prima scribendi.*

37 Nicholas Hudson, *Writing and European Thought, 1600–1830* (Cambridge: Cambridge University Press, 1994), 33–34.

38 Postel, *Linguarum*; Theodore Bibliander, *De ratione communi omnium linguarum* (Zurich: Christophe Frosch, 1548); Scaliger, *Opus novum*; and Angelo Rocca, *Bibliotheca apostolica Vaticana* (Rome: Typographia Apostolica Vaticana 1591).

39 Bibliander, 39.

40 This sometimes makes tracking them difficult at several centuries' remove.

41 Duret, *Le thrésor.*

42 Duret, 643–44.

43 Duret, 643–44.

44 Duret, 116–18.

45 While most Cabalistic (Christian) and Kabbalistic (Hebrew) literature was composed in the late Middle Ages, mainly from the twelfth century onward in Spain, the *Sefer Yetzirah* is generally dated to at least as early as the second century CE, and possibly earlier. What is clear is that Clement of Alexandria's writings from that period contain statements that are similar to those in the *Sefer* and appear to be based in part on a reading of that text.

46 Classical and patristic authors were often indicated in shorthand, and dates, editions, and page or verse numbers were generally absent. Duret's conventions were not yet those of modern scholarship.

47 For example, in his 1672 publication, *Chronicus canon Aegyptiacus, Ebraicus, Graecus, & disquisitiones*, John Marsham mentioned Thoth/Mercury as the inventor of writing, but he also cited Pliny's opinion that the letters were Assyrian, noted that others say they came from Egypt, or were Syrian, and then finished by saying that "among the Jews, the tradition is that Seth, son of Adam, inscribed two columns," for which point he cited, of course, Josephus. The chain of citation here, like that of classical sources, repeated and reiterated the information of earlier authorities.

48 Duret, *Le thrésor*, 129.

49 James G. Fraser, "A Checklist of Samaritan Manuscripts Known to Have Entered Europe before AD 1700," *Abr Nahrain* 21 (1982–83): 10–27; and M. Gaster, "Jewish Knowledge of the Samaritan Alphabet in the Middle Ages," *Studies and Texts* (London: 1928), 1:600–613.

50 Until the finding of the Dead Sea Scrolls, no earlier manuscripts of the Old Testament were known other than Greek ones from early in the Common Era.

51 Daniel Defoe, *An Essay upon Literature, or An Enquiry into the Antiquity and Original of Letters* [. . .] (London: Thomas Bowles, 1726).

52 Approximately three hundred years, according to chronologies that date Creation at 4004 BC, or as much as six hundred years. See William Austin, "The Hebrew Chronology Corrected for Half-Years and Synchronized to Mesopotamian and Egyptian History," (2016), https://www.academia.edu/20426570/The_Hebrew_chronology_from_Noah_to_Moses_corrected_for_half_years.

53 Defoe, *An Essay*, 3.

54 Defoe, 4.

55 Defoe, 10.

56 The earliest accepted date for Phoenician coins is about 450 BCE, and they often bear a dolphin motif, or that of an owl, sometimes without inscriptions. Mike Markowitz, "CoinWeek Ancient Coin Series—Coinage of the Phoenicians," *CoinWeek*, February 29, 2016, https://coinweek.com/ancient-coins/coinweek-ancient-coin-series-coinage-of-the-phoenicians/. Defoe might well have had access to numismatic collections in which these featured.

57 Defoe, *An Essay*, 15.

58 Defoe, 20.

59 Defoe, 20.

60 James Ussher, *Annales veteris testamenti, a prima mundi origine deducti* (London, 1650), would have been the commonly used source for biblical chronology, but he put the date of Exodus at 1446 BC, so Defoe must have drawn on another authority.

61 Sir Walter Raleigh, *The Historie of the World in Five Books* (London: William Stansby for Walter Burre, 1614).

62 Defoe, *An Essay*, 38.

63 Defoe, 38.

64 Defoe, 43.

65 Defoe, *An Essay*, 50, cites Thomas Bang, Checking Bang's own text, we find a long list of alphabets presented, those associated with: Adamus, Adami filii, Sethus, Sethus filii, Henochus, Chaldiai, Assyrii, Syri, Phoenices, Aegyptii, Aethiopes, Moses, Abraham, Mercurius, Memnon, Isis, Esdras, Cadmus, Linus Thebanus, Phoenix, Cecrops Diphyes, Evander, Nicostrata, Saturnus, Pythagoras, Epicharmus Siculus, Simonides Melicus, Palamedes, Claudius Imperator, Hieronymous, Chrysostomus, Ulphilas.

66 Duret, Rocca, Teseo Ambrogio, Johannes Pantheus, and Bonaventure Hepburn, among others.

67 Defoe, *An Essay*, 79.

68 The number of scholars working in this domain proliferates in the eighteenth century, and the list given in the summary of Charles Toustain's references later in this chapter gives a hint of the scope.

69 Bayly, *An Introduction*, 38.

70 Bayly, 27.

71 In particular, on page 27 Bayly cites Pierre Besnier, *La Réunion des Langages* (Paris, 1674) and Brian Walton, *Biblia sacra polyglotta* (London: Thomas Roycroft, 1657). Walton's polyglot printing included fonts in Syriac, Arabic, Greek, Hebrew, Samaritan, and Latin.

72 Bayly, *An Introduction*, cites his sources, 30–31: (*Nat. Hist.* b. 5, c. 12, c. 56; Siciulus, B.5; Eusebius, *Praep. Ev.* l. 10; Clem, *Strom* l. 1; Augustine, *De Civ Dei.*; Dr. John Owen, *Theol.* l. 4, c. 3; Gale, *In the Court of the Gentiles*, part 1, b. 1, c. 10; Wolseley, *Reasonableness of Christian Belief*; Johnson, *Preface to a Sermon*).

73 Bayly, 33.

74 Bayly, 33.

75 Bayly, 34.

76 Bayly, 38.

77 Bayly might have seen coins from the second to the first centuries BCE, considered by L. Kadman to be an "artificial revival of the ancient Hebrew alphabet." L. Kadman, "The Hebrew Coin Script: A Study in the Epigraphy of Ancient Jewish Coins," *Israel Exploration Journal* 4, nos. 3/4 (1954): 168.

78 Jackson's reference was to the Septuagint, the Greek translation of the Old Testament, and the reference to the Hebrew copy Josephus might have consulted was unclear. Jackson, *Chronological Antiquities*, xi.

79 Jackson, 85.

80 Jackson, 87.

81 Jackson, 87.

82 Jackson, 90.

83 Charles Toustain, *Nouveau traité de diplomatique* (Paris: Guillaume Desprez and Pierre Guillaume Cavelier, 1750), 572.

84 The authors Toustain lists include the following, some of whom are easier to identify than others: Genebrand, Bellarmin, Arias Montanus, le Père Etienne Morin, M. Huet, Montfaucon, Calmet, Renaudot, Willalpandus, Scaliger, Grotius, Hottinger, Casaubon, Drusius, Waser, Brerewood, Capelle, Walton, Bouchard, Vossius, Prideaux, Shuckford, Edouard Bernard, and Simon.

85 Toustain, *Nouveau traité*, 594.

86 Astle, *The Origin*, 11. Astle's list of learned men also contained many familiar names (Eusebius, Clement, and Isidore), as well as now-obscure modern authorities: Mr. Wise, Mr. Windar, and a Mr. Costard, famous for his Letter to Mr. Halhed.

87 Astle, 11.

88 Astle, 11.

89 Astle, 12.

90 Astle, 12.

91 Astle, 12.

92 Astle, 12–13.

93 Astle, 13.

94 Astle, 14.

95 Astle, 15.

96 Astle, 25.

97 Astle, 20.

98 Richard Pococke, *A Description of the East and Some Other Countries* (London: 1743).

99 Pococke, 142.

100 See Douglas Petrovich, *The World's Oldest Alphabet* (Jerusalem: Carta, 2016); and Christopher Rollston's refutation of his claims in Rollston Epigraphy, http://www.rollstonepigraphy.com/?p=779.

CHAPTER THREE

1 Gideon Bohak's "The Charaktêres in Ancient and Medieval Jewish Magic," *Acta classica universitatis scientiarum debreceniensis* 47 (2011): 25–44 and *Ancient Jewish Magic: A History* (Cambridge: Cambridge University Press, 2008); Michael W. Herren's

Cosmography of Aethicus Ister: Edition, Translation, and Commentary (Turnhout: Brepols, 2011) and Malcolm Letts's *Mandeville's Travels: Texts and Translations*, vols. 1 and 2 (Milton Park, Abingdon: Routledge, 2011), on the alphabets of John Mandeville, as well as the scholarship of others cited in the chapter, have been invaluable in sorting out the lineages of these graphical alphabets.

2 Mystical interpretation of the letters of the alphabet is associated with Marcus the Gnostic in the second century CE, for instance. Lynn Thorndike, *A History of Magic and Experimental Science*, vols. 1–2, *The First Thirteen Centuries of Our Era* (New York: Columbia University Press, 1923), 370.

3 Deborah Hayden, "Language and Linguistics in Medieval Europe," in *Oxford Research Encyclopedias* (New York: Oxford University Press, 26 April 2017), https://doi.org/10.1093/acrefore/9780199384655.013.380, notes that the study of vernaculars, and grammars for them, increased and that Irish, Welsh, and Old Norse began to be studied and have grammars.

4 Hayden, n.p.

5 The position was held by the biblical scholar Edward Pococke, who had studied Arabic in Aleppo and traveled extensively in the East. He was a distant relative of Richard Pococke, the eighteenth-century traveler whose *Description of the East* was mentioned in Chapter 2. Both are distantly related to the nineteenth-century writer Edward Pococke, whose *India in Greece*, published in 1852, argued for Indian origins and influences on Greek culture.

6 Peter N. Miller, "The 'Antiquarianization' of Biblical Scholarship and the London Polyglot Bible (1653–57)," *Journal of the History of Ideas* 62, no. 3 (July 2001): 463–82.

7 Miller, 468.

8 Horst Weinstock, "Roger Bacon's Polyglot Alphabet," *Florilegium* 11 (1992): 160–78. Little organized means of learning Hebrew existed in medieval England. Weinstock's discussion of the context in which Bacon might have acquired Hebrew is detailed and includes a careful analysis of the way Bacon's use of the Hebrew letters shows a lack of understanding of the structure of the Semitic Hebrew language.

9 Weinstock, 162: "He could have acquired his knowledge of Hebrew either in England before 1240 as well as between 1247 and 1257, or in France between 1240 and 1247 as well as between 1257 and 1268." Weinstock is extending his earlier comments: "Abraham ben Meir ibn Ezra's stay in and around London after 1158 must have established and promoted Hebrew studies in the Middle English period." The "monastic scholars of Saint Victor" were called out by Richard the Lionhearted for "Judaizing tendencies."

10 See Cairo Genizah manuscripts from the sixth century onward: "Cairo Genizah," University of Cambridge Digital Library, accessed May 17, 2021, https://cudl.lib.cam.ac.uk/view/MS-TS-K-00001-00064/1.

11 Bohak, "The Charaktêres," 27–28.

12 Bohak, 27.

13 Bohak, 27–28.

14 Bohak, 34.

15 Venetia Porter, "The Use of Arabic Script in Magic," in *The Development of Arabic as a Written Language*, ed. M. C. A. Macdonald, *Supplement to the Proceedings of the Seminar for Arabian Studies* 40 (Oxford: Archaeopress, 2010), 131–40.

16 Bohak, "The Charaktêres," 36. He cites a manuscript in the New York Public Library as one of his sources, Heb.190 (olim MS Sassoon 56) (1460s), and MS Geneva 145 (olim MS Sassoon 290) (early sixteenth century).

17 Many of these are codified in the writings of the fifteenth-century alchemist Paracelsus.

18 Marco Moriggi, *A Corpus of Syriac Incantation Bowls* (Leiden: Brill, 2014) deals with slightly later practices.

19 Henry Austen Layard, *Discoveries in the Ruins of Nineveh and Babylon; with Travels in Armenia, Kurdistan and the Desert, Being the Result of a Second Expedition Undertaken for the Trustees of the British Museum* (London: John Murray, 1853), 518.

20 David Jackson, "The aljamiadas of Spain," *Medieval Musings*, May 24, 2015, http://www.davidjackson.info/voynich/2015/05/24/the-aljamiadas-of-spain/.

21 A. G. Avilés, "Alfonso X y el Liber Razielis: Imágenes de la magia astral judia en el scriptorium alfonsi," *Bulletin of Hispanic Studies* 74, no. 1 (1 January 1997): 21–39.

22 Daniel Harms, "Magical Manuscripts Online at the University of Leipzig," *Papers Falling from an Attic Window*, August 10, 2013, https://danharms.wordpress.com/2013/08/10/magical-manuscripts-online-at-the-university-of-leipzig/.

23 J. H. Chajes, *Between Worlds: Dybbuks, Exorcists, and Early Modern Judaism* (Philadelphia: University of Pennsylvania Press, 2011), 64.

24 Chajes, 209.

25 Gaffarel took issue with Postel's assertion that there was an Arabic language older than Hebrew, an argument laid out in Postel's *De foenicvm literis, seu, de prisco Latinae & Graecae linguae charactere, eiusq[ue], antiquissima origine & vsu* (1552).

26 Jacques Gaffarel, *Unheard-of Curiosities: Concerning the Talismanical Sculpture of the Persians and the Reading of the Stars; Englished by Edmund Chilmead* (London: Humphrey Moseley, 1650), author's additions, n.p. The list is useful because of the way it indicates direct lineages: Trithemius, Pico, Albertus Magnus, Roger Bacon, Pantheus, Marsillo Ficino, Reuchlin, Agrippa, Fludd, Bang, and many more. In another section, he also cites Rabbi Moses ben Nachman (sic) and other Jewish rabbis (263).

27 Gaffarel, 433.

28 Gaffarel, 303.

29 Porter, "The Use of Arabic Script," 136.

30 Abu Bakr Ahmad ibn Ali Ibn Wahshiyyah, *Ancient Characters and Hieroglyphics Explained*, trans. Joseph Hammer von Purgstall (London: Bulmer, 1806), iv. Some record of that manuscript should exist.

31 Porter, "The Use of Arabic Script," 136.

32 Porter, 136, citing *The Encyclopedia of Islam* (Leiden: Brill, 1971), 963–65.

33 Patricia Cone and Michael Cook, *Hagarism: The Making of the Islamic World* (Cambridge: Cambridge University Press, 1977), 209–10.

34 Ibn Wahshiyyah, *Ancient Characters*, iv.

35 Ibn Wahshiyyah, 41.

36 Ibn Wahshiyyah, 117–18.

37 An Arabic manuscript version exists in the Bayerische Staatsbibliothek. [BSB-Hss Cod. arab. 789] Ibn-Wahsiya, Ahmad Ibn-×Ali: Kitab Sauq al-mustaham fi ma×rifat rumuz al-aqlam—BSB Cod.arab. 789, Constantinople, 1791, Bavarian State Library, Digitale Bibliothek, accessed June 12, 2021, https://www.digitale-sammlungen.de/en/view/bsb00037029?page=,1.

38 References to Aben Vaschia appear in various places, including Richard Rolt Brash, *The Ogham Inscribed Monuments of the Gaedhill* (London: George Bell and Sons, 1879), 368.

39 Ibn Wahshiyyah, *An Explanation of Ancient Alphabets and Hieroglyphics* [Kitab Shawq al-Mustaham], trans. Joseph von Hammer-Purgstall, ed. Jason Colavito, on the website of Jason Colavito, accessed June 25, 2021, http://www.jasoncolavito.com/ancient-alphabets-explained.html.

40 Porter suggests that the real author of this book may be "Abu Talib al-Zayyat." She bases her suggestion on T. Fahd, "Ibn Wahshiyyahh," in *Encyclopedia of Islam*, new ed., iii (Leiden: Brill 1971), 963–65. Porter cites work that compares Wahshiyyah and other Arabic magical scripts at Bib.Nat.Folio 90 from BN 2676 and BN 2675. The *Kitab miftah* 1303–4 consists of twenty-four alphabets, many of them imaginary, where there are symbols with Arabic letter equivalents in the *abjad* order of the alphabet.

41 The *Sepher Raziel* was partially based on the *Sepher ha-Razim*, in the manner of late medieval texts that have absorbed earlier fragments and traditions.

42 Johannes Trithemius, *Steganographia* (Francofvrti: Ex officina typographica Matthiæ Beckeri, sumptibus Ioannis Berneri, 1608).

43 Joseph Peterson states, "According to historian Lynn Thorndike, the attribution of the text [Heptameron] to the famous physician Peter de Abano (1250–1316) 'seems quite certainly spurious.'" Joseph Peterson, *Peter of Abano: Heptameron, or Magic Elements*, with his commentary, accessed June 10, 2021, http://www.esotericarchives.com/solomon/heptamer.htm. Peterson is citing Thorndike, *A History of Magic*, 2:912.

44 See Abraham ben Meir de Balmes, *Mikneh Avram-Peculium Abrae* (Venice: Bomberg, 1523), for a copy of the script, beautifully made in metal.

45 Ibn Wahshiyyah, *Ancient Characters*, 118.

46 Thorndike, *A History of Magic*, 340–47.

47 Enoch is identified as an "extra-biblical" text.

48 See Thorndike, footnote 341, for bibliography of the Book of Enoch.

49 James C. VanderKam, "The Book of Enoch and the Qumran Scrolls," in *The Oxford Handbook of the Dead Sea Scrolls* (New York: Oxford University Press, 2010), https://www.oxfordhandbooks.com/view/10.1093/oxfordhb/9780199207237.001.0001/oxfordhb-9780199207237-e-11.

50 Martin Findell, "The Book of Enoch, the Angelic Alphabet and the 'Real Cabala,'" *Henry Sweet Society Bulletin*, May 2007, 7–22.

51 Findell, 12, citing Peterson, *John Dee's Five Books of Mystery* (York Beach, ME: Weiser, 2003), 268–71.

52 Findell, 13.

53 Several of the manuscripts in the British Library were part of John Dee's library and are classified among the Sloane manuscripts [3188][3189][Sloane 3846 fol. 154r-158v Royal MS17Axlii]. They can be searched at https://www.bl.uk/manuscripts/ for individual manuscripts, such as, https://www.bl.uk/manuscripts/FullDisplay.aspx?ref=Sloane_MS_3188&index=53.

54 See Donald Laycock, *The Complete Enochian Dictionary* (York Beach, ME: Weiser, 1994) on the Angelic language.

55 Meric Casaubon, *A True and Faithful Relation of What Passed for Many Years between John Dee and Some Spirits* (London: D. Maxwell, 1659), preface, n.p.

56 Nick Pelling, "The Voarchadumia & John Dee," *Cipher Mysteries*, May 23, 2009, http://ciphermysteries.com/2009/05/23/the-voarchadumia-john-dee.

57 Herren, *Cosmography*, facing pages 216 and 217; Herren cites both Ister manuscripts, The "Murbach hymnal," fol. 2, "The Cosmography of Aethicus," Oxford Bodleian Library, Junius 25, fol. 59v and Aethicus Ister, "Cosmographia," Leiden, Universiteitsbibliotheken, Voss. Lat. F 113, fol. 30r.

58 René Derolez, *Runica manuscripta* (Brugge: De Tempel, 1954), chap. 3, appendix, 274–78.

59 Abbey of St. Gall, Codex Sangallensis 878, 321–22, http://www.e-codices.unifr.ch/en/csg/0878.

60 Derolez, *Runica manuscripta*, xliv. For a detailed discussion of the history of scholarship on runic manuscripts, Derolez's text is still unsurpassed.

61 E. J. Christie, "By Means of a Secret Alphabet: Dangerous Letters and the Semantics of Gebregdstafas," *Modern Philology* 109, no. 2 (2011): 145–70, https://www.jstor.org/stable/10.1086/663211?seq=1#metadata_info_tab_contents. The observation about the anachronism is mine, the mention of St. Jerome is Christie's.

62 Hrabanus Maurus, "De inventione," German National Museum (MS 1966 fol. 121v–122r), cited by Derolez, 308.

63 St. John's College, Oxford, Byrhtferth manuscript, c.1110 (St. John's 17_005v).

64 Melchior Goldast, *Rerun alamannicarum scriptores aliquot vetusti* (Frankfurt: Wolffgang Richter, 1606); again, see Derolez, *Runica manuscripta*, for detailed discussion.

65 Derolez, *Runica manuscripta*. Several editions of this work focus on Nordic, English, and Germanic traditions.

66 Iain Macleod Higgins, *The Book of John Mandeville* (Indianapolis, IN: Hackett Publishing, 2011), xii–xiii.

67 Letts, *Mandeville's Travels*, xxxix.

68 Derolez, *Runica manuscripta*, 136.

69 Geraldine Heng, *Empire of Magic: Medieval Romance and the Politics of Cultural Fantasy* (New York: Columbia University Press, 2003), 459.

70 Marcia Kupfer, "'. . . lectres . . . plus vrayes': Hebrew Script and Jewish Witness in the *Mandeville* manuscript of Charles V," *Speculum* 83 (2008): 60.

71 Heng, *Empire*, 458–59, citing Letts, *Mandeville's Travels*, 152.

72 Heng, 459–60.

73 Kupfer, "'. . . lectres . . . plus vrayes,'" 59.

74 Kupfer, 58–111.

75 Kupfer, "'. . . lectres . . . plus vrayes,'" 65, citing Judith Olszowy-Schlanger, the Hebrew paleographer.

76 Kupfer notes a northern French copy, c. 1370–80, of Moses ben Jacob's *Great Book of Precepts* (Paris, BnF, MS hébr. 375).

77 Kupfer, 84.

78 Kupfer, "'. . . lectres . . . plus vrayes,'" 67. The commissioned copy is dated to about 1371, the Expulsion is two decades later, but anti-Semitism was active throughout the period. Kupfer notes that a horde of Jewish books that had been seized at the beginning of the fourteenth century was given by Charles to the Jews of Paris in his own attempts at a conciliatory gesture and that he also made attempts to ameliorate some of the suspicions and charges leveled against the Jewish population. Charles died in 1380, before the Expulsion.

79 I have never seen any, however.

80 Elmar Seebold, "Mandeville's Alphabets," in *Beitrage zur Geschichte der deutschen Sprache und Literatur* (Paris: Niemeyer, 1998), Band 120, 435–49. Seebold's inventory is useful, and he tracks the Egyptian to Isidore of Seville and one Saracen to the oldest English manuscript of Mandeville (BL, Add 17335 fol 29nr), which I have not been able to track. A Persian is actually Chaldean, and so on. The point is that enough copies and versions of scripts, or approximations and imitations of them, existed to provide exemplars, even if they were corrupted in copying, renamed, or otherwise altered.

81 Most authorities seem to believe that the text may have been written by Martin Roth.

82 Bernhard von Breydenbach, *Prefatio in opus transmarine peregrinations ad venerandum et gloriosum spulcrum Dominicum in Iherusalem* (Mainz: Erhard Reuwich, 1486).

83 Gloss written by Helga Rebhan, Bavarian State Library, World Digital Library, Library of Congress, https://www.wdl.org/en/item/18395/.

84 For another case study, see Sebastian Kempgen, "The Mysterious 'Alphabetum Iliricum Sclavorum,'" (University of Bamberg, 2015), https://kodeks.uni-bamberg.de/slavling/downloads/SK_IllyrianSlavicAlphabet.pdf, which traces the development of this "other" Slavic alphabet as a possible derivation of Glagolitic.

CHAPTER FOUR

1 I have not been able to locate any incunabula that contain alphabet compendia. Trithemius's *Steganographia* was composed in 1499 but not published until 1606 and picked up the manuscript transmissions of the De Inventione alphabets.

2 According to Saverio Campanini, the collecting passion for exotic scripts, particularly "oriental" scripts, peaked in Europe with the beginnings of global expansion to the New World. One center of this activity was Venice, which sat in an opportune position with regard to trade. Campanini, "The Quest for the Holiest Alphabet in the Renaissance," in *A Universal Art: Hebrew Grammar across Disciplines and Faiths*, ed. Nadia Vidro, Irene E. Zwiep, and Judith Olszowy-Schlanger (Leiden: Brill, 2014), 196–245.

3 Conrad Gessner, *Mithridates* (Tiguri: Excudebat Froschouerus, 1555).

4 Gessner, 1.

5 Erich Poppe, "The Celtic Languages in Conrad Gessner's *Mithridates* (1555)," *Zeitschrift fü celtische Philologie* 45, no. 1 (2009): 240.

6 Conrad Gessner, *Bibliotheca universalis* (Zurich: Christophorum Froschouerum, 1545).

7 Campanini, "The Quest."

8 Charles Forster, *The One Primeval Language Traced Experimentally*, 3 vols. (London: Richard Bentley, 1851).

9 See Derolez, *Runica manuscripta*, for discussion of alphabet specimens in manuscript transmission.

10 Edmund Fry, *Pantographia: Containing Accurate Copies of All the Known Alphabets in the World; Together with an English Explanation of the Peculiar Force or Power of Each Letter: To Which Are Added, Specimens of All Well-Authenticated Oral Languages; Forming a Comprehensive Digest of Phonology*. (Printed by Cooper and Wilson, for John and Arthur Arch, Gracechurch-Street; John White, Fleet-Street; John Edwards, Pall-Mall; and John Debrett, Piccadilly, 1799).

11 Daniels and Bright, *The World's Writing Systems*.

12 *Congregatio de Propaganda Fide* (Rome: Vatican, 1636).

13 Johannes Reuchlin (1455–1522), Petrus Galatin (1460–1540), Joseph Scaliger (1540–1609), John Buxtorf (1564–1629), and later Ezechiel Spanheim (1629–1710) are frequently invoked. Interestingly, though Isidore of Seville and Clement of Alexandria are also sometimes mentioned, Hrabanus Maurus (780–856) is not, except in the context of runes.

14 Johannes Trithemius, *Polygraphia* (Oppenheim: Ioannis Hasebergi de Aia, 1518); Johannes Pantheus, *Voarchadumia* (Venetiis: Diebus Aprilis, 1530); Heinrich Cornelius Agrippa von Nettesheim, *De occulta philosophia*, (Cologne: 1531); Guillaume Postel, *Linguarum duodecim characteribus differentium alphabetum introductio* (Paris: Apud Dionysius Lescuier, 1538); and Teseo Ambrogio, *Introductio in Chaldaicum linguam* (Pavio: Excudebat Papiae Ioan. Maria Simoneta Cremonen[sis] in canonica Sancti Petri in caelo aureo, su[m]ptibus & typis, authoris libri, anno à Virginis partu, 1538).

15 Giovanni Battista Palatino, *Libro nuovo* (Stampata in Roma: Appresso Campo di Fiore, nelle case di m. Benedetto Gionta: Per Baldassarre di Francesco Cartolari perugino, 1540); Urbanus Wyss, *Das Schreibbuch* (Zurich, 1549); and Theodor de Bry and Israel de Bry, *Alphabeta et charactères* (Frankfurt, 1596).

16 Claude Duret, *Le thrésor de l'histoire des langues de cest univers* [. . .] (Cologny: par Matth. Berjon, pour la Societé Caldoriene,1613).

17 Joannes Baptista Gramaye, *Specimen litterarum & linguarum universi orbis* [. . .] (Ath: Ionannes Masius, 1622); Samuel Purchas, *Hakluytus posthumus, or Purchas His Pilgrimes* (London: Henry Fetherston, 1624).

18 Blaise de Vigenère, *Traicté de chiffres* (Paris: Chez Abel L'Angelier, au premier pillier de la grand' salle du Palais, 1586); and François Colletet, *Traittez des langues estrangères, de leurs alphabets, et des chiffres* [. . .] (Paris: Jean Promé, 1660).

19 Trithemius, *Polygraphia*.

20 David A. King, *The Ciphers of the Monks: A Forgotten Number Notation of the Middle Ages* (Stuttgart: F. Steiner, 2001).

21 Trithemius, *Polygraphia*, 281–288.

22 Trithemius, 281–288.

23 Trithemius, *Polygraphia*.

24 Johannes Trithemius, *Polygraphie* (Paris: Jacques Kerver, 1561), 178–79.

25 Trithemius, 179.

26 Trithemius, 180.

27 Edward Edwards, *Memoirs of Libraries: A Handbook of Library Economy* (London: Trübner, 1859), 265–67. Edwards said no catalogue of the collection still exists, though Trithemius supposedly started to prepare one around 1502.

28 M. Dorothy Neuhofer, *In the Benedictine Tradition* (Lanham, MD: University Press of America, 1999), 40; *Nepiachus*, in Johann Georg von Eckhart, Origine Germanorum eorumque vetustissimis coloniis, migrationibus ac rebus gestus (Gottingen: J. G. Schmid, 1750) l.c. II, p.1828, quoted in Roland O. Behrendt, O.S.B., *The Library of Sponheim Abbey under Abbot Trithemius (1483–1506)* (Latrobe, PA: American Benedictine Academy, Library Section, St. Vincent's Archabbey, August 1958), 8.

29 Neuhofer, 40; she cites R. W. Seton-Watson, "The Abbott Trithemius," *Tudor Studies* (London, 1924) and also Behrendt, "The Library of Sponheim Abbey," 6.

30 WorldCat lists approximately a dozen editions in French and Latin within about a century of the original publication.

31 Trithemius, *Polygraphia*, 181. See Johann Eckhart, *De origine Germanorum* (Goettingae: Sumptibus Ioh. Guil. Schmidii, 1750) for comparison, but none of Trithemius's samples match Eckhart's.

32 Trithemius, 182. Doracus is mentioned in a passage of Louis Ellies Du Pin, *A New History of Ecclesiastical Writers* (London: Tim Child, 1710) that is drawing on Agrippa as a source (403).

33 Trithemius, *Polygraphia*, 183.

34 Hichus is mentioned in Arthur Machen, *The Enchanted Treasure, or The Spagyric Quest of Beroaldus Cosmopolita* (London: Thomas Marvell, 1888) in a summary of Trithemius's book.

35 Runic scripts in variant forms are found in medieval manuscripts in the British Isles and resemble the versions printed in Trithemius, which suggests that he took them from texts by Bede and others. See Kate Thomas, "How Many Alphabets?," *Medieval Manuscripts Blog*, May 10, 2019, https://blogs.bl.uk/digitisedmanuscripts/2019/05/how-many-alphabets.html.

36 Trithemius, *Polygraphia*, 186.

37 Trithemius, 186.

38 Pantheus, *Voarchadumia*, 12–13.

39 Cornelius Agrippa, *Three Books of Occult Philosophy*, trans. J. French (London: Gregory Moule, 1651), 438.

40 Agrippa, 162.

41 Agrippa, *De occulta philosophia*.

42 I have been unable to find any trace of a manuscript of de Abano with this script, but that is, of course, not conclusive evidence that it did not exist.

43 Leonhard Thurneysser, *Onomasticum* (Berlin: Nicolaum Voltzen, 1583), 181.

44 Agrippa, *Three Books*, 160.

45 Agrippa, 316.

46 Agrippa, 439.

47 Postel, *Linguarum*.

48 Brandon Wheeler, "Guillaume Postel and the Primordial Origins of the Middle East," in *Method and Theory in the Study of Religion* (Leiden: Brill, 2012), https://www.academia.edu/14955597/Guillaume_Postel_and_the_Primordial_Origins_of_the_Middle_East.

49 Wheeler, 4.

50 Wheeler, 8.

51 Postel, *Linguarum*.

52 James G. Fraser, "Epigraphy and Paleography as Scientific Disciplines," *Perspectives on Language and Text: Essays and Paper in Honor of Francis I. Anderson's Sixtieth Birthday, July 28, 1985* (Winona Lake, IN: Eisenbrauns, 1987), 27, cites François Secrete, *Bibliographie des manuscrits de Guillaume Postel* (Geneva: Droz, 1970) and identifies the manuscript Postel acquired as authored by Ya'qub b. Mahasin, written between 1482 and 1486.

53 Alan David Crown, *Samaritan Scribes and Manuscripts* (Tübingen: Mohr Siebeck, 2001), 270. Crown suggests that the first characters in the column on Postel's page are copied from coins, not from the manuscript, because they are so misshapen.

54 Crown, 271.

55 Crown, 274.

56 Nathan Shur, "The Return of the Diaspora Samaritans to Nablus at the End of the Middle Ages," http://members.tripod.com/~osher_2/html_articles/Diaspora.htm.

57 Pietro della Valle bought a Samaritan Pentateuch in Damascus in 1616, and this is the source for the Morin publication in 1631.

58 Fraser, "Epigraphy."

59 Campanini, "The Quest," 209.

60 Campanini, 201.

61 Campanini, 201.

62 Campanini, 207–8.

63 Campanini, 209–11. In Balmes's opinion, the people of Israel had taken that script and the Hebrew language while leaving the (old) Hebrew characters and the Aramaic language behind for "simpletons—Cutheans" (where Cuthean is synonymous with Samaritan).

64 Abraham de Balmes, *Mikneh Avram* (Venice: Daniel Bomberg, 1523).

65 Campanini, "The Quest," 214.

66 Campanini, "The Quest," 214.

67 Campanini, "The Quest," 227.

68 Ambrogio, *Introductio*, 196–97.

69 Palatino, *Libro nuovo*.

70 Wyss, *Das Schreibbuch*.

71 Israel de Bry and Theodor de Bry, *Alphabeta*.

72 Thomas Harriot, *A Briefe and True Report of the New Found Land of Virginia* (Francoforti ad Moenvm: Typis I. Wecheli, svmtibvs vero T. de Bry, 1590).

73 Bartolomé de las Casas in *Narratio Regionum indicarum per Hispanos Quosdam devastatarum verissimai* (Oppenheim: John-Theod. De Bry, 1614); a translation of *Tyrannies et cruatez des Espagnols* (Antwerp: Ravelenghien, 1579).

74 de Bry, n.p.

75 Scripts in de Bry, *Alphabeta*: Antique Chaldean, Abraham (Syriac) (*elpha*), Syriac (*olaph*), Phoenician (the two-line split *alpha*), Siriorum (*alyn*), Hebrew before Ezra (Aleph with some celestials, running *aleph*), Celestial (bent back of *beth*), Malachim (from Agrippa), Esdras (square Hebrew), Moses (Paleo-Hebrew), Hebrew (script/brush square), Thoth, Aegyptiarum (same as in Thomas Bang, *Caelum orientis et prisco mundi triade exercitatio literarium repraesentatum curisque* [Hauniae: Petri Morsingi, 1657], 114), Aegyptiorum (Athemus) Aegyptiacum (*a*, *j* shapes), Arabum (*elaf*), Arabicum (*eliph*), Samaritan (*aleph*), Cyrillic, Greek, Cadmus Phoenicis Frater (shows *y* added by Pythagoras, four letters added by Simonides, two by Epicharmus Siculus, four by Palamedes), Jacobitan (Alfa Veda), Hieronymus (Illyricarum), and St. Cyrillus, Sclavorum (Ac, Buc), Sclavor, Croaticum, Muscovitium, Armenica, Chrysostomus, Indicum, Hetruscum, Demaratus Corinth, Uphilas (Gothicum), Saracen, Roman and then twelve different national hands, all Latin letters, but stylistically distinct—black letter, etc.

76 Duret, *Le thrésor*.
77 Duret, title page.
78 Duret, 6.
79 Duret, 6.
80 Duret, 28.
81 Duret, 6.
82 Duret, 42–43.
83 Duret, on Adam, 39–40, though this does not have the reference to how long he lived.
84 Duret 42.
85 Duret, 117.
86 Duret also had access to the Grimani Library before it burnt and to collections assembled by de Fanti. Campanini, "The Quest," 228–29.
87 The *Virga Aurea* published by James Bonaventure Hepburn in 1616 presents seventy-two alphabets on his plate. Adam McLean, "The Virga Aurea," The Alchemy Website, first published in the *Hermetic Journal*, 1980, http://www.levity.com/alchemy/virga_aurea.html. The number seventy-two is redolent with symbolism from Old and New Testament references.
88 His Syrian script was taken from Ambrosius, and a Phoenician (a variant termed "Ionic" recognizing the Greek adoption) is followed by discussion of Egyptian, which is a version of Coptic, and a description of the religion and beliefs of the Egyptians. The Phoenician and Ionic are given on 366.
89 Duret, *Le thrésor*, 589.
90 Duret, 314.
91 Duret, 324.
92 Vigenère, *Traicté*; and Colletet, *Traittez*.
93 Vigenère, 288–89.
94 Vigenère, 337–40.
95 Vigenère, *Traicté*.
96 Colletet, "Advis du lecteur," in Colletet, *Traittez*, n.p.
97 In his "Advis au lecteur," Colletet references Fulvio Montaury as a source for his own work, but I have not been able to locate Fulvio Montaury, or his manuscript, under any title or variant spelling.
98 Simon is citing a study by Bernard Colombat and Manfred Peters. Simon points out that among others composed of "parts of texts," such large-scale appropriation was not uncommon. Citing a bibliometric study of Gessner's *Mithradates*, he notes that 47 percent of that text was quotations, 11 percent was language samples, and that only 42 percent of the text was written by the author. He thus places the work within a tradition of commonplace books. Fabien Simon, "Collecting Languages, Alphabets and Texts: The Circulation of 'Parts and Texts' among Paper Cabinets of Linguistic Curiosities (Sixteenth-Seventeenth Century)," in *Pieces and Parts in Scientific Texts*, vol. 1, ed. Florence Bretelle-Establet and Stéphane Schmitt (New York: Springer, 2018), 310.
99 Purchas, *Hakluytus posthumus*.
100 Gramaye, *Specimen litterarum*.
101 Purchas, *Hakluytus posthumus*, 1:1.
102 Purchas, *Hakluytus posthumus*.
103 Purchas, 1:93.
104 Purchas, 1: 176–77.
105 Purchas, 1:178.
106 Bang, *Caelum orientis*.
107 Adam, the sons of Adam, Seth, the sons of Seth, Enoch, the Chaldeans, Assyrians, Syrians Phoenicians Aegyptians, Aethiopians, Moses, Abraham, Mercury, etc.
108 Bang, *Caelum orientis*, 100.

109 Bang, 104, 105.
110 Bang, 106.
111 Bang, 125.
112 Fry, *Pantographia.*
113 Fry, *Pantographia.*
114 Conspicuously absent from Fry's bibliography were de Bry, Rocca, Bang, Schrader, and a handful of others. Here is the list of sources for Fry's Chaldeans:

Ibn Wahshiyya (trans. Joseph Hammer von Purgstall, 1801, originally from ninth-tenth century)
Picatrix (MS in British Library, later tenth or eleventh century grimoire)
Sefer Raziel, thirteenth century Latin MS earliest surviving version
Sworn Book of Honorius, Liber Juratus, thirteenth century grimoire
Petro d'Abano (1250–1316)
Trithemius, *Steganographia*, 1499
Trithemius, *Polygraphia*, 1518
Guillaume Postel, 1538
Theseus Ambrosius, 1539
Paracelsus, 1530s
Cornelius Agrippa, *De Occulta* (1509–10, published 1531)
Palatino, 1540
Johannes Pantheus, 1530, *Voarchadumia*
John Dee, Enochian Script 1580s
Fazellus 1579
Virga Aurea, 1616
Claude Duret, *Thrésor* 1619
Jacques Gaffarel, 1629
Athanasius Kircher, 1643–9
Ezechiel Spanheim, 1671
Pierre Simon Fournier, Le Jeune, 1766
De Sivry, 1778
Edmund Fry, 1799

115 Bright and Daniels, *The World's Writing Systems.*

CHAPTER FIVE

1 Joseph Levine, *Battle of the Books: History and Literature in the Augustan Age* (Ithaca, NY: Cornell University Press, 2018), 3.
2 Cyril Mango, "The Triumphal Way of Constantinople and the Golden Gate," *Dumbarton Oaks Papers* 54 (2000): 183–84.
3 Isabel Yaya, "Wonders of America: The Curiosity Cabinet as a Site of Representation and Knowledge," *Journal of the History of Collections* 20, no. 2 (November 2008): 173–88.
4 Bernard de Montfaucon, *Antiquité expliquée et representée en figures* (Paris: F. Delaulne, 1719).
5 Comte de Caylus, *Recueil d'antiquités égyptiennes, étrusques, grecques et romaines* (Paris: Chez Desaint et Saillant, 1752–57), ii.
6 William Massey, *The Origin and Progress of Letters* (London: Printed for J. Johnson, 1763), 24.
7 Vivian Salmon, "The Study of Foreign Languages in 17th Century England," *Histoire épistémologie langage* 7, no. 2 (1985): 45–70, https://www.persee.fr/doc/hel_0750-8069_1985_num_7_2_1314.
8 Otto Zwartjes, "Portuguese Missionary Grammars in Asia, Africa, and Brazil, 1500–1800,"

Historiographia Linguistica 39, nos. 2–3 (January 2012): 383–92, https://doi.org/10.1075/hl.39.2-3.11fer.

9 Salmon, "The Study of Foreign Languages," 45–70.

10 Christian Ravis, *Discourse of the Oriental Tongues* (London: Thomas Slater and Thomas Huntington, 1649), 3.

11 Ravis, 5.

12 Ravis, 5. Salmon, "The Study of Foreign Languages," 59–60, also remarks that Ravis recognized the family resemblance among the Afro-Asiatic languages of Hebrew, Chaldean, Samaritan, Syriac, Arabic, and Ethiopic, though he did not call them by that name.

13 Gaster, "Jewish Knowledge."

14 Jean Morin, *Exercitationes ecclesiasticae in utrumque Samaritanorum Pentateuchum* (Paris: Antonius Vitray, 1631).

15 Peter Miller, *Peiresec's Orient: Antiquarianism as Cultural History in the Seventeenth Century* (Abingdon, Oxfordshire: Routledge, 2012), 167.

16 Anthony Grafton, "Joseph Scaliger and Historical Chronology: The Rise and Fall of a Discipline," *History and Theory* 14, no 2 (May 1975): 156–83.

17 Sir Walter Raleigh, *The Historie of the World* (London: William Stansby for Walter Burre, 1614).

18 Raleigh, 250.

19 James Ussher, *Annales veteris testamenti, a prima mundi origine deducti* (London: J. Flesher, J. Crook, and J. Baker, 1650).

20 James Ussher, *Annals of the World* (London: J. Flesher, J. Crook, and J. Baker, 1650).

21 Sir Isaac Newton, *The Chronology of Antient Kingdoms Amended* (London: J. Tonson, 1728).

22 John Jackson, *Chronological Antiquities* (London: Printed for the author, 1752).

23 Jackson cites *De.Civ.Dei.*, 15:1.

24 Jackson, xii.

25 Jackson, 109.

26 He cited Morin and Kircher in support.

27 Jackson, *Chronological Antiquities*, 82.

28 Jackson, 82–83.

29 Jackson, 87.

30 Jackson, 88.

31 Jackson, 90.

32 It is unclear whether Jackson saw the original tablets. The earliest publication of the inscriptions seems to be mid-nineteenth century.

33 Levine, *Battle*, 170.

34 See E. L. Hicks et al., *Greek Inscriptions in the British Museum* [*GIBM*] (Oxford: Clarendon, 1874–1916), 3:149–50 for a detailed description.

35 Levine, *Battle*, 169.

36 A trove of Greek coins assembled by Consul Raye, slightly earlier than the discovery of the Sigean inscription, was sent to the Bodleian around 1704. Their description is detailed in the *Annals* and makes amusing reading for the controversies they sparked. William Dunn Macray, *The Annals of the Bodleian Library, Oxford* (Oxford: Clarendon Press, 1890), 173.

37 James Henry Monk, *The Life of Richard Bentley: With an Account of His Writings* (London: J. G. and F. Rivington, 1833), 2:157.

38 For a detailed analysis of the inscription, dating debates, and letterforms, see Hicks et al., *GIBM*, 149–50.

39 Dr. Bentley to Dr. Mead (CCXXV), in *The Correspondence of Richard Bentley*, ed. Christopher Wordsworth (London: John Murray, 1842), 581–90.

40 Dr. Bentley to Dr. Mead (CCXXV), 581–90.

41 Dr. Bentley to Dr. Mead (CCXXV), 582.

42 R. G., Correspondence addressed, "Mr. Urban," and dated November 20 describes the inscription pictured in the engraving in Plate III on the facing page. *Gentleman's Magazine* 85 (January 1799): 25, https://archive.org/details/sim_gentlemans-magazine_1799-01_69_1/page/n33/mode/2up.

43 The author is identified only by initials, as R. G.

44 Levine, *Battle*.

45 Bernard de Montfaucon, *Palaeographia Graeca* (Paris: L. Guerin, 1708) and *Antiquity Explained* (London: J. Tonson and J. Watts, 1721).

46 Cited by Levine, *Battle*, 174.

47 Cited by Levine from Montfaucon, *Antiquity Explained*, 4:28–30.

48 Montfaucon, *Paleographia*, 304.

49 Montfaucon, facing 123.

50 Montfaucon, facing 123.

51 Montfaucon, *Antiquity*, preface. n.p.

52 Montfaucon, preface, n.p.

53 Montfaucon, introduction, vol. 1.

54 Ezechiel Spanheim, *Dissertationes de præstantia et usu numismatum antiquorum*, (Amstelodami: Daniel Elsevir, 1671).

55 Godwin, *Romanae historiae*.

56 Godwin, 248.

57 Godwin, 249.

58 Edward Stillingfleet, *Origines sacrae, or A rational account of the grounds of Christian faith* (London: R.W. for Henry Mortlock, 1662).

59 Samuel Shuckford, *The Sacred and Prophane History of the World Connected, from the Creation of the World to the Dissolution of the Assyrian Empire at the Death of Sardanapalus, and to the Declension of the Kingdoms of Judah and Israel, under the Reigns of Ahaz and Pekah* (London: R. Knaplock and J. Tonson, 1731).

60 For emphasis on the British context, see William Stukeley, *Palaeographia Britannica, or Discourses on Antiquities in Britain* (London: Printed for R. Manby, 1743).

61 Shuckford, *The Sacred and Prophane*, 220.

62 Shuckford, 228.

63 Shuckford, 254.

64 Charles Davy, *Conjectural Observations on the Origin and Progress of the Alphabet* (London: T. Wright for T. Cadell, 1772), 5.

65 Davy, 9.

66 Davy, 105.

67 Johanna Drucker, *The Alphabetic Labyrinth: The Letters in History and Imagination* (London: Thames and Hudson, 1994); Alexander Melville Bell, *Visible Speech* (London: Simkin, Marshall, 1867).

68 Jean Mabillon, *De re diplomatica* (Luteciæ Parisiorum: Sumtibus Ludovici Billaine, 1671).

69 Randolph Head, "Documents, Archives, and Proof around 1700: Diplomatics, the *ius archivi* and State Practice in the Seventeenth and Eighteenth Centuries," *Historical Journal* 56, no. 4 (2013): 909–30.

70 Mabillon, *De re diplomatica*, preface, n.p.

71 Another practical manual, Augustin Aldenbruck, *In artem diplomaticam isagoge* (Col. Claud. Aug. Agripp.: Ludovicum Schorn, 1765), introduced the principles of paleographic diplomatics through a question and answer format.

72 Toustain, *Nouveau traité de diplomatique* (Paris: Guillaume Desprez, P.-G. Cavelier, 1750), 559.

73 Toustain, 572.
74 Toustain, 577.
75 Toustain, 585–86. The reference to *Paleographia* probably refers to the inscriptions from Delos and Sigea reproduced in that volume, which was not authored by Shuckford. On the following page, Toustain describes the engraving in Shuckford's *Sacred and Prophane History of the World* (London: Printed for R. Knaplock and J. Tonson, 1728–30) in some detail, and cites 1:260 of that title.
76 Toustain, 585.
77 Toustain, 592.
78 Kaspar Waser, *De antiquis Numis Hebraeorum, chaldaeorum, et Syrorum S. Biblioa et Rabbinorum scripta meminerunt* (Switzerland: Officina Wolphiana, 1605).
79 From an online exhibit at the Israel Museum, "More than Money," curated by Haim Gitler, accessed June 13, 2021, https://museum.img.org.il/coins.
80 Yosef Ofer, "The Half Shekel, Nahmanides, and Ancient Coins," Bar-Ilan University. Link not retrievable.
81 Ofer, "The Half Shekel."
82 Caylus, *Recueil d'antiquités*.
83 Caylus, vi.
84 Caylus, xii.
85 Caylus, xiii.
86 Caylus, 74.
87 Caylus, 75.
88 Poinsenet de Sivry, *Nouvelles recherches sur la science des medailles* (Maestricht: Jean-Edme Dufour and Phillippe Roux, 1778), 88–89.
89 Velásquez de Velasco, *Ensayo sobre los alphabetos de las letras desconocidas* (Madrid: Antonio Sanz, 1752).
90 Velasco, 7.
91 Velasco, 7.
92 Velasco, 7.
93 From sources on medals and authorities, he pulls Strabo, Philostrato, Modern Greek, Primitive Greek, Etruscan, Arcadian, Pelasgican, Ancient Latin, Gothic, Runic, Phoenician and Samaritan (according to Montfaucon), Samaritan and Phenician (according to Edward Bernard), Syriac, Caldean, Hebrew, Spanish Phenician (according to Rhenvord), Punic, Phenician (Swinton), Phenician (Chishull), Samaritan (Walton), Samaritan/Phonecian according to Bochart, Phonecian of Scaliger, Celtiberico, Turdetano, Bastulo-phenicio.
94 Velasco, *Ensayo*, 51.
95 Astle, *The Origin*.
96 Astle, ii.
97 Astle, iv.
98 Astle, 66–67; He supplies extra information in (2) on the city of Laconia and then (3) cites Court de Gébelin, who suggests the text was written "two hundred years before the Trojan war."
99 Astle, 70.
100 Astle, ii.
101 Gébelin, *Le monde primitif*, 119.
102 Astle, 50.
103 Astle, 5.
104 Thomas Astle, *On the Radical Letters of the Pelasgians* (London: Printed by J. Nichols, 1785), 5.
105 Astle, 6.
106 Astle, *The Origin*, v–xii.

107 Francis Grosse and Thomas Astle, *The Antiquarian Repertory* (London: Edward Jeffery, 1807), iii.

108 Gosse and Astle, iv.

109 Massey, *The Origin*, 19–20.

110 Massey, 20–21.

111 Massey, 31–33.

112 Bayly, *An Introduction*, 33.

113 Bayly, 34.

114 Bayly, 35.

115 Bayly, 38.

116 Ole Worm, *Runir, seu, Danica literature antiquissima* (Hafniae: Melchiorus Martzan, 1651) and Eckhart, *De origine Germanorum*.

117 L. D. Nelme, *An Essay towards an Investigation of the Origin and Elements of Language and Letters* (London: T. Spilsbury for S. Leacroft, 1772).

118 Johannes Goropius Becanus, *Origines Antwerpianae, sive Cimmeriorum Becceselana novem libros complexa: Atvatica I. Gigantomachia II. Niloscopivm III. Cronia IV. Indoscythica V. Saxsonica VI. Gotodanica VII. Amazonica VIII. Venetica & Hyperborea IX* [. . .] (Antwerp: Christophori Plantin, 1569).

119 Becanus, discussion of Adam, 3.

120 "Johannes Goropius Becanus," *Wikipedia*, accessed June 26, 2021, https://en.wikipedia.org/wiki/Johannes_Goropius_Becanus.

121 Albert Schultens, *Origines Hebraeae sive Hebraeae Linguae antiquissima natura et indoles* (Lugduni Batauorum: Samel et Joannem Luchtmans et Joannem le Mair, 1761).

122 See Michael Covington, "Albert Schultens on Language Relationship," *Linguistics* 17, nos. 7–8 (1979), https://doi.org/10.1515/ling.1979.17.7-8.707.

123 Henri de Bukentop, *Alphabetum Graecum & Hebraïcum: Quo singularum litterarum utriusque linguae figura proponitur, genuinus sonus adstruitur, legendi methodus traditur* (Louvain: Typis viduae Henrici van Overbeke, Anno 1704).

124 Rowland Jones, *A Postscript to the Origin of Language and Nations* [. . .] (London: J. Hughes, 1764), 13.

125 Charles Vallancey, *Prospectus of a Dictionary of the Language of the Aire Coti, or Ancient Irish, Compared with the Language of the Cuti, or Ancient Persians, with the Hindoostanee, the Arabic, and Chaldean Languages* (Dublin: Graisberry and Campbell, 1802).

126 Edward Lhuyd, *Archaeologica Britannica* (London: 1707), preface, n.p.

127 Richard Verstegan, *A Restitution of Decayed Intelligence in Antiquities concerning the Most Noble and Renowned English Nation* (Antwerp: Robert Bruney, 1605).

128 Verstegan, 188.

129 George Jones, *The History of Ancient America prior to the Time of Columbus Proving the Identity of the Aborigines with the Tyrians and Israelites* (London: Longman, Brown, Green, and Longmans, 1843).

130 Nicholas Hudson, *Writing and European Thought, 1600–1830* (Cambridge: Cambridge University Press, 1994).

CHAPTER SIX

1 Willem Goeree, *Voor-Bereidselen tot de bybelsche Wysheid, en Gebruik der heilige en kerklijke Historien: Uit de alder-oudste Gedenkkenissen der Hebreen, Chaldeen, Babyloniers, Egiptenaars, Syriers, Grieken en Romeinen* (Utrecht: Anthony Schouten and Hermannus Ribbius Boeckverkoopers, 1700).

2 Athanasius Kircher, *Turris Babel* (Amstelodami: Janssonio-Waesbergiana, 1679).

3 Agrippa, *De occulta philosophia*.

4 David A. King, "The Ciphers as Presented by Agrippa of Nettesheim," in *The Ciphers of the*

Monks: A Forgotten Number Notation of the Middle Ages (Stuttgart: Franz Steiner Verlag, 2001), 196–97, offers specific possible sources for these scripts in medieval manuscripts.

5 Interestingly, for all his comprehensiveness, Edmund Fry does not cite either of these plates nor the other published work of Rocca, which suggests they were not available to him since he culled samples from every other conceivable source in this period.

6 Angelo Rocca, *Variarum linguarum alphabeta et inventores* (Rome: Ex typographia Dominici Basae, 1595).

7 Rocca notes the addition made by Epicharmus Siculus (to augment the letters brought by Cadmus), the favorite letter of Pythagoras.

8 Angelo Rocca, *Bibliothea apostolica Vaticana Sixto V* (Rome: Typographia Apostolica Vaticana, 1591). This book served as the basis for the iconography of the fresco cycles in the Vatican Library. See Paul Nelles, "The Vatican Library Alphabets, Luco Orfei, and Graphic Media in Sistine Rome," in *For the Sake of Learning*, ed. Ann Blair and Anja-Silvia Goeing (Leiden: Brill, 2016), n4.

9 WorldCat lists one in the Uffizi Gallery Library, one in Harvard's Houghton Library, and one in the Zentralbibliothek, in Zurich.

10 Nelles, "The Vatican Library Alphabets," 441–68.

11 Nelles, 447. Nelles, rightly in my opinion, aligns this sheet with writing manuals.

12 Nelles, 441–68.

13 Hepburn had published a Hebrew grammar in 1591 as a very young man.

14 Hepburn, *Virga Aurea*.

15 Adam McLean, "The Virga Aurea," *The Alchemy Website*, first published in the *Hermetic Journal* (1980), contains useful contextual information on Hepburn, hermeticism, and the symbolism of the plate: http://www.levity.com/alchemy/virga_aurea.html.

16 Kircher, *Turris Babel*.

17 Goeree, *Voor-Bereidselen Tot*.

18 By the author, with assistance from Google Translate.

19 Goeree cited the usual authors: Pliny, the rabbis, Plutarch, Cicero, Diodorus Siculus, and Plato.

20 *Aleph* was at the bottom right, the top row began with *T* and ended with some diphthongs, and the middle row started with *K* and *L*.

21 Athanasius Kircher, *Oedipus Aegyptiacus* (Rome: Mascardi, 1652).

22 For instance, Bibliander, *De ratione communi*; Luca Orfei, *De caracterum et litterarum inventoribus* [. . .] (Rome: Gio. Batt. Rossi, 1589), and Bang, *Caelum orientis*. The list of cited authorities, while long, becomes familiar.

23 Edward Bernard, *Orbis eruditi literarum* (Oxoniae: Apud Theatrum, 1689) n.p.

24 Jackson, *Chronological Antiquities*.

25 Deirdre Jackson, "Humfrey Wanley and the Harley Collection," *eBLJ* (*British Library Journal*), article 2 (2011), https://www.bl.uk/eblj/2011articles/pdf/ebljarticle22011.pdf.

26 Edmund Chishull, *Antiquitates Asiaticæ Christianam æram antecedents* (London: William Bowyer, 1728).

27 Giovanni Bianconi, *De antiquis litteris Hebraeorum et Graecorum Libellus* (Bononiae: Apud Thoman Colli ex typographia S. Thomae Aquinatis, 1763); a 1748 edition also exists.

28 Toustain, *Nouveau traité*, table 1, "Alphabet General."

29 Toustain, 594, gives a long list of scholars who provide this authority, all of whom are involved in heated debates about which is the oldest script: Genebrand, Bellarmin, Arias Montanus, le Pere Etienne Morin, M. Huet, Montfaucon, Calmet, Renaudot, Willalpandus, Scaliger, Grotius, Hottinger, Casaubon, Drusius, Waser, Brerewood, Capelle, Walton, Bouchard, les Vossius, Prideaux, Shuckford, Edouard Bernard, Simon, Spanheim, Meier, Conringius, Buxtorf, Schickard, Fuller, Brougthon, Junius, Lightfoot, and so on.

30 This information is from the 1911 *Encyclopedia Britannica* online, on Gébelin.

31 Court de Gébelin, *Le monde primitif* (Paris, 1777–96), 11–13.

32 James Knowlson, *Universal Language Schemes in England* (Toronto: University of Toronto Press, 1975).

33 Ignace Gelb, *A Study of Writing* (Chicago: University of Chicago Press, 1952) is the oft-cited example but it is typical, not unique.

34 Gébelin, *Le monde primitif*, 119–20.

35 Astle, table 1, facing page 64.

36 Charles Forster, *A Harmony of Primeval Alphabets* (London: Richard Bentley, 1852).

37 *Journal of the Royal Geographical Society of London* 13–14 (1843): l–li.

38 Forster, *A Harmony*, 6.

39 Forster, 1.

40 Recent discovery of the "Cascajal Block" in Veracruz suggests a date as early as 900 BCE.

41 Isaac Taylor, *The Alphabet* (London: Kegan Paul, Trench, 1883).

42 Taylor, 18, 39.

43 Taylor, 121. The Eshmunazar sarcophagus had been discovered near Sidon in 1855.

44 Driver, *Semitic Writing*.

CHAPTER SEVEN

1 The official inventory of Canaanite and Aramaic inscriptions is just over three hundred. The Sinai inscriptions total about fifty, and many of these consist of just a few letters. Herbert Donner, Wolfgang Röllig, and O. Rössler, *Kanaanaische und aramaische Inschriften* (Wiesbanden: Harrassowitz, 2002–).

2 Benjamin Sass and Israel Finkelstein, "Epigraphic Evidence from Jerusalem and Its Environs at the Dawn of Biblical History: Facts First," *New Studies in the Archaeology of Jerusalem and its Region* 11 (2017): 21–26, 25.

3 Sass and Finkelstein, 25.

4 Forster, *The One Primeval Language*, 1:1.

5 See Seth Sanders, *The Invention of Hebrew* (Urbana: University of Illinois Press, 2011) for a discussion of language and national identity formation.

6 Samuel Bochart, *Geographia sacra, cuius pars prior Phaleg de dispersion Gentium et terrarium divisione facta in aedification turris Babel pars posterior Chanaan de coloniis et sermone Phoenicum* (Frankfurt on Mainz: Impensis Johannis Davidis Zunneri, typis Balthasaris Christophori Wustii, 1674); originally published 1646.

7 Bochart, *Geographia sacra*.

8 The citation is from (François-Marie Arouet) Voltaire's *Philosophical Dictionary (Dictionnaire Philosophique)* (1764), under the entry "Augure" 297, https://archive.org/details/dictionnairephi05beucgoog; see the Wiki entry on Samuel Bochart, accessed June 15, 2021, https://en.wikipedia.org/wiki/Samuel_Bochart.

9 Adriaan Relaant, *Antiquitates sacrae veterum Hebraeorum* (Lipsiae: Apud Joh. Fridericum Wehrmannum; Typis Jo. Heinrici Richteri, 1713).

10 Frederick Jones Bliss, *The Development of Palestine Exploration* (New York: Scribner, 1907) is a published version of 1903 Ely lectures. Bliss begins with biblical descriptions of the geography, followed by records of Egyptian exploration and the Tell el-Amarna letters (cuneiform) from about 1500 BCE, and attends to the classical writers' accounts—those of Josephus, Eusebius, Jerome, and various Christian pilgrims—and other works in his meticulous inventory. See chap. 1, "The Dawn of Exploration," and chap. 2, "The Age of Pilgrimage."

11 Bliss, citing Dr. Roswell D. Hitchcock, 189.

12 Relaant, *Antiquitates sacrae*; Karl von Raumer, *Palästina* (Leipzig: F. A. Brockhaus, 1835); John Lewis Burckhardt, *Travels in Arabia* (London: H. Colburn, 1829); and Léon Mar-

quis de Laborde, *Journey through Arabia Petra to Mount Sinai* (London: John Murray, 1836).

13 Bliss, *The Development*, on Robinson, 195.

14 Mike Markowitz, "CoinWeek Ancient Coin Series—Coinage of the Phoenicians," *CoinWeek*, February 29, 2016, https://coinweek.com/ancient-coins/coinweek-ancient-coin-series-coinage-of-the-phoenicians/.

15 The site is known as Magharat Abloun.

16 The sarcophagus is carved from amphibolite, a stone related to basalt, and mined in an eastern area of Egypt.

17 Notes of the meeting in the Institute Rooms, April 3, 1855, *Transactions of the Albany Institute* 4, art. 4 (1855): 68–69; reports that the Secretary "laid before the meeting" a communication from Dr. C. V. A. Van Dyck, who was in Syria.

18 *Transactions*.

19 William T. Turner, "Remarks on the Phoenician Inscription of Sidon," presented to the Society, October 26, 1859, in *Journal of the American Oriental Society* 7, no. 48 (1860): 50.

20 M. L'Abbé J. J. L. Bargès, *Mémoire sur le sacrophage et l'inscription funéraire d'Eschmounazar roi de Sidon* (Paris: Benjamin Duprat, Libraire de l'Institut de la Bibliothèque Impériale des Sociétés Asiatiques, de Paris, de Londre, de Madras et de Calcutta, etc., 1856).

21 Reinhard Lehmann, "Much Ado about an Implement!," in *Understanding Relations between Scripts II, Early Alphabets*, ed. Philip J. Boyes and Philippa M. Steele (Oxford, UK: Oxbow Books, 2020), 72.

22 Bargès, *Mémoire*.

23 Bargès, 1.

24 Turner, "Remarks," 48–59.

25 Turner, "Remarks."

26 Turner, 50.

27 Turner, 57.

28 Turner, 57.

29 Turner, 58.

30 Biblical Hebrew is one of those problematic terms, since the word Hebrew is anachronistic, Canaanite being the term used in biblical references. The script used to write Canaanite is almost identical to Phoenician in this period from about 1000 BCE to the beginning of the Common Era.

31 Reverend James King, *Moab's Patriarchal Stone: Being an Account of the Moabite Stone, Its Story and Teaching* (London: Bickers, 1878), 1.

32 King, 5.

33 King, 7, whose vivid details are paraphrased throughout.

34 A. H. Sayce *Fresh Light from Ancient Monuments* (London: Religious Tract Society, 1883), 77.

35 Sayce, 76–77.

36 King, *Moab's Patriarchal Stone*, 21.

37 King, 21.

38 King, 22.

39 Charles Warren, "The Moabite Stone: Captain Warren's First Account of the Inscription from the Moab," *Quarterly Statement of the Palestine Exploration Fund*, January 21, 1870, 169–83, https://www.biblicalstudies.org.uk/pdf/pefqs/1869-71_169.pdf. Contains multiple documents, letters, and accounts relevant to the discovery and analysis of the stone.

40 Warren, n.p.

41 Sayce, *Fresh Light*, 169.

42 Sayce, 169.

43 Sayce, 169.

44 Christopher Rollston, *Writing and Literacy in the World of Ancient Israel* (Boston: Brill, 2010).
45 Anson Rainey, *The Sacred Bridge: Carta's Atlas of the Biblical World* (Jerusalem: Carta, 2006).
46 Daniel Silas Adamson, "The Men Who Uncovered Assyria," *BBC Magazine*, March 22, 2015, https://www.bbc.com/news/magazine-31941827.
47 Gareth Brereton, "Lion Hunting: The Sport of Kings," *The British Museum Blog*, January 4, 2019, https://blog.britishmuseum.org/lion-hunting-the-sport-of-kings-2/.
48 Layard, *Discoveries*.
49 Layard, 155n.
50 Layard, *Discoveries*.
51 Naveh, *The Early History*, 30–32.
52 Eric Burrows, "The Origin of the Ras Shamra Alphabet," *Journal of the Royal Asiatic Society of Great Britain and Ireland* 68, no. 2 (April 1936): 271–77. Burrows surveys the various theories of derivation that had sprung up in response to the discovery, including work by M. Sprengling, J. G. Feverie, T. Gaster, M. Virolleaud, A. Sayce, and other prominent authorities of the era.
53 J. Philip Hyatt, "The Ras Shamra Discoveries and the Interpretation of the Old Testament," *Journal of Bible and Religion* 10, no. 2 (May 1942): 67–75. The tablets were not immediately published, and Hyatt made many cautionary statements about their use: fragmentary translation, uncertain readings, lacunae in our knowledge, and other matters. But, he emphasized, this material was still an improvement since this was some of the first genuine primary material for Old Testament study (before this, he notes, there had been much reliance on classical authors).
54 Alfred Weidemann, *Ägyptische Geschichte* (Gotha: F. A. Perthes, 1884).
55 Pierre Montet, *Byblos et l'Egypte, Quatre Campagnes des Fouilles, 1921–1924* (Paris: P. Geuthner, 1928–29), 228–238, Tafel CXXVII–CXLI.
56 Reinhard G. Lehmann, "Wer war Aḥīrōms Sohn (KAI 1:1)? Eine kalligraphisch-prosopographische Annäherung an eine epigraphisch offene Frage," in *Neue Beiträge zur Semitistik: Fünftes Treffen der ArbeitsgemeinschaftSemitistik in der Deutschen MorgenländischenGesellschaft vom 15.–17. Februar 2012 an der Universität Basel* (AOAT 425), ed. V. Golinets et al. (Münster: Ugarit-Verlag, 2015), 163–80.
57 Edward M. Cook, "On the Linguistic Dating of the Phoenician Ahiram Inscription (KAI 1)," *Journal of Near Eastern Studies* 53, no. 1 (January 1994): 33.
58 Charles C. Torrey, "The Ahiram Inscription of Byblos," *Journal of the American Oriental Society* 45 (1925): 269–79, https://www.jstor.org/stable/pdf/593505.pdf.
59 Christopher Rollston, "The Dating of the Early Royal Byblian Phoenician Inscriptions: A Response to Benjamin Sass," *Maarav* 15, no.1 (2008): 57–93.
60 Rollston, 59.
61 Edith Porada, "Notes on the Sarcophagus of Ahiram," *Journal of the Ancient Near East Society* 5, no. 1 (1973): 354–72.
62 Porada, "Notes."
63 Ben Haring, "Ancient Egypt and the Earliest Known Stages of Alphabetic Writing," in *Understanding the Relations Between Scripts II, Early Alphabets*, ed. Philip J. Boyes and Philippa M. Steele (Oxford, UK: Oxbow Books, 2020), 62.
64 W. M. Flinders Petrie, *Inductive Metrology, or The Recovery of Ancient Measures from the Monuments* (London: Hargrove Saunders, 1877).
65 W. M. Flinders Petrie, *Tell el-Hesi* (London: Published for the Committee of the Palestine Exploration Fund, 1891).
66 Petrie, *Tell el-Hesi*.
67 Petrie, 50.

68 Julian Obermann, "A Revised Reading of the Tell el-Hesi Inscription, with a Note on the Gezer Sherd," *American Journal of Archaeology* 44, no.1 (January–March 1940): 93–104.

69 Obermann, 99.

70 "Gezer Calendar," Jewish Virtual Library, accessed June 23, 2021, https://www.jewishvirtuallibrary.org/gezer-calender. Cites *Encyclopedia Judaica*, 2008, as the source.

71 Naveh, *The Early History*, 26.

72 Sariel Shalev, *Swords and Daggers in Late Bronze Age Canaan* (Stuttgart: Franz Steiner Verlag, 2004), 12.

73 Ben Haring, "Ancient Egypt," 58–60.

74 Harry Torczyner et al., *The Lachish Letters* (Oxford: Oxford University Press, 1938); W. F. Albright, "The Oldest Hebrew Letters: The Lachish Ostraca," *Bulletin of the American Schools of Oriental Research* 70 (April 1938): 11–17.

75 Dennis Pardee, "Lachish Ostraca (3.42)," *Context of Scripture* 3, no. 42 (2002): 78.

76 Edward Robinson and Eli Smith, *Biblical Researches in Palestine and the Adjacent Regions, Journal of Travels in the Year 1838* (Boston: Crocker and Brewster, 1841), 1:596.

77 Diodorus Siculus, *Bibliotheca historica*, 60–30 BCE, book 3, section 42, from the Thomas Browne Website, by William Thayer, http://penelope.uchicago.edu/Thayer/E/Roman/Texts/Diodorus_Siculus/3C*.html.

78 Forster, *The One Primeval Language*, 1:2.

79 Forster, 3.

80 Forster, 3. Apparently, it was the peculiar anti-Ptolemaic approach in Cosmas's work that kept it from finding broader acceptance and audience.

81 Pococke, *A Description*.

82 Lottin de Laval, *Voyage dans la peninsule arabique du Sinai et l'Egypte moyenne, histoire, geographie, epigraphie* (Paris: Gide, 1855), introduction.

83 Laval, 24.

84 Laval, 353.

85 Laval, 353.

86 Laval, 353.

87 Arthur Stanley, *Sinai and Palestine in Connection with Their History* (London: John Murray, 1857) and Samuel Sharpe, *Hebrew Inscriptions: From the Valleys between Egypt and Mount Sinai* (London: John Russell Smith, 1875).

88 Robinson and Smith, *Biblical Researches*.

89 Eduard F. F. Beer, *Studia Asiatica* (Leipzig: Joannis Ambrosii Barys, 1840) and Forster, *The One Primeval Language*.

90 G. F. Grey, "Inscriptions from the Waady El Muketteb, or The Written Valley; copied, in 1820, by the Rev. G. F. Grey, and communicated to the Royal Society of Literature in 1830," *Transactions of the Royal Society of Literature of the United Kingdom*, vol. 1, part 2 (1830): 147–48; N. N. Lewis and M. C. A. MacDonald, "W. J. Bankes and the Discovery and Identification of the Nabataean Script," *Syria* 80 (2003): 41–110.

91 Sharpe, *Hebrew Inscriptions*, iii.

92 Forster, *The One Primeval Language*, 1:2.

93 Sharpe, iv.

94 Sharpe, iv.

95 Sharpe, iv.

96 Sharpe, 11.

97 Sharpe, 11–12.

98 Sharpe, 15.

99 Grey, "Inscriptions."

100 Sharpe, *Hebrew Inscriptions*, 30.

101 Sharpe describes the geographic location, speculates on the identity of the carvers as

persons coming to the spot in a pilgrimage from Egypt and returning, not passing through (1–2).

102 Sharpe, 2.

103 Sharpe, 9.

104 Sharpe, 8.

105 Sharpe, 11.

106 Sharpe, 13. He suggests that the author of the Book of Job, which he attributes to a sixth-century BC writer (538 BC to be precise), "describes these inscriptions on and near Mount Serbal."

107 Forster, *The One Primeval Language*.

108 Forster, *The One Primeval Language*.

109 Forster, 3:iv.

110 Forster, 3:7.

111 Forster, 3:41–42.

112 Forster makes this argument repeatedly on 1:58–65, though I cannot locate these precise phrases.

113 Forster, 1:58–59.

114 Forster, 1:62.

115 Forster, 1:58, "The People kicked like an ass."

116 Jane Taylor, "The Writing on the Rocks," *Al-Ahram Weekly Online*, post no. 620, January 9–15, 2003. Reference no longer online.

117 Kirsopp Lake and Robert P. Blake, "The Serâbît Inscriptions: I. The Rediscovery of the Inscriptions," *Harvard Theological Review* 21, no.1 (January 1928): 1–8.

118 W. M. Flinders Petrie, *Researches in the Sinai* (London: John Murray, 1906).

119 Beginning with one authored by Alan Gardiner and T. Eric Peet, *The Inscriptions of Sinai* (London: Egypt Exploration Fund, 1917). Revised by Jaroslav Cerny, *The Inscriptions of Sinai, II*, Egypt Exploration Society Memoir 45 (London: Egypt Exploration Society, 1952–55).

120 Petrie, *Researches*, vii.

121 Petrie, 130.

122 Petrie, 131–32.

123 Petrie, 132.

124 W. M. Flinders Petrie, *The Formation of the Alphabet*, British School of Archaeology in Egypt 3 (London: Macmillan; Bernard Quaritch, 1912), 1.

125 Petrie, 2.

126 Petrie, 2.

127 Petrie, 8.

128 Petrie, 2.

129 Petrie, 7.

130 Petrie, 19.

131 David Diringer, "The Palestinian Inscriptions and the Origin of the Alphabet," *Journal of the American Oriental Society* 63, no. 1 (March 1943): 24–30.

132 Diringer, 24.

133 Diringer, "The Palestinian Inscriptions," 24.

134 A. Biran and Joseph Naveh, "The Tel Dan Inscription: A New Fragment," *Israel Exploration Journal* 43 (1993): 81–98. Reprinted in Joseph Naveh, *Studies in West-Semitic Epigraphy* (Jerusalem: The Hebrew University; Magnes Press, 2009), 256–73.

135 Ron E. Tappy et al., "An Abecedary of the Mid-Tenth Century B.C. from the Judaean Shephelah," *Bulletin of the American Schools of Oriental Research* 344 (November 2006): 5–46.

136 David M. Carr, "The Tel Zayit Abecedary in (Social) Context," in *Literate Culture and Tenth-Century Canaan: The Tel Zayit Abecedary in Context*, ed. Ron E. Tappy and Peter

Kyle McCarter (Winona Lake, IN: Eisenbrauns, 2008), 113–29; Peter Kyle McCarter, "Paleographic Notes on the Tel Zayit Abecedary," in Tappy and McCarter, *Literate Culture*, 45–60.

137 Ministry of Tourism, "Earliest Known Hebrew Text Unearthed at 3,000 Year Old Judean Fortress," *Israel Ministry of Foreign Affairs*, October 30, 2008, https://mfa.gov.il/MFA/IsraelExperience/History/Pages/Earliest_Hebrew_text_unearthed_3000-year-old_Judean_fortress_30-Oct-2008.aspx (link no longer works); Yosef Garfinkel et al., "The Eshbaal Inscription," Khirbet Qeiyafa Archaeological Project, Hebrew University of Jerusalem, accessed June 15, 2021, http://qeiyafa.huji.ac.il/eshbaal.asp.

138 Alan Millard, "The New Jerusalem Inscription—So What?" *Biblical Archaeology Review* 40, no. 3 (May–June 2014), https://www.baslibrary.org/biblical-archaeology-review/40/3/6.

139 Douglas Petrovich, "The Ophel Pithos Inscription: Its Dating, Language, Translation, and Script," *Palestine Exploration Quarterly* 147, no. 2 (2015): 130–45; Eilat Mazar and David Ben-Shlomo, "An Inscribed Pithos from the Ophel, Jerusalem," *Israel Exploration Journal* 63, no. 1 (January 2013): 39–49.

140 Albert de Luynes, *Mémoire sur le sarcophage et l'inscription funéraire d'Esmunazar, roi de Sidon* (Paris: Henri Plon, 1856), 65.

141 Bruce Zuckerman, Marilyn Lundberg, and Leta Hunt, "Inscriptifact Digital Image Library," accessed June 23, 2021, http://www.inscriptifact.com/.

CHAPTER EIGHT

1 Benjamin Sass and Israel Finkelstein, "The Swan-Song of Proto-Canaanite in the Ninth Century BCE in Light of an Alphabetic Inscription from Megiddo," *Semitica et Classica, International Journal of Oriental and Mediterranean Studies* 9 (2016): 19.

2 Sass and Finkelstein, 19–43.

3 Sass and Finkelstein, 19.

4 Sass and Finkelstein, 19.

5 Benjamin Sass, *The Alphabet at the Turn of the Millennium: The West Semitic Alphabet, c.1150–850* (Tel Aviv: Emery and Claire Yass Publications in Archaeology, 2005).

6 Sass, 26.

7 While Joseph Scaliger, Ezechiel Spanheim, and other scholars were important influences in the sixteenth and seventeenth centuries, epigraphy as a field belongs to the late eighteenth and early nineteenth centuries.

8 Frank Moore Cross, *Leaves from an Epigrapher's Notebook* (Winona Lake, IN: Eisenbrauns, 2002) and Jo Ann Hackett and Walter E. Aufrecht, eds., *"An Eye for Form": Epigraphic Essays in Honor of Frank Moore Cross* (Winona Lake, Indiana: Eisenbrauns, 2014).

9 Charles Toustain, *Nouveau traité*, 653–54, cites Père Souciet, Athanasius Kircher, Samuel Petit, Bernard de Montfaucon, Joseph Scaliger, Samuel Shuckford, Gerardus Vossius, and many others. This intellectual lineage is clearly established and regularly cited, as is the work of Etienne Morin and Rabbi Azarias. Toustain also cites Edmund Chishull and Edward Bernard.

10 Mark Lidzbarski, George A. Combe, William Albright, Frank Moore Cross, Godfrey Driver, P. Kyle McCarter, Joseph Naveh, Benjamin Sass, Israel Finkelstein, Christopher Rollston, and many others have extended this work into the present.

11 Through the efforts of Christopher Rollston, Douglas Petrovich, Émile Puech, and many others.

12 Reinhard G. Lehman, "Wilhelm Gesenius and the Rise of Phoenician Philology," *Bieheste zur Zeitschrift für die alttestamentliche Wissenschaft*, Band 427 (Berlin: De Gruyter, 2013).

13 Identified as Isaac Newton, Keynes MS 28, in *The Chymistry of Isaac Newton*, ed. By

William R. Newman, June 2010, http://webapp1.dlib.indiana.edu/newton/mss/dipl/ALCH00017.

14 Heinrich Khunrath *Amphitheatrum saptientiae aeternae, solvis verae* (Hanoviae: Excudebat Guilielmus Antonius, 1609).

15 Iulia Millesima, "Kriegsmann: Sun, Moon, Wind and Earth in Tabula Smaragdina," 2021, https://www.labyrinthdesigners.org/alchemic-authors-1598-1832/kriegsmann-sun-moon-wind-earth-in-tabula-smaragdina/.

16 Roberto Weiss, "The Study of Ancient Numismatics during the Renaissance (1313–1517)," *Numismatic Chronicle* 8 (1968): 177–87.

17 Lehman, "Wilhelm Gesenius."

18 Lehmann, "Wilhelm Gesenius," 213–14.

19 L'Abbé Jean-Jacques Barthélemy, "Réflexions sur quelques monuments phéniciens, et sur les alphabets qui en résultent," *Memoires de l'Académie des Inscriptions et Belles Lettres* 30 (1764): 405–26.

20 Lehmann, "Wilhelm Gesenius."

21 Johannes Franz, *Elementa epigraphices Graecae* (Berolini: F. Nicolai, 1840).

22 John McClintock, *Cyclopedia of Biblical, Theological, and Ecclesiastical Literature*, vol. 8 (New York: Harper and Brothers, 1881).

23 Mark Cartwright, "Trade in the Phoenician World," *Ancient History Encyclopedia*, April 1, 2016, https://www.ancient.eu/article/881/trade-in-the-phoenician-world/.

24 Wilhelm Gesenius, *Scripturae linguaeque Phoeniciae monumenta quotquot supersunt* (Leipzig: Vogel, 1837).

25 P. Kyle McCarter, *The Antiquity of the Greek Alphabet*, Harvard Semitic Monographs 9 (Cambridge, MA: Harvard College, 1975), 3.

26 Wilhelm Gesenius, *Hebräische Grammatik* (Halle, 1813), went into dozens of editions and translations.

27 Gesenius, *Scripturae*.

28 McCarter, *The Antiquity*, 3.

29 See Naveh, *The Early History*, 8–9, for a clear discussion of the division of Semitic languages into eastern (Akkadian, Babylonian, Assyrian), western (Canaanite, including Hebrew, Phoenician, Moabite, Ammonite, and probably Ugaritic), Aramaic, and southern (South Arabian, Ethiopian, Arabic). Semitic scripts are not parallel to languages.

30 Eduard Friedrich Ferdinand Beer, *Inscriptiones et papyri veteres semitici* [. . .] (Leipzig: Typographia Fridericines 1833).

31 Eduard F. F. Beer, *Inscriptiones veteres litteris et lingua hucusque incognitis ad Montem Sinai* (Leipzig, 1840).

32 Beer, "Theses," *Inscriptiones et papyri*, 22.

33 Pococke, *A Description*; Carsten Niebuhr, *Travels through Arabia* (Edinburgh: R. Morison and Son, 1792); Grey, "Inscriptions."

34 Erik Iversen, *The Myth of Egypt and Its Hieroglyphs in European Tradition* (Copenhagen: Gad, 1961).

35 Kircher, *Oedipus*.

36 Ingrid D. Rowland, "Athanasius Kircher and the Egyptian Oedipus," Fathom Archive, accessed June 15, 2021, https://fathom.lib.uchicago.edu/1/777777122590/.

37 François Joseph Chabas, "Le plus ancien livre du monde: Étude sur le Papyrus Prisse," *Revue archéologique* 15ième Année, no. 1 (avril à septembre 1858): 1–25; Franz Joseph Lauth, *Papyrus Prisse* (Munich: Bayerischen Akademie der Wissenschaften, 1869).

38 For an image of the manuscript, see "Papyrus Prisse," on the website of the Bibliothèque Nationale, accessed May 12, 2021, https://gallica.bnf.fr/ark:/12148/btv1b8304609v.image.

39 Taylor, *The Alphabet*, 95–96.

40 Taylor, 95–96.
41 Taylor, 96.
42 Taylor, 98. See Sass, *The Alphabet*, 141, for discussion of the specifics of hieratic.
43 C. W. Goodwin, "Hieratic Papyri," in *Cambridge Essays: 1858*, Members of the University (London: Parker and Sons, 1858), 276.
44 Emmanuel de Rougé, "Mémoire sur l'origine égyptienne de l'alphabet phénicien," reviewed in *Comptes rendus des séances de l'Académie des Inscriptions et Belles-Lettres* (1859): 115.
45 De Rougé, 115.
46 De Rougé, 116.
47 De Rougé, 117.
48 These citations are my translations and paraphrases of the account.
49 De Rougé, *Mémoire sur l'origine égyptienne de l'alphabet phénicien* (Paris: Maisonneuve, 1874), 11.
50 De Rougé (table is at end, after 110).
51 Friedrich Ballhorn, *Grammatography: A Manual of Reference of the Alphabets of Ancient and Modern Languages* (London: Trübner, 1861), 8–9.
52 Rev. A. H. Sayce, *The Archaeology of Cuneiform Inscriptions* (London: Society for Promoting Christian Knowledge, 1908), v.
53 Sayce, vi.
54 Pietro della Valle, *Viaggi di Pietro Della Valle* (Rome, 1650).
55 Carsten Niebuhr, *Travels through Arabia* (Edinburgh: R. Morison and Son, 1792).
56 Sayce, *The Archaeology*, 10.
57 Georg Grotefend, *Neue Beiträge zur Erläuterung der persepolitanischen Keilshrift* (Hannover: Hahn, 1837).
58 Sayce, *The Archaeology*, 4–15.
59 Sayce, 19.
60 Sayce, 36.
61 Sayce, 36.
62 Sayce, 37.
63 Philippe Berger, *L'histoire de l'écriture dans l'antiquité* (Paris: L'Imprimerie Nationale, 1891).
64 Berger, dedication, n.p.
65 Ernest Renan, *Mission de Phénicie* (Paris: Imprimerie Imperiale, 1864). Renan's work was controversial, particularly because he had negative views of Jews, and though he eschewed strict biological racism, he espoused anti-Semitic positions that were reprehensible to some but not virulent enough for others.
66 Berger, *L'histoire*, vii.
67 Berger, 164.
68 Berger, 164.
69 Berger, 165. Berger also mentions the works of various authors as of particular importance but without fuller citation: those of d'Arnaud, de Fresnel, de Saulcy, de Longpérier, de Vogüé, and Waddington, as well as that of Renan.
70 Berger, 165–66.
71 *Corpus inscriptionum semiticarum* (Paris: Académie des Inscriptions et Belles-Lettres, Reipublicae Typographeo, 1881).
72 Berger, *L'histoire*, 169.
73 Berger, 175.
74 Berger, 183.
75 Berger, 189. The substance of this paragraph is paraphrased and translated directly from Berger.
76 Mark Lidzbarski, *Handbuch der Nordsemitischen Epigraphik* (Weimar: Emil Felber, 1898).

77 S. A. C., "Obituary," *Journal of the Royal Asiatic Society of Great Britain and Ireland*, no. 4 (October 1929): 872–74.

78 G. A. Cooke, *A Text-book of the North Semitic Inscriptions* (Oxford: Clarendon Press, 1903), is an English language handbook that covers much of the same materials.

79 Alan Gardiner, "The Egyptian Origin of the Semitic Alphabet," *Journal of Egyptian Archaeology* 3, no. 1 (January 1916): 1–16.

80 Gardiner, 1.

81 Gardiner, 1.

82 Gardiner, 1–2. His discussion is slightly more detailed and lists several advocates for the Babylonia position—Ball, Delitzsch, and Hommel. He gives Gesenius-Kautzsch's *Hebräische Grammatik*, 28th edition (!), as the source. He notes René Dussaud's contribution to the argument for Cretan/Minoan scripts.

83 Gardiner, 2–3.

84 Gardiner, 7.

85 Gardiner, 5.

86 Gardiner, 5.

87 Gardiner, 6.

88 Gardiner, 8–9, shreds a discussion by Macalister that suggests the Hebrew names were taken from the Greek.

89 Gardiner, 11.

90 Gardiner, 14.

91 Gardiner, 14.

92 Gardiner, 16.

93 Arthur Evans, *Scripta Minoa* (Oxford: Oxford University Press, 1909) sections on the Phoenician alphabet.

94 Hackett and Aufrecht, *"An Eye for Form,"* ix. In their preface, they note that the phrase "an eye for form," uttered by Cross, drove at least one of his students into the college town seeking an "eifferform" in one shop after another.

95 Albright was idealistic and religious and argued passionately that the Holyland and its antiquities were the possession of the whole world. Other archaeological approaches, such as those of the University of Chicago's Oriental Institute, sponsored, for instance, by the Rockefeller Foundation, stressed more secular interpretations of evidence.

96 Benjamin Sass, *The Genesis of the Alphabet and Its Development in the Second Millennium BC* (Wiesbaden: Otto Harrassowitz, 1988), 2.

97 Sass, 1.

98 Sass, 2.

99 Cross's revision was informed by Albright's change to his own work, a paper published in 1948, "The Early Alphabetic Inscriptions from the Sinai and Their Decipherment." The date resonates, of course, because it coincides with the discovery of the Dead Sea Scrolls in whose authentication Albright played a key role in validating those artifacts, but by 1954, his focus on epigraphic evidence brought other objects into the foreground.

100 Frank Moore Cross, "The Origin and Early Evolution of the Alphabet," *Eretz-Israel* 8 (Israel Publication Society, 1967), in Cross, *Leaves*, 309. Cross discusses the Lachish ewer and bowl found in the 1930s, an ostracon from Beth Shemesh, and a sherd from Tell es-Sarem, three examples of geographically distributed evidence.

101 Cross, "The Origin and Early Evolution," in Cross, *Leaves*, 310.

102 Cross revisited these arguments in his 1975 paper "Early Alphabetic Scripts," in *Symposia Celebrating the Seventy-Fifth Anniversary of the Founding of the American Schools of Oriental Research (1900–1975)*, ed. F. M. Cross (Cambridge, MA: ASOR, 1979).

103 Frank Moore Cross, "Alphabets and Pots: Reflections on Typological Method in the Dating of Human Artifacts," in Cross, *Leaves*, 344. Originally delivered as the W. F. Al-

bright Lecture at Johns Hopkins University, April 14, 1980; he is citing his own *Yahweh and the Gods of Canaan* (Garden City, NY: Doubleday, 1968).

104 Cross, "Alphabets and Pots," in Cross, *Leaves*, 347.

105 Jason Colavito, trans., "Eumalos of Cyrene on Atlantis," in "Discourse Composed for the Asiatic Society," by Fortia d'Urban, for the meeting of February 4, 1828, http://www.jasoncolavito.com/eumalos-on-atlantis-hoax.html.

106 Thomas Crawford Johnston, *Did the Phoenicians Discover America?* (San Francisco, CA: Geographical Society of California, 1892) is one example of the popular interest in the idea that America was discovered by the Phoenicians. Arguments for Phoenician settlements in England, Ireland, Spain, and elsewhere spring up throughout the late eighteenth and nineteenth centuries.

107 The Paraiba inscription, *Life*, June 10, 1968, and Cyrus H. Gordon, "The Canaanite Text from Brazil," *Orientalia*, n.s., 37, no. 4 (1968): 425–36.

108 Frank Moore Cross, "The Phoenician Inscription from Brazil: A Nineteenth-Century Forgery" *Orientalis* 37, no. 4 (1968), in Cross, *Leaves*, 238–49.

109 Cross, "The Phoenician Inscription," 238.

110 Cross, 238.

111 Cross, 240.

112 Cross, 239.

113 Cross, 239.

114 Cyrus H. Gordon, "The Authenticity of the Phoenician Text from Parahyba," *Orientalia*, n.s., 37, no.1 (1968): 75–80.

115 For details, see Gordon, 75.

116 Gordon, 80, cites Zelia Nuttall, *The Fundamental Principles of Old and New World Civilizations* (Cambridge, MA: Peabody Museum, 1901).

117 Standard references like Hubert Grimme, *Althebräische Inschriften vom Sinai* [. . .] [Old Hebrew inscriptions from Sinai] (Hannover: H. Lafaire, 1923); Eckard Unger's *Babylonian Writing* (reference is unclear); David Diringer's *The Antique-Hebrew Inscriptions from Palestine* (I can locate only the Italian edition, *Le iscrizioni antico-ebraiche palestinesi* [Firenze: F. Le Monnier, 1934]); and other inventories of the known corpus by Obermann, Sprengling, Dunand, Butin, G. A. Cooke, and others.

118 Naveh, *The Early History*.

119 Gelb, *A Study*.

120 Gelb, *A Study*.

121 David Diringer, *The Alphabet: A Key to the History of Mankind* (New York: Philosophical Society, 1948).

122 Driver, *Semitic Writing*. Published in 1954, the text was revised in 1976 by S. A. Hopkins.

123 Driver, 99.

124 Diringer, "The Palestinian Inscriptions," 24–30.

125 Lehmann, "Much Ado."

126 Driver, *Semitic Writing*, 138.

127 Driver, 187.

128 Driver, 197.

129 Sass, *The Genesis*.

130 Sass, *The Alphabet*, 147.

131 Sass, *The Genesis*, 145.

132 Sass, 4. Also Herbert G. May, "Moses and the Sinai Inscriptions," *Biblical Archaeologist* 8, no. 4 (December 1945): 93–99, described Grimme's work as "the product of a too-fertile imagination and utter disregard of established philological principles" (98).

133 Sass, *The Alphabet*.

134 Sass, 47.

135 Sass, 1.

136 Sass, *The Genesis*, 2.
137 Sass, *The Alphabet*, 148.
138 Sass, 135.
139 Sass, 149.
140 Sass, 149.
141 Sass, 150.
142 Sass, *The Genesis*, 4.
143 Sass, 5.
144 Sass, 5.
145 Sass, 5.
146 Frank Moore Cross, "Newly Found Inscriptions in Old Canaanite and Early Phoenician Scripts," *Bulletin of the American Schools of Oriental Research*, no. 238 (Spring 1980): 1–20, in Cross, *Leaves*, 213.
147 John Coleman Darnell et al., "Two Early Alphabetic Inscriptions from the Wadi el-Hôl," *Annual of the American Schools of Oriental Research* 79 (2005): 73.
148 John Coleman Darnell, "Wadi el-Hol," *UCLA Encyclopedia of Egyptology* (*UEE*), May 26, 2013, 3, https://escholarship.org/content/qt1sd2j49d/qt1sd2j49d.pdf?t=qlp9at. Citation is from Darnell et al., "Two Early Alphabetic Inscriptions," 74.
149 Darnell et al., "Two Early Alphabetic Inscriptions," 74.
150 Darnell, "Wadi el-Hol," 6.
151 Darnell, 7.
152 Darnell et al., "Two Early Alphabetic Inscriptions," 75.
153 John Noble Wilford, "Discovery of Egyptian Inscriptions Indicates an Earlier Date for Origin of the Alphabet," *New York Times*, Science, November 13, 1999, https://archive.nytimes.com/www.nytimes.com/library/national/science/111499sci-alphabet-origin.html.
154 Wilford, "Discovery."
155 Elizabeth J. Himelfarb, "First Alphabet Found in Egypt," *Archaeology* 53, no. 1 (2000): n.p.
156 Wilford, "Discovery."
157 Darnell, "Wadi el-Hol," 7.
158 Darnell, 7.
159 Darnell, 7. Darnell's comments here are a response to and refutation of Orly Goldwasser's assertions that unlettered people created these signs.
160 Darnell et al., "Two Early Alphabetic Inscriptions," 83–84.
161 Darnell et al., 86.
162 Darnell et al, 86.
163 Orly Goldwasser, "How the Alphabet Was Born from Hieroglyphs," *Biblical Archaeology Review* 36, no. 2 (March–April 2010): 40–53.
164 Darnell et al., "Two Early Alphabetic Inscriptions," 90.
165 Petrovich, *The World's Oldest Alphabet*, 1.
166 Petrovich, 1.
167 Petrovich, 5.
168 Petrovich, 6, paraphrased almost directly.
169 Petrovich, 10.
170 Joseph Naveh, "The Scripts in Palestine and Transjordan in the Iron Age," in *Studies in West-Semitic Epigraphy* (Jerusalem: Hebrew University; Magnes Press, 2009), 3; original publication of paper, 1970.
171 Naveh, 3.
172 Naveh, 3.
173 Christopher Rollston, "The Proto-Sinaitic Inscriptions 2.0: Canaanite Language and

Canaanite Script, Not Hebrew," *Rollston Epigraphy*, December 10, 2016, http://www.rollstonepigraphy.com/?m=201612.

174 Rollston also points to a precedent for this interpretation in the work of Grimme, *Althebräische Inschriften* (Hannover, 1923), which was also incorrect.

175 Naveh, *The Early History*, 26, cited by Rollston.

176 Rollston suggests that the words in the inscriptions could be Phoenician, Aramaic, Edomite, Hebrew, Moabite, or Ammonite.

177 Rollston's list: W. F. Albright, *The Proto-Sinaitic Inscriptions and Their Decipherment* (Cambridge, MA: Harvard University Press, 1966); Cross, *Leaves*; McCarter, *The Antiquity*; Sass, *The Genesis*; Gordon Hamilton, *The Origins of the West Semitic Alphabet in Egyptian Scripts* (Washington, DC: Catholic Biblical Association, 2006); and Sanders, *The Invention*.

178 For detailed discussion of particular letter forms, combinations, and words, see Rollston, "Proto-Sinaitic Inscriptions."

179 Rollston, *Writing and Literacy*.

180 Rollston, 1.

181 Rollston, 39.

182 Bruce Zuckerman, *West Semitic Research Project*, USC, Dornsife, https://dornsife.usc.edu/wsrp/.

183 Bruce Zuckerman, Marilyn Lundberg, and Leta Hunt, InscriptiFact, http://www.inscriptifact.com/aboutus/index.shtml.

184 Absent from mention are Ada Yardeni, Orly Goldwasser, Ben Mazar, Seth Sanders, and others. An entire book could be devoted simply to development and history of Semitic epigraphy.

CHAPTER NINE

1 Israel Finkelstein and Benjamin Sass, "The West Semitic Alphabet Inscriptions," *HeBAI* 2 (2013): 149–220.

2 The Ugaritic syllabary on the Ras Shamra tablet and the Izbet Sartah ostracon provide two examples, one in cuneiform script and the other Proto-Canaanite. Naveh, *Studies in West-Semitic Epigraphy*, 94.

3 See the West Semitic Research Project, USC Dornsife, https://dornsife.usc.edu/wsrp/.

4 Arthur de Gobineau, *Essai sur l'inégalité des races* (Paris: Firmin Didot, 1853–55).

5 Isaac Taylor, *The Origin of the Aryans*, 2nd ed. (London: W. Scott 1892), 3–5.

6 Taylor, 49.

7 Taylor, 49–50.

8 The Mitanni occupied Syria, and their kingdom stretched north into Anatolia and southeast into Mesopotamia. They may have migrated into the Indus valley region about 1500 BCE. Joshua J. Mark, "Mitanni," *World History Encyclopedia*, April 28, 2011, https://www.ancient.eu/Mitanni/. They are considered a blend of Hurrians and Indo-Aryans.

9 Tracking early language sources and their spread is difficult, with estimates on the earliest use among humans varying from fifty thousand to two million years ago. See Michael Balter, "Human Language May Have Evolved to Help Our Ancestors Make Tools," *Science*, January 13, 2015, https://www.sciencemag.org/news/2015/01/human-language-may-have-evolved-help-our-ancestors-make-tools.

10 Salomon Reinach, "Le mirage orientale," in *L'anthropologie* (Paris, 1893), 540. For a complete and nuanced discussion of Reinach's work, see Aron Rodrigue, "Totems, Taboos, and Jews: Salomon Reinach and the Politics of Scholarship in Fin-de-Siècle France," *Jewish Social Studies*, n.s., 10, no. 2 (Winter 2004): 1–19.

11 Reinach, 540.
12 Reinach, 723.
13 Rodrigue, "Totems," 1–19.
14 Rodrigue, 14.
15 McCarter, *The Antiquity*.
16 Laurence A. Waddell, *The Aryan Origin of the Alphabet* (London: Luzac, 1927).
17 Waddell, 1.
18 Waddell, 63.
19 Waddell, 64.
20 Waddell, 67.
21 Waddell, 2.
22 Alex Boese, "The Myserious Glozel Finds," *Museum of Hoaxes*, accessed June 15, 2021, http://hoaxes.org/archive/permalink/the_mysterious_glozel_finds.
23 Waddell, *The Aryan Origin*, 72.
24 Waddell, 6.
25 Waddell, 3, 13, and throughout.
26 Waddell, 9.
27 Waddell, 15.
28 Waddell, *The Aryan Origin*.
29 Waddell, 66.
30 Waddell, 66.
31 Waddell, 67.
32 Waddell, 71.
33 Waddell, 73.
34 Waddell, *The Aryan Origin*.
35 Bernal, *Cadmean Letters*, 7.
36 Bernal, 7.
37 Discussion of the development and spread of the discourse on the supposed superiority of the Aryan race is beyond the scope of this study.
38 Bernal, *Cadmean Letters*.
39 Bernal, 6.
40 For instance, work by David Reich, at the Harvard Medical School. See Reich, "Ancient DNA Tells Tales of Humans' Migrant History," *Science Daily*, February 21, 2018, https://www.sciencedaily.com/releases/2018/02/180221131851.htm.
41 Woodard, *Greek Writing*, vii.
42 Woodard, vii.
43 Woodard, vii.
44 Robert Logan, *The Alphabet Effect* (New York City: Morrow, 1986).
45 Milman Parry, "Studies in the Epic Technique of Oral Verse-Making: I. Homer and Homeric Style," *Harvard Studies in Classical Philology* 41 (1930): 73–148.
46 These concepts weave through Eric Havelock's titles, including *Prologue to Greek Literacy* (Cincinnati: University of Cincinnati Press, 1971) 2; *Origins of Western Literacy* (Toronto: Ontario Institute for Studies in Education, 1976); *The Literate Revolution in Greece and Its Cultural Consequences* (Princeton, NJ: Princeton University Press, 1981) 82; and *The Muse Learns to Write: Reflections on Orality and Literacy from Antiquity to the Present* (New Haven, CT: Yale University Press, 1986).
47 Eric Havelock, *Preface to Plato* (Cambridge, MA: Harvard University Press, 1963).
48 John Halverson, "Havelock on Greek Orality and Literacy," *Journal of the History of Ideas* 53, no. 1 (1992): 148; Havelock, *Literate*, 82.
49 Havelock, *The Muse*, 114.
50 Havelock, *Prologue*.

51 Eric Havelock, "Prologue to Greek Literacy," talk delivered at the University of Cincinnati, November 17, 1970, 1.

52 Havelock, *Prologue*, 3.

53 Havelock, 9.

54 Havelock, 10.

55 Havelock, 6–7.

56 Havelock, *Origins*, 39.

57 Havelock, 42.

58 Havelock, *Prologue*, 6; *Literate*, 330.

59 Leonard Shlain, *The Alphabet versus the Goddess* (New York: Viking, 1998).

60 Martin Bernal, *Cadmean Letters*, 2.

61 Havelock, *The Muse*, chapter 10, "The Special Theory of Greek Literacy," 98–116.

62 Havelock, 114.

63 Havelock, 114.

64 Havelock, 1.

65 Oscar Ogg, *The 26 Letters* (New York: T. Y. Crowell, 1948); Hans Jensen, *Sign, Script, and Symbol* (New York: Putnam, 1969); and Berthold Ullmann, *Ancient Writing and Its Influence* (New York: Cooper Square Publishers, 1963).

66 Harold Innis, *Empire and Communication* (Oxford: Clarendon, 1950) and *The Bias of Communication* (Toronto: University of Toronto Press, 1951). For a discussion of Innis in relation to Kittler and German Media Theory, see Till A. Heilman, "Innis and Kittler: The Case of the Greek Alphabet," in *Media Transatlantic: Developments in Media and Communication Studies between North American and German-Speaking Europe*, ed. Norm Freisen (Cham: Springer International Publishing, 2016), 91–110. First published online May 10, 2016. Kittler stated that since the alphabet denotes numbers, music, and speech and thus has multimedia capacity, it can function to represent "being as a whole . . . articulated through a single code" (91).

67 Harold Innis, *The Bias of Communication* (Toronto: University of Toronto Press, 1951).

68 The work of Harold Lasswell and the Institute for Propaganda Analysis, for instance, in the 1930s.

69 Other twentieth-century figures (e.g., Roger Chartier, Marcel Cohen, Friedrich Kittler, Lisa Gitelman) extended arguments about materiality into highly refined and specific studies. See also Johanna Drucker, *The Visible Word* (Chicago: University of Chicago Press, 1994).

70 Harold Innis, *Empire and Communications* (Oxford: Oxford University Press, 1950), 64.

71 Innis, 77.

72 Marshall McLuhan, *Understanding Media* (New York: McGraw-Hill, 1964), 8, 82.

73 McLuhan, 85.

74 Robert Babe, *Canadian Communication Thought: Ten Foundational Writers* (Toronto: University of Toronto Press, 2000) and Lester Faigley, "Material Literacy and Visual Design," in *Rhetorical Bodies*, ed. Jack Selzer and Sharon Crowley (Madison: University of Wisconsin Press, 1999), 171–201.

75 Innis, *The Bias*.

76 Jean Bottero, Clarisse Herrenschmidt, and Jean-Pierre Vernant, *Ancestor of the West* (Chicago: University of Chicago Press, 2000).

77 Jack Goody and Ian Watt, "The Consequences of Literacy," *Comparative Studies in Society and History* 5, no.3 (April 1963): 304–45.

78 Lucien Levy-Bruhl, *How "Natives" Think* (London: G. Allen and Unwin, 1926); originally published in French as *Les fonctions mentales dans les sociétés inférieures* (Paris: F. Alcan, 1910).

79 Goody and Watt, "The Consequences of Literacy," 313.

80 Goody and Watt, 317.
81 Goody and Watt, 319.
82 Goody and Watt, 320.
83 Jack Goody, *Domestication of the Savage Mind* (Cambridge: Cambridge University Press, 1977).
84 Goody, 5.
85 Goody, 6.
86 Goody, 7.
87 Cameron McEwen, "Writing and the Alphabet in Innis and McLuhan," *McLuhan's New Sciences*, July 26, 2017, https://mcluhansnewsciences.com/mcluhan/2017/07/writing-and-the-alphabet-in-innis-and-mcluhan/.
88 Derrick de Kerckhove, "A Theory of Greek Tragedy," *SubStance* 9, no. 4 (1980): 24.
89 De Kerckhove, 24.
90 De Kerckhove, 27.
91 De Kerckhove, 28.
92 De Kerckhove, 32.
93 De Kerckhove, 33.
94 De Kerckhove, 12.
95 De Kerckhove, "Critical Brain Processes Involved in Deciphering the Greek Alphabet," in *The Alphabet and the Brain: The Lateralization of Writing*, ed. Derrick de Kerckhove and C. J. Lumsden (Berlin: Springer, 1988), 401.
96 Derrick de Kerckhove and Charles J. Lumsden, introduction to *The Alphabet and the Brain* (Berlin: Springer, 1988).
97 De Kerckhove, "Critical Brain Processes," 412.
98 H. M. McLuhan and R. K. Logan, "Alphabet, Mother of Invention," *Et Cetera* 34 (December 1977): 373–83.
99 Logan, *The Alphabet Effect*, 23–24.
100 Logan, 35.
101 Daniels and Bright, *The World's Writing Systems*.
102 Logan, *The Alphabet Effect*, 21.
103 Logan, 21.
104 Logan, 21.
105 Logan, *The Alphabet Effect*. The argument weaves throughout, particularly in chapter 3, "A Comparison of Eastern and Western Writing Systems and Their Impact on Cultural Patterns" (46–58).
106 Logan, 51.
107 Dominic Yu, "Thoughts on Logan's 'The Alphabet Effect,'" last modified January 3, 2003, https://web.archive.org/web/20160413133632/http://rescomp.stanford.edu/~domingo2/zok/logan.html. Accessed on *Wayback Machine*, June 15, 2021.
108 Logan, *The Alphabet Effect*, 55.
109 Logan, 69.
110 Yu, "Thoughts."
111 Sanders, *The Invention of Hebrew*.
112 Logan, *The Alphabet Effect*, 103.
113 Logan, 103.
114 Logan, 121.
115 Paul Grosswiler, "Dispelling the Alphabet Effect," *Canadian Journal of Communication* 29, no. 2 (2004) 145–58.
116 Grosswiler, "Dispelling."
117 Michael Ridley, "Are Reading and Writing Doomed?," in *Proceedings, ACRL Fourteenth*

National Conference, March 12–15, 2009, 210–13, https://www.ala.org/acrl/sites/ala.org.acrl/files/content/conferences/confsandpreconfs/national/seattle/papers/210.pdf.

118 Grosswiler, "Dispelling," 145.

119 Grosswiler, 145.

120 See Jack Gernet, *A History of Chinese Civilization* (Cambridge: Cambridge University Press, 1982); Derk Bodde, *Chinese Thought, Society, and Science* (Honolulu: University of Hawaii Press, 1991); and Sylvia Scribner and Michael Cole, *The Psychology of Literacy* (Cambridge, MA: Harvard University Press, 1981). Gernet says more people have been educated in China than in the West. Chinese writing is unchanged since the third century BCE and can be read even if the language can't be spoken (the characters are the same). One can read a second-century BCE text as easily as a contemporary one. China also developed the first shorthand, and Bodde suggested a relationship between characters and ways of thinking—ambiguity, multiple meanings of Chinese, parallelism and not clarity.

121 Marshall McLuhan, *War and Peace in the Global Village* (New York: McGraw-Hill 1968).

122 Jack Goody, *The East in the West* (New York: Cambridge University Press, 1996).

123 Grosswiler, "Dispelling," 57, referring to Jack Goody, *The Interface between the Written and the Oral* (New York: Cambridge University Press, 1987), 56.

124 Bernal, *The Cadmean*.

125 Bernal, 9. See his citation of J. B. Bury, *History of Greece*, to the effect that there is "no reason to think that Canaanites . . . introduced Semitic blood into the population of Greece."

126 Bernal, 3.

127 Ivan Illich and Barry Sanders, *ABC: The Alphabetization of the Popular Mind* (New York: Random House, 1998), 9.

128 Illich and Sanders, 9.

129 Illich and Sanders, 10.

130 Illich and Sanders, 11.

131 Bernal, *The Cadmean*.

132 Robert Fraser, *Book History through Post-colonial Eyes* (New York: Routledge, 2008).

133 Leonard Shlain, *The Alphabet*.

134 Shlain, 6.

135 Shlain 66.

136 Shlain, 67.

137 Shlain, 430.

138 Sanders, *The Invention of Hebrew*.

CODA

1 Judith Flanders, *A Place for Everything* (New York: Basic Books, 2020).

2 Luther Marsh, "The Alphabet—The Vehicle of History" (New York: New York Historical Society, November 17, 1885), 6.

3 Marsh, 9.

4 Marsh, 8.

5 Marsh, 8.

6 Marsh, 15.

7 Marsh, 19.

8 Marsh, 25.

9 Donald Knuth, *TEX and METAFONT: New Directions in Typesetting* (Providence, RI: American Mathematical Society, 1979).

10 Douglas Hofstadter, "Metafont, Mathematics, and Metaphysics: Comments on Donald Knuth's Article 'The Concept of a Meta-Font.'" *Visible Language* 16, no. 4 (Autumn 1982): 309–38.

11 Unicode Consortium, History of Unicode, last updated November 18, 2015, https://unicode.org/history/.

12 Unicode Consortium, https://home.unicode.org/basic-info/overview/. For an interesting exchange of correspondence about Imperial Aramic script encoding see Deborah Anderson et al., "Script Encoding Initiatve," July 29, 2007, http://unicode.org/L2/L2007/07236-aramaic-support.pdf.

13 See Peter Kirk, response to revised "Final Proposal for Encoding the Phoenician Script in the UCS," June 7, 2004, https://www.gentlewisdom.org/qaya/academic/hebrew/Phoenician.html.

14 Jukka K. Korpela *Unicode Explained* (Boston: O'Reilly, 2006), 3, and following is my source throughout these two paragraphs.

15 Because it was the first to be encoded, Basic Latin used 128 code points, while the full Latin alphabet set is about 1374 points.

16 Korpela, *Unicode Explained*, 17.

17 David Liedle, "A Brief History of Optical Character Recognition," *Filestack* (blog), November 9, 2018, https://blog.filestack.com/thoughts-and-knowledge/history-of-ocr/.

18 Margaret Rouse, "OCR (Optical Character Recognition)," TechTarget, updated April 2019, https://searchcontentmanagement.techtarget.com/definition/OCR-optical-character-recognition.

19 Mohamed Cheriet, et al., *Character Recognition Systems* (Hoboken, NJ: John Wiley and Sons, 2007).

20 Patricia Crain, *The Story of A* (Palo Alto: Stanford University Press, 2001).

21 Preston R. Salisbury, "Analysis of Primers in the de Grummond Children's Literature Collection," *SLIS Connecting* 3, no. 2 (2014), https://aquila.usm.edu/cgi/viewcontent.cgi?article=1067&context=slisconnecting.

22 Alex Q. Arbuckle, "1899: An ABC for Baby Patriots," *Mashable*, accessed May 14, 2021, https://mashable.com/2016/08/27/abc-for-baby-patriots/.

23 Craig Brandist, *The Dimensions of Hegemony: Language, Culture, and Politics in Revolutionary Russia* (Chicago: Haymarket Books, 2016), 168.

24 Tom Mullaney, *The Chinese Typewriter: A History* (Cambridge, MA: MIT Press, 2017), 9.

25 Mullaney, 10–11.

26 Mullaney, 239.

27 Mullaney, 239.

28 Mullaney, 239.

29 Mullaney, 110.

30 From a description of a presentation Tom Mullaney, "Computer Wars: Chinese script in the age of alphanumeric hegemony," MIT Events Calendar, October 5, 2017, https://calendar.mit.edu/event/computer_wars_chinese_script_in_the_age_of_alphanumeric_hegemony#.XVagsZNKiqA.

Selected Bibliography

PRIMARY SOURCE WORKS

The works listed in this section are all themselves objects of study for the historiography of the alphabet. A full listing of all primary works in this area would be considerably longer. I have only included objects about which I have written in this study.

The works listed in the second section, "Key Reference Materials," are significant scholarly resources on which I have drawn but not written about as primary objects.

Agrippa von Nettesheim, Henry Cornelius. *De occulta philosophia*. Paris, 1531.

———. *Three Books of Occult Philosophy*. Translated by J. French. London: Gregory Moule, 1651.

Albright, William Foxwell. "The Oldest Hebrew Letters: The Lachish Ostraca." *Bulletin of the American Schools of Oriental Research* 70 (April 1938): 11–21.

———. *The Proto-Sinaitic Inscriptions and Their Decipherment*. Cambridge, MA: Harvard University Press, 1966.

Aldenbruck, Augustin. *In artem diplomaticam isagoge*. Col. Claud. Aug. Agripp; Ludovicum Schorn, 1769.

Ambrogio, Teseo. *Introductio in Chaldaicum linguam* [. . .]. Pavio: Excudebat Papiae Ioan. Maria Simoneta Cremonen[sis] in canonica Sancti Petri in caelo aureo, su[m]ptibus & typis, authoris libri, anno à Virginis partu, 1538.

Astle, Thomas. *The Origin and Progress of Writing, as well Hieroglyphic as Elementary*. London: T. Payne and Son, 1784.

Ballhorn, Friedrich. *Grammatography: A Manual of Reference to the Alphabets of Ancient and Modern Languages*. London: Trübner, 1861.

Balmes, Abraham de. *Mikneh Avram: Peculium Abrae; Grammatica Hebraea una cum Latino nuper edita*. Venice: Daniel Bomberg, 1523.

Bang, Thomas. *Caelum orientis et prisci mundi triade exercitationum literariarum repraesentatum curisque*. Hauniae: Petri Morsingi, 1657.

Bargès, M. L'Abbé J. J. L. *Mémoire sur le sacrophage et l'inscription funéraire d'Eschmounazar, roi de Sidon*. Paris: Benjamin Duprat, Libraire de l'Institut de la Bibliothèque Impériale des Sociétés Asiatiques, de Paris, de Londre, de Madras et de Calcutta, etc., 1856.

Barthélemy, L'Abbé Jean-Jacques. "Réflexions sur quelques monuments phéniciens, et sur les alphabets qui en résultent." *Mémoires de l'académie des inscriptions et belles lettres* 30 (1764): 405–26.

Bayly, Anselm. *An Introduction Literary and Philosophical to Languages*. London: John Rivington, 1756.

Becanus, Johannes Goropius. *Origines Antwerpianae, sive Cimmeriorum Becceselana novem libros complexa: Atvatica I. Gigantomachia II. Niloscopivm III. Cronia IV. Indoscythica V. Saxsonica VI. Gotodanica VII. Amazonica VIII. Venetica & Hyperborea IX* [. . .]. Antwerp: Christophori Plantin, 1569.

Beer, Eduard Friedrich Ferdinand. *Inscriptiones et papyri veteres semitici* [. . .]. Leipzig: Typographia Fridericines, 1833.

———. *Inscriptiones veteres litteris et lingua hucusque incognitis ad Montem Sinai*. Leipzig, 1840.

———. *Studia Asiatica*. Leipzig: Joannis Ambrosii Barys, 1840.

Bentley, Richard. *The Correspondence of Richard Bentley*, edited by Christopher Wordsworth. London: John Murray, 1842.

Berger, Philippe. *L'histoire de l'écriture dans l'antiquité*. Paris: L'Imprimerie Nationale, 1891.

Bernal, Martin. *Cadmean Letters*. Winona Lake, IN: Eisenbrauns, 1990.

Bernard, Edward. *Orbis eruditi literarum*. Oxoniae: Apud Theatrum, 1689.

Bianconi, Giovanni. *De antiquis litteris Hebraeorum et Graecorum Libellus*. Bononiae: Apud Thoman Colli ex typographia S. Thomae Aquinatis, 1763.

Bibliander, Theodore. *De ratione communi omnium linguarum*. Zurich: Christoph Frosch, 1548.

Bliss, Frederick Jones. *The Development of Palestine Exploration*. New York: Scribner, 1907.

Bochart, Samuel. *Geographia sacra, cuius pars prior Phaleg de dispersion Gentium et terrarium divisione facta in aedification turris Babel pars posterior Chanaan de coloniis et sermone Phoenicum*. Frankfurt on Mainz: Impensis Johannis Davidis Zunneri, typis Balthasaris Christophori Wustii, 1674; original publication 1646.

Breydenbach, Bernhard von. *Prefatio in opus transmarine peregrinations ad venerandum et gloriosum spulcrum Dominicum in Iherusalem*. Moguntino: Erhard Reuwich, 1486.

Bukentop, Henri de. *Alphabetum Graecum & Hebraïcum: Quo singularum litterarum utriusque linguae figura proponitur, genuinus sonus adstruitur, legendi methodus traditur*. Louvain: Typis viduae Henrici van Overbeke, Anno 1704.

Burckhardt, John Lewis. *Travels in Arabia*. London: H. Colburn, 1829.

Carpenter, Rhys. "Letters of Cadmus." *American Journal of Philology* 56, no.1 (1935): 5–13.

Casas, Bartolomé de las. *Narratio Regionum indicarum per Hispanos Quosdam devastatarum verissima*. Oppenheim: John-Theod. De Bry, 1614; a translation of *Tyrannies et cruatez des Espagnols* (Antwerp: Ravelenghien, 1579), itself a translation of *Brevissima relaçion* (Seville: Sebastian Trugillo, 1552).

Caylus, Comte de. *Recueil d'antiquités égyptiennes, étrusques, grecques et romaines*. Paris: Chez Desaint et Saillant, 1752–57.

Chabas, François Joseph. "Le plus ancien livre du monde: Étude sur le Papyrus Prisse." *Revue archéologique* 15, no. 1 (avril à septembre 1858): 1–25.

Champollion-Figeac, M. (Jacques-Joseph). Introduction to *Universal Palaeography, or Facsimiles of Writings of All Nations and Periods*, by J. B. Silvestre, xvii–lxix. Translated by Frederic Madden. London: H. G. Bohn, 1849.

Chishull, Edmund. *Antiquitates Asiaticæ Christianam æram antecedentes*. London: William Bowyer, 1728.

———. *Inscriptio Sigea antiquissima Boustrophedon exarata*. London: William and John Innys, 1721.

Christmas, Henry. *Universal Mythology*. London: John W. Parker, 1838.

Clermont-Ganneau, Charles Simon. *Inscription égypto-phénicienne de Byblos, comptes rendu, Académie des inscriptions et belles-lettres*. Paris, 1903.

Colletet, François. *Traittez des langues estrangères, de leurs alphabets, et des chiffres* [. . .]. Paris: Jean Promé, 1660.

Congregatio de Propaganda Fide. Rome: Vatican, 1636.

Cooke, G. A. *A Text-book of the North Semitic Inscriptions*. Oxford: Clarendon Press, 1903.

Corpus inscriptionum semiticarum. Paris: Académie des Inscriptions et Belles-Lettres, Reipublicae Typographeo, 1881.

Cross, Frank Moore. *Leaves from an Epigrapher's Notebook*. Winona Lake, IN: Eisenbrauns, 2002.

———. "Newly Found Inscriptions in Old Canaanite and Early Phoenician Scripts." *Bulletin of the American Schools of Oriental Research*, no. 238 (Spring 1980): 1–20.

Cross, Frank Moore. "The Phoenician Inscription from Brazil: A Nineteenth-Century Forgery." *Orientalia* 37, no. 4 (1968): 437–60.

Crown, Alan David. *Samaritan Scribes and Manuscripts*. Tübingen: Mohr Siebeck, 2001.

Daniels, Peter, and William Bright. *The World's Writing Systems*. New York: Oxford University Press, 1996.

Darnell, John Coleman, F. W. Dobbs-Allsopp, Marilyn J. Lundberg, P. Kyle McCarter, and Bruce Zuckerman with the assistance of Colleen Manassa. "Two Early Alphabetic Inscriptions from the Wadi el-Hôl." *Annual of the American Schools of Oriental Research* 79 (2005): 65–123.

Davis, Thomas W. *Shifting Sands: The Rise and Fall of Biblical Archaeology*. Oxford: Oxford University Press, 2004.

Davy, Charles. *Conjectural Observations on the Origin and Progress of the Alphabet*. London: T. Wright for T. Cadell, 1772.

De Bry, Theodor, and Israel De Bry. *Alphabeta et charactères*. Frankfurt, 1596.

Defoe, Daniel. *An Essay upon Literature, or An Enquiry into the Antiquity and Original of Letters* [. . .]. London: Thomas Bowles, 1726.

de Kerckhove, Derrick, and C. J. Lumsden, eds. *The Alphabet and the Brain: The Lateralization of Writing*. Berlin: Springer, 1988.

DeLooze, Laurence. *The Letters and the Cosmos*. Toronto: University of Toronto Press, 2016.

de Mely, Fernand. *La Virga Aurea du J-B Hepburn*. Milan: Arche Milan, 1984.

de Rougé, Emmanuel. "Memoire sur l'origine égyptienne de l'alphabet phénicien." *Comptes rendus des séances de l'Académie des Inscriptions et Belles-Lettres* (1859): 115–24.

Derolez, René. *Runica manuscripta*. Brugge: De Tempel, 1954.

Diringer, David. *The Alphabet: Key to the History of Mankind*. New York: Philosophical Society, 1948.

———. *Le iscrizioni antico-ebraiche palestinesi*. Firenze: F. Le Monnier, 1934.

———. "The Palestinian Inscriptions and the Origin of the Alphabet." *Journal of the American Oriental Society* 63, no. 1 (March 1943): 24–30.

Donner, Herbert, Wolfgang Röllig, and O. Rössler. *Kanaanaische und aramaische Inschriften (KAI)*. Wiesbanden: Harrassowitz, 2002– .

Driver, Godfrey. *Semitic Writing from Pictograph to Alphabet*. Oxford: Oxford University Press, 1954.

Duret, Claude. *Le thrésor de l'histoire des langues de cest univers* [. . .]. Cologny: Matt. Berjon, pour la Société caldoriene, 1613.

Eckhart, Johann Georg von. *De origine Germanorum*. Goettingae: Sumptibus Ioh. Guil. Schmidii, 1750.

Edwards, Edward. *Memoirs of Libraries: A Handbook of Library Economy*. London: Trübner, 1859.

Evans, Arthur. *Scripta Minoa*. Oxford: Oxford University Press, 1909–52.

Finkelstein, Israel, and Benjamin Sass. "The West Semitic Alphabet Inscriptions." *HeBAI* 2, no. 2 (2013): 149–220.

Fischer, Steven R. *A History of Writing*. London: Reaktion, 2001.

Flanders, Judith. *A Place for Everything*. New York: Basic Books, 2020.

Forster, Charles. *The One Primeval Language Traced Experimentally*. 3 vols. London: Richard Bentley, 1851.

Franz, Johannes. *Elementa epigraphices Graecae*. Berolini: F. Nicolai, 1840.

Fry, Edmund. *Pantographia: Containing Accurate Copies of All the Known Alphabets in the World; Together with an English Explanation of the Peculiar Force or Power of Each Letter: To Which Are Added, Specimens of All Well-Authenticated Oral Languages; Forming a Comprehensive Digest of Phonology*. Printed by Cooper and Wilson, for John and Arthur Arch, Gracechurch-Street; John White, Fleet-Street; John Edwards, Pall-Mall; and John Debrett, Piccadilly, 1799.

Gaffarel, Jacques. *Curiositez inouyes hoc est curiositates inauditae de figuris Persarum talismannicis, horoscopo patriarcharum et characteribus coelestibus*. Paris: Hervé du Mesnil, 1629.

———. *Curiositez inouyes hoc est curiositates inauditae de figuris Persarum talismannicis, horoscopo patriarcharum et characteribus coelestibus*. Paris: Hervé du Mesnil, 1631.

———. *Unheard-of Curiosities: Concerning the Talismanical Sculpture of the Persians and the Reading of the Stars; Englished by Edmund Chilmead*. London: Humphrey Moseley, 1650.

Gardiner, Alan. "The Egyptian Origin of the Semitic Alphabet." *Journal of Egyptian Archaeology* 3, no. 1 (January 1916): 1–16.

Gardiner, Alan, and T. Eric Peet. *The Inscriptions of Sinai*, Egypt Exploration Society Memoir. London: Egypt Exploration Society, 1917.

------. *The Inscriptions of Sinai*. Revised by Jasolav Cerny. Egypt Exploration Society Memoir 45. London: Egypt Exploration Society, 1952–55.

Gébelin, Antoine Court de. *Le monde primitif*. Paris: Chez l'auteur, 1777–96.

Gelb, Ignace. *A Study of Writing*. Chicago: University of Chicago Press, 1952.

Gesenius, Wilhelm. *Hebräische Grammatik*. Halle, 1813.

———. *Scripturae linguaeque Phoeniciae monumenta quotquot supersunt*. Leipzig: Vogel, 1837.

Gessner, Conrad. *Bibliotheca universalis*. Zurich: Christophorum Froschouerum, 1545.

———. *Mithridates*. Tiguri: Excudebat Froschouerum, 1555.

Gobineau, Arthur de. *Essai sur l'inégalite des races humaines*. Paris: Firmin Didot, 1853–55.

Godwin, Thomas. *Romanae historiae anthologia recognita et aucta*. London: Printed for Henry Cripps, 1661–62.

Goeree, Willem. *Voor-Bereidselen tot de bybelsche Wysheid, en Gebruik der heilige en kerklijke Historien: uit de alder-oudste Gedenkkenissen der Hebreen, Chaldeen, Babyloniers, Egiptenaars, Syriers, Grieken en Romeinen*. Utrecht, 1700.

Goldast, Melchior. *Rerun alamannicarum scriptores aliquot vetusti*. Frankfurt: Wolffgang Richter, 1606.

Goodwin, C. W. "Hieratic Papyri." In *Cambridge Essays: 1858*, 226–82. London: Parker and Sons, 1858.

Goody, Jack. *The East in the West*. New York: Cambridge University Press, 1996.

Gordon, Cyrus H. "The Authenticity of the Phoenician Text from Parahyba." *Orientalia*, n.s., 37, no. 1 (1968): 75–80.

———. "The Canaanite Text from Brazil." *Orientalia*, n.s., 37, no. 4 (1968): 425–36.

Gramaye, Joannes B. *Specimen litterarum & linguarum universi orbis* [. . .]. Ath: Ionannes Masius, 1622.

G., R. Letter addressed to Mr. Urban, *Gentleman's Magazine*, volume 85, January 1799, 24–27.

Geisler, Wilhelm. *De literaturae phoneticae origine atque indole [electronic resource] : disseruit tabulis literas veterum semitarum indorum graecorum italorum himjaritarum normannorum anglosaxonum ulfilae scripturam cuneatam iranicam exhibentibus*. Berolini: Apud Ferd. Duemmlerum, 1858.

Grey, Rev. G. F. "Communicated to the Royal Society of Literature in 1830." *Transactions of the Royal Society of Literature of the United Kingdom* 1, no. 2, 147–48.

Grimme, Hubert. *Althebräische Inschriften vom Sinai* [. . .]. Hannover: H. Lafaire, 1923.

Grose, Francis, and Thomas Astle. *The Antiquarian Repertory*. London: Edward Jeffery, 1807.

Grotefend, Georg. *Neue Beiträge zur Erläuterung der persepolitanischen Keilschrift*. Hannover: Hahn, 1837.

Gutwein, Johann Balthasar. *Alphabeta varia ex antiquis diplomatis et codicibus mss.: Diversorum saeculorum excerpta et adfacilem eorum lectionem conducentia*. Würzburg, 1765.

Hamilton, Gordon. *The Origins of the West Semitic Alphabet in Egyptian Scripts*. Washington, DC: Catholic Biblical Association, 2006.

Harriot, Thomas. *A Briefe and True Report of the New Found Land of Virginia*. Francoforti ad Moenvm: Typis Ioannis Wecheli, svmtibvs vero T. de Bry, 1590.

Havelock, Eric. *The Literate Revolution in Greece and Its Cultural Consequences*. Princeton, NJ: Princeton University Press, 1981.

———. *The Muse Learns to Write: Reflections on Orality and Literacy from Antiquity to the Present*. New Haven, CT: Yale University Press, 1986.

———. *Origins of Western Literacy*. Toronto: Ontario Institute for Studies in Education, 1976.

———. *Preface to Plato*. Cambridge, MA: Harvard University Press, 1963.

———. *Prologue to Greek Literacy*. Cincinnati: University of Cincinnati Press, 1971.

Hepburn, James Bonaventure. *Virga Aurea*. Rome, 1616.

Herodotus. *Histories*. Book V, translated by A. D. Godley. Loeb Classical Library. Cambridge, MA: Harvard University Press, 1920–25.

Hicks, E. L., C. T. Newton, Gustav Hirschfeld, and F. H. Marshall. *Greek Inscriptions in the British Museum* [*GIBM*]. 4 vols. Oxford: Clarendon, 1874–1916.

Hugo, Hermannus. *De prima scribendi origine* [. . .]. Antwerp: Officina Plantiniana, 1617.

Humphreys, Henry Noel. *The Origin and Progress of the Art of Writing*. London: Ingraham, Cooke, 1854.

Ibn Wahshiyyah, Ahman ibn Ali, *Ancient Characters and Hieroglyphics Explained*. Translated by Joseph Hammer von Purgstall. London: Bulmer, 1806.

Illich, Ivan, and Barry Sanders. *ABC: The Alphabetization of the Popular Mind*. New York: Random House, 1998.

Innis, Harold. *The Bias of Communication*. Toronto: University of Toronto Press, 1951.

———. *Empire and Communications*. Oxford: Oxford University Press, 1950.

Jackson, John. *Chronological Antiquities, or The Antiquities and Chronology of the Most Ancient Kingdoms, from the Creation of the World, for the Space of Five Thousand Years: In Three Volumes* [. . .]. London: Printed for the author, 1752.

Jeffery, Lilian. *Local Scripts of Archaic Greece*. Oxford: Clarendon Press, 1961.

Jensen, Hans. *Sign, Script, and Symbol*. New York: Putnam, 1969.

Johnston, Thomas Crawford. *Did the Phoenicians Discover America?* San Francisco, CA: Geographical Society of California, 1892.

Jones, George. *The History of Ancient America prior to the Time of Columbus Proving the Identity of the Aborigines with the Tyrians and Israelites*. London: Longman, Brown, Green, and Longmans, 1843.

Jones, Rowland. *A Postscript to the Origin of Language and Nations* [. . .]. London: J. Hughes, 1764.

Josephus, Flavius. *Of the Antiquities of the Jews, Book I, Containing the Interval of 3833 years from the Creation to the Death of Isaac*. London, 1737. http://penelope.uchicago.edu/josephus/ant-1.html.

King, James. *Moab's Patriarchal Stone: Being an Account of the Moabite Stone, Its Story and Teaching*. London: Bickers, 1878.

Kircher, Athanasius. *Oedipus Aegyptiacus*. Rome: Mascardi, 1652.

———. *Turris Babel*. Amstelodami: Janssonio-Waesbergiana, 1679.

Kirchhoff, Adolf. *Studien zur Geschichte des griechischen Alphabets*. Berlin: F. Dümmler, 1877.

Knuth, Donald. *TEX and METAFONT: New Directions in Typesetting*. Providence, RI: American Mathematical Society, 1979.

Korpela, Jukka K. *Unicode Explained*. Boston: O'Reilly, 2006.

Laborde, Léon Marquis de. *Journey through Arabia Petra to Mount Sinai*. London: John Murray, 1836.

Lake, Kirsopp, and Robert P. Blake, "The Serâbît Inscriptions: I. The Rediscovery of the Inscriptions." *Harvard Theological Review* 21, no. 1 (January 1928): 1–8.

Lauth, Franz Joseph. *Papyrus Prisse*. Munich: K. Bayerischen Akademie der Wissenschaften, 1869.

Laval, Lottin de. *Voyage dans la peninsule arabique du Sinai et l'Egypte moyenne*. Paris: Gide, 1855.

Layard, Austen Henry. *Discoveries in the Ruins of Nineveh and Babylon; with Travels in Armenia, Kurdistan and the Desert, Being the Result of a Second Expedition Undertaken for the Trustees of the British Museum*. London: John Murray, 1853.

Lenormant, François. *Essai sur la propogation de l'alphabet phénicien dans l'ancien monde*. Paris: Maisonneuve, 1872–1875.

Lhuyd, Edward. *Archaeologia Britannica*. London: 1707.

Lidzbarski, Mark. *Handbuch der Nordsemitischen Epigraphik*. Weimar: Emil Felber, 1898.

Logan, Robert. *The Alphabet Effect*. New York: Morrow, 1986.

Lucan. *Pharsalia*. Book III, Massilia, translated by Sir Edward Ridley. London: Longmans, Green, 1905.

Luynes, Albert de. *Mémoire sur le sarcophage et l'inscription funéraire d'Esmunazar, roi de Sidon*. Paris: Henri Plon, 1856.

Mabillon, Jean. *De re diplomatica*. Luteciæ Parisiorum: Sumtibus Ludovici Billaine, 1681.

Machen, Arthur. *The Enchanted Treasure, or The Spagyric Quest of Beroaldus Cosmopolita*. London: Thomas Marvell, 1888.

Macray, William Dunn. *The Annals of the Bodleian Library, Oxford, A.D. 1598–A.D. 1867*. Oxford: Clarendon Press, 1890.

Marsh, Luther. "The Alphabet—The Vehicle of History." New York: New York Historical Society, November 17, 1885.

Marsham, John. *Chronicus canon Aegyptiacus, Ebraicus, Graecus et disquisitiones*. London: T. Roycroft, 1672.

Massey, William. *The Origin and Progress of Letters*. London: Printed for J. Johnson, 1763.

McCarter, P. Kyle. *The Antiquity of the Greek Alphabet*. Harvard Semitic Monographs 9. Cambridge, MA: Harvard College, 1975.

McLean, Adam. "The Virga Aurea." *Hermetic Journal* (1980). Reproduced by Adam McLean on The Alchemy Website. http://www.levity.com/alchemy/virga_aurea.html.

McClintock, John. *Cyclopedia of Biblical, Theological, and Ecclesiastical Literature*. Vol. 8. New York: Harper and Brothers, 1879.

McLuhan, Marshall. *Understanding Media*. New York: McGraw-Hill, 1964.

Monk, James Henry. *The Life of Richard Bentley: With an Account of His Writings*. London: J. G. and F. Rivington, 1833.

Montet, Pierre. *Byblos et l'Egypte, Quatre Campagnes des Fouilles, 1921–1924*. Paris: P. Geuthner, 1928–29.

Montfaucon, Bernard de. *Antiquité expliquée et representée en figures*. Paris: F. Delaulne, 1719.

———. *Palaeographia Graeca*. Paris: L. Guerin, 1708.

Morin, Jean. *Exercitationes ecclesiasticae in utrumque Samaritanorum Pentateuchum*. Paris: Antonius Vitray, 1631.

Mullaney, Tom. *The Chinese Typewriter: A History*. Cambridge, MA: MIT Press, 2017.
Naveh, Joseph. *The Early History of the Alphabet*. Jerusalem: Hebrew University; Magnes Press, 1982.
———. *Studies in West-Semitic Epigraphy*. Jerusalem: Hebrew University; Magnes Press, 2009.
Nelme, L. D. *An Essay Towards an Investigation of the Origin and Elements of Language and Letters*. London: T. Spilsbury for S. Leacroft, 1772.
Newton, Sir Isaac. *The Chronology of Antient Kingdoms Amended*. London: J. Tonson, 1728.
Niebuhr, Carsten. *Travels through Arabia*. Edinburgh: R. Morison and Son, 1792.
Notes of the meeting in the Institute Rooms, April 3, 1855. *Transactions of the Albany Institute* 4, art. 4 (1855): 68–69.
Nuttall, P. Austin. *A Classical and Archaeological Dictionary* [. . .]. London: Whittaker; Oxford: J. H Parker, 1840.
Nuttall, Zelia. *The Fundamental Principles of Old and New World Civilizations*. Cambridge, MA: Peabody Museum, 1901.
Ogg, Oscar. *The 26 Letters*. New York: T. Y. Crowell, 1948.
Orfei, Luca. *De caracterum et litterarum inventoribus* [. . .]. Rome: Gio. Batt. Rossi, 1589.
Palatino, Giovanni Battista. *Libro nuovo d'imparare a scrivere*. Stampata in Roma: Appresso Campo di Fiore, nelle case di m. Benedetto Gionta: Per Baldassarre di Francesco Cartolari perugino, 1540.
Pantheus, Johannes. *Voarchadumia*. Venetiis: Diebus Aprilis, 1530.
Parry, Adam. *The Making of Homeric Verse: The Collected Papers of Milman Parry*. Oxford: Clarendon Press, 1971.
Parry, Milman. "Studies in the Epic Technique of Oral Verse-Making: I. Homer and Homeric Style." *Harvard Studies in Classical Philology* 41 (1930): 73–148.
Petrie, W. M. Flinders. *The Formation of the Alphabet*, British School of Archaeology in Egypt 3. London: Macmillan; Bernard Quaritch, 1912.
———. *Inductive Metrology, or The Recovery of Ancient Measures from the Monuments*. London: Hargrove Saunders, 1877.
———. *Researches in the Sinai*. London: John Murray, 1906.
———. *Tell el-Hesi*. London: Published for the Committee of the Palestine Exploration Fund, 1891.
Petrovich, Douglas. "The Ophel Pithos Inscription: Its Dating, Language, Translation, and Script." *Palestine Exploration Quarterly* 147, no. 2 (2015): 130–45.
———. *The World's Oldest Alphabet*. Jerusalem: Carta, 2016.
Pico della Mirandola, Giovanni. *Opera*. Venice: Bernardinus Venetus, de Vitalibus, 1498.
Pococke, Edward. *India in Greece*. London: John Griffin, 1852.
Pococke, Richard. *A Description of the East and Some Other Countries*. London: 1743.
Postel, Guillaume. *De originibus seu de Hebraicae linguae & gentis antiquitate, deque variarum linguarum affinitate liber*. Paris: Apud Dionysium Lescuier, 1538.
———. *Linguarum duodecim characteribus differentium alphabetum, introductio, ac legendi modus longè facilimus*. Paris: Apud Dionysium Lescuier, 1538.
Purchas, Samuel. *Hakluytus posthumus or Purchas His Pilgrimes*. London: Henry Fetherston, 1625.
Raleigh, Sir Walter. *The Historie of the World in Five Books*. London: William Stansby for Walter Burre, 1614.
Raumer, Karl von. *Palästina*. Leipzig: F. A. Brockhaus, 1835.
Ravis, Christian. *A Discourse of the Oriental Tongues*. London: Thomas Slater and Thomas Huntington, 1649.
Rawlinson, Henry. *A Commentary on the Cuneiform Inscriptions of Babylonia and Assyria, including Readings of the Inscription of the Nimrud Obelisk and a Brief Notice of the Ancient Kings of Nineveh and Babylon*. London: John W. Parker, 1850.
Reinach, Salomon. "Le mirage orientale." In *L'anthropologie*, 4:539–578. Paris, 1893.

Relaant, Adriaan. *Antiquitates sacrae veterum Hebraeorum*. Lipsiae: Apud Joh. Fridericum; Wehrmannum: Typis Jo. Heinrici Richteri, 1713.

Renan, Ernest. *Mission de Phénicie*. Paris: Imprimerie Imperiale, 1864.

Robinson, Edward, and Eli Smith. *Biblical Researches in Palestine and the Adjacent Regions, Journal of Travels in the Year 1838*. Boston: Crocker and Brewster, 1841.

Rocca, Angelo. *Bibliotheca apostolica Vaticana Sixto V*. Rome: Typographia Apostolica Vaticana, 1591.

———. *Variarum linguarum alphabeta et inventores*. Rome: Ex typographia Dominici Basae, 1595.

Rollston, Christopher. "The Dating of the Early Royal Byblian Phoenician Inscriptions: A Response to Benjamin Sass." *Maarav* 15, no. 1 (2008): 57–93.

———. "The Proto-Sinaitic Inscriptions 2.0; Canaanite Language and Canaanite Script, Not Hebrew." December 10, 2016. http://www.rollstonepigraphy.com/.

———. *Writing and Literacy in the World of Ancient Israel*. Leiden: Brill, 2010.

Rose, Hugh James. *Inscriptiones Graecae vetustissimae*. London: John Murray, 1825.

Sampson, Geoffrey. *Writing Systems*. Stanford: Stanford University Press, 1985.

Sass, Benjamin. *The Alphabet at the Turn of the Millennium: The West Semitic Alphabet, c.1150–850*. Tel Aviv: Emery and Claire Yass Publications in Archaeology, 2005.

———. *The Genesis of the Alphabet and Its Development in the Second Millennium BC*. Wiesbaden: Otto Harrassowitz, 1988.

Sass, Benjamin, and Israel Finkelstein, "Epigraphic Evidence from Jerusalem and Its Environs at the Dawn of Biblical History: Facts First." *New Studies in the Archaeology of Jerusalem* 11 (2017): 21–46.

———. "The Swan-Song of Proto-Canaanite in the Ninth Century BCE in Light of an Alphabetic Inscription from Megiddo." *Semitica et Classica, International Journal of Oriental and Mediterranean Studies* 9 (2016): 19–43.

Sanders, Seth. *The Invention of Hebrew*. Urbana: University of Illinois Press, 2011.

Sayce, A. H. *The Archaeology of Cuneiform Inscriptions*. London: Society for Promoting Christian Knowledge, 1908.

———. *Fresh Light from Ancient Monuments*. London: Religious Tract Society, 1883.

Scaliger, Joseph. *Opus novum de emendatione temporum*. Lutèce: Mamert Pattison for Sebastien Nivelle, 1583.

Schultens, Albert. *Origines Hebraeae sive Hebraeae Linguae antiquissima natura et indoles*. Lugduni Batauorum: Samel et Joannem Luchtmans et Joannem le Mair, 1761.

Sharpe, Samuel. *Hebrew Inscriptions: From the Valleys between Egypt and Mount Sinai*. London: John Russell Smith, 1875.

Shlain, Leonard. *The Alphabet versus the Goddess*. New York: Viking, 1998.

Shuckford, Samuel. *The Sacred and Prophane History of the World Connected, from the Creation of the World to the Dissolution of the Assyrian Empire at the Death of Sardanapalus, and to the Declension of the Kingdoms of Judah and Israel, under the reigns of Ahaz and Pekah*. London: R. Knaplock and J. Tonson, 1731. First edition 1728.

Siculus, Diodorus. *Bibliotheca Historica*. Book 3, section 42. http://penelope.uchicago.edu/Thayer/E/Roman/Texts/Diodorus_Siculus/3C*.html.

Sivry, Poinsenet de. *Nouvelles recherches sur la science des medailles*. Maestricht: Jean-Edme Dufour and Phillippe Roux, 1778.

Spanheim, Ezechiel. *Dissertationes de præstantia et usu numismatum antiquorum*. Amstelodami: Daniel Elsevir, 1671.

Stanley, Arthur. *Sinai and Palestine in Connection with Their History*. London: John Murray, 1857.

Stillingfleet, Edward. *Origines sacrae, or a Rational Account of the Grounds of the Christian Faith*. London: Printed by R. W. for Henry Mortlock, 1662.

Stukeley, William. *Palaeographia Britannica, or Discourses on Antiquities in Britain*. London: Printed for R. Manby, 1743.

Tappy, Ron E., and Peter Kyle McCarter, eds. *Literate Culture and Tenth-Century Canaan: The Tel Zayit Abecedary in Context*. Winona Lake, IN: Eisenbrauns. pp. 113–129.

Taylor, Isaac. *The Alphabet*. London: Kegan Paul, Trench, 1883.

———. *The Origin of the Aryans*, 2nd ed. London: W. Scott, 1892.

Taylor, Jane. "The Writing on the Rocks." *Al-Ahram Weekly Online*, post no. 620, January 9–15, 2003. Reference no longer online.

Thurneysser, Leonhard. *Magna alchymia*. Cöln, 1583.

———. *Onomasticum*. Berlin: Nicolaum Voltzen, 1583.

Top, Alexander. *The Olive Leafe*. London: W. White for George Vincent, 1603.

Torczyner, Harry, Lankester Harding, Alkin Lewis, and J. L. Starkey. *The Lachish Letters*. Oxford: Oxford University Press, 1938.

Torrey, Charles C. "The Ahiram Inscription of Byblos." *Journal of the American Oriental Society* 45 (1925): 269–79. https://www.jstor.org/stable/pdf/593505.pdf.

Toustain, Charles. *Nouveau traité de diplomatique*. Paris: Guillaume Desprez and Pierre Guillaume Cavelier, 1750.

Trithemius, Johannes. *Polygraphia*. Oppenheim: Ioannis Hasebergi de Aia, 1518.

———. *Steganographia*. Francofvrti: Ex officina typographica Matthiæ Beckeri, sumptibus Ioannis Berneri, 1608.

Turner, William T. "Remarks on the Phoenician Inscription of Sidon." Presented to the Society, October 29, 1855. *Journal of the American Oriental Society* 7 (1860): 48–59.

Ullman, Berthold. *Ancient Writing and Its Influence*. New York: Cooper Square Publishers, 1963.

Ussher, James. *Annales veteris testamenti, a prima mundi origine deducti*. London: J. Flesher, J. Crook, and J. Baker, 1650.

Vallancey, Charles. *Prospectus of a Dictionary of the Language of the Aire Coti, or Ancient Irish, Compared with the Language of the Cuti, or Ancient Persians, with the Hindoostanee, the Arabic, and Chaldean Languages*. Dublin: Graisberry and Campbell, 1802.

Valle, Pietro della. *Viaggi di Pietro Della Valle*. Rome, 1650–58.

Velasco, Velásquez de. *Ensayo sobre los alphabetos de las letras desconocidas*. Madrid: Antonio Sanz, 1752.

Verstegan, Richard. *A Restitution of Decayed Intelligence in Antiquities concerning the Most Noble and Renowned English Nation*. Antwerp: Robert Bruney, 1605.

Vigenère, Blaise de. *Traicté de chiffres*. Paris: Chez Abel L'Angelier, au premier pillier de la grand' salle du Palais, 1586.

Waddell, Laurence A. *The Aryan Origin of the Alphabet*. London: Luzac, 1927.

Warren, Charles. "The Moabite Stone: Captain Warren's First Account of the Inscription from the Moab." *Quarterly Statement of the Palestine Exploration Fund*, January 21, 1870, 169–83. https://www.biblicalstudies.org.uk/pdf/pefqs/1869-71_169.pdf.

Waser, Kaspar. *De antiquis Numis Hebraeorum, chaldaeorum, et Syrorum S. Biblioa et Rabbinorum scripta meminerunt*. Switzerland: Officina Wolphiana, 1605.

Weidemann, Alfred. *Ägyptische Geschichte*. Gotha: F. A. Perthes, 1884.

Woodard, Roger D. *Greek Writing from Knossos to Homer*. New York: Oxford University Press, 1997.

Worm, Ole. *Runir, seu, Danica literature antiquissima*. Hafniae: Melchiorus Martzan, 1651.

Wyss, Urbanus. *Libellus valde doctus elegans et utilis, multa et varia scribendarum literarum genera complectens*. 1549.

Zuckerman, Bruce. *West Semitic Research Project*. USC, Dornsife. https://dornsife.usc.edu/wsrp/.

Avilés, A. G. "Alfonso X y el Liber Razielis: Imágenes de la magia astral judia en el scriptorium alfonsi." *Bulletin of Hispanic Studies* 74, no. 1 (1 January 1997): 21–39.

Barney, Stephen A., W. J. Lewis, J. A. Beach, and Oliver Berghof. *The Etymologies of Isidore of Seville*. Cambridge: Cambridge University Press, 2006.

Barrett, Rob. "Johann Reuchlin, Philologist and Mystic: The Christian Recovery of Hebrew." Vancouver: Regent College, 2001. https://www.academia.edu/333690/Johann_Reuchlin_Philologist_and_Mystic_The_Christian_Rediscovery_of_Hebrew.

Biran, A., and Joseph Naveh. "The Tel Dan Inscription: A New Fragment." *Israel Exploration Journal* 43 (1993): 81–98.

Bodde, Derk. *Chinese Thought, Society, and Science*. Honolulu: University of Hawaii Press, 1991.

Bohak, Gideon. *Ancient Jewish Magic: A History*. Cambridge: Cambridge University Press, 2008.

———. "The Charaktêres in Ancient and Medieval Jewish Magic." *Acta classica universitatis scientiarum debreceniensis* 47 (2011): 25–44.

Bottero, Jean, Clarisse Herrenschmidt, and Jean-Pierre Vernant. *Ancestor of the West*. Chicago: University of Chicago Press, 2000.

Brandist, Craig. *The Dimensions of Hegemony: Language, Culture, and Politics in Revolutionary Russia*. Chicago: Haymarket Books, 2016.

Brash, Richard Rolt. *The Ogham Inscribed Monuments of the Gaedhill*. London: George Bell and Sons, 1879.

Brereton, Gareth. "Lion Hunting: The Sport of Kings." *The British Museum Blog*, January 4, 2019. https://blog.britishmuseum.org/lion-hunting-the-sport-of-kings-2/.

Burrows, Eric. "The Origin of the Ras Shamra Alphabet." *Journal of the Royal Asiatic Society of Great Britain and Ireland* 68, no. 2 (April 1936): 271–77.

Campanini, Saverio. "The Quest for the Holiest Alphabet in the Renaissance." In *A Universal Art: Hebrew Grammar across Disciplines and Faiths*, edited by Nadia Vidro, Irene E. Zwiep, and Judith Olszowy-Schlanger, 196–245 (Boston: Brill, 2014).

Cartwright, Mark. "Trade in the Phoenician World." *Ancient History Encyclopedia*, April 1, 2016. https://www.ancient.eu/article/881/trade-in-the-phoenician-world/.

Chajes, J. H. *Between Worlds: Dybbuks, Exorcists, and Early Modern Judaism*. Philadelphia: University of Pennsylvania Press, 2011.

Cheriet, Mohamed, Nawwaf Kharma, Chen-Lin Liu, and Ching Y. Suen. *Character Recognition Systems*. Hoboken, NJ: John Wiley and Sons, 2007.

Christie, E. J. "By Means of a Secret Alphabet: Dangerous Letters and the Semantics of Gebregdstafas." *Modern Philology* 109, no. 2 (2011). https://www.jstor.org/stable/10.1086/663211?seq=1#metadata_info_tab_contents.

Christin, Anne-Marie. *L'histoire de l'écriture*. Paris: Flammarion, 2001.

Colavito, Jason, trans. "Eumalos of Cyrene on Atlantis." In "Discourse Composed for the Asiatic Society," by Fortia d'Urban, for the meeting of February 4, 1828. http://www.jasoncolavito.com/eumalos-on-atlantis-hoax.html.

———. "An Explanation of Ancient Alphabets and Hieroglyphics." A transcription of Ibn Wahshiyyah, *Kitab Shawq a-Mustaham*, translated by Joseph Hammer von Purgstall, http://www.jasoncolavito.com/ancient-alphabets-explained.html.

Cone, Patricia, and Michael Cook. *Hagarism: The Making of the Islamic World*. Cambridge: Cambridge University Press, 1977.

Cook, Edward M. "On the Linguistic Dating of the Phoenician Ahiram Inscription (KAI 1)." *Journal of Near Eastern Studies* 53, no. 1 (January 1994): 33–36.

Courdert, Allison. *The Impact of the Kabbalah in the Seventeenth Century: The Life and Thought of Francis Mercury van Helmont (1614–1698)*. Leiden: Brill, 1999.

Covington, Michael. "Albert Schultens on Language Relationship." *Linguistics* 17, nos. 7–8 (1979). https://doi.org/10.1515/ling.1979.17.7-8.707.

Crain, Patricia. *The Story of A*. Palo Alto: Stanford University Press, 2001.

de Kerckhove, Derrick. "A Theory of Greek Tragedy." *SubStance* 9, no. 4 (May 1981): 23–36.

Denecker, Tim. "The Origin and Nature of Language." In *Ideas on Language in Early Latin Christianity from Tertullian to Isidore of Seville*, Vigiliae Christianae, Supplements, vol. 142 (Boston: Brill, 2017). https://brill.com/abstract/book/9789004276659/B9789004276659_003.xml.

Doumas, Christos G. "Aegeans in the Levant: Myth and Reality." In *Mediterranean People in Transition: Thirteen to Early Tenth Century BCE*, edited by S. Gitin, A. Mazar, and E. Stern, 129–37. Jerusalem: Israel Exploration Society, 1998.

Drucker, Johanna. *The Alphabetic Labyrinth: The Letters in History and Imagination*. London: Thames and Hudson, 1994.

———. *The Visible Word*. Chicago: University of Chicago Press, 1994.

Du Pin, Louis Ellies. *A New History of Ecclesiastical Writers*. London: Tim Child, 1710.

Fahd, T. "Ibn Wahshiyyah." In *Encyclopedia of Islam*, 2nd ed., edited by P. Bearman, Th. Bianquis, C. E. Bosworth, E. van Donzel, and W. P. Heinrichs, 3:963–65. Leiden: Brill 1971.

Faigley, Lester. "Material Literacy and Visual Design." In *Rhetorical Bodies*, edited by Jack Selzer and Sharon Crowley, 171–201. Madison: University of Wisconsin Press, 1999.

Findell, Martin. "The Book of Enoch, the Angelic Alphabet and the 'Real Cabala.'" *Henry Sweet Society Bulletin*, May 2007, 7–22.

Fraser, James G. "A Checklist of Samaritan Manuscripts Known to Have Entered Europe before AD 1700." *Abr Nahrain* 21 (1982–83): 10–27.

———. "Epigraphy and Paleography as Scientific Disciplines." *Perspectives on Language and Text: Essays and Paper in Honor of Francis I. Anderson's Sixtieth Birthday, July 28, 1985*. Winona, IN: Eisenbrauns: 1987.

Fraser, Robert. *Book History through Post-colonial Eyes*. New York: Routledge, 2008.

Gaster, M. "Jewish Knowledge of the Samaritan Alphabet in the Middle Ages." In *Studies and Texts*, 600–613. 2 vols. London, 1928.

Gaur, Albertine. *A History of Writing*. London: British Library, 1984.

Gernet, Jack. *A History of Chinese Civilization*. Cambridge: Cambridge University Press, 1982.

Goldwasser, Orly. "How the Alphabet Was Born from Hieroglyphs." *Biblical Archaeology Review* 36, no. 2 (March–April 2010): 40–53.

Gonzalez, Elena Martin. "The Drawings on the Rock Inscriptions of Archaic Thera." *Inscriptiones Graecae* (*IG* XII3, 536–601; *IG* XII3 Suppl. 1410–93). Berlin-Brandenburg Academy, Society for Classical Studies.

Goody, Jack, and Ian Watt. "The Consequences of Literacy." *Comparative Studies in Society and History* 5, no. 3 (April 1963): 304–45.

Grafton, Anthony. "Joseph Scaliger and Historical Chronology: The Rise and Fall of a Discipline." *History and Theory* 14, no. 2 (May 1975): 156–83.

Grosswiler, Paul. "Dispelling the Alphabet Effect." *Canadian Journal of Communication* 29, no. 2 (2004): n.p. Accessed June 17, 2021. https://cjc-online.ca/index.php/journal/issue/view/108.

Hackett, Jo Ann, and Walter E. Aufrecht, eds. *"An Eye for Form": Epigraphic Essays in Honor of Frank Moore Cross*. Winona Lake, IN: Eisenbrauns, 2014.

Haring, Ben. "Ancient Egypt and the Earliest Known Stages of Alphabetic Writing." In *Understanding the Relations Between Scripts II, Early Alphabets*, edited by Philip J. Boyes and Philippa M. Steele, 53–68. Oxford, UK: Oxbow Books, 2020.

Hayden, Deborah. "Language and Linguistics in Medieval Europe." In *Oxford Research Encyclopedias*. New York: Oxford University Press, 2017. https://doi.org/10.1093/acrefore/9780199384655.013.380.

Head, Randolph. "Archives, Documents, and Proof around 1700: Diplomatics, the *ius archivi* and State Practice in the Seventeenth and Eighteenth Centuries." *Historical Journal* 56, no. 4 (2013): 909–30.

Healey, John F. *The Early Alphabet*. Berkeley: University of California Press, 1990.

Heilman Till A. "Innis and Kittler: The Case of the Greek Alphabet." In *Media Transatlantic: Developments in Media and Communication Studies between North American and German-speaking Europe*, edited by Norm Friesen, 91–110. Cham: Springer International Publishing, 2016.

Heng, Geraldine. *Empire of Magic: Medieval Romance and the Politics of Cultural Fantasy*. New York: Columbia University Press, 2003.

Herren, Michael W. *Cosmography of Aethicus Ister: Edition, Translation, and Commentary*. Turnhout: Brepols, 2011.

Higgins, Iain Macleod. *The Book of John Mandeville*. Indianapolis: Hackett Publishing, 2011.

Himelfarb, Elizabeth J. "First Alphabet found in Egypt." *Archaeology* 53, no. 1 (2000): n.p. Accessed June 17, 2021. https://archive.archaeology.org/0001/newsbriefs/egypt.html.

Hofstadter, Douglas. "Metafont, Mathematics, and Metaphysics: Comments on Donald Knuth's Article 'The Concept of a Meta-Font.'" *Visible Language* 16, no. 4 (Autumn 1982): 309–38.

Hudson, Nicholas. *Writing and European Thought, 1600–1830*. Cambridge: Cambridge University Press, 1994.

Hyatt, J. Philip. *The Journal of Bible and Religion* 10, no. 2 (May 1942): 67–75.

Iversen, Erik. *The Myth of Egypt and Its Hieroglyphs in European Tradition*. Copenhagen: Gad, 1961.

Jackson, David. "The almajiadas of Spain," *Medieval Musings*, May 24, 2015. http://www.davidjackson.info/voynich/2015/05/24/the-aljamiadas-of-spain/.

Jackson, Deirdre. "Humfrey Wanley and the Harley Collection." *eBLJ* (*British Library Journal*), article 2 (2011). https://www.bl.uk/eblj/2011articles/pdf/ebljarticle22011.pdf.

Johnston, A. W. "The Alphabet." In *Sea Routes from Sidon to Huelva: Interconnections in the Mediterranean*, edited by N. Stampolidis and V. Karageorghis, 263–76. Athens: Museum of Cycladic Art, 2003.

Kadman, L. "The Hebrew Coin Script: A Study in the Epigraphy of Ancient Jewish Coins." *Israel Exploration Journal* 4, nos. 3/4 (1954): 150–69.

Kalvesmaki, Joel. "The Orthodox Possibilities of the Theology of Arithmetic." Clement of Alexandria, *Stromates*, 6.140.4–6.141.1. https://chs.harvard.edu/CHS/article/display/6309.7-the-orthodox-possibilities-of-the-theology-of-arithmetic-clement-of-alexandria.

Kempgen, Sebastian. "The Mysterious 'Alphabetum Iliricum Sclavorum.'" University of Bamberg, 2015. https://kodeks.uni-bamberg.de/slavling/downloads/SK_IllyrianSlavicAlphabet.pdf.

King, David A. *The Ciphers of the Monks: A Forgotten Number Notation of the Middle Ages*. Stuttgart: F. Steiner Verlag, 2001.

Kirk, Peter. Response to revised "Final Proposal for Encoding the Phoenician Script in the UCS." June 7, 2004. https://www.gentlewisdom.org/qaya/academic/hebrew/Phoenician.html.

Knowlson, James. *Universal Language Schemes in England*. Toronto: University of Toronto Press, 1975.

Kupfer, Marcia. "'. . . lectres . . . plus vrayes': Hebrew Script and Jewish Witness in the *Mandeville* manuscript of Charles V." *Speculum* 83 (January 2008): 58–111.

Laycock, Donald. *The Complete Enochian Dictionary*. York Beach, ME: Weiser, 1994.

Lehmann, Reinhard G. "Much Ado about an Implement!" Chap. 5 in *Understanding Relations between Scripts II, Early Alphabets*, edited by Philip J. Boyes and Philippa M. Steele. Oxford, UK: Oxbow Books, 2020.

———. "Wer war Aḥīrōms Sohn (KAI 1:1)? Eine kalligraphisch-prosopographische Annäherung an eine epigraphisch offene Frage." In *Neue Beiträge zur Semitistik. Fünftes Treffen der ArbeitsgemeinschaftSemitistik in der Deutschen MorgenländischenGesellschaft vom 15.–17. Februar 2012 an der Universität Basel* (AOAT 425), edited by V. Golinets, H. Jenni, H.-P. Mathys, and S. Sarasin (Hg.), 163–80. Münster: Ugarit-Verlag, 2015.

———. "Wilhelm Gesenius and the Rise of Phoenician Philology." In *Bieheste zur Zeitschrift für die alttestamentliche Wissenschaft*, 209–66. Band 427. Berlin: De Gruyter, 2013.

Letts, Malcolm. *Mandeville's Travels: Texts and Translations.* 2 vols. Milton Park, Abingdon: Routledge, 2011.

Levine, Joseph. *Battle of the Books: History and Literature in the Augustan Age*. Ithaca, NY: Cornell University Press, 2018.

Lewis, Jesica Jayd. "A *History of the Histories*: From Papyrus to Codex, From Codex to Today." *A&P: Antiquorum et Praesentis*, December 20, 2014. www.antiquorumetpraesentis.com.

Lewis, N. N., and M. C. A. MacDonald. "W. J. Bankes and the Discovery and Identification of the Nabataean Script." *Syria* 80 (2003): 41–110.

Levy-Bruhl, Lucien. *How "Natives" Think*. London: G. Allen and Unwin, 1926; originally published in French as *Les fonctions mentales dans les sociétés inférieures* (Paris: F. Alcan, 1910).

Liedle, David. "A Brief History of Optical Character recognition," *Filestack* (blog), November 9, 2018. https://blog.filestack.com/thoughts-and-knowledge/history-of-ocr/.

Mango, Cyril. "The Triumphal Way of Constantinople and the Golden Gate." *Dumbarton Oaks Papers* 54 (2000): 173–88.

Markowitz, Mike. "CoinWeek Ancient Coin Series—Coinage of the Phoenicians." *CoinWeek*, February 29, 2016. https://coinweek.com/ancient-coins/coinweek-ancient-coin-series-coinage-of-the-phoenicians/.

May, Herbert G. "Moses and the Sinai Inscriptions." *Biblical Archaeologist* 8, no. 4 (December 1945): 93–99.

Mazar, Benjamin. "The Phoenician Inscriptions from Byblos and the Evolution of the Phoenician-Hebrew Alphabet." In *The Early Biblical Period: Historical Studies*, edited by S. Ahituv and B. A. Levine, 231–247. Jerusalem: *IES*, 1986 (originally published 1946).

Mazar, Eilat, and David Ben-Shlomo. "An Inscribed Pithos from the Ophel, Jerusalem." *Israel Exploration Journal* 63, no. 1 (January 2013): 39–49.

McLuhan, Marshall. *War and Peace in the Global Village*. New York: McGraw-Hill 1968.

McNeal, R. A. "On Editing Herodotus." *L'antiquité classique* 52 (1983): 110–29.

Millard, Alan. "The New Jerusalem Inscription—So What?" *Biblical Archaeology Review* 40, no. 3 (May–June 2014). https://www.baslibrary.org/biblical-archaeology-review/40/3/6.

Miller, Peter N. "The 'Antiquarianization' of Biblical Scholarship and the London Polyglot Bible (1653–57)." *Journal of the History of Ideas* 62, no. 3 (July 2001): 463–82.

———. *Peiresec's Orient: Antiquarianism as Cultural History in the Seventeenth Century*. Abingdon, Oxfordshire: Routledge, 2012.

Millesima, Iulia. "Kriegsmann: Sun, Moon, Wind and Earth in Tabula Smaragdina." *Labyrinth Designers and the Art of Fire*, 2021. https://www.labyrinthdesigners.org/alchemic-authors-1598-1832/kriegsmann-sun-moon-wind-earth-in-tabula-smaragdina/.

Nelles, Paul. "The Vatican Library Alphabets, Luco Orfei, and Graphic Media in Sistine Rome." In *For the Sake of Learning*, edited by Ann Blair and Anja-Silvia Goeing, 441–68. Leiden: Brill, 2016.

Neuhofer, M. Dorothy. *In the Benedictine Tradition*. Lanham, MD: University Press of America, 1999.

Niesiolowski-Spano, Lukasz. "Early Alphabetic Scripts and the Origin of Greek Letters." In *Haec mihi in animis vestris templa: Studia Classica in Memory of Professor Lesław Morawiecki*, edited by Piotr Berdowski and Beata Blahaczek, 47–63. Rzeszów: Institute of History, University of Rzeszów, 2007.

Nothaft, C. P. E. "Josephus and New Testament Chronology in the Work of Joseph Scaliger." *International Journal of the Classical Tradition* 23, no. 3 (2016): 246–51.

Obermann, Julian. "A Revised Reading of the Tell el-Hesi Inscription, with a Note on the Gezer Sherd." *American Journal of Archaeology* 44, no. 1 (January–March 1940): 93–104.

Papadopoulos, John K. "The Early History of the Greek Alphabet: New Evidence from Eretria and Methone." *Antiquity* 90, no. 353 (October 2016): 1238–54.

Pardee, Dennis. "Lachish Ostraca." *Context of Scripture* 3, no. 42. From The Interactive Bible Website. Accessed June 17, 20221. https://www.bible.ca/ostraca/Ostraca-Lachish-Letters-Jeremiah-YHWH-Egypt-Fire-Signals-Azekah-weakening-hands-nebuchadnezzar-587BC.htm.

Pelling, Nick. "The Voarchadumia & John Dee." *Cipher Mysteries*, May 23, 2009. http://ciphermysteries.com/2009/05/23/the-voarchadumia-john-dee.

Pingree, David. "Some of the Sources of the Ghāyat al-hakīm." *Journal of the Warburg and Courtauld Institutes* 43 (1980): 1–15.

Poppe, Erich. "The Celtic Languages in Conrad Gessner's *Mithridates* (1555)." *Zeitschrift fü celtische Philologie* 45, no. 1 (2009): 240–50.

Porada, Edith. "Notes on the Sarcophagus of Ahiram." *Journal of the Ancient Near East Society* 5, no. 1 (1973): 354–72.

Porter, Venetia. "The Use of Arabic Script in Magic." In *The Development of Arabic as a Written Language*, edited by M. C. A. Macdonald, *Supplement to the Proceedings of the Seminar for Arabian Studies* 40, 131–40. Oxford: Archaeopress, 2010.

Rainey, Anson. *The Sacred Bridge: Carta's Atlas of the Biblical World*. Jerusalem: Carta, 2006.

Reich, David. "Ancient DNA Tells Tales of Humans' Migrant History." *Science Daily*, February 21, 2018. https://www.sciencedaily.com/releases/2018/02/180221131851.htm.

Ridley, Michael. "Are Reading and Writing Doomed?" In *Proceedings, ACRL Fourteenth National Conference*, March 12–15, 2009, 210–13. https://www.ala.org/acrl/sites/ala.org.acrl/files/content/conferences/confsandpreconfs/national/seattle/papers/210.pdf.

Robinson, Andrew. *The Story of Writing*. London: Thames and Hudson, 2007.

Rodrigue, Aron. "Totems, Taboos, and Jews: Salomon Reinach and the Politics of Scholarship in Fin-de-Siècle France." *Jewish Social Studies*, n.s., 10, no. 2 (Winter 2004): 1–19.

Rouse, Margaret. "OCR (Optical Character Recognition)." TechTarget, updated April 2019. https://searchcontentmanagement.techtarget.com/definition/OCR-optical-character-recognition.

Rowland, Ingrid. "Athanasius Kircher and the Egyptian Oedipus." *Fathom Archive*, University of Chicago, 2004. http://fathom.lib.uchicago.edu/1/777777122590/.

Salisbury, Preston R. "Analysis of Primers in the de Grummond Children's Literature Collection." *SLIS Connecting* 3, no. 2, article 7 (2014). Accessed June 17, 2021. https://aquila.usm.edu/slisconnecting/vol3/iss2/7/.

Salmon, Vivian. "The Study of Foreign Languages in 17th Century England." *Histoire épistémologie langage* 7, no. 2 (1985): 45–70.

Scribner, Sylvia, and Michael Cole. *The Psychology of Literacy*. Cambridge, MA: Harvard University Press, 1981.

Seebold, Elmar. "Mandeville's Alphabets." In *Beitrage zur Geschichte der deutschen Sprache und Literatur*, 366–77. Paris, Niemeyer, 1998.

Shalev, Sariel. *Swords and Daggers in Late Bronze Age Canaan*. Stuttgart: Franz Steiner Verlag, 2004.

Shur, Nathan. "The Return of the Diaspora Samaritans to Nablus at the End of the Middle Ages." http://members.tripod.com/~osher_2/html_articles/Diaspora.htm.

Simon, Fabien. "Collecting Languages, Alphabets and Texts: The Circulation of 'Parts of Texts' among Paper Cabinets of Linguistic Curiosities (Sixteenth-Seventeenth Century)." In *Pieces and Parts in Scientific Texts*. Vol. 1, edited by Florence Bretelle-Establet and Stéphane Schmitt, 297–346. New York: Springer, 2018.

Tappy, Ron E., P. Kyle McCarter, Marilyn J. Lundberg, and Bruce Zuckerman, "An Abecedary of the Mid-Tenth Century B.C. from the Judaean Shephelah." *Bulletin of the American Schools of Oriental Research* 344 (November 2006): 5–46.

Thomas, Kate. "How Many Alphabets?" *Medieval Manuscripts Blog*, May 10, 2019. https://blogs.bl.uk/digitisedmanuscripts/2019/05/how-many-alphabets.html.

Thorndike, Lynn. *A History of Magic and Experimental Science during the First Thirteen Centuries of Our Era*. 8 vols. New York: Columbia University Press, 1923.

VanderKam, James C. "The Book of Enoch and the Qumran Scrolls." In *The Oxford Handbook of the Dead Sea Scrolls*. New York: Oxford University Press, 2010. https://www.oxfordhandbooks.com/view/10.1093/oxfordhb/9780199207237.001.0001/oxfordhb-9780199207237-e-11.

Waal, Willemijn. "On the 'Phoenician Letters': The Case for an Early Transmission of the Greek Alphabet from an Archaeological, Epigraphic, and Linguistic Perspective." *Aegean Studies* 1, no. 4 (December 2018): 83–125.

Weinstock, Horst. "Roger Bacon's Polyglot Alphabet." *Florilegium* 11 (1992): 160–78.

Weiss, Roberto. "The Study of Ancient Numismatics during the Renaissance (1313–1517)." *Numismatic Chronicle* 8 (1968): 177–87.

Wheeler, Brandon. "Guillaume Postel and the Primordial Origins of the Middle East." In *Method and Theory in the Study of Religion*. Leiden: Brill, 2012. https://www.academia.edu/14955597/Guillaume_Postel_and_the_Primordial_Origins_of_the_Middle_East.

Wilford, John Noble. "Discovery of Egyptian Inscriptions Indicates an Earlier Date for Origin of the Alphabet." *New York Times*, Science, November 13, 1999. Accessed June 17, 2021. https://archive.nytimes.com/www.nytimes.com/library/national/science/111499sci-alphabet-origin.html.

Winslow, Alexander, "The Pillar in the Land of Siriad." Squires Publishing, 1998–2009. http://www.squirespublishing.co.uk/files/syriad.htm.

Wirszubski, Chaim. *Pico della Mirandola's Encounter with Jewish Mysticism*. Cambridge, MA: Harvard University Press, 1989.

Yaya, Isabel. "Wonders of America: The Curiosity Cabinet as a Site of Representation and Knowledge." *Journal of the History of Collections* 20, no. 2 (November 2008): 173–88.

Yu, Dominic. "Thoughts on Logan's 'The Alphabet Effect,'" last modified January 3, 2003. https://web.archive.org/web/20160413133632/http://rescomp.stanford.edu/~domingo2/zok/logan.html.

Z

Index

Page numbers in italics refer to illustrations.